Successful School Leadership

Planning, Politics, Performance, and Power

JAMES W. GUTHRIE

Peabody College at Vanderbilt University

PATRICK J. SCHUERMANN

Peabody College at Vanderbilt University

Allyn & Bacon

Boston   New York   San Francisco
Mexico City   Montreal   Toronto   London   Madrid   Munich   Paris
Hong Kong   Singapore   Tokyo   Cape Town   Sydney

Executive Editor and Publisher: Stephen D. Dragin
Series Editorial Assistant: Anne Whittaker
Marketing Manager: Jared Brueckner
Production Editor: Gregory Erb
Editorial Production Service: Nesbitt Graphics, Inc.
Composition Buyer: Linda Cox
Manufacturing Buyer: Megan Cochran
Electronic Composition: Nesbitt Graphics, Inc.
Interior Design: Nesbitt Graphics, Inc.
Cover Designer: Linda Knowles

For related titles and support materials, visit our online catalog at www.pearsonhighered.com.

Between the time website information is gathered and then published, it is not unusual for some sites to have closed. Also, the transcription of URLs can result in typographical errors. The publisher would appreciate notification where these errors occur so that they may be corrected in subsequent editions.

Library of Congress Cataloging-in-Publication Data

Guthrie, James W.
   Successful school leadership: planning, politics, performance, and power / James W. Guthrie, Patrick J. Schuermann.
      p. cm. – (The Peabody education leadership series)
   Includes bibliographical references and index.
   ISBN 0-205-46999-X
   1. School management and organization–United States.   2. Educational leadership–United States.
   I. Schuermann, Patrick Jude.   II. Title.
LB2805.G883 2010
371.200973–dc22   2008027172

Printed in the United States of America
10 9 8 7 6 5 4 3 2 1 HAM 12 11 10 09 08

**Allyn & Bacon
is an imprint of**

www.pearsonhighered.com

ISBN 10: 0-205-46999-X
ISBN 13: 978-0-205-46999-4

Contents

Preface

If you liked playing in fast-moving traffic, climbing dangerously tall trees, or wrestling with exasperatingly complex puzzles when you were a child, it may be that education leadership is your field. Today's school leaders are expected to be forward looking and capable of planning for change; politically astute; knowledgeable regarding learning; and expert in managing the day-to-day operations of an organization, be it a school, district, union, or some related education organization. This book provides knowledge and ideas about how to succeed amid an often-frustrating cacophony of modern educational expectations. The book strives to make sense of what is taking place now and likely to take place in the future that will affect education and education leaders.

The book is divided into four functional frames of reference: Planning, Politics, Performance, and Power. These are the functions with which education leaders now must continually grapple. However, whereas the chapter headings and discussions of subjects are separate, the majesty of successful leadership is blending these functional elements into the smooth amalgam of strategic and applied activity needed for modern leadership. It is the manner in which a reader molds these capacities and manifests their practical elements that will define his or her unique leadership style and likely contribute substantially to leadership success or failure.

■ ELCC STANDARDS AND THEIR CENTRALITY FOR THE SERIES AND FOR THIS VOLUME

This specific volume and the Peabody Education Leadership Series generally are undertaken in a manner consistent with and intended to promote the Educational Leadership Constituent Consortium (ELCC) standards for the advanced preparation of education leaders. These standards, developed under the auspices of the National Policy Board for Educational Administration, specify the knowledge and skills needed by a modern school leader. This book explicates and illustrates this package of knowledge and skills and is intended to facilitate the acquisition of such knowledge by practicing and aspiring school leaders of all kinds. The organizing matrix appearing on the inside cover specifies the detailed content of the book that corresponds to each of the six ELCC standards. Additionally, the introductory material in each section of this text highlights specific ways that text content is aligned with the ELCC standards.

ELCC Standards

Effective education leaders are presumed to have the knowledge and ability to promote the success of all students by:

Standard 1: facilitating the development, articulation, implementation, and stewardship of a school or district vision of learning supported by the school community

Standard 2: promoting a positive school culture, providing an effective instructional program, applying best practices to student learning, and designing comprehensive professional growth plans for staff

Standard 3: managing the organization, operations, and resources in a way that promotes a safe, efficient, and effective learning environment

Standard 4: collaborating with families and other community members, responding to diverse community interests and needs, and mobilizing community resources

Standard 5: acting with integrity, fairly, and in an ethical manner

Standard 6: understanding, responding to, and influencing the larger political, social, economic, legal, and cultural context

■ PEABODY LEADERSHIP PRECEPTS

Peabody College's research efforts and professional development programs have evolved a set of principles or precepts regarding education leadership to which this book and the entire book series adhere. These precepts are consistent with the leadership encouraged by the ELCC standards. They are derived from scholarship, cognitive science, organizational theory, and professional practitioners' distilled experience and are woven into the professional preparation activities operated by Peabody's Leadership Development Center and the Peabody Professional Institutes. Peabody leadership principles are as follows.

- Learning is at the heart of leadership and an education organization.
- Leaders can be created and improved through learning, and are not simply born to the challenge.
- Learning for leadership should itself mirror learning in a leader's organization.
- Leadership is a continuum from novice to expert.
- Appropriate mentoring can accelerate learning along this continuum toward becoming an "expert" leader.
- Leadership is a continuous learning process for a leader and his or her organization.
- Effective leadership necessitates learning about oneself and being amenable to continual personal growth and change.
- Leaders must learn both what is the "right" thing to do and how to do things right.
- Leader effectiveness is enhanced by knowledge of an organization's community and societal context.
- Leaders must know sources of appropriate data and possess data analytic capacity.

■ PUTTING LEARNING FIRST: PRACTICING WHAT PEABODY PREACHES

Each of these precepts is addressed throughout this text, and the precepts are also woven into discussions of topics relevant to the previously mentioned ELCC standards. In addition, this volume, as with all Peabody Series texts, is engaged in ongoing efforts to unravel what is meant by and how to assess student understanding. Whereas the mere recital of discrete tidbits of knowledge and facts by students was once accepted as an appropriate indicator of student understanding, more contemporary approaches stress such elements as conceptual clarity, real-world application, critical analysis, and reflection to appraise student understanding. In an extension of those approaches, this textbook strives to enhance reader learning and performance through an innovative assessment technique called *Understanding by Design*, which promotes deep understanding and meaningful application by students.

Understanding by Design

The approach to learning employed within these pages is grounded in the performance assessments developed by Grant Wiggins and Jay McTighe, two leading thinkers who advocate situating student understanding at the core of curricular, assessment, and instructional designs. In 1998, Wiggins and McTighe published the highly acclaimed *Understanding by Design*, a resource book for educators that sponsors performance assessment as a means to promote deep understanding of content by students. Wiggins and McTighe assert that an individual truly understands when he or she (1) can explain, (2) can interpret, (3) can apply, (4) has perspective, (5) can emphasize, and (6) has self-knowledge. This textbook draws upon Wiggins and McTighe's six facets of understanding through use of discussion questions, case studies, and articles from mainstream media to enhance student understanding of topics under consideration.

Using this approach to enhance reader understanding yields a standard chapter outline that will guide users through the remainder of this text. Each chapter begins with a thoughtful list of learning objectives. Throughout the chapter, readers will encounter material that will be used to guide discussion. Often, this material will refer readers back to one of the section-opening case studies. In addition, each chapter will have an "In the News" feature that highlights a newspaper article, journal article, press release, or similar piece of media that presents the issues in each chapter within a real-world context. The end of each chapter contains a chapter summary, a list of discussion questions, and a list of resources and suggested readings.

Because of their intended use for professional practitioners, books in the Peabody Education Leadership Series deliberately include only a few footnotes and scholarly references. An exception to this practice is made when there is a particularly important piece of research or a classic reference on a topic. For example, the 1966 study of *Equality of Educational Opportunity* or the 1983 report *A Nation at Risk* each triggered such important changes in the course of modern American education that they are explicitly cited and explained.

Principles and concepts upon which each Peabody Series volume rests are grounded in solid scholarship and practical reality. Bibliographic references to guide a reader to seminal related writings and research studies are provided at the end of each chapter. For those readers seeking additional insights, each volume includes a subject/author index to assist in referring to important topics and influential individuals.

■ PLAN FOR THIS BOOK

Leaders of our nation's schools are confronted with a new educational era of high expectations for learning and intensifying performance accountability. The purpose of this book is to enable aspiring and practicing school leaders and other interested individuals to understand and successfully confront the multiple educational challenges posed by twenty-first-century conditions and contexts. The format and flow of the book are consciously designed to facilitate this purpose.

The book is divided into four sections. These sections are presented as essential frames of reference, or domains of understanding and action, for current and aspiring education leaders. The frames are (1) Planning: defining and applying strategic leadership; (2) Politics: comprehending contextual knowledge regarding political systems, governance, law, and resources; (3) Performance: explaining learning, educational programs, performance measurement, and problem solving through data analyses; and (4) Power: undertaking day-to-day operations in which leaders must successfully persuade others to do what is right—for example, personnel management and incentives, community partnerships, and practical operations and decision making.

The sections are far more than simply alliterative means to divide a great deal of content. The four sections also serve several major operational and pedagogical functions for the book. Each section opener specifies the content in the section, describes the relationship of that content to ELCC standards, and then provides case studies that can act as discussion launching pads linking the content of the section to the actual practices of leadership. Throughout the content of each section, a reader gains insights important in fulfilling both traditional leadership and management components of guiding an education organization. A strategic approach to leadership applies to both the visionary components of leadership and the daily operations essential for moving an organization toward the realization of state, district, or school goals.

■ A GENERAL NOTE REGARDING EDUCATIONAL ADMINISTRATION TEXTBOOKS

In 2006, Fredrick M. Hess and Andrew P. Kelly published an analysis of educational administration textbooks.[1] They sorted through eleven of the most commonly used administration preparation texts to determine the intensity with which these publications addressed important contemporary topics such as performance accountability, personnel incentives, data use, teacher termination, school efficiency, and resource sufficiency. Many of these topics, functions for which education leaders are now clearly held responsible for addressing successfully, were found to be lacking or seldom mentioned in the books analyzed by Hess and Kelly. All of these topics reside close to the core of strategic leadership and modern management, and consequently are covered in depth in this text. A primary concern elevated by Hess and Kelly is that principals are not being sufficiently exposed to the full range of management practices necessary to thrive in the current education policy context. As such, it is imperative that leadership preparation programs and texts be constructed to provide experiences and knowledge that are more closely aligned with the realities of what it takes to lead today's schools. This foundational volume of the Peabody Educational Leadership Series makes a concerted effort to address these thoughtful concerns.

■ ACKNOWLEDGMENTS

The series originator and editor, and first author of this specific volume, is James W. Guthrie, professor of public policy and education at Peabody College, chair of the Leadership, Policy, and Organizations department, director of the Peabody Center for Education Policy, director of the National Center on Performance Incentives, and policy director for the Center on Educator Compensation Reform.[2] Peabody's Department of Leadership, Policy, and Organizations is among the most highly rated academic units in the nation concerned with the preparation of education leaders[3] and offers advanced degree programs for both researchers and professional practitioners.

The second author of this volume is Patrick J. Schuermann, a research assistant professor at Peabody College, director of technical assistance for the Center on Educator Compensation Reform, and coordinator of the Independent School Leadership Institute, which is a joint venture between the National Research and Development Center on School Choice and the Peabody Professional Institutes.

Much of the underlying knowledge of education leadership and successful school operation upon which all Peabody Education Leadership Series volumes rest was pioneered through decades of research and design efforts undertaken at Peabody College with the financial support of the Institute of Education Sciences of the United States Department of Education, the Office of Elementary and Secondary Education within the United States Department of Education, the Tennessee State Education Department, the Tennessee Department of Human Services, the Texas Education Agency, Metropolitan Nashville Public Schools, and national philanthropic foundations, prominent among which have been the Bill and Melinda Gates Foundation, the Ball Foundation, the Stewart Foundation, the William and Flora Hewlett Foundation, the Wallace Foundation, W. T. Grant Foundation, and the Public Education Foundation of Nashville. While deeply appreciative of the resources and opportunities all of these agencies have contributed, the series editor and individual authors are responsible for the content and recommendations contained in this and other series volumes.

We wish to express our appreciation to Peabody College's Dean Camilla P. Benbow. Further, we are thankful to Arnis Burvikovs, Steve Dragin, Gregory Erb, and Anne Whittaker of Allyn & Bacon, whose encouragement rendered this project doable. Linda Zuk and her team of editors provided guidance throughout the editing stages of the process for which we are thankful. Also during the editing stages of manuscript production, Merrie Clark served as an expert resource to the authors, and for this we are very grateful. Additionally, Peabody College staff members Lia Fisher, Suzanne Vahaly, Jacob Thornton and Peter Witham were a continual source of unselfish assistance. Also in this regard, Joyce Hilley, who has managed the Peabody Center for Education Policy for thirteen years, kept the writing and production processes connected with this book on track and on time.

The authors are especially appreciative of the contributions of their Peabody College and Vanderbilt University faculty colleagues Kathryn H. Anderson, R. Dale Ballou,

Steven R. Baum, Leonard Bickman, Leonard K. Bradley, Timothy C. Caboni, Robert L. Crowson, Mark D. Cannon, Janet S. Eyler, John G. Geer, Ellen B. Goldring, Stephen P. Heyneman, Michael K. McLendon, Joseph F. Murphy, Bruce I. Oppenheimer, Cynthia D. Prince, Daniel J. Reschly, Pearl G. Sims, Matthew G. Springer, and Thomas T. Ward. Additionally, the authors are grateful to Gareth P. Fowles of Lynn University for his contributions to the text.

As well, authors have benefited from the advice and friendship of a number of professional colleagues, among whom are Jake P. Abbott, California independent education executive search consultant; Jacob E. Adams, Claremont Graduate University; Jane Best and Gina E. Burkhardt, Learning Point Associates; Sir Clive Booth, Oxford Brookes College; Devin Brown, Asbury University; Sharon Brown, Transylvania University; Charles W. Cagle, Lewis, King, Krieg & Waldrop, P.C.; Geraldine J. Clifford, University of California, Berkeley; Robert M. Costrell, University of Arkansas; Ric Dressen, Edina Public Schools, Minnesota; Christopher T. Cross, Cross & Joftus, LLC; Vincent Durnan, University School of Nashville; John W. Evans, Educational Testing Service; Pedro E. Garcia, University of Southern California; Jay P. Greene, University of Arkansas; William Green, Minneapolis Public Schools; Babette Gutmann, Westat; Eric A. Hanushek, Hoover Institution of Stanford University; Janet S. Hansen, Committee for Economic Development; Gerald C. Hayward, California Community College System; Allison Henderson, Westat; Carolyn D. Herrington, University of Missouri-Columbia; Frederick M. Hess, American Enterprise Institute; Paul T. Hill, University of Washington; Eric A. Houck, University of Georgia; Joseph Jaconette, Orinda, California; Sally Kilgore, Modern Red SchoolHouse, Michael W. Kirst, Stanford University; Julia E. Koppich, J. Koppich & Associates; Richard Laine, Wallace Foundation; Sabrina Laine, Learning Point Associates; April Lee, United States Department of Education; Alfred A. Lindseth, Sutherland, Asbill & Brennan, LLP; Goodwin Liu, University of California, Berkeley School of Law (Boalt Hall); Susanna Loeb, Stanford University; Robert H. Meyer, University of Wisconsin-Madison; J. Dennis O'Brien, Office of the Governor, Minnesota; Allan R. Odden, University of Wisconsin-Madison; Jennifer L. Osterhage, Hanover College; David H. Monk, Pennsylvania State University; Paul Peterson, Harvard University; Darcy Pietryka, Westat; Michael J. Podgursky, University of Missouri-Columbia; R. Anthony Rolle, Texas A&M University; Kevin M. Ross, Lynn University; Richard Rothstein, Economic Policy Institute; Roger Sampson, Education Commission of the States; Kevin Skelly, Palo Alto, California, Neil Slotnick, Alaska attorney general's office; James R. Smith, Management Analysis and Planning (MAP); Robert E. Stepp, Sowell, Gray, Stepp & Laffitte, LLC; Rocco E. Testani, Sutherland, Asbill & Brennan, LLC; Christopher A. Thorn, University of Wisconsin-Madison; Jason L. Walton, Lynn University; Jerry D. Weast, Montgomery County Maryland; Elizabeth Witt, United States Department of Education; and Patrick J. Wolf, University of Arkansas.

This volume was written while E. Gordon Gee was the chancellor of Vanderbilt University. Seldom have the authors witnessed an individual who so fully and genuinely pursued and exemplified the strategic leadership principles and practices described and espoused in this book. Few leaders think as globally and act as personally as Gordon Gee. We were fortunate to have had him as an exemplar from which we could learn so much and employ as a favorable model so often.

Patrick Schuermann would like to thank his immediate family, extended family, and school families from whom he has learned much by example about leadership and the importance of integrity in action.

As authors, we are flattered at reader interest in this volume and welcome suggestions for improving its accuracy and utility. As should be obvious in such ventures, errors and omissions are the responsibility of authors alone.

James W. Guthrie   Peabody College
Patrick J. Schuermann   Vanderbilt University
                                                        Nashville, Tennessee

Notes

1. Hess, F. M., and Kelly, A. P. What school leadership texts teach: An analysis of leadership volumes used in principal preparation. *Education Working Paper Archive*: Washington, DC, April 4, 2006.
2. www.Performanceincentives.org and http://cecr.ed.gov
3. Leadership, Policy, and Organizations was ranked number one in the nation by *U.S. News and World Report* in 2008, and Peabody College was ranked the number-two school of education.

About the Authors

James W. Guthrie is a professor of public policy and education, chair of Leadership, Policy and Organizations, and director of the Peabody Center for Education Policy at Peabody College of Vanderbilt University. He instructs both undergraduate and graduate courses, and conducts research on education policy and finance. He also is the founder and chairman of the board of Management Analysis & Planning, Inc. (MAP), a California private sector management consulting firm specializing in public finance and litigation support. Previously a professor at the University of California, Berkeley for 27 years, he holds a BA, MA, and PhD from Stanford University and undertook postdoctoral study in public finance at Harvard. He also was a postdoctoral Fellow at Oxford Brookes College, Oxford, England, and the Irving R. Melbo Visiting Professor at the University of Southern California. He is the author or co-author of ten books and more than 200 professional and scholarly articles. He was the editor-in-chief of the *Encyclopedia of American Education*, published in 2002.

Patrick J. Schuermann is a research assistant professor of educational leadership and public policy at Peabody College of Vanderbilt University. He serves as the director of technical assistance for the Center for Educator Compensation Reform (CECR), the comprehensive assistance center for the federally funded Teacher Incentive Fund (TIF) grant. He developed and serves as the faculty chair for one of the Leadership Institutes at Peabody College. For several years, Patrick worked in conjunction with the Leadership Development Center at Vanderbilt University on several professional development initiatives for local and state education leaders. Previously a teacher, tutor, and leader at the elementary, middle, and high school levels for 8 years, he holds BS and MA degrees from Furman University and an Ed. D. degree from Vanderbilt University.

PART ONE

Planning for Change
Understanding Strategic Leadership

This first part of the text stresses the significance of strategy, strategic planning, and strategic thinking for modern school leaders. Here, the emphasis is upon a modern leader understanding the consequences for his or her organization of the influence of external events upon internal operations.

This book part comprises three chapters that form a foundation for subsequent discussions of strategic leadership knowledge and actions. These chapters discuss the contextual factors influencing schools and education leaders and provide operational insights from formal theories of leadership and organization behavior. Chapter 1 discusses the historical, contextual, and organizational factors that help answer the question, Why is a strategic approach to education leadership needed and needed now? Chapter 2 examines the qualities of organizational dynamics and education leaders and endorses a strategic approach to school leadership. Chapter 3 provides detailed explanations of the steps involved in undertaking strategic planning in an education organization. Throughout this book, boldface words denote glossary terms.

■ APPLICABILITY OF PART 1 CONTENT TO ELCC STANDARDS

As described in the Preface to this book, this text contains content that aligns with all six of the ELCC Standards. An overview of how text content aligns with the ELCC Standards is provided on the inside front cover. At the outset of each part of the text, the alignment between the ELCC Standards and chapter content will be described. Content in this first part of the text is most applicable to ELCC Standards 1, 3, 5, and 6. For example, when describing the attributes of strategic leaders, Chapters 2 and 3 emphasize vision, the focus of ELCC Standard 1, and the values of integrity and fairness, the focus of ELCC Standard 5. By discussing the manner in which a broad spectrum of contextual factors influence schools and school leaders, Chapter 2 deals substantially with ELCC Standard 6. All three chapters, which provide insights about strategic organizations, provide a significant amount of content pertinent to ELCC Standard 3, which concentrates upon the organizational management of learning environments.

■ CASE STUDIES

For each part of the text, case studies have been constructed so readers can consider how text content might inform real-life situations. To facilitate the application of knowledge to practice, several "flashbacks" to case studies will be provided in each chapter. Within the first part of the text, the following two case studies will be referred to as a way to encourage the application of content to real-life situations. The case studies do not involve actual people or places. They do, however, involve actual challenges that leaders routinely face and must overcome. In addition to these two introductory case challenges, some chapters will include separate case studies, which are challenges particularly appropriate to the subject matter under discussion in that chapter. Reflection points are provided at the conclusion of each of the following case challenges as one way to facilitate group discussion and encourage individuals to apply their practical expertise to these leadership dilemmas.

 CASE 1 ————————————————————————————————

A Profile of Strategic Planning Failure: A Case of Foreshortened Vision

Things are not always as they appear.

Daniel Bowles was, until recently, CEO of a major Madison Avenue advertising company, Omnibus Marketing Inc. (OMI). To all outward observers, he was remarkably successful.

U.S. News & World Report rated the firm as number four in the nation in its business category. Clients continued to seek the company's marketing and advertising services. The company had no difficulty in attracting talented artists, technicians, and other employees upon which it crucially depended to serve its clients. It regularly upgraded the technological bases upon which it conducted its business.

Company profits were slightly up, returns on investment were steady, if not spectacular, and the company's stock price and price–earnings ratio both remained stable when similar firms' values plummeted after September 11, 2001. The company had financial reserves that, while not growing, were not being tapped.

Daniel was himself tall, slender, intelligent, handsome, athletic in appearance, well educated, well dressed, happily married, a father of several successful children, and about to become a grandfather. He was a loving spouse and parent to members of his family, civil in his public discourse, and concerned when it came to his employees' and clients' well-being. He was civic minded, religiously tolerant, and attentive to his own parents.

He was known among his staff for his keen understanding of finances. He could read and analyze a balance sheet and statement of accounts faster and more accurately than anyone they had ever seen. He also was known to have high ethical standards and regularly to act upon them. He possessed a powerful internal gyroscope upon which he depended for knowing right from wrong. He was known among his managers as a perfectionist. Whatever he did, he strived to do right.

So what was the problem here? Did Daniel abuse his wife or children? Did he use contraband drugs? Was he a compulsive gambler or womanizer? Was he an agent of a foreign or terrorist power? Did he "cook" the company accounts for personal gain or stock leverage? No to all of the above. Indeed, as noted, what Daniel did was known to be right and good. The problem was not in what Daniel did, but rather in what he did not do.

Daniel's firm was maintaining the momentum that others before him had initiated. He had become the CEO five years before. Previously he was a successful bond manager and venture capitalist. He had never managed an operating firm such as OMI. He knew money. However, he did not know the core activities of his new business. He did not know and could not easily communicate or socialize with the firm's employees or clients. He spent his days in his office. He seldom walked among the creative staff and artists on the floors below. He seldom met with executives of similar companies. He did not participate intensely in the professional organizations of his field.

The firm was coasting on its reputation and was not making new investments in people or infrastructure needed to keep pace with rivals. Daniel had little clue regarding where the advertising field was headed. He could not formulate a vision of where his company should be going. Perhaps more dangerous yet, he steadfastly refused to surround himself with talent that could see the field and could shape a vision for the company's future. He continued to rely upon managers who had brought the firm to where it was but who had hardly any idea about what it could or should become.

Daniel used as measures of company success conventional financial figures. He knew and understood accounting fundamentals and counted on this knowledge to enable him to manage by the numbers. As long as these numbers were okay, then he assumed the company was okay.

Daniel was fundamentally a shy man. He was honest, straightforward, and, as specified above, had many sterling qualities. However, he could not easily mix with outsiders, could not easily ask for advice, could not easily listen to others around him, and he could not easily delegate authority. Moreover, he was unable to see over the horizon. He did not solicit the views of subordinates, and thus continually restricted himself to the observations of those close to him who depended upon his constant approval for their jobs and status.

Consequently, Daniel was surprised to read in the *Wall Street Journal* that two smaller competing firms were merging, were adapting to online technologies, and were about to expand into the European Community. Moreover, several of his most talented creative staff members announced that they were joining the new firm. The new firm announced that many of OMI's major clients had already agreed that they would go with the new firm.

Daniel was about to preside over an empty shell. Just as things looked good, they turned bad. What had he done wrong?

Daniel had been proud of his ability to do things right. In the process he forgot the other half of the crucial leadership equation: it is necessary not only to do things right, but also to determine continually the right things to do.

Discussion Questions for Case 1

1. What should Daniel have been doing? Could he have acted differently? Should Daniel have been fired?
2. Could Daniel likely have changed his behavior, learned new skills, and become the CEO his company needed to meet the challenge of the future?
3. What should the board of directors of OMI have done when they selected Daniel? Could they have headed off this downward turn of events?
4. What are the key parallels between Daniel and a school district CEO or principal?

 CASE 2

Enlivening "LEARNing"

Richard Ray was deep in thought and engulfed in melancholy on a beautiful late-November afternoon, pondering what to do next. Thanksgiving break was the next week, but it seemed as if the break could not come soon enough. Richard was the principal for a newly opened public school. The school was in its second year and had sixty-seven fifth-grade students and fifty-nine sixth-grade students. The school was part of a national network of highly visible schools that had a presence nationwide called LEARN (Leading Education Achievements 'Round the Nation). LEARN was a public school network for the elementary, middle, junior high, and high school levels. LEARN schools were located in inner cities and designed to enroll students that were failing in the public school system. The LEARN network was the brainchild of a nationally prominent education-school dean who had made a big name for himself by writing books and appearing on television. He was a smart man, but Richard wished he were around more frequently to actually help him solve problems instead of pontificating about education reform.

Richard had just received word from two of his six teachers that they would be leaving the school at the end of the semester. With an exceptionally tight budget and strict network school guidelines as outlined by LEARN, Richard wondered how he would be able to replace these two teachers and, more importantly, stop the worrisome attrition that the school had experienced in its brief history.

As Richard was pondering these challenges, he reflected back on his career and the path that had led to his involvement in the LEARN program. Richard was an educator at heart. He had always known that he wanted to be a teacher and, having grown up in the Midwest, placed a high degree of value on a solid education. After graduating from Central High School, Richard attended Midwest University and majored in secondary education. Because of a state scholarship that Richard received while attending Midwest University, he had a four-year teaching commitment, which he fulfilled at East High School, located in a large inner city.

Richard truly enjoyed his teaching at East High School and developed a real love for helping underprivileged teens reach their potential. He found he was particularly successful at helping refocus students on school with a goal of attending college. By spending extensive time after school with children and challenging them with academic problems, Richard genuinely inspired and personally assisted many students in realizing their goal of attending the college or university of their choice. Richard found it particularly gratifying to see these students reach significant milestones in their lives.

Despite his success at sending students from the inner city to college, Richard became extremely frustrated with his school system and disheartened that he was not able to spend more time with more students. He was also disappointed that there was not an official program to motivate more students to attend college. As a result of his tremendous success, Richard proposed a new curriculum to the principal. The proposal drew on his personal experiences and theories of challenging the students and lengthening the school day. He felt this would keep the students out of trouble and provide them with the extra time and energy to mature academically. He also felt that increased discipline and dedication to education was what had made the difference for those who successfully made it to the collegiate level.

The principal of East High School did not see the same benefits in the proposed curriculum as Richard did and dismissed the idea with little discussion. However, the more Richard thought through his curriculum, the more persuasive he found its unique way of influencing the lives of these high school students and helping them reach their goals of attending the university of their choice. Richard took his ideas on the road to see if other principals in the district would concur. To Richard's dismay, no one was interested or would even take note. Feeling like his reputation was tainted in the local school district, Richard decided he needed a fresh start. As a result, he relocated his family to Bayou Bay, where he took a job at a public middle school in the north part of the city in a southern state.

The education system was generally not as strong in the South as compared to where he had grown up in the Midwest, and Richard was invigorated by the challenge of changing the system. Teaching middle school ended up becoming a very beneficial experience for Richard. Although he enjoyed the maturity that high school students had in learning, Richard fell in love with teaching middle school. He felt that this was the critical time really to help students begin to value education and form habits that could actually get them to college. Although he was not able to send his students directly to college, he felt he could more successfully reach and affect them. After teaching at the middle school for five years, Richard decided to see if the curriculum ideas he had developed earlier would be more welcome in the South by testing them in the Bayou Bay public school system.

Again, to Richard's disappointment, the proposal was not thought of favorably and was disregarded without much thought. However, in the process of discussing his idea with another teacher, Bill Mitchell, Richard found a quick friend and ally. Bill had discovered the national program called LEARN. He had always wanted to start a LEARN school in east Bayou Bay but lacked the courage to go out on his own, not feeling quite confident in his own abilities. Upon hearing about the program, Richard was energized to know that others across the nation had had the same experiences he had and had put together a proven curriculum very similar to his own. Together, Richard and Bill decided that they could successfully start a LEARN network school in east Bayou Bay for middle school–age children. Richard and Bill quickly contacted the LEARN organization and began negotiating with the Bayou Bay public school system for support.

Richard and Bill spent a lot of time trying to figure out exactly how to make the LEARN program work in east Bayou Bay. The first step was getting students. There was limited time to get the word out before the new school year began, so in early May, Richard and Bill started knocking on doors in east Bayou Bay neighborhoods to find students who were "educationally underprivileged" and who were willing to make the sacrifices and commitments for the LEARN curriculum. To find fifty-nine students, Richard and Bill knocked on close to 1,000 doors. After looking over the students they had recruited for the first year, they noticed that the student-body demographics included 75 percent black, 15 percent Hispanic, and 10 percent white. Eighty-five percent of the students qualified for free or reduced lunch. The student body was also spread over a seventeen-mile radius from the school, which had the potential to cause major transportation issues for the parents and ultimately for LEARN Bayou Bay.

The time investment required of Richard and Bill to get LEARN Bayou Bay off the ground averaged out to nearly sixteen hours a day, six days a week, for the months of April through August. Heated negotiations were required with the Bayou Bay public school system to receive permission and find an "adequate" building for the middle school. Richard and Bill did the best they could to establish a strong relationship with Bayou Bay Public Schools' central office and felt they made progress over the months, despite the slow movement to resolution on the building issue. However, after months of bargaining, a dilapidated building that had not been used since the mid-1990s was set aside and became the future home of LEARN Bayou Bay.

After the building was secured and students recruited, the next step was getting the right teachers. Bill and Richard figured that if they could split time filling one teacher's role, they could get by with hiring only two other teachers. Close to seventy-five applications came in, and Richard and Bill then began the tedious process of interviewing each candidate to make sure they found the two very best teachers to take care of the fifty-nine fifth-grade students they had enrolled. After several rounds of interviews, two teachers were selected: Dan Harmon and Casey Houston. Both were highly energetic, in their mid-twenties, and experienced in teaching at inner-city public schools. Richard and Bill were confident they had a solid team in place for the upcoming school year.

The school year kicked off with significant amounts of excitement, anticipation, and anxiety. The long-term viability of LEARN Bayou Bay was a question definitely still in the air. The first year had begun, but the school was squeaking by with just barely enough resources. The first year for LEARN Bayou Bay was indeed a successful one, although not without a lot of hard work. The building they obtained from Bayou Bay Public Schools was in bad repair and often caused problems that forced the entire school to be flexible as workers came in to make repairs. The relationship with Bayou Bay Public Schools grew stronger, and Richard and Bill were more confident than ever in the backing they were receiving from the public school system. In the end, ultimate success was determined when the State Comprehensive Assessment

Program scores came back very high—15 percent higher than the fifth-grade average for the school district. It made all the hard work put into the first year worth it, despite the roller-coaster ride.

Midway through the first year, Richard and Bill had found it extremely difficult to share a teacher's spot and do all the other necessary things, such as fund-raising, that were of equal importance to the school's long-term vitality. As a result, they decided that Bill would take on the role of business manager and would step out of teaching completely to secure necessary operating funds and focus on school strategy. Bill found a fair amount of success, getting donations from companies like The Building Store, which agreed to donate items or supplies to "spruce up" the school. Bill also sought out longer-term partnerships with other corporations. Richard became the principal and ran the day-to-day affairs of the school and essentially took on a full teaching load. Both Bill and Richard devoted twelve to fourteen hours a day over the course of the year in their efforts to get the school off the ground. Although they enjoyed their work immensely, both men struggled to find balance in their lives and often felt as if they were neglecting their families. Bill had about a forty-five-minute commute to the school, which only added to the long days away from his family.

Dan and Casey both excelled in the classroom and loved their LEARN Bayou Bay experience. Richard and Bill were extremely pleased with their hires and Dan's and Casey's phenomenal dedication to LEARN Bayou Bay. While Dan and Casey both loved their LEARN Bayou Bay experience, both teachers struggled with different elements of the program. Dan had no problem putting in a full day and found his time with the students to be tremendously rewarding. He even looked forward to the calls at night from the students regarding homework questions. However, Dan struggled to accept the need for Saturday school. Dan was married with no kids, and he and his wife loved to travel as much as possible. Casey did not mind working on Saturdays, but she dreaded the evening calls that she would get from her students each night. Although she adored each student, Casey felt as if she could mentally never get away from school. She was physically at the school until 5 p.m. each day, and then available by phone until 8 p.m. (although calls always seemed to trickle in until 9). Casey liked to hang out with her friends at night and found it particularly difficult to help students with their homework when she was on a date with her boyfriend. Despite their issues with the LEARN program, Dan and Casey said nothing to either Richard or Bill, feeling it was something that they would just get used to as time went on.

Although LEARN Bayou Bay was far from being "out of the woods" in terms of long-term survival, things looked especially positive as the first school year ended. Bill had secured some more one-time donations from local companies and had even negotiated with the Bayou Bay public school district to share two transportation routes that would expand the reach of the school. As a result, enrollment for the new class of fifth-graders went up to sixty-seven students. Word of mouth had spread in the local community, and due to the publicity and solid test scores students received in the first year, little effort was necessary to recruit the second LEARN Bayou Bay class. Along with the increase in students came the need to staff the school with more teachers. A new cadre of teachers was brought in that Richard and Bill were confident would match or exceed the level of achievement established by Dan and Casey.

It was just at that moment, when things looked the brightest, that things began to spiral out of control. It started when Bill approached Richard in early August right before the national LEARN conference. Bill informed Richard that although he was enthralled by the work they were doing together, he could not continue onward in his current capacity. Things happening at home in his personal life, specifically his relationship with his wife, had taken a backseat for more than a year to LEARN Bayou Bay. Bill had simply burned out and had neglected other parts of his life for an overdue amount of time. Bill agreed to stay with the school until the school year started in late August. Richard was taken aback. LEARN Bayou Bay was something both Richard and Bill were so passionate about and had worked so hard to achieve. Richard completely understood Bill's rationale for leaving LEARN but struggled with emotions of frustration and loneliness as he realized that he was now the only one in charge. He felt nauseous as he contemplated the implications of running LEARN all by himself. Richard also struggled with the guilt of not being a good husband and parent, as he was usually gone before his kids woke up and came home minutes before they went to bed.

The second school year kicked off more easily than expected, especially considering Bill's recent exit. The students were performing well, and the sixth-grade class was doing a superb job of training the new fifth-grade class to the rules and the LEARN program. There were still issues to deal with, as the four new teachers were still learning the ropes and getting used to the LEARN Bayou Bay program. Bayou Bay Public Schools also backed out of their agreement to share transportation routes with LEARN Bayou Bay, which caused Richard to scramble to find buses they could lease to provide ways for the kids to get to school. The teachers took turns running the morning and evening routes, which added one more burden onto an already-overworked staff. However, Richard felt comfortable stepping out of the classroom a bit more and felt that he was doing a better job of being principal now, although he still spent a significant amount of time in the classroom.

All indications seemed to be pointing to the fact that LEARN Bayou Bay was in good shape, had recovered from an indefinite beginning, and was well into another successful year. Then, in the matter of a week, Richard's two most experienced teachers, Dan and Casey, each turned in their letter of resignation, without knowledge of the other's resignation. Both were feeling overworked and unbalanced in their work and home lives. Dan needed his weekends, and Casey needed her evenings. Neither had any idea that the other had resigned until Richard pulled them both into his office late on a November afternoon. Feeling puzzled about the timing and their reasoning for leaving LEARN Bayou Bay, Richard began to probe. Both Dan and Casey were open and candid about their reasons for leaving. Neither planned on getting another teaching job. Dan's friends had convinced him to give an "office job" a try, and Casey had recently gotten engaged and decided that she wanted to start a family.

As Richard sat pondering the events that had just transpired, Thanksgiving break could not come soon enough. He dreaded the thought of announcing Dan's and Casey's resignations to the other teachers after the Thanksgiving holiday and quickly put it out of his mind. He continued thinking. In LEARN Bayou Bay's short eighteen-month existence, three of the original four employees had left, so the school had an overall attrition rate of nearly 38 percent. Richard was torn as to the real causes of attrition and wondered what he could do about it. If he was going to make LEARN Bayou Bay a viable educational solution for the educationally under-privileged in the Bayou Bay area, Richard knew he had to solve his staffing and teacher attrition issues. He quickly got on the Internet to do some basic research on national teacher attrition so that he could better understand what was happening to the industry as a whole. Richard found the results below:

State	Total Number of Teachers*	Teachers Leaving the Profession**	Cost Related to Teachers Who Leave the Profession***	Teachers Transferring to Other Schools**	Cost Related to Teachers Who Transfer to Other Schools**	Total Teacher Turnover Cost (Not Including Retirements)
SC	43,723	2,822	$ 30,551,316	4,067	$ 44,026,758	$ 74,578,074
SD	11,538	611	$ 5,328,932	868	$ 7,569,478	$ 12,898,410
TN	58,275	2,971	$ 32,378,057	5,090	$ 55,472,856	$ 87,850,913
TX	266,661	19,034	$214,509,448	25,768	$290,407,937	$504,917,385
UT	23,346	1,736	$ 18,203,284	1,426	$ 14,944,657	$ 33,147,941

Source: Alliance for Excellent Education, Issue Brief, August 2005, *Teacher Attrition: A Costly Loss to the Nation and to the States,* Washington, DC.

*U.S. Department of Education, National Center for Education Statistics Schools and Staffing Survey, 1999–2000 ("Public School Teacher Questionnaire," "Private School Teacher Questionnaire," and "Public Charter School Teacher Questionnaire") and 2000–1 Teacher Follow-up Survey ("Questionnaire for Current Teachers" and "Questionnaire for Former Teachers," Table 1.01), Washington, DC.

**State estimations are based on analysis by Richard Ingersoll, professor of education and sociology, University of Pennsylvania, from the National Center for Education Statistics Schools and Staffing Survey and therefore include a slight margin of error. Additional data available at www.gse.upenn.edu/faculty_research/Shortage-RMI-09-2003.pdf.

***The Department of Labor conservatively estimates that attrition costs an employer 30 percent of the leaving employee's salary. Teacher salary data were taken from the National Education Association's Estimates of School Statistics, 1969–70 through 2002–3, and prepared August 2003. Available online at http://nces.ed.gov/programs /digest/d03/tables/dt078.asp.

He quickly learned that teacher attrition had a significant financial impact and learned some interesting statistics about national attrition in the teaching industry, such as:

- The rate of attrition is roughly 50 percent higher in poor schools than in wealthier ones[1].
- Teachers new to the profession are far more likely to leave than are their more experienced counterparts[2].

• Nearly half of all teachers who enter the field leave it within a mere five years, and the best and brightest teachers are often the first to leave[3].

While Richard found the financial costs of teacher attrition relevant and interesting, the last point caught his attention most. After reviewing this statistic even more, he quickly realized that both Dan and Casey, being in their mid-twenties, were part of the national statistical group that was leaving teaching after five or fewer years of teaching. Richard instantly questioned whether or not compensation had anything to do with many of the nation's best and brightest teachers' leaving the profession so quickly. Like everyone else, Richard had always known that teaching was a low-paying profession as a whole, and he felt strongly that most teachers chose their profession for other reasons than pay. Some more quick research on the Internet helped him to find out what state averages were for teachers.

2002–2003 K–12 Salary Allocation Table for Certificated Instructional Staff

Years of Service	BA+0	BA+15	BA+30	BA+45	BA+90	BA+135	MA+0	MA+45	MA+90 or PhD
0	28,300	29,064	29,856	30,649	33,196	34,836	33,929	36,476	38,118
1	28,680	29,455	30,257	31,086	33,659	35,291	34,306	36,879	38,510
2	29,327	30,117	30,936	31,837	34,428	36,093	35,025	37,616	39,280
3	30,293	31,107	31,950	32,899	35,536	37,274	36,089	38,725	40,464
4	30,975	31,833	32,690	33,681	36,360	38,129	36,840	39,519	41,288
5	31,682	32,553	33,427	34,483	37,179	39,001	37,610	40,307	42,129
6	32,091	32,943	33,847	34,956	37,639	39,470	38,023	40,706	42,537
7	33,139	34,012	34,937	36,118	38,868	40,769	39,185	41,934	43,836
8	34,202	35,122	36,069	37,348	40,135	42,106	40,414	43,202	45,172
9		36,272	37,266	38,591	41,443	43,481	41,656	44,510	46,548
10			38,477	39,898	42,788	44,894	42,964	45,855	47,960
11				41,243	44,196	46,344	44,309	47,263	49,410
12				42,545	45,642	47,854	45,707	48,708	50,921
13					47,123	49,401	47,154	50,189	52,467
14					48,611	51,006	48,644	51,775	54,073
15					49,876	52,333	49,908	53,121	55,479
16 or more					50,873	53,379	50,906	54,183	56,588

Source: Washington State Professional Educator Standards Board, Olympia, WA, www.leg.wa.gov/legislature.
Note: Column heads represent degrees earned and graduate course hours accumulated.

However, after spending time reviewing the data gathered in his quick re-search, Richard determined that there was more to the national problem, and in particular his problem, than just pay (although he figured total compensation ulti-mately plays into the equation at some point). Thinking back to his conversation earlier that afternoon with Dan and Casey, Richard tried to think about what he could have done differently to have made their teaching experience better. Here were two of the best and brightest teachers Bayou Bay had, and both were leaving the teaching profession. Richard acknowledged that the national LEARN curriculum was demanding of its teachers and required a lot of dedication. However, during the hiring process it seemed that Dan and Casey would make teaching their career. What had changed during the course of their LEARN Bayou Bay experience? Richard decided to take his research one step further. He contacted the national LEARN office in Libertyville, Pennsylvania, in order to get national attrition numbers for LEARN. To Richard's surprise, he learned that nationally LEARN had a teacher attrition rate of just over 33 percent. While this made him feel better about his own high attrition rate, Richard quickly realized that although LEARN's nationally acclaimed curriculum was getting the results in the classroom with students, a lot of refinement was needed quickly. With an overall declining teacher workforce, if LEARN schools were to be staffed properly in future years with the types of teachers that the LEARN program needed to make it successful, something would have to change.

General Discussion Questions

1. Are network or charter schools effective? Are they a sustainable model for education long term? Why or why not?
2. Why would network or charter schools and public school systems have a hard time getting along?
3. Should the Bayou Bay public school system do more to support LEARN Bayou Bay? If so, what could the public school system do to make the charter school more successful?

Discussion Questions Focused on Teacher Attrition

1. What do you think Richard should do to address the retention issues at LEARN?
2. Do you think teacher attrition is higher than or different from that of other labor-intensive professions, such as nursing? Does attrition always cost a school or school district something? Could it be that some level of attrition is actually advantageous for a school or district?
3. How does traditional education look at teachers' schedules? Do new methods/paradigms regarding education need to look at new ways to schedule teachers? What schedules would be most beneficial to students?
4. With limited resources, how can you keep the energy teachers bring but allow them more balance in their lives to prevent burnout? How can Richard decrease the rate of burnout among his teachers and staff?
5. How can the principal create continuity in the school/classroom with teachers lasting two to five years on average? Why do teachers leave teaching for other careers?
6. Given the overwhelming success of the LEARN program nationally, how can LEARN Bayou Bay keep the rigor and prestige of the national program but reduce its teacher attrition?

7. How can the education system better mirror the trend corporate America has set in terms of offering a variety of flex schedules to meet the needs of its workforce? What are practical ways of incorporating these principles into education? How can the school better accommodate teachers who would like to have families but would also like to teach?

8. What role, if any, does compensation play in teacher attrition? in teacher burnout?

Source: Adapted from Knowledge Is Power program Web site: www.kipp.org.

Notes

1. National Commission on Teaching and America's Future (2003).

2. Ingersoll, R. (2003). *Is there really a teacher shortage?* Consortium for Policy Research in Education, University of Pennsylvania. "Beginning teachers (under five years) leaving at a rate that outpaces experienced teachers is a long-noted phenomenon, with most research upholding that teaching has always had a higher rate of attrition among newcomers." Study available online at www.gse.upenn.edu/faculty_research/ShortageRMI-09-2003.pdf.

3. Henke, R. R., Chen, X., & Geis, S. (2000). *Progress through the teacher pipeline: 1992–93 college graduate and elementary/secondary school teaching as of 1997*. Statistical analysis report. National Center for Education Statistics, Washington, DC, 10.

CHAPTER ONE

The Evolving Context of Leadership

What Strategic Leadership Is and Why It Is Needed Now

LEARNING OBJECTIVES

By the end of this chapter, you should be able to

- understand the evolving global context of twenty-first-century society and its consequences for education;
- identify forces shaping, including those opposing, the new globalism;
- define strategic leadership, and explain what it is not.

INTRODUCTORY CASE

Excellence Is Seemingly No Longer Sufficient: A True Case of How "Times They Are a-Changing"

Harold Halley (not his real name) was a principal in a semi-rural South Carolina high school. His school had 1,500 students in grades 9 through 12. Harold had been the principal for three years. Prior to that, he had been a successful high school chemistry teacher in another district and an assistant principal in his current district. As a youth he had been a good, if not outstanding, student and an unusually strong high school athlete for whom much was expected, perhaps even an NBA contract. A damaging knee injury in his junior year of college foreclosed professional stardom, and Harold eventually turned his attention to identifying a career in science and preparing to be a teacher.

Harold was 6'2", well muscled, and almost movie-star handsome. He took good care of himself physically. He exercised early every morning in the high school weight room, and he jogged two to three miles each day. He still could play pickup ball in the gym with his high school students, and they could see just how good he must have been in his youth. They admired him professionally, liked him personally, and easily took him as a role model.

His superintendent, his teachers, parents, community leaders, and others also liked Harold. His personal poise, proud bearing, good taste in clothes, personal openness, and articulate manner infused confidence in others. He also had acquired a reputation for being a good listener and for not being one to offer outrageous opinions in matters about which he was uninformed.

In the three years that Harold had been a principal, he was widely perceived as successful. He had inherited what was generally accorded to be a beautiful physical plant with a totally dysfunctional culture. Student discipline was borderline criminal. The school's faculty was discouraged, and high teacher turnover was a huge problem. Academic achievement was below the radar screen, and parents played every game known in the Western world to keep their children from being assigned to that school. Harold inherited a school of last choice for students whose parents could not afford to live elsewhere or who did not know how to manipulate the system to gain admission for their children elsewhere.

Now the school was clean, teachers were eager to work for Harold, parents increasingly were seeing that the school no longer deserved its past poor reputation, and mean test scores on the Palmetto Academic Competency Test were inching their way up.

Imagine Harold's surprise the day he was summoned to the central office for an unscheduled talk with the new superintendent. Whereas he walked in expecting to be congratulated for his past accomplishments, he was knocked off his feet by her torrent of criticism. She acknowledged all that he had done to turn the school around, but she made it clear that the school, under his leadership, had to achieve far higher standards of student performance if he was to remain as principal.

The superintendent was armed with table after chart after graph after report regarding student achievement in his school. Whereas he had previously been satisfied to trumpet the gains in mean test scores, he was now bombarded with finely tuned evidence of failure for students below the mean. He had been patting himself on the back for creating a productive culture. Now, the superintendent was criticizing him for not elevating the achievement of those below the mean, mostly students of color and from low-income families.

Harold found himself shell-shocked. He had done all he knew to do, and he had done it right. His was a textbook case for turning a school around. He had expected to be celebrated, not criticized. He left her office crestfallen at first, and then, as he drove home, he became angrier and angrier. How dare she diminish what he had done? He had devoted every fiber of himself to taking a terrible school and turning it into a desirable place for student learning. Who was she, and how could she be so arrogant? He was at once hurt, angry, disappointed, dumbfounded, and at a loss to know what to do next. In fact, he went home, not back to his school.

The next day, he phoned the superintendent and asked to talk with her again. She quickly altered her schedule to meet with him. He walked in, expressed his shocked reaction to her statements and attitude of the prior day, and asked what in the world was behind her vastly elevated expectations for his school. Had he not done a good job? Why did she now want so much more? He asked if she would like him to resign.

His superintendent was patient and did not flare defensively. Rather, she explained that the state now was operating under the far higher achievement mandates embedded in the recently enacted No Child Left Behind federal legislation. She went further to explain that the state's new testing program offered far more finely grained student achievement analyses than were ever before possible.

She sympathized with his posture and said she did not want him to resign. She explained that in her view he was a good principal. However, what he now had to realize was that what was once good enough was no longer sufficient. American education generally, and right down to his school and to his teachers' classrooms particularly, was now being held to a far higher standard, and the new world of American education was about performance, not processes.

It has never been easy to be a leader in American education. Being a school principal, a district superintendent, a central office administrator, a teacher organization executive, or a private or independent school head—or holding any number of other responsible roles in the nation's schooling spectrum—has always involved meeting multiple expectations and being accountable to multiple constituencies. Often, expectations from varying client groups are in conflict. Satisfying one set of constituents may mean alienating or at least disappointing another set. Indeed, satisfying some expectations may even be impossible because of a lack of resources or authority.

Time to Reflect

- Based on your prior experiences, to what degree can you relate to the situation between the superintendent and Harold?
- Should the superintendent have been more encouraging in their first meeting? Why or why not?
- In what important ways is Harold's superintendent encouraging him to become a more strategic education leader?
- What if Harold had not requested the second meeting? What might have been the result?
- In what ways have you struggled to meet the shifting expectations of your key education constituents?

What has happened in Harold Halley's world? What are the emerging conditions that impel leaders such as Harold to alter their conventional behavior and begin, more than ever, to pay attention to both external societal conditions and internal organizational dynamics? The simple, single-word answer to this rhetorical question is *globalization*.

Globalization is a central feature of this chapter, and this book, because the new worldwide interdependence and its accompanying economic and social imperatives likely make up a significant change in the trajectory of human history. Prior shifts include the movement from hunting and gathering to agriculture and domestication of animals, the transformation from a rural and agricultural society to an urban and manufacturing way of life, and then the more recent shift from manufacturing to an electronic-, entertainment-, and service-oriented economy. What happens now in faraway places matters more to local settings than ever before in the history of the world. This is true of climate, economics, technology, politics, education, and peace.

In an earlier time, a principal could succeed by merely keeping his or her eye on the day-to-day operation of the school. Running a good ship was what was expected, as evidenced by Harold's frustrations above. In today's world, a leader needs split vision. One can no longer survive or succeed by simply focusing on what is occurring internally and immediately. External and extended events, be they local, state, national, or international, can have remarkable consequences for an education organization.

The following questions illustrate important issues that routinely confront education leaders. These questions call for strategic responses.

- How does one lead a successful or high-performing modern-day educational organization?
- How does a leader cope with a constantly shifting set of performance expectations?
- What do you do when public preferences are at odds with professional practices or personal precepts?
- What are proper roles for administrators with respect to policy-setting bodies, such as boards of directors?
- What are the most important decisions on which a leader should concentrate?
- How can an organization ensure that it is pursuing its mission effectively, satisfying its clients' expectations, and meeting its obligations to the general public?
- Given the political complexity engulfing American education, including federal, state and local regulations, how can a leader exercise initiative?

Education leaders, anyone aspiring to become one, or those responsible for preparing them, should constantly be mindful of questions such as these. Of course, for many of these kinds of inquiries there are no enduring answers. Societal conditions change, public purposes vary, and private interests evolve. New technologies emerge, resources ebb and flow, and political alignments shift.

Modern leaders can safely assume only two conditions. One, they will almost always have to operate within the context of an organization or within a set of rules established or heavily shaped by another agency. Second, change appears to be the only contemporary condition that is constant, and thus, organizations and their leaders must continually adapt.

Nevertheless, even if it is unrealistic to expect the rules of organizational operation to be unchanging, there are enduring leadership principles that can be applied and that usefully transfer across many different kinds of education organizations. For that matter, many of these principles, and day-to-day practices logically associated with them, also apply to groups, agencies, and institutions beyond schools and colleges. However, leadership within education organizations is the topic of concern in this book, and that is where the spotlight will remain.

■ LOOKING BACK: A HISTORICAL NOTE

Being an effective leader has probably never been easy, but it certainly has not become easier over time. In earlier historic periods leadership more frequently depended upon individual actions and interactions between individuals. However, at least since World War II, effective leadership has relied less upon isolated individual initiative and more upon the ability of a leader to mobilize and direct organizational activities. The last half of the twentieth century marked a transition to the modern-era pattern of large, complicated, multilayered organizations. Big companies, big government, big universities, big school systems, big conglomerates, big multinational corporations, big bureaucracies, and seemingly big everything dominate our work lives and influence what we eat, wear, watch on TV, read, and possibly, what we think.

Once upon a time, or at least once upon a simpler, less complicated, and less interdependent time, one could lead an organization through individual intelligence and personal force of will. Leaders often could exercise command simply because they held the status of a leader; they had been designated, usually by an outside authority, as the leader. In recent times, the end of the twentieth century, this changed. Democracy is a major, though not always dominant, understanding throughout most of the world. Increasingly, a leader is an individual who can sense and manifest hopes and feelings of followers.

Today, one leads not only with time-tested traditional traits, but also by understanding complexities of organizational dynamics and gaining the confidence of others, both subordinates within the organization and influentials outside the organization, in seeking a shared **goal**.

Two individuals well known from history represent models of modern **strategic leadership**. While vastly different in background, temperament, style, and personal tastes, each crafted a crucially needed long-range vision and had a personal capacity to persuade others that the vision was the right one for the time and worthy of being pursued.

General Dwight David Eisenhower, the Supreme Allied Commander in Europe for the planning of the D-Day Normandy invasion, was a great general and a great leader not simply because he had been named the leader by President Roosevelt or because he was powerful physically, had a commanding personal presence or a loud voice, was a brilliant tactician, or could shoot accurately in battle. He was an effective leader because he could weave a determined course through complicated bureaucratic interstices of government, military organizations, armament manufacturers, and private sector suppliers and simultaneously maintain effective diplomatic relationships with the U.S., English, Soviet, Canadian, and French exile governments.

In accomplishing his goals, effecting a successful surprise landing of hundreds of thousands of soldiers from several nations, off-loading hundreds of thousands of tons of equipment, and establishing a second battlefront in Europe, Dwight Eisenhower was the prototype of today's successful strategic leader. He was an "organization man." He had to determine both what to do and how to do it.

England's World War II leader, Eisenhower's colleague for strategic planning purposes, offers an interesting comparison. Winston Churchill was brilliant by virtually any appraisal and when seen from virtually any angle. With few resources other than his knowledge of history, global perspective, and awesome command of the English language, he was able to inspire his fellow citizens and sustain their hopes in the darkest hours of the war, before the United States entered the fray against the Axis powers. Certainly he had to render numerous tactical decisions, select subordinates, and undertake a host of actions befalling conventional leaders. However, his leadership anticipated the twenty-first century.

To be a successful leader in the twenty-first century, it will be necessary to be an "organizational person," a superb motivator of others, and more. The "more" involves constantly surveying a rapidly changing external world, interpreting the consequences of changes for one's organization, and mobilizing the will of followers to pursue agreed-upon ends. Technical understanding of an organization's tasks, as crucial as such is and will continue to be, will not likely suffice by itself for the future. An effective leader will also have to be a strategic leader, exhibiting traits of both Eisenhower and Churchill—combining vision, analysis, technical knowledge, and action, and usually doing so in a complicated, multilayered organizational setting.

Leadership's Contemporary Societal Context: Illustrating Unceasing Change

A Tale of Modern Service. The November 1, 2002, *Wall Street Journal* contained an article describing efforts of two reporters who strove to travel 2,500 miles via airplane from Los Angeles to Washington, DC, without benefit of human service intervention. Online ticket purchases, automated baggage check-in, electronic package scanning, explosive-detection machines, video surveillance, agentless boarding-pass kiosks, online rental car reservations and vehicle assignment, and automated hotel reservation and room registration almost fulfilled their quest. They were foiled only at a rental-car parking lot exit gate when an optical scanner failed and an actual agent intervened. Otherwise, from the time they departed their Los Angeles garage with their infrared door-closing device until they used their plasticized hotel-room entry key in Washington, DC, they experienced no human contact for reasons of service or information.

A Tale of Modern Business. "Big Box" retailers (discount stores operating in warehouses, such as Wal-Mart, Target, Costco, and Toys R Us) account for approximately one out of every five retail sales dollars in America. Indeed, it is estimated that 40 percent of American women between 18 and 70 shop at Wal-Mart at least once a week.

Their gigantic sales volume provides Big Box retailers with enormous leverage with suppliers. Modern electronic inventory systems, linked to point-of-sale checkout register data, enable retailers to order and replace inventory only when they need it. In fact, with just-in-time delivery strategies, retailers are forcing suppliers to bear carrying costs and sales risks of inventory. Now most goods are not credited to a producer until they are sold over the retail counter. Even when they are on the shelf, a retailer may not have accepted formal financial delivery from a wholesaler or producer. Until they are sold, the goods are still owned by and are the financial responsibility of suppliers. Strong-armed accounting procedures, such as "damage discounts," often confront suppliers with the unanticipated choice of losing a huge customer or even lower profit margins for themselves.

A Tale of Modern Medicine. Whirr, glide, clunk, glide, whirr, plop. This is an automated pharmacy in operation in Los Angeles. It is filling prescriptions faster, more accurately, and at far less cost, even after having paid off its $250,000 purchase price, than can human pharmacists. In addition, it contributes to inventory information, controlled substance security, patient billing, and insurance regulation. A supervisor oversees the machine. There is no pharmacist present.

One floor above the automated pharmacy, a robotic surgery is about to begin. Here an orderly is precisely placing a patient under the electric "scalpel and suturing machine's" three-dimensional grid coordinates. A trained technician is overseeing testing of the remote cameras and computerized surgery controls. A nurse-anesthetist is present and monitoring the patient. The surgeon, wearing his virtual sight-magnifying goggles, is sitting at the robot's computerized controls, 2,000 miles away in Nashville. The surgeon has never seen the patient in person. He did talk with her yesterday on a videophone.

What Is Going On Here? These examples are from modern transportation, retailing, and health care. One just as easily could have described Internet banking; remote-control military attack vehicles, ships and aircraft; online university degree programs; electronic monitoring of indicted criminals; online book sales, catalog ordering, antiques auctions; Internet church attendance, etc.

Modern economic imperatives represent an advanced stage of a global transition from a manufacturing and trade era to a technological information–based economy. This change has come to be labeled *postindustrialism*. This transition is similar to other historic paradigm shifts in its dislocating effects on human interaction.

In each prior societal transition, humans' material well-being improved. Farmers led more settled, safe, and comfortable lives than hunters. Manufacturing employees eventually came to live more comfortably than farmers. Knowledge workers are already coming to live more commodiously than manually engaged assembly-line workers.

Transition from one economic paradigm to another triggers alterations in social interactions. Humans become subject to new roles. Hunting and gathering tribes forewent constant travel and wandering for the disciplined stability of raising crops and domesticating animals. An agricultural economy contributed to permanent shelter and predictable food supplies. These, in turn, led to expanded communal life and collective stability. Differing work and survival skills and knowledge bases contributed to different status hierarchies and patterns of human interaction. Still, interpersonal behavior and ethical conduct were regulated principally by perceptions of reciprocal dependence.

In none of the foregoing modern-technology illustrations pertaining to travel, retailing, or medicine is a customer, patient, or client particularly harmed. On some dimensions, they may be better off. The airline ticket and rental car rate may have been less expensive because of the automation involved in moving travelers across the country. Big Box retailer prices are certainly low. The surgery patient may otherwise not have had access to the level of medical expertise and operating-room precision that a remote cutting-and-sewing surgical surrogate rendered possible.

There may not have been a net displacement of employment. It is possible that the design, manufacturing, and maintenance of the systems and machines involved in delivering such modern services may necessitate a workforce that matches or exceeds replaced employees. Once we somehow account for the anxiety and distress of displaced travel agents and airline ticket counter employees, supplier sales agents and brokers, and pharmacists and nurses, labor-force supply and demand may be in equilibrium. Other, and almost assuredly more skilled, positions are typically created by the new technology.

Moreover, the airplane still needs a pilot, the Big Box retail store still needs a manager, and the cutting-and-sewing surgical robot still needs a guiding physician, or at least all of these skilled professionals are needed until the next round of automation enhancement and productivity gains.

So if clients and customers do not lose benefits from automation and workers do not suffer, at least when labor-force equilibrium is restored, then what is the change? The transition from manufacturing to a new technologically reinforced information era appears to have a qualitatively different consequence for education.

In a way far different than ever before in human history, the quality of an individual's material well-being, and possibly his or her personal fulfillment, is crucially linked to obtaining and continually renewing a thorough education.

Similarly, societies once flourished or foundered based on what their citizens could harvest from the ground. Today's societies survive and flourish based on what they can harvest from the minds of their citizens.

Education now matters in a way that is being felt not only throughout a household's daily life and the practical operation of the nation's overall economy, but throughout the dynamics of the policy system as well. Public officials have received the citizenry's forceful message and are striving mightily for means by which schools can be rendered more effective and more productive.

It is a transition from a time when one could have little schooling and still high wages to the condition today where insufficient schooling virtually condemns one to a lower level of material comfort and restricted opportunity for personal fulfillment. These realities have created new needs for education, and they have triggered a need for a "new" kind of education leader.

▪ EVOLVING CONTEXTUAL DETAILS

Six macro sociodemographic, economic, environmental, and political currents are dramatically altering the conditions within which educational institutions, and education leaders, must operate. These conditions render it insufficient for a leader to be a "great" individual or to be knowledgeable about technical matters or organizational dynamics alone. These conditions render a strategic approach to leadership imperative.

The primary forces altering the external context in which educators increasingly operate are global in scope. These worldwide conditions are interrelated and reciprocally reinforcing. Ironically, they are also antithetical and inconsistent. One of these sets of forces draws the world closer together. These are the centripetal conditions of international economic competitiveness, cultural globalism, and ecological interdependence. The other conditions, which exert a fragmenting force in this equation, are increasing demographic diversity, intensified ethnic and religious consciousness, and political fragmentation.

The following descriptions treat each contextual dimension separately. However, it should be understood from the outset that the six conditions are intensely intertwined and self-reinforcing. The conditions are graphically depicted in Figure 1.1 with those forces drawing the world together highlighted in gray.

1. An Internationally Competitive Economy and the Human Capital Imperative

Rapid communication, expanding information, and modern organizational arrangements are transforming national economies. They are now global in their competitive outlook, internationally interdependent, insatiable in their quest for technological innovation, and crucially dependent upon availability of human talent. Reliance on a narrow management elite appears increasingly outmoded. Modern manufacturing and service-industry techniques demand a labor force capable of adjusting to new technologies and making informed production decisions. Educated and highly skilled human intelligence is increasingly

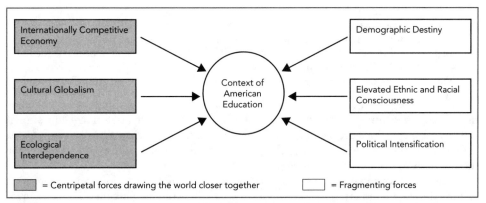

FIGURE 1.1 Six Global Forces Shaping the Context of American Education

viewed as a nation's and an organization's primary economic resource, and it is needed in large quantities.

Throughout history, technological innovations have redistributed power, enabling a tribe, a people, or a nation to vie for and gain dominance. Fire, ferrous metal, and farming are historic discoveries that transformed nations and transferred power. Modern examples include internal combustion engines, interchangeable parts, electrical energy, and electronic components. The list is longer, but the point is the same. Significant technological revolutions formerly were founded upon sporadic scientific discoveries. Increasingly, such shifts are now crucially dependent upon systematic inventions. Nations currently compete to create inventions and be the first to rush into the market with products and services based upon invention. They believe that elevating or sustaining their standard of living depends crucially upon being competitive in this regard.

Modern economies, however, are not simply boosting or gently nudging an already-initiated notion that education systems should enhance a nation's human capital resources. Rather, competitive economic forces are rapidly and intensely reshaping forms of schooling across national boundaries. This globalization of educational expectations is occurring primarily because nations no longer can easily protect their domestic producers from international economic forces. Failure to respond quickly to technological and organizational inventions can rapidly jeopardize a people's standard of living and a government's political future. Increasingly, even former Soviet Union, Eastern Bloc nations find that they are no longer immune to or can wall themselves off from the rapid ebb and flow of international trade and monetary, technological, and financial developments.

The following quotation from an *Atlantic* article on economic development crystallizes the complex, intertwined, and rapidly evolving nature of international manufacturing and services industries.

> Ford, with one third of its sales from outside the United States, owns 25 percent of Mazda. Mazda makes cars in America for Ford, Ford reciprocates by making trucks for Mazda, and the two companies trade parts. Each owns a piece of Korea's Kia Motors, which produces the Ford Festiva for export to the United States. Ford and Nissan, Japan's No. 2, swap vehicles in Australia and are planning a joint minivan program in America. Ford and Volkswagen have merged into a single company in Latin America that exports trucks to the United States.

General Motors holds a 41.6 percent stake in Isuzu, which is starting a joint venture in America with Subaru, which is partly owned by Nissan. GM also owns half of Daewoo Motors, Hyundai's major competitor in Korea. Daewoo makes Nissan cars for Japan and Pontiacs for America; soon it will be selling cars that were primarily designed by GM-Europe to Isuzu in Japan. GM has also teamed with Japan's No. 1, Toyota, to produce cars under both companies' labels in America and Australia.[1]

As convoluted as the above-encapsulated explication is, it probably captures the continued economic future for the industrialized world. Consequently, traditional educational values and institutions are being crowded by government officials who, in response to competitive economic imperatives, believe that new educational policies are necessary for their nations to become or remain vital.

Specific educational reform tactics may differ from nation to nation, depending upon historic development patterns, contemporary politics, current resource levels, and operating structures. For example, in national systems emphasizing an elitist schooling model— such as France, England, and historic members of the British Commonwealth—the clear long-run education reform goal is to expand the numbers of individuals eligible for and interested in seeking higher levels of schooling. In egalitarian-oriented systems, such as the United States, the long-run goal of education reform is to elevate achievement standards such that there are larger numbers of well-educated citizens and workers.

Regardless of the variety of national tactics, the objective of much of the industrialized world is the same. The long-run goal is to utilize educated intellect as a strategic means for a nation to gain or retain an economically competitive position in the global marketplace. The new human capital imperative does not apply simply to nations. It also will apply, perhaps painfully in some instances, to individual citizens. Failure to obtain an education may relegate an individual to a revolving chain of never-ending low-level, low-paying, unfulfilling jobs, or even sustained unemployment.

2. Cultural Globalization

It is not only that economic endeavors are now international in nature; so also is our culture. Pervasive electronic communication, inexpensive worldwide transportation, and international marketing of consumer products are shrinking the world dramatically. It is not simply that radio and television enable worldwide viewers to be informed almost firsthand about distant events. Ironically sometimes, such as in disasters like the March 2005 Indonesian earthquake and resulting tsunami, remote viewers and listeners actually may be better informed than many of those immediately on the scene who are deprived of electrical power and other resources. Rather, some far more fundamental dynamic is at work. It is not only "news" that is spreading with the speed of the electromagnetic spectrum, but also ideas, opinions, fears, and aspirations.

Ideas about what exists elsewhere, what is possible, what is right and what is wrong, and about who does what to whom are no longer easily restricted to a geographic locality or narrowly defined region. A global community is being constructed electronically, and the availability of rapid and inexpensive transportation is reinforcing this condition personally. Despotic leaders could once wall off their followers from the "dangerous" influence of outside ideas. Such a practice increasingly is now impossible. Not only is there a flourishing international market for popular consumer goods, but also citizens of one nation are ever more intensely informed regarding the beliefs, hopes, and conditions of citizens of all other nations. Their own ideas and dreams are forcefully shaped as a consequence.

Globalization has consequences for leaders. Not only must they now be attuned and responsive to the ebb and flow of forces immediately connected with constituents, but they must also be ever attentive to events and views throughout the world. Queen Anne learned of the Duke of Marlborough's August 13, 1704, victory over Louis XIV's armies at Waterloo ten days after the event. A modern nation's leader would be informed almost immediately. The new "global dynamic" means that local conditions can rapidly be transformed by distant circumstances. Teachers in Germany now know of job openings in Greece and Georgia, and parents in Oxfordshire, England, have an interest in school-site management reforms in Miami and Chicago. Worldliness and breadth of understanding no longer are simply desirable qualities. Increasingly, they are imperatives of leadership.

3. Ecological Interdependence

The fragility of the physical environment is ever more evident scientifically, ever more apparent internationally, and ever more compelling politically. Globalized economic forces are consuming awesome levels of raw materials, and sophisticated production technologies are resulting in heretofore-never-seen environmental reactions. Ozone depletion, acid rain, soil erosion, radiation leakage, pesticide saturation, rain forest destruction, hazardous waste accumulation, overfishing and overgrazing, air and water pollution, greenhouse effects, and disappearing species are no longer problems limited to a few highly industrialized nations.

Environmental problems triggered by actions of one nation can spill over national boundaries and rapidly become a danger to the citizens of many nations, perhaps the entire world. There is a paradox involved. The forces of global communication and internationalized economies exacerbate environmental problems and, simultaneously, render the world's population better informed about them. There is little choice regarding the eventual outcome. The need for environmental regulation will become a larger part of the political agenda of virtually all nations, at least the industrialized nations. The global effects of modern production and consumption will reinforce international communication and cooperation. Education systems will be expected to intensify their instruction regarding environmental issues.

4. Demographic Destiny

The United States continues to be a nation of immigrants. However, the "newest" Americans are not simply from Western Europe; they come from many other regions of the world, particularly Asia and Middle and South America. California is already a "majority" of "minorities" insofar as its schools are concerned. Other states may be slower to follow. Nevertheless, ethnic, racial, and national diversity is clearly a growing characteristic of the United States, and other industrialized societies as well.

What are the consequences of growing demographic diversity for leaders? The first response is that extreme personal views regarding cultural supremacy and any desire for insularity and isolation are outmoded, dysfunctional, and ultimately doomed. Education leaders must come not simply to accept demographic diversity, but also to enhance their professional knowledge to cope with and take advantage of it. Eventually, well-informed prospective leaders will come to understand that such diversity, appropriately appreciated and orchestrated, represents a potential wellspring of creativity and strength for their organization particularly and for the nation as a whole.

Additionally, education leaders must face the fact that added diversity may, at least initially, render it more difficult to gain consensus among stakeholders regarding goals.

In the News

Cobb County is no longer a majority-white school system, according to enrollment data released this month in the district's 2006 annual report.

Last school year, the system changed from being predominantly white to majority minority. White enrollment dipped to 49.9 percent of the 105,885 total for 2005–6. Ten years ago, 74.1 percent of Cobb's students were white.

The school system has seen a decline in white enrollment over the past 10 years, dropping from 62,726 to 52,936 by 2005–6. Overall enrollment has grown by 25 percent.

Part of that growth has been because of Hispanic enrollment, which shot up from 2,849 to 13,422. Hispanics showed the greatest gains, but black students still account for the second-largest demographic group with 31,030 students, compared with 52,936 white, 13,422 Hispanic, 4,290 Asian, 3,975 multiracial, and 232 American Indian, according to the ten-year enrollment history contained in the report.

Black enrollment jumped by 101.1 percent, from 15,425 to 31,030, quadruple the district's overall growth rate. Other highlights in the report show that 29 percent of Cobb's students are in special education (14,554) or gifted (15,653) programs.

The shift in demographics of Cobb's student population is not mirrored in the staff. Ethnic breakdown of staff shows that 78.3 percent are white, 17.6 percent are black, and 2.2 percent are Hispanic.

About 81 percent of 2006 graduates reported they planned to attend four-year colleges, and 8 percent chose two-year colleges. About 11 percent were bound for technical schools, according to the report.

By Diane Stepp, March 22, 2007, "Demographic shift evident in schools; Minorities now find they are majority," published in the *Atlanta Journal-Constitution*.

Additional effort may have to be expended in gaining agreement on a mission and aggressively attempting to build a community of shared values.

There are two other demographic trends of note. One additional trend is internal. The United States is engaged at the beginning of the twenty-first century in one of its three largest population migrations. The first was in the middle of the nineteenth century with the westward movement. The second took place during World War II with movement from the agricultural South to the war industries of the North and West. The third and current movement is a return from the north to the south. Southern state educators can expect the nation's greatest population growth in the first part of the twenty-first century.

The other demographic trend of note is external; it is the birthrate explosion in the southern hemisphere. Whereas many northern industrialized nations are experiencing birthrate and overall population declines, South American and sub-Saharan African nations are experiencing explosive rates of birth, despite the pandemic of the HIV infection. Unless the birthrate in the southern hemisphere slows dramatically, the earth is on a trajectory of doubling its current six billion inhabitants in the next quarter century. One can hardly imagine the consequences for the environment, human suffering, expansionist warfare, and political and social instability.

5. Elevated Ethnic and Racial Consciousness

Geographic locations with which Americans have had to become familiar. Somalia, Bosnia, Haiti, the Israeli West Bank and Hebron, Lebanon, Darfur, Kazakhstan, Rwanda, Iraq, North Korea, include Zimbabwe, among others. These are not simply geographic labels, either. In another era, few Americans would have recognized rebel groups such as Al Quaida, Hamas, or Hezbollah or have known of the differences between Shiite and Sunni Moslems. What were once ill-known names for exotic or remote locations now command nightly news attention and possibly the time, or even the life, of a relative or friend. When the former Soviet Union and United States each dominated a geographic and economic sphere of influence, regional strife and ethnic conflict were less apparent, and lines of international responsibility more controlled. Today there is only one superpower, the United States. Regions, nations, and localities where centuries of racial, ethnic, and religious conflict have been simmering but suppressed by Cold War–dominated tensions are now continually erupting, and the United States must determine what role to play.

This situation would be merely a foreign policy matter, and perhaps a concern for domestic versus military budget priorities, except that underlying dynamics of these global conflicts are also present in our daily domestic life. For example, consider the small-town U.S. middle school vice principal who must constantly mediate between Hmong and Hispanic students at his school, the supervisor of attendance and security of what was once a quiet middle class suburban school district who now keeps track of twenty-seven known teenage gangs representing multiple ethnic and racial factions, and the superintendent who weekly must resolve conflicts between Christian and Islamic fundamentalists. These individuals are daily wrestling with worldwide problems that manifest themselves in local public schools. These school administrators do not need to be reminded of today's enhanced sense of ethnic identification, religious righteousness, and racial conflict that characterize modern America as well as the remainder of the globe.

A major condition that separates modern America from international trouble spots listed at the beginning of this section is a two-hundred-year tradition of representative government and widely understood civil procedures for resolving citizen conflict and maintaining domestic order. As important as these notions of governance are, they are but fragile barriers that can quickly and painfully be penetrated by mass rioting and civil unrests. Moreover, whatever racial and religious tensions exist can be rubbed even more raw by the presence of economic depression, widespread disparity in living conditions, and loss of hope.

Education leaders must understand that these conditions, both global and domestic, influence their worlds. They also should realize that the broader American society will expect them to contribute to solutions for these problems.

6. Political Intensification and Politics as Entertainment

Increased efforts by policy makers to utilize education systems to enhance national economic productivity, a desire by environmentalists that schools assume a larger role in sensitizing students to the fragility of the Earth's ecology, and tradeoffs between economic development and worldwide ecological balance are drawing education ever more tightly into the realm of political debate.

What once were primarily the domains of professional educators and academics increasingly are subsumed into the realm of policy makers and government officials. Central-government specification of curricula goals, widespread use of standardized tests for measuring "productivity" of an educational system, added emphasis upon science and mathematics courses, the welding of individual higher education institutions into larger state and national systems, and efforts to link higher education more tightly to business and economic development are all trends developing throughout Western nations. These are actions generally imposed on educators by public officials. They exemplify the trend toward education policy increasingly as part of the larger political agenda. Moreover, the larger political agenda attracts an intensified audience. Network and print media now encourage a protracted presidential campaign, actually years in advance of national, state, and local elections, in order to have twenty-four-hour news about celebrity-candidates, their positions, and in many instances, their foibles.

Even before the end of the twentieth century, the insightful author Gail Sheehy anticipated the aforementioned global complexity. In the opening to her book *Character: America's Search for Leadership*, Sheehy writes:

> We live in a global electronic marketplace where money now moves faster than the human mind, where terrorism can now hold a whole nation hostage to an aggrieved group whose name we can't even pronounce, where missiles are programmed to lift off in a matter of minutes after the command is given. In a world so often electrified by the suddenness and the swiftness of change, a great burden is placed on our leaders.[2]

What are the consequences of these trends for education leaders? Should all education executives strive to become walking encyclopedias of world events, ecological and technological trends, and political power? Clearly not. However, these forces hold profound implications for the preparation and performance of future education leaders.

No longer can an education leader assume that his or her exclusive focus is upon what transpires inside, or even in the immediate community of, a school, a college, or an education system. Henceforth, what takes place inside is as likely to be a function of what occurs outside, and throughout the world, as it is likely to be a result of internal dynamics among teachers, students, and others located immediately nearby. The pace of change and the influence of the external world are forces that will increasingly play a potent role in the lives of educational leaders.

It is these forces that require that education executives adopt a mode of "strategic thinking," that they become strategic education leaders.

Education leaders should come to understand that the only constant will be change. External conditions will continue to shift in a kaleidoscopic manner. Only those leaders who anticipate change and possess sufficiently broad intellectual categories to make sense of it can reasonably expect to guide their organizations successfully through the almost-inevitable torrent of communication and the whirlpool of political and economic forces that already characterize the twenty-first century.

▮ STRATEGIC LEADERSHIP: WHAT IT IS AND WHY IT IS NOW NEEDED

What *strategic* means in this context is that a twenty-first-century leader, to cope with the complexity of globalization and to manage its local effects, must continually undertake two operations simultaneously. He or she must have split vision, at once looking outward toward the larger society and inward toward the operation of the organization itself.

There Has Always Been an "In." Organizations have their own unique purposes, internal operations, specific cultures, systems of personnel incentives, employee regulations, and overall character. This amalgam of day-to-day internal activities taking place inside an organization is responsible for its production of goods and services. It is an organization's internal character that renders it successful, efficient, profitable, productive, admired, friendly, envied, successful, or failed. This unique internal environment has material components such as its physical appearance, visual icons and logos, and aesthetic qualities. In addition, it has less palpable, but no less real, features such as the way it operates its production processes or goes about its business with clients; the manner in which its employees and clients interact; the way bosses treat subordinates; and the way in which employees interact with each other. All of these features, material and social, make up the internal environment or operational composite of every organization, including schools.

There Also Has Always Been an "Out." Additionally, organizations have external contexts, outside conditions or environments to which they must be sensitive. It is the external environment that provides resources and legitimates an organization's very existence. Almost every organizational leader is now, and long has been, aware that organizations operate within a larger social, economic, and political context. Schools have always had to be concerned with the concerns of parents, the views of a board of education or a board of directors, the presence of a county office of education, a state education department, federal courts, Congressional acts, and world events.

So What Is New? If there has always been an "in" and there has always been an "out," then what is different now? Until recently, it is an organization's internal environment to which education leaders have been advised or admonished to pay the most attention: recruiting and evaluating teachers, scheduling classes, ordering books and supplies, greeting parents, enforcing discipline, policing hallways, supervising bus pickups and drop-offs, monitoring the content of the student newspaper and the daily use of the public address system, overseeing maintenance, ensuring the timely release of grades and report cards, ensuring that there are athletic events and public theatrical productions, and planning commencements. These day-to-day operations, however pedestrian in appearance or sometimes mechanical in their expression, were once seen as the stuff of operating a school or school district.

The above list of activities and conditions, and the pages of additions that could be made to it, continues to be important. There is no effort here to belittle or diminish these activities or those who conduct or oversee them. They all continue to be important elements of shaping and operating a school or school district.

However, there is something now new. Something has happened that renders the above, or any other list of operational details, by itself insufficient for successful leaders. What is new is that the external environment now counts just as much. Today, attention to the internal environment is, by itself, no longer sufficient. A successful education leader, principal, superintendent, union leader, and so on must have the split vision to which reference was previously made. One must simultaneously operate the internal machinery of an education organization and, additionally, continually undertake the adjustments imposed on that organization by a fluid, almost ever-changing external environment.

Even tribal leaders from Paleolithic times, leaders in prehistoric hunting and gathering and agricultural eras, or leaders in modern manufacturing societies have had to be attentive to both internal and external conditions. What is new for today, in the rapidly emerging modern era of an information-driven global economy, is the frequency and significance of external influences. Throughout the initial section of this book, a reader's attention will be drawn to the pace and impact of external influences upon education. However, suffice it here to illustrate the point by listing the following conditions externally imposed upon schools and school leaders.

State learning standards, performance accountability requirements, **Adequate Yearly Progress**, highly qualified teachers, statewide testing, performance pay, supplemental educational services, value added testing, homeschooling, a renewed interest in school uniforms, the resurgence of physical education, individualized education programs, least restrictive environment, mainstreaming, and parental **choice** are illustrative of conditions, situations, and regulations to which today's education leaders must continually pay a great deal of attention. These conditions did not originate in a local school or school district and then gradually spread by word of mouth or professional proclamation across the education landscape because principals, teachers, superintendents, and union leaders thought they were good or productive practices. Rather, they have come quickly from federal legislation, court cases, state legislative actions, and more informal avenues (such as testing companies and book publishers). They are illustrative of school practices that are now commonly accepted, or at least commonly accommodated, and that have been imposed by the external environment upon individual schools, both public and private.

But not all externally influenced changes come by way of formal conditions, statutes, or regulations. The enrollment composition of a school, newly arrived Bosnians or Kurds, the prevalence of nationalistic adolescent gang activity, parent expectations for remedial or gifted courses, and the need for bilingual or English Language Learning classes are all conditions that might well be necessary for a principal, superintendent, or another education leader to confront, and they may all have been conditions that were generated overseas and that came to the schools as a consequence of world events. This combination of forces from the internal and external environments is what makes a strategic approach to school leadership imperative. Successful school leaders must rely upon a split vision, at once looking outward toward broad contextual factors and inward toward the operations of the school itself.

Modern Emphasis on Academic Achievement. Contemporary concerns for high academic achievement are the single most important consequence of rapidly evolving external forces. Up until the last quarter of the twentieth century, the United States could operate its major institutions (e.g., government, the military, academia, religion, and business) with the talents of a well-educated elite. About 10 percent of the working population was extensively schooled. The globalization that began to grow so intensely in the final quarter of the last century has changed all of that.

An American worker could once enter and remain in the middle class by holding a manufacturing job. Johnny could drop out of school, get a job, and still earn a sufficient amount on an assembly line to marry Mary and maintain the material American dream. One can seldom expect such comfortable economic circumstances today. The queue for good jobs demands a good education. Parents and citizens understand this transformation. Consequently, schools today have the heretofore-unimaginable national goal of educating

Leaders and Strategy

This book makes frequent reference to **strategy**, and hence the origins of the term are deserving of mention. The etymological roots of *strategy* stretch to classical Greece, where the original term concerned military leadership. A *stratagem* was a means for gaining the upper hand over an enemy. Often this involved an artifice or a major element of deceit. The deceptively hollow wooden horse used by Spartan soldiers to gain access to the city of Troy was a stratagem. Gaining higher or more easily defended ground, surprising an unprepared combatant, or severing an opponent's vital supply route are examples of military strategies. The Allied invasion at Normandy, France, in the summer of 1944 was a strategy to force the German army to further divide its

attention and spread its ever-withering resources so widely that the Allies could prevail.

A modern "strategic leader," someone who guides organizations, has a broader role to play than connoted by Greek or modern military parallels alone. A contemporary strategic leader is one who understands not only that change is always present, but also that the external environment of an educational institution will continually impose new challenges. A strategic leader is one who realizes that his or her organization must constantly be appraising the external world, assessing its own purposes and performance in light of those findings, and systematically altering its internal procedures accordingly.

virtually every child to a high standard. Such is an absolutely new circumstance in the history of the world. No nation of the magnitude and expanse of the United States has ever set for itself the goal of educating virtually everyone to a high standard. It is a goal that is so ambitious, it will occupy professional educators for decades as they strive to find the techniques and political support necessary to accomplish such a challenge. It is to the preparation of a leadership cadre capable of surmounting this challenge that this book is dedicated.

A strategic leader successfully blends effective internal management with the rapid recognition of and accommodation to externally imposed conditions.

▪ WHAT A STRATEGIC LEADER IS NOT

No effort is made here to pose strategic leadership as somehow different than or a substitute for some other kind of formal brand of **leadership** such as transformational, transactional, situational, and so on. All of these conventional definitions and characterizations of leadership are worthy of consideration and will be addressed in the following chapter. What is advocated here is the addition of a strategic perspective for leaders. One is not either a strategic leader or a transformational leader. One can, and probably should, be both. Strategic leadership is a frame of mind expressed through a new habit of continually scanning the external environment to distill and comprehend its consequences for the

TABLE 1.1 Contrasting Leadership Dimensions

Leadership Dimensions and Operational Orientation	20th-Century School: "Inclusivity" or "Equality" as Dominant Objectives	21st-Century School: Organizational "Effectiveness" as a Dominant Objective
1. Leadership Outlook	Incremental and tactical	Strategic
2. Dominant Organizational Consideration	Regulatory compliance	Performance enhancement
3. Administrative and Authority Structure	Centralized, hierarchical, and bureaucratically specialized	Horizontal, school centered, distributed decision discretion
4. Relations and communication with parents and students	Paternalistic and directive	Customer or client orientation
5. Service Provision	Virtual public monopoly	Mixture of public and private
6. Source of Innovation	Central authority	Operating units
7. Resource Allocation Decisions	Made centrally	Operating unit discretion
8. Accountability	Bureaucratic and procedural	Professional and outcome driven

operation of one's organization. Table 1.1 summarizes and contrasts "old" expectations of leaders with those views currently emerging from the previously described new global reality and the organizational realities that will be described in Chapter 2.

Summary

This introductory chapter provides a reader with a broad contextual understanding of the evolving global context of twenty-first-century society and discusses its consequences for education leaders. In doing so, the chapter identifies six forces shaping, including those opposing, a new globalism. These economic, environmental, and political currents are dramatically altering the conditions within which educational institutions, and education leaders, must operate. Related to an increasingly internationally competitive marketplace, education leaders are charged with the goal of elevating achievement levels for all students in order to ensure a large number of well-educated citizens and workers. Cultural globalism is making it essential for school leaders to be attuned to events and views throughout the world. Further, schools and their graduates will be expected to contribute to solutions facing society and the world. Our ecological interdependence requires that school leaders help education systems intensify their instruction and action surrounding environmental issues. Amidst a growing demographic diversity, education leaders are charged with the important task of orchestrating this potential wellspring of creativity and strength for their schools. As education increasingly occupies a prominent place within the larger political agenda, school leaders are relied upon to assess and respond to national and international conditions impacting their school community. It is these conditions that render a more strategic approach to leadership imperative. This strategic orientation to education leadership, one that combines a continual scanning of the external environment with the ability to comprehend the consequences of such for the internal operations of a school, is the focus of the next chapter.

Discussion Questions

1. A strategic approach to education leadership involves constantly surveying a changing external world, interpreting the consequences of changes for one's organization, and mobilizing the will of followers to pursue agreed-upon ends. From your professional experience in education, describe an example of a time when a leader has demonstrated the ability to do this.
2. In what ways will the twin components of strategic leadership, the continual scanning of the external environment and applying this information to the internal environment, challenge you as an education leader?
3. In what ways have you seen the trend toward globalization impact classrooms, teaching, and education leadership?
4. Choose two of the six global forces shaping the context of American education and discuss the impact that these forces have had upon your students, faculty, community, and school.
5. Within the context of increasing demographic diversity, how would you as a school leader propose to engage all stakeholders in a process of agreement on school mission and goals and to build a community of shared values?
6. As an education leader, do you, or do you think you will, struggle more with managing the "internal" or the "external" contexts of education? Explain.

References and Suggestions for Further Reading

Friedman, T. (2005). *The world is flat: A brief history of the twenty-first century*. New York: Farrar, Straus & Giroux.

   Friedman's text is an essential update on globalization and its effects on countries, economies, institutions, governments, and the individual.

Leavitt, S., and Dubner, S. (2005). *Freakonomics: A rogue economist explores the hidden side of everything*. New York: William Morrow/Harper Collins.

   This unique take on economics makes data intriguing, confounds conventional wisdom, and uncovers insights the reader may have ignored as the authors focus attention on more intimate real-world issues.

Marshall, R., and Tucker, M. (1992). *Thinking for a living: Education and the wealth of nations*. New York: Basic Books/Harper Collins.

   This book documents the disparity between the needs of our economy and what our educational system supplies to our workforce.

Naisbitt, J. (1982). *Megatrends: Ten new directions transforming our lives*. New York: Warner Books.

   In a classic that rightfully deserves to sit alongside Whyte's *The Organization Man* and Toffler's *Future Shock*, Naisbitt captures the transition of the American economy from industrial production to tendering information and services, and what it means to the individual.

Wolf, C., Jr. (1997). *Markets or governments: Choosing between imperfect alternatives* (2nd ed.). Cambridge, MA: The MIT Press.

Wolf analyzes problems frequently used in understanding market failures to supply the reader with a formal theory of nonmarket failure in institutions such as universities, foundations, and governments.

Notes

1. Morris, C. R. (1989). The coming global boom. *Atlantic, 264*(4), 53–54. If he had been writing one month later, the author could have mentioned that Ford planned to purchase England's number-one luxury car producer, Jaguar, and the James Bond-made-famous auto badge, Aston Martin.
2. Sheehy, G. (1990). Character: America's search for leadership. New York: Bantam Books, p. 1.

CHAPTER TWO

Strategic Leadership in an Organizational Context

LEARNING OBJECTIVES

By the end of this chapter, you should be able to

- identify varying conceptions of leadership;
- recognize the significance of nature and nurture in shaping leaders;
- envision the linkage between organizational theories and concepts of leadership;
- explain the added functions expected of strategic leaders.

Harold Halley, a school principal whose professional-leader case was described in Chapter 1, was in good physical condition and in his youth had been a superb athlete. However, that is not likely what imbued him with leadership potential. An effective organizational leader is seldom possessed of remarkable genetically endowed capabilities. Highly visible luminaries, towering historic figures, media celebrities, high-level political officials, military heroes, corporate titans, religious visionaries, military geniuses, scientific wizards, and athletic notables often shape popular perceptions of leadership. However, the overwhelming majority of organizational leaders almost never are widely known and only rarely become heroes, at least not in a historic or media sense. They are otherwise quite normal individuals to be found in every walk of life who consistently perform leadership roles with relatively quiet effectiveness. They have existed across time and across cultures, and there are no boundaries regarding their race, age, or gender.

Leaders exhibit a remarkably wide range of psychological and physical characteristics. To emulate Dr. Seuss: some leaders are big and some are small, some are short and some are tall, some have deep booming voices, and others hardly speak at all. Now, having commented on their diversity and specified what they are not confined to being, it is appropriate to offer a first definition of what legitimately constituted leaders are.

A leader is an individual who accepts authoritative expectations of others to guide activities responsibly and to enhance the performance of an organization.

Components of this definition will be explained and expanded upon in detail throughout this book. Suffice it to mention here that a strategic leader, the kind of leader with which this book is principally concerned, is one who attempts to meet these expectations for guiding an organization by incorporating into his or her day-to-day thinking and overall management posture the constellation of practices that strategic thinking and strategic planning comprise.

■ THEORETICAL VIEWS OF ORGANIZATIONS AND THEIR RELEVANCE FOR A STRATEGIC LEADER

As is obvious, this is not the world's first book to consider the interactions between leadership practices, external conditions, and internal organizational dynamics. For literally centuries, these have been crucial topics for all sectors of society, including education and leadership. However, in light of the preceding descriptions of six globalizing conditions impacting American education and school leaders, academically constructed theoretical considerations of organizational dynamics and leadership practices sometimes prove deficient. The principal weakness of classical organizational theories is insufficient attention to the sustained need for a leader not simply to grasp and improve the internal dynamics of his or her organization but also continually to reposition that organization so as to be aligned with ever more rapidly evolving external events.

Classical organizational theories attempt to distill the essence of human behavior in collective settings. If one could unlock the DNA code or identify the Rosetta stone for collective human behavior, then one would know better how to act as a leader. Thus, a leader's actions flow from and crucially depend upon an assumed concept of organizational dynamics. If one can discern organizational dynamics correctly, then one has a better chance of being an effective leader. However, if one's understanding of organizations is in some crucial ways disoriented or deficient, then as a leader, one is at risk. Therefore, this chapter provides readers with a solid overview of organizational theory as it applies to strategic education leadership.

Hoy and Miskel[1] describe three developmental phases of organizational theory. These are (1) a classical organization phase, starting roughly in 1900 and pioneered by Taylor, Fayol, Gulick, and Urwick; (2) a human relations phase, starting in 1930 with Follett, Mayo, and Roethlisberger as early advocates; and (3) a behavioral science phase, initiated in 1950 by Barnard and Simon.

Classical Approach to Organizations and Leadership

Basic features of the traditional or classical management model include:

- **Time and motion studies.** Tasks are conducted in a way that minimizes time and effort.
- **Division of labor and specialization.** Subdividing operations into basic components so as to ensure effective worker performance can best attain efficiency.
- **Standardization of tasks.** Disaggregating tasks into component parts allows for routinized performance.
- **Unity of command.** To coordinate an organization, decision making should be **centralized**, with responsibility flowing from top to bottom.
- **Span of control.** Unity of command and coordination is possible only if each superior at any level has a limited number of subordinates (five to ten) to oversee.
- **Uniqueness of function.** One department of an organization should not, knowingly or unknowingly, duplicate functions performed by another.

- **Formal organization.** The focus of analysis is on the official organizational blue-print; semiformal and informal structures created by dynamic interactions among individuals within the formal organization go unanalyzed.

When surveyed from the perspective of strategic leadership, this classical model suffers from organizational rigidity and a lack of recognition of the effect of events external to the organization, as well as conditions and events that are poorly coordinated internally.

Human Relations Approach to Organizations and Leadership

The human relations approach evolved as a reaction to the rigidity of the classical model. Among its early proponents was Mary Parker Follett (1941), who wrote a series of papers concentrating upon the human side of management. She contended that the fundamental challenge influencing the performance of all organizations was developing and maintaining dynamic and harmonious employee and management relationships.

The empirical research studies that stimulated the human relations phase of management theory were those undertaken in the Hawthorne plant of the Western Electric Company, located in New Jersey. These three studies, although inconclusive as to results, prompted substantial additional research. The Hawthorne studies suggested that workers react positively to management attention. Furthermore, workers can endure some degree of discomfort if they are involved in the decision process.

Hoy and Miskel summarize the Hawthorne study results as follows[2]:

- Economic incentive is not the only significant motivator. In fact, noneconomic social sanctions limit the effectiveness of economic incentives.
- Workers respond to management as members of an informal group, as well as individuals.
- Production levels are limited as much by the social norms of the informal organization as by collective physiological capacities.
- Specialization does not necessarily create the most efficient organization of the work group.
- Workers rely upon informal organizational behaviors to protect themselves against arbitrary management decisions.
- Informal social organizations interact with management.
- A narrow span of control is not a prerequisite to effective management.
- Informal leaders are often as important as formal supervisors.
- Individuals are active human beings, not passive cogs in a machine.

Behavioral Science Phase of Organizations and Leadership

The writing of Chester I. Barnard and Herbert Simon originated much of the behavioral science methodology. Barnard and Simon drew upon the ideas of Max Weber, particularly the view that organizations are social systems that interact with and are dependent on their external environments. Historically, organizations were seen as closed systems with a set of interdependent elements forming an organized whole. By the early 1960s, behavioral scientists began to focus attention on the fact that organizations not only are influenced by their external environments, but also are dependent upon them. This open-system definition has now become the norm, so that today few, if any, organizational theorists accept the premise that organizations can be understood in isolation from external conditions and events.

Within the broad field of organizational theory, three competing systems perspectives have emerged and continue today, each with its share of advocates. Scott and Davis label them the rational systems, the natural systems, and the open systems perspectives.

Rational Systems. Stemming from the early classical organizational thought of **scientific-management theorists**, rational systems view the behavior of organizations as purposeful, disciplined, and rational. The concerns and concepts of rational systems theorists are conveyed by such terms as information, efficiency, effectiveness, optimization, implementation, rationality, and design.

Rational systems are best described by their emphasis on goal specificity and on formalization. Examples of technical tools used by managers to facilitate rational decision making are **management by objective**; planning, programming, and budgeting systems; and performance evaluation and review techniques.

Natural Systems. In contrast to the rational systems perspective, the natural systems view stems from the human relations approach of the 1930s. While natural systems proponents agree that goal specificity and formalization are characteristics of organizations, they argue that other **attributes** such as similarities among social groups and survival are of far greater importance. Natural systems adherents stress the individual over structure.

Open Systems. Open systems theory holds that it is unrealistic to assume that organizational behavior can be isolated from external forces. Indeed, the open systems model views organizations as not only influenced by environments, but also dependent on them. For example, schools are social systems that absorb resources such as labor, students, and community directions from the environment and blend these inputs into an educational transformation process to produce literate and educated students and graduates.

Open systems tend to move toward a state of equilibrium by exporting and importing energy from the environment. Open systems are able to adapt to changing environments by responding to demands with a variety of means and mechanisms. Thus, the open system is better able to survive because its structure is not fixed and it can change roles and relationships to meet changing environments.

Establishment of Management Sciences

Peters and Waterman, in their classic work *In Search of Excellence*, claim four stages in the development of the field of management science.[3] Each of the stages or eras contributed a set of major premises to the field. The period from 1900 to 1930 is the closed system–rational actor era. The two main proponents were Max Weber, a German sociologist, and Frederick Taylor, an American engineer who put Weber's theories to the test with time and motion studies. They attempted to formulate a finite set of rules and techniques to be learned and mastered about maximum span of control and about matching authority and responsibility to solve problems of managing large groups of workers.

The next era, that of the closed system–social actor, spanned the period from 1930 to 1960. Among the chief spokespersons for this era were Elton Mayo, Chester Barnard, Philip Selznick, and Douglas McGregor. Mayo was the father of the Hawthorne experiments, which suggested that by giving personal attention to individuals and groups, production can be increased.

McGregor is known chiefly for his development of **Theory X and Theory Y**. Theory X holds that people have an inherent dislike for work and they must be coerced, controlled, directed, and threatened to work toward an organization's goals, while Theory Y holds that humans like work, that commitment to objectives is satisfying to the ego and is the direct product of efforts directed to an organization's purposes, and that the capacity to exercise a relatively high degree of imagination, ingenuity, and creativity is widely distributed in the population.

Barnard and Selznick focused on the role of the **chief executive officer** as the shaper and manager of shared values in an organization. They stressed managing the whole enterprise and emphasized the nature of the organization as a set of social interactions.

Stage three, the open system–rational actor era, lasted from 1960 to 1970 and was dominated by scholars such as Alfred Chandler, Paul Lawrence, and Jay Lorsch. They viewed a company as part of a competitive marketplace, shaped and molded by forces outside itself. They were the first to notice that in fast-developing businesses a more decentralized form of organization enabled quick responses to emerging situations.

Stage four, starting in 1970 and continuing today, is described as open system–social actor. In the view of today's theorists, everything is in flux, including ends, means, and the storm of external change. Leading theorists are Karl Weick and James March. The dominant theme of this era is informality, individual entrepreneurship, and evolution. Weick is convinced that military metaphors are a bad choice when it comes to managing a commercial enterprise because someone always wins or loses in the military scenario. Additionally, the military metaphor limits the solutions to a problem and the ways of organizing for delivery of services.

Peters and Waterman suggest four elements of the new theory: (1) people's need for meaning; (2) people's need for a medium of control; (3) people's need for positive reinforcement, to think of themselves as winners in some sense; and (4) the degree to which actions and behaviors shape attitudes and beliefs rather than vice versa. They also stress the notion of companies as distinctive **cultures** and the emergence of the successful company through purposeful but specifically unpredictable evolution.

Public versus Private Organizations

Perhaps the biggest distinction between private and public sector management is the realization that the public sector is just that—public—and all the issues, decisions, and deliberations are made in the full view of the public. Open meetings, laws of various types, and the heightened interest and focus of the media also contribute to the involvement of the citizens of a community in school organizations.

Also contributing to the interest of the citizenry is awareness of the educational reforms of the late 1990s and the crucial nature of the educational system to the general well-being of a town, city, state, and nation. In addition frequently to being a city's largest employer and often having the largest budget of any organization, the school system holds the keys to success or failure for the young people of a community.

However, regardless of their public nature, educational organizations are more alike than different from any other organization. Schooling is labor intensive like many business and commercial organizations, is a provider of services like many organizations, is a multi-building, multi-unit organization like many other organizations, and is diverse and serves a varied clientele like other organizations. While it is not possible to measure by counting the number of "widgets" manufactured, individual and group academic growth is capable and worthy of being measured.

Whereas the business, commercial, or industrial organization is organized to produce the greatest profit, and the military organization is organized to produce the strongest and most effective army, the educational organization must produce the greatest academic growth possible on a cost-effective basis. The business administrator, particularly, is crucial to the application of cost-effectiveness techniques to the educational enterprise.

While it is much more difficult to generate profit-and-loss statements in the educational enterprise, it is possible to generate progress toward academic objectives and to indicate the cost-effectiveness of the organization in meeting those objectives. Comparative data between similar districts and between units within districts can be used to discern the full story. The significant difference, of course, is that every citizen of the community is a stockholder in the organization and deserves the full report of progress or lack thereof.

What Are the Implications for Organizations and Leadership?

Whether labeled *learning systems, learning organizations,* or *open systems,* organizations that continually appraise their external environment, revitalize their missions when needed, systematically design and appraise new techniques and products, embrace employees with aberrant, even weird ideas, and repeatedly ask themselves, "Is this working?" are the organizations most likely to be successful in the modern world.[4] In the language of this book, these are strategic organizations. *A strategic leader should orient his or her efforts toward creating this vision of an organization. The remainder of this book provides a leader, or an aspiring leader, with the knowledge and skills useful in creating such a strategic organization.*

Before addressing these topics, however, it is important to realize that the following leadership descriptions and explanations are constructed around a fundamental assumption. Effective strategic leadership is a set of skills and understandings that are not contingent upon an individual executive being endowed with Herculean physical and intellectual abilities. *What is necessary to know for one to be an effective strategic leader can be learned.*

No longer can an education leader assume that his or her exclusive focus is upon what transpires inside, or even in the immediate community of, a school, a college, or an education system. Henceforth, what takes place inside is as likely to be a function of what occurs outside, and throughout the world, as it is likely to be a result of internal dynamics among teachers, students, and others located immediately nearby. The pace of change and the influence of the external world are forces that will increasingly play a potent role in the lives of education leaders. It is these forces that require that educational executives adopt a mode of *strategic thinking,* that they become strategic leaders.

Are leaders born or made? This is an enduring but a quickly answered question. In those few instances where leadership requires a towering intellect or a rare gift of artistic genius or physical prowess, the prerequisites for leadership may be genetically influenced and thus conferred on only a few. However, in the overwhelming proportion of organizational settings, effective leaders need not possess exotic innate abilities. No one can be a leader in every setting. However, almost everyone can become a leader in a setting appropriate to his or her talents, training, and interests.

Few persons could successfully replace an NFL quarterback in leading a last-minute Super Bowl touchdown drive or substitute for the league's Most Valuable Player during an NBA championship game. Similarly, it is not certain that unusually capable athletic leaders could sustain success as a high school principal, teacher union official, school district superintendent, or college president. Leadership is situational.

Effective leadership entails the successful chronological coincidence of a constellation of individual characteristics and an appropriate institutional context in which to exercise them. Moreover, this amalgam of individual skills, abilities, and understandings can be learned. Diligence, discipline, and devotion may be necessary to comprehend and polish these characteristics, but these are traits well within the range of most human beings to acquire.

▪ LEADERSHIP THEORIES AND STYLES

As highlighted in the previous section and chapter, a leader's actions flow from and crucially depend upon assumed concepts of external contexts and internal operational dynamics. It is from within an organizational context that education leadership is practiced, for as no man is an island, entire of itself, no school leader operates in isolation from the relational and organizational dynamics of the school community. While it is imperative for current and aspiring school leaders to understand organizational theory, it is likewise important for one to have knowledge of leadership theory. This section of text outlines a few of the key theoretical constructs within the leadership literature and situates the idea of strategic leadership within this evolving field of study. It should be noted that the field of leadership theory and styles is very broad and rich. Many scholars have devoted their careers to articulating the nuances of various approaches to leadership. The purpose of this section of the text is to provide an overview of several key leadership theories that have particular application to education organizations.

Leadership Theories

Theoretical constructs of education leadership emerged during the late nineteenth century as an attempt to define the nature of school leadership. From that time, common approaches to classify leadership theories include trait theories, behavior theories, and situational theories.[5]

Trait and Attribution Theories. The earliest theories of education leadership focused exclusively upon the physical, social, and personal characteristics of leaders. By focusing on the innate attributes of individuals, early studies dismissed the host of contextual and relational variables at play in leader-follower interactions. Within these theories, hereditary traits such as height, gender, appearance, and intelligence, along with good fortune in a Darwinian survival of the fittest, were the means by which one rose to the rank of leader.

While subsequent research has dispelled the notion of leadership being exclusively innate and has endorsed the importance of situational variables, trait theory still impacts current views of leadership. For example, consider the new superintendent who steps into an underachieving school district and succeeds in moving school performance from significantly underperforming to highly successful in a short period of time. The media buzz surrounding such a turnaround often emphasizes the heroic acts of a leader who rose to the occasion and stepped forward to rescue a drowning organization by virtue of his or her personal integrity, intelligence, vision, and **charisma**.

Behavior Theories. A second strand of leadership theory made a clean separation from focusing exclusively on who a leader innately is to an emphasis on the behaviors with which a leader is engaged. The behaviorist theory builds upon the premise that leadership is seen as a set of observable actions and, as such, focuses upon the interactions between leaders and subordinates in various organizational contexts. In addition to studying the overt actions of leaders, behaviorist researchers also strive to discern the psychological motivations and historical influences of action. Not surprisingly, this vein of research was grounded in the scholarship of individuals such as Sigmund Freud and Carl Jung, as it sought to explain leader behaviors related to associations, interpretations, and analyses of prior experience.

Within the behaviorist camp, theorists propose that leadership is a combination of two kinds of behaviors and that a leader's effectiveness depends on using the best combination of behaviors appropriate to the circumstances. The two kinds of behaviors are described as being either (1) task focused, where a leader initiates actions for the purpose of goal attainment (nomethetic) or (2) relationship focused (ideographic), where leaders primarily show consideration for people and interpersonal dynamics. While behaviorists contend that leaders might have a preference for one particular dimension, they do not believe that leaders function in one dimension exclusively, but rather toggle between the two as appropriate for the circumstance.

Situational and Contingency Theories. Another group of leadership theories contends that situational context is a formative component of leadership emergence. This line of research directly contrasts with the trait theorists who viewed leadership in isolation from contextual variables. While the situational theory contends that leadership is contingent upon context, it is the interaction of personal traits and the situational context that mutually determines leadership action. It is this interplay between situations and individuals that is at the core of the situational and **contingency theories**. As a result, much research by situation theorists seeks to determine the optimal matching of individual traits, skills, and background experiences to particular job requirements and contexts. Within the broad base of the situational theory camp there are several subdivisions, each with its own focus and conceptual understandings. These will be briefly described below.

The *interaction theory* views leadership through the lens of leader-subordinate relationships, where leaders demonstrate behaviors based on how they perceive that others see them as leaders. *Attainment theory* focuses on who emerges as a leader in various situations and why and asserts that leadership roles are defined by organizational expectations. The *political theorists* view leadership in terms of an individual's ability to utilize **power** to exert influence within organizations. The notion that leaders are able to alter the behaviors of others to bring about organizational change is the central tenet of the *reinforced change theory*. In this theory, a leader is successful to the degree that leadership actions are congruent with followers' expectations for rewards and punishments within the organization. The primary aim for leaders in *path-goal theory* is to move subordinates along a desired path of behaviors toward attainment of organizational goals. In this theory, leaders assess work and worker needs and adjust their own behaviors based on these situational variables.

Leadership Styles

While leadership theories provide explanations of leadership based on traits, behaviors, or situational variables, leadership styles refer to patterns of behaviors demonstrated by leaders as they influence others and provide organizational direction. The study of leadership style provides a framework for assessing various approaches to and orientations of leadership behavior. A wide array of leadership styles is discussed in the educational literature.

Here, five global categories of leadership styles will be presented. These include authoritarian, transformational, transactional, participative, and instructional.

Authoritarian Leaders. When one considers the type of leader suited to McGregor's Theory X, which holds that people have an inherent dislike for work and they must be coerced, controlled, directed, and threatened to work toward an organization's goals, one can easily imagine an authoritarian leader. Such leaders rely on hierarchical, top-down organizations with clear levels of authority and chains of command. The primary management strategy employed by authoritarian leaders is not collegiality or cooperation, but control. While often viewed as overly objective and insensitive to the human facets of organizations, authoritarian leaders often prevail amidst excessive accountability demands when one must get an organization back on track or else.

Transformational Leaders. In sharp contrast to the authoritarian approach, transformational leaders create environments in which each individual feels empowered to fulfill his or her needs as a member of a productive learning community. Transformational leaders articulate a purpose for individuals within an organization in a manner that transcends short-term goals while focusing on higher-order intrinsic needs. This results in followers identifying with the needs of the leader. According to James Burns, who first introduced the concept of transformational leadership in 1978, the four primary dimensions of transformational leadership are

- **Charisma or idealized influence.** This is understood as the degree to which a leader behaves in admirable ways that cause followers to identify with the leader. Charismatic leaders display convictions, take stands, and appeal to followers on an emotional level. Transformational leaders espouse a clear set of values and demonstrate them in every action, providing a role model for their followers.
- **Inspirational motivation.** This entails the degree to which a leader articulates a vision that is appealing and inspiring to followers. Leaders with inspirational motivation challenge followers with high standards, communicate optimism about future goals, and provide meaning for the task at hand. Followers need to have a strong sense of purpose if they are to be motivated to act.
- **Intellectual stimulation.** This refers to the degree to which a leader challenges assumptions, takes risks, and solicits followers' ideas. By doing this, transformational leaders stimulate and encourage creativity in their followers.
- **Individualized consideration or individualized attention.** This is displayed as the degree to which a leader attends to each follower's needs, acts as a mentor or coach to the follower, and listens to the follower's concerns and needs. This also encompasses the need to respect and celebrate the individual contribution that each follower can make to the team.

Transactional Leaders. Complementary to transformational leadership is the theory of transactional leadership, which identifies the leader as the articulator of expectations and goals and the provider of recognition and rewards when a task is completed. The transactional leader style is described as an exchange of rewards contingent upon successful performance and the use of positional resources in order to encourage desired behaviors. This style of leadership requires a balancing of organizational goals with the expectations of people doing the work. In this approach to leadership, employees receive rewards in exchange for their collaboration and assistance. As such, transactional leaders are essentially pursuing a cost-benefit, economic exchange with followers. According to Bernard Bass, who was integral in articulating the theory of transactional leadership, the two primary components of the theory include

- **Contingent reward.** This is understood as the process whereby leaders recognize individual talents and contributions by providing employee rewards in a manner that promotes compliance to organizational objectives.
- **Management by exception.** This is evidenced by the implicit trust that leaders have in their workers to finish a job to satisfactory standards. Here, the leader avoids giving directions if the old ways are working and allows followers to continue doing their jobs as always if performance goals are met. While this approach should not be construed as an abdication of leadership, such management by exception rarely inspires workers to achieve beyond the stated expectations. As long as organizational goals are achieved, employees are rewarded, and both parties have benefited.

Participative Leaders. This category of leadership style is one that recognizes the important contributions made by multiple individuals at different levels of the school organization. Participative leadership acknowledges that it is no longer feasible for one administrator to serve as the leader for a school community without the substantial participation of other educators. Within this domain of leadership style are such approaches as **distributed leadership**, shared leadership, and teacher leadership. Each of these is described in Table 2.1. Within the domain of participative leadership, one particularly well-researched construct is distributed leadership. Since 1998, James Spillane and his colleagues have continued to build a theory that captures the evolving understanding of distributed leadership. In this theory, leadership activity is distributed across an interactive web of leaders, followers, and contextual conditions. A distributed perspective on leadership moves us beyond seeing leadership as synonymous with the work of the principal and therefore recognizes that the work of leadership involves multiple individuals including teacher leaders and key constituents. Hence, the distributed leadership frame shifts the level of analysis from the individual actor or group of actors to the web of leaders, followers, and situations that gives activity its form.[6]

Instructional Leaders. Instructional leadership views the principal as the primary source of educational expertise in a school. Instructional leaders focus on leadership functions that are directly related to teaching and that contribute to student learning. In continual reviews and syntheses of the literature on instructional leadership, Peabody professor Joseph Murphy contends that instructional leaders emphasize four sets of activities that center on instruction:

- Developing the school **mission** and goals
- Coordinating, monitoring, and evaluating curriculum, instruction, and assessment
- Promoting a climate for leaning
- Creating a supportive work environment

Effectively, instructional leadership is a professional orientation or a decision to focus efforts on supporting the achievement of students and the ability of teachers to teach. Based on a principal's behavioral preference and the specific initiative requiring leadership, instructional leadership might take on a more authoritarian or hierarchical mode or utilize more participative means to accomplish instructional goals. The notion of shared instructional leadership is an approach compatible with competent, professional, and **empowered**

TABLE 2.1 Definitions for Leadership Approaches Related to Participative Leadership

Leadership Style	Definition
Participative Leadership	An umbrella term that encompasses any number of efforts to engage a broad and diverse set of actors in the processes of leadership. As such, all of the constructs defined below are different methods of operationalizing a participative leadership model.
Distributed Leadership	An approach that understands school leadership to be distributed across the school's social and situational contexts. Leadership tasks are often distributed across multiple leaders in school, including principals, curriculum specialists, and classroom teachers. The emphasis is on the delivery of the educational program—as the expertise in a school is distributed, so is the leadership.
Shared Leadership & Professional Learning Communities	A school community where the professional staff is learning together while directing all their efforts toward improved student learning. Within professional learning communities, shared leadership involves the sharing of the authority, power, and control to make decisions that will maximize student progress. This leadership model is most often discussed within the context of professional learning communities and emphasizes broad-based, skillful participation in the work of leadership.
Teacher Leadership	An approach to school leadership that is primarily concerned with enhanced leadership roles and decision-making powers for teachers without taking them out of the classroom. Of these roles, the mentoring, induction, and continual professional development of colleagues and development of collaborative relationships within the community in order to positively impact the school are central.
Site-Based Management / School-Based Decision Making	An approach to school management that shifts responsibility for the governance and control of schools from the central school district authorities into the hands of administrators, teachers, community members, and others at the level of the individual school.

teachers. Whereas the principal remains the educational leader of the school, teachers, who possess essential knowledge and expertise, exercise leadership collaboratively with the principal. Therefore, shared instructional leadership is not dependent on role or position, but rather its currency lies in the personal resources of participants and is deployed through interaction.

Several Peabody professors, with funding support of the Wallace Foundation, have made substantial progress on further defining the concept of instructionally focused leadership and have created an assessment tool to determine the degree to which a school principal is exhibiting learning-centered leadership. This work, undertaken by Murphy, Goldring, Porter, and Elliot, is described in detail in Chapter 10.

■ THE IDEA OF STRATEGIC LEADERSHIP

As the description of shared instructional leadership attests, no single theory or leadership style is sufficient to rely upon to lead a complex modern educational organization. A full range of leadership theories and styles exists, each one analytically distinct. Certainly, an effective school principal operates simultaneously in transformational, transactional, and instructional modes. The key is how one draws upon them to construct a coherent, integrated model of leadership appropriate for each unique situation, dilemma, individual, or action.

Little research has been done to analyze the impact of leadership styles across various individuals, schools, and situations. Yet personal and professional experience suggests that some leaders are better than others in assessing their environments, analyzing alternatives, and adjusting their styles successfully to address issues. As no single theory can define or predict the best leadership approach for a given situation, it is essential that school leaders are strategic in their thinking and action.

A strategic leader is one who realizes that his or her organization must constantly be appraising the external world, assessing its own purposes and performance in light of those findings, and systematically altering its internal procedures accordingly. Strategic leadership necessitates constant measurement and evaluation of conditions both external and internal to an organization. Information regarding external and internal conditions should constantly be collected, compiled, synthesized, and analyzed in a strategic organization. The point is to determine whether or not changes in the external or internal environments, or the interactions between the two, have implications for the organization's mission and goals. As such, a strategic leader is obligated to ensure that "action" is consistent with organizational goals and is as finely tuned as appropriate analyses and feedback can make it.

Strategic leadership, the theme around which this book is organized, is not a theory or a style. Rather, it involves a mind-set, or viewpoint, or orientation to leadership that allows one to draw upon all of the prospective theories and styles and integrate them based on a cycle of appraisal and analysis before launching into action.

■ STRATEGIC THINKING APPLIED TO EDUCATION LEADERSHIP

Successful leaders in the future will be distinguished by the degree to which they understand that there no longer exists a static world. Organizations must comprehend and cope with the continual changes that occur in their external environment, and successful leaders will be those that are able to make sense of change and interpret it meaningfully for their organizations.

Strategic leaders engage in a constant appraisal of the external environment and unceasingly ask, "What does this fluctuating or evolving condition mean for my organization?" They understand external changes eventually permeate the internal world of organizations and promote or provoke dislocations and discontinuities that, if not appropriately recognized and rationalized, will impede an organization's effectiveness and sooner or later render it dysfunctional. The purpose of strategic leadership is not organizational change. Change is everywhere, and of their own accord or even against their will, organizations will change. The question is whether or not change will be purposeful, productive, consistent with the organization's objectives, and to the benefit of students, teachers, communities, and society.

▪ COMBINING APPRAISAL AND ACTION

Strategic leadership is characterized by a self-conscious, self-initiated, self-critical, continuous, and interactive cycle of appraisal and action. It involves strategic planning but encompasses much more. An organization can episodically engage in strategic planning or arrange to have it performed by a team of outside planning experts. Strategic leadership is built upon strategic planning and incorporates these activities into the regular rhythm of organizational life.

Moreover, a strategic organization eventually develops a planning and analytic capability internally and for planning purposes is relatively independent of outsiders. Lastly, a strategic organization does not depend exclusively upon strategic leadership. Rather, strategic thinking begins to permeate the entire institution. Leaders, managers, and almost all employees come to think and act continuously in terms of appraisal, analysis, and action.

Strategic leadership involves a set of cyclical activities portrayed in Figure 2.1. As with all cycles, it is incomplete and eventually collapses if one phase is continually omitted or ineffective. Thus, beginning a description at this point is not meant to convey a message that appraisal is the primary or most important component of the cycle. Rather, it simply is necessary to begin somewhere, and this component is a convenient beginning. Keep in mind, however, that organizations exist to accomplish purposes, and doing so ultimately depends upon action. Thus, if one could begin with a discussion of the action phase of the cycle, eventually the question would have to be posed as to whether or not it was the right action. That is the question that most distinguishes a strategic organization from one that is moribund.

Appraisal. To appraise is to measure and assign a value. Strategic leadership necessitates constant measurement and evaluation of conditions both external and internal to an organization. The dimensions that should be appraised are illustrated below. Keep in mind, however, that "appraisal" involves more than simply applying an empirical yardstick to these conditions. It also entails placing a value upon them, rendering a judgment regarding their significance, and placing them in an evaluative context so that their significance

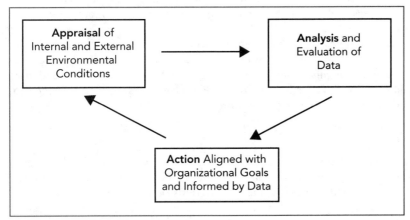

FIGURE 2.1 Strategic Leadership Cycle of Appraisal, Analysis, and Action

for the organization can be determined. If measurement were all that was necessary, then measurement experts alone could perform the task. However, it is the combination of measurement and wisdom that characterizes an effective strategic leader.

The external and internal dimensions that should systematically be appraised will vary depending upon an organization's nature. Private-sector firms may be oriented more toward market conditions, and public-sector organizations more toward politics. Higher education may be oriented more toward state and federal government, and public schools more toward local and state governments. Private schools may concentrate more on philanthropy, and public schools more on tax rates. One of the important responsibilities of a strategic executive is to determine and periodically review dimensions to be appraised. However, the following list illustrates concepts involved.

External Dimensions

- **Demographics.** An educational organization should regularly appraise relevant demographic conditions. What is the shape of forthcoming age cohorts? What is the ethnic, racial, and gender composition of school or college age groups? These data make a crucial base from which to extrapolate many other useful data such as future facilities needs, financial projections, and personnel needs.
- **Economics.** What trends are developing in an education organization's immediate locality, region, or state? This is particularly important for vocational training institutions. However, it is also of concern for secondary schools, community colleges, and postsecondary institutions that orient themselves toward a region. Attention should be paid to likely effects of these trends upon the availability of future revenues and likely consequences of trends for employment or matriculation of the institution's graduates.
- **Public opinion.** Attention should be given to two kinds of public opinion. One is the general public's attitude about education. An effort should be made to develop precursors of public views, to grasp possible changes in citizen outlook that might shape expectations they hold for educational institutions. A second dimension of public opinion consists of views of an institution's more immediate clients, pupils, parents, employees, public officials, and so on regarding the effectiveness of the organization.
- **Sociopolitical dynamics.** What forces in operation in the larger society are likely to influence the organization? Are there technological innovations that may alter employment, leisure, or family conditions? Are demography and economics combining to shift political priorities? Are international events changing such as to influence domestic political outlooks regarding education?

Internal Conditions

- **Finances.** Projections, usually employing a five-year rolling horizon, should annually be undertaken of an organization's likely revenues and expenditures. When undertaken systematically and repeatedly, these projections can become sufficiently honed to provide organizational decision makers with advance knowledge of likely opportunities for growth and improvement or the possibility of retrenchment.
- **Employee morale.** What employees think and feel is crucial to the successful operation of an organization, and a variety of methods should be used to appraise this

dimension. Leaders and managers should always be sensitive to what is developing around them, among those employees closest to them. By itself, however, such first-hand opinion is insufficient. Systematic polling under conditions that pose no threat to respondents should also take place. Also, behaviors such as grievances filed, work stoppages, absenteeism, and turnover rates should all be recorded as possible indicators of employee morale and opinion.

- **Outcome measurement.** An educational organization should rely upon systematic accumulation of outcome data. This should include, but not be limited to, student test scores, persistence or dropout rates, graduation levels, degree completions, and downstream performance (at the next level of schooling or employment).
- **Process measures.** What are patterns of student course enrollments? Do students pursue curricular or vocational objectives by gender, race, or socioeconomic levels? What are time-to-completion rates of students, and do they form patterns? What times of day or week are courses offered? What are library usage rates? What are tardiness and absenteeism rates? What are extracurricular participation rates?
- **Operational costs.** What are the cost profiles of various programs and organizational subunits? How do these profiles compare with historic trends and with the same operations in comparable institutions? For example, what are the relationships of administrative to instructional costs? Are the costs of substitute teachers climbing or decreasing over time? What about utility costs?
- **Organizational structure.** Are subcomponents within an organization arranged in a manner that facilitates communication, enhances accountability, and reduces unnecessary duplication? Are reporting lines clear, spans of control reasonable, and client convenience maximized?

Analysis. Information regarding external and internal conditions should constantly be collected, compiled, synthesized, and analyzed in a strategic organization. However, the uses to which such data are put are crucial. An organization can easily suffer from informational paralysis, collecting more data than can be used and incurring excessive operational costs as a consequence. Information for its own sake has little value and can become dysfunctional. Thus, it is critical that a strategic executive know the purposes for which data are collected and ensure that those purposes are met. If an information item cannot be justified, then resulting data should not be collected.

One of the important reasons for strategic education leaders to be constantly engaged in measurement and analysis of organizational data is to assess the currency and appropriateness of an organization's objectives. The point is to determine whether or not changes in the external or internal environments, or the interactions between the two, have implications for the organization's mission and goals and the manner in which it pursues its mission. This is a complex set of deliberations typically involving collaboration with public representatives and policy-setting bodies. Topics for such deliberations include the following: Have regional demographics shifted such that school attendance boundaries should be redrawn for fear of unreasonably contributing to racial segregation? Has the regional economy changed sufficiently that a district's secondary school instructional strategy should be altered? Do new state-issued curriculum guidelines necessitate new testing or textbook policies? Are faculty members aging at a rate necessitating a major out-of-state recruitment program for new personnel? Are categorical programs interfering with core functions of the schooling process?

These and dozens of similar questions should regularly be posed by educational policy makers and strategic executives. Answers to such questions may suggest that the status quo continues to be appropriate. Nevertheless, an organization is the better for having asked and answered the questions. The answers either dictate a change in mission or operation, or they reaffirm and reinforce what currently is being done. In either instance, the organization is more confident of its purpose than was previously the case.

Action. Strategic leadership is not all evaluation and planning. It is every bit as important to know "how to do it right" as it is to know "what is right to do." A leader's principal responsibility is to determine the right thing to do and to motivate organizational members to achieve the goal; hence the stress here upon vision, appraisal, analysis, and assessment. However, it should be remembered that organizations exist to accomplish goals, not simply to set them. Action is thus the flywheel that maintains an organization's forward momentum. A strategic leader is obligated to ensure that "action" is consistent with organizational goals and is as continually and finely tuned as appropriate analyses and feedback can make it. However, action must take place.

Doing things "right" demands that a strategic leader know how to motivate individuals and groups and be able to mobilize coalitions. Moreover, these are not activities that a leader does once, and then they are "done." Motivation and mobilization are the essence of the internal organizational responsibilities of a strategic leader. These two activities never stop; they must be done again, again, and again. Still, motivation and mobilization toward what end? Here is the point at which a leader's concerns and activities come full circle to a reconsideration or reappraisal of organizational aims and goals.

 CASE 1 REVISITED

> Considering the dual focus required of strategic leaders, do you consider that CEO Daniel Boyle's more detrimental shortcomings were those pertaining to his focus and interactions within his organization, or his lack of paying adequate attention to the forces at play external to his organization? From your years of experience in education, are you familiar with a leader who possessed this dual focus? What did you learn from this leader that will help you take a strategic approach to education leadership?

Summary

This chapter began with a discussion of theoretic views of organizations and their implications for strategic leadership. During the past one hundred years, a variety of theories and approaches to organizations and leadership have shaped the educational landscape of our nation. It is important for current and aspiring leaders to have knowledge of these theories, as they can serve as lenses with which to view organizational dynamics. Yet this knowledge is not all that is needed to ensure that school leaders are effective. The current pace of societal change makes it necessary for leaders not only to grasp the internal dynamics of their organization, but also continually to ensure their organization is aligned with rapidly evolving external events. This chapter also provides insight about the many leadership theories and styles that impact education. Here one sees there are multiple ways that educational researchers have sought to understand and describe the interaction between leaders, organizations, and constituents. Given the growing demographic diversity discussed in the previous chapter, it is apparent that no single theory or leadership style is sufficient to rely upon to lead a complex modern educational organization. Yet it is imperative that school leaders are strategic in their approach to leading educational organizations. By strategic we mean that a leader works to ensure that action is consistent with organizational goals and is as continually and finely tuned as appropriate appraisals, analyses, and feedback can make it.

Discussion Questions

1. Is the classical, human relations, or behavioral sciences approach to organizations and leadership most aligned with your preferences and understandings?
2. Do you think the rational, natural, or open systems approach has the most applicability to your current educational organization?
3. If asked to describe the general public and then specifically those who work in schools, do you think there is a difference between the two groups in terms of McGregor's Theories X and Y?
4. Which of the leadership theories do you think most accurately captures the essence of leadership in your current educational organization?
5. Which of the leadership styles is most closely aligned with your personal philosophy of leadership? Which most closely resembles that of your current supervisor?
6. ELCC Standard 5 describes the importance of school leaders acting with integrity, fairness, and in an ethical manner. Do you think that any of the leadership theories or styles discussed in this chapter facilitate or impede a leader's ability to live up to this standard?
7. This chapter describes several global forces impacting the educational landscape of our nation. ELCC Standard 6 takes into consideration the various external contexts that influence educational organizations and thus school leadership. Choose one political, social, economic, or cultural trend, and describe the ways in which you feel it is impacting your current school.

References and Suggestions for Further Reading

Bolman, L. G., & Deal, T. E. (2003). *Reframing organizations: Artistry, choice, and leadership*. San Francisco: Jossey-Bass.

    This book has proven useful for practicing education leaders because of the suggestion that leadership involves overlapping and sometimes conflicting purposes involving political, technical, and social objectives.

Burns, J. M. (1978). *Leadership*. New York: Harper & Row.

    Since its appearance more than three decades ago, this monumental summary of leadership literature and research has been a classic reference displaying the evolution of the field. The unique contribution of Burns is to claim that successful leadership necessitates a moral or spiritual component. If such a component is absent, then leadership is too narrowly interpreted as a set of mechanical activities.

Collins, J. (2001). *Good to great: Why some companies make the leap and others don't.* New York: Harper Collins.

One of the rare empirical studies of successful leaders. Collins and colleagues studied the chief executive officers of unusually successful companies and arrive at unexpected results. Successful CEOs are not necessarily charismatic or self-aggrandizing. They often are quite modest and quick to give credit for successes to subordinates.

Peters, T. J., & Waterman, R. H. (2004). *In search of excellence: Lessons from America's best-run companies.* New York: Harper Collins.

Classic analysis of large and prominent private sector corporations in search of organizational structure and leader actions associated with success. Some, but not all, of the authors' lessons are enduring.

Senge, P. H. (2006). *Fifth discipline: The art and practice of the learning organization* (5th ed.). New York: Doubleday.

Another classic analysis of successful organizations.

Notes

1. This classification of organizational theory is a distillation of ideas provided by Hoy, W. K., & Miskel, C. J. (2005). *Educational theory, research, and practice* (7th ed.). New York: McGraw-Hill.
2. Ibid.
3. Peters, T. J., & Waterman, R. H. (2004). *In search of excellence: Lessons from America's best-run companies.* New York: Harper Collins Publishers.
4. In his 2005 book *Re-Imagine*, author and management guru Tom Peters makes much of the utility of modern organizations to identify the maverick employee, one who is dissatisfied with the status quo, one who continually seeks another way, the one who marches to a different drummer. It is this creative employee, Peters contends, who is most likely to point the way to new products and new procedures that can capture future markets and pioneer future products and services.
5. This classification of leadership theory is a distillation of ideas provided by Williams, F., Ricciardi, D., & Blackbourn, R. (2006). *Encyclopedia of educational leadership and administration.* Thousand Oaks: Sage.
6. Spillane, J. (2004). Educational leadership. *Educational Evaluation and Policy Analysis, 26*(2), 169–172. Spillane, J., Halverson, R., & Diamond, J. (2001). Investigating school leadership practice: A distributed perspective. *Educational Researcher, 30*(3), 23–28.

CHAPTER THREE

Planning Operational Details

LEARNING OBJECTIVES

By the end of this chapter, you should be able to

- define strategic planning and the tactical components that make up the planning process;
- recognize strategic planning as a dynamic management instrument for an education agency;
- engage the correct actors in planning;
- determine a reasonable planning time frame and time horizon.

Preceding and following chapters provide key components of a knowledge base for strategic leaders, a necessary precursor to taking action. This chapter explains the strategic planning process in detail. The conduct of strategic planning initially assists an organization in identifying the "right things to do." Having accomplished that purpose, strategic planning also can assist a leader in getting things done. The purpose of strategic planning is to render an organization more effective and to enable it to achieve its goals more completely and respond more efficiently to its clients.

Strategic **planning** entails systematic review, and possible redeployment, of an agency's resources. This is often a remarkably complicated and resource-consuming undertaking. It can involve sophisticated analytic and technical procedures, political acumen, widespread employee participation, forceful leadership, and a measure of intuition.

Inclusion of the word *planning*, however, should not deceive a reader. Strategic planning of the variety described and illustrated in this book is far from a hollow or bureaucratic paper-and-pencil exercise.

Certainly, planning reports can be ignored—"put on the shelf" to gather dust. However, if undertaken with appropriate expertise and commitment, the strategic planning process has the potential to rattle an organization to its fundamental roots and render it dramatically more responsive and effective. A strategic plan is a powerful tool by which policy makers and leaders can fine-tune an already-responsive and achieving agency or re-orient a runaway organization.

▪ WHAT IS STRATEGIC PLANNING?

As specified in Chapter 1, etymological roots of *strategy* stretch to classical Greece, where the original term concerned military leadership. A *stratagem* was a means for gaining the upper hand over an enemy or severing an opponent's vital supply route. Achieving a strategic objective often requires substantial forethought. Through the planning process, numerous detailed actions are specified and are often referred to as tactics. As an aside, the Eisenhower-planned 1944 Normandy invasion may well represent the most complicated human planning effort in history. Staying with this example, troop movements, logistical arrangements, aerial bombardment, compilation of intelligence, sabotage, civilian propaganda efforts, and so on may represent tactical details. However, many and varied as they may be, when motivated by an overarching strategy, the cohesive purpose of aligned tactics is to achieve an organization's goals.

Developing strategic objectives and the means for achieving them, what this chapter refers to as strategic planning, has evolved substantially from its Greek and military origins. Strategic planning presently is employed by a wide spectrum of private, not-for-profit, and public-sector organizations in order to achieve objectives more effectively; for example, to enhance profits, expand services to clients, and be more responsive to constituent preferences.

What is strategic planning? It is a composite of sociopolitical processes and analytic techniques designed to enhance an organization's performance and relationships with its external environment, and to ratchet up the efficiency of its internal resource allocation. It combines **analysis** with more generally obtained information and judgments regarding matters such as demographics, politics, and technology. The outcome is an organizational **action plan** that takes into account likely future changes and orients the agency's resources toward achievement of mutually agreed-upon organizational objectives. A good strategic plan can congeal an organization and concentrate the energies of personnel at all levels upon the organization's path to success. Obviously, such a plan has implications for a strategic leader's actions.

Any effective organization, that is, one that purposefully is pursuing and achieving its announced objectives, engages in planning. A simple business with only five or ten employees, in order to remain effective, must plan. A small, locally operating social agency, in order to fulfill its mission or adjust to a changing environment, must assess its current status and give thought to the future. Not to do so risks becoming an anachronism and obsolete. Even a household must occasionally undertake planning in order to satisfy current desires and secure the future for its members.

Planning, in these instances, may be informal and unilateral. The head of a household simply may take stock of current family needs, speculate regarding future desires, assess current and prospective resources, and arrive at a conclusion regarding next-needed actions. All of this might be done without once putting pencil to paper.

Similarly, the head of a small business may undertake an informal assessment of sales trends, current operating costs, personnel performance, and profits; stir into the mixture an informed appraisal of market developments; and arrive at a conclusion regarding future business directions.

Such simplified and informal efforts contain many elements of strategic planning, and they may suffice to promote the ends of the organizations involved—in these examples, a family and small business. These planning exercises involve important dimensions such as assessing the current status of the "organization," determining desired performance levels, possibly altering the external environment, and arriving at a set of alternative actions. However, these simplified efforts are missing several critical components that characterize strategic planning for a large organization.

Effective strategic planning for a complex agency depends additionally upon the presence of (1) specific organizational goals, (2) a capacity for objective, independent judgment, and (3) technical expertise. In other words, in order to be effective, a strategic planning effort must be oriented toward achievement of explicit organizational goals, undertaken in circumstances that permit analytic objectivity and independence, and must involve appropriate levels of technical sophistication.

Making Organizational Goals Explicit

The head of a household might assume that family happiness and security are important goals. The owner of a small business might assume that making sufficient profit is the major objective. However, for larger organizations, particularly public-sector agencies, strategic planning necessitates that goals be made explicit. Only in this way is it possible to assess organizational performance and subsequently align or realign resources effectively.

In the News

With many problems on its plate, the Minneapolis School District is inching toward its first attempt in a quarter-century at a broad strategic plan for improvement. That plan could address some of the tough issues the district faces, such as stopping the flight of students to other schools and disparate rates of academic progress among students by race.

Key participants say they expect it will take at least eight months to come up with a plan to chart district goals for the next five years or more. The school board is expected to get a blueprint in early August for planning activities. It's expected to cover digging out statistics, forming a core team of insiders and outsiders to guide the process, and increasing internal staffing. With a majority of board seats turning over in this fall's elections, the current board's goal is to make the preparations for planning to be done by the new board that starts in January. Candidates say they favor long-range planning. At stake is what the face of education in Minneapolis will look like in the years to come.

"This is 'big questions'; this is not the little things," said board chairman Joseph Erickson. "This is about what we want the future of Minneapolis education to be like." But just how far is the board willing to go? So far it has only tiptoed in the direction of planning. Judy Farmer, the only board member around for the last thorough round of planning—in the early 1980s—campaigned on the issue when reelected in 2002. But her nagging has been slow to produce results. That's despite the recommendations from the board's last extensive community listening sessions in 2004, in which people said they wanted stability from long-range planning rather than year-to-year planning and reactive decisions.

(continued)

More than a year ago, the board budgeted more than $200,000 to start up an internal planning office, but most of that remains untouched. The district is likely to turn to outside private funding if it decides to hire a consultant to guide it through a strategic plan, just as then-superintendent Richard Green did in the early 1980s.

That plan led to the closing of twenty-two schools to offset an enrollment decline as the last of the baby boomers finished school. Over the past two years, the board has closed about half that many elementary schools because of lower birth rates and students leaving for suburban and charter alternatives. But those closings dealt only with enrollment losses expected through 2008, and sagging enrollments now are reaching middle and high schools.

Farmer suggests that planners examine such issues as the role of magnet schools, small learning communities in high schools, completion of middle-school reform, the effect of race and class on school performance, and whether integration with suburbs can affect that. But the board also may need to reform itself. Many meetings focus more on staff recognition and administrative minutiae than the policy decisions critical to

regaining public confidence. "The board should really talk about the role of the board," said Farmer, who would like to see planners force it through a series of tough choices on priorities. "If the board members are not really involved in the hard work, they won't do squat with it and they'll put it on a shelf."

But that's not all. Stephen Barone, an outside planning consultant who met with the board in April, told it that continuity of leadership for several years is critical to making sure whatever plan is adopted is used. And he said leadership needs to be developed from within, something that observers such as longtime education activist Sue Eyestone fault the district for not doing. The district has had five superintendents—three of them interim—in less than three years. That's one reason that the board hopes to institutionalize an internal planning capacity the district has lacked for several years now.

From "Minneapolis schools seek strategic plan: It's the first attempt in a quarter-century toward a broad map for improvement," by Steve Brandt, published July 31, 2006, © 2006 Star Tribune, Minneapolis, MN. Reprinted with permission.

The objectives of an education system or agency can be classified either as *end goals* or *instrumental goals*. Ends are the final outcomes or products that the system or agency attempts to achieve. High academic achievement, vocational preparation, good citizenship, and ethnic understanding are all potential end purposes of a school or school district.[1] These can be regarded as strategic objectives. An organization's progress in achieving such objectives can be systematically assessed. Also, such objectives should determine rational allocation of organizational resources.

Instrumental goals, or means, are those outcomes that, while perhaps being desirable in themselves, are pursued by an organization because their accomplishment facilitates achievement of end goals. For example, a school district might regard parent participation or citizen satisfaction as objectives it desires to maximize. These probably are good things to do regardless, but there exists an additional motivation to accomplishing them. Arguably, parent participation is a means that might enhance student achievement, an end goal. Increased citizen satisfaction with schools might secure a stable stream of local property-tax resources for the district. In this light, parent participation and citizen satisfaction are instrumental objectives. Ends are *strategic goals* and means are *instrumental goals.* The latter are intended to promote the former.

In the absence of explicit ends or strategic goals, it is not possible to undertake a complete strategic planning effort for a large organization. At a minimum, strategic goals are needed by an organization as (1) criteria with which to determine the degree to which it currently is succeeding in its mission or missions, (2) targets toward which to orient subsequent allocations of resources, and (3) foci around which to organize personnel and incentives.

■ IMPACT OF POLITICS ON GOAL SETTING AND STRATEGIC PLANNING

Establishing an organization's purposes, particularly a public organization's purposes, often involves politics. There exists an infinite range of useful things to do in this world and a finite quantity of resources, including human time, with which to accomplish such good purposes. Consequently, decisions almost inevitably must be made regarding ends to be pursued and resources to be allocated. Who will pay, who will benefit, and who will participate are important questions, and they are the stuff of politics. If it is a public organization receiving and responsible for allocating public resources, such as tax revenues, then goal setting is subject to the added complexity of government regulation regarding both rightful participants and the decision process.

Because of the political complexity involved, simply admonishing policy makers and managers to make organizational goals explicit is probably insufficient. Frankly, specifying goals is difficult, and the larger and more heterogeneous the public served by an organization, the more difficult it becomes to reach agreement among participants and to be specific. Also, reaching agreement regarding goals is frequently more difficult to accomplish in a public-sector agency than in the private or not-for-profit sectors. Lastly, the more directly linked the agency is to the electoral process, the more complicated goal setting can become.

As vast and complex as it is, General Motors Corporation probably can establish its strategic goals more readily than the National Aeronautic and Space Administration (NASA). Though not directly linked to the electorate, NASA, a federal executive-branch agency, is nevertheless subject to the political pressures of the presidency and Congress and the perceptions of the general public. A locally elected school board, especially for a medium or large city school district, may have even greater difficulty than NASA in agreeing upon its strategic agenda. This is so because at least NASA has the luxury of a relatively prescribed zone of activity: space exploration. It also has a powerful scientific and technical base undergirding its operations. A local school district seems to have to wrestle with virtually every issue but space exploration. Moreover, it has to undertake the complicated deliberations without the solid base of science that one would hope, someday, might characterize education.

In a small, specialized government agency such as a mosquito control or a transportation district, it may be relatively easy for elected policy makers to reach consensus regarding goals. However, in a general government such as a county or municipality, or even a value-laden special service such as a public school district, community college, or university, efforts to reach agreement on or to establish priorities among specific purposes can provoke intense conflict.

Public agencies are intended to be sensitive to the needs of their clients, and elected officials generally desire to be responsive to constituent preferences. If the policy charter for a government agency is broad, as in the case of a city, or if the population to be served is large and possessed of diverse views regarding the nature of the service, as is generally the case in a heterogeneous or big city school district, there is an opportunity for substantial disagreement about goals. Ironically, the more democratic and inclusive the political process, and the more representative the resultant policy-making body, the greater the prospect of disagreement regarding agency goals.

A reader unfamiliar with the political dynamics of a public K–12 or higher education agency in the United States might be surprised at the potential range of disagreement regarding organizational purposes. At first glance, it might appear reasonable to expect schools to be concerned with maximizing student academic achievement. However, American society expects much more of schools and colleges, both explicitly and implicitly. Societal cohesion, civic participation, economic productivity, national defense, patriotism, social mobility, employment opportunities, and moral integrity are all social purposes to which schools are expected to contribute. Reasonable people can arrive at varying conclusions regarding which of these goals is of greater or lesser significance.

Implicitly, schools may be expected to meet yet another agenda of objectives. Some cynics assert that policy makers desire schools to serve unseemly purposes such as ladders to further the policy makers' personal political careers, pulpits for publicly promoting privately held ideologies, "warehouses" for youth until they are acceptable to the labor market, or as trainers of an unquestioning and docile workforce.

The spectrum of potential purposes for a K–12 or higher education agency, public or private, is remarkably broad. The intent here is not to suggest that one goal or set of goals is to be preferred over another. Rather, the point is that the objectives an organization attempts to maximize, either through a set of explicit decisions or by default by making no decisions, will influence internal allocation of resources.

A school district or college that desires to enhance student academic achievement, promote acceptance of its graduates to colleges and universities, encourage graduate school enrollments, or reduce student dropout rates may allocate its funds and efforts quite differently from one that has as its prime, if unprofessed, purpose serving as the employer of last resort for a labor pool of unskilled political constituents.

Small agencies, or those serving homogeneous populations, are likely to reach agreement with relative ease. In more complicated settings, a set of political compromises must be struck in order to reach accord on organizational purposes. This should not be interpreted as improper or bad. Indeed, a political system is operating effectively when it resolves disagreements peacefully that otherwise might escalate into painful or protracted conflicts.

Political compromise may necessitate multiple or vaguely worded agendas for an organization. For example, many school districts specify that their purpose is educating the whole child. This is at once a noble and an empty statement. No one can easily argue with such a high-minded aspiration. On the other hand, how would an organization know if it achieved its purposes?

However, from the perspective of strategic planning, even amorphous goals are to be preferred over the condition where no explicit agreement is reached regarding agency objectives. In the latter situation, an organization either pursues too many goals or has no direction whatsoever. In such anarchical situations, an agency frequently will fragment its resources to the point of being ineffective. In not being able to pursue a reasonably concentrated explicit agenda, it risks not being able to achieve any purposes.

Under ideal conditions, an organization will already have derived an explicit agenda of purposes that can be used to guide a strategic planning effort. In the absence of such an agenda, planners may have to stimulate policy makers and managers to make their goals explicit. The least desirable scenario entails strategic planners, engaged from outside an organization, having to assume or infer an organization's purposes. This involves substantial risks. A resource mobilization plan directed at maximizing externally imputed objectives might be rejected by those in power as inconsistent with their implicit purposes. Under these conditions, strategic planning can dissolve into a hollow paper-and-pencil undertaking. It is strategic plans imposed from the outside of an organization that are most at risk of being placed on a shelf and gathering dust.

Even though less than fully desirable, when planners have to assume organizational objectives, all is not necessarily lost. Sometimes policy makers, themselves unable to craft an agreement, will acquiesce to or adopt goals specified by a group of outsiders in whom they have confidence. A highly stressful alternative is for strategic planners to impose direction, or purposes, on an organization through external political pressures. Here, a planner leaves the domain of the technician and dramatically enters the realm of planner as politician.

These political machinations are described in greater detail in Chapter 5. Suffice it to say here that, on occasion, public officials are badly embarrassed, and may even have to resign, because they fail to understand that an appropriately legitimated, comprehensive strategic-planning effort can create a potent wave of unfavorable political momentum capable of unseating those in power. This is true even if the planning team comprises individuals from outside the operating agency itself.

Because of possible political consequences, a policy maker or public-sector manager is well advised to utilize strategic planning for purposes of his or her own, as well as the organization's well-being. If a strategic planning effort is mandated from the outside, then accede to it gracefully, cooperate with it, shape it for productive purposes, perhaps attempt appropriately to influence it, but do not resist it unless prepared to expend substantial political resources, and perhaps even lose.

If an organization's political leaders believe their agency is performing well and simply desire an affirmation of this condition, then they should seek strategic planners from outside whose legitimacy or credentials are impeccable.

Even here there is risk, however. Such outsiders may uncover some heretofore unknown and unfavorable condition. The answer in such uncomfortable circumstances is to know the planners sufficiently to have confidence that they will bring the bad news carefully to the attention of organizational leaders and discuss its consequences before informing others outside the organization.

▪ KEY CONSIDERATIONS IN THE PLANNING PROCESS

When a strategic education leader is to engage in the planning process, three key considerations must be made. These include a regard for the level of intergovernmental complexity at play in the endeavor, the need for objectivity in the planning process, and the degree of technical sophistication essential to approach the enterprise thoughtfully.

Intergovernmental Complexity

Public schools particularly, and to some degree private and independent schools as well, seldom have the luxury of freely determining their own purposes. They operate in a complicated federal matrix. As specified in Chapter 5, the United States is a mosaic of overlapping **authorities**, national, state, and local. Consequently, a strategic planning effort in a school district or school should be unusually mindful of the purposes that are imposed at higher government levels, state and federal. For example, states have statutorily specified learning objectives, objectives reflected in state standardized achievement tests. Similarly the federal **No Child Left Behind Act** demands of states and local districts that they achieve adequate yearly progress, measured in terms of academic achievement. No strategic planning endeavor can bypass or neglect these high-level mandates. This ability to focus both within the school context and simultaneously on issues within the external environment is a key principle of strategic education leadership.

Objectivity

In addition to relying upon explicit objectives, full-blown strategic planning projects undertaken for formal organizations differ from ad hoc assessments and seat-of-the-pants extrapolations of a household or small business on yet another dimension: efforts to achieve objectivity. "*Objectivity*," in this context, refers to the absence of prejudice, a condition of independence, a lack of conflicting interests, or an open-mindedness on the part of those conducting analyses and generating alternative recommendations.

Ensuring objectivity has important implications for the *who* of planning, a topic covered later in this chapter. However, a reader should keep in mind that at crucial junctures, independent judgment is an indispensable aid to strategic planning.

Planning rests on several platforms, where obtaining informed, unbiased counsel may be crucial for the success of the undertaking. Examples include assessing potential markets for service, measuring current productivity, evaluating congruence between present personnel and those likely to be needed in the future, judging relations between an organization and its clients, and predicting future regulatory environments. A few illustrations may assist in making the point more concrete.

Enrollment projections are pivotal for understanding the numbers of students likely to present themselves for educational services in the future. Demographic and market share analyses are equally crucial for a college or university. These projections are also fundamental for extrapolating likely future revenues and expenditures and the need for personnel and facilities. Given the crucial nature of this technical planning dimension, it is important not only that those entrusted with the tasks be competent and experienced, but also that they not have a tightly vested interest in the outcome. It would be inappropriate to rely upon building contractors and architects to undertake enrollment projections or teacher or faculty bargaining agents or citizen tax relief representatives to undertake revenue projections.

Technical Sophistication

When undertaken appropriately, strategic planning also relies upon a degree of technical sophistication that surpasses the ability of many informal or small organizations to obtain. Much of the "technology" is involved in two components of strategic planning: (1) understanding an organization's relationship to specific dimensions of its external environment and (2) understanding the internal allocation of an organization's resources.

External Environments. Ways to assess an organization's relation to specific dimensions in the external environment are varied. The following questions illustrate the type of considerations a strategic leader must make in regard to the broader environmental context. What is the current market for a product or service, and how might it change in the future? Is there a new technology on the horizon that will likely eliminate the demand or perhaps create a demand for a different set of goods or services? What portion of existing and likely future demands can an organization control and under what conditions? What do current clients think about an organization's products or services? How do they perceive the organization? What changes would customers or clients like to see undertaken to serve them better?

Questions such as these lend themselves to technically derived answers. These dimensions can be made more specific for educational organizations and can be contrasted with a different set of questions that generally must be answered in other ways.

For an operating educational organization, the clientele to be served drives the system. Consequently, having adequate knowledge of the current cohort of students and projections of future cohorts is critical. Enrollment projections and student **flow models** can be constructed and regularly updated. No school, district, or educational system should be without such systematically generated information.

In the United States, where elementary school attendance is virtually universal, projecting enrollments in the early grades is a relatively easy undertaking. This is particularly true in large districts or in a state as a whole. In-and-out migration, private school enrollments, and possible fluctuations in birthrates must all be taken into account, but these are not difficult technically, assuming adequate information. These data must, of course, be finely tuned by the addition of information regarding building permits, developer plans, housing starts, interest rates for housing loans, and an assortment of local particulars.

Predicting enrollments for secondary schools, private schools, and higher education institutions is more difficult but still can be accomplished with great accuracy. Indeed, predictions can be, and are, made for all such institutions by entire states and nations. Technical projections of future school populations serve as an important basis for revenue and expenditure analyses as well as assessments of future personnel and facility needs.

Enrollments can be thought of as an "input" to schools and colleges from the external environment. Another component of the external environment to which education systems must be alert is the "market" for education products. Here the concern is the relationship between the external environment and school "outputs." What kinds of jobs are likely to develop, and how should educational institutions react to future labor needs? What are the views of parents, citizens, and employers regarding the current performance of schools? Various analytic and survey techniques can be employed to answer questions such as these.

Internal Environments. Technical procedures also assist in better understanding internal allocations of an organization's resources and the status of its "productivity." A private-sector firm may desire information regarding internal allocations in order to reduce production costs and overhead and thereby improve profits. A not-for-profit or public-sector organization may wish to assess internal allocations in order to determine if it can improve or expand the range of services offered to clients. Here the analytic techniques of the cost accountant come into play.

Ratio analyses are particularly useful. Here, an organization can make three kinds of comparisons. It can compare its costs for an operation or object with what it paid for the same undertaking in the past—historical comparison. Another kind of comparison, horizontal comparison, is between an organization's costs for an operation or object and the expenditure figures from a similar organization—for example, another school district or college of similar size and purpose. A third kind of comparison involves assessing an organization's cost for an operation or object with expenditures for similar endeavors but in different agencies. For example, a school or college can compare its food costs on a unit basis with those of a hospital.

An organization also may desire to examine the extent to which it is currently meeting its strategic goals, and frequently this may involve substantial technical sophistication. This is especially true with schools. Measuring student outcomes can involve awesome complexity regarding sampling, item selection, test construction, and analysis of out-of-school influences on achievement.

Technical sophistication thus has a role in strategic planning in order to understand both internal and external conditions of an organization. Moreover, techniques such as demographic analyses, flow models, financial accounting, ratio analysis, survey research, opinion polling, and outcome measurement may be applied both to current and future conditions. Taken in isolation, absent consideration for an organization's purposes, politics, and people, these technological dimensions may prove relatively useless. However, when combined appropriately with other planning components, technical tools can crucially strengthen final strategic plan analyses and outcomes.

Timing: When Should Strategic Planning Be Undertaken?

Planning is, or at least should be, a cyclical activity. To be maximally effective, a strategic plan should be systematically revisited. Not only does this enable planners to update data and extend projections, but also it enables policy makers and organizational leaders to reassess the assumptions upon which a strategic plan is based. It probably is better for an organization to construct a strategic plan at one point in time, than never to do it at all. However, the primary benefit of a strategic planning effort is not only initially to chart but also thereafter to maintain a direction for an agency. When an organization continually engages in planning, the chance is good that it is transforming itself into a strategic organization. In these instances, strategic planning morphs into strategic thinking, the ultimate goal of an effective agency.

If strategic planning, when undertaken at its best, is cyclical, when should the cycle begin? The easy response is "at any point, and perhaps the sooner the better." This may not be the most realistic or even the best answer. There are stages in the life of an organization when initiating a comprehensive strategic planning effort makes more sense than at other times. Also, initiating a comprehensive strategic planning undertaking has symbolic and political consequences. Therefore, selection of the starting point, and the manner in which it is announced, should be carefully considered.

If an organization is judged to be out of control, ineffective, or unresponsive to client expectations and constituent preferences, then launching a strategic planning project with substantial publicity may be desirable. High visibility and use of a prestigious planning team can focus attention on, and build and create, a powerful anticipation for improved project or agency results. All this in turn may assist in changing an organization. When radical reform is the purpose, then finding the most appropriate time to announce the planning project is crucial.

Leadership transitions offer a particularly attractive opportunity in the life cycle of an organization to launch a planning project intended to create major change. For example, a dramatic planning point occurs when a major management shift takes place (a new school board majority is elected or a new superintendent is selected, replacing a long-term incumbent) or a dramatic organizational shock has occurred or is about to occur (a drastic revenue ceiling has been imposed, enrollments are predicted suddenly to explode, or consolidation with a neighboring district has been mandated).

The foregoing examples represent major organizational shifts and are relatively infrequent events. They offer particularly attractive opportunities for policy makers and leaders to gain leverage for organizational change. An alert leader will be quick to take advantage of such openings and use them to launch a comprehensive planning effort.

If no dramatic public event appears available as a coincidental opportunity to begin a planning project, there is an alternative. Make announcement of the planning project itself the major feature. Those initiating the plan, desiring the organizational reforms, can utilize the planning project and the identification of the planning team as a publicity centerpiece. However, leaders should be sensitive to the fact that one or a series of highly visible events creates expectations for change that can be damaging to an organization and its leadership, if not fulfilled.

If an organization is judged to be performing reasonably well and strategic planning is envisioned as a tool for fine-tuning its operation, then a less-dramatic launching may be appropriate. Here the intent is not to use the plan for major reform leverage, but simply for minor course redirection. In such circumstances, it is often useful to begin the planning project coincident with natural recurring events in the life cycle of the organization. In this manner, no undue publicity is accorded the event, and anxiety levels are not elevated unproductively.

Among the less dramatic and naturally occurring openings for educational organizations is the beginning of the school year. Educational organizations generally are oriented to an academic year beginning in the autumn and ending in late spring or early summer. It makes good sense to initiate a comprehensive planning project so as to permit its recommendations to be considered and acted upon by all appropriate constituents in time for implementation at the beginning of the academic year. This often means launching the undertaking the preceding summer.

An added advantage of beginning during the summer is that this is frequently the least busy time for various administrative officials and professional educators. In the absence of the day-to-day pressures of dealing with pupils and parents, they may be able to devote time and reflection to planning and analysis that otherwise would not easily be available.

In addition, budget cycles, legislative openings, calendar years, and other naturally recurring organizational beginnings offer additional points at which to initiate a planning project. The downside of a summer launch is the possible vacation absence of crucial staff, some of whom may have data badly needed for determining how well the organization is performing or how it is allocating its resources.

A strategic action plan is usually based upon a medium-length time horizon—for example, five years. That means projections, analyses, and goals are oriented toward a period five years into the future. For example, a planning team engaged by an education agency might begin enrollment projections for the year 2010 and carry them through to 2015.

Pupil projections act as a foundation for many other planning components, and five years is a reasonable basis upon which to project dynamic conditions such as an organization's revenues and expenditures. Personnel planning (hiring instructors) may necessitate longer-range projections. In this case a ten-year horizon may be appropriate. Facilities' planning often requires an even more extended set of projections—fifteen or twenty years.

As is probably obvious, the further into the future a projection extends, the greater the kind and range of undetermined events that can influence the outcome and the less accurate predictions are likely to be. In order to be maximally useful, a strategic plan should be updated on a regular basis so as to take into account dimensions such as new instructional techniques, intensified state or local mandates, alterations in the environment, or changes in client preferences. Systematically reassessing the information upon which a strategic plan is based reduces the range of unknown factors, renders projections more accurate, and thus enhances the utility of the plan.

Whom Should the Planning Team Comprise?

Before answering this question, it is important to distinguish between the "planning team" proper and the many other individuals and groups who because of their positions will participate in the planning process.

If appropriately conducted, a comprehensive strategic planning process will involve almost all top-level policy makers and leaders and managers in an organization and a representative sample of other employees, clients, and, in a public-sector organization, citizens as well. All of these individuals will be needed to supply information, offer opinions, and make decisions; however, these are not necessarily members of the planning team.

A Planning Team

The planning team should consist of a group of individuals selected for the skills, knowledge, and experience they can contribute to the undertaking. The team leader, head planner, should possess a comprehensive understanding of the institution involved, be it a corporation, a state education agency, a school district, or an individual school. In addition, the team leader should possess knowledge of the components of a strategic planning project, both technical and procedural. It is not necessary that the leader be able himself or herself to conduct every part of the study. However, this leader should have sufficient management skill and experience to know quickly if a member of the team is not performing correctly or is incapable of completing an assignment.

In addition to a head planner, a strategic planning team in education should comprise individuals with technical talents in enrollment forecasting, demographics, finances, personnel systems, pupil outcome measurement, survey research and opinion polling, data management, research design, statistical methods, curriculum and instruction, graphic design, and report writing.

Each of these competencies need not represent a separate full-time individual. One person can sometimes encompass more than one field of expertise. Also, experts can be engaged on a part-time or consulting basis. However, regardless of how many individuals, or how much of the time of any one individual is occupied by a planning assignment, a comprehensive strategic planning effort is likely to draw upon all the above-listed technical areas prior to completion.

In addition to leadership and technical expertise, a strategic planning team needs individuals on it who are insightful regarding organizational and political dynamics. Such individuals can contribute productively to analyzing the results of technical studies. Also, periodically it is useful to conduct a policy audit. This is an analysis of an organization's effectiveness in communicating and implementing policy directives.

Inside or Outside?

From where should the planning team come, inside or outside an organization? An answer to this question depends upon several conditions. The purposes for which a strategic planning project is being initiated will necessarily influence the prospective composition of the planning team.

Assuming a large organization possessed of substantial technical capability, it still may be advisable to rely upon outsiders to undertake the planning. The decision revolves around the degree to which radical change is envisioned or the added legitimacy of an objective outside observer is desired. Depending too heavily upon insiders risks a conflict of interest and a desire on the part of those currently employed to protect the status quo. On the other hand, if marginal or incremental changes and modest redirection are the anticipated end product, then relying upon insiders may prove appropriate. In the latter case, the assumption of available inside expertise is crucial.

If an organization does not possess on its staff the previously listed range of technical skills, then there is little recourse but to engage the services of outsiders. However, when the decision is made to utilize outside planners to obtain technical competence, gain outside legitimacy, stimulate change, or all three, then the bona fides of those involved are critical. Keep in mind that comprehensive strategic planning, particularly in the public sector, is also a political undertaking. The qualifications, experience, and institutional affiliation of the planning team, particularly its leader, will enter into the political equation. They will influence not only the quality of the strategic planning effort, but also the manner in which its recommendations are accepted and eventually implemented.

Of course, a compromise or fusion of inside and outside talent is possible. Here again, the anticipated or desired strategic planning outcome is an important influence on the decision. Radical reform suggests exclusion of insiders below the policy or highest management levels. Findings and recommendations of the planning team are too subject to insider influence to take the risk, if substantial organizational change is desired.

Public or Secret?

To what degree should organizational leaders reveal the existence of a strategic planning effort and the composition of the team? In fact, a comprehensive strategic planning project is sufficiently visible throughout an organization that there is little realistic prospect of disguising its existence. This is true even in a private-sector agency, but particularly accurate in a public-sector organization. Furthermore, the more troubled the organization, the more widely observed is the fact that it is not meeting its goals or serving its clients and the less likely a strategic planning project can be kept secret.

When chief executives or policy boards desire new ideas or suggestions for new direction, they can sometimes convene a high-level task force and, if they want, keep it a secret. In such circumstances, secrecy protects the initiators from embarrassment. If they do not desire to adopt the suggested ideas, they are not saddled subsequently with having to explain publicly why they rejected the advice of a prestigious body of individuals.

Of course, secrecy in such instances also has its costs. In addition to the usual tension accompanying surreptitious activities, keeping a high-level organizational task force secret often squanders the visibility and legitimacy to be gained from the prestige of its members, if the initiators in fact turn out to concur with its recommendations. As is often the case, there are trade-offs, and decision makers are called upon to anticipate the future without complete information.

Unlike task force activities, strategic planning can seldom take place surreptitiously. Data gathering, analyses, inquiries regarding outcomes and opinions, and the overall sweep of employee and client involvement militate against secrecy. An organizational leader probably errs in attempting to engage in strategic planning secretly. The covert effort will eventually be discovered, and the planning team's outcomes compromised by the subsequent suspicions. Strategic planning is better conducted openly, and members of the team should be known to those involved and with whom they will interact.

Why Undertake Strategic Planning?

In the most global terms, planning is done to render an organization more effective. However, there are more detailed responses to such an inquiry. Strategic planning is appropriate for undertaking an assessment of an organization's performance and ensuring that it is headed in desired directions. In this fashion, policy makers and managers fulfill their multiple responsibilities to owners, shareholders, or the general public.

An organization that is unevaluated risks being out of control. Private-sector firms expected to generate profits for their owners have a more universal criterion, namely money, against which to assess their success. Even so, private-sector agencies can stray off course—for example, lose their market share, fall prey to shoddy production quality, or lag behind competition in customer service. Consequently, the evaluation that a comprehensive strategic planning project can offer is of value in ensuring sustained productivity. Strategic planning has an added feature beyond assessment. It not only provides policy makers and managers with a scorecard on past effectiveness, but it also can suggest a map for future direction.

All that has been stated immediately above regarding private-sector firms is especially true in public-sector organizations where the "bottom line," expected outcomes, is not nearly so easily specified or measured. Every organization should have a regularly employed evaluation system, a feedback loop that continually informs policy makers and managers of the level of performance. Strategic planning extends the usefulness of such an evaluation mechanism by systematically linking organizational outcomes to specific agency purposes, internal resource allocation, and consumer or client satisfaction and preferences.

Strategic planning is also appropriate for determining whether or not the external or internal environment is undergoing changes that potentially could alter an organization's purposes or the manner in which it operates. It is important for an organization to undertake a periodic assessment of the external environment in which it operates. Only in this manner can it be assured of anticipating important changes in sufficient time to adjust to them successfully.

Rapid influx of non-English-speaking students, construction of a nearby public community college, growing taxpayer resentment, or dramatically expanding use of charter or nonpublic schools illustrate environmental alterations with significant portent for a local school district's operation. Strategic planning involves systematically scanning an organization's environmental horizon for trends and developments with potential influence. This is the case for changes likely to occur in both internal and external environments.

Systematic planning can inform an organization of important pending developments within itself. For example, a school district learning that 25 percent of its teacher workforce will reach retirement age within the next five years is in a position to plan and mount a comprehensive recruitment program. With sufficient advance notice, a school board perhaps can allocate funds to plan a recruitment campaign, develop an appropriate orientation for new teachers, inform master teachers of forthcoming training responsibilities and schedule their time accordingly, establish new linkages with teacher training institutions, and so on.

Changes in the external environment can also mean important future changes for an organization. For example, for a school district to have to accommodate an enrollment decline of 20 percent over the next five years undoubtedly would be difficult. Layoffs, possible school closures, and declining revenues all provoke policy and management headaches, not to mention personal hardship for individual employees, parents, and possibly pupils. However, as painful as contraction can be for an organization, forewarning is far more likely than ignorance to facilitate planning that can mitigate distressing developments.

Knowing that a major change is going to occur does not by itself ensure ability to cope. However, ignorance of a pending development almost inevitably guarantees inability to formulate and mobilize resources in support of a timely and rational solution. The larger the organization, the longer it typically takes to change direction. Thus, large organizations, such as school districts, particularly should utilize strategic planning in order to sense pending changes in their environment.

Strategic planning is appropriate when an organization's effectiveness is in question and those responsible for its management, its leaders, desire reform. Organizations can drift for a variety of reasons: lack of vision on the part of policy makers, poor leadership, lack of appropriate incentives, poor employee selection and training, misreading of client preferences, failure to adjust to environmental shifts, and so on. Regardless of the explanation, dissatisfaction may begin to build: elected officials are unhappy; stockholders become distressed at low returns to their investment; parents express dissatisfaction with pupil academic performance or discipline; or employers become disturbed with the level of training they experience with entry-level employees.

On occasion, the dissatisfaction may be irrational. In 1957 the Soviet Union launched its first orbital space vehicle, Sputnik. The United States was caught technologically flat-footed by a series of prior federal government decisions regarding space. National embarrassment dictated a scapegoat be found, and schools' alleged lack of academic rigor and discipline eventually was the target. A result was an awesome outpouring of school reform rhetoric and a flurry of high-level task forces, Congressional bills, and school district flagellation. A similar set of activities ensued in the aftermath of the 1983 public release of

A Nation at Risk, a high-level U.S. Department of Education report that triggered education alarm bells that have echoed for decades, most recently setting the stage for the 2001 enactment of the No Child Left Behind Act.

Aside from the source of displeasure, or its validity, organizations come under fire from time to time. Strategic planning offers a systematic and comprehensive means for assessing the degree to which an agency really is off course and generates alternative means by which redirection and reform may occur.

Lastly, an organization may genuinely and accurately believe itself to be operating effectively and, nevertheless, desire the reassurance and feedback of an outside assessment. Under such circumstances, all or a portion of a strategic planning endeavor may be useful.

Summary

Strategic planning is a tool by which education policy makers and leaders can assess an organization to determine whether it is performing appropriately and thereafter decide either that only fine-tuning and minimal redirection are in order or that substantial reform is needed. Strategic planning relies upon a mix of technically sophisticated procedures and social and political analyses to arrive at a picture of an organization's current performance relative to its goals, the manner in which it allocated its resources internally, its relationship to external environments, and likely alterations in its external and internal conditions. The outcome of these procedures is a strategic plan that, if propelled forcefully by an agency's policy makers and managers or by outside political pressures, can result in sustained productivity or dynamic reform for an organization. Whether comprising outside experts, employees of the organization itself, or some combination, a strategic planning team consists of individuals knowledgeable about a wide range of technical procedures as well as experts in organizational dynamics and politics. A respected team leader certainly is a crucial component.

The timing of a strategic planning effort is also important. Major transitions in the life of an organization often provide particularly advantageous openings to launch a planning project. Similarly, the completion of a planning effort should be timed to coincide with events that encourage change. In another sense, strategic planning should never stop. A plan, once forged, should be systematically updated and, where appropriate, altered. Once under way, comprehensive strategic planning insinuates itself so deeply into the important interstices of an organization that any posture other than openness regarding the undertaking would be ill advised. Finally, the ultimate organizational objective is not so much formal planning, though such is good. Rather, the ultimate goal is to imbue an organization and its employees, particularly its leaders, with a predisposition to strategic thinking.

Discussion Questions

1. As a litmus test for readiness to embark upon strategic planning, to what degree does your current education organization benefit from (1) specific organizational goals, (2) a capacity for objective judgment, and (3) technical expertise? In which of these dimensions would your organization be most challenged? What can you as a strategic leader do to ameliorate this condition?

2. Reflect on your career in education leadership. List one significant end goal that you have for yourself and several supporting instrumental goals that will help you achieve it.

3. Based on your past experiences with strategic planning or goal-setting activities, in what ways have you felt the impact of politics on the process and outcomes of these goal-setting endeavors?

4. When considering the technical sophistication necessary for successful strategic planning, both internal and external environments need to be considered. Provide one example of how you can assess an important aspect of your current organization's external and internal environment for the purpose of meeting current goals.

5. At this point in the life cycle of your organization, do you feel your institution would benefit from a new strategic planning initiative? Why or why not?

6. ELCC Standard 1 places a vision for learning at the center of a school. What role has a vision for learning played in previous planning initiatives at your school? As a current or aspiring school leader, how might you utilize your school's vision for learning when in the planning or developmental stages of initiatives and programs?

References and Suggestions for Further Reading

Blau, P. M., and Scott, W. R. (1962). *Formal organizations: A comparative approach*. San Francisco: Chandler Publishing Company.

This text presents a sociological analysis of some of the main facets of organizational life, including the nature and types of formal organizations, the connections between them and the larger social context of which they are a part, and the various aspects of their internal structure.

Gergen, D. (2000). *Eyewitness to power*. New York: Touchstone/Simon & Schuster.

Gergen, a White House adviser to four presidents, takes the reader inside the administrations of Nixon, Ford, Reagan, and Clinton and offers a vivid, behind-the-scenes account of their struggles to exercise power while drawing from them key lessons for leaders of the future.

Goldstein, L., Nolan, T., and Pfeiffer, J. (1993). *Applied strategic planning: How to develop a plan that really works*. New York: McGraw-Hill.

This primer provides a model for transforming organizations through the involvement of all employees.

Kaplan, R. S., and Norton, D. P. (2000). *The strategy focused organization: How business score cards thrive in the new business environment*. Boston: Harvard Business School Press.

Culled from the research of 200 companies, this book develops a strategic planning process that requires the inclusion of all employees versus just the top management.

Kirst, M. W. (1984). *Who controls our schools?* Stanford, CA: Stanford Alumni Association.

This text places in historical perspective concerns with how well American schools perform their function and also seeks to move beyond the history of education to an understanding of modern education policies.

Mintzberg, H., Lampel, J., and Ahlstrand, B. (2005). *Strategy safari: A guided walking tour through the wilds of strategic management.* New York: Free Press.
These management scholars take ten different models of creative planning strategies and analyze the contributions and limitations of each approach.

Notes

1. A reader may recognize quickly that what constitutes an *end* for an education system may be an *instrumental* objective for the larger society. Whether the goal is related to a strategy or a tactic is always a matter of perspective.

PART TWO

Politics

Policy Knowledge Needed
by Strategic Leaders

■ INTRODUCTION

Part II of the text provides an overview of several key domains of political and policy-related knowledge that are crucial in enabling strategic leaders to become more effective in leading educational organizations. For example, Chapter 4 provides an overview of the governance mechanisms that exert influence on American education systems. Chapter 5 provides conceptual lenses through which leaders can understand school politics while providing a brief history of key American education policies. Chapter 6 examines the evolution of U.S. education finance and postulates regarding the future fiscal landscape that education leaders will likely confront. Chapter 7 considers the role of school law in shaping the operational context for education leaders and notes the constitutional and jurisprudential underpinnings of American education.

A Caveat

Politics and education are often said to be separate. Yet such a statement cannot possibly be taken seriously. The U.S. education system, including elementary and secondary and postsecondary levels, annually expends almost a trillion dollars. It involves more than seventy million students and a hundred million households, employs seven to eight million individuals, and occupies 8 to 10 percent of the gross domestic product. It is unreal to think that any endeavor involving this many resources and holding such significance to the people in general and individuals in particular could possibly avoid the scrutiny and involvement of the political system. It then follows, obviously, that a strategic leader should be well aware of political dynamics, policy processes, governance conditions, legal and financial principles, and significant education policies themselves.

■ APPLICABILITY OF PART II CONTENT TO ELCC STANDARDS

Content in Part II of the text is most closely aligned with ELCC Standards 2, 3, 5, and 6. By considering the organization and control of American education, the treatment of governance issues in Chapter 4 has implications for ELCC Standard 3. Chapters 5, 6, and 7 provide important contextual knowledge for school leaders that is applicable to ELCC Standard 6. Additionally, the legal insights offered in Chapter 7 provide school leaders with the knowledge necessary to ensure school policies and practices are implemented in a fair manner, consistent with ELCC Standard 5.

■ CASE STUDIES

 CASE 3 ———————————————————————————————

A Profile of Leadership Complexity

A Case of Evolving and Conflicting Cultures and Expectations

Shannon Cantrell is the superintendent in Lake City, a 15,000-student district on the outskirts of one of the nation's major metropolitan areas. It was once a recreational area with a great deal of productive farmland but morphed into an upper-class enclave.

While having remained relatively stable for generations, the district's demographics have recently been changing. Developers have purchased large tracts of unincorporated farmland and have been constructing relatively inexpensive rental units and starter homes. While the population of Lake City for many years was quite homogeneous, it is rapidly becoming more diverse. These changes have been facilitated by increasing numbers of families from Mexico and Middle Eastern nations—Kurds, Afghanis, and others.

Shannon has been superintendent in Lake City for fifteen years. She has served as the district's only superintendent, ever since it was formed as a district. She had previously been a teacher in another state. She returned to graduate school, received a doctorate, worked in a central office in a nearby district, and then, when she turned forty-nine, assumed Lake City's superintendency.

Shannon is well educated, experienced, disciplined, sociable, and continually engaged in efforts to enhance her knowledge and expand her professional skills. She is particularly knowledgeable regarding learning, curriculum matters, the application of technology to instruction, and testing and measurement. When the district was formed, her background, interests, and expertise seemed perfectly suited for the challenge of an academically oriented elite district.

Lake City started as a posh suburb. Parents purchased expensive homes on or near the lake, and they wanted the public-sector equivalent of private schooling. Shannon fit their needs well. She knew about instruction, and she knew well how to select good principals and good teachers who could facilitate the college aspirations of her high-expectation parents.

She has experienced only minor conflicts with her school board or her staff. Lake City was a community with a coherent social structure, and Shannon was an integral part of it, considering her membership in Rotary and her easy access to the city's power elite.

Shannon also has been attentive to another facet of her community's expectation. Her community wanted a good basketball team, and year after year her high school coach has fulfilled the expectation. Lake City has had good players, many of whom actually moved into or otherwise used a Lake City address to gain admission to a highly regarded high school and then play basketball on what proved year after year to be a championship team.

Lake City's new children, those moving into the burgeoning rental community and inexpensive starter homes, are far less affluent and far more in need of remedial classes and English language training. In addition, newly arrived parents seem less oriented toward college for their children and more concerned about vocational training. In sports, it is soccer that interests them far more than basketball.

Shannon is well informed regarding social change, and she is an astute student of demography. She understands well that her district is undergoing a transition, and she is confident in her ability to steer a new course, paying respect to the old while paying productive attention to what needs to change to accommodate the new.

However, regardless of Shannon's best intentions, No Child Left Behind Act (NCLB) standards, when coupled with her state's learning objectives and her vocal and upwardly mobile middle class parents' demands, place Shannon in an awkward spot. Her town's power structure is not eager to raise the tax rate. She cannot otherwise generate additional funding. Yet she somehow needs to train her workforce in the ways of their new students. She sees a need for added services, particularly around language and vocational training. She also sees the need for an adult education program, something that Lake City never before considered.

Still, she constantly is wondering how she can reallocate resources to (1) ensure that the district's academically talented and highly aspiring middle class students still get the hands-on attention to which their parents have become accustomed; (2) provide the district's new lower socioeconomic students with the remedial preparation needed for NCLB proficiency ratings and adequate yearly progress; (3) cater to the vocational aspirations of her new students; and (4) accommodate the now-expanded sports programs that she feels her community desires.

At a Rotary meeting, one of her friends has suggested that the Lake City old-guard power structure, while opposing a tax increase, might well accept a major private fund-raising campaign. Perhaps they would start and annually ensure funding for a school district foundation. The condition would be that the money generated would have to support advanced placement and other elite programs that the moneyed crowd preferred, and the basketball team. It would be unlikely that they would want their charitable donations to subsidize vocational courses, remedial activities, English as a Second Language, or soccer.

Shannon believes she is caught between old and new, academic and vocational, classroom instruction and athletics, old money and newly arrived low-income residents, demands for added resources and resistance to higher taxes, and federal and state requirements and local district preferences; and now she must decide if she should engage in community fund-raising for a select group of beneficiaries. She believes she and the school board face some tough choices. Of course, she is coming close to retirement age. That in itself could be a choice for her.

Discussion Questions for Case 3

1. Can a medium-size district adequately balance such growing and dramatic differences in its residents and their expectations?
2. What are a few reasonable solutions to Lake City's growing challenges?
3. Should Lake City be divided into two districts to better serve its two populations?
4. Should the school board accept the idea of highly targeted charitable contributions, resources likely to favor only a portion of the district's students?
5. Would such an action buy any peace by enabling the district to cater to two populations better?
6. Does No Child Left Behind make matters better or worse in Lake City?
7. Should Shannon just retire and let a successor wrestle with these issues?
8. What are the parallels between Shannon Cantrell and Daniel Bowles, the private-sector CEO in Case 1 in Part I?

CASE 4

A State Official's Challenge

Seeking a Political Solution to Facilitate a Technical Improvement

Mary Kay Porter was the chief state school officer of one of the nation's largest states. She had been a highly renowned teacher and had subsequently managed a private-sector firm delivering supplemental education services to underperforming students in local school districts. Her business had done well, and she was moderately wealthy.

Mary Kay was a single mother who raised her son virtually without support from her former husband. She was a good mother, and her son had been a star high school athlete and was now the quarterback on the bowl-bound state university football team. It was hard to know who was the celebrity, politico mom or likely NFL Hall of Fame offspring.

She was dynamic on virtually every dimension. Her business employees were unusually fond of her. In addition she was poised and telegenic. She was physically fit, stylish, articulate, fast on her feet, and a political campaign manager's dream. She had run for school board in the large urban district in which she resided and became a regular fixture on local television. In time, local business and political officials persuaded her to run for state office, and she did, easily winning a race to be the state's superintendent of public instruction. She ran for a nonpartisan office, not having to proclaim her allegiance to either major party. However, both Republicans and Democrats lusted after her as prospectively one of their own in a downstream governor's race.

Mary Kay easily trumped all opponents in the primary and, after the election, moved to the state capital. She inherited a large and dispirited bureaucracy that had been overseen by her predecessor and run as a feudal fiefdom devoted to his personal well-being and political career and only remotely concerned with the achievement of the state's school systems and its students.

Mary Kay was at once idealistic and pragmatic. She wanted change, and she wanted it fast. After all, if she was going to run for reelection, four years was not a long time in which to turn the agency around and elevate school standards in her state. She had work to do.

Mary Kay's view of the world, her philosophy, had been shaped both by her formal education, including several dynamic college professors, and by her experience as a teacher and successful businesswoman. She came to believe that it was important to be conservative at the core of an organization's activities, risking little, and progressive on the periphery, experimenting with new activities and items that did not jeopardize the fundamental operation of the organization.

State superintendent Mary Kay Porter also knew instinctively of the significance of hiring the right people. In her early months on the job she spent endless hours perusing job applications and résumés searching for the subordinates that could enforce her will, without her having to supervise them every moment. If she was to succeed, she would continuously have to be mobilizing public understanding and external political support, and she would not have the time constantly to oversee the day-to-day actions of a bureaucracy. For supervision and implementation, she wanted smart subordinates in whom she could trust and to whom she could confidently delegate authority and assignments. She wanted a team of able lieutenants.

Mary Kay had another management tool important to her. From running her business she had come to understand the crucial significance of accurate data, not simply regarding resource inputs, with which she thought educators seemed to be obsessed, but also with process measures and multiple performance indicators.

Mary Kay wanted a first-rate management information system that would enable her, the state legislature and governor, professional educators, and the public accurately to know just where the state's schools stood. Getting such an information system would become her challenge. It was upon this sword that she was prepared to fall because she knew both instinctively and intellectually that this is what her state needed most.

A principal problem in setting her sights on constructing an information system was that information had little political sex appeal. Providing new services to constituents, reducing class size, constructing new buildings, adding preschool classes, expanding vocational classes, and ensuring teachers had large salary increases were the pork-barrel staples of long-term political success. These were the types of activities to which one could point when running for higher office and proclaim leadership success.

Still, Mary Kay had a strong internal gyroscope. She took Margaret Thatcher as a role model. Mrs. Thatcher repeatedly rowed upstream against public opinion and took political risks to turn around the English mind-set and unleash the island nation on a remarkable thirty-year trajectory of economic success and modern well-being. That was the way in which Mary Kay Porter saw herself.

Mary Kay set about the design and acquisition of a modern state education data system in a most thoughtful manner. First, she spoke extensively with important political officials, including the governor and the officers of both state legislative houses. Next, she made the rounds of the state's business elites and was quick to include teacher and administrator leaders in her planning conversations. She also fully informed herself regarding the technical parameters of a modern data system.

Then she launched her effort via the appointment of a highly visible blue-ribbon state education data commission, chaired by a famous electronics company executive with a track record of public service. On her commission was the right combination of public, private, political, and other constituents. She knew how to balance these efforts, and she knew to supply her commission with able staff. She went further and procured private-foundation financial support for the endeavor so that no future political opponent could accuse her of foolishly expending public funds in pursuit of a frivolous pipe dream.

Here is what Mary Kay eventually encountered: when it became evident that a comprehensive modern data system would have to have an individual identifier for each student enrolled in school, the American Civil Liberties Union immediately objected on grounds that such bar-codes thinking would infringe on personal privacy and surely contribute to the coming of a Big Brother dictator–led state.

When it also became evident that a modern education data system would have to connect students to their teachers in a data link, the teacher unions objected on grounds that such a bridge would lead down a slippery slope in which teachers would be held accountable for their students' academic performance, even when students did not want or were ill equipped to learn.

Further evidence that a modern data system would also link student test scores to the teachers under whom they studied triggered the opposition not only of teachers but also of administrators. The latter claimed that the next step would be to judge principals by the performance of their students, collectively for a school; that seemed unfair to them given that they had so little control over assignment of students, the operation of their school, and access to the resources needed to achieve academic success and to operate schools in the manner they knew was right.

When Mary Kay's commission went even further and made the case for tying dollars spent to performance results by classroom, school, and district, the entire education establishment proclaimed the effort to be ill conceived and inspired by a fanatic who wanted control.

Once control was mentioned, the state association of local school boards began to pay careful attention. Their fear was that the creation of a comprehensive data system would facilitate greater authority from the capital, and local preferences would more easily be overrun by state officials.

Once strong political opposition to a data system—something that initially seemed so safe and sanitary in the abstract—began to emerge, opponents visited with the governor and other political leaders and suggested that Mary Kay's idea had gone far enough. Mary Kay was thereafter visited by these officials, who advised her that her long-run political career was at stake and the best action was to accept the commission report graciously and then let it molder on the shelf of virtuous ideas. She was sufficiently distant from her reelection that the media and public would quickly forget about the commission report, and she could claim victory and pursue other more popular reforms such as reducing class size.

Mary Kay was a strong person. Her natural instinct was to fight and strive to win. Yet she knew that if she lost, all the other goals she hoped to pursue would go down with her. She had to think strategically. Should she stand and fight now, or come back another day?

Discussion Questions for Case 4

1. Should Mary Kay give up her aspirations for a modern education data system and succumb to political pressure?
2. Did Mary Kay make a mistake by launching her effort with political and media fanfare?
3. Might she have made more progress by simply requesting state education department technical staff to draw up specifications for a modern data system and then selling it piece by piece to the legislature and governor?
4. When compared to other changes such as charter schools, class-size reduction, teacher professional development, or higher teacher salaries, what kind of impact would a data system make?

CHAPTER FOUR

Governance

LEARNING OBJECTIVES

By the end of this chapter, you should be able to

- understand the organization and control of American education;
- identify the never-ending layers of statutory and legal authority that impinge on education leaders;
- recount the multiple constituencies with which education leaders are inevitably involved.

Organizational structure, as well as **governance** mechanisms and other control features, are relatively static components of American education. To be sure, the number of **school districts** and individual schools is large and ebbs and flows over time, and historically there has been a persistent increase in the range of services schools offer—for example, preschool, kindergarten, meals, transportation, after-school care, and summer tutorials.

Still, the fundamental organizational scaffolding of American education has been in place for more than a century and is unlikely to change dramatically, at least for decades and perhaps never in a reader's professional lifetime. Nevertheless, the relative immutability of education's organizational architecture does not automatically imply that the leadership context of schooling is also static. Indeed, education leadership is subject to an ever-moving set of altered societal conditions, expectations, and regulations. One need only refer to Figure 4.1 to see poignant evidence of this constant fluidity.

■ THE SEEMINGLY SEAMLESS SPECTRUM OF SCHOOLING STAKEHOLDERS

Almost no school leader—no principal, superintendent, headmaster, teacher union president, central office supervisor or director, nor other school official—has the luxury of administrative autonomy. Public schools serve a multitiered clientele. They are instruments of a larger society. Thus, they and their leaders have multiple masters. Moreover,

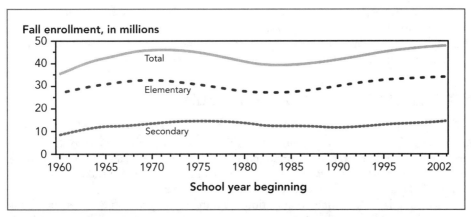

Fall enrollment, in millions

FIGURE 4.1 Enrollment Trends in American Public Elementary and Secondary Schools

Source: U.S. Department of Education, National Center for Education Statistics, *Statistics of State School Systems,* 1959–60 through 1969–70; *Statistics of Public Elementary* and *Secondary School Systems,* 1970 through 1980; *Revenue and Expenditures for Public Elementary and Secondary Education,* 1970–71 through 1980–81; and The NCES Common Core of Data (CCD), "State Nonfiscal Survey of Public Elementary and Secondary Education," 1981–82 through 2002–03, and "National Public Education Financial Survey," 1989–90 through 2000–01; and unpublished data.

an individual school, often even an independent, proprietary, or religious school, nests within multiple tiers of formal authority: local, state, federal, or national.

This chapter explains the complex formal and informal governance and control networks to which public and many nonpublic schools are continually subject. Before beginning, however, a reader should be conscious of the following audiences to which schools are expected to pay attention. This accounting prepares one's consciousness for the complexity regarding leadership challenges that follows.

Students and parents are obvious school stakeholders. However, there are many others. School district administrative authorities; teacher unions; county offices of education or other intermediate authorities; state officials, including governors and legislators; state and federal administrative agencies; the entire judicial system, including the criminal justice system; and various municipal and other civic, state, and federal officials responsible for enforcing rules regarding health, safety, and building codes all come into play.

The above list becomes more complicated when less-formal influences, such as athletic leagues, religious or ideological interest groups, philanthropic foundations, private-sector financial lending institutions and investment banks, bond rating firms, and civic booster and charitable agencies, are taken into account.

The examples can be extended, but the point is the same. Schools are the target of numerous expectations, influences, and interventions. Some of these influences are formal and stem from substantial structural or chartered authority—for example, superintendents, school boards, and state and federal government education departments. Others may have little formal authority but may nevertheless exert substantial influence by virtue of resources they distribute or withhold (e.g., philanthropic foundations) or political capital they carry.

While complicated, these interactions are not necessarily fearsome. An adroit school leader often can harness external forces, shape them toward a collective purpose, and take advantage of their financial capital, organizational energy, and political momentum to gain significant improvements for his or her school, school district, or other agency.

■ SCALE AND SCOPE OF U.S. SCHOOLING

When viewed from an overseas or global perspective, schooling in the United States has three unusual governance and organizational features. First is the degree to which decision making is multilayered and compounded. Schools are the focus for governance and political forces that are simultaneously centrifugal and centripetal, centralized and decentralized, all described in a subsequent section of this chapter.

A second relatively unique organizational feature is American education's magnitude. This is true regardless of the dimension under consideration: pupils, districts, schools, teachers, decision makers, size of administrative units, or financial resources.

A third unique feature is the diversity that characterizes the system. The United States seems to have the largest and smallest; the best and sometimes worst; highest- and lowest-spending districts; and on and on.

Scale. One way to understand the growing scope of our nation's education system is to look at trend data collected over the past several decades. Figure 4.1 displays over forty years' worth of statistics regarding U.S. K–12 enrollments. Figure 4.2 depicts the number of public school teachers, as well as the per-pupil ratios in the United States over the same period of

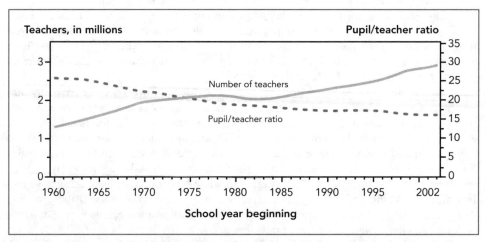

FIGURE 4.2 **Trends in the Number of Teachers and Pupil/Teacher Ratio in American Public Elementary and Secondary Schools**

Source: U.S. Department of Education, National Center for Education Statistics, *Statistics of State School Systems, 1959–60 through 1969–70; Statistics of Public Elementary and Secondary School Systems, 1970 through 1980; Revenue and Expenditures for Public Elementary and Secondary Education, 1970–71 through 1980–81;* and The NCES Common Core of Data (CCD), "State Nonfiscal Survey of Public Elementary and Secondary Education," 1981–82 through 2002–03, and "National Public Education Financial Survey," 1989–90 through 2000–01; and unpublished data.

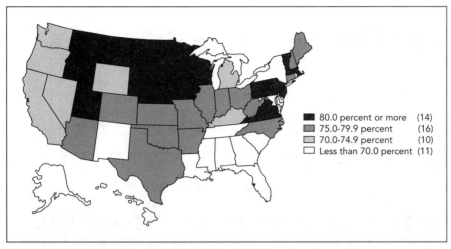

FIGURE 4.3 High School Completion Rates

Source: Seastrom, M., Hoffman, L., Chapman, C., and Stillwell, R. (2005). *The Averaged Freshman Graduation Rate for Public High Schools from the Common Core of Data: School Years 2001–02 and 2002–03* (NCES 2006-601), tables 2 and 3 and previously unpublished tabulation (September 2005). Data from U.S. Department of Education, National Center for Education Statistics, Common Core of Data (CCD), "State Nonfiscal Data File: School Years 1996–97 through 2003–04."

time. Figure 4.3 provides a national picture of recent public high school completion rates. Figure 4.4 illustrates the enrollment in both public and private colleges during the past forty years. Figures 4.5 and 4.6 highlight the trends of degrees attained and expenditures associated with our nation's public and private colleges. Figure 4.7 extends the picture of finances associated with our nation's schools by including K–12 institutions. Finally, Figure 4.8 depicts forty-five years of data looking at the years of school completed by persons twenty-five years and older in our nation.

Demography and Migration. Figures 4.1 through 4.8 illustrate both the current magnitude of the U.S. education system and its explosive post–World War II growth. Enrollments skyrocketed for two decades immediately following the war. As a result, local school districts were hard pressed to maintain pace with the growth. Indeed, one of the costly items for districts today is the physical maintenance of many hurriedly constructed post–World War II buildings. In the 1970s and for two decades thereafter, enrollments declined. By the 1990s enrollments again began to zoom. This latter increase is instructive because it displays the cyclical effects of demography upon schools.

The 1990s enrollment spurt is a function of what demographers label the Baby Boom Echo. These children are the offspring of post–World War II baby boomers. These younger mothers are not themselves having many children each. Indeed, their families average fewer than two children (2.1 children per each adult female is population balance, assuming no in or out migration). However, because there is such a large bulge of baby boomers themselves, even though they do not have large families, their offspring still account for a sizable portion of the current enrollment increase.

However, turn-of-the-twenty-first-century enrollment increases are only partially a consequence of Baby Boom Echo children. They also are a result of one of the nation's

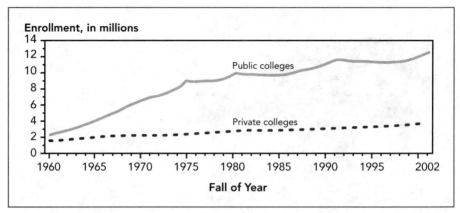

FIGURE 4.4 **National Enrollment Trends in Public and Private Colleges**

Source : U.S. Department of Education, National Center for Education Statistics, *Opening Fall Enrollment in Higher Education,* 1960 through 1965; *Financial Statistics of Institutions of Higher Education,* 1959–60 through 1964–65; *Earned Degrees Conferred,* 1959–60 through 1965–66. Higher Education General Information Survey (HEGIS), "Fall Enrollment in Institutions of Higher Education," 1966 through 1985; "Degrees and Other Formal Awards Conferred," 1986–87 through 1985–86; and "Financial Statistics of Institutions of Education," 1966–67 through 1985–86 and 1986–87 through 2002–03. Integrated Postsecondary Education Data System, "Fall Enrollment Survey" (IPEDS-EF:86–99), "Completions Survey" (IPEDS-C:87–99), "Finance Survey" (IPEDS-F:87–99), Fall 2001 through Fall 2003 and Spring 2001 to 2003.

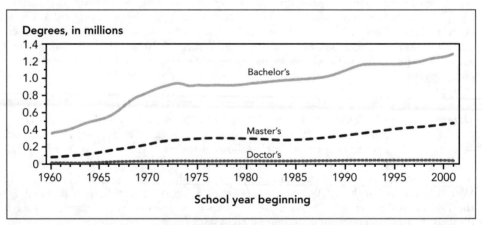

FIGURE 4.5 **Trends in Degrees Awarded at American Universities**

Source : U.S. Department of Education, National Center for Education Statistics, *Opening Fall Enrollment in Higher Education,* 1960 through 1965; *Financial Statistics of Institutions of Higher Education,* 1959–60 through 1964–65; *Earned Degrees Conferred,* 1959–60 through 1965–66. Higher Education General Information Survey (HEGIS), "Fall Enrollment in Institutions of Higher Education," 1966 through 1985; "Degrees and Other Formal Awards Conferred," 1986–87 through 1985–86; and "Financial Statistics of Institutions of Education," 1966–67 through 1985–86 and 1986–87 through 2002–03. Integrated Postsecondary Education Data System, "Fall Enrollment Survey" (IPEDS-EF:86–99), "Completions Survey" (IPEDS-C:87–99), "Finance Survey" (IPEDS-F:87–99), Fall 2001 through Fall 2003 and Spring 2001 to 2003.

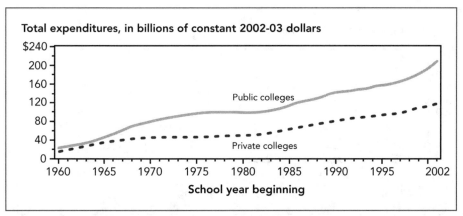

Total expenditures, in billions of constant 2002-03 dollars

FIGURE 4.6 National Expenditures on Private and
Public Postsecondary Education

Source : U.S. Department of Education, National Center for Education Statistics, *Opening Fall
Enrollment in Higher Education,* 1960 through 1965; *Financial Statistics of Institutions of Higher
Education,* 1959–60 through 1964–65; *Earned Degrees Conferred,* 1959–60 through 1965–66.
Higher Education General Information Survey (HEGIS), "Fall Enrollment in Institutions of Higher
Education," 1966 through 1985; "Degrees and Other Formal Awards Conferred," 1986–87
through 1985–86; and "Financial Statistics of Institutions of Education," 1966–67 through 1985–86
and 1986–87 through 2002–03. Integrated Postsecondary Education Data System, "Fall
Enrollment Survey" (IPEDS-EF:86–99), "Completions Survey" (IPEDS-C:87–99), "Finance
Survey" (IPEDS-F:87–99), Fall 2001 through Fall 2003 and Spring 2001 to 2003.

largest-ever immigration waves. Most newcomer students are Hispanic in origin, their
families coming to the United States from Mexico and other Latin American locations.
In addition, however, there are millions of Asian immigrants. Also, the late-twentieth-
century collapse of the Soviet Union triggered an exodus of Eastern European and Middle Eastern immigrants, attracted by greater opportunities afforded by United States employment and citizenship. This in-migration has fueled the traditional American melting
pot of immigrant energy and talent. However, it has also provided U.S. schools with multiple challenges. There is a third immigration dynamic in operation that also shapes education resource distribution. Beginning in the latter decades of the twentieth century,
U.S. residents began another mass migration, moving to southern states in huge numbers. In part, this north-to-south migration is baby boomers retiring. In part, also, it is a
reflection of the availability of lower-priced land and better employment opportunities in
the South.

Taken together, these migration patterns have implications for schools beyond a need
for added buildings. The United States has been experiencing a vastly expanded need for
teachers who know foreign languages and who are qualified to instruct. When it comes to
a language as widespread as Spanish, there is a reasonably available pool of bilingual instructors. However, there are many less widely spoken languages (e.g., Hindi and Taga-
log) that pose a far larger challenge to local superintendents and principals. Moreover,
federal and state accountability regulations permit a transition period for non-English-
speaking students. Yet eventually, these students too are expected to exhibit adequate
yearly progress in their academic performance.

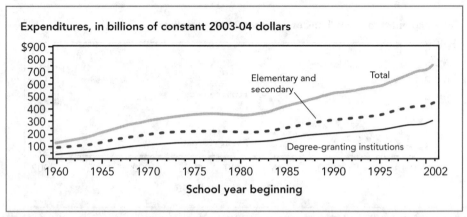

Expenditures, in billions of constant 2003-04 dollars

Elementary and secondary

Total

Degree-granting institutions

School year beginning

FIGURE 4.7 Trends in National Expenditures at Elementary, Secondary, and Postsecondary Institutions in Constant 2003–04 Dollars

Note: Data for 2002–03 and 2003–04 are estimates.

Source: U.S. Department of Education, National Center for Education Statistics, *Statistics of State School Systems,* 1959–60 through 1969–70; *Statistics of Public Elementary and Secondary School Systems,* 1970 through 1980; *Revenues and Expenditures for Public Elementary and Secondary Education,* 1970–71 through 1987–88. (CCD) The NCES Common Core of Data "State Nonfiscal Survey of Public Elementary and Secondary Education," 1981–82 through 2002–03; "National Public Education Financial Survey," 1988–89 through 2001–02; "Statistics of Nonpublic Elementary and Secondary Schools," 1970–71 through 1980; "Private School Universe Survey (PSS)," 1989–90 through 2001. Higher Education General Information Survey (HEGIS), "Fall Enrollment in Institutions of Higher Education," 1959–60 through 1985–86; "Financial Statistics of Institutions of Higher Education," 1959–60 through 1985–86 and 1986–87 through 2002–03. Integrated Postsecondary Education Data System (IPEDS), Fall Enrollment surveys 1985 through 1999, Spring 2001 to 2004 surveys, and Fall 2001 to 2004 surveys; and *Projections of Education Statistics to 2014.*

 CASE 3 REVISITED

> Recall the contextual issues challenging Shannon Cantrell, the superintendent of the Lake City school district currently undergoing a significant demographic transition. Assuming that the demographic trends discussed in this chapter will continue impacting school districts in the foreseeable future, discuss a few proactive steps that district and school leaders can take to minimize conflicts associated with increasingly heterogeneous school cultures.

Private Schools. Most American elementary and secondary enrollees attend public school. Only 10 percent attend private or independent schools. This percentage has remained remarkably stable during the past century. During the post–*Brown v. Board of Education* era, when many southern states were reluctant to desegregate previously racially divided school systems, segregated private schools (so-called "white academies") flourished, and nonpublic school enrollments zoomed to 14 percent of the school age–eligible population. However, by the end of the 1960s, this reactionary phenomenon had dampened, private

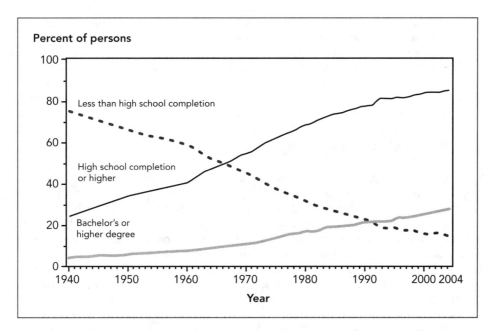

FIGURE 4.8 Years of School Completed by Persons 25 Years Old and Over

Source : U.S. Department of Commerce, Census Bureau, *1960 Census of Population,* Volume 1, part 1; and *Current Population Reports, Series P-20. Educational Attainment in the United States,* various years; and Current Population Survey, unpublished data.

school enrollments dropped to their contemporary percentages, and public school districts (and sometimes even individual schools) began to be racially desegregated.

Ironically, the region of the nation that presently displays the most racially integrated school populations is the U.S. South. However, for the moment discounting the post-*Brown* era, private school enrollments do not account for much of the U.S. enrollment, and their share of the market appears stable. The 90 percent of enrollments they control, for many practical purposes, place U.S. public schools in a monopoly setting. The consequences of this condition, both positive and negative, are topics to which this book will return in subsequent chapters.

Even if the overall nonpublic school enrollment pattern has been steady, the composition of nonpublic school enrollees has changed dramatically in the last half-century. In the decades of the 1950s, 1960s, and 1970s, the overwhelming percent of nonpublic school enrollees were Catholic school students. Beginning in the 1980s, and continuing ever since, Catholic schools have been closing. In their stead, at least statistically, has been the growth in popularity of self-identified "Christian schools."

Rising Academic Expectations. School enrollments are growing both horizontally and vertically. Not only is an expanding population affecting enrollments, but the United States also has expanded its expectations for going to school. This applies at an early age, with the availability and expansion of enrollments in kindergarten and in preschools. It also applies to students staying in school. Whereas an eighth-grade expectation was the norm, and later even some high school, most contemporary American families expect high school graduation and college attendance for their children. Figures 4.3 and 4.4 depict this societal change in schooling expectation.

Figure 4.2 makes it clear that the United States has expanded its capacity to offer instruction in response to enrollment and expectation increases. The United States now employs over four million teachers. There are more individuals in the teaching force than there are immediately engaged in agriculture. There are also millions of other school employees: administrators; specialists of various kinds and "classified" employees; and those who perform crucial tasks, such as custodians, cafeteria workers, bus drivers, and so on.

Scope and Diversity. As mentioned above, it is not simply the magnitude of America's education system that is daunting; so also is its scope and diversity.

At any one time, approximately 20 percent of the U.S. population is formally enrolled in or employed by an educational institution pre-kindergarten through postsecondary. Public and private institutions, K–12 and postsecondary, serve children as young as three years of age and adults ten and twenty times that number. Elementary and secondary instruction is delivered by districts as large as New York City with more than 1.1 million students enrolled in a thousand schools or Los Angeles with approximately 700,000 students in 650 schools.

At the opposite end of the district-size spectrum are rural school districts in the contiguous forty-eight states, which have almost as many **school board** members as students, often offering instruction across all grade levels in a single building to a dozen or fewer students in total. The Alaskan "bush" offers a particularly dramatic example of such small and remote schools. Often, air or boat travel is the only connection between these unusually small and remote settlements and the larger outside world.

Small rural districts aside, most U.S. public school students are schooled in concentrations of urban and suburban districts. Fifty percent of all public school students are enrolled in only 5 percent, approximately 750, of the nation's largest school districts. Population-dense big city districts often operate large schools—elementary schools of a thousand or two thousand students and high schools of equal or larger size. Suburban districts seldom approach such large school sizes. Indeed, one of the conditions that middle class households seek for their children when they leave the city for suburbia is smaller, presumably more personable, schools and smaller classes. Much the same can be said of households that rely upon private and independent schools. In part, they are paying tuition on top of their public school taxes to obtain smaller schools and smaller classes that they believe are advantageous to their children's learning.

Of the nation's slightly more than 14,000 public school districts, most—75 percent—serve fewer than five hundred students. Whereas big city districts often suffer from **diseconomies of scale** in their operation since they are too large to be economically or instructionally efficient, rural districts often suffer from diseconomies of scale due to their small size. They cannot easily afford to offer specialized courses to secondary students, unless they creatively rely upon distance learning. Rural district costs of providing teachers for specialized courses (e.g., calculus or advanced placement courses) may exceed available revenues.

Diversity does not adhere to organizational size alone. Student academic achievement also runs the gamut from unusually high performance in big city academic specialty high schools, residentially exclusive suburban schools, and costly private independent schools, to abysmally low standardized test scores in big cities and rural areas characterized by high levels of household poverty. Table 4.1 displays state-by-state scores in reading and mathematics on the 2003 National Assessment of Educational Progress exam. Here can be

TABLE 4.1 Average Math and Reading Scores for
Public-School Eighth Graders in 2003

State or Jurisdiction	Math Average Scale Score in 2003	Reading Average Scale Score in 2003
National Average	276	261
Alabama	262	253
Alaska	279	256
Arizona	271	255
Arkansas	266	258
California	267	251
Colorado	283	268
Connecticut	284	267
Delaware	277	265
Florida	271	257
Georgia	270	258
Hawaii	266	251
Idaho	280	264
Illinois	277	266
Indiana	281	265
Iowa	284	268
Kansas	284	266
Kentucky	274	266
Louisiana	266	253
Maine	282	268
Maryland	278	262
Massachusetts	287	273
Michigan	276	264
Minnesota	291	268
Mississippi	261	255
Missouri	279	267
Montana	286	270
Nebraska	282	266
Nevada	268	252
New Hampshire	286	271
New Jersey	281	268
New Mexico	263	252
New York	280	265
North Carolina	281	262
North Dakota	287	270
Ohio	282	267
Oklahoma	272	262
Oregon	281	264
Pennsylvania	279	264
Rhode Island	272	261
South Carolina	277	258
South Dakota	285	270
Tennessee	268	258
Texas	277	259
Utah	281	264
Vermont	286	271
Virginia	282	268
Washington	281	264
West Virginia	271	260
Wisconsin	284	266
Wyoming	284	267

seen the range of performance differences among states. The range among individual school districts is wider yet.

Finally, school spending also varied in 2003 from a nationwide low in Mississippi of $6,199 per pupil to New Jersey's $13,338. Even when these figures are adjusted for regional purchasing-power differences, Mississippi students are disadvantaged. The upcoming revenue generation and resource distribution chapter explores these and related spending differences in greater depth.

■ CONSTITUTIONAL UNDERPINNINGS OF EDUCATION'S COMPLEXITY AND DIVERSITY

How did such enormity evolve? What could trigger such massive diversity? These are good questions. Answers reside in large measure within the mind-sets of Constitutional Convention participants and the federal government charter they constructed. By spreading authority, protecting individuality and liberty, encouraging multiple political voices, and eschewing uniformity, this founding charter facilitated today's diversity and growth.

Among the historic Constitutional conditions important for understanding U.S. education was a fear of large formal government and a strong distaste for concentrating power in the hands of those connected with government. To counter these anxieties, Constitutional framers (1) honed a set of philosophical abstractions regarding human nature into a new, applied, and anti-monarch Social Contract Theory of the State; (2) limited central government to the role of facilitating commerce and sustaining personal freedom; and (3) diluted what little government power they were willing to authorize by distributing formal authority in almost every possible direction to avoid concentration.

A New "Social Contract Theory of the State"

American revolutionaries, or at least the more extreme rebels among them, did not want simply to replace England's King George III with another authority, even if closer to home. They wanted complete independence from England. They had a multipronged rationale for fearing a powerful government. First, they were reacting to what they perceived as the autocratic reign of King George III, rebelling against what they asserted was taxation without representation and the unfair imposition of distant English authority. To justify abrupt change, to counter literally centuries of dominance by monarchies, they needed a new rationale.

Prior to the American Revolution, the dominant theory of the state assumed that the right to govern was ceded by a deity to a head of state. In Western cultures, this was referred to as the Divine Right of Kings, which on occasion covered queens as well. A crucial assumption was that the right to govern, being God-given, was indisputable. To question state authority was not simply to risk the monarch's ire, but also to jeopardize one's place in an afterlife. Conversely, to do a monarch's bidding was tantamount to obeying God's will and gaining a comfortable place in the hereafter.

Constitutional framers adopted a different view of the state. They continued to anchor the concept of government in the powers of a supreme being. Thereafter, however, they turned centuries of conventional governance thinking on its head. Drawing upon Western-European eighteenth-century ideas of Locke, Rousseau, and Montesquieu, they adopted a notion by which the God-given right to govern was embodied in commoners, not monarchs. In effect, the new theory of the state postulated that all humans were inalienably endowed with the right to govern.

Fear of "Big" Government

Constitutional framers had a multipronged strategy for reorienting and restricting government. First, they limited the formal role of government. Their contention was that central government would possess only that authority explicitly granted to it. Authority not specified as a federal government power was assumed to reside with subordinate units of the federation (initially the thirteen colonies, later states) or the people themselves. The **social contract** notion of limited federal government authority, and state and citizen empowerment, is expressed formally in the Tenth Amendment: "The powers not delegated to the United States by the Constitution, nor prohibited by it to the states, are reserved to the states respectively, or to the people."

The Social Contract and Tenth Amendment Subtlety

If all were endowed by their creator with the right to govern, then direct **democracy** was possible. Such direct and personal participation in government might have been attractive as an abstract Athenian ideal. However, in the geographic vastness of the new nation, complicated by large numbers of voters, great distances, and more than a little elite suspicion of the common man's wisdom on matters of government, direct democracy seemed impractical and awkward. Hence, the Constitution relies upon the idea of a social contract by which citizens cede immediate right to govern to duly elected representatives but retain the right to recall representatives if authority is abused or inappropriately expressed. It is this social contract that empowers today's republican form of U.S. government, with elected officials presumably representing popular will.

One of the consequences of a social contract is a supposition of substantial citizen equality. However, the early Constitution was not as democratic as American ideals have subsequently evolved. Voting was thought to be the privileged preserve of white male landowners, and slaves were not originally accorded full status as humans, let alone given rights as voting citizens.

Diluting the Prospect of Power

Constitutional framers were highly conscious of what they perceived as an abuse of power by the English monarchy and parliament. They understood that securing liberty and facilitating commerce necessitated a degree of central control—government. They were not anarchists. However, they were eager to ensure that what limited power was necessary could not easily be usurped or accumulated in the hands of a few. Their formula for preserving liberty was to restrict authority, distribute power widely, and establish competing spheres of influence.

Resorting to both horizontal and vertical distribution of decision authority also restricted federal power. Three competing branches of government—legislative, executive, and judicial—were established, each with its domain of authority and with a conscious understanding that on occasion these branches would conflict. An interesting historical aside is that Constitutional framers imagined the final arbiter, when conflicts between governmental branches were otherwise unresolved, would be the people. American government has evolved so that the Supreme Court has come to occupy the role of final arbiter. As evidence for this assertion, take the U. S. Supreme Court's decision over Florida votes in the 2000 Gore versus Bush presidential election dispute.

Federal power was also restricted by empowering states and, through states, localities. This is vertical decentralization. The Tenth Amendment's specification that those powers not enumerated for the federal government were not only denied the federal government but also accorded to states makes clear that there is an authoritative role for other levels of government.

Omission of Education

A trick question to pose to laypersons is, what part of the U.S. Constitution specifies arrangements for education and schooling? This is an unfair question because the nation's Constitution makes no direct mention of education or schooling. Such a condition is in stark contrast to most other nations wherein formal government charters assume national responsibility for education. The United States is among the few industrialized nations to omit education in its foundation charter and to forgo a national system of public schooling as a consequence. Australia, Canada, and Germany, like the United States, delegate education authority to the state or provincial level. Most other large nations, however, retain school control as a national government endeavor.

Why no Constitutional mention of schooling and no federal system of education? This, too, is a good and not fully understood question. Those present in Philadelphia at the signing of the Declaration of Independence, many of whom were subsequently present for the framing of the Constitution some five years later, were among the most sophisticated and competent individuals in the world. They were, collectively, well educated. However, Madison's diary of the Constitutional Convention records only one debate, and a short one at that, regarding education. It was a discussion, and an eventual denial, of the idea of establishing a national university. Otherwise, original Constitutional framers busied themselves with other issues.

Education Governance: State Plenary Authority

The Tenth Amendment's reservation of authority to states and the people and the absence, deliberate or not, of education as an enumerated federal government power leaves education policy to states. These default conditions, when coupled with the affirmative acceptance of responsibility for education by state constitutions, render states the most responsible actors when it comes to education in the United States. States are said to have **plenary authority**. *Plenary* is Latin for "ultimate."

Such state responsibility accounts for the lack of a national system of education in the United States. In effect, there are fifty systems, even more if one considers the District of Columbia and the various federally overseen trust Territories and the Department of Defense schools, both domestic and overseas. Add to this the many private religious and independent schools, and one can see the remarkable complexity to which this chapter has continually referred. It is a complicated mosaic indeed; one unmatched by any other nation in the world.

■ INFORMAL CENTRALIZATION

Lest the foregoing analysis of constitutional authorities and government decentralization leave a sense that U.S. education is awash in an uncharted sea of exceptions and eccentricities, consider the following centralizing conditions. Even if formal authority is widely distributed, there are many centripetal forces. Among these are the forceful presence of nationally marketed textbooks; nationally active professional organizations for teachers, administrators, and local school board members; nationally similar teacher credentialing and licensing procedures and examinations; ubiquitous and relatively similar college entrance examinations and admissions requirements; national education media, professional publications, and honor societies; and the ever-watchful competitive eye of one state versus another, each often reluctant to permit another to gain a competitive advantage in the attraction of industry, national projects, or prestige.

Such informal centralizing forces are sufficiently powerful to provoke complaints among public school critics regarding bland and stifling uniformity of schooling. Indeed, extreme critics cite uniformity as a justification for encouraging a far greater element of market competition in education, in hopes of generating greater diversity and wider choice for consumers.

■ STRUCTURE OF STATES FOR GOVERNING EDUCATION

Simply specifying that states have plenary authority over education insufficiently describes the situation. State governance and control of U.S. education is itself an enormously layered phenomenon. State constitutions, as a condition of admission into the Union, accept education as a state responsibility. State constitutions routinely specify that the state is responsible for ensuring a "thorough and efficient" or "general and uniform" system of schools. A sampling of state education language clauses is provided in Table 4.2.

A major portion of state control is undertaken through general government. These are the constitutional officers and agencies that make and administer policy generally. A complementary set of specialist agencies and officers will be described later.

■ GENERAL GOVERNMENT AND EDUCATION

At the highest formal levels of state government are three primary actors, most prominent of which are state legislative bodies. Here is lodged constitutional authority to enact policy. However, as education has ascended as a priority issue for the American people, increasing numbers of governors have taken education reform as a major element of their policy portfolio. For example, Jimmy Carter, William Clinton, and George W. Bush, prior to becoming presidents of the United States, were forceful education reform champions

TABLE 4.2 Sample State Education Clause Language

Language	Sample States
Thorough and efficient system	WV, NJ, OH
Efficient system	KY, TX
Liberal system	AL
General and uniform system	AZ, NC
Complete and uniform system	WY
System of free public schools	NY, CT, SC
Equal educational opportunity	MT
Paramount state duty	WA
Legislature must "cherish" education	MA, NH

in their respective states. Indeed, Jimmy Carter served as a local school board member in Plains, Georgia. As a governor in Texas, George W. Bush was instrumental in proposing state education reforms that subsequently became the spine of the No Child Left Behind Act. Then, too, state courts are increasingly active in overseeing education matters within a state, particularly on matters of education finance and equality of opportunity.

These formal bodies, legislative and executive, depend heavily upon the expertise and energy of staff members. It is typical for a governor, particularly in a large state, to have an aide who specializes in education policy and acts as a liaison to **state education agencies** and to education interest groups. Such informal officials are often highly influential on policy, and even a few are influential also on administrative matters.

Similarly, legislatures rely upon both member and committee staff. The latter can comprise remarkably expert individuals. Moreover, as selected states have adopted term limits for elected officials, these staff members have ascended in importance, serving as an institution's memory and maintaining policy continuity between what is often otherwise a very fluid situation with elected policy makers frequently moving in and out of office and legislative dominance sometimes shifting from one party to another.

State Education Officials

There is another tier of more specialized state education officials, drawing their authority more from statute and less from a state constitution. These are chief state school officers (CSSOs)[1] and state boards of education. In selected states, the CSSO is an elected official, often exhibiting a level of media prominence equal to that of other statewide elected officials, even the governor. In other states, the CSSO is selected by and more beholden to the state's governor or state board of education.

Every state has one of these latter bodies; however, the manner in which members are selected varies. In some instances, such as in New York, state education board members are elected from Congressional districts or geographic regions throughout a state. In other settings, such as Alaska or California, state board members are appointed by the governor or appointed by the governor and approved by legislative bodies.

In many states, serving as a member of the board of education is a prestigious position. For example, Florida has a small but influential gubernatorially appointed state board of education, and governors have ensured that appointees are prominent members of their political party. New York State has what may be the most prestigious state board of education in the nation. This is the New York Board of Regents. Appointment to this body is complicated, occurs by legislative district, and requires legislative approval. Its members serve for a long time and have often become quite prominent in setting education policy for the state, even becoming nationally visible.

These complicated and sometimes conflicting mechanisms for selecting education officials blur accountability. Presumably the CSSO is the administrative officer for the state education department. If he or she is a statewide elected official, as in South Carolina, the individual may rely upon state education department resources to further an expanded political career. Also, if elected from a statewide constituent base, a CSSO may not easily acquiesce to the policy-making authority of a gubernatorially appointed state board of education. The situation can be fraught with frustrating conflict regarding accountability. Education professionals are often befuddled regarding lines of state authority, and the public can be excused if it is baffled also.

State Education Departments

Every state has a department of education. Its functions are broad—for example, overseeing distribution of finances to local districts, monitoring quality of local district performance, overseeing statewide achievement examinations, licensing teachers, accrediting teacher training institutions, ordering textbooks in some states, and providing advice on matters such as school facilities and buses. State education departments in California, New York, Texas, Illinois, and Florida are large institutions staffed with hundreds of professionals. These individuals often are highly expert in their areas of specialization.

Despite the significance of these agencies and officials, for the operation of education in a state, the resources of state education departments are conventionally thin and seldom sufficient to perform their many responsibilities to a high standard. They often have restricted pay scales for their executives and thus experience intense difficulty recruiting high-quality personnel. They cannot compete easily with local school districts when it comes to professional salaries. State education departments routinely are supported, up to 50 percent or more of budgeted revenues, by federal funds. These federal funds are present to assist states in monitoring local district and school **compliance** with federal programs such as the Education for All Handicapped Children Act and the No Child Left Behind Act. These are examples of federally funded national school programs about which more will be specified later.

Other State Agencies

Additional state officials and agencies have responsibility for education matters. However, these usually are tangential to instruction and to school operation. For example, it is usual for a state architect's office to collaborate in the approval of plans for new school facilities. A state treasurer may be active in the approval and sale of local district facility construction bonds. The state highway patrol may be active in overseeing school bus safety and bus driver training. A state agriculture department may act as a broker between federal and local school officials to facilitate school breakfasts and lunch programs. State welfare or child protection agencies may assist in the development and oversight of day-care and preschool programs in districts. Interacting with these state agencies usually becomes a responsibility of school district officials, while a principal may not sense their immediate presence.

Intermediate Units

Thirty-five states, particularly states of larger population or geographic size, rely upon intermediate government units, midway between the state and local school districts. These intermediate agencies principally perform administrative and service tasks, particularly those for which scale economies exist. They are important but are not a dominant feature of American education's organizational landscape. A few state examples suffice to convey their purposes and operation. However, these agencies assume a wide variety of forms, and one has to be careful not to overgeneralize about them.

For example, California relies upon statutorily authorized **county offices of education,** some with elected county superintendents. These agencies can generate revenues from property taxation. They are important in that they conduct budget reviews of local school districts and offer a wide variety of scale economy support services to local districts.

In Texas, by contrast, there are statutorily authorized Regional Service Centers whose state-provided operating revenues are remarkably slender. The existence of these organizations depends crucially upon the entrepreneurial capacities of their staff. Still, several Texas Regional Service Centers are nationally famous for the quality of their administrative advice and operational service to local districts as well as their ability to broker bulk purchases, evoke administrative efficiencies, and elevate the quality of their personnel development for teachers and others.

New York State relies upon BOCES, Boards of Cooperative Education Services. Here local districts cooperate to secure provision of specialized services, the high unit cost of which would virtually prohibit any one of them individually from acquiring that service. Iowa depends upon Area Education Administrations (AEAs) that assist local school districts in the provision of services amenable to scale economies. Many southern states organize their local school systems along county lines, as described in the forthcoming section of this chapter. Florida is here a good example. In these instances, county offices of education would be superfluous.

School District Organization

The United States is characterized by two dominant patterns of school district organization, a "New England" model and a "Mid-Atlantic" or "Southern" model. There are states where these are blended. First, however, here is a description of the pure prototypes.

New England School District Organization Model. America's school organizational roots are deep, extending back in time four centuries. In 1647, the Massachusetts Commonwealth enacted Ye Olde Deluder Satan Act, the title of which, by itself, suggests education's major purpose at the time. This statute has had long-run ramifications for school organization. It specified each township would have a school. In effect, here is the origin of America's local schools. Further, it specified that the township would form a special governmental body (local school board in effect) to oversee operation of the school. Finally, the school board was not to comprise religious, military, or education professionals. Rather, it was to be composed of laypersons. Here are the foundations to America's long-standing tradition of local control over schools through a specially selected government body, separate from municipal or county government and overseen by laypersons, not clerics or professional educators. The New England model of schooling spread westward through federally promulgated late-eighteenth-century land ordinances. Most western territories, including most states added by the Louisiana Purchase, as far as California, Oregon, and Washington, adopted this model. It is the dominant model still today.[2]

Mid-Atlantic or Southern Model. A minority of states pursued a different organizational path. In mid-Atlantic and southern colonies, religious organizations, the Church of England generally and the Catholic Church in the instance of Louisiana, were dominant institutions. Thus, when lay government evolved, it tended to emerge consistent with church parish lines. Today, much of the South's education is still organized on county lines or may have both county and municipally aligned school districts with a larger county system.

On the topic of educational organization, Figure 4.9 depicts the structure of our nation's educational system.

School District Numbers and Consolidation

Regardless of New England or southern roots, the United States has many local school districts, slightly in excess of 14,000. This national condition, however, needs some clarification. Five states—California, Illinois, Nebraska, New York, and Texas—account for one-third of these districts. The remaining nine thousand districts are distributed over forty-five

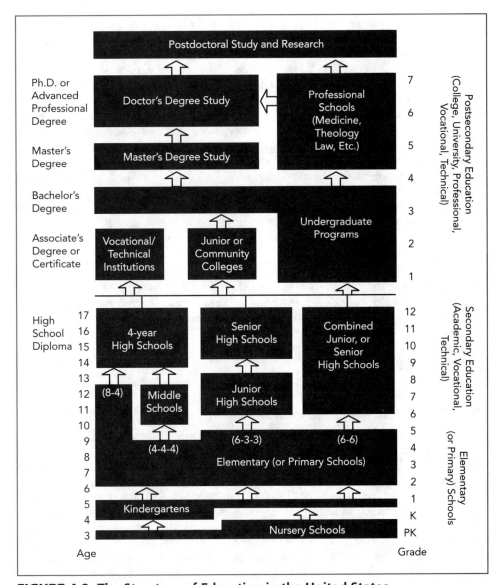

FIGURE 4.9 The Structure of Education in the United States

Note: Audit education programs, while not separately delineated above, may provide instruction at the elementary, secondary, or postsecondary education level. Chart reflects typical patterns of progression rather than all possible variations.

Source: U.S. Department of Education, National Center for Education Statistics, Annual Reports Program.

states. As mentioned previously, southern states tend to be organized along county lines. The consequence is that they typically have geographically larger and numerically fewer districts. Florida, for example, the nation's fourth most populous state, has only sixty-seven county-organized districts. Maryland has only twenty-four county-aligned districts.

Hawaii is a particular exception to all other patterns. It is a statewide system with no conventional local government school districts.[3]

Once, a century ago, the United States had almost nine times as many local school districts. In 1920, there were 127,000 local districts. Most of these were rural in nature. Many had only one school and a one-room school at that. In a bizarre way, some of these districts operated no schools. They were tax havens formed by large landholders who relied upon puppet school boards to dampen the prospect of having to pay significant school taxes.

By the first quarter of the twentieth century, a coalition of business leaders and university officials began a political campaign to consolidate these rural agencies into larger districts. In a remarkably successful reform effort, they lobbied legislatures, arguing that small districts offered inferior education and were economically inefficient. The campaign also had unanticipated and possibly deleterious and long-lasting effects. It created larger, sometimes inefficiently large, school districts; separated schools from the local citizen communities they served; and did not demonstrably produce cost savings.

 CASE 4 REVISITED

> Recall the motivated, pragmatic chief state school officer Mary Kay Porter. Based on the governance issues presented in this chapter, can you propose an alternate route to establishing a politically viable and uniformly endorsed state-wide data system? What do you see as her most daunting governance-related obstacles? What entity might intervene or weigh in with an objective view of such sensitive proposals?

Fiscal Dependence and Independence

When school districts are statutorily granted taxing authority, almost always property-taxing authority, they are said to possess "fiscal independence." This is something of a misnomer because state legislatures seldom empower local districts with unfettered taxing authority. It is usually bounded. Still, approximately 75 percent of U.S. school districts, through their elected school boards or through direct citizen vote, have authority to levy property taxes.[4]

Districts that submit annual spending plans, or budgets, to other governmental bodies for approval and revenue generation are said to be "fiscally dependent." This usually involves large cities (e.g., New York) and southern districts that have to submit their proposed budgets to mayors, city councils, or county boards of supervisors. Washington, D.C., schools and the Department of Defense schools are special cases because they receive funding directly from Congress.

School Boards

School boards draw formal authority from legislative statutes. Their primary, but not exclusive, function is employing and evaluating a chief executive officer, a superintendent of schools. In addition, they have authority over individual school attendance boundaries, budgetary approval, and curriculum authority, within the boundaries of state specifications regarding what is to be taught.

Boards vary in their membership size. Most have five members, a few have only three, and some have more, as many as fifteen in several large cities. Generally, 80 percent of the time, these are elected positions. Where boards are appointed, it generally is by mayors, sometimes requiring city council advice and consent. A few unusual circumstances exist. In Pennsylvania, for example, justices of the Court of Common Pleas appoint large city board members.

Superintendents

Occupants of this position serve as the chief executive for local school districts. A few experiments have been undertaken by which districts had both a superintendent for instruction and an organizationally parallel business manager. Such bifurcation almost always leads to a lack of accountability. Superintendents sometimes serve more than a single district, in the instance of sparsely populated rural areas. However, usually a district has its own executive, selected by the school board.

The position has a great deal of authority, perhaps the most important of which are selecting and evaluating school principals and recommending an annual spending plan, a district budget. The superintendency is a difficult task. Occupants find themselves simultaneously pinched by school board member expectations and the expectations of subordinates, principals, and teachers. This may be one reason superintendents' tenure in many districts is notoriously short lived.

Individual School Organization

In contrast to entire states and school districts, schools themselves are usually relatively simple organizations. This is particularly true of elementary schools. Middle and senior high schools may rely upon subject-matter departments (e.g., history, mathematics, and physical education). However, elementary schools, unless unusually large, are typically operated by a principal, an all-important school clerk, classroom teachers, and a custodial staff. Also, depending upon the district, there will be various licensed specialists such as counselors, department chairs, and school psychologists. The presence of additional administrators in a school, an assistant principal for example, is almost always a function of enrollment size. When elementary enrollments are in excess of five or six hundred students, districts will frequently assign an assistant principal, or some variant, to support the principal. Middle and senior high schools, being larger in almost every instance, will be assigned one or more additional administrators to assist the principal.

Whatever the particulars of school administrative staff, the school generally draws its authority from and operates within policy parameters specified by district, state, federal, and judicial officials. Schools seldom are otherwise empowered, beyond matters regarding student discipline. Indeed, this is one of the issues to be subsequently addressed in this book. Selected reformers believe that schools would be more effective organizations if principals, perhaps teachers, and others that operated them were more fully empowered to make decisions regarding personnel and performance incentives.

Private and Independent Schools

As previously mentioned, 10 percent of America's K–12 children attend nonpublic schools. These may include private, even proprietary, profit-seeking schools. They may be independent, having their own board of directors, financial assets, and so on. Additionally, they may be religiously affiliated (e.g., Catholic, Methodist, Jewish, or Christian).

Sometimes, as in large city Catholic systems, these schools may themselves be part of a hierarchy that, while almost always much smaller, is fashioned after a public school bureaucracy. The New York City and Chicago diocesan schools are huge. Sometimes a religious order or a regional or nationwide system oversees the schools' general operation. Usually, however, private and independent schools are operated with a substantial degree of autonomy.

There are many operating similarities between public and nonpublic schools. However, here is a place to emphasize distinctions. First, the nonpublic schools do not have to accept or retain as students anyone who shows up at their door and is interested in attending. Private and independent schools have flexibility in which applicants they accept and retain (public school advocates make much of this, claiming that in a competitive free-market setting, discretion over admission and continued enrollment provides an unfair advantage to nonpublic schools). Second, private school budgets are tightly tied to enrollment levels. Too few students, and the school may have to close. Public schools also are sensitive to enrollment ebb and flow. However, financial effects seldom are as immediate as they are for nonpublic schools losing students. Third, a headmaster or headmistress has more discretion over how to spend money and whom to hire and fire than does the archetypal public school principal.

Federal Government Education Structures

Given that it has little explicit authority for education, it is remarkable how much influence the federal government has over U.S. K–12 schooling. Since adoption of the federal Constitution, courts have concurred that the General Welfare clause[5] empowers Congress to undertake actions and activities that, presumably, are in the public's interest. This is the justification for literally dozens of federal programs, and billions of federal dollars directed at public, generally public, education support. (A small portion of federal funding does support private and religious school activity.)

Federal government apparatus for overseeing education programs is similar to what one finds for states. There are executive and legislative branch components. The Office of the President, like the office of a governor, has ability to initiate or vitiate (through veto) policy proposals. Congress can do the same. Generally both must agree for a proposal to become law. Within the executive branch, there is a Department of Education. The secretary of this agency, appointed by the president with the advice and consent of the U.S. Senate, is a cabinet-level official.

Congress, both the House and the Senate, relies heavily upon a committee system for initial deliberation over legislative proposals and for program oversight. These committees have expert staff. Also, committee chairs, usually of the majority party, are themselves often knowledgeable regarding legislative programs the committee oversees.

The U.S. Department of Education has regional offices located throughout the United States. However, most federal education programs are overseen through state education departments and operated by local school districts. Federal officials certainly exercise oversight, but they seldom engage in actual organizational operations.

Any discussion of federal government organization matters in education would be remiss without mention of the U.S. Supreme Court. In Chapter 7, substantial emphasis will be allotted to influential Supreme Court decisions (e.g., *Brown v. Board of Education*). Suffice it here, however, to bring to a reader's attention that this third branch of government, while not having enumerated educational responsibilities, nevertheless has exerted remarkable influence on the operation of America's schools.

Residual Issues of Control

The preceding description of structure and control is merely a summary. Regardless of the level or branch of government, describing control of American education is much like peeling an onion. There is always another layer. Many of these governance and organizational subtleties will be specified in greater detail in subsequent chapters. Suffice it here to acknowledge that there is untapped complexity and to extend a caveat to unwary readers who falsely believe the foregoing is a full or fixed description of the control of U.S. schooling.

Summary

In Chapter 4, the reader addressed the issues of the organization and control of American education, the never-ending layers of statutory and legal authority that impinge on education leaders, and the multiple constituencies with which education leaders are inevitably involved. Understanding the complex and dynamic organizational structures of education is important for educational leaders. Through this chapter, the reader learned that the governance mechanisms and other control features are relatively static components of American education. Within this context, education leadership is subject to an ever-moving set of altered societal conditions, expectations, and regulations.

Discussion Questions

1. The text and graphics in the chapter provide insights regarding the demographic trends impacting public education. Describe one such demographically related challenge and your educational institution's solution.
2. Describe the level of cooperation and/or competition between the public and nonpublic educational institutions in your region.
3. To what degree do charter and magnet schools generate greater diversity and wider choice for educational consumers?
4. Discuss one benefit and one drawback of the governance structure in which your educational organization is situated.
5. What do you think are the key similarities and differences between strategic education leadership within the public and nonpublic school arenas?
6. If you could go back in time and alter the Constitution, and the amendments impacting education, what, if anything, would you change?
7. ELCC Standard 3 focuses on the work that school leaders do to manage the school organization and resources in a way that fosters an effective learning environment. Choose one insight from this chapter, and describe how it will help you more efficiently or effectively manage an education organization.

References and Suggested Readings

Fuller, E., & Pearson, J. (1969). *Education in the states: Nationwide development since 1900: A project of the Council of Chief State School Officers.* Washington, D.C.: National Education Association of the United States.

    A seminal report from the National Education Association focusing on sixteen areas of educational concerns, examining the historical, existing, and future directions of the organization and financing of public education.

Goodwin, D. K. (2005). *Team of rivals: The political genius of Abraham Lincoln.* New York: Simon & Schuster.

Goodwin provides a stunning portrait of a political genius as she recounts Lincoln's ability to bring disparate individuals, factions, and egos into his presidency, masterfully using their talents to hold the country together.

Notes

1. Also known as superintendent of public instruction or commissioner of education in some states.
2. Nevada's county system of school organization is a western-state anomaly resulting from a post–World War II consulting report submitted by a team of southern model–oriented faculty from Peabody College.
3. Hawaii entered statehood in 1959, having previously been a monarchy consolidated under King Kamehameha. It had no continental tradition of municipal or county government around which to organize schools. It is a highly centralized system operated by a state board of education, a chief state school officer, and a state education department.
4. California is an interesting outlier. Each of the state's almost one thousand school districts has nominal property-taxing authority. However, the overwhelming majority of districts are prevented from exercising this authority by virtue of the 1978-enacted **Proposition Thirteen**, the nation's leading tax limitation initiative that restricts property taxation to 1 percent of a property's purchase price.
5. "We the People of the United States, in Order to form a more perfect Union, establish Justice, insure domestic Tranquility, provide for the common defense, *promote the general Welfare*, and secure the Blessings of Liberty to ourselves and our Posterity, do ordain and establish this Constitution for the United States of America." (Emphasis added)

CHAPTER FIVE

Politics and Education Policy Issues

LEARNING OBJECTIVES

By the end of this chapter, you should be able to

- understand the history of key American education policies;
- apply systems theory to politics and education policy;
- explain a systems paradigm of political actions;
- conceive of multiple lenses through which a leader might view policy.

To a principal in Seattle the U.S. Congress may appear uninvolved with education, or to a schoolteacher in Topeka the U.S. Supreme Court may seem remote. In fact, however, much of America's day-to-day school activity is shaped strongly by the **policy** dynamics that take place in and among physically and psychologically distant individuals and institutions. In terms of the intensity and immediacy of their operational impact, these external policy pressures can be virtually next door to the school. Moreover, the policy context that is remotely constructed—in state capitals, Washington, D.C., and in courts—is additionally compounded by local actors such as school boards, mayors, municipal and county officials, and local courts.

As introduced earlier, a strategic education leader draws frequently upon an understanding of the complicated dynamics through which the education policy context evolves. Before entering the realm of policy system dynamics, however, a reader should also understand that schools are not simply inert or empty vessels open to the value vicissitudes and willy-nilly whims of other institutions and actors. Schools, and school system officials, have positive policy energy of their own. To be sure, schools must acquiesce to various higher government policy proscriptions. However, there are plentiful and positive mechanisms by which feedback from school officials can have a reciprocal impact on policy.

Here is an illustration. School board members, whatever their immediate policy connection with a community's schools, can also be deeply engaged in the broader currents of the political stream. One should remember, for example, that Jimmy Carter was a public school board member prior to becoming Georgia's governor and president of the United

States, and Lewis Powell was a school board member before ascending to the U.S. Supreme Court. Also, the influence of schools can be indirect, but still significant. For example, schools are among the agencies, along with families and peer groups, that shape political attitudes and predispositions of students who, when they eventually reach the age of consent and act politically, have an opportunity to influence other public institutions, as well as schools. The bottom line is that schools are influenced by the policy system and have multiple reciprocal opportunities to influence the larger policy system themselves, both directly and indirectly. What follows are selected illustrations of education policy that have had, and continue to have, a deep impact upon the day-to-day activities of education leaders.

▪ ILLUSTRATING HOW POLICY MATTERS FOR EDUCATION LEADERS

This chapter opened with an assertion that matters of policy may appear remote to those operating districts and schools, but in fact, policy influences their day-to-day leadership actions and the quality of their work life. What follows are powerful examples from history of policy movements and their operational consequences.

Bigger But Not Necessarily Better: The School District Consolidation Movement[1]

America continues to be a nation of relatively small school districts. In 2000, 90 percent of the local school districts in the nation each enrolled five thousand or fewer students. Smaller yet, 80 percent of all districts each enrolled fewer than 2,500 students. What, then, is the problem?

The problem is on the other end of the distribution. Fifty percent of the nation's public school pupils are enrolled in only 5 percent of the nation's school districts. These large districts include the nation's premier cities such as New York, Los Angeles, Chicago, Miami, and Dallas. They also contain the largest concentrations of low-income, dropout-prone, and low-achieving students. These are the very districts whose upper-income populations have come most to depend upon private schooling. These are the districts most jeopardized by past and impending middle-class flight from public schooling. These are the very districts whose pupil populations are at the greatest risk of educational failure and for whom one could argue the nation should have the greatest concern. Yet these are the very districts in which the governance impasse is the most intense. The further irony is that the reforms that led to this condition were intended originally to make everything better.

In 1931 there were 127,531 U.S. local school districts.[2] Thereafter, state officials responded to a coordinated plea by business leaders, college professors, and National Education Association experts to eliminate small, usually rural school districts and consolidate them into larger administrative units. The campaign was remarkably successful. Consolidation advocates made a commonsensical appeal asserting that small districts were educationally ineffective and economically inefficient. They amassed almost no empirical data in support of their position. Nevertheless, within a fifty-year period, even with major distractions such as the Great Depression, World War II, and the postwar baby boom, the number of local districts was reduced eightfold. This figure has continued to shrink, though at a slower rate. Today, there are estimated to be approximately 14,631 local school districts. Figure 5.1 displays how these districts are

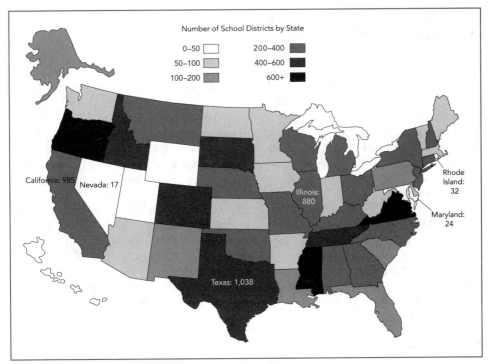

FIGURE 5.1 Number of School Districts by State

distributed across our nation by providing a national picture of the number of school districts by state.

Among the less-heralded consequences of this dramatic reduction in units of government is the status of representativeness. The number of school board members nationwide was reduced accordingly from a pre-reform estimate of more than 300,000 to today's level of approximately 50,000 to 55,000. Of course, the nation's population increased along the way. Thus, whereas there used to be a school board member for every 300 or so citizens, each such office holder today must represent approximately 5,000 constituents. The distribution around such mean figures is enormous. Central city school board members in districts such as New York and Los Angeles represent millions of constituents. A few small districts conceivably have more school board members than students.

The school district consolidation movement may have created larger numbers of larger districts; however, it did not create large cities. Big cities existed before the 1930s, and their school districts already had large numbers of students for whom they were responsible. Something more must have been operating to transform these systems, which at the turn of the century were thought to have the nation's best schools, into the stultifying bureaucracies that critics claim they have become. The something more came in two waves. The first wave, before World War II, came with formation of a cadre of professional administrators and growth of political centralization. The post–World War wave came in the form of judicially imposed racial desegregation plans and a spate of Johnson Era categorical aid programs.

"Scientific Management" and the Growth of Educational Administration

Frederick Taylor, an industrial engineer who pioneered widespread employment of time and motion studies and efficiency applications to business production, was a cult hero in his time. He was a turn-of-the-twentieth-century counterpart of contemporary business advisers and organizational gurus such as Jim Collins, Edwards Deming, Tom Peters, and Stephen Covey.[3]

Taylor's and his colleagues' efficiency and time use notions, which came to be labeled Scientific Management, were quick to be adopted by the fledgling field of school administration. Who could resist rendering schools more efficient, and who better to apply the new efficiency principles than trained school administrators? Yet long-lasting effects upon instruction were few.

Nevertheless, Taylorism had a dramatic impact on the broader educational landscape. It vastly abetted school administration as a profession. While growth of big city schools had already created the need for managers, which further diluted the sovereignty of school board members, it had not yet spawned a "profession." Early big city administrators were mere civil service clerks. Scientific Management assisted the field in transforming itself into one that had professional legitimacy. Because they "knew" how to operate schools efficiently, they could command authority and in that way began to draw power away from school board members.[4]

Progressive Era Reforms

The excesses uncovered by turn-of-the-century literary "muckrakers" were not restricted to the meat-packing industry scandals disclosed in Upton Sinclair's famous novel *The Jungle*. Public institutions, particularly in cities managed by big political machines, were found to suffer from similar corrupt practices such as rampant nepotism, illegal rebates, and sweetheart contracts. Progressive Era reformers diagnosed the problem as an excess of partisan politics and prescribed a heavy dose of government centralization as a cure. Their reasoning was that if small, relatively invisible, ward-based decision-making bodies were consolidated into highly visible and socially prominent central city school boards, often appointed or selected in a manner that would separate their members from the day-to-day, down-and-dirty partisanship politics of machines, they would attract citizens of a higher caliber, more likely to make decisions in the best interest of the overall community.

As a consequence, big city school districts all over the nation, but most particularly on the eastern seaboard and in the Midwest, underwent a series of governance changes. Ward-based elected school boards generally were eliminated. Central city boards, often appointed, replaced them. Corruption, at least petty corruption, probably was diminished. However, yet greater authority came to rest in the hands of fewer individuals. Close links to parent and citizen constituents probably suffered in the process. The biggest winners of all may have been the professional school managers just then beginning to burgeon as a profession. They now had school board bosses who were knowledgeable about and comfortable with the private-sector management model that turned the detailed operation of an organization over to professional administrators.

Racial Desegregation

The Warren Court's unanimous 1954 decision to render racially segregated dual school systems unconstitutional must surely be one of the most significant domestic decisions of the twentieth century.[5] Repercussions are still being experienced decades later. However, once the judicial genie of desegregation was released, it could not be contained in the South. The legal logic that impelled the U.S. Supreme Court to find explicitly segregated schools to be unconstitutional also persuaded state and federal district courts that more subtle forms of segregation were also illegal.

Hence, cities as far from the Confederate South as Boston, Denver, and San Francisco found themselves wrestling with court-ordered desegregation plans. Desegregation opponents resisted both militantly and passively. White-dominated southern state legislatures rescinded compulsory school attendance statutes. One Virginia county (Prince Edward) actually suspended public schooling. White students flowed in droves to private, racially segregated "white academies." Resistance outside the South was frequently more subtle, but often more effective. Many middle-income white families sought refuge in the **de facto segregated** public schools located in suburban districts.

Where desegregation actually occurred, it was often black households that bore the brunt of transportation burdens. They disproportionately rode buses to attend schools outside their immediate neighborhoods.[6] Numbers of black and white students attending school together increased. However, there was a price to pay. Particularly for many black households, an easy interaction with a conveniently located neighborhood school was no longer possible. Also, from the standpoint of many desegregating school districts, there was a new government authority with overarching power, a federal judge. Each federal judge was not simply another elected official with whom one negotiated on matters in conflict. Unlike a fellow school board member, a city council, or a mayor, these judges held all the cards. Negotiations were not typically a part of their modus operandi. Some courts transformed themselves into monitors of day-to-day school operation. School governance was all the more complicated, and accountability was diluted as a consequence.

Federal and State Categorical Aid Programs

The early years of Lyndon Johnson's administration benefited from a remarkable coincidence of political and economic circumstances. Johnson's 1964 landslide presidential victory over Barry Goldwater provided him with a hundred-seat Democratic margin in the House of Representatives as well as a comfortable Senate majority. The economy, fueled by a Vietnam War military buildup, had recovered from a recession. These conditions, when mixed with Johnson's master command of the political process, provoked an outpouring of social legislation such as had not been seen since the Great Depression.[7]

Among the bills ushered into legislation during this period were many that concentrated on education, and K–12 schooling particularly. The centerpiece was the 1965 **Elementary and Secondary Education Act (ESEA)**. Additionally, professional development, vocational education, international education, bilingual education, and migrant education were also included in the president's portfolio. The momentum was sufficient that even when Johnson forwent a second elected term, the bills kept coming under President Nixon. For example, as an aid to racial desegregation the Nixon administration sponsored the Emergency School Assistance Act and education research initiatives. Subsequently, President Carter endorsed the Education for All Handicapped Children Act and the formation of a separate federal Department of Education.[8]

While federal authorities were enacting new school programs, state officials were similarly engaged. Thus, the decade from the mid-1960s through the middle of the 1970s witnessed literally dozens of new categorical aid programs, some state, some federal, intended to aid local school districts in coping with specialized problems.

An unanticipated outcome of this proliferation of special programs was a substantial increase in special program administrators. Both federal and state governments were eager to ensure their funds were appropriately deployed. Hence, they promulgated rules, and the rules had to be properly overseen. Most federal and state categorical programs required a local school district's central office administrators to assist individual school sites. These administrators derived their managerial or regulatory **legitimacy** not from the district superintendent or local school board, but from more remote authorities in state capitals and Washington, D.C. School principals now were beholden not only to the conventional chain of command, running up through their central office to the superintendent, but also to a categorical chain of command running from their central office, bypassing the superintendent, and leading to a state or the nation's capital. Administrative complexity resulted, and accountability at the school level was dealt yet another body blow.

The cumulative impact of these centralizing conditions has itself been reinforced by other conditions. For example, the expansion of teacher unions in the latter portion of the twentieth century and their insistence on district-wide contracts and district-wide enforcement mechanisms have further impeded the operating integrity of individual schools.[9] To some degree, the same thing has happened in states with court decisions regarding school finance equity. Such judicial decisions generally have increased overall spending for education.[10] However, where courts have called for greater statewide equality, it generally has come at the expense of local district authority to elevate tax rates and exert local discretion over levels of spending.

■ EXPLAINING THE FORMATION OF POLICY

Social scientists and other research scholars often rely upon a systems paradigm as a means for mapping elements of a social activity and for determining possible dimensions of organizational influence and causality. This is particularly true when it comes to understanding education and education policy. Prior to the application of modern systems theory to educational policy, the human body with its circulatory, digestive, reproductive, skeletal, immune, and nervous subsystems provided a good "systems" example. Damage to any one component may have ill effects upon other parts or subsystems. Heart damage can affect not only the circulatory system but also limit ability of kidneys to filter waste and of lungs to acquire oxygen. A toxic buildup from kidney malfunction can affect the liver, and this can alter digestive processes and reduce both energy and disease resistance. If a subsystem is damaged or altered, other components attempt to compensate. If a kidney fails, the heart rate may increase. Also, if the system is thrown out of synchrony, it attempts to redefine and reestablish a new equilibrium. For example, if infected with a bacteria or virus, the human body will elevate in temperature and then, upon the surmounting of the foreign element, return to normal body temperature. Finally, as marvelously adapted as are human subsystems, they cannot operate without resources, air, food, and water, from the larger external environment.

The economic system and its sensitivity to component change provide another good example. Interest rate increases, sometimes undertaken by the Federal Reserve to ward off inflation, or dramatic petroleum price escalation can dampen consumer confidence and curtail retail purchasing, resulting in reduced manufacturing demand, reduced exports, increased unemployment, and overall economic retrenchment.

Schools as "Systems"

Schools and school districts meet most of the definitions of social systems. However, they are not perfect systems. The organizational sociologist Karl Weick was among the first to note that school systems are "loosely coupled." By this is meant that alterations to one system component do not automatically trigger change to another component.

For example, a school board may expect curriculum or personnel changes to be made or even vote on the matter in public. However, a politically entrenched and secure superintendent may refuse to comply or act in a recalcitrant manner, eviscerating a school board's authority in the process. Further, a principal might admonish teachers to instruct more effectively so that, presumably, students will learn more or score higher on state academic achievement tests. However, if the principal is unpersuasive, and teachers are tenured or otherwise have employment protection, they may choose to ignore admonitions or comply only in the most superficial manner.

Many effective organizations, particularly in the private sector, arrange their incentives, both positive and negative, to gain tight coupling and empower managers and leaders effectively to shape subordinate behavior. For reasons of history and politics, school leaders typically have weak incentive systems at their disposal for these purposes.

Still, whatever their operational deficiencies, school districts and schools can productively be conceptualized as a system. Here, then, are several key implications of systems theory for school leaders. A leader should understand that

- as a consequence of past actions and decisions, an organization already has a direction and has amassed a momentum that may have to be redirected before a new direction can be established;
- one can seldom undertake a single change, attempt just one thing, or try to change simply one component of a school or an educational institution's operation;
- one can rarely single-handedly impose significant change upon a school or larger educational organization;
- it is difficult accurately or fully to anticipate all ramifications of a proposed change; and
- one should not view change as a one-time-only undertaking.

■ POLICY, PUBLIC POLICY, EDUCATION POLICY, AND A POLICY SYSTEM PARADIGM

This section applies the principles of systems theory to public policy generally and education policy specifically.

Defining "Policy"

A **policy** is a uniform plan or course of action intended to guide organizational behavior or agency practice. Policy can be formal, a written rule or distributed action guidelines. It can also be informal, a social or organizational norm that is generally followed, even if not codified. Policy exists in both public and private settings. Even a family can have a "policy"

In the News

The board of education Tuesday adopted a new policy that requires alcohol detection devices to be used at school events. In a 6-3 vote, the board approved the policy, which requires the screening at school-sponsored events on or off campus. The policy takes effect immediately.

Under the policy, students will have to be tested by the device before being allowed into an event. Students who refuse will not be allowed to attend the activity and will not receive a refund. Those who test positively for use of alcohol will have their parents called to pick them up from the event, and the student will face other disciplinary action.

Board Vice Chairman Al Harrison said that since its introduction, the measure has stirred a lot of media attention, and other school systems, such as Windsor Locks, have asked for copies of the policy. Harrison said he and other school officials have heard only positive comments about the policy from students and the public.

One of the devices is an enlarged flashlight that includes a passive detection function that can detect alcohol on a person's breath or even in a beverage. If a student gets a negative reading twice on the passive device, then an active detector, which is a Breathalyzer, will be used, Harrison said.

The devices were used in trials at the Enfield and Enrico Fermi high schools' junior proms in March. No positive readings from students were detected at the events, Harrison said. "Both of them reported back very positively on their experiences," Harrison said. Superintendent of Schools John Gallacher recommended using the devices on a test basis so the two high school principals can get input from students, parents and chaperones on how they work.

Three board members—Chuck Johnson, Susan Lavelli-Hozempa and Andre Greco—voted against the measure after the defeat of an amendment by Johnson to include the testing of chaperones. Harrison said including chaperones might create a problem with labor agreements for school employees who are usually the chaperones.

There are school policies in place concerning employees and the use of alcoholic beverages, he added. Board Chairwoman Sharon Racine said she doesn't believe chaperones need to be tested because it has not been an issue. Greco said not including chaperones, who are not school employees, does students a disservice.

Fermi Principal Paul Newton and Enfield Principal Thomas Duffy said they only use faculty members as chaperones at the schools' proms.

From "Alcohol Screening Policy OK'd; Board of Education Approves Plan 6-3" by Larry Smith, published April 26, 2006, by the *Hartford Courant* (Connecticut), www.courant .com/about/custom/the/hc-all-reprints, 0,3780706.htmlstory

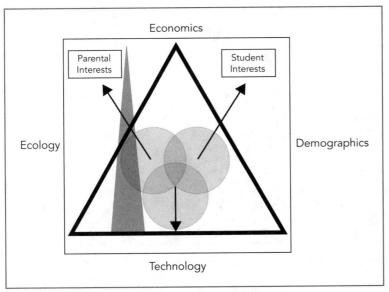

FIGURE 5.2 Contributors to Public Policy

regarding children's bedtime or rules for earning a weekly allowance. Private-sector corporations have policies regarding conflicts of interest, work rules, workplace behavior, and so on. Of course, governments have policies too.

Public Policy. When a policy is a product of government and draws upon public resources for its implementation, operation, or oversight, then it is said to be a public policy. Here, the range of actions and activities is enormous. As will be described in connection with Figure 5.2, public policy encompasses all manner of activities, including regulatory, symbolic, and operational. Indeed, every session of the U.S. Congress is marked by submission of, though not necessarily deliberation about or enactment of, literally tens of thousands of bills, proposed alterations, or additions to policy. Though the scale may be smaller, state legislatures, county boards, city councils, and other deliberative bodies are no different.

Education Policy. An education policy is presumed to be a public policy, one especially affecting education, schooling, instruction, or something related to these activities. For historic, Constitutional reasons described in the preceding chapter, the United States has chosen to offer education principally through the public sector. Thus, education policy is more often than not a subset of public policy. To understand how these decision rules are derived and to understand eventually their impact upon education leadership, it is necessary to comprehend the dynamics of the public policy system and the way these political and governmental actions particularly influence education.

Policy Systems. A policy system meets most of the definitions and characteristics of systems theory presented in the prior section. Individual policy system components are depicted in Figure 5.2. Each of these will be explained in greater detail below. Here,

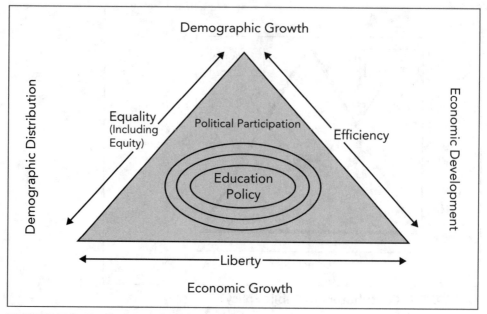

FIGURE 5.3 Preliminary Policy Paradigm

however, the point to be taken is that a policy system nests within, and interacts with, the large environment, the polity. The policy system is dependent upon the polity, the larger society, for supporting resources. It is also from the external environment that the policy system periodically receives "stimuli." These external stimuli can cause internal imbalance and trigger a search for a new system-wide homeostasis.

Value Shifts and Policy Change. Imbalance among core values can trigger a policy change. This causal chain for policy system change can be understood in this manner. Figure 5.3 depicts a triangle within a rectangle. Each side of the triangle represents a core value crucial to democracy: equality, efficiency, and liberty. These three values are deeply embedded in the public ideology and political ecology of the United States, and each is continually and collectively reinforced in the nation's symbols and political rhetoric.

In reality, the three values can be in conflict. For example, to pursue equality to its absolute metaphysical limit is violently to restrict liberty. Similarly, to eschew equality and pursue only choice, or liberty, runs the risk of creating such wealth and social class extremes as to jeopardize stability of the polity. Finally, efficiency may well be furthered by choice and liberty. However, unfettered efficiency may jeopardize equality.

Liberty is often seen as the higher goal, as equality for its own sake can be empty. To be sure, a democracy must strive to achieve and maintain equality of opportunity. However, few contend that absolute material equality, with all of its trappings of drab sameness, is an end in itself. If everyone had only the same clothes, cars, houses, and food, there might be equality, but tedium might well be the order of the day. Absolute equality, or at least the pretense of such, was the hallmark of the former Soviet Union. Its ultimate downfall was a function of an inept system of individual and collective performance incentives, distance between ideological aspirations and the material corruption of its leaders, and its inability to provide consumers with choice.

Similarly, efficiency usually is taken to be an instrumental or mediating goal. As such, or for its own sake, it has little value. Conversely, the conservation of resources so as to have more of something, be it material or psychic, would seem to be a useful end toward enhanced choice or liberty.

Equilibrium Theory. A major function of the policy system is to maintain a balance among these core values. Too much emphasis, for example, upon equality, and perhaps an erosion of liberty, may provoke a pendulum swing. Similarly, too great a concern for liberty may alienate those who perceive that unfettering of choice disadvantages them, and they push politically for a restoration of concern for equality.

There exists a set of dynamics that can upset the value balance, a set of dynamics that can shift the emphasis of a political system, resulting in new or altered policies. Returning to Figure 5.2, one can see a rectangle, each side of which represents a change vector: technology, economy, demography, and ecology. A significant change on any particular dimension can distort the public value balance, triggering altered policies, and eventually provoke a search for a new policy equilibrium. Following are illustrations of this process at work.

Technological innovation is a major source of system imbalance and, hence, a principal trigger of new policies. Here is a dramatic example: reliable birth control pills for women were a 1950s biochemical invention by Stanford researcher Carl Dierassi. Few could have predicted the eventual consequences, including a sustained decline in the birthrate, vastly expanded workforce participation by women, increased demand for out-of-home child-care services, reliance upon television for entertaining children and youth, possible erosion of the two-parent nuclear family or at least a diminution in the proportion of such units, widespread relaxation of prior prohibitions regarding premarital and extramarital sex, and a reduction of the ratio of children to adults in society.

These changes themselves contributed to policy demands for publicly subsidized child care, extension of public school kindergarten and preschool programs, new child welfare laws, added reliance on equal protection laws to ensure women equal treatment in the workplace, increased regulation of television offerings, and a greater openness to overseas immigration to enable the workforce to keep up with the job demands of a vastly expanding economy resulting from two income earners in many households.

Examples abound of the reciprocal effects of technological innovation and economic change, and the combined effect of these two forces upon policy demands. The acceleration of a global economy in the 1990s resulted from the convergence of a number of electronic innovations leading to formation of the World Wide Web and the Internet. These new communication and information-transfer technologies disconnected capital, creative ideas, and talent from national boundaries. Companies and other organizations, including even international terrorist groups, could now draw upon ideas and recruits from overseas, in a never-ceasing quest for means to lower manufacturing and production costs. The outsourcing of jobs itself reverberated through the U.S. policy system as electoral candidates and government officials debated and sought means for regulating or limiting the flow of jobs overseas.

Policy System Paradigm. By what processes and through what institutions are value imbalances addressed, policies enacted, and equilibrium restored? Figure 5.4 depicts a policy system paradigm developed by University of Chicago political scientist David Easton.

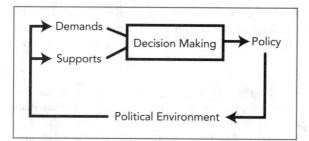

FIGURE 5.4 Easton's Policy System Model

▪ CULTURES OF POLICY

The policy system has five identifiable cultural components, five ways of viewing reality and attempting to shape it. These policy cultures influence the manner in which
advocates for a particular change will define a problem or design solutions. The unique
components of each culture also shape the instruments and processes by which participants attempt to implement and oversee policy.

The five policy cultures are as follows.

Political. This culture conventionally associated with policy making is **political culture**.
Deliberative bodies, such as legislatures, city councils, and school boards, confer about issues and render recorded decisions. These politically made rules may have been the focus
of intense controversy or of complicated and protracted lobbying by various parties and
interests. The activity may have been partisan, linked to identifiable political parties. The
newly enacted policy may alter some existing circumstance, add a new service, elevate
taxes, or acknowledge some important symbolic issue. Whatever the policy, its construction is characterized by the principal components of the political process, coalition building and bargaining.

Regulative. This too is a widely perceived component of policy. However, many individuals
misperceive regulation. They believe that regulations derive singularly from enactments
by deliberative bodies. In short, they think of regulations as detailed rules authorized by
and flowing from relatively abstract policy enactments, something of a bureaucratic
follow-on to politics. There is some accuracy to this perception. However, by itself, it is
insufficient.

Bureaucratic executive-branch operating agencies also have a momentum of their
own. Some of the rules they develop and promulgate stem solely from the momentum of
bureaucratic practices, and only remotely from political enactments. There is a large
organization imperative specifying that if there is to be a hierarchy of authority with some
individuals in greater positions of decision-making power than others, a division of labor,
specialization of tasks, and an expectation that all similarly situated clients will be treated
similarly, then there must be rules to enforce all of this.

The distinguishing characteristics of the regulatory policy culture are codification, rationality, rigidity, specialization, hierarchy, standardization, and efforts to appear objective
and independent. Anyone who has had military experience will have encountered a regulatory policy culture. Military procedures may eventually be linked to statutory authority,
but often one must follow the policy "food chain" to very high levels to identify the

overarching authority. In fact, the military is quite capable of generating many rules all by itself, as are educational institutions. Public universities and school districts have many sets of rules that, however well intentioned and effective, are a product of bureaucratic, and thus not necessarily openly political, processes.

Legal. Courts and legal procedures make up a third major cultural component of the policy system. The identifying features are an ability to frame an issue in keeping with long-standing, judicially sanctioned doctrines; a resort to adversarial techniques; adherence to precedent; appeals to higher authority; and proscribed sets of procedural activities known only to a restricted cadre of certified technicians, lawyers.

Professional. This is the policy culture that may be least visible to the general public. From this culture stem procedures and decisions derived from self-reinforcing sets of beliefs of professional participants, not necessarily from court decisions, bureaucratic rules, or political enactments. Distinguishing characteristics are actions taken to protect clients, enhance standards, advance knowledge in a field, and insulate the profession from partisan or selfish interests. Examples include peer evaluation procedures for assessing performance of university professors, peer review among research organizations to determine a manuscript's publishability or fundability of a proposed project, or grading policies for student performance in an institution of higher education or a secondary school.

Markets. This policy culture is distinguished by a fundamental belief that clients are sufficiently informed and motivated to operate in their own self-interests and that, in the process of doing so, will promote the public long-run interests as well. Market-oriented policy cultures certainly have room for rules generated in other spheres. For example, few who believe in deregulating the airline industry would also completely eliminate Federal Aviation Administration rules regarding pilot training. However, the weight of an argument from a marketplace advocate's point of view must be heavily in favor of regulation. Further, open choice among services or products, open competition for consumers' resources, access to capital, and a free flow of information are seen as the *sine qua non* that should shape policy.

 CASE 4 REVISITED

> Recall from Case 4 chief state school officer Mary Kay, the action-oriented leader with a desire for a first-rate management information system capable of measuring multiple performance indicators across her state's schools. In her desire for progress, however, she ran into resistance amidst the five policy cultures of her organization. Choose one of the policy cultures and discuss the nature of her difficulties as well as potential win-win solutions.

Confluence and Confusion of Reality

Those affected by policy, and almost everyone is, can benefit from understanding each of the five separate policy cultures and their identifying components. In reality, however, parents, students, school administrators, teacher leaders, education reformers, public officials, and interested laypersons may become engaged in a real-life educational policy matter and thus find themselves caught in a whirling vortex of perceptions and predetermined processes from more than one policy culture. There are many intersections at which two or more of the policy cultures collide or combine, each imparting its flavor to the whole, but the whole itself can be identifiably different than any one of its parts.

For example, legalistically defined policy problems may eventually be addressed through reform legislation that, in turn, may be implemented through bureaucratically shaped rules. These new rules may subsequently serve as the basis for added amounts of litigation or even market-oriented solutions. The logjam of *de jure* racial segregation was broken in 1954 by a U.S. Supreme Court decision in *Brown v. Board of Education*. However, the court's admonition that the nation's dual school systems be eliminated with "all deliberate speed" ultimately contributed to federal legislation and that, in turn, ultimately led to a set of executive-branch regulations regarding school desegregation. These agency rules have themselves served as bases for litigation and appeals and in other settings have shaped the formation of organizational rules in school districts.

Thus, only rarely will one see a "pure" policy representing only one culture. Nevertheless, each archetype to be explained and explored in this book has a quintessential core of assumptions, beliefs, tenets, and historical roots that, if understood, will enable a reader, an analyst, a policy maker, or an activist to comprehend more fully the policy reality whirling around him or her in both his or her private and professional worlds.

■ INSIDE THE "MODERN" EDUCATION REFORM POLICY PARADIGM

Two principal school improvement or education reform strategies—systems alignment and economic dynamics—have emerged since 1983 to build a foundation for elevating student academic performance.

Systems Alignment. One major reform strategy hinges upon the presence of measurable academic expectations or curriculum standards and an assortment of instructional and accountability components aligned in pursuit of these standards. The "production" components in this model involve dimensions such as educator time, class size (a dimension of teacher time spent with students), instructional materials and textbooks, student achievement testing, time on learning tasks, preservice teacher training, parent and community engagement, leadership training, personnel and institutional performance reports, professional development, in-school peer group characteristics, and in-school and out-of-school **extracurricular** activities for students.

This systems alignment strategy presumes that much regarding good instruction is already known and that appropriate coherence between various instructional components can result in higher levels of student academic learning. Also, components of this strategy lend themselves to being operationalized into an instructional alignment measure that can be considered either as a dependent variable, in an effort to discern policy system conditions providing the greatest or best alignment, or an independent variable to determine alignment consequences for pupil performance.[11]

Economic Incentives. The other principal reform model takes schooling and instruction to be a black box, perhaps a currently impenetrable or unknowable black box. Market and economic incentive advocates contend that a specification of expected outcomes and an appropriate system for measuring and sanctioning school success in producing desired student outcomes will productively guide actions of those inside the black box. Under such assumptions it is less necessary than in a systems alignment strategy to understand the nature of "throughputs." However, it is still crucial to understand the nature of outputs. It is also more important to understand interactions of various market components, (e.g., supply; consumer information; performance incentives for students, teachers, schools, and districts; competition effects; and market regulation) than in the systems alignment model.

Competition is often posed in policy circles as an alternative reform strategy since market dependence is seen as a major incentive. The ability of clients to seek different schools, presumably schools more consistent with personal preferences, is taken to be a market incentive to motivate instructional providers. In essence, providers either perform to clients' expectations or lose market share and accompanying resources.

While it is important to distinguish between these two intervention models—each implies a partially different set of tools to determine its effectiveness—a reader should not gain a misimpression that the two models are mutually exclusive. There are ways by which they can be combined. For example, an operator of a private school presumably is interested in having instructional components aligned, in order to be effective. Although a systems alignment strategy does not preclude reliance upon client choice systems or performance awards and punishments for teachers or schools in the public sector, systems alignment advocates seldom recommend performance incentives for students, teachers, schools, or school districts.

 CASE 3 REVISITED

Recall the multiple factors converging on Superintendent Shannon Cantrell's school district. Amidst significant demographic change, her district is having to contend with both No Child Left Behind standards and her state's learning objectives. While her historic student population would not hinder her district in meeting either of these expectations, that is not the case today. Which of the education reform policy paradigms do you feel would be most successful in helping Shannon move her district in a positive direction? Explain your thinking.

Summary

In this chapter, the reader learned about the politics, policy, and policy issues in American education. Given the degree to which education leaders are impacted by federal, state, and district policy, it is important for a strategic leader to understand the complex dynamics of education policy and develop strategies to navigate and influence education policy. One of the largest contextual variables for public schooling is that schools exist in a policy environment of increasing consolidation, as the numbers of school districts, state officials, and school board members have diminished dramatically. The complexity created through the history of education policy makes the use of systems theory a helpful tool for future education leaders to unravel policy. Another important concept introduced in this chapter was that any policy system can be conceptualized through a variety of lenses. Since the goal of policy systems is to maintain balance (equilibrium theory) and direction toward a given set of goals, it is important to understand the different paradigms through which policy is interpreted. These frameworks were referred to in this chapter as policy cultures and include political, regulative, legal, professional, and market. Each of these policy cultures influences the manner in which advocates for a particular change will define a problem or design a solution. Strategic education leaders are able to navigate through each of the policy cultures in a manner that engages key constituents and keeps the organization aligned with its core mission and vision.

Discussion Questions

1. This chapter describes schools and school districts as "loosely coupled" organizations. From within your current education organizational context, describe one benefit and one challenge associated with such loosely coupled systems.
2. The chapter discusses five major implications of systems theory for school leaders. Choose one, and describe the impact that it will have upon your leadership approach or style.
3. Figure 5.3 presents three values that are deeply embedded in the public ideology. Reflect on a policy initiative at your education institution, and discuss the tensions between equality, efficiency, and liberty inherent in the policy. What, if anything, did the leaders in your organization do to recognize and stabilize the competing tensions?
4. As highlighted in the chapter, the number of school districts, and thus local school boards, has dramatically declined nationwide over the past fifty years. At the same time, population growth has increased. In your local region, what impact has this had upon the ability of school board members to adequately represent community constituents? What solutions can you offer to amend this situation?
5. ELCC 6 expects school leaders to understand, respond to, and influence the larger political context. As described in this chapter, the policy system has five identifiable cultural components, five ways of viewing reality and attempting to shape it. These policy cultures influence the manner in which advocates for a particular change will define a problem or design solutions. As a current or aspiring school leader, which of the five cultural components do you think will be most beneficial when formulating, implementing, and overseeing educational policies in your school or district?

References and Suggested Readings

Curtis, M. (1976). *The great political theories: A comprehensive selection of the crucial ideas in political philosophy from Burke, Rousseau and Kant to modern times.* New York: Avon Books.

　　This well-organized anthology shows the evolution of political thinking through the thoughts of individual men, the patterns of thought emerging from their writings, and the possible influence one theorist had on another.

Dahl, R. A. (2005). *Who governs: Democracy and power in an American city.* New Haven, CT: Yale University Press.

　　A classic work offering a comprehensive interpretation of where the political power in America's urban communities resides.

Kennedy, J. F. (2003). *Profiles in courage*. New York: Harper Collins.

  The famous study of eight historical figures in their acts of political courage and integrity when faced with vast opposition.

Notes

1. Data in this paragraph were derived from the U.S. Department of Education. National Center for Education Statistics, *Digest of Education Statistics, 2000*, NCES 2001-034, by Thomas D. Snyder and Charlene M. Hoffman. Washington, D.C.: 2001.

2. These and other data in this paragraph are derived from 1991–92 and 2004–2005 *Estimates of School Statistics* (Washington D.C.: National Education Association 1992, 2005).

3. Peters, Thomas, J., and Waterman, R. H. (1984). *In search of excellence: Lessons from America's best run companies*. New York: Warner Books. Also, Covey, S. (1990). *The seven habits of highly effective people*. New York: Firestone Pub.

4. Tyack, D. B. (1974). *The one best system*. Cambridge, Mass: Harvard University Press. Also, Eaton, W. E. (1990). *Shaping the superintendency: A reexamination of Callahan and the cult of efficiency*. New York: Teachers College Press.

5. Kluger, R. *Simple justice*. New York: Vintage Books, 1975. Also, Horowitz, D. L. *The courts and social policy*, Washington D.C.: The Brookings Institution, 1977. Also, Wolters, R. *The burden of brown: Thirty years of school desegregation*, (Knoxville, University of Tennessee Press, 1984). Tyack, D, Thomas, J., and Benavot, A. *Law and the shaping of public education: 1785–1954* (Madison: University of Wisconsin Press, 1987). Also, Guthrie, J., & Springer, M. (2004). Returning to square one: From *Plessy* to *Brown* and back to *Plessy*. *Peabody Journal of Education*. *79*(2), 5–32.

6. Pride, R., & Woodard, J. (1995). *The burden of busing: The politics of desegregation in Nashville, Tennessee*. Knoxville, TN: University of Tennessee at Knoxville. Also, Orfield, G. (1978). *Must we bus? Segregated schools and national policy*. Washington, D.C.: The Brookings Institute.

7. Guthrie, J. W. A political case history: Passage of the ESEA. *Phi Delta Kappan*, *49*(6), February 1968, 302–6.

8. Graham, H. D. (1984). *The uncertain triumph: Federal education policy in the Kennedy and Johnson years*. Chapel Hill, NC: University of North Carolina Press.

9. Kerchner, C. T., Koppich, J. E., and Weeres, J. G. *United mind workers: Representing teaching in the knowledge society*, San Francisco: Jossey-Bass, 1997.

10. Murray, S., Evans, W., & Schwab, R. (September 1998). Education-finance reform and the distribution of education resources. *American Economic Review*. *88*(4), 789–812.

11. For more information on means for measuring "alignment" and the metrics involved, see Andrew C. Porter, "Measuring the Content of Instruction: Uses in Research and Practice," *Educational Researcher*, *37*(7), pp. 3–14.

CHAPTER SIX

Finance

LEARNING OBJECTIVES

By the end of this chapter, you should be able to

- comprehend the financial magnitude of the U.S. education system;
- explain means by which revenues are generated and distributed to support public schools in the United States;
- identify mechanisms by which resources are allocated (budgeted) within school districts and schools;
- understand inefficiencies inherent in the operation of school fiscal management;
- identify factors contributing to the stasis in educational accounting practices;
- describe the fiscal landscape that education leaders will likely confront in the upcoming decades.

Imagine the year 2020 when the following three scenarios could occur in the United States:

State Senator Jeffrey LaMorte is sitting at the Apple computer in his Atlanta legislative office. He chairs the Senate Appropriations Committee, and the markup session for the fiscal 2021 budget begins the next morning. He is working on a spreadsheet that displays a ten-year pattern of public school spending by subject matter and grade level. He is networked to the state education database that enables him to access categories of spending data and an assortment of school process and outcome data, such as student performance on state subject matter achievement tests. These data are stored in a manner that permits disaggregation to the school site of origin.

The Georgia Association for Guidance, an intensely focused interest group representing guidance counselors in the state, contends that added spending for counselors would enhance the proportion of female students majoring in math and science. They are lobbying for a categorical spending feature in the upcoming appropriations bill.

Generally, Senator LaMorte detests earmarked spending limitations on school site personnel. Nevertheless, he decides to explore the matter. Both of his sisters were themselves quite gifted mathematically, and he always has been interested in expanding the career opportunities of women. Consequently, he is open to any reasonable means that would enhance gender equity on this dimension.

Senator LaMorte asks himself the question, Will added spending on counselors likely enhance female science and math enrollments and achievement levels? If the answer is yes, he is quite willing to increase state **appropriations** for these purposes. To answer this question, he accesses ten years of school spending data and an assortment of other input and output information from the state education department data file. He makes the keystrokes necessary to array these data on a school-by-school basis, scrolls to the new Super Social Science Statistical Program (S4P) under TOOLS, and applies the programmed weighting controls for student social background characteristics. He then begins to search for Georgia high schools with the highest and lowest proportions of female science and mathematics majors.

Once identifying these top and bottom ten secondary schools on this dimension, he quickly computes the mean per-pupil guidance expenditure in each set of schools. He uses his S4P again to control for student achievement levels and concludes, alas, that higher levels of guidance spending bear no relationship either to gender decisions or achievement levels.

Ten years of precise accounting for functional and subject matter spending, school-by-school, simply does not reveal any systematic relationship between added levels of spending on guidance counselors and student decisions about academic major, number of courses taken, or subject matter achievement. All of these results hold even after having applied the most stringent statistical controls for student characteristics.

Senator LaMorte searches further through his database, looking for possible relationships to high levels of student math and science achievement, and finds that the most likely spending-linked variable is teacher training in advanced science and mathematics courses and in-service education in these areas.

Senator LaMorte firmly believes in permitting school site professional educators to make resource allocation decisions. Further, he has little doubt that literally dozens of Georgia principals have already done the kinds of analyses that he has just conducted in the last fifteen minutes. However, he has now verified for himself that added resources, if allocated in a **categorical aid** bill directed specifically at guidance spending, would unlikely lead to the intended outcomes. He now will have an answer when he meets the next morning with guidance association advocates. They will not be happy with his response and his refusal to include them in an earmarked section of the appropriations bill. Still, he thinks to himself, the data he has just analyzed would be every bit as available to them as to him. Why did they not do the analyses themselves? If they did, then they might have proposed an alternate appropriation.

Concurrently, the following scenario unfolds twenty-seven hundred miles to the west:
In his office in the Los Angeles Municipal Court building, the facility that had been made famous twenty-five years before by the trial of O. J. Simpson, Anthony Serrano is sitting at his networked computer. Almost two decades have passed since the Los Angeles Unified School District consented, in *Rodriguez v. Los Angeles USD*, to allocate financial resources on an equal per-pupil basis. Serrano, the grandson of a lead plaintiff in a famous interdistrict equal protection school finance suit, is a court-appointed master charged with ensuring that the school district has been complying with the intradistrict equal protection agreement.

The school district had been fumbling for years in achieving per-pupil spending parity. To do so had been an intense challenge because senior teachers had filed their own suits claiming a violation of union contractual agreements regarding seniority transfer privileges. The school-by-school budgeting that had resulted from the original Rodriguez consent decree had left many schools in the San Fernando Valley, which were in the upper-income reaches of the city, short of the resources to employ senior teachers with their higher salaries. In effect, parents on school site councils had generally opted for smaller class sizes, in contrast to higher-paid, more senior teachers and the inevitable concomitant of large classes. Many of the district's more senior teachers were finding that they were having to accept the forced-choice positions available to them in central city schools, and they were not pleased with the prospect of having either to move their residences or undertake a long daily commute. Of course a number had resigned, but a significant percent had filed suit and had delayed the consent decree implementation as a result.

By 2010, the court had resolved most of these problems, and Serrano is now using the LAUSD data bank to test for anomalies in school site budgets. The consent decree still permitted a degree of disparity. Judge Lance Ito, formerly of the criminal justice division but now hearing civil cases, has decided that the same decision rule that applied to school spending for the state of California and stipulated that 95 percent of all pupils in the state had to fall within a prescribed per-pupil spending band will also hold inside a school district. It is the young Serrano's task to monitor this spending band and report to the court if resource allocation disparities exceed the limit. He is now preparing his quarterly report for the court.

Meanwhile, in midcontinent:

In a Chicago suburb, Theresa Coons sits at her computer. The screen is filled with school-by-school **budget** and program comparisons. As she scrolls through available data regarding spending and program profiles of Chicago-area secondary schools, she reflects fondly upon the distinguished career of her grandfather, Robert E. Coons, a forceful and thoughtful advocate for school choice plans. Here she is, a school choice adviser, living out the hopes of her famous relative by advising families regarding the fit between their schooling preferences and the offerings of area public and private schools.

The widespread availability of school-by-school accounting data, and the later addition of program information coded by school, has created a remarkable opportunity to enable parents to make informed choices about schooling for their children. Theresa is one of thousands of certified school choice advisers who, for a fee, counsel households regarding the relative advantages of particular individual schools.

▪ PROVIDING STRATEGIC LEADERS WITH THE FINANCE KNOWLEDGE THEY NEED

This chapter will return to each of the preceding three hypothetical scenarios and trace their links to contemporary leadership issues. Meanwhile, here is the broad context of this chapter. First, a strategic education leader can benefit from possessing a generalized understanding of the means by which the United States generates and distributes revenues for the operation of its K–12 schools and the myriad policy issues that accompany these arrangements.

Second, understanding the sheer magnitude of the resources involved is important as professional background knowledge. Few other endeavors, public or private, absorb resources as does education. The immediate upcoming chapter section addresses this topic. Third, strategic leaders need to understand the broad mechanisms by which revenues are generated and distributed for schooling in America. This does not require detailed understanding of **property tax** technicalities and state distribution formula nuances. A more stratospheric comprehension will suffice. Knowing this big picture advantages a leader in conceptualizing the entire system of education, engaging with members of the public and the media, and partaking in informed exchanges with state and federal policy makers. Such professional knowledge is the topic of the third portion of this chapter.

The fourth section focuses on budgeting and thus explains the processes by which resources are and might better be allocated within an education organization. This skill set is of central importance to a strategic education leader. The final sections of this chapter explain the evolving policy context of education finance. These sections examine the inherent inefficiencies in education finance, explore reasons for the stasis within educational accounting practices, and suggest what strategic leaders are likely to encounter in the next decade as they strive to improve education.

■ EDUCATION FINANCE OPERATIONAL MAGNITUDE

In the past half-century, **per-pupil expenditures** in public elementary and secondary schools have more than quadrupled, even after adjusting for **inflation**. This chapter section discusses some of the reasons.

In 2007, the United States spent more than $3.5 billion per operating day to support K–12 schools. This was more than was spent on national defense, more than almost anything but health care and debt, in terms of its costliness.

Public elementary and secondary schools account for almost one-third of all state government expenditures and almost half of all local government expenditures, plus 2 percent of all money annually appropriated by the federal government. These amounts, and possibly proportions, likely will increase in the future due to projected population growth. In addition, the per-pupil expenditure rate has risen continuously for most of the last fifty years. These sustained trends and the awesome magnitude of the total education enterprise highlight the need to understand the finances of public schools. Here is a quick summary of spending increases.

- A significant share of the increase is due to an 86 percent inflation-adjusted increase in teacher salaries between 1949–50 and 1971–72, although teacher salaries have changed little, except for inflation-adjusted increases, in the years since.
- The ratio of students to school employees has become more favorable by half, due to declining class sizes and more nonteaching school employees, which significantly affects costs.
- A substantial part of the increase in per-pupil spending is due to expansions in services provided by the schools. More expensive, specialized classes for high school students, compensatory education for students from disadvantaged backgrounds, special education and related services for students with disabilities, and racial desegregation efforts all contribute to higher costs.
- Efforts to improve funding **equity** have led to increased expenditures. When faced with equity court decisions, rather than transferring funds from wealthier districts,

most states prefer to raise the funding available to schools at the bottom and the middle of the spending scale, increasing total spending.
- A share of the total increase must be attributed to the workings of the political system governing schools.

A Half-Century of Spending Increases. The National Center for Education Statistics calculates that the average per-pupil expenditure (excluding capital expenditures), in constant 2003 dollars, has risen from $1,299 in 1949–50 to $8,224 in 2004–05.[1] Table 6.1 illustrates the changes in enrollment, number of teachers employed, average teacher salary, and cost per pupil from 1949–50 to 2004–05.

It is also important to keep in mind that, while the cost of education per pupil has risen, the American economy has also expanded significantly. As portrayed in Figure 6.1, total spending, expressed as a percentage of gross domestic product (GDP), has followed enrollment closely.

TABLE 6.1 Changes in Enrollment, Number of Teachers Employed, Average Teacher Salary, and Cost per Pupil from 1949–2006

Year	Public K–12 Enrollment (X 10,000)	Number of K–12 Teachers	Average Teacher Salary ($)	Per Pupil Cost ($)
1949–50	2,511	914,000	18,580	1,299
1951–52	2,656	963,000	19,190	1,369
1953–54	2,844	1,032,000	20,800	1,440
1955–56	3,116	1,149,000	21,760	1,600
1957–58	3,353	1,238,000	23,140	1,747
Fall 1959	3,609	1,355,000	24,860	1,867
Fall 1961	3,825	1,458,000	26,830	2,038
Fall 1963	4,103	1,568,000	2,8420	2,182
Fall 1965	4,207	1,711,000	29,720	2,464
Fall 1967	4,389	1,864,000	31,920	2,830
Fall 1969	4,555	2,023,000	33,390	3,158
Fall 1971	4,607	2,070,000	34,490	3,517
Fall 1973	4,545	2,136,000	33,780	3,786
Fall 1975	4,482	2,198,000	33,220	3,964
Fall 1977	4,358	2,209,000	33,150	4,255
Fall 1979	4,165	2,185,000	30,080	4,279
Fall 1981	4,004	2,118,000	29,960	4,236
Fall 1983	3,925	2,139,000	31,530	4,561
Fall 1985	3,942	2,206,000	33,870	5,047
Fall 1987	4,001	2,279,000	35,380	5,352
Fall 1989	4,054	2,357,000	36,130	5,715
Fall 1991	4,205	2,432,000	36,040	5,737
Fall 1993	4,347	2,505,000	35,820	5,825
Fall 1995	4,466	2,634,000	37,640	5,989
Fall 1997	4,654	2,746,000	39,350	6,320
Fall 1999	4,737	2,910,000	41,820	6,940
Fall 2001	4,789	2,999,000	44,680	7,256
Fall 2003	4,823	3,067,000	46,870	7,727
Fall 2005	4,957	3,132,000	48,320	8,224
Fall 2006	5,103	3,207,000	49,760	8,990

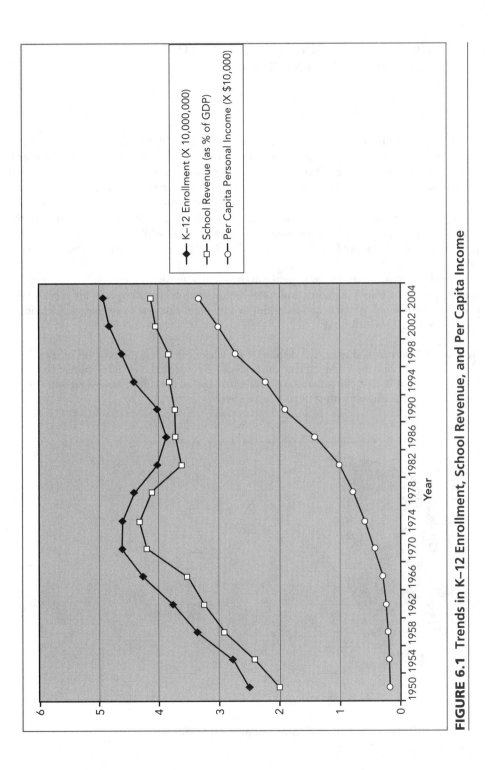

FIGURE 6.1 Trends in K–12 Enrollment, School Revenue, and Per Capita Income

Legend:
- ◆ K–12 Enrollment (X 10,000,000)
- ☐ School Revenue (as % of GDP)
- ○ Per Capita Personal Income (X $10,000)

Year

■ GENERATING AND DISTRIBUTING STATE AND FEDERAL EDUCATION REVENUES

It is convenient for descriptive purposes to divide revenue discussions into (1) government levels and processes responsible for generating and, separately, for (2) distributing school revenues.[2]

It is also useful to keep in mind that revenues come in classifications. There exist operational funds, of which there are two kinds: general and categorical. The first, **general funds**, are monies that local district revenue recipients are free to expend, within legal boundaries, in a manner of the school board's choosing. These are discretionary dollars. Revenues also come from higher levels of government, federal and state, and are labeled categorical. In these instances, the money is accompanied by regulations that specify the purpose, the program, or the personnel that can benefit from the dollars involved or that can actually be purchased. Local districts are legally obligated to adhere to these categorical spending rules.

Finally, revenues can be for capital purchases that are of an enduring nature, such as school or administrative facilities and long-lasting equipment. Revenues for capital purposes are distributed by states and localities in a manner different from that of operational (general and categorical) funds.

Revenue Generation. Figure 6.2 displays a pie chart capturing the portion of total U.S. K–12 spending contributed by each of three levels of government (federal, state, and local). What is evident is that the federal government is by far the junior revenue-contributing partner when contrasted with state and local governments.

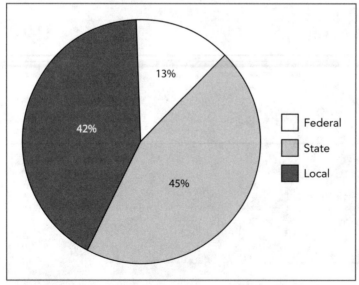

FIGURE 6.2 Percentage of State, Local, and Federal Contributions to Education

However, these contribution proportions should not easily deceive a reader. Federal regulations for the use of categorical revenues ensure that the practical influence of federal funding far outstrips its actual dollar contributions to operation. One need only be conscious of NCLB as a dominant influence over the nation's education system, even if providing to local districts but a small proportion of the resources expended. What revenues it contributes are generated by the federal government, principally through personal and corporate income tax proceeds.

State-contributed revenues to school operation are usually generated through personal income tax receipts, sales taxes, or both. Locally contributions stem principally from property tax receipts.

Nationwide, state revenues conventionally comprise about forty-five cents out of every school-operating dollar. Local contributions are usually in the 42 percent range. The long-term trend since World War II, and particularly since the advent in the 1970s of equal protection suits, about which more will be said in the succeeding chapter on legal matters, has been for the state share to increase and the local share to decrease. The federal share has been stable for a quarter of a century. However, the distribution of state and local contributions surrounding this national norm is wide. In Hawaii, for example, there are only state (and federal) revenues for school support. The local property tax plays little part in school support. By contrast, in New Hampshire, local contributions are the major source of school revenue, with the state contributing a minor share.

Property taxation necessitates a multistage process for (1) identifying and recording ownership of property, (2) determining its taxable value (**assessment**), (3) **levying** a tax (always undertaken by an elected body), (4) collecting tax receipts (tax collectors), (5) ensuring compliance and hearing appeals (state boards of equalization), and (6) means for handling payment delinquencies (sheriffs).

Capital funds for construction usually are generated through debt instruments, **bonds**, and are repaid by revenues from specifically levied local property taxes or from state general fund revenues. There is a justification for funding capital activities differently than funding operating activities. Capital projects usually serve multiple generations of users. Hence, it makes sense to repay their costs over time, not asking a single user cohort to bear the unusually heavy burden of a building, but rather to spread the costs over the multiple generations of those likely to benefit from the facility.

Distribution: Flat Grants and Foundation Programs.[3] Initially, during the colonial and early federal periods, efforts to fund public schools by first territories and later states involved distribution of operating revenue dollar grants to local school districts. The purpose of a flat grant of money, later adjusted to be a flat grant per pupil, was to induce and to assist local districts to operate schools. These dollar amounts were legislatively established and were seldom distributed in connection with local school district or community property wealth. The absence of consideration of local wealth led, in time, to substantial disparities in school district capacity to operate schools.

George D. Strayer and Robert M. Haig were among the first to address the issue of local district wealth disparity. In 1923, in a report to the Educational Finance Inquiry Commission, they proposed a system that had the effect of capturing a portion of the local property tax for state purposes without that being openly evident. Their proposal subsequently became known as a foundation program, or the Strayer-Haig plan.

Under the Strayer-Haig formulation, the state specifies a dollar amount per student to which each school district is entitled. Presumptively, this is the amount of money per pupil necessary to guarantee an adequate education. At the time of the foundation plan's invention or conception, there were few systematic efforts to ensure that the dollar amount prescribed, in fact, was sufficient to provide a foundational level of schooling. More often than not, the foundation dollar amount was a political product. Knowing what it was willing to tax or what level of revenue was available, state legislatures would first establish the revenue pool and then, through division, determine the per-pupil amount of the foundation. More will be said regarding this situation when the topic of **adequacy** is raised in subsequent chapters.

The state requires each district to levy a property tax at a fixed rate (called required local effort) and provides only the difference between the amount raised by that tax and the guaranteed expenditure level. Thus, a property-poor district will generate little with the tax at the specified rate, and the state will provide generously. A district wealthier in property will generate almost as much or even more as the dollar guarantee and will receive little **equalization aid** from the state. An unusually property-wealthy district will generate more than the guarantee and will receive no subsidy from the state.

If the state requires each district to levy a property tax at a specified rate in order to receive state money and counts proceeds of that local tax as a part of the guarantee, the required property tax is, in effect, a state tax. If the required local **tax rate** is relatively high, a substantial amount of money will be raised. This, combined with state money, enables the legislature to establish a guarantee level sufficient for what is assumed to be a minimal education. Some states do not require the district actually to levy the tax at the specified rate, calling it instead a computational tax. It is then a device used only in determining dollar amount of state aid to a district. A few districts may then levy a lower tax than this, raising less money per child than the guarantee and subverting the intent of the foundation concept.

The manner in which foundation programs operate is illustrated in Figure 6.3. The horizontal line LE depicts the dollar amount of the foundation guarantee, supposedly representing the cost of a minimal program. The section labeled Required Local Effort is the amount raised by the local property tax at a required rate of ten **mills**. The section labeled State Aid is supplied by the state, at a foundation level of $2000. For District A, the required local effort (RLE) raises little money, and the state contribution is high. District B raises most of the guarantee locally, and District C raises more than the guarantee and receives nothing from the state. The solid sloping line at the top is the total amount that would be raised if all districts chose to levy an optional local tax at the rate of five mills, in addition to the required tax. District B can raise more than District A, and District C can raise more than District B. The line becomes steeper at point M because districts beyond that point already raise more than the guarantee by using only the required rate, thus making the total amount they collect that much higher. That is, the slope of the line 0K is ten mills, the slope of the line LM is five mills, and the slope of the line MN is the sum of those, or fifteen mills.

It may be argued that it is unfair that some districts, because they happen to be rich in property, have more money to spend from levying the required tax rates than do property-poor districts. If the required tax is indeed a state tax, then the amounts raised above the

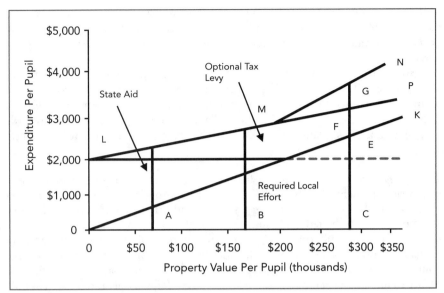

FIGURE 6.3 **Financial Considerations for Foundation Programs in Education**

guarantee should be returned to the state to be used elsewhere. This concept is called **recapture**, and the dashed lines in Figure 6.3 show the effect of it. District C would raise, at the required rate, the amount shown by the line CF. It would return to the state the amount EF, leaving it exactly as much as every other district. Because of this, if it levied an additional optional tax at the same rate as the other districts, it would raise the amount EG. With recapture on the ten mills of RLE, the line LMGP shows the amount generated by districts at a fifteen-mill tax rate.

The underlying philosophy of the foundation plan is that the state should provide for an adequate educational program, defined as a specified number of dollars per student, and districts may raise money above that guarantee if they wish, as a local luxury, without help from the state.

A state education financing system such as this, including recapture, would provide complete wealth equalization if the underlying philosophy were accepted. States, however, have been unwilling typically to employ the recapture concept. To do so is to admit publicly that the required property tax is a state tax rather than a mechanism open to local option. In addition, the amount of taxes exported from a local district is highly visible. Recapture has been attempted in only a few states and repealed in some of those. For example, in the 2006 trial court decision in *West Orange Cove Independent School District v. Nelson*, the Texas statewide recapture and redistribution plan was declared a statewide property tax, prohibited constitutionally in Texas, and voided.

An alternative, of course, would be simply to levy a statewide property tax at the RLE rate and use proceeds to finance a flat grant system. Looked at this way, one can see that the flat grant is simply a special case of the foundation program, in which the required local tax rate is zero.

As with the flat grant (and indeed with all school finance schemes), there are practical problems with the foundation plan. The plan assumes that the foundation amount is the amount necessary for an adequate education, although there is no way of determining this with accuracy.

Another problem is the minimum grant, or residual flat grant, that usually accompanies a foundation program. The reason for this grant is that it is not only unpopular to recapture excess tax money generated by districts; it is even unpopular to grant them nothing. As a result, each district receives at least a minimum dollar amount of state aid per pupil regardless of its wealth. Since this minimum aid flows only to the wealthy districts, it is obviously disequalizing.

Federal Funding Distribution. Federal funds are distributed through categorical programs, statutory enactments specifying dollar amounts (appropriation acts) to which states and districts are eligible and the operating purposes (authorization acts) for which states and local districts can use the federal funds.

The federal categorical programs are for the support of vocational preparation, poverty enhancement, and assistance with the financing of schooling for disabled students. Federal funds also flow to states and local school districts to compensate local districts for their inability to impose property taxes on federal lands or federal operations (such as military bases). These in lieu of tax acts are known as **impact aid**.

▮ ALLOCATING RESOURCES PRODUCTIVELY IN AN EDUCATION ORGANIZATION

Financial administration of a school district, as with almost any formal organization, consists of two conceptually distinct activities: budget planning and budget administration. In a district such as New York City, separate specialized teams, involving hundreds of officials, may perform each of these activities. In a small school district, the superintendent and secretary may perform all functions. Regardless of how many or how well-trained and specialized the actors or participants, neither budget planning nor administration typically involves schools as a unit of accounting control or analysis.

Planning and accounting are far more likely to be undertaken districtwide. It is unusual to be able to read a school district budget and determine the amount of money spent in a school. When a superintendent is asked, "What do you spend at X school?" the likely answer is to name a figure that specifies the amount of discretionary funding for instructional supplies and expense. This typically is only 1 or 2 percent of the total spending at a school. The overwhelming proportion of resources allocated for operating the conventional school is linked to professional and classified salaries and fringe benefits. It is unusual for these personnel-related spending amounts to be specified on a school-by-school basis. The few districts that do, however, are an unusually avant-garde cadre.

Budget Planning

This is the forward-looking component of the budget cycle. Here an organization determines what it intends to spend in a forthcoming fiscal year.

School districts with a thousand or more enrolled students frequently resort to a mechanical or formulaic budget format. They rely upon uniform allocation rules that provide an illusory appearance of treating each school, and by deduction each student, equally. A district will formulate allocation rules, such as each twenty-five enrolled students will generate a teaching position at a school site; every four hundred students entitles a school to a librarian, or a counselor, an assistant administrator, and so forth; every fifteen students generates a teacher aide; so many square feet of building generates a custodial position; and so many school site acres generate a groundskeeper or gardener.

In addition to these full-time equivalent (FTE) personnel allocations, the formulae will distribute a specified amount of **revenue per pupil** for discretionary items such as textbooks, instructional supplies, and perhaps field trips and consultant days. A school's "budget" is the aggregate of the personnel positions and discretionary funding it is due by virtue of such uniform decision rules.

The allocation of revenues to cover activities such as employing substitute teachers, paying utilities, covering legal costs, paying for maintenance, and engaging consultants is likely to remain centrally budgeted. It is an unusual principal who has detailed and usable knowledge of how much is annually being spent on these items for his or her school.

These uniform distribution decision rules are often reinforced by state statutory components (for example, maximum class sizes specified by a state legislature), collective bargaining contracts, and historic precedent, either in the district or in its surrounding region.

However rational these decision rules appear (and they may even square with the experience of educators), they are not scientifically validated and have little or no basis in research.

Uniform allocation rules have two principal advantages. First, they give the appearance of equality. Everyone appears to be treated the same way. A principal, a parent, a teacher, or someone else is provided with little apparent reason to complain. Any question regarding equity of treatment can be answered with, "Well, we have an allocation rule. Your school was treated like every other school. If you do not like the result, then you can ask the school board, legislature, or Congress for an exception." Such an admonition generally serves to discourage debate.

The other advantage to formulaic allocation is that it centralizes authority. In U.S. public schools, mechanical allocation norms are, in fact, followed for allocating personnel. Consequently, for every twenty-five (or whatever number) of students generating an FTE teaching position, the school is likely to be allocated a teacher.

Of course, the alternative is to utilize uniform decision rules to determine the resources for which a school is eligible, convert this result to actual dollar resource levels, and then permit the operating unit, the individual school, to determine how it chooses to allocate the resources. An individual school under such a plan might choose to trade people for things, things for people, or people for different kinds of people. However, such school-site decision making is quite unusual in the United States. This alternative approach is sometimes referred to as a weighted pupil allocation formula or school site budgeting.

Outmoded, But Still Existing, Budget Models

Budget processes can be plotted on a continuum ranging from a centralized set of processes that rely little upon strategic planning to an emerging set of decentralized concepts that emphasize educational planning and evaluation as the basis for budget development. The discussion that follows contrasts centralized budgeting systems with decentralized procedures now being pioneered by adventurous and experimental districts throughout the nation.

Mechanical Budget. The mechanically operated budget can be set forth on two sheets of paper—one presenting the estimated yearly receipts of an institution and the other displaying how the money can be divided to operate a school. Under this concept, budgeting is strictly a revenue-and-expenditure operation, a bookkeeping chore required by law that is the product of intense activity near the end of the fiscal year and then is quickly forgotten until the end of the next year. This type of budgeting forces expenditures to fit income expectations and pays little attention to needs. Any planning done is negative, calculating what can be eliminated or what can be padded so that the budget will balance. The object of this budgeting mind-set often is to keep costs at a minimum without regard for needs or educational achievement. Mechanical budgeting is the antithesis of strategic leadership.

Yearly Budget. The annual budget approach attempts to construct a school budget in a short (three- to four-week) period for presentation to the board of education and to the community. It is a refinement of the mechanical type, in that it necessitates quick decisions on expenditures and revenues, and little effort is made to evaluate its impact. Decisions on staffing, salaries, programs, supplies, and services are often made with little consideration of educational needs or evolving educational opportunities. The challenge is to get the budget document completed and approved before the deadline date. Usually, this method attempts to adjust the previous year's document to include items such as pay increases, enlarged staff, and increased numbers of students but does not consider changes in program, availability of new materials, differing needs, and emerging concepts. Once completed, this type of budget may become a straitjacket that provides little opportunity for strategic shifts in priority.

Administration-Dominated Budget. This concept views the development of the budget as strictly a management responsibility. Little or no staff help is requested. The central office provides an impression that budgeting is a dauntingly complex process and that only a "chosen few" are sufficiently sophisticated to participate. The prevailing philosophy seems to be that if fewer people know, and do not know much, about the budget, there will be less conflict and fewer questions. Often, value judgments are made without proper evaluation and with few options offered to those immediately affected. This tight-ship approach is symptomatic of authoritarian systems and hastened the coming present of collective bargaining, citizen involvement, and student awareness.

Centralized Budget. The centralized concept of budgeting treats all schools in a system as if they were only one. *It regards the district as a school system, not a system of schools.* While it is an efficient way of developing a budget, little consideration is permitted for differing needs among the various schools and communities served. Allocations are made on a mechanical per-pupil basis, and little attention is given to existing resources or to any backlog of requests. Decisions concerning such issues as teacher-pupil ratio, supplies, materials, texts, and curriculum are made by formula at the central office, and all schools must conform. This concept tends to treat the entire system as a homogeneous unit rather than recognize that even the smallest systems are heterogeneous, made up of diverse communities with unique needs, abilities, and capacities.

Budget Administration

The purpose of budget administration is to ensure that an organization adheres to whatever budget plan it develops. Budget administration calls for a series of "control" points.

These are the domains of accountants, auditors, payroll specialists, and purchasing agents. Spending decisions are controlled by such agents who use the budget, and by reference all appropriate laws, to ensure that a proposed expenditure is, in fact, both approved by the budget as an organizational spending plan and legal. The overwhelming result of this is a centralization of control.

Public school accounting practices in the United States are principally a product of advisory publications of the U.S. Department of Education. These advisories regarding accounting procedures have been adopted and, in many instances, adapted by state agencies. The consequence is an almost uniform school accounting system across the United States.[4]

This relatively uniform code of accounts serves at least two purposes admirably. First, it accurately tracks revenue sources, ensuring that categorical funds are separated from general discretionary revenues. This enables governmental agencies to ensure that revenues are deployed in the manner, and for the purposes, that governments decree.

A second purpose served by existing accounting procedures is ensuring that school revenues are expended in a legal manner. Current functional and object codes permit careful tracking of expenditures, should such detailed **auditing** be necessary.

■ WHAT IS WRONG WITH THIS (FINANCIAL) PICTURE?

The inability to obtain revenue and spending data school by school is a major impediment to efficient planning, equitable distribution, good school management, and client choice. In effect, the inability to determine precisely what is spent at a school prevents American education from being efficient, fair, or just. Few seemingly simple matters have such far-reaching consequences. More accurate spending information is an unusually small reform step possessing a potential for huge policy and practical rewards. Of course, such a small step might also trigger substantial added conflict. However, about that more will be said later.

The Impediment to Efficiency. The absence of school-by-school revenue and spending data and accompanying program information imposes so many barriers to rational operation and determination of efficiencies that it will be difficult to catalog them all here. Suffice it to say that research, effective practice, and realistic accountability are all handicapped by the absence of sensible and accurate disaggregated data.

An Illustration about Production Function Research. In 1966, the *Coleman Report* was released by what was then known as the United States Office of Education.[5] This endeavor, authorized by Congress as a part of the 1964 Civil Rights Act, was then the largest social science undertaking in history. The world-famous sociologist Jeffery S. Coleman led the analytic team. The Congressional charge was to map the extent of educational inequality in the United States.

Among its activities, the Coleman team attempted to understand the relationship between financial resources and student achievement. Even though Coleman and his colleagues attempted to control for student background characteristics, their research effort proved badly flawed. For financial data, they used what was available to them: district-wide, highly aggregated expenditures per pupil. These proved to be quite inaccurate portrayals of the levels of resources actually expended on particular pupils. Consequently, out of ignorance, not malice, the Coleman Report finding that financial resources had little relationship to level of pupil performance, separate from the social background of students, was simply unsupportable. Inaccurate data eroded the nature of the finding; however, this did not impede the acceptance of the finding itself. The prestige of Coleman, the massive data sets involved, the sophistication, for the time, of the analytic techniques utilized, and possibly, a predisposition by policy makers to believe that schools waste money combined to create a receptive audience, even if the message had not properly been proved.

Despite the inaccurate information, the Coleman findings were widely trumpeted by the popular press and widely misinterpreted by the policy community. For literally decades following issuance of the report, it has been cited as evidence that added financial resources make little or no difference in pupil performance. Other researchers have attempted valiantly to employ more sophisticated models with more accurate data. Nevertheless, it is still difficult to conduct the research in the manner needed because of the widespread absence of school-by-school and student-by-student financial data.

Professional Ineffectiveness through Uniformity. The absence of school-by-school data, along with spending discretion on the part of school executives, renders American education unnecessarily ineffective. Essentially, currently employed aggregated budgeting and accounting procedures reinforce a virtual uniform blanket model of schooling. Levels of experimentation are unusually limited by the dictates of uniform allocation rules. Principals and staffs are stifled in whatever creative efforts they might desire to make to re-arrange resources.[6]

Ill-Conceived Process Accountability. The absence of school-by-school data and school site budgeting eviscerates useful accountability. By budgeting and accounting for resources centrally, school districts provide administrators with a built-in excuse for lack of pupil performance. Under current arrangements, school decisions are, effectively, central office decisions, perhaps even school board and state legislative decisions. It is thus easy for a principal to hide behind such centrally promulgated rules and explain that a lack of student achievement is not his or her fault. Rather, the absence of results is a consequence of the district's decision rules. The principal is only acting as a conduit, overseeing educational and operational decisions made elsewhere.

School-based management exposes dramatically the decisions of those at schools. Principals, teachers, parent councils, whoever are subject to careful scrutiny in a system that simultaneously measures student performance and permits school-based decisions. The threat of such true accountability may well explain the absence of enthusiasm on the part of professional educators for school-by-school data and school-based management.

The Impediment to Equality. Present-day budgeting procedures disguise dramatic spending disparities. Certainly aggregating spending to district level means disguising the high spending on legally protected categories such as the handicapped. However, less well understood are the dynamics of intradistrict spending disparities that penalize low-income students.

The principal "culprit" in intradistrict unequal spending, or at least a silent accomplice, is the aggregated spending means kept by districts and the use of previously described uniform allocative criteria. By relying upon uniform personnel allocation rules and then driving the decision rule through to practice by allocating actual positions rather than revenues, school districts disguise spending inequities accompanying teacher salaries.

In most school districts, particularly in large districts where disproportionate percentages of low-income youngsters attend, teachers' pay is a function of number of years of service and numbers of college credits beyond a bachelor's degree. These two factors have little bearing upon instructional proficiency. However, they possess the advantage of being measurable. Thus, they are widely used, regardless of their validity in measuring competency or **productivity**.

Also as a frequent product of collective bargaining, teachers have often gained the right to transfer to open teaching positions based on their seniority of service. This condition frequently permits teachers with the greatest years of service to transfer to schools within a district with high-achieving students or working conditions that are the most comfortable. Aside from whatever just deserts are involved for individual teachers, the system constitutes a conspiracy, however unintended, to defraud inner city students of a just share of revenues or high-quality personnel. In those unusual instances in which actual accounting has taken place school-by-school, low-income students often find themselves in schools with lower-paid teachers. This is true simply because their teachers are the least senior, and thus the least paid.

A few court cases have questioned the equity of such arrangements. The earliest was *Hobson v. Hansen*, a Washington, D.C., intradistrict equity case. The court decided in favor of plaintiffs and required that the Washington, D.C., school district reallocate teachers so that their salary distributions were more equitably aligned with the socioeconomic status and race of school children. The court stopped short of mandating an imaginative reform such as school site budgeting that offered the prospect of achieving both greater equality and greater efficiency. A more recent West Coast consent decree is *Rodriguez v. Los Angeles Unified School District*. Here the school district agreed to make a transition to school-based budgeting and accounting.

The regular practice of school-by-school accounting and school-based decision making, coupled with other reforms, might actually rectify these types of intradistrict injustices and simultaneously render schooling more effective.

The Impediment to "Liberty." Private schooling has a long history in the United States. Nevertheless, as discussed earlier, almost 90 percent of America's students attend public schools. Many individuals cannot afford otherwise. Many of those who can afford a choice of schools have exercised their option by purchasing a home in a desirable public school district. They exercise choice through their pocketbook. Thus, there remains a substantial residue of less-than-wealthy households who use assigned public schools but who might prefer a choice, if they could afford it.

Increasingly, public school districts attempt to accommodate this desire for greater choice by using magnet schools, charter schools, or some other optional assignment mechanism. This may prove to be more satisfying than simply assigning schools to households. However, a school choice plan would be measurably enhanced by providing school-by-school financial and program information to families in the district. Such an arrangement would enable households to make more informed choices. They could choose the school with a resource allocation pattern most to their liking. Parents and students preferring more senior teachers might be willing to trade larger classes for their preference. Conversely, households favoring small class size might trade teacher experience. Still other sets of parents might choose a school heavily invested in technology. Whatever the customer preferences, they would all be better served with better information.

┌─── CASE 4 REVISITED ────────────────────────────────

Recall the opposition to State Superintendent Porter's proposed disaggregated management information system. Given the substantial and sustained disadvantages accompanying aggregated, school district–wide data, why has there not been a sustained outcry for change? Why have not public officials demanded more precise and disaggregated information? Why has not school-by-school accounting been higher on the reform agenda?

└───

More definitive answers to these and related questions will no doubt have to be provided by historians writing in some future time. Meanwhile, it is possible to pose several hypotheses to explain the absence of more policy-relevant financial data. Before offering these tentative explanations, it is of importance to note that these hypotheses are tightly tied to political conditions. Technically, it has been practical to account for school spending in a more precise manner for literally decades. There is little by way of technical planning or accounting complexity in providing decision makers with school-by-school financial information. The problem is one of political will, not practical way.

■ POSSIBLE EXPLANATIONS FOR THE FINANCIAL ACCOUNTING STATUS QUO

Progressive Era Residue. "Scientific management" and "depoliticization discouragement" were the watchwords of a sweeping set of turn-of-the-century reforms that dramatically altered the governance and management landscape of American public education. The full range of changes is chronicled by historians such as David Tyack in *The One Best System* or Raymond Callahan in *The Cult of Efficiency*. Suffice it to summarize here that a coincidence of events tied Progressive Era political reforms, industrial engineer Frederick Taylor's "scientific management," school district consolidation, and the advent of urban school district professional administration into a forceful reform package. One component of this package was a redefinition and restriction of decision-making legitimacy for school board members. They were intensely socialized to avoid the prerogatives of management and repeatedly admonished only to make policy. Detailed decisions regarding what should be allocated or the manner in which it might be allocated to a school were surely regarded as intrusions on management prerogatives. Hence, asking that a new accounting system concentrate on school-by-school measures would probably have been used as a threat to mount a recall election.

Present-Day Political Homeostasis. School-by-school financial information holds the prospect for upsetting the political status quo. System ignorance of detailed distributional consequences enables teachers and their unions to adhere to the above-described transfer privileges. Principals make few requests for more complete disaggregated financial data because such an information flow might expose them to greater accountability expectations. Superintendents and central office staff may believe that their currently held decision-making prerogatives would be threatened by greater school-site autonomy. Similarly, parents of upper-socioeconomic-status students may not be eager to have the existing balance changed out of a belief that they are currently advantaged. In short, the political system has accommodated to ignorance. Added information threatens this balance. Hence, there is no great clamor for change.

Sheer Ignorance and Naiveté. Few school board members assume their public office positions having had experience with the financial side of organizations. Their training and expertise reside in other areas. Hence, they seldom know to ask for disaggregated data. For their part, business experts may often assume that school data are arrayed in a disaggregated manner. They are used to cost centers and **decentralized** management. Many of them may simply assume that such procedures are commonplace. Of course, in schools they are not. However, only those individuals close to school decision making know of the absence of disaggregated data. The president of a large local business is seldom sufficiently engaged with schools to learn the difference.

■ SO WHAT IF THINGS WERE DIFFERENT?

More and more-accurate knowledge of the manner in which education resources were allocated could be a mixed blessing. The prospect is favorable if the policy system links disaggregated budget information with disaggregated decision making, school site budgeting with school-site decision making. However, if the policy community used school site financial data simply to make more proscriptive decisions from the center, to invent even more narrow programs of categorical aid, then more accurate information may serve only to rigidify American education even further.

Positive Policy Possibilities. The favorable consequences are in the realms of efficiency, equity, and possibly liberty. Accurate school-by-school, classroom-by-classroom, or even student-by-student data would permit far more research about education "production." This would be particularly true if schools were sufficiently unfettered, even encouraged by incentive systems, to experiment with far wider models of instruction than now generally exist. Researchers would have more settings, more accurate information, and possibly a wider range of instructional models to assess.

More accurate and more appropriate information would also create an opportunity for greater strategic leadership on the part of educators. Having knowledge of, and greater control over, resource decisions would empower leaders and enable them more productively to match resources to the needs of students.

More accurate information would also create the possibility of an effective accountability system, an accountability system that placed responsibility for results at schools. Similarly, as illustrated in the opening fictional Serrano scenario, more accurate and disaggregated data would permit far greater monitoring of equality of opportunity. Finally, more accurate information, particularly regarding school-level spending, would permit more accurate matching of client preference with the offerings of schools. This could serve as a productive platform for enhancing the choices of households.

Possible Dysfunctional Policy Outcomes. More accurate data might well provoke more sophisticated debates among the public and its representatives regarding the purposes of schooling. If hypothetical Senator LaMorte wanted to know how much money was being spent on science instruction in Georgia, in contrast with home economics or social studies, he might have stirred a controversy regarding the question, What knowledge is of most worth?

Under current arrangements, the United States can claim to include virtually every subject in the public school curriculum. All one has to do is mention or mandate that subject X should be taught. With a disaggregated, accurate, school-by-school accounting system, one could subsequently proceed further to explore how much money was actually being allocated for and spent on the instruction of subject X. Under such circumstances, the prospect is elevated that spending on subject X conflicts with the spending priorities of others who would like more spent on subject Y. Proponents of subject Y, once understanding that their interests were being slighted in terms of resource flows, might well complain and undertake some form of political action in behalf of their interest. Few spending-priority protests currently occur because there is seldom any accurate information regarding spending level on particular subjects or activities.

Such political controversy need not be negative. Indeed, one can argue that it is good. An appropriate role of the political system is to resolve conflicts regarding the allocation of values. Hence, if more accurate information provokes conflict regarding values, then the political system can accommodate the interests involved, and the polity enjoys the added commitment of participants.

Nice talk. Tell it to the residents of Bosnia, Rwanda, Iraq, or Lebanon—nations torn by conflict because the political system could not resolve questions of values and allocation of scarce resources. The question is the level of conflict provoked. If it becomes too intense, it could prove dysfunctional. Public schooling would become even more politicized, losers would be less willing to allocate resources to its support, and social cohesion might be jeopardized as a result.

Accurate information, if mishandled, also could lead to greater levels of rigidity in schools. If education leaders took the opportunity resulting from accurate resource-flow information to proscribe even more tightly the uses of resources, to direct that spending per pupil in each school not only be equal but also be equal for science, math, social studies, home economics, foreign language, and so on, the system would lose what little flexibility now exists. The opportunity to tailor resource flows to the needs and preferences of individual students could be reduced even further. Incentives for educators to exercise professional discretion would be further diminished, and the productivity of the system could be decreased.

■ LIKELY FUTURE CONTEXT OF EDUCATION FINANCE

The most powerful policy stimulus for organizational and control changes, at least for the foreseeable future, is that the judicial system is beginning to take state constitutions at their word. Judges are no longer simply asserting that education funding must be equitable and sufficient. Increasingly they claim that it is a state's responsibility to ensure that school services are of a specified quality, a quality sufficient to ensure that a student is capable of good citizenship, empowered to participate productively in the economy, and personally fulfilled. Formerly, legislators and governors met state constitutional requirements by compelling school attendance, ensuring free schooling, and inducing formation of districts.

From such restricted policy beginnings sprang a minor branch of educational governance theology that came to be known as **local control**. It was the local control mantra more than any other that provided a framework for education policy choices and judicial remedies in the nineteenth and twentieth centuries. Now, however, it is this time-honored mantra that is most at risk of succumbing to other values in the twenty-first century.

The old equity issues have not disappeared. It is simply that emerging adequacy and efficiency considerations must now be addressed in addition.

Twenty-first-century court decisions in Massachusetts, Wyoming, Alabama, Arkansas, Wisconsin, New York, and North Carolina have held the state responsible not simply for ensuring that local schools are funded equitably or even sufficiently. In addition, they proceed to hold the state responsible for (1) ensuring that schools pursue higher than heretofore codified standards, (2) providing disproportionate resources to disadvantaged students, and perhaps through direct provision or intense oversight, (3) guaranteeing that instruction is of a high quality.

For example, a Wisconsin Supreme Court decision holds the state accountable for ensuring schooling "will equip students for their roles as citizens and enable them to succeed economically and personally."

The Court specifies that the purpose of an adequacy criterion must be to "adopt a standard that will equalize outcomes, not merely inputs."

In a January 2001 decision, New York trial judge Leland DeGrasse rejected as insufficient for the twenty-first century a conventional state constitutional standard of "basic literacy" and specified instead the necessity of schooling for civic engagement: "productive citizenship—not just voting or sitting on a jury—but doing so capably and knowledgeably."

He proceeds to charge schools with closing "the disconnect between the skills of the State's and City's labor force and the skills of the high technology sector."

In the Leandro case in North Carolina, trial judge Manning rejected the state defense that passage of a standardized test at the eighth-grade level met constitutional requirements. Instead, Judge Manning's opinion insists that performance "at grade level" on state-specified curriculum standards is the minimum now acceptable. The Leandro decision proceeds further to insist that "economically disadvantaged students need services and opportunities above those provided to the general student population."

The Wyoming Supreme Court, in its 2002 *Campbell II* decision, makes clear that it is the state's responsibility not simply to ensure funding is sufficient to provide Wyoming with a "proper" and "unsurpassed" education system, but also that the state must itself take responsibility for ensuring the best educational opportunities are made available to disadvantaged students, be they poor, non–English speaking, or disabled.

In short, the judicial system, unencumbered by narrow political constraints often felt by more directly elected public officials, is taking state constitutions literally. If a constitution charges the state with provision of schooling, then the state must ensure that such schooling is of a quality tailored to twenty-first-century needs.

If states are to be held accountable to new and higher education standards, then states are being goaded into far more intense actions about the actual provision of schooling. What once was the clear and protected domain of local school board members and superintendents is now increasingly the responsibility of state officials. Thus, here is the challenge facing strategic leaders and policy system participants in the early part of the twenty-first century.

Summary

A strategic leader should be aware that the pattern in which his or her organization expends resources reflects the organization's priorities. If a school district's priorities involve elevating student academic performance, then it makes little sense to pay teachers and others for qualities and conditions that reveal little relationship with student achievement. A strategic leader should carefully think through what matters most for his or her organization and then ensure that the organization's resources are aligned with those objectives.

Discussion Questions

1. Federal funds provide but a sliver of the nation's educational dollars, yet federal policies such as NCLB have a tremendous impact on educational institutions. What is your opinion of this apparent discrepancy?
2. Discuss the relative merits of foundation programs and flat grants, the two primary revenue distribution methods we have learned about in this chapter.
3. After weighing the positive possibilities with the possible dysfunctional outcomes associated with a more disaggregated understanding of allocated education resources, propose a rationale for or against such a policy.
4. As public education in the United States becomes increasingly subject to market forces, the ability of school leaders to meet the economic demands of ELCC Standard 6 are paramount. Given the evolution of the fiscal landscape confronting American education, articulate how one key concept from this chapter will help you position your school or district on a more economically sound foundation.
5. In an analysis of the patterns by which your school and district expends resources, what priorities would be reflected?

References and Suggested Readings

Guthrie, J. W., Springer, M. G. Rolle, R. A., Houck, E. A. (2007). *Modern education finance and policy*. Peabody Education Leadership Series. Boston: Allyn & Bacon.
   In-depth explanation of means by which K-12 education is supplied with revenues and the policy issues associated with taxation and distribution of school funds.

Ladd, H. F., and Fiske, T. A. (2008). *Handbook of education finance and policy*. American Education Finance Association. New Jersey: Lawrence C. Erlbaum Associates.
   This is the most comprehensive and current reference regarding education finance, K-12 and postsecondary, and the policy issues associated with these activities.

Notes

1. Per-pupil expenditures 2004-05: *Rankings & Estimates: Rankings of the States 2004 and Estimates of School Statistics 2005*, Highlights Table 2. Summary of Selected Estimates Data for 2004–05. Data from *Rankings of the States 2004 and Estimates of School Statistics 2005*, used with permission of the National Education Association © 2005. All rights reserved.
2. A reader desirous of detailed knowledge of these processes should see Guthrie, J. W., Springer, M. G., Rolle, R. A., and Houck, E. *Modern education finance and policy*. Boston: Allyn & Bacon, 2006.
3. A history of education finance is provided in Chapter 1 by Matthew G. Springer, Eric C. Houck, and Jeffery W. Guthrie, of the American Education Finance Association

Handbook on Education Finance, Helen Ladd and Theodore Fiske Eds. Lawrence Erlbaum Associates, New Jersey, 2008.

4. However, even if fundamentally part of the same genus, for those who attempt to interpolate finance data across state boundaries, accounting system idiosyncrasies and definitional differences can be maddening.

5. It was elevated to cabinet status as the Department of Education in 1979 by the Carter administration.

6. This matter is apparently more complicated than it might initially seem. Lack of school-based budgeting and decision making might well be crucial impediments to developing mixed models of education. However, there is some other dynamic at work also. Otherwise, why is there allegedly so little innovation among private schools, which presumably are not hindered by the need to rely upon mechanical allocation formulae? The probable answer is that such schools are evaluated by the satisfaction of their client parents. They are seldom driven by more precise measures of student performance, particularly some kind of "value-added" performance measures. If they were, and if they had actually to account for students' gains in achievement, they might find themselves more motivated to experiment with a wider variety of "production" techniques.

CHAPTER SEVEN

Law

LEARNING OBJECTIVES

By the end of this chapter, you should be able to

- understand the role of law in shaping the operational context for education leaders;
- explain constitutional and jurisprudential underpinnings of American education;
- identify court cases of historic significance for American education, and hence of professional importance for leaders;
- list criteria for judicial intervention in an issue;
- identify cases illustrating students' and employees' judicially protected and restricted rights.

A strategic education leader operates within a larger societal context. Among the features of this contextual landscape are laws and legal procedures. Legal matters are particularly important in shaping the landscape of school leadership because K–12 education is lawfully compelled everywhere in the United States. Once school compulsion is in play, an imposition upon the freedom of families and their children found in few other instances in American society, then the oversight and intensity of the court's interaction with the activity is elevated substantially.

Timid, or perhaps insufficiently informed, education leaders can mistakenly view the law and courts as constraints, narrowly concentrating only on the limits courts impose upon their authority and viewing laws as impediments to their otherwise legitimate need to change their organizations. Such a negative view is reinforced by the heavy presence of the law when it comes to elementary and secondary education. Because K–12 schooling is compelled by society, courts are quick to ensure that those subjected to this compulsion, namely students and parents, are fairly treated and protected when it comes to their fundamental liberties. A K–12 school administrator is influenced substantially more by an applicable body of law than, for example, is a postsecondary administrator or private-sector manager. However, going to college or working at Wal-Mart is a voluntary act. Going to elementary and secondary school is not an option open to individuals of school age in the United States.

Thus, through one set of lenses, courts and the law can be viewed as a restriction. However, a strategic leader must be confident that he or she is not simply hiding behind the skirts of the court, using the fear of law and litigation as pretexts for passivity. There are multiple conditions in which the law can be seen as a facilitator of, not simply an impediment to, change.

In reality, a strategic leader who is well informed regarding the law and judicial dynamics might better see the legal glass as half full. Properly approached, the law may provide an otherwise hard-to-identify lever for removing impediments. For example, at one time, a good portion of the nation maintained legislatively approved racially segregated schools, students with identifiable handicaps did not have regular access to schooling, students routinely subjected to abusive parents or teachers were unprotected, public financial aid to nonpublic schools was illegal, teachers who voted "incorrectly" in school board elections for a candidate opposed by their boss were routinely at risk of being fired, and the children of illegal immigrants were denied access to schooling. These deficit conditions, while surely not yet fully rectified, would unlikely have been addressed at all without the interventions of courageous plaintiffs and inventive attorneys operating through the legal system.

The purpose of this chapter is to provide a strategic leader or aspiring leader with a sufficient grasp of legal fundamentals to understand where useful leverage for thoughtful change may exist and how to avoid arbitrary and capricious actions that may prove professionally and institutionally disadvantageous. A strategic leader's best defense, if confronted with a legal challenge, is to ensure that he or she knew existing law and acted both in good faith and in a thoughtful and rational manner. If one has good knowledge, good reason, and good motives and has given due consideration to alternatives, then chances are good that one has performed legally. However, simple exposure to this chapter is by no means a substitute for obtaining appropriate legal advice when faced individually with the details of a potentially litigious situation. As a chapter in a foundational text on education leadership, the following content will focus on cases of significant historical magnitude. In the appendix, the reader will find a list of court cases of more contemporary, if not yet historical, interest.

■ CONVENTIONS, CONSTITUTIONS, CASES, COURTROOMS, AND CLASSROOMS

The fundamental charter by which the United States governs itself comprises the Constitution and accumulated legal interpretations of its various provisions. This overarching governance document, framed in Philadelphia during the summer of 1787 at the Federal Convention, specifies important governing matters, such as the form of the federal government, enumerated powers of each branch of government, and eligibility for holding federal office, and contains in its first ten amendments a set of especially protected personal liberties, the so-called Bill of Rights. The document also makes clear that the source of its authority is the people of the member states whose duly elected representatives have agreed to abide by, sustain, and promote the principles involved.

The Federal Convention

The colonial delegates who convened at the Federal Convention on May 25, 1787, rejected the idea of merely revising the formerly operative Articles of Confederation and agreed to construct a new framework for a national government. Throughout the summer months at the convention in Philadelphia, delegates from twelve states debated the proper form such a new government should take, but few questioned the need to establish a more vigorous government to preside over the union of states. The thirty-nine delegates who signed the Constitution on September 17, 1787, expected the new charter to provide a permanent guarantee of the political liberties pursued in the victorious Revolutionary War against England.

Prior to the adoption of the Federal Constitution, the Articles of Confederation, drafted by the Continental Congress and approved by thirteen colonies, provided for a union of the former British colonies. Even before Maryland became the last state to accede to the Articles in 1781, a number of Americans, particularly those involved in the Revolutionary War, recognized the inadequacies of the Articles as a basis for a national government. In the 1780s these nationally minded convention delegates became increasingly disturbed by the Articles of Confederation's failure to facilitate formation of a central government with authority to raise revenue, regulate international and interstate commerce, or enforce treaties.

Despite repeated proposals that the Continental Congress revise the Articles, the movement for a new national government began outside the Congress. Representatives of Maryland and Virginia, meeting at Mount Vernon to discuss trade problems between the two states, agreed to invite delegates from all states to discuss commercial affairs at a meeting in Annapolis, Maryland, in September 1786. Although delegates from only five colonies reached the Annapolis Convention, that group issued a call for a meeting of all colonies to discuss necessary revisions of the Articles of Confederation. Responding to this call and the endorsement of the Continental Congress, every state except Rhode Island selected and sponsored delegates for the Federal Convention in the State House at Philadelphia.

The resulting document, the U.S. Constitution, was the product of nearly four months of deliberations. The challenging task before the delegates was to create a republican form of government that could encompass the thirteen states and accommodate the anticipated expansion to the West. The distribution of authority between legislative, executive, and judicial branches was a boldly original attempt to create an energetic central government while at the same time preserving the sovereignty of the people and the accumulated governing rights of each of what had been the individual founding colonies.

The longest debate of the Convention centered on the proper form of representation and election for the Congress. The division between small states that wished to perpetuate the equal representation of states in the Continental Congress and the large states that proposed representation proportional to population threatened to bring the Convention proceedings to a halt. Over several weeks the delegates developed a complicated compromise that provided for equal representation of the states in a Senate elected by state legislatures and proportional representation in a popularly elected House of Representatives.

The conflict between large and small states declined substantially in the early years of the republic. The large state–small state compromise was a success. More lasting was the regrettable division between slave and free states that had been a disturbing undercurrent in the Federal Convention debates. The Convention's strained attempt to avoid using the word *slavery* in the articles granting recognition and protection to that institution scarcely hid the regional divisions that would remain unresolved under the terms of union agreed to in 1787.

Of course, the Federal Convention's failure forthrightly to address slavery permitted the issue to fester for decades thereafter and eventually contributed to the most deadly war in the nation's history, the Civil War. Even a North, or Union-preserving, victory did not fully resolve the issues at hand. As late as 1954, in *Brown v. Board of Education*, and into the last quarter of the twentieth century, the judicial system was still making episodic corrections to a policy of racially unequal treatment that had persisted for hundreds of years.

There exists here a strategic issue for leadership consideration. On one hand, if founding fathers had striven with greater resolve to settle the issue of slavery once and for all, they may never have reached any accord whatsoever regarding the formation of a new nation. Their disagreements regarding this issue were so fundamental that after a debate regarding slavery, any chance of consensus on other matters may have been impossible. On the other hand, failure to resolve the slavery issue not only postponed the seemingly inevitable conflict, but also perhaps rendered it not simply a protracted political debate, but far worse, facilitated a full-blown war. The absence of a Federal Convention resolution of the issue of slavery contributed to an eventual armed battle of greater intensity and brutality than any other in our nation's history and worse than might otherwise have had to occur. It was a question of priorities.

Time to Reflect

If you had been a Federal Convention participant, would you so easily have acquiesced to the interest of slave states, or would you more forcefully have faced the slavery issue at the time? What was ultimately more important, the formation of a new union or the abolition of slavery?

The Resulting Constitution

Aside from slavery, for professional educators, the U.S. Constitution represents several enigmas. The United States is one of the world's few modern industrial democracies that operates a decentralized education system. Only Canada and Australia, and in some ways Germany, even approximate this pattern. Most of the world's modern nations rely upon a national education system. However, the federal constitution makes no provision for a national education system. Indeed, it makes no provision for education or schooling whatsoever. This seems peculiar since the thirty-nine convention delegates were among the best-educated individuals in the world at the time. Regardless, the absence of any formal consideration precludes education as an enumerated federal government function.

The Tenth Amendment, ratified on December 15, 1791, is also important here. It specifies:

> *The powers not delegated to the United States by the Constitution, nor prohibited by it to the States, are reserved to the States respectively, or to the people.*

The Tenth Amendment makes clear that if a power is not explicitly delegated by the Constitution to the federal government, or prohibited by the Constitution to states, it is thus, by default, a state function. Education finds itself defined by these boundaries. It is for this reason that states are said to have *plenary*, meaning ultimate, authority over education.

The Tenth Amendment, however nuanced and understated, contains another important point. By reference in the final clause to "or the people," the Tenth Amendment expresses the *social contract* theory of government upon which the U.S. Constitution rests. The intellectual revolution embedded here is that, whereas the right to govern may be

God given, it is practically ceded to citizens, the people, not to a historically enfranchised, divinely empowered monarch.

A Digression Regarding State Constitution Education Clauses

The fundamental authority of states in education is reinforced by state constitutional clauses. Forty-nine of fifty states have constitution clauses requiring the state to maintain a public school system.[1]

Some scholars maintain that education clauses can be classified, based upon particular language, into four categories. These categories attempt to array state constitutions in order of the intensity of the duty placed upon the state. Category I clauses are the weakest, insofar as the language employed in those clauses appears to impose only a minimal duty. Category I education clauses require the state provide only a system of public schools, and the clause does not elaborate on the scope of the requirement. The Connecticut and New York state constitutions provide examples of Category I education clauses.

Connecticut's Constitution states:

There shall always be free public elementary and secondary schools in the state.

New York State Constitution at Article 11, Section 1:

The legislature shall provide for the maintenance and support of a system of free common schools, wherein all the children of this state may be educated.

Category II clauses exceed Category I requirements by requiring an explicit commitment to public education. Category II clauses may often require that the public education system be "thorough," "efficient," or both as found in the New Jersey state constitution. Essentially, the Category II clauses require that a state meet a minimal level of quality in their public education system.

In Category III clauses a state includes a more specific mandate or objective that education is to achieve, while Category IV clauses impose the strongest requirements on states. Category IV clauses are buttressed by language such as "primary," "fundamental," or "paramount." Essentially, Category IV clauses impose an explicit and affirmative duty on the state to support public education.

For example, the Washington state Constitution states, "It is the paramount duty of the state to make *ample provision* for the education of all children residing within its borders . . ." (emphasis added).

Presumably strong education clauses should aid in legal challenges to state action, or inaction. However, evidence suggests that there is little correlation between strength of education clauses and education-related decisions by state courts.

Returning to the United States Constitution and Its Interpretation

Judicial interpretations of the Constitution, not simply the Constitution itself, have had dramatic effects upon education governance and practice. For example, an informed reader will almost assuredly be wondering if the Constitution is silent regarding education and schooling, since Congress has enacted such significant education policies as the Elementary and Secondary Education Act, the Education for All Handicapped Children Act, and the No Child Left Behind Act. The justification for such federal action is through liberal judicial interpretations of the General Welfare Clause.

The U.S. Constitution's preamble reads as follows:

We the People of the United States, in Order to form a more perfect Union, establish Justice, insure domestic Tranquility, provide for the common defense, promote the general Welfare, and secure the Blessings of Liberty to ourselves and our Posterity, do ordain and establish this Constitution for the United States of America.[2]

Embedded in the Preamble is the "promote the general Welfare" language that subsequently has been interpreted to provide Congress with far-reaching authority to promote the long-run well-being of the nation. This, and the following parts of the Preamble, are the culmination of everything that came before it—the whole point of having tranquility, justice, and defense was to promote the general welfare—to allow every state and every citizen of those states to benefit from what the government could possibly provide. The majority of Constitutional framers looked forward to the expansion of landholdings, industry, and investment, and they knew that a strong national government could be the beginning of that.

The General Welfare Clause was initially accompanied by controversy. Forceful Federalists such as Alexander Hamilton preferred a liberal interpretation so as to enable the fledgling government to become a strong nation, active in regulating finance, promotive of international trade, and capable of defending itself. Others, such as Thomas Jefferson, enamored of a farmer-patriot model of a democratic citizenry, were less comfortable with the concept of a powerful central government and argued for more limited interpretations. Over time, the Hamiltonian view has prevailed. The Federal Reserve banking system, federal income tax, voluminous pieces of New Deal legislation, as well as the various specific education acts, are all products of generous interpretation of the welfare clause.

Significant Federal Court Cases

The following cases are illustrative of a set of U.S. Supreme Court decisions that, over time, have had a significant influence over American education policy and practice. The cases are presented below in chronological order. Principles from these cases make up a portion of a strategic education leader's portfolio of professional knowledge. A prior caveat bears repeating. The point here is not to transform a reader into an attorney. Rather, these cases represent important general knowledge for a strategic education leader.

Pierce v. Society of Sisters. The landscape of American education governance is complicated further by the existence of a wide spectrum of nonpublic schools. These range from sectarian religious institutions, to elite independent schools, some with histories extending to the colonial era, to proprietary schools. Throughout most of the nation's history from World War II to the present, approximately 10 percent of the school-age population has attended these private, parochial, and sometimes profit-making institutions. However, despite their long-standing history and their widespread use, it is only since 1925, with the U.S. Supreme Court's decision in the above-mentioned case, that the right of parents to choose nonpublic schools has been legally assured.

On November 7, 1922, at the urging of nativist advocates and the Ku Klux Klan, Oregon voters passed a referendum amending the state's Compulsory Education Act. Under this new law, attending a private school no longer would fulfill the state's compulsory school attendance mandate. Private schools viewed this as an attack on their right to enroll students and do business in the state of Oregon.

Two sorts of opposition to the law emerged. Nonsectarian private schools, such as the Hill Military Academy, were primarily concerned with the loss of revenue. This loss was felt almost immediately, as parents began withdrawing children from private schools in the belief that these would soon cease to exist. In addition, religious private schools such as those operated by the Society of Sisters of the Holy Names of Jesus and Mary were concerned about the right of parents to send their children to such schools as they saw fit, including religious schools.

The Society of Sisters and Hill Military Academy separately sued Walter Pierce, the Oregon governor, and other named state officials as defendants.

The two cases, heard and decided together, were slanted along slightly different lines. The Society's case alleged that the enactment conflicted with the right of parents to choose schools where their children would receive appropriate mental and religious training, the right of the child to influence the parents' choice of a school, and the right of schools and teachers therein to engage in a useful business or profession. The Society's primary allegation was that the state of Oregon was violating specific First Amendment rights (such as the right to freely practice one's religion). Their case alleged only secondarily that the law infringed on Fourteenth Amendment rights regarding protection of property (namely, the school's contracts with the families). The Hill Military Academy, on the other hand, proposed this latter view as its major allegation.

The case eventually reached the U.S. Supreme Court in 1925, and the Court unanimously decided against the amended Compulsory Attendance Act. The court stated that children were not "mere creature[s] of the state" and that by its very nature, the traditional American understanding of the term *liberty* prevented the state from forcing students to accept instruction only from public schools. The court opinion states that this responsibility belonged to the child's parents or guardians and that the ability to make such a choice was a "liberty" protected by the Fourteenth Amendment.

Brown v. Board of Education.[3] This is perhaps the most important U.S. Supreme Court decision of the twentieth century. The Court's 1954 ruling closed the door on legally condoned racial segregation by declaring the previously prevailing "separate but equal" doctrine unconstitutional.

In 1951, a class action suit was filed against the Board of Education of the City of Topeka, Kansas. Plaintiffs were thirteen Topeka parents on behalf of their twenty children. The suit called for the school district to reverse its policy of racial segregation. The Topeka Board of Education operated separate elementary schools under an 1879 Kansas law that permitted (but did not require) districts to maintain separate elementary school facilities for black and white students in twelve communities with populations over 15,000.

At trial, the district court ruled in favor of the Board of Education, citing the U.S. Supreme Court precedent in *Plessy v. Ferguson* (1896), which had upheld an Alabama state law requiring "separate but equal" segregated facilities for blacks and whites in railway cars. The three-judge district court found that segregation in public education had a detrimental effect upon black children but denied relief on the ground that black and white schools in Topeka were substantially equal with respect to buildings, transportation, curricula, and qualifications of teachers.

The decision was **appealed**, and the case of *Brown v. Board of Education* was heard before the Supreme Court. It combined four cases: *Brown* itself, *Briggs v. Elliott* (filed in South Carolina), *Davis v. County School Board of Prince Edward County* (filed in Virginia), and *Gebhart v. Belton* (filed in Delaware). All were NAACP-sponsored legal suits. The Kansas case was unique among the group in that there was no contention of gross inferiority of the segregated schools' physical plant, curriculum, or staff. The district court found substantial equality as to all such factors. The Delaware case was unique in that the district court judge in *Gebhart* ordered that the black students be admitted to the white high school due to the substantial harm of segregation and the palpable differences that made the schools separate but not equal. The NAACP's chief counsel, Thurgood Marshall—later elevated to the U.S. Supreme Court in 1967—argued the case before the Supreme Court for the plaintiffs.

On May 17, 1954, the Warren Court handed down a 9-0 decision that stated that "separate educational facilities are inherently unequal." Chief Justice Warren wrote:

> *Today, education is perhaps the most important function of state and local governments. Compulsory school attendance laws and the great expenditures for education both demonstrate our recognition of the importance of education to our democratic society. It is required in the performance of our most basic public responsibilities, even service in the armed forces. It is the very foundation of good citizenship. Today it is a principal instrument in awakening the child to cultural values, in preparing him for later professional training, and in helping him to adjust normally to his environment. In these days, it is doubtful that any child may reasonably be expected to succeed in life if he is denied the opportunity of an education. Such an opportunity, where the state has undertaken to provide it, is a right that must be made available to all on equal terms.*

San Antonio Independent School District v. Rodriguez.[4] This is the most important U.S. Supreme Court case regarding the financing of public schools. With the exception of Hawaii,[5] all states fund public schools with local taxes assessed upon property values within local school districts. However, as explained in detail in the preceding chapter, states' financing methods aim to achieve a greater equality in resources than that which would occur if schools were funded by local property taxes alone. Concurrently, state plans aim at retaining local control of schools through retaining locally imposed property taxes.

Maintaining local control is often at the center of judicial decisions that uphold state school-finance systems. If all school funds were distributed by states, local school boards might be at risk of sacrificing a degree of control currently held over neighborhood schools. Not only does the issue of local control involve decision making, but also "freedom to devote more money to the education of one's children." Some state constitutions have specific clauses that cite, and thus preserve, the value of local control. Therefore, balancing a mix of local and state revenues regularly results in funding inequalities and, consequently, litigation.

📁 CASE 4 REVISITED ────────────────────────────────

Recall State Superintendent Porter's plan to create a statewide information system able to disaggregate data to the student level. As soon as the issue of control was raised, a fear grew across the state that the comprehensive data system would facilitate greater authority from the capital, and local preferences would more easily be overrun by state officials. Reflect and comment on why, whether it pertains to fiscal or programmatic decisions, the issue of control is such a tender subject within K–12 public education.

The context of the *Rodriguez* case provides an opportunity to discuss the manner in which the judicial system ensures equal protection under the law. There are two principal arguments upon which challenges rely in education finance litigation. The first line of argument is a suit that seeks to establish education as a fundamental right because of public education's individual and collective impact on social and economic structures within society. Education articles of state constitutions must be used to demonstrate that education is a fundamental right.

The other main argument in a suit seeks to show how funding disparities result in unequal opportunities by treating students in low-wealth or low-spending school districts differently from students with greater access to fiscal resources. In other words, legal challenges rely upon standards created within the **equal protection clauses** of federal and state constitutions.

Equal Protection Analysis. According to equal protection guarantees, individuals in similar situations must be treated the same. Therefore, differential treatment of individuals will only be upheld if such treatment is not arbitrary or irrational according to the law. Typically a multitiered test has been the method used by courts for equal protection claims. The possible levels of the test in ascending order of rigor are rational basis, intermediate scrutiny, and strict scrutiny.

- *Rational Basis.* Under a rational basis test, the court examines whether or not the classification is related to a legitimate or reasonable governmental objective. Therefore, to uphold the challenged policy, the government must merely show that a rational relationship exists between the classification and the governmental purpose of the law.

    The rational basis test has been chosen to be the appropriate test by many courts, including the U.S. Supreme Court, in school finance challenges. Although school finance policies may permit significant fiscal disparities among districts, several courts have reasoned that policies were reasonably related to the states' interests in maintaining local control of education; therefore, financial policies are constitutional since they further the interest of liberty through local control.
- *Intermediate Scrutiny.* This is the middle level of scrutiny applied by courts deciding constitutional issues through judicial review. The intermediate scrutiny test applies not only to federal, state, and local judiciary proceedings, but also to legislative and executive action. Examples of classifications that have undergone intermediate scrutiny include sex-based classifications and affirmative action programs established through the federal government.
- *Strict Scrutiny.* This heightened level of review is employed to determine violations of equal protection when a policy treats some people differently solely because they belong to a suspect classification or when a fundamental right guaranteed by the Constitution is violated. In order to survive the critical analysis of strict scrutiny, the classification or denial of a fundamental right must be necessary to further a compelling objective of the state or federal government. Moreover, under a strict scrutiny test, government has the burden of showing that there is no less intrusive method to achieve the government's purpose.

In general, the level of scrutiny utilized by courts will determine the outcome of litigation. The following describes the properties of strict scrutiny—suspect classification and fundamental rights.

Suspect Classification. In education finance litigation, plaintiffs often maintain that a school financing system classifies districts, taxpayers, or students according to the value of the local property wealth, which may result in a suspect classification. Wide variations in property wealth among school districts across a state can result in disparities that are inadequately dampened by state aid. Therefore, arguably, available revenues per student and educational opportunities may vary among the school districts in each state. Plaintiffs contend that a classification system predicated on wealth, resulting in significant wealth-related revenue disparities, constitutes illegal discrimination against students and taxpayers in property-poor districts.

Courts have the ultimate responsibility for deciding what constitutes a suspect classification. However, plaintiffs often encounter difficulties in convincing courts that low-wealth-district students constitute a class for equal protection purposes. The case of *San Antonio v. Rodriguez* illustrates this variation in the courts' recognition of wealth-based discrimination as a suspect classification.

Fundamental Rights. Similar to the disagreement of the status of wealth discrimination as a suspect classification, courts do not agree as to whether education is a fundamental right. The U.S. Supreme Court defines a fundamental right as one "explicitly or implicitly guaranteed by the Constitution".[6] In the previously mentioned *Rodriguez* case, the U.S. Supreme Court, upon examining the Constitution literally, did not determine that education is a fundamental interest.

In its *Rodriguez* opinion, the U.S. Supreme Court even specified "though education is one of the most important services performed by the state, it is not within the limited category of rights recognized by this Court as guaranteed by the Constitution." The *Rodriguez* decision, at least for now, ensures that school finance litigation will be addressed by state courts and thus, until and unless overturned, limits the possibility of school finance reform at the federal level. If it were not for the *Rodriguez* decision, U.S. education fiscal policies might have evolved into a quite different system than that in existence today.

Plyler v Doe.[7] This is a 1982 case in which the U.S. Supreme Court struck a Texas statute denying funding for education to children who were illegal immigrants. The court found that where states limit rights based on individuals' status as aliens, this limitation must be examined under an intermediate scrutiny standard to determine if it furthers a substantial state goal.

Revisions to education laws in Texas in 1975 withheld state funds for educating children who had not been legally admitted to the United States and authorized local school districts to deny enrollment to such students. A 5–4 majority of the Supreme Court found that this policy was in violation of the Fourteenth Amendment, as illegal immigrant children are people "in any ordinary sense of the term" and therefore had protection from discrimination unless a substantial state interest could be shown to justify it.

The court majority found that the Texas law was "directed against children, and impose[d] its discriminatory burden on the basis of a legal characteristic over which children can have little control"—namely, the fact of their having been brought illegally into the United States by their parents. The majority also observed that denying the children in question a proper education would likely contribute to "the creation and perpetuation of a subclass of illiterates within our boundaries, surely adding to the problems and costs of unemployment, welfare, and crime." The majority refused to accept that any substantial state interest would be served by discrimination on this basis, and it struck down the Texas law.

The Court's dissenting minority agreed in principle that it was unwise for illegal alien children to be denied a public education, but the four dissenting justices argued that the Texas law was not so objectionable as to be unconstitutional; that this issue ought to be dealt with through the legislative process; that "[t]he Constitution does not provide a cure for every social ill, nor does it vest judges with a mandate to try to remedy every social problem"; and that the majority was overstepping its bounds by seeking "to do Congress' job for it, compensating for congressional inaction."

Zelman v. Simmons-Harris.[8] This was a 2002 case decided by the U.S. Supreme Court that tested the permissibility of school vouchers in relation to the "separation of church and state" clause in the First Amendment. The Ohio General Assembly passed a bill creating the Ohio Pilot Scholarship Program, which established school vouchers allowing K–12 students to attend private schools. The program provides tuition assistance to children in kindergarten through eighth grade within certain school districts to attend private schools or provides financial assistance for tutoring students who choose to remain in public schools. It gives preference to students from low-income families.

Susan Tave Zelman was the superintendent of public instruction for Ohio. In 1999, the U.S. Court of Appeals for the Sixth Circuit heard the case and ruled the program was unconstitutional. The case was later appealed to the U.S. Supreme Court, which reversed the appeals court judgment. Approximately 96 percent of the children on Ohio's vouchers attended religious schools. The court attempted to resolve the question of whether the funds paying tuition at religious schools violated the U.S. Constitution's First Amendment. Since a majority of schools participating in the voucher program were religious schools (82 percent), the parents claimed that there was really no legitimate secular choice.

The Supreme Court ruled that the Ohio program did not violate the Establishment Clause of the First Amendment to the U.S. Constitution because it passed a five-part test developed by the court. The decision was 5-4, with moderate justices Anthony Kennedy and Sandra Day O'Connor and conservative justices William Rehnquist, Antonin Scalia, and Clarence Thomas in the majority.

The test developed by the Supreme Court in this case can be called the Private Choice Test, and five parts must be passed for a voucher program to be constitutional. The five conditions are (1) the program must have a valid secular purpose, (2) aid must go to parents and not schools, (3) a broad class of beneficiaries must be covered, (4) it must be neutral with respect to religion, and (5) there must be adequate nonreligious options. The Court found that the program in question passed all of these tests.

Chief Justice Rehnquist, writing for the majority, stated that "the incidental advancement of a religious mission, or the perceived endorsement of a religious message, is reasonably attributable to the individual aid recipients not the government, whose role ends with the disbursement of benefits." They found that, in theory, there is no need for parents to use religious schools, and so long as the law does not especially encourage the use of vouchers for religious schools, the fact that most parents do choose parochial schools is irrelevant. Indeed, the fact that in this case, the funding was given to the parents to disburse as they chose, whereas in *Lemon v. Kurtzman*[9] the funding at question was given directly to the schools, was a key part of the Private Choice Test. The majority held, therefore, that the intent of the law was the important thing.

In his concurring opinion, Justice Thomas emphasized that voucher programs like the one in this case were essential because "failing urban public schools disproportionately affect minority children most in need of educational opportunity." He stated that vouchers and other forms of publicly funded private school choice are necessary to give families an opportunity to enroll their children in more effective private schools. Otherwise, "the core purposes of the Fourteenth Amendment" would be frustrated.

The dissenting opinions, on the other hand, disagreed with Chief Justice Rehnquist. Justice Stevens wrote that "the voluntary character of the private choice to prefer a parochial education over an education in the public school system seems to me quite irrelevant to the question whether the government's choice to pay for religious indoctrination is constitutionally permissible." Justice Souter's opinion questioned how the Court could keep *Everson v. Board of Education*[10] on as precedent and decide this case in the way they did, feeling it was contradictory. He also found that religious instruction and secular education could not be separated, and this itself violated the U.S. Constitution's First Amendment Establishment Clause.

Courts and Classrooms

The judicial branch is now, and long has been, a major force in shaping U.S. education. Courts play a fundamental role by establishing boundaries, by intervening between the rules of government and the rights of individuals. As such, courts are a major balancing force. This equilibrium is subject to constant adjustment. It is not fixed at one point in time and thereafter immutable. Times change, technology changes, and courts adapt their positions to new circumstances.

In the News

Can you hear me now?

That's what parents, students and lawmakers who want a school cell phone ban lifted asked Mayor Michael Bloomberg's administration at a city council hearing Wednesday, but the city is refusing to budge. The prohibition on cell phones in the nation's biggest school system has been in place for years, but students have mostly carried the phones without consequence.

When the city began random security checks in late April as part of a weapons crackdown, authorities began finding and confiscating hundreds of cell phones, prompting a fierce battle over the no-phone policy. "This involves our safety and our rights," said high school sophomore Seth Pearce, one of three students who lobbied for a change on Wednesday. New York schools have one of the toughest such bans among the nation's large districts, but similar debates have bubbled up in school systems elsewhere.

Parents and students insist the right to carry mobile phones is a matter of safety; they must be able to get in touch at any hour of the day for emergencies. They have written letters, staged rallies and repeatedly called the mayor's weekly radio show to demand that he reconsider.

No chance, says the mayor. Bloomberg, the former chief executive of a financial information company, has a certain obsession with technology and communications. He and his aides are never without their Blackberries, but he has a similar fixation on efficiency and order.

He says cell phones are disruptive in schools, where students can use them to cheat on exams, take inappropriate photos and waste time chatting and text messaging instead of learning.

Students took issue with that before the council on Wednesday. Pearce noted wryly during his testimony: "All three of us have cell phones right now in City Hall, and it seems to me the city is running just fine." The City Council took up the dispute even though it is not clear whether it has much say on the matter. While the school system of 1.1 million students is under the mayor's management, it is regulated by the state.

Still, council members have introduced legislation that would guarantee parents the right to provide their children with cell phones to carry to and from school and prohibit anyone from interfering with that right. The council appears to have enough votes to override a likely mayoral veto, but the bill's supporters acknowledged that the point of the Wednesday hearing was not necessarily to push the law, but rather to nudge a compromise.

While some lawmakers cried that the mayor had "drawn a line in the sand" and warned they were prepared to "stage a battle" and go to court, others said they are hopeful that all sides could work it out. "I would like to change this policy with the mayor, not over the mayor," Councilman Lewis Fidler said. But the Bloomberg administration shows no room for compromise. Deputy Mayor Dennis Walcott described the policy as "non-negotiable."

From "Families, lawmakers plead to change cell phone ban; city refuses" by Sara Kugler, published June 14, 2006, by the Associated Press (New York).

Courts ensure that education policies satisfy constitutional provisions calling for efficiency, equity, and adequacy and stimulate appropriate policy revisions. Courts also may be called upon to decide whether policies satisfy federal or state constitutions. However, at least in the abstract, courts do not initiate policy issues for judicial review; courts may only react to challenges brought forth by affected citizens or government jurisdictions.

Below are illustrated the conditions that come into play when a court might, or might not, engage in reviewing an education leader's actions.

Jurisdiction. In order to consider merits of a case, a court must have appropriate jurisdiction over the matter of the suit and parties involved. Jurisdiction means that the court has prescribed authority to hear and determine a judicial proceeding.

Justiciability. A justiciable issue is one that is "appropriate for judicial determination." For example, a justiciable issue requires (1) parties have genuine, not hypothetical, rights and interests; (2) a judgment by the court may effectively rectify the dispute, and it is not purely a political, philosophical, or academic debate; (3) a court ruling would have the effect of a final judgment; and (4) proceedings are advanced by parties with sufficient interest to produce a thorough analysis of the issues, and parties must be genuinely adversarial in nature.

Standing. Plaintiffs must also have standing to bring forth an education finance challenge. Standing means "a party has sufficient stake in an otherwise justiciable controversy to obtain judicial resolution of that controversy." Typically in education finance litigation, school officials, taxpayers, students, and parent groups all have the necessary standing to bring forth legal challenges.

Mootness. A moot case "no longer presents a justiciable controversy because issues involved have become academic or dead" and are "not entitled to judicial intervention unless the issue is a recurring one and likely to be raised again between parties."

Ripeness. Ripeness concerns timing of a judicial action. The court must consider whether a case has matured or ripened into a controversy worthy of judicial review.

Political Neutrality. If issues pled by plaintiffs are perceived as purely political, courts may refuse to rule on the matter. According to the doctrine of separation of powers, the legislative, executive, and judicial branches may not encroach on the domain of the others. Therefore, courts may not rule for the legislature to enact or not enact any law. Essentially, as long as a court limits the ruling or decision to constitutional interpretations, there should be no violation of the separation of powers doctrine. However, judicial system authority to affect educational systems should not be underestimated; as this chapter progresses, strength and evolution of judicial activism in education litigation become evident.

■ PROTECTING (AND SOMETIMES RESTRICTING) STUDENTS' RIGHTS

This is an unusually full field of law. There are administrative-rights proponents who proclaim that the judicial system has intruded too far in the operation of schools. Of course, there are those who dissent from such a view; often the American Civil Liberties Union represents the dissenters.

What follows is agnostic regarding the issue of intrusion. Moreover, this section is not intended to be comprehensive, but rather it is illustrative. What is being illustrated is that schools, despite, or more aptly because of, their compulsory nature, do not have an unfettered charter to transgress upon the civil rights of students and their families. There are dimensions on which school administrators must tread with caution in order not to violate student rights regarding matters such as religion, possession of illegal or contraband items, expression of political dissent, and individual behavior.

It must be noted at the outset that there are multiple dimensions of schooling on which courts have displayed remarkable understanding and restraint. For example, operating a school, particularly a large public school, necessitates a modicum of order. If a student's actions can be shown directly to interfere with or materially threaten a minimal level of physical order needed to facilitate instruction, protect student safety and well-being, and serve other school purposes, courts generally will tolerate restrictions on student behavior.

Similarly, if an administratively imposed restriction upon students can be rationally demonstrated to facilitate or to further instruction, the core function of schools, then the weight of any argument shifts to plaintiffs. Under circumstances wherein instruction is closely at issue, it is those who question who must demonstrate the substantial derogation of some important freedom.

The following cases from the legal history of education illustrate protected freedoms, and allowable administrative restrictions, for students on dimensions such as religious expression, political protest, and rights to due process in disciplinary instances, as well as dress and grooming.

Wisconsin v. Yoder, 406 U.S. 205 (1972). Here is a case that illustrates the protection of student rights and the complex interaction between freedom of religion and compulsory school attendance.

Three Amish students from three families stopped attending high school in the New Glarus, Wisconsin, school district at the end of the eighth grade, all for the same reason. Defendants believed that a high school education would endanger their own salvation and that of their children. Jonas Yoder was one of the fathers involved when the case went to trial.

The families were convicted in the Brown County Court, and that ruling was upheld in the appeals court. Each defendant was fined the sum of five dollars each. Thereafter, the Wisconsin Supreme Court overturned the lower court opinions and found in Yoder's favor. At this point Wisconsin appealed the ruling in the U. S. Supreme Court.

The defendant parents and students were Amish, a religion whose members seldom believe in going to court to settle disputes but instead follow the biblical command to "turn the other cheek." However, a Lutheran minister took an interest in Amish legal difficulties from a religious freedom perspective and founded the National Committee for Amish Religious Freedom (partly as a result of this case) and then provided defendants with legal counsel.

The U. S. Supreme Court ruled in favor of Yoder in a 6-1 decision. The Court found that "the evidence showed that the Amish provide continuing informal vocational education to their children designed to prepare them for life in the rural Amish community. The evidence also showed that respondents sincerely believed that high school attendance was contrary to the Amish religion and way of life and that they would endanger their own salvation and that of their children by complying with the law." The U. S. Supreme Court also "sustained respondents' claim that application of the compulsory school-attendance law to them violated their rights under the Free Exercise Clause of the First Amendment, made applicable to the states by the Fourteenth Amendment."

The dissenting opinion by Justice William O. Douglas was interesting. Justice Douglas was concerned with protecting the interests of the child. While not disputing that Amish beliefs were sincere, he posed a question regarding the welfare of a student who, contrary to Amish practical engagement, preferred to be a ballerina, an astronaut, or a cellist.

Tinker v. Des Moines Independent Community School District, 393 U.S. 503 (1969). This case is important because of the role it played in defining the constitutional rights of students in U.S. public schools. It is considered one of the Court's more controversial decisions of the 1960s regarding freedom of speech. The Tinker test is still used by courts today to determine whether or not a school's disciplinary actions violate students' First Amendment rights. However, subsequent judicial decisions have restricted or placed boundaries around Tinker. These cases are discussed near the end of this section.

In December 1965, Des Moines, Iowa, residents John (fifteen years old) and Mary Beth Tinker (thirteen years old) and their friend Christopher Eckhardt (sixteen years old) decided to wear black armbands to their schools (high school for John and Christopher, junior high for Mary Beth) in protest of the Vietnam War. The school board apparently heard rumor of this and chose to pass a policy banning the wearing of armbands to school. Violating students would be suspended and allowed to return to school after agreeing to comply with the policy. Mary Beth Tinker and Christopher Eckhardt chose to violate this policy, and the next day John Tinker also did so. All were suspended from school until after New Year's Day 1966 when their protest had been scheduled to end.

Their parents, in turn, filed suit in U.S. District Court, which upheld the decision of the Des Moines school board. A tie vote in the U.S. Court of Appeals meant that the school board's decision continued to stand and forced the Tinkers and Eckhardts to appeal to the Supreme Court directly. The case was argued before the court on November 12, 1968.

The U.S. Supreme Court's 7-2 decision was handed down on February 24, 1969. It held that the First Amendment applied to public schools and that administrators would have to demonstrate constitutionally valid reasons for any specific regulation of speech in the classroom. Justice Abe Fortas wrote the majority opinion, holding that the speech regulation at issue in Tinker was "based upon an urgent wish to avoid the controversy which might result from the expression, even by the silent symbol of armbands, of opposition to this Nation's part in the conflagration in Vietnam" and finding that the actions of the Tinkers in wearing armbands did not cause disruption, held that their activity represented constitutionally protected symbolic speech.

Justices Hugo Black and John Marshall Harlan II dissented. Black, who had long believed that disruptive "symbolic speech" was not constitutionally protected, wrote, "While I have always believed that under the First and Fourteenth Amendments neither the State nor the Federal Government has any authority to regulate or censor the content of speech, I have never believed that any person has a right to give speeches or engage in demonstrations where he pleases and when he pleases." Black argued that the Tinkers' behavior was indeed disruptive and declared, "I repeat that if the time has come when pupils of state-supported schools, kindergartens, grammar schools, or high schools can defy and flout orders of school officials to keep their minds on their own schoolwork, it is the beginning of a new revolutionary era of permissiveness in this country fostered by the judiciary." Harlan dissented on the grounds that he "[found] nothing in this record which impugns the good faith of respondents in promulgating the armband regulation."

Though *Tinker* remains one of the most frequently cited Court opinions in society today, some argue the ruling's applicability has been limited by subsequent decisions. In *Bethel School District v. Fraser*[11], a 1986 case, the Supreme Court held that a high school student's sexual innuendo–laden speech during a student assembly was not constitutionally protected. While the Fraser court distinguished Tinker, the Fraser court carved out an exception for "indecent" speech. *Hazelwood v. Kuhlmeier*,[12] where the court ruled that schools have the right to regulate, for legitimate educational reasons, the content of non-forum, school-sponsored newspapers, also limits Tinker's application. The court in *Hazelwood* clarified that both *Fraser* and *Hazelwood* were decided under the doctrine of *Perry Education Association v. Perry Local Educators Association*.[13] Such a distinction keeps undisturbed the Material Disruption doctrine of *Tinker*, while deciding certain student free-speech cases under the Nonpublic Forum doctrine of *Perry*.

Zorach v. Clausen, 343 U.S. 306 (1952).

When is it okay to pray? Not publicly before a public school football game, according to the U.S. Supreme Court. The Court ruled (6-3) in this case that students cannot lead prayers over the public-address system before public school football games. The Supreme Court said prayers broadcast before public school football games violate this constitutionally required separation of government and religion.

The issue is not whether individual students can pray before the game—they can. This case asked whether a student-led prayer could be broadcast to everyone at a sporting event.

"God, thank you for this evening. Thank you for all the prayers that were lifted up this week for me. I pray that you'll bless each and every person here tonight . . . In Jesus' name, I pray. Amen." (public prayer said by Texas student before game)

In this case, initial plaintiffs alleged that the school district's policy of allowing students to lead prayers at home football games violated the First Amendment by creating a religious atmosphere. The trial court agreed in principle.

A federal appeals court ruled that student-led prayers that are "nonsectarian (not limited to one specific religion) and non-proselytizing (do not attempt convert)" are allowed at graduations, but banned before football games—which the court said are not sufficiently serious to be "solemnized with prayer."

The school district responded to the lower court ruling by implementing strict guidelines banning pregame prayer and warned senior Marian Ward, elected by fellow students to deliver religious messages before football games, that she would be disciplined if she prayed.

Ward's family filed suit, arguing that the guidelines violated her free speech rights. A U.S. District Court judge agreed that the guidelines the school had written were unconstitutional and ruled that the school could not censor Ward's speech. However, this view was overturned by the U.S. Supreme Court's subsequent opinion in the appeal.

The issue involved Supreme Court justices' interpretation of the First Amendment to the Constitution. This amendment specifies principles regarding religion, speech, press, assembly, and petition. Basically, it protects an individual's right to worship, speak, publish, gather in groups, and petition government. It also prohibits the government from identifying with a particular religion, effectively separating church and state. On this basis, the school district rules banning public prayer before games were upheld.

In the News

SYRACUSE, New York (AP)—A school district violated a fourth-grader's constitutional rights to free speech and equal protection by refusing to allow her to distribute "personal statement" fliers carrying a religious message, a federal judge has ruled.

The Liverpool Central School District in upstate New York based its restrictions on "fear or apprehension of disturbance, which is not enough to overcome the right to freedom of expression," Chief U.S. District Judge Norman Mordue wrote in a 46-page decision Friday.

"School officials had no right to silence Michaela's personal Christian testimony," attorney Mat Staver said Monday. Staver is executive director of Liberty Counsel, the Orlando, Florida-based conservative legal group that represented Michaela Bloodgood and her mother, Nicole.

Liverpool school district lawyer Frank Miller said the school district was studying the decision and "reviewing its options." According to the family's 2004 lawsuit, Nicole Bloodgood tried three times to get permission for Michaela to pass out the homemade fliers to other students at Nate Perry Elementary School. The flier, about the size of a greeting card, started out: "Hi! My name is Michaela and I would like to tell you about my life and how Jesus Christ gave me a new one."

Bloodgood's requests to school officials said that her daughter, now a sixth-grader, would hand them out only during "non-instructional time," such as on the bus, before school, lunch, recess and after school.

The lawsuit noted that Michaela had received literature from other students at school, including materials for a YMCA basketball camp, a Syracuse Children's Theater promotion and Camp Fire USA's summer camps.

Liverpool officials said at the time there was "a substantial probability" that other parents and students might misunderstand and presume the district endorsed the religious statements in the flier, according to the lawsuit.

"The court cannot say the danger that children would misperceive the endorsement of religion is any greater than the danger that they would perceive a hostility toward religion as a result of the district's denial," Mordue wrote.

Nicole Bloodgood said Mordue's decision vindicated her daughter and set a strong precedent for protecting students' free speech rights. "It's taken 2½ years to get justice . . . but our prayers were answered," Bloodgood said.

From " N.Y. school district violated students' rights by banning fliers about Jesus, Judge says," by William Kates, published April 2, 2007, by the Associated Press, New York.

Goss v. Lopez, 419 U.S. 565 (1975). In 1971, widespread student unrest took place in the Columbus, Ohio, public schools. Students who either participated in, or were present at, demonstrations held on school grounds were suspended. Many suspensions were for a period of ten days. Students were not given a hearing before suspension, although at a later date some students and their parents were given informal conferences with the school principal. Ohio law provides free education to all children between the ages of six and twenty-one. A number of students, through their parents, sued the board of education, claiming that their right to due process had been violated when they were suspended without a hearing.

In *Goss v. Lopez,* the Supreme Court decided that students who are suspended for ten days or less are entitled to certain rights before their suspension. These rights include (1) oral or written notice of the charges, (2) an explanation (if students deny the charges) of the evidence against them, and (3) an opportunity for students to present their side of the story.

The U.S. Supreme Court stated that in an emergency, students could be sent home immediately and a hearing held at a later date. The court did *not* give students a right to a lawyer, a right to cross-examine witnesses, a right to call witnesses, or a right to a hearing before an impartial person.

This case fundamentally involves issues of due process. *"No person shall be . . . deprived of life, Liberty, or property without due process of law . . ."* (Fifth Amendment).

No State shall deprive any person of life, liberty, or property, without due process of law . . . (Fourteenth Amendment).

Procedural due process of law refers to the fair procedures that must be followed when a citizen's rights are to be infringed upon by a government agent. The Constitution protects the rights of individuals (including children) against an infringement of life, liberty, or property without fair government procedures. In actuality, the government takes many actions that may deprive people of life, liberty, or property. Yet in each case, some form of due process is required. For example, a state might fire someone from a government job, revoke a prisoner's parole, or eliminate someone's Social Security payments.

Due process does not prohibit these actions, but it does require that certain procedures be followed before any action is taken.

If an individual has a right to due process, the next issue is this: What process is due? Due process is a flexible concept. The procedures required in specific situations depend on several factors: (1) the seriousness of the harm that might be done to the citizen; (2) the cost to the government, in time and money, of carrying out the procedures; and (3) the risk of making an error without the procedures.

In *Goss*, the Court considered the due process interests of harm, cost, and risk. The Court ruled that reputations were harmed and educational opportunities were lost during the suspension; that an informal hearing would not be overly costly for the schools; and that while most disciplinary decisions were probably correct, an informal hearing would help reduce the risk of error.

New Jersey v. T. L. O., 469 U.S. 325 (1985). This case involves the search of a high school student for contraband after she was caught smoking. She was charged as a juvenile for the drugs and paraphernalia found in the search. She fought the search, claiming it violated her Fourth Amendment right against unreasonable searches. The U.S. Supreme Court, in a 5-4 ruling, held that the search was reasonable under the Fourth Amendment.

A fourteen-year-old New Jersey high school freshman, known by the initials T. L. O., was caught by a teacher smoking in a bathroom with another girl at Piscataway Township High School in Middlesex County, New Jersey. The teacher took both students to the principal's office, where they met with assistant vice principal Theodore Choplick. The vice principal questioned them about violating a school rule by smoking in the bathroom. The other girl admitting to smoking, but T.L.O. denied smoking in the bathroom and stated she had never smoked in her life. Choplick then requested that T. L. O. come into his private office and demanded to see the contents of her purse. Upon opening the purse, he observed a pack of cigarettes; while removing the cigarettes, he noticed a package of rolling papers. Based on his experience, the possession of rolling papers by high school students was closely tied to the use of marijuana. Choplick then began a more thorough search for the evidence of drugs. His search revealed a small amount of marijuana, a pipe, empty plastic bags, a large quantity of money in one-dollar bills, an index card that appeared to list students who owed T. L. O. money, and two letters that implicated T. L. O. in drug dealing.

Choplick then notified T. L. O.'s mother and the police, to whom he turned over the evidence of drug dealing. The police requested that the mother take her daughter to police headquarters. T. L. O. and her mother went to the police station, where T. L. O. confessed to selling marijuana at the high school. Using the confession and the evidence obtained by Choplick's search, the state brought delinquency charges against T. L. O. in Juvenile and Domestic Relations.

T. L. O. claimed the assistant principal's search violated the Fourth Amendment. She moved to suppress the evidence found in her purse as well as her confession, arguing that the evidence was "fruit of the poisonous tree." The juvenile court denied the motion to suppress. Although the court concluded that the Fourth Amendment did apply to searches carried out by school officials, it held:

> A school official may properly conduct a search of a student's person if the official has a reasonable suspicion that a crime has been or is in the process of being committed, or reasonable cause to believe that the search is necessary to maintain school discipline or enforce school policies.

The Supreme Court of the United States ruled that the search and seizure by school officials without a warrant was constitutional, as long as the search was deemed reasonable. This overturned the New Jersey Supreme Court ruling. The case is also important because of the court's statement that states have a duty to provide a safe school environment.

Bannister v. Paradis et al., 316 F.Supp. 185 (1970). A school had instituted a dress code banning jeans, and a student was sent home for wearing them. The U.S. District Court, District of New Hampshire, held that "a person's right to wear clothes of his own choosing provided that, in the case of a schoolboy, they are neat and clean is a constitutional right protected and guaranteed by the Fourteenth Amendment." It also said, "Prohibition of high school dress code against wearing of dungarees was unconstitutional and invalid, in absence of showing that wearing of dungarees in any way inhibited or tended to inhibit the educational process."

However, a school can, for its own preservation, exclude persons who are unsanitarily, obscenely, or scantily clad. Moreover, school boards have power to adopt reasonable restrictions on dress as part of the educational policy and as an educational device; however, the board's power must be limited to that required by its function of administering public education.

For example, in California, a trial court, noting that the Clovis Unified School District had gone to great effort to engage the community in the formation of a school dress and grooming code, had reason to limit the hair length of male students on grounds that it was a part of the decorum the community expected and had a useful additional purpose in assisting district security officers in determining *who was and was not a member of the student body*.

■ PROTECTING (AND SOMETIMES RESTRICTING) EMPLOYEE RIGHTS

While falling short of the volume of case law regarding student protections and restrictions, school district employees also have been the subject of multiple court opinions. These opinions range from matters of teacher attire, freedom of expression, employment discrimination, use of instructional materials, sexual conduct, and collective bargaining. What follows is but a sample of the voluminous case law applicable in these settings. The point here is not to provide a leader with an encyclopedic understanding of the issues, but rather to illustrate that there is a rational underpinning to the manner in which the judicial system approaches issues of school governance and operation.

Pickering v. Board of Education, 391 U.S. 563 (1968). This is a case in which the Supreme Court of the United States held that in the absence of proof of a teacher knowingly or recklessly making false statements, a teacher had a right to speak on issues of public importance without being dismissed from his position.

In February 1961, the Township Board of Education asked the voters of Township High School District 205 to approve a bond issue to raise $4,875,000 to erect two new schools, which was defeated. In December 1961, the board again submitted a bond proposal to the voters for $5,500,000 to build two new schools, which passed; the two schools were built with the money. In May 1964, the board proposed and submitted to the voters an increase in the tax rate for educational purposes, which was defeated. On September 19, 1964, a second proposal to increase the tax rate was submitted by the board and was similarly defeated.

Prior to the vote on the September 1964 tax increase proposal, various newspaper articles appeared in the local paper that were attributed to the District 205 Teachers' Organization. Those articles urged passage of the proposal and stated that failure to pass the increase would result in a decline in the quality of education afforded children in the district's schools. Also, a letter making the same point from the superintendent of schools was published in the paper two days before the election, and copies of the letter were given to the voters the following day.

After the proposal failed, Marvin L. Pickering, appellant and a teacher in the district, wrote a letter to the editor in response to the material from the teachers' organization and the superintendent. The letter was an attack on the board's handling of the 1961 bond proposals and its subsequent allocation of financial resources between the schools' educational and athletic programs. It also charged the superintendent of schools with trying to prevent teachers from speaking out against the proposed bond issue. Pickering was dismissed by the board for writing and publishing the letter.

Under Illinois law, the board was then required to hold a hearing on the dismissal, where it stated that numerous statements in the letter were false and that the publication of the statements "unjustifiably impugned the 'motives, honesty, integrity, truthfulness, responsibility and competence' of both the board and the school administration. The board also charged that the false statements damaged the professional reputations of its members and of the school administrators, would be disruptive of faculty discipline, and would tend to foment 'controversy, conflict and dissension' among teachers, administrators, the board of education, and the residents of the district."

A variety of witnesses testified as to the truth or falsity of the particular statements in the letter with which the board took issue. The board found the statements to be false as charged. However, the board made no further findings nor introduced evidence that went beyond the falsity of Pickering's statements.

Pickering claimed that his writing of the letter was protected by the First and Fourteenth Amendments. This argument was rejected by the board of education. He appealed the board's action to the Circuit Court of Will County and then to the Supreme Court of Illinois, which both affirmed his dismissal. However, the Supreme Court of the United States agreed that the teacher's First Amendment right to free speech was violated and reversed the decision of the Illinois Supreme Court.

East Hartford Education Association v. Board of Education. May a teacher wear clothing not approved by a teacher dress code? Probably not. The few published court decisions dealing with teacher dress codes have sided with school officials.

The 1970s case of Richard Brimley is instructive. Brimley, an English teacher in a Connecticut high school, challenged a reprimand he received for violating the teacher dress code by refusing to wear a necktie. The school board argued that its tie code supported its interest in maintaining a professional image for its teachers and for engendering respect and discipline from the students. Brimley, through the teachers union, argued that his failure to wear a necktie implicated his First Amendment free expression rights in several ways, including (1) presenting himself as someone not tied to "establishment conformity" and (2) showing his students that he rejected many of the values associated with the older generation.

A panel of three federal judges in the Second Circuit struck the balance in favor of Brimley, finding that the case implicated both a Fourteenth Amendment liberty interest and a First Amendment free speech interest.

However, the full panel of the Second Circuit reversed in *East Hartford Education Association v. Board of Education*. "The very notion of public education implies substantial public control," the full appeals court wrote. "Educational decisions must be made by someone; there is no reason to create a constitutional preference for the views of individual teachers over those of their employers." The appeals court concluded, "If Mr. Brimley has any protected interest in his neckwear, it does not weigh very heavily on the constitutional scales."

Other courts have reached similar results in teacher dress code cases. For example, a federal court in Mississippi upheld the discharge of a teacher's aide for refusing to abide by the dress code of the school. The aide asserted she had a constitutional right to wear berets to show her African American heritage and her religious beliefs. The school district countered that the berets were "inappropriate attire." Ultimately, the court sided with the school board, finding that the teacher failed to communicate to school district officials that she had a religious basis for her conduct. However, the court noted that the "[d]istrict is required, under the First Amendment and Title VII, to make some accommodation for the practice of religious beliefs when it pursues an end which incidentally burdens religious practices."

Despite this statement in the *McGlothlin* case, other courts have rejected claims that state statutes restricting teachers from wearing religious clothing are unconstitutional. In *United States v. Board of Education*, for example, the Third Circuit rejected a Title VII religious discrimination claim against a school board for prohibiting a Muslim substitute teacher from wearing her religious clothing.

The case originated with a Pennsylvania statute, called the Garb Statute, which provided that "no teacher in any public school shall wear. . .or while engaged in the performance of his duty as such teacher any dress, mark, emblem or insignia indicating the fact that such teacher is a member or adherent of any religious order, sect or denomination." In its ruling, the Third Circuit determined it would impose an "undue hardship" on the school to require it to accommodate the Muslim teacher's request to wear her religious clothing. Such an accommodation, according to the court, would represent a "significant threat to the maintenance of religious neutrality in the public school system."

Similarly, the Oregon Supreme Court rejected a free exercise challenge—under the First Amendment and a provision of the state constitution—to an Oregon statute prohibiting teachers from wearing religious clothing. The teacher, who was an adherent to the Sikh religion, argued against the constitutionality of a state law that provided: "No teacher in any public school shall wear any religious dress while engaged in the performance of duties as a teacher." The Oregon high court upheld the statute, writing that "the aim of maintaining the religious neutrality of the public schools furthers a constitutional obligation beyond an ordinary policy preference for the legislature."

It should be noted that although these decisions permit states and school districts to restrict the wearing of religious garb, they do not require such restrictions. Two states, Arkansas and Tennessee, have statutes explicitly allowing teachers to wear religious garb in public schools. In states without such laws, the vast majority of state courts have held that public schools may allow teachers to wear religious clothing.

Summary

Since a strategic education leader operates within a larger social context than his or her individual school, it is important to understand the specific contextual features of law and legal procedures. Through this chapter's content and themes, a reader should come to understand how legal matters are particularly important in shaping the landscape of school leadership and providing an aspiring leader with a sufficient grasp of legal fundamentals.

This chapter also introduces an illustrative set of U.S. Supreme Court decisions that have had a significant influence over American education policy and practice. Each of these cases provides future education leaders with an understanding of the legal landscape and prepares them for potential legal issues that may arise in their school.

Discussion Questions

1. Conduct a library or Internet-based search for your state constitution's education clause. Summarize the clause, and provide a rationale for assigning it to one of the four categories discussed in the chapter.
2. If instead of the Hamiltonian view prevailing, the more limited Jeffersonian interpretation of the General Welfare Clause had won out, how might our nation's education system be different today?
3. Drawing upon either *Pierce*, *Brown*, *Rodriguez*, or *Plyler*, explain how the outcome of this court decision has impacted your current educational institution and the educational experience of someone you know personally.
4. To what degree have the elements of justiciability, standing, and political neutrality been demonstrated in a recent dispute at your education organization?
5. As a professional educator, you have come across a variety of student and parent personalities. Discuss your ability to relate to the lone dissenting opinion in the *Yoder* case, that of Justice William O. Douglas.
6. The *New Jersey v. T.L.O.* case was decided by one vote in the U.S. Supreme Court. If you had had to cast the deciding vote in this case, what rationale would have guided your decision?
7. ELCC Standards 5 and 6 deal with the need for education leaders to act in ways that are guided by the law, integrity, fairness, and ethics. To what extent do you feel your understanding of school law permits you to meet these standards? What additional support structures will be most valuable for you as an education leader to ensure that your actions are in compliance with these two standards?

References and Suggested Readings

Hazard, W. R. (1978). *Education and the law: Cases and materials on public schools* (2nd ed.). New York: The Free Press.

> This book shows the interaction of law with public schooling by dealing primarily with state and federal statutory and case law affecting the operations of elementary and secondary schools.

Horowitz, D. (1977). *The courts and social policy*. Washington, D.C.: The Brookings Institution.

Through an examination of four cases, involving either urban affairs, educational resources, juvenile courts, or police action, the author presents a comprehensive study of the power of courts to create and order the implementation of social policy.

La Morte, M. W. (2004). *School law: Cases and concepts* (9th ed.). Englewood Cliffs, NJ: Prentice Hall.

The presentation of actual education-law case studies combined with explanatory comments in this book enable the reader to learn both the legal rationale and the reasoning grounding the decisions and dissents of important legal cases facing our schools.

Yudof, M., Kirp, D., & Levin, B. (1997). *Educational policy and the law* (4th ed.). St. Paul, MN: West Publishing Company.

Through cases and analysis, Yudof et al. show that law should not be regarded as an isolated entity, but rather a player in the creation of policy, legal decisions, and educational practices.

Notes

1. Only Mississippi does not have an education clause. However, there is disagreement regarding this point. The language of the constitution contains language about schools; however, some experts maintain that this language does not impose an obligation on the state and should not be considered an education clause. See Molly McUsic, The use of education clauses in school finance reform litigation, 28 *Harvard Journal on Legislation 307*, 311 n. 5 (1991); and William E. Thro, Note, To render them safe: The analysis of state constitutional provisions in public school finance reform litigation, 75 *Virginia Law Review* (1989).
2. Several spellings in the original Constitutional wording were more British than modern English. *Defense* would be the modern spelling.
3. *Brown v. Board of Education of Topeka*, 347 U.S. 483, 74 S.Ct. 686, 98 L.Ed. 873 (U.S. 1954).
4. *San Antonio v. Rodriguez*, 411 U.S. 1, 93 1278 (S. Ct. 1973).
5. After collecting all local and state taxes, Hawaii centrally distributes monies to local schools.
6. *Rodriguez v. San Antonio*, 411 U.S. at 33-4.
7. *Plyler v. Doe*, 457 U.S. 202 (1982).
8. *Zelman v. Simmons-Harris*, 536 U.S. 639 (2002).
9. *Lemon v. Kurtzman*, 403 U.S. 602 (1971).
10. *Everson v. Board of Education*, 330 U.S. 1 (1947).
11. *Bethel School District No. 403 et al. v. Fraser* et al., 478 U.S. 675 (1986).
12. *Hazelwood School District v. Kuhlmeier*, 484 U.S. 260 (1988).
13. *Perry Education Association v. Perry Local Educators Association*, 460 U.S. 37 (1983).

PART THREE

Performance

What a Strategic Leader Needs to Know Regarding Knowing

This third section of the text provides a reader with knowledge of several key domains that are crucial in enabling strategic leaders to become more effective in successfully leading educational organizations. For example, Chapter 8 discusses an array of topics central to human learning theory, a subject at the core of schooling. Chapter 9 provides insights regarding several issues pertinent to the role of school programs, while Chapter 10 describes approaches to assessing the performance of students, schools, and education leaders. Chapter 11 concludes this section by providing knowledge about the important tasks of problem solving and making data-based decisions in schools.

■ APPLICABILITY OF SECTION III CONTENT TO ELCC STANDARDS

Content in Part III of the text is most closely aligned with ELCC Standards 1, 2, 3, and 6. As the chapters on learning and problem solving relate directly to the core mission and vision of schooling, content here is applicable to ELCC Standard 1. By focusing on many issues central to teaching and learning and the overall instructional program, all four chapters in this section align substantially with the goals of ELCC Standards 2 and 3, which pay attention to school culture, the instructional program, and professional development issues. Within the content of the performance chapter, attention is paid to the importance of personal ethics and consistent behavior, two dimensions of ELCC Standard 5. Finally, multiple chapters within this section speak to the broader contextual factors that shape the practice of leadership within schools, thus addressing ELCC Standard 6.

■ CASE STUDIES

 CASE 5

A Principal's Professional Challenge

Instruct Those Who Elevate a School or Elevate Those Who Need Instruction

Frank Gomez was the principal of the Carter Middle School. He had performed a minor miracle in turning the school into a place where academics counted. Where once dropout rates were high and scores on statewide achievement tests were low, matters were now headed in the opposite direction.

Frank had a soft spot in his heart for the students that populated his school. Most were from Hispanic families. They were first- or second-generation Americans. Their parents worked hard, and many of the students themselves held an after-school job or otherwise had to assist at home with chores and child care, as both parents were employed.

They were working people who lived simple lives, even if their lives were far better now than in the nations from which they emigrated to the United States. While these families had a strong work ethic and were adapting to the American dream, they still did not see the value of completing school to the extent that Frank knew was important for them and their children.

Frank was always at work with the students and in the community, advocating for the importance of education and staying in school until completion. He did not meet with opposition. It was just that these families had many other pressures, many of them economic, to which they were continually subjected. For many of these families, life was a continual balancing act.

Fortunately, Frank had an ally. Not all his teachers or even all the administrators in his district agreed with or liked the ally. It was the No Child Left Behind Act. From Frank's perspective, this was a breakthrough piece of legislation. Many hailed it for rearranging the outlook of schools, forcing them to concentrate upon outcomes and performance rather than inputs.

Frank agreed with that perspective. However, he liked NCLB for an entirely different reason. He liked it because it required a disaggregated view of test scores and made visible the low achievement of the Hispanic children for whom he saw himself as an advocate. While he liked to use NCLB as a whipping boy, blaming the federal government for paperwork, testing, and attention to basics, he knew in his heart that these were the right things to do and the right students upon whom the system should concentrate. Hence, he was an NCLB fan, even if a somewhat quiet one.

However, as much as Frank approved of NCLB, he was faced with something of a dilemma. Carter Middle School had been placed on a list of inadequately per-forming schools. His school had not made Adequate Yearly Progress for two years in a row. He had to do something to elevate the test scores in reading and mathe-matics. If he did not, then not only would his school be shamed and his reputation tarnished, but also his students' parents would be receiving information regarding the reputation of the school that would unnerve them and trigger a diminution in community confidence.

Frank did not mind that students might become eligible for federally funded supplemental educational services or tutoring. Many might benefit from the right kind of added instruction. What concerned him more was the prospect of parents utilizing vouchers and opting into another school. He knew that Carter ultimately would be the right place for students, and he did not want them leaving.

Frank had this problem: he had to raise the test scores. Otherwise his school was in jeopardy. He thought he knew how to elevate the mean score. What he did not know was whether he should do this by concentrating on a select few students at each grade level who were just below the proficiency cutoff point, or by directing the added resources and instructional intensity at the lowest-scoring students. He knew it was the latter who needed the most help. However, it might well be that he could assist his school best in the long run by concentrating on those closer to success. If he could boost them over the proficiency threshold, then his school would be less in jeopardy and he could take a longer-range view.

Frank did not want to discuss this dilemma with any district administrator or with his teaching staff. He did not want to be boxed in by the advice of others or to give an impression that he was willing to "game" the system. He was compelled to figure this out by himself, and there was much riding on his decision.

Discussion Questions for Case 5

1. Was Frank Gomez according NCLB too much credit? Why or why not?
2. Is the legislation really likely to help poor children, or is it just another gimmick or fad that will pass in time?
3. Was Frank framing the issue the right way? Was it either–or? Couldn't he boost mean achievement by helping all children?
4. Should Frank have sought advice, against his own instincts, without being secretive?

 CASE 6

Cameron Campbell's Calculation Challenge

Cameron Campbell, a former nationally ranked skier and Olympic hopeful, had been drawn to the Lake Tahoe area of California by the beautiful scenery, winter sports, and active lifestyle. After his serious ski career was ended by a bad injury, he applied to be a high school science teacher and was quickly hired. In time, he married another teacher, had a family, and continued his love affair with the outdoors. Along the way, his leadership talents were noticed, and he rose in a conventional career path to be a school counselor, principal, central office administrator, and then, eventually, to become the superintendent of the five thousand–pupil Mountain Union School District.

Mountain Union, or at least a significant component of Mountain Union, was a posh place. It consisted of vastly expensive resort homes, second homes for many owners, and a spectrum of luxury recreation resorts that catered to skiers in the winter and boaters, bikers, and hikers during the summer. The district covered a great deal of ground and consequently operated a large bus fleet.

The district was divided into quite clear geographic and socioeconomic settlements. The many mountains and valleys both facilitated and accentuated this separation. In one valley were the exclusive homes of the wealthy, both permanent and seasonal residents, and in another section were the far more modest residences of those who worked in the resorts, cooking, cleaning, and maintaining hotels, ski and boat rentals, and so forth. There was also a small community of craftsmen, plumbers, carpenters, mechanics, and other technicians who maintained the ski facilities in the winter and boats and homes in the summer.

In the past fifteen years, this residential segregation had been rendered more complicated by the arrival of many Hispanic workers who quickly found employment in construction and in the hospitality industry that was starting to expand. In several of Mountain Union's schools, Spanish was now the first language of most students.

Mountain Union had long benefited from a civic-minded elite who took government and schools to be a serious matter. Many of these individuals were old-line San Francisco families who had made their money in an earlier industrial and financial era, before the post–World War II population expansion and the late-twentieth-century Silicon Valley technology boom. They took their California pioneer roots seriously. Many were environmentalists who worked assiduously to preserve the pristine beauty of the lakes, streams, and mountains that characterized the area. They would consent periodically to thinning the deer population, but not much else about nature was to be disturbed. They were against overdevelopment, overgrazing, overpopulation, and, when it came to government, overspending.

Indeed, this civic elite had long dominated the Mountain Union school board. That is not to say that they were necessarily public school products themselves. Many had attended the West's, and the nation's, most exclusive independent schools. Still, they believed in education. In addition, they carried with them onto the school board their concerns for the environment, for academic high standards, for moderate tax rates, and for returns on investment. Assuredly they were responsible citizens, environmentalists too. But foremost, they were hardheaded managers who wanted the Mountain Union district operated as though it were a business. Teachers should teach. Students should study. Books should be balanced. Buses should run on time.

Cameron Campbell was well regarded by the area's civic community. His reputation as a world-class skier stood him in good stead, even though he was now in his early fifties. He was a welcome member of the local community organizations such as the Rotary Club. His six-figure salary was high by superintendent standards, and this reflected the board's and community's confidence in his leadership. He enjoyed good relations with his board, with his community, with other elected officials in the area, and with his teachers and parents.

Then it happened. One night, midway through a school board meeting, the board president, William Hopkins, began ruminating about the district's teacher contracts and teacher salaries. He inquired of Cameron:

Do we have to pay all teachers the same? Cannot we pay the good ones more and the less effective ones less? I do that in my business. Jack Welch sure does that at General Electric. I do not know why we cannot follow more modern pay practices and pay teachers based on their demonstrated performance. What evidence is there, Cameron, that years of experience and education-school graduate courses are the primary contributors to a teacher's effectiveness?

To Cameron's surprise, the conversation went round the bend and went fast. Before he could begin to respond or control what was being said, a five-to-two board majority had framed and enacted a resolution calling upon the administration to return at the next month's meeting with a pay-for-performance plan that rewarded the most effective teachers and held steady the least effective. It was all Cameron could do to close off discussion about a proposed amendment that would have called for firing 10 percent of the district's least effective teachers each year, the "GE way."

After the meeting, at home having a glass of wine with his veteran teacher wife, Cameron recounted events. In his six years as superintendent, he had never seen a board take the bit in its teeth and virtually disregard the administration's views. He was taken aback. Moreover, he saw that he would have to educate himself and his district rapidly about pay for performance. He knew from his reading of professional publications that it was rapidly heating up as a topic of discussion. However, he had never envisioned that it would influence his district so fast. Phew!

His wife suggested that he phone the district union president and brief her on events first thing in the morning. He had usually seen eye to eye with the union. He had been fair with them, and they had reciprocated. He did not want to move too fast without union consultation. Still, the board had issued him a mandate, and he was not absolutely sure that he could produce a union-acceptable plan in a month. After all, it was summer, and he did not even know how many union representatives were in town. It looked like a tough assignment.

Cameron cleared his calendar and met first thing with Colleen Bonnet, the union president. He did not have to explain to her what had occurred the preceding evening. The union representative covering the school board meeting had already briefed her down to the last detail.

Cameron could see that the pay-for-performance issue was going to place a strain on labor and management relationships. Colleen bristled at the slightest reference to performance pay. The Mountain District had a quite traditional pay schedule, with teachers slotting into cells on a set of horizontal and vertical scales representing years of service and number of graduate units taken. A beginning teacher's salary was almost precisely half of the announced salary of the district's most senior teachers. If one taught in Mountain Union for twenty years and obtained a master's degree in that period of time, one generally earned twice what was paid to a beginning teacher. It had been that way since Cameron was himself employed. Teacher salaries had stayed abreast of inflation in the intervening twenty years since he was initially employed, but teachers had not reaped any reward from the economic boom of the 1990s. Colleen was quick to remind him that teachers in Mountain Union were, comparatively speaking, not among the state's highest paid. Indeed, few teachers, unless they had a high-earning spouse, could afford to live within Mountain Union's finest neighborhoods.

Cameron thought he would use the perception of low pay as an opening wedge with Colleen. He suggested that whatever pay for performance meant, it would sit on top of, and thus be in addition to, the regular salary schedule. With this as a starting point, Colleen said she was willing to talk. To Cameron, this was progress. If he could design an acceptable bonus system, he thought he might get the board to go along on grounds that it was progress, even if not precisely what they might have in mind. He suggested that Colleen meet with her bargaining team and discuss some ways in which they might fit a performance bonus system on top of what existed. They agreed to meet in a week.

When Cameron and Colleen met again, she suggested that they pattern Mountain Union's bonus pay after many of the pay-for-performance plans being discussed around the nation. She liked the idea that teachers would be eligible for an annual bonus if they sought added professional development consistent with district goals and if they had high performance evaluations from a group of peer re-viewers. She also liked the idea of providing teachers with an annual bonus if they qualified for National Board of Professional Teaching Standards certificates.

Cameron allowed that he did not object to such plans, but that he did not think they went far enough. He suggested bonuses for teachers willing to transfer to the district's least desirable schools and for teachers who qualified for slots in hard-to-fill subjects such as the sciences, foreign languages, and special education. Colleen said she would think about it, but that she did not really favor paying some teachers more than others because they were teaching in a war zone, her term for the tough schools. She said such bonuses stigmatized students in such schools. That per-plexed Cameron. He thought the stigma for such students stemmed from their low achievement, not their teachers' pay.

Colleen was even more discouraging regarding premiums for hard-to-recruit science teachers and others. She said it was not fair to history and art teachers. After all, were those subjects not as important as science? If the district wanted to pay science teachers more, why not pay all teachers more?

Cameron suggested that principals' judgments of teachers be an element in determining their performance ratings and eligibility for annual bonuses. Colleen countered that they had tried such a scheme twenty-five years ago, just before he was hired. She claimed it did not work well because principals were known to be prejudiced, favoring some teachers over others regardless of their ability as instruc-tors. She would not agree to a plan that enabled principals unfairly to reward their favorites.

Finally Cameron asked about rewarding teachers based on the academic achievement of students in their classrooms. He proposed using state test scores as the metric for making such judgments. This is when Colleen really came apart. She claimed that such a plan was wildly unfair, particularly in Mountain Union, when the differences in student capacity for achieving high scores were well known histori-cally. She pointed out to Cameron what he already knew. The students in the desir-able schools in town routinely achieved high scores and many academic honors. Students in the less desirable schools routinely received low scores and few honors. Colleen asked how any plan could be more unfair than that. Cameron had to admit that giving the teachers of high-scoring students a bonus for their classrooms being filled with highly motivated students seemed unfair to him too.

They talked further but made little progress. Thus, three weeks later, Cameron attended the school board meeting and proposed all that he could gain agreement upon: a plan for annual bonuses based upon added professional development and teacher peer reviews. His board pushed and pushed, and he explained the union leader's and teachers' objections. When Colleen saw his explanations as insufficient, she took the microphone and became adamant in exclaiming the unfairness of any plan but hers.

During the meeting, Cameron went on to raise the issue of using test scores as a bonus element. He mentioned that there was a problem in that not all teachers taught subjects that the state tested. However, he mentioned that having whole-school performance bonuses might mitigate this problem.

Colleen again addressed the board and explained how unfair it was to reward teachers who were assigned traditionally high-achieving classes and neglecting teachers who did the Lord's work by teaching hard-to-instruct children.

At this point, the school board president, William Hopkins, had heard all he could tolerate. He explained that he had been studying the matter deeply and had been reading about the use of various psychometric and econometric mechanisms by which the socioeconomic status of students could be mitigated as an influence in performance measurement. He asked if either Colleen or Cameron could explain these techniques to the public and asked further what objections they had to them. He asked specifically whether or not Colleen and Cameron knew of "gain scores" and "value-added" measurement. Neither could give a satisfactory explanation and asked for time to study more.

The board president made it clear that his patience with Colleen was exhausted and that he was losing confidence in Cameron as well for not having done his homework completely. He said he had hoped for more imagination and cooperation from both of them.

Soon thereafter, the board held a discussion, in public to be sure, but among themselves. Neither Colleen nor Cameron was asked to participate. At the conclusion of this discussion, the board voted five to two to adopt a value-added performance bonus system, the details of which they expected the administration to design and report back in a month. The teachers in the room walked out of the public meeting, threatening that such a pay-for-performance plan would violate their contract and that they would take some kind of job action.

Cameron went home, again to talk to his wife. As he saw the situation, his position with the board was eroding, and the years of cooperative relations he had cultivated with the teacher union were evaporating. What could he do? He liked his job. He liked his staff. He liked his community. He was well paid. He was not ready to retire, and yet he disliked the conflict into which he now felt locked.

Cameron distilled his options into the following:

He could resign, explaining that the board's and union's lack of confidence left him little choice.

He could flail out at the union, alleging that they were uncooperative and the root cause of the problems with the board.

He could attempt to fuel a recall against several board members, claiming that they were asking more than science could now deliver and had violated the public's trust in the process.

He could meet with the board president, ask for more time, and seek technical assistance from outside experts to see if they could in fact construct a district pay-for-performance scheme that fairly treated teachers by taking into account prior student knowledge and likely effects of social and economic influences.

Discussion Questions for Case 6

1. Propose what you think are the immediate and long-term effects of each of the options Cameron has distilled above.
2. At the end of the case study, Cameron is in a difficult place. If you were Cameron, what would you have done differently? What would your next steps be?
3. As a teacher or administrator, have you had any experiences with performance-based compensation systems? If so, how would you characterize your experiences?
4. What is your local union perspective on the merits of pay for performance? How does this differ from your personal views?
5. What do you feel are the strongest and weakest components of Colleen's argument against performance-based compensation?
6. What do you feel are the most and least valid measures of a teacher's performance?
7. What are the pros and cons of individual and group-based awards?
8. Do you think performance-based compensation is a good mechanism for increasing student achievement?

CHAPTER EIGHT

Learning

LEARNING OBJECTIVES

By the end of this chapter, you should be able to

- recognize the significance of instructional time in schools;
- understand the links between academic standards, curricula, and learning;
- identify theories of how people learn;
- distinguish between acquiring skills and deep understanding;
- understand discipline domains and types of knowledge;
- comprehend approaches to motivating learners;
- specify teachers' roles in the learning process;
- appreciate **multiculturalism** and learning environments.

Teaching and **learning** make up the **core competencies** of schooling. Whatever else schools strive to accomplish, from providing meals to arranging transportation, promoting athletics, ensuring employment, providing health care, inducing parental engagement, and encouraging community development, the principal function of schooling is still enhancing the academic aspirations and achievement of students. As evidenced by the diversity of state education clauses described in Chapter 4, the ultimate purposes of education are manifold, yet all rely resolutely on the intellectual, physical, moral, and social learning experiences facilitated in our nation's schools.

To be sure, the vast majority of a student's time is spent outside of school, as depicted in Figure 8.1. Assuredly, students learn much that is valuable outside of the school day and beyond the borders of the classroom. Even so, there is much that students do learn while in school. Thus, an education leader or aspiring leader is required to have a solid grasp of human learning theories, understand pedagogical dimensions that influence the processes of teaching and learning, and value the role of the policy environment in shaping the educational experiences of students.

This chapter provides readers with an overview of topics that are central to the issue of student learning in schools. However, as is or will be obvious, the sheer magnitude

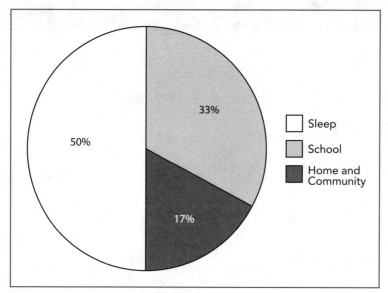

FIGURE 8.1 Comparison of Time Spent in School, Home, Community, and Sleep

of topics, approaches, and issues that could be addressed in the domain of human learning is well beyond the scope of any book chapter, and a reader is provided resources at the end of the chapter for further reading to encourage the pursuit of this subject in greater depth.

While it is imperative for school leaders to understand how state standards are constructed, rated, and assessed for alignment to state tests (the focus of Chapter 9), an equally critical domain of knowledge and skill for school leaders occurs at the intersection of these statewide realities and the curriculum and instruction enacted in schools. State standards and assessments provide benchmarks and an accountability structure, while the instructional program serves as the vehicle responsible for ensuring student learning. Sections of this chapter will focus on several school-level approaches to enhancing school programs and thus student learning. Specifically, sections deal with the issue of **alignment** between facets of the school program and state standards, provide insights about the use of instructional time in schools, and recognize the importance of considering cultural diversity in the school program.

■ IMPORTANCE OF INSTRUCTIONAL TIME

A school year comprises approximately five thousand hours, administered for the most part in short bursts of class time that last under an hour. When one considers the realm of possible school-based alterations that might benefit students and teachers, the words of Milton Goldberg, director of the National Education Commission on Time and Learning, provide one viable option: "Time is a resource that must be used more creatively and effectively."[1] This section of the chapter provides suggestions on how school leaders can address the issue of using time as a resource for teaching and learning in schools by drawing out several insights from the commission's recently rereleased report *Prisoners of Time*. This is especially important given our nation's emphasis on a standards-based reform agenda, which calls for new ways to use time to achieve powerful learning.

Interestingly, the profound changes our nation has experienced in the realms of technology, demographics, and the economy have had minimal effect on either the amount of time or manner in which students spend it engaged in school. Additionally, in comparison to the educational systems on which we base international measures of student performance, America's teachers have less time to plan, collaborate, and assess instruction. More flexible time for teacher personal and professional development might assist educators in meeting the increased demands for accountability in our nation's education system. Even with the articulation and growing importance of standards for student learning, analysis of how instruction is structured leads to a conclusion that boundaries for student growth are defined more by schedules for bells, buses, and vacations than they are by goals for student learning. Take, for example, the following observations noted by the commission:

- With few exceptions, schools open and close their doors at fixed times in the morning and early afternoon—generally between 7:30 a.m. and 3:30 p.m.
- With few exceptions, the school year lasts nine months, beginning in late summer and ending in late spring.
- According to the National Center for Education Statistics, schools typically offer a six-period day, with about 5.6 hours of classroom time a day.
- No matter how complex or simple the subject—literature, shop, physics, gym, or calculus—the schedule assigns each an impartial national average of 51 minutes per class period, no matter how well or poorly students understand the material.
- The norm for required attendance, according to the Council for Chief State School Officers, is 180 days.
- Secondary school graduation requirements are based universally on seat time expressed in **Carnegie units**, with one credit representing a one-year course meeting daily.
- Staff salary increases are typically tied to time—to seniority and the number of graduate courses completed.
- Of the forty-two states examined by the commission, on average, only 41 percent of secondary school time is spent on core academic subjects.

Based on these findings, the commission concludes that the school clock governs how administrators oversee their schools and how teachers progress through the curriculum, by influencing how material is presented to students and the opportunity they have to comprehend and master it. Has this always been the case? In 1894, the U.S. Commissioner of Education, William T. Harris, calculated that due to recent reductions in class time, students at the advent of the 1900s would have to spend more than eleven years in school to receive as much instruction as students fifty years earlier received in eight years. In recent years, the reductions have only become more dramatic in our nation. This has not been the case in other countries and thus may serve as one potential contributor to unfavorable international comparisons of student achievement. For example, in a review of other nations, the commission found

- students in other postindustrial nations receive twice the instruction in core academic areas during high school;
- many overseas schools protect academic time by differentiating between the "academic day" and the "school day";
- many of our international economic competitors supplement formal education with substantial out-of-school learning time;
- in many nations, school performance has serious implications for further educational opportunities and employment.

While schools in the United States occupy approximately the middle of the distribution in terms of number of annual "instructional hours," only 41 percent of these hours are devoted to core academic subjects (literature, mathematics, languages, history, and science). A comparison of time devoted to core academic subjects in the United States, Japan, France, and Germany is provided in Figure 8.2. Here we see that students in the United States spend less than half of the time devoted to core academic subjects that students do in select international countries. From this perspective, in order for American students to score comparably to those in Japan, France, and Germany, they would need to learn as much as their foreign peers in half the time. Based on such analyses, the commission distilled five significant time-related challenges facing American education. These include:

- the fixed clock and calendar are a fundamental design flaw that must be changed;
- academic time has been encroached upon to make room for a host of nonacademic activities;

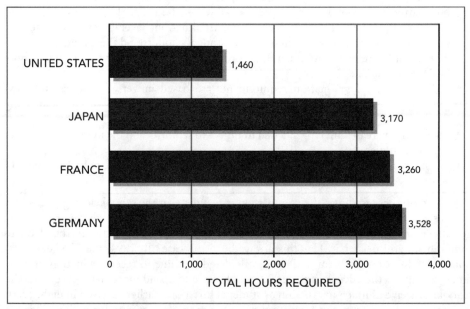

FIGURE 8.2 International Comparison of Time Devoted to Core Academic Subjects during the Final Four Years of Secondary School

Source: Prisoners of Time, report of the National Education Commission on Time and Learning.

- today's public school schedule must be modified to respond to the great changes that have reshaped American life outside school;
- educators do not have the time they need to do their job properly;
- mastering rigorous standards will require more time for almost all students.

In an effort to address these issues and to assist our nation in the attainment of the goals at the center of our standards-based educational system, the National Commission on Time and Learning offered the following recommendations:

1. Reinvent schools around learning, not time. Effectively, there is little use in merely adding more time to schools if it is not used in new ways to promote greater learning. School communities are encouraged to redesign educational programs and experiences so that time becomes a factor supporting learning, not a boundary making its limits.
2. Establish an academic day. In order to assist students in meeting current academic standards, the commission suggests schools daily provide at least 5.5 hours of core academic instruction time. Within the confines of a 180-day school year, this alone would nearly double the amount of time devoted to mathematics, English and language arts, science, history, the arts, and foreign language.
3. Keep schools open longer to meet the needs of children and communities. If more time during the traditional school day is devoted to core academics, supplemental student activities, compensatory programs, and additional efforts for special education and gifted students could be provided during an extended school day. While schools cannot single-handedly solve all of the needs of today's families, an extended school day would allow schools to serve as community learning centers for a broader array of citizen educational needs.
4. Provide teachers with the professional time and opportunities they need to perform their functions effectively. Teachers, individually and collectively, might well benefit from systematic and continuous opportunities for preparation, planning, reflection, collaboration, and professional development. This could be done by extending the school day or the contract year, or through the systematic use of well-prepared, full-time substitute teachers.
5. Districts and school communities should engage a wide constituent base in dialogue about the shape and future of its schools. Local school leaders can help school communities crystallize a vision for their schools and develop action plans to transform schools. These discussions should focus on learning time and may result in the provision of multiple school calendars from which parents, students, and teachers could choose the optimal arrangement.

Certainly, many challenges face schools and school leaders in our nation. In many ways we have led the world in providing our citizens access to education. Yet there are many ways in which our education system can better meet the diverse needs of our student population. As language formation and reading comprehension skills have significant implications for the successful acquisition of knowledge in all subject areas, many schools have undertaken special efforts to allocate a significant portion of the school day to the development of these skills.

Efforts to "protect" time are more commonplace in elementary and middle schools than in high schools. These programs stipulate that a significant portion of each school day is dedicated exclusively to the study or act of reading. These programs ensure that reading time is prioritized and protected from trivial interruption and provide a forum for supplemental programs for students not making adequate progress. The efficacy of such programs depends on careful planning and design. School leaders can help school communities articulate needs and define goals for such programs, determine the best time of day and week to offer the programs, discern the optimal amount of time to be added to these targeted learning opportunities, and weigh the benefits of such programs with competing instructional issues.

 CASE 5 REVISITED

> Recall principal Frank Gomez of Carter Middle School. He is faced with the prospect of not meeting Annual Yearly Progress for the third year in a row. How might he and his faculty restructure the use of time to target the academic needs of those students in the most dire need, as well as those who are almost at the proficient level?

■ SIGNIFICANCE OF SPECIFYING WHAT IS TO BE LEARNED

A Nation at Risk (1983) stimulated an era of heightened accountability on the educational landscape of our nation. No less influential is the more recent No Child Left Behind (2001) legislation that has promoted a prominent role for **academic standards** and **accountability** in our nation's public school system. Specific components of the NCLB legislation include annual testing aligned with state content standards in reading and mathematics for all students in grades 3 through 8. However, even before this federal legislation, many state education departments and school districts were beginning to set standards for student performance and to create standardized measurements for assessing student performance. As such, in today's policy environment, it is increasingly important to understand what content students have been exposed to and thus have had an opportunity to learn.

Academic standards address the critical issues of what should be taught and in what sequence. In essence, the introduction of academic standards should ensure that what students are taught comprises a coherent opportunity to master challenging academic content. Therefore, in order to remain instructionally focused, education leaders should systematically assess the academic program by leading the faculty in reflection and action on such questions as these:

- Does learning at our school progress in a coherent manner and provide increasingly challenging expectations?
- Do learning goals provide students with an opportunity to master challenging academic content?

Such faculty reflection, and subsequent action, is one strategy to ensure that a school is delivering a coherent curriculum, with the appropriate level of skill building, without significant overlap or gaps.

For students in urban schools, or for those from disadvantaged backgrounds, this issue is especially important. That is, disadvantaged students are likely to be more dependent on schools for their academic learning than are children from more socially advantaged backgrounds. Educational researchers at Johns Hopkins undertook a small study in Baltimore and found that by the end of fifth grade the cumulative impact of the summer break was related to a forty-seven-point gain for "relatively well educated and economically secure homes" while low-income students lost two points from summer deficit. Dramatically increasing and sustaining achievement without longer days and years seems doubtful. In addition, however, solid academic standards assist in establishing generalized principles that can guide the construction of specific learning activities, and good instruction is the vehicle that teachers employ to help students meet the learning objectives contained within the state standards.

Well-developed academic standards are associated with increasingly sophisticated mastery of skills and subject matter and the formation of a coherent academic program. Unfortunately, analysis of the academic program at many elementary schools reveals that grades 3 through 6 are providing instruction with very similar levels of complexity (or lack thereof). That is, sixth-grade teachers expected no more sophistication in the task than third-grade teachers. Endorsing this claim, David Gordon, writing about the research from the Consortium on Chicago Schools, found that schools introducing lessons on the parallelogram were teaching essentially the same thing in the second-, fifth-, eighth-, and tenth-grade classes, offering lessons of comparable complexity to students at all grade levels. These examples show possible missteps in the formation of a learning sequence that is not a coherent whole nor is taught in a sequenced manner to ensure that students have the necessary prior knowledge and encounter new concepts that are increasingly sophisticated. More will be said about the topic of state standards and their relation to school programs in the following chapter. Here we turn our attention to the alignment of state or local standards with instructional programs in schools.

▪ INSTRUCTIONAL PROGRAM ALIGNMENT

It only makes sense that the more efficient an organization is, the greater the payoff will be from organizational efforts. In the case of schools, coherence between academic expectations (expressed in the standards and assessments) and educational experiences (expressed in the curriculum and instruction) is a primary mechanism to enhance efficiency. While it is important for an organization to articulate a mission, establish challenging goals, and set rigorous standards, these are essentially a proposed destination. Without ensuring that the curriculum and instruction are harnessed in a way to reach this destination, the goals and standards will only serve as a reminder of what might have been. As such, it is important that education leaders facilitate a high degree of alignment between the instructional program, the destination articulated in the standards, and the methods for assessing performance. Figure 8.3 displays various levels of alignment that call for strategic education leadership. This figure highlights the need for both horizontal alignment, which ensures within-sector integration of activities, and vertical alignment, which ensures that state, district, and school-level initiatives inform each other.

Figure 8.4 provides another view of the benefit of alignment between key elements of the instructional program. For example, in many education organizations, there is a

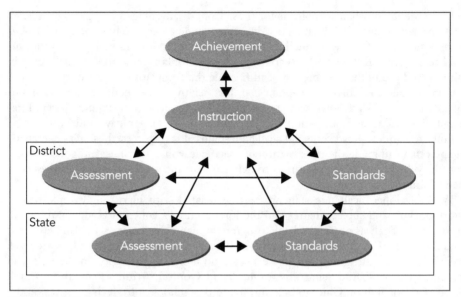

FIGURE 8.3 Various Levels of Alignment

Source: Porter, A. C. (2002), Measuring the content of instruction: Uses in research and practice, *Educational Researcher, 31*(7), 3–14.

considerable discrepancy between what the formal **curricular guide** proposes and what is actually taught in classrooms. Further, it is possible that what is tested does not necessarily align with the curriculum that students are actually engaged in during classroom instruction. One practical and reliable way to determine the degree of alignment between

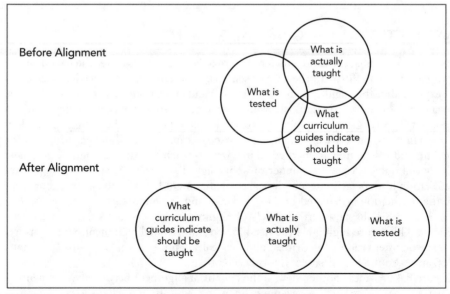

FIGURE 8.4 Alignment of the Instructional Program

facets of the instructional program is by utilizing the Surveys of Enacted Curriculum (SEC) that has been developed by educational researcher Andrew Porter and a team of curricular specialists. The SEC is a set of data-collection tools being used in the domains of mathematics, language arts, and science to collect and report data on instructional practices and the content being taught in classrooms. These data provide an objective method for school leaders and teachers to assess the degree of alignment between state standards, assessments, curricular guides, and classroom instruction.

School leaders and teachers are inundated with resources and suggestions regarding what needs to be taught in various subjects and at various grade levels. Yet many school leaders do not know if teachers are teaching what is described in the content standards, if they are teaching what is in the textbooks, and if they teach in ways aligned with state testing.

When all is said and done, classroom teachers are the ultimate negotiators of what content is covered, how much time is devoted to particular topics, when and in what order material is taught, to what standards of achievement, and to which students. It is imperative that education leaders have accurate information about these important classroom dynamics, including the degree to which there is overlap among what is taught at various grade levels, what is tested, and what the state and local standards require. The primary ways that the SEC can assist school leaders are summarized below.[2]

- *Alignment of instruction, standards, and assessments.* For example, states, districts, and schools can use the SEC to explore the alignment of their instruction with the state standards and/or assessments. This particular application assists these SEC users in answering the following types of questions: To what degree are the content topics and expectations of the state standards being taught in the classroom? Is the content being taught with sufficient rigor or depth? Are the expectations for students, as reported by their teachers, consistent with the defined expectations on the state assessment? To what degree might the misalignment of instruction be related to lower student achievement?
- *Improvement of instruction.* For example, SEC leaders who are using the SEC for this purpose frequently find themselves addressing questions such as, How do instructional practices differ for teachers of the same subject at the same grade level? How are data on differences in instruction useful in developing consistent approaches to improved achievement? How are data helpful as a foundation for beginning discussions on instruction among colleagues? Over time, does instruction within a school become more aligned to standards?
- *Needs assessment and program evaluation.* Frequently states and districts turn to the SEC as a tool for identifying areas of instructional strengths and weaknesses, as well as a tool for identifying progress against specific project benchmarks (e.g., Reading First). For this purpose, SEC users often address specific educational questions such as, What do the data suggest about the current status of teaching and learning in classrooms across the state and/or district? In what content areas or instructional practices are teachers well or poorly prepared? What are the major areas of content or instruction that would best be served by professional development programs?
- *Indicator system for monitoring change.* State, district, or school projects can use SEC data to identify the indicators that they will use to monitor change toward a specific vision or goal(s), for example, focusing on increased student engagement in science by periodic review of SEC data related to laboratory experiences, students working in groups to solve problems, and use of field studies. Questions that are addressed for

this purpose include, What goal(s) are being targeted, and what specific data should be reviewed to identify progress toward this goal(s)? What do the selected indicators reveal relative to the effects of improvement projects or initiatives on improving instruction across a sample of teachers?

- *Professional development.* States, districts, and schools can use SEC data to address professional development in two ways:

  - First, SEC data are used as a vehicle for delivering professional development. Because SEC data engage teachers and specialists in deeply exploring questions about their content, their expectations for students over time, and so on, they meet the requirements necessary for high-quality professional development. During the course of these experiences, educators ask questions such as, What content am I teaching? At what level of cognitive demand am I challenging my students? How aligned is my content with my colleagues'? To what degree does the content that is being taught at this grade level relate to what is being taught at the previous and next grade levels? Is the content that I am teaching aligned with the state standards and assessment expectations for these students?

  - Second, SEC data are used as a vehicle for designing high-quality professional development programs that are tied directly to teacher needs and student learning. Questions explored when addressing this purpose include, In which content areas are teachers showing strength or weakness? Which instructional strategies are demonstrated and used well, and which are not? Where do the professional development efforts need to focus? What data identify the indicators that will be used to monitor the impact of professional development on the classroom?

Examples of the type of data that are available to school leaders through the SEC are provided in Figures 8.5 and 8.6. The sample content map displayed in Figure 8.5 provides data on the English language arts/reading (ELAR) curricular area. Content maps provide a three-dimensional representation of instructional content using a surface area chart resulting in a graphic very similar to a topographical map. The grid overlaying each map identifies a list of topic areas (indicated by horizontal grid lines) and five categories of cognitive expectations for students (indicated by vertical lines). The intersection of each topic area and category of cognitive expectation represents a measurement node. Each measurement node indicates a measure of instructional time for a given topic area and category of cognitive expectation based on teacher reports. Figure 8.5 depicts the concentration of content contained in the fourth-grade standards for ELAR and on the state assessment. This graphic illuminates several areas of content concentration on the standards, specifically *explaining comprehension*, *explaining language study*, *explaining speaking and presenting*, *creating speaking and presenting*, and *creating writing* applications. Yet the analysis yields only two significant areas of focus on the assessment, namely *analyzing comprehension* and *explaining language study*. What implications do these data have for school leaders and teachers? Would language arts teachers be advised to cover the broader domains of content articulated in the standards or be encouraged to focus instructional time in the areas most pertinent to the assessment?

The data provided in Figure 8.6 also illuminate a substantial amount of misalignment. This time, however, it is between the state standards and the instruction taking place in classrooms. While the seventh-grade math standards are skewed heavily toward *geometric concept procedures*, the seventh-grade mathematics program shows no evidence of mirroring this focus. Instead the actual instruction is distributed among several different content

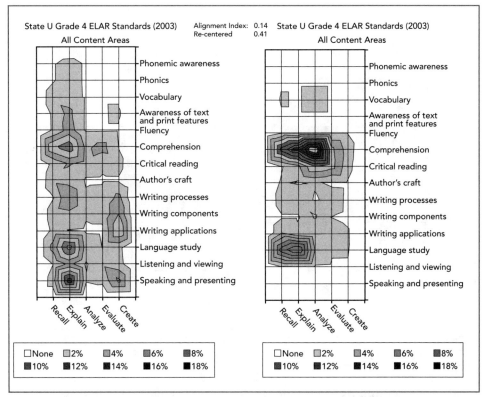

FIGURE 8.5 Comparison of Fourth-Grade Language Arts Standards and Assessment Content

Source: Blank, R. (2005). Surveys of enacted curriculum: A guide for SEC state and local coordinators. CCSSO SEC Collaborative Project.

areas and certainly lacks an emphasis on the domain targeted in the standards. This again raises important questions for education leaders. For example, given the various ability levels and prior mathematics experiences of seventh-grade math students, is a more broad-based approach appropriate, or should math classrooms be brought into closer alignment with the content focus articulated in the standards?

While a strategic education leader works within the guidelines of the state or district academic standards to create a coherent, appropriately sequenced academic program, he or she must concurrently address the "how" of teaching. And if school leaders are to have a positive influence on the teaching at their school, they must understand how students learn. Toward that end, an overview of several learning theories is presented below.

■ LEARNING THEORIES

Throughout the course of human history, many individuals have ruminated about the nature of learning. Three dominant theories of learning have evolved.

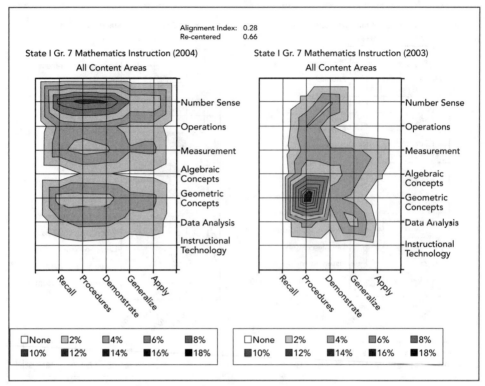

FIGURE 8.6 Comparison of Seventh-Grade Mathematics Standards and Instructional Content

Source: Blank, R. (2005). *Surveys of enacted curriculum: A guide for SEC state and local coordinators.* CCSSO SEC Collaborative Project.

Behaviorism. **Behaviorism** is a learning theory that can be traced to Aristotle, and the threads of this evolving concept are woven through the work of Hobbes, Hume, Pavlov, Thorndike, Watson, and Skinner. Behaviorism is based on observable changes in behavior and focuses on human or animal behavioral patterns being repeated until they become automatic. As such, this theory of learning has concentrated on the study of overt behaviors that can be observed and measured. In terms of how the mind is understood within this theory, the brain essentially is viewed as a mysterious, opaque, and perplexing black box, with the emphasis on responses to stimuli, thus minimizing any thought processes going on in the mind.

Central to behaviorism is the view of learning as the formation of a connection between stimulus and response. Formation of these impulse-reaction associations is regulated by confirmation, such as rewarding the desirable reaction and not rewarding undesirable reactions.

All of us have firsthand experience of many school-based processes and approaches that have their roots in the behaviorist theory of learning. For example, it was Skinner's research that brought us the notion of reinforcement schedules, be they fixed or variable-interval, or fixed or variable-ratio schedules. Within the behaviorist framework, it is held that if learning is divided into small segments and teaching is planned accurately to reward the desired reaction, then any preferred behavior can be conditioned. This notion is roughly the equivalent of training a pet to behave.

Cognitivism. As with behaviorism, the cognitivist theory of learning can be traced to the ancient Greeks. However, it was during the mid-twentieth century that this theory became a more formalized understanding of human learning, due in large measure to the writing of Jean Piaget. Like the behaviorists, the cognitivists are concerned about observable behaviors; but unlike behaviorists, they use those behaviors to make inferences about underlying mental processes that, unlike behaviors, cannot be directly observed. While behaviorists are comfortable with the human mind as a black box, the cognitivists are focused on shedding light on the internal cognitive processes that are concerned with processes inside the black box, processes intertwined in the action of human learning.

The cognitive theory of learning asserts that each of us has existing internal knowledge structures, or schemas, to which new information is compared. When we approach a new situation or concept, our schemas are altered to accommodate the new information. A simplified view of how this occurs is that new information first enters our sensory register, is then processed in short-term memory, and is then transferred to long-term memory for storage and retrieval. Research conducted by cognitive psychologists has found that meaningful information is easier to learn and remember, that it is easier to remember items from the beginning or end of a list instead of the middle, and that categorization of input makes items easier to learn. These findings have resulted in the inclusion of such pedagogical tools as mnemonic devices and advance organizers.

Constructivism. The seeds of **constructivism** can be found in the writings of such people as Kant, Kuhn, and Dewey, yet the major influencers of this theory were Bartlett and an extension of the work of Jean Piaget by Smorgasbord. This theory contends that knowledge does not move into a learner; instead, a learner has to "construct" knowledge from his or her experiences. Learning is an active process requiring individual effort, and conceptual growth comes from changing our internal representations through collaborative learning and environmental interaction.

In this view, cognition is the process by which learners eventually construct mental structures that correspond to external structures located in the environment. As every building has a foundation, a central idea in constructivism is that knowledge is not transmitted, but constructed by building upon the learner's prior knowledge. In the constructivist view, learning is understood to be a self-directed process, in which the learner plays an active role in designing, evaluating, and developing learning strategies. Learners, therefore, are not sponges or empty barrels that can passively be filled with knowledge. Rather, learning is a result of social and environmental interaction and is thus bound to the culture in which it occurs, as student identities affect their experiences both in and out of school. This theory, more than behaviorism or cognitivism, understands learning to be a social activity that is enhanced by shared inquiry. The diversity of personal histories represented in a class, and the spontaneous nature of social interaction, can result in varied and unpredictable outcomes of constructivist learning processes.

▪ DIMENSIONS OF KNOWLEDGE

A core purpose of learning is the development of knowledge. Yet, as with theories of learning, there are many conceptions of knowledge. Table 8.1 provides definitions for several types of knowledge that are derived from learning experiences.

In addition to the forms of knowledge outlined in Table 8.1, there are three primary states of knowledge. The nature of each state, along with the implications for teaching and assessment, are described in Table 8.2.

Considering the intersection of the forms of knowledge from Table 8.1 with the states of knowledge in Table 8.2 shows how educators can provide students with many

TABLE 8.1 Definitions of Select Knowledge Constructs

Form of Knowledge	Definitional Statements and Associated Research
Conceptual	Knowledge of ideas, including what they are, how they function, and the conditions under which they are used (Carey, 1985; Ryle, 1949)
Conditional	Knowledge of when and where knowledge could or should be applied (Alexander & Judy, 1988; Lipson & Wixson, 1983)
Declarative	Factual information; sometimes described as "knowing what" (Anderson, 1983)
Discipline	Highly formal subset of domain knowledge from a particular field of study or branch of learning (Bazerman, 1981)
Domain	A realm of knowledge that broadly encompasses a field of study or thought. Synonymous with domain-specific, content-specific, or subject knowledge (Glasser, 1984; Rabinowitz & Chi, 1987)
Explicit	Knowledge that one has analyzed to the point of easy explication and that directly guides ongoing interactions with the world (Prawat, 1989)
Metacognitive	Knowledge about one's own thinking and the regulation of that cognition (Flavell, 1987; Garner, 1987)
Prior	The sum of what an individual knows. Also known as background knowledge, experiential knowledge, world knowledge, preexisting knowledge, and personal knowledge (Lipson, 1983; Shuell, 1986)
Procedural	Knowledge one has of certain processes. Also known as "knowing how" (Anderson, 1983; Ryle, 1949)
Sociocultural	Attitudes and beliefs about the world and how to interact with it that arise from a person's membership with a particular social group or culture (Heath, 1983; Rosenblatt, 1978)
Strategic	Knowledge of processes that are effortful, planful, and consciously invoked to facilitate the acquisition and utilization of knowledge (Alexander & Judy, 1988)
Tacit	Knowledge of which we are currently or normally unaware; unanalyzed knowledge (Schon, 1988)
Task	An understanding of the cognitive demands of a task (Doyle, 1983; Garner, 1987)
Topic	The intersection between one's prior knowledge and the content of a specific passage or discourse (Freebody & Anderson, 1983; Hare & Borchardt, 1984)

Source: Adapted from Murphy & Alexander's (2005) adaptation of Alexander, P., Schallert, D., & Hare, V. (1991), Coming to terms with the terminology of knowledge, *Review of Educational Research*, 61, 315–343.

TABLE 8.2 Comparison of Three States of Knowledge

	States of Knowledge		
	Declarative	Procedural	Conditional
Description	Factual, or *what* knowledge, useful in describing, labeling, or explaining	Actions, routines, or *how* knowledge that is useful in demonstrating or performing	Knowing *how, when,* or *why* other two states of knowledge should be applied
Implications for Teaching	Provide students with opportunities to define, explain, recall, and illustrate terms and concepts	Provide students with opportunities to engage in hands-on demonstrations of procedures or steps in a process	Allow students to implement procedures in multiple settings to determine when best to use certain procedures
Implications for Assessing Students	Assess specific factual content through recognition and recall	Use performance-based assessments and simulations, allow demonstration of mastery via simulations, problem solving, or decision making	Assess student ability to articulate explanation for choices via problem solving. Incorporate self-evaluative measures

Source: Adapted from Murphy, K., Alexander, P. (2005). *Understanding how students learn: A guide for instructional leaders*, Thousand Oaks, CA: Corwin.

opportunities to encounter information in all of its states. School leaders can work with individuals and teams of teachers to encourage student learning experiences that will result in the development of various categories of knowledge by utilizing a range of pedagogical techniques.

As discussed at the outset of the chapter, the core technology of schools involves helping students to build a knowledge base. As the next section illustrates, it is imperative that this building process begin with an assessment of students' prior knowledge. As the sum of what an individual knows and believes, however accurate or inaccurate, prior knowledge forms the basis upon which an individual will construct new knowledge. Thus, the role that it plays in future academic endeavors is paramount.

▮ IMPLICATION OF BRAIN-BASED LEARNING THEORY AND COGNITIVE SCIENCE FOR LEARNING ENVIRONMENTS[3]

While the previously discussed theories of learning have roots stretching back for decades, even centuries, the immediate past thirty years of cognitive development, neuroscience, and social psychology have generated a wealth of scientific information about human learning. The research report of the National Academy of Sciences, *How People Learn*, draws upon this research and discusses the instructional implications of new insights in the realms of memory and the structure of knowledge, problem solving and reasoning, expert performance, **metacognitive** processes, and community participation. Specifically, these insights are synthesized into the *How People Learn* framework, and they have important implications for the design of learning environments.

Theoretical physics does not prescribe the design of a spacecraft, yet it does constrain the design of a successful vehicle. Similarly, a synthesis of all available learning theory provides no magic formula for the design of learning environments and experiences, yet it does constrain the design of effective ones. Fundamental tenets of contemporary learning theory assert that different kinds of learning goals require different pedagogical approaches and that the design of learning environments can be enhanced by insights about the processes of learning, transfer, and competent performance. Those processes, and the core competency of schooling, in turn are affected by the degree to which learning environments are student centered, knowledge centered, assessment centered, and community centered.[4] Together, these four components make up the *How People Learn* framework shown in Figure 8.7.

Learner-Centered Environments. Effective instruction begins from the foundation of what learners bring to the setting. This includes cultural practices and beliefs, as well as knowledge of academic content. A focus on the degree to which environments are learner centered is consistent with the evidence showing that learners use their prior knowledge to construct new knowledge and that what they know and believe at the moment affects how they interpret new information. Sometimes learners' current knowledge supports new learning; sometimes it hampers learning. People may have acquired knowledge yet fail to activate it in a particular setting. This is congruous with a learner having declarative or procedural knowledge, without yet developing conditional knowledge. Learner-centered environments attempt to help students make connections between their previous knowledge and their current academic tasks. Naturally, parents are especially good at helping their children make connections. Teachers have a harder time because they do not

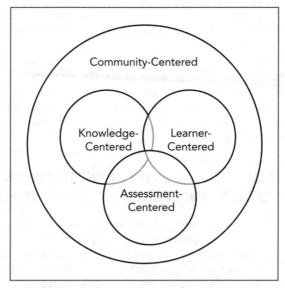

FIGURE 8.7 The *How People Learn* Framework

share the life experiences of all of their students. Therefore, in order to enhance the learner-centeredness of their classrooms, teachers must invest the time and effort required to become familiar with their students' special interests and strengths.

Knowledge-Centered Environments. The ability to think and solve problems requires knowledge that is accessible and applied appropriately. An emphasis on knowledge-centered instruction raises a number of questions, such as the degree to which instruction focuses on ways to help students use their current knowledge and skills. New knowledge about early learning suggests that young students are capable of grasping more complex concepts than was believed previously. However, these concepts must be presented in ways that are developmentally appropriate by linking learning to students' current understanding.

A knowledge-centered perspective on learning environments highlights the importance of thinking about designs for curricula. To what extent do they help students learn with understanding versus promote the acquisition of disconnected sets of facts and skills? As discussed earlier, the domain of educational standards plays a role in determining the content, or knowledge-centeredness, of the academic program. Curricula that are a mile wide and an inch deep run the risk of developing disconnected rather than connected knowledge.

Assessment-Centered Environments. Issues of assessment also represent an important perspective for viewing the design of learning environments. Feedback is fundamental to learning, but feedback opportunities are often scarce in classrooms. Imagine you are an archery student seeking to hone your skills with the bow and arrow. Would mere practice help? What if you practiced for an entire day but were blindfolded? Would you improve? Or rather, is it a combination of practice and feedback (seeing your performance relative to the target) that allows you to develop your archery skills? Students may receive grades on tests and essays, but these are summative assessments that occur at the end of projects. What are needed are formative assessments that provide students with opportunities to revise and improve the quality of their thinking and understanding. Assessments must reflect the learning goals that define various environments. If the goal is to enhance understanding and applicability of knowledge, it is not sufficient to provide assessments that focus primarily on memory for facts and formulas.

Community-Centered Environments. The fourth important perspective on learning environments is the degree to which they promote a sense of community. Students, teachers, and other interested participants share norms that value learning and high standards. Norms such as these increase people's opportunities and **motivation** to interact, receive feedback, and learn. The importance of connected communities becomes clear when one examines the relatively small amount of time spent in school compared to other settings, as highlighted in Figure 8.1. Activities in homes, community centers, and after-school clubs can have important effects on students' academic achievement. Each of us can cite an example of the positive impact that being a part of a caring community has had on our development. Although it is very challenging, education leaders must ensure that their schools and classrooms provide a caring community of learning to students—all students.

Intersection of Learning Theory and the Needs of Diverse Learners

The insights gained from years of cognitive science research intersect with several enduring and emerging issues in education. Two of these will be discussed below. They include the issue of **learning styles** and **multiple intelligences** and the emerging emphasis on tailoring the instructional program to meet the needs of learners from diverse socioeconomic backgrounds.

Learning Styles and Multiple Intelligences (MI). As no two people have exactly the same taste in clothes or food, places to travel, and what to do once they get there, so too no two people have exactly the same learning style or combination of intelligences that are relied on to make sense of the world. Each individual has a host of mental, physical, social, and emotional tools to gain knowledge and interact with other individuals. In the classroom, teachers must be cognizant of the diversity of learning styles that students call upon to understand content and apply to solving problems. One theory that highlights the diversity of tactics drawn upon in such endeavors is Howard Gardner's theory of multiple intelligences (1983).[5] In this theory, Gardner explains that humans have a host of ways in which to understand or make sense of the world and make valued contributions to our society. The eight dominant intelligences that Gardner has articulated include:

- *Linguistic intelligence.* This is understood to include a host of verbal and "word-smart" skills.
- *Logical-mathematic intelligence.* This includes number and reasoning skills.
- *Spatial intelligence.* This is described as *picture smart* or seeing the patterns and relationship between items in the spatial domain.
- *Bodily-kinesthetic intelligence.* This is synonymous with body smarts, coordination, and knowing by doing.
- *Musical intelligence.* This is understood to be the skills needed to appreciate and create music.
- *Interpersonal intelligence.* This is known as being people smart, the ability to relate well to others, socially and emotionally.
- *Intrapersonal intelligence.* This is the skill of introspection and reflection necessary to know oneself.
- *Naturalist intelligence.* This is understood as the ability to recognize patterns within one's natural environment and craft products valued by society.

Gardner contends that schools focus primarily on the linguistic and logical-mathematical intelligences. Within our current policy environment of heightened accountability mandates, one would think that the focus would become, or has become, nearly exclusive. Yet this theory proposes a transformation in the ways that school environments are constructed and learning experiences are created. In order to present material that is equally accessible to students across a broader spectrum of learning styles, or intelligences, school leaders and teachers must expand their pedagogical toolbox.

Intersection of Instruction and Socioeconomic Conditions. As students have preferred learning styles that impact how they understand and assimilate information, so too are children influenced by a host of socioeconomic conditions. Children growing up in poverty are not a phenomenon relegated to elementary- and secondary-age students in other countries. Ruby Payne has articulated one framework for understanding the implications of poverty for educating students in our nation's schools. Similar to MI theory, Payne draws attention to the varying perspectives that teachers must consider when constructing learning experiences. The vast majority of schoolteachers, and education leaders, are situated comfortably in the middle and upper-middle class. Thus, educators

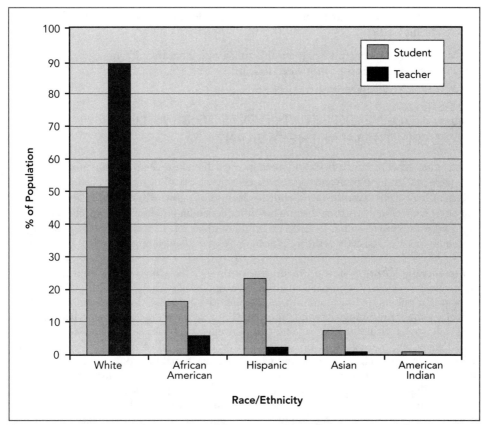

FIGURE 8.8 Projected Demographic Comparisons between Teacher Workforce and Student Population for the Year 2025

Source: *Statistical Abstract of the United States: 1997,* 117th ed., Washington, DC: U.S. Government Printing Office, 1997:20–27.

have a very hard time relating to the rules, values, and essential survival knowledge that make up the cultural landscape of those living in poverty. As highlighted in Figure 8.8, there is often a significant disconnect between the cultural life experiences of educators and those of their socioeconomically disadvantaged students. As such, extra effort must be taken to ensure that these disparities do not persist between school expectations and students' needs. While some educators do this instinctively, others do not. Therefore, it is imperative that successful school leaders are continually appraising the school community, analyzing the needs of all constituents, and then harnessing the collective energy of the community toward productive action. Such a strategic approach to education leadership can ensure that the needs of all students are considered in the construction of learning experiences.

Debates about pedagogy, the *how* of teaching, challenge educators, researchers, parents, and the public. Educators, as well as the public, often have strong convictions about how students should or should not be taught. The debates on pedagogy revolve around three enduring issues:

- What do we expect students to be able to do with what they learn?
- How should students be motivated to learn?
- What is the role of a teacher in the learning process?

■ WHAT DO WE EXPECT STUDENTS TO BE ABLE TO DO WITH WHAT THEY LEARN?

In the larger scheme, students should learn in ways that allow them to remember what they have learned for a long time and to use whatever they "know" in future academic pursuits as well as in their daily lives. Research evidence from the cognitive and neurosciences suggests that best practices in instructional strategies differ depending on how one expects the learners to use what they are learning. Does one want them to be able to recite, upon request, a given procedure or set of facts? Or is the intention for them to do well on next week's history test?

Remembering Things. Steven Pinker, author of *How the Mind Works*, notes that human brains are marvelously efficient machines. We remember what we use frequently, be it telephone numbers or basic addition facts. Cognitive scientists find that rehearsals are a critical activity for recalling facts and procedures. Rehearsal strategies include what educators often refer to as "drill and kill," a label that conveys a derogative opinion. Bad reputation notwithstanding, there are appropriate times to use rehearsal strategies: when the knowledge or skills need to be automatic and when the same signal or prompt will be used when that skill or knowledge is needed. Playing a musical instrument, driving a car, keyboarding, dribbling a basketball, and multiplying numbers as part of a larger mathematical problem all require one to recall facts and procedures automatically. Drivers who need to think through the physics of motion before they apply the brakes are dangerous. Applying brakes at the right time needs to be automatic.

Procedural knowledge is usually acquired through rehearsals. "*I* before *E* except after *C* or when sounding like *A* as in *neighbor* and *weigh*" is a sentence that many have learned in lieu of rehearsing every single word with adjacent *I*s and *E*s. And silly as it seems, as a rule it proves to be fairly effective. One can apply the rule in writing until the spelling becomes automatic. Rehearsing this procedure allows one to manage arbitrary spelling rules. Having math facts available automatically can be important in consumer transactions, and they are essential in many negotiations in commerce. And of equal importance, automaticity of specific skills is required for advanced learning in many fields. Thus, one should not believe that all learning involves the exhilaration of discovering new understandings about the universe. Some essential parts of learning are about drill, diligence, and discipline.

Educators need to remember, moreover, that learning how to make one's brain do what is wanted is empowering. Students who learn strategies, rather than just drills for recalling information, allow themselves to win twice. First, they remember what they need to know; second, they have strategies for the future. Expert chess players, for instance, have an advantage because they rely upon recognizing the patterns of pieces on the board, not individual moves or the position of particular pieces. Similarly, practice in recall that includes seemingly silly strategies can be applied in a variety of adult situations. Almost anyone would welcome a strategy for remembering the names of new acquaintances.

Relying exclusively, however, upon rehearsals can be a time-consuming way to teach and thus is often inefficient. Moreover, only a limited part of what students are expected to know and need to do comes with the same signal or prompt in everyday life. So before relying solely on rehearsal of facts or procedures, educators should evaluate carefully how students will use the knowledge.

Early neuroscience experiments on memory sought to evaluate the effectiveness of various strategies that people use to remember things. Such research uncovered three strategies for enhancing memory: mnemonic, structural, and semantic tactics. Using a mnemonic strategy, people grouped the words they were to recall by sound (e.g., can, pan, ran, and so on). Using structural tactics, participants grouped the words alphabetically. With semantic approaches, words were grouped by meaning; for instance, all animal names into one group, cooking utensils into another. Across a broad spectrum of individuals, organizing words semantically proved to be the superior method for assisting with memory. Thus, rates of memory are substantially better when words are grouped into categories with meaning. This experiment is one of many that point to one general finding: improving memory begins by improving understanding. Thus, if you need to remember something for a long time, but it does not need to be automatic, then understanding it (giving it meaning) is the best way to do it.

In the cognitive sciences, the value of meaning in recall has long been in evidence. Katona's classic studies from the 1960s, reported in *Organizing and Memorizing* (1967), provide some of the clearest evidence that if one understands a principle, one can remember it for a longer time than if one has merely memorized a procedure by repeating it numerous times. Using card tricks, Katona conducted a series of experiments on long-term recall in an attempt to evaluate the efficacy of memorization versus understanding. He summarized the issue quite succinctly: in memorizing, the time required for learning depends on the number of repetitions. Learning takes longer for much material than for a small amount. On the other hand, learning by understanding is independent of the amount of material, since the understanding of a trick with a very few cards is sufficient to ensure knowledge of the trick with a very large number of cards. Therefore, memorizing is a quicker method of learning only when a small amount of material is concerned. For a large amount and for more complex material, meaningful learning is much easier and much more acceptable to the subjects than memorizing (Katona, 1967).

Thus, research evidence is fairly clear: nothing beats repetition, drill, and practice for those less complex tasks one needs to do almost automatically long into adulthood. When material is extended or complex, however, teaching for understanding is much more efficient; that is, ability to remember is strong for a longer period of time with this method, and it takes less time to learn it than with rehearsal strategies. Considering this, most of the class time that requires all students to focus on the same activity should be devoted to interactions, presentations, and discussions that advance the understanding of concepts, where both long-term memory and the ability to use what has been learned are achieved.

Using What Has Been Learned. Behaviorists conducted some of the first scientific research on learning in the early part of the twentieth century. They began their research seeking to discover what types of rewards (or punishments) were most effective in creating desired responses. Thus, Pavlov's famous dogs. Later, though, as researchers tightened their focus on human learning, they sought to determine what types of stimuli brought the desired "response," where the stimuli could be a question or a problem. Researchers consistently failed to find evidence that people could transfer what they had learned in one context to a new situation. Research showed that one needed to use the same stimuli to evoke the response, whether they were facts or procedures. So, for instance, a word problem used to evaluate mathematical knowledge needed to look quite similar to the problems students were given during instruction. In fact, some thought it was unfair to evaluate student learning unless the test used the same stimuli as those used when teaching the student.

Not surprisingly, researchers and educational practitioners did not find this a satisfying outcome. That is why research such as Katona's was so important. After all, what is the use of learning something if you are not able to apply it to new situations? Thus, researchers began to focus on the problem of **transfer**, not only because adults who had learned many mathematical principles in formal schooling were seldom able to apply them in everyday life, but also because people who had never been to school developed some fairly sophisticated ways of counting things in daily life, yet they, too, could not apply their strategies to new situations. Clearly, just learning about numbers in a "real-life" situation would not create transfer any better than formal schooling.

The process of transfer has analogies to a subject catalog at a library or a search engine for the Internet. In each case, a keyword or phrase should link a learner to relevant information. If the linkages in a catalog or search engine use only books (not journals, video, or other media) and only the titles of those books, a significant amount of relevant information is omitted. So a person interested in finding information about children's health would learn only about books that had those two words in the title, and a good deal of information about children's health would be left out. Similarly, human brains may supply only a few of the connections possible when asked to relate what is known about a topic. What is forgotten, to use the terminology of cognitive scientists, is "inert" or inaccessible. And what good does it do to know something you cannot call up when you need it?

■ HOW SHOULD STUDENTS BE MOTIVATED TO LEARN?

Learning is ultimately a voluntary act. Listening, observing, and thinking are essential activities in learning that no one can force upon another person. One can look attentive, for instance, yet not hear a word spoken. One must somehow be motivated to learn for critical acts of learning to occur. When discussing motivation in the realm of education, the question typically is framed as follows: to what degree should teachers rely upon intrinsic versus extrinsic rewards to encourage student learning?

Early in the twentieth century, behavioral researchers focused on **extrinsic rewards** educators could use. Public schools often were organized to provide rewards to learners, such as grades and recognition ceremonies. Eligibility requirements for sports exist because of an assumption that students need some reward, or extrinsic motivation, to learn. While these practices may have had a powerful effect on many students in earlier generations, they seldom have engaged a significant portion of the population of low-achieving students from disadvantaged circumstances.

Progressives in education, most often associated with the writing of John Dewey, approached motivation differently. They argued that learning occurs best when students are motivated **intrinsically**; that is, a student's natural curiosity should direct his or her learning. The intrinsic interest in the subject or the pleasure that arises from mastery will, they argue, facilitate learning. In fact, when people of any age are motivated intrinsically to learn, they do listen and read more carefully and work longer and harder to understand something.

While learning that is led by a student's current interest is certainly a powerful experience that in many cases provides a learner with deep understandings, students must have sufficient prior knowledge to understand complex principles. Gaps in knowledge can and do occur, and the ability of teachers to build upon children's prior knowledge is especially challenged when each student arrives with a unique "package" of prior knowledge. Evidence from the 1980s suggests that relying on intrinsic motivation alone has limitations in general practice. In the late 1970s, high school students had a broad range of courses from which they could choose to enroll. Academic requirements were at a minimum. By 1979, 42 percent of U.S. high school students were enrolled in a general track with few required courses, and it prepared them neither for entry into the workforce nor for college completion (National Commission on Excellence in Education, *A Nation at Risk*, 1983). Many disadvantaged students did not have information about the importance of academic learning with regard to their future options.

The evidence would suggest that the nation's most economically disadvantaged youth seldom enter schools with intrinsic motivation sufficiently cultivated to drive their efforts, nor do they respond predictably to traditional forms of extrinsic rewards. Moreover, adolescents from all walks of life are often more concerned about the more immediate pleasures of clothes and cars than their long-term opportunities as adults. Thus, the dilemma. If one accepts that a standards-driven system is the preferred method of determining what should be taught and acknowledges the power of intrinsic motivation in the learning process, then one must accept that educators have an essential role in cultivating an intrinsic obligation to motivate learning within students.

If one does not insist upon drawing the boundaries between extrinsic and intrinsic motivation with too fine a line, teachers can, in fact, affect the degree to which a student becomes intrinsically motivated to learn. The oldest research tradition on student motivation has repeatedly shown that teachers who are passionate about the subjects they teach have a contagious effect on their students. Passion, however, is quite like charisma. It is hard to train people to become "passionate." Unlike charisma, which, by definition, is visible to other people, passion about learning can be invisible, as in some otherwise-shy teachers, for instance. It is unrealistic to expect all teachers to be able to demonstrate passion with overt enthusiasm, and thus other strategies must also be considered.

Motivation is better when educators treat mistakes as a normal part of learning, and their feedback reflects an absolute goal rather than some accomplishment relative to other students. Consider the aerobics instructor who has students with wide ranges in **proficiency**. Those with low levels of proficiency are encouraged to understand that people have different levels of experience with athletic challenges and that, with extra effort, they can demonstrate an adequate level of proficiency. The confidence that the instructor exhibits actually creates a commitment among those with lower levels of proficiency to persist and make the extra effort they will need to show proficiency; in this case, completing all the routines proposed by the instructor. Progress toward that goal is praised just as often as exceeding it. Educators who consider mistakes as part of learning and demonstrate confidence that students' efforts will lead to mastery actually affect students' beliefs and their motivation to learn.

CASE 6 REVISITED

As Cameron and his district grapple with the construction of a pay-for-performance program, in what way should the ability to measure such characteristics as teachers' ability to motivate students to learn enter into the discussion or plan?

Finding ways to link what needs to be learned with students' existing interests is another obvious way to cultivate a student's intrinsic interest in learning. To make those linkages, an educator must be fluent in the social history and cultural milieu in which his or her students live. For example, elementary school teachers in Harlem teaching about the European Renaissance can integrate the history of the Harlem Renaissance and thereby stimulate their students' interest in that period of history while deepening their understanding of the concept of renaissance. Similarly, the pop culture of students, from SpongeBob SquarePants to Powerpuff Girls, holds numerous resources for motivating students in their academic learning. An important implication of this motivational challenge is that schooling must be organized in ways that provide teachers sufficient freedom to construct learning experiences that incorporate such culturally meaningful motivation. Districts and schools that restrict instruction to scripts developed for the "average student" fail to provide that freedom.

Finally, assessment strategies also can cultivate motivation. Learning that leads to a public performance or a product that will be appreciated in the community, such as the newspaper, can be especially motivating. Publishing a paper or magazine, for instance, provides a wealth of opportunity for instruction, and it also results in an activity and product that can excite otherwise-indifferent students. Designing and planning a community garden can be rich with opportunities in science and mathematics. With proper guidance, such activities can be a way to partner meaningfully with individuals and businesses in the community, as volunteers and sponsors can help translate such plans into reality. Such activities can be especially effective for students who have come to ignore traditional incentives, such as grades. Learning opportunities in these situations, however, must be carefully planned to ensure that students extract general principles and acquire competencies to meet academic standards, a problem discussed earlier. Within today's accountability environment, teachers are all too aware that each student must be able to demonstrate that he or she has mastered the essential concepts outlined in the state standards, or at least those tested on the state assessments.

Motivation, then, becomes an important element in a standards-driven environment. Teachers can employ a variety of strategies in this domain, ranging from the convictions they demonstrate in their daily teaching, to the links they can make with a student's interests and cultural milieu, to the types of activities they construct for learning. The pedagogical challenge is to integrate these opportunities into the routines and organizational context of teaching and learning.

■ WHAT IS THE ROLE OF THE TEACHER IN THE LEARNING PROCESS?

Efforts to transform classroom instruction into powerful education experiences have led theorists of learning to look at classroom practices along a continuum from teacher-centered to student-centered instruction. Teacher-centered instruction occurs when instruction proceeds in a manner that is overtly guided by the instructor, such as presenting lecture-style delivery to a class. Given the organization of schooling into classes of students, the tremendous time constraints placed on teachers, and the ever-looming presence of accountability demands, teacher-driven instruction is a common, if not essential, mode of instruction in our nation's schools. In reality, most classroom instruction proceeds with a combination of teacher-centered elements and student-centered elements. The appropriate balance can be dictated by such considerations as grade level of student, subject matter, and the social dynamics of a particular class of students.

Teacher-led learning involves five critical actions: linking new learning with prior knowledge; providing students with "the big picture" and where what they are learning fits into it; establishing opportunities for students to experience, organize, and apply new concepts; uncovering (and correcting) misconceptions students may have about the concepts, principles, or facts; and nurturing their understanding of excellence.

Teachers must take responsibility for providing students with the big picture; that is, how what they are learning fits into the landscape of that discipline. (Why are we doing this? How does this fit with what we already know?) Experts in any given field have an organized body of knowledge in their discipline. Cognitive scientists refer to the mastery of a field as "knowing the landscape," which is to say that an expert knows the relationships among various concepts and pieces of knowledge and understands how the big ideas in that discipline fit together in that landscape.

Student-centered instruction begins with the proposition that all learners construct their own knowledge and that the role of the teacher is to provide experiences and activities that allow students to develop their own understanding of how things work. Cognitive science research has produced evidence that suggests students learn best, meaning they are able to form associations between new knowledge and prior knowledge and are able to apply new knowledge to situations, when they actively construct their own understandings. Critics of student-centered learning contend that such learning leads to an unacceptably high number of students who are "off task," wallowing in misconceptions that are never corrected and treating differences in perceptions and conclusions as mere differences of opinion.

Research evidence is clearly supportive of two principles of instruction associated with student-centered pedagogical approaches: new learning must be linked with prior experience, and students have a deeper understanding of concepts and retain what they learn when they are co-constructors of the learning themselves. That said, "prior experience" is a much broader concept than advocates of student-centered theory often allow. It includes prior academic knowledge, social experiences outside the classroom, as well as experiments or activities within the classroom. In essence, teachers must link the new with the familiar. Similarly, actively "organizing material" may be strictly an intellectual task that reconstructs or rearranges the "new material" into a meaningful set of connections using outlines, webs, path diagrams, matrices, or other tools for systematizing and visualizing patterns and relationships.

Research evidence, summarized in *How People Learn*, points to both strengths and potential drawbacks associated with teacher-centered and student-centered approaches to instruction. Clearly, teaching strategies that rely upon both methods are more likely to give students the capability of applying what they have learned as well as remembering what they have learned. Research from cognitive psychology and neuroscience contends that in order for students to understand, apply, or even just remember something, they need to be able to make sense of it using their prior experiences. Thus, instruction must be student centered insofar as the prior experiences and culture of students are used to help students make sense of whatever scientific principle or historical issue one hopes for students to master. On the other hand, the research on the importance of prior learning often has been misinterpreted. The research does not find that students can learn only something that is overtly linked to their everyday experiences, but rather that teachers must make the link between the new and the familiar.

Research also suggests that teachers must actively seek to uncover misconceptions. H. Jackson Brown in *Live and Learn and Pass It On* (1992) entertains us with what children think they have learned at various ages. One seven-year-old reports, "I've learned that when I eat fish sticks, they help me swim faster, because they are fish." Research on teaching, especially science, demonstrates how misconceptions, much less humorous than the effects of fish sticks, create barriers to understanding principles or concepts. Teachers cannot teach by just telling students something, or even just demonstrating. Effective instruction must be inquisitive, asking students to explain, clarify, or make predictions about the concept under scrutiny. Only then can teachers uncover the particular misconceptions hiding in the minds of their students. For example, John Bransford and colleagues asked more than one hundred fifth-graders to solve this problem: *There are twenty-six sheep and ten goats on a ship. How old is the captain?* More than three-quarters of students tried to provide an answer. One fifth-grader explained his conclusion that the captain was thirty-six years old this way: "Well, you need to add, subtract, or multiply in problems like this, and this one seems to work best if I add."

■ CULTURAL DIVERSITY AND INSTRUCTIONAL ENVIRONMENTS

In the United States, the percentage of children from racial and ethnic minority groups[6] has increased over the past decade and is projected to continue to increase at least for the next twenty years. According to the *Statistical Abstracts of the United States*, by the year 2020, approximately 40 percent of school-age children are expected to be of nonwhite racial or ethnic backgrounds. Projections for the year 2025 estimate that the student population will consist of 15.8 percent blacks, 23.6 percent Hispanics, 1.1 percent American Indian/Native Alaskans, 6.9 percent Asian/Pacific Islanders, and 52.6 percent whites. Yet the current and projected racial distribution of teachers and school leaders does not approach the degree of diversity in the student population. As has been the case for the past forty years, approximately 90 percent of the teaching workforce is white, 6 percent is composed of African Americans, and the remaining 4 percent denotes "other" in the racial category. Therefore, during the next twenty years, the disparities between the racial and ethnic mix of the student population and that of their teachers and principals can be expected to widen substantially. Figure 8.8 depicts these demographic trends.

The increasing cultural diversity of our nation's population has significant implications for the teaching workforce and for the provision of educational services. There is a need for a teaching workforce that is more racially and ethnically diverse and educated to recognize and address the needs of the increasingly diverse student population. Increased diversity and cultural sensitivity in the teaching workforce and in the leadership of our education organizations can promote an appreciation for cultural distinctions and enhance the cultural effectiveness of schools. Such understanding would take into account the beliefs, values, actions, customs, and unique needs of distinct population groups. These understandings would in turn enhance interpersonal and communication skills, thereby strengthening teacher, student, and family relationships and maximizing the benefit of educational opportunities.

Given the growing gap between teacher and student ethnic composition, it is becoming increasingly important that education leaders examine the influence of school norms and assumptions about race, social class, ability, and language on the access, opportunities, and educational outcomes of local minority students. In this domain, a key task facing school leaders is to link the analyses of the aforementioned issues to the conceptualization of a culturally responsive educational program. This would entail efforts to:

- Understand education as an evolving and changing discipline based on philosophies, evidence-based principles and theories, relevant laws and policies, and diverse and historical points of view. Then, use this knowledge to examine the philosophies of education guiding the instructional program.
- Recognize the factors that influence the overrepresentation of culturally/linguistically diverse students in programs for individuals with mild and moderate disabilities. Then, use this knowledge to ameliorate this situation.
- Understand that families, students, educators, and communities may perceive the notion of "competence" differently depending upon cultural processes and historical legacies. Then, seek to use these insights when working with students and their families.
- Understand that cultural, racial, social class, gender, and linguistic differences may be confused with or misinterpreted as manifestations of a disability, and take actions to guard against inappropriate assessment and over- and under-identification of students for special education services.
- Foster environments in which diversity is valued and individuals are taught to live harmoniously and productively in a culturally diverse world.
- Reflect on the interaction between students' cultural and historical experiences and institutional forces that influence student learning.

One can take several philosophical approaches toward embracing multiculturalism. It is beyond the scope of this text to deal with these various theories in detail, yet it is important to outline several variations in approaching diversity within schools. Awareness of such is important for school leaders because, as sociologist Pierre Bourdieu asserts, schools act as markets that are not necessarily neutral, but value and confer status on students who display particular knowledge, linguistic behavior, styles, dispositions, and modes of thought and expression.

One approach to multiculturalism entails school efforts to honor and be sensitive to specific holidays, celebrate different cultural traditions, eat foods of various countries, and read about historical figures that have impacted the broader civil rights movement. The pedagogical purpose of this human relations approach is to reduce negative attitudes, prejudices, and cultural biases that can get in the way of cross-cultural understanding. Yet schools often see themselves as socializing agents and thus responsible for helping diverse students fit into the mainstream. As such, schools can fall into the habit of seeing culturally different children as deficient and thus in need of remediation. This deficiency approach to multiculturalism presumes a lack of ability, resources, and congruity between school culture and the home culture of students. To minimize such incongruence, it is not schools but students who must do the difficult work of adaptation and acculturation.

A third approach sees the cultural dynamics active in schools as part of a larger societal context that privileges certain groups, perspectives, and ideas while silencing, marginalizing, and repressing others. This social reconstructionist approach moves beyond issues of diversity and difference by focusing on issues of power, privilege, ideology, and social structures. Unlike the human relations approach, this view does not seek comfort or cross-cultural dialogue that would only substantiate the power relationships in the larger society.

Further, unlike the deficit model, this approach does not see cultural minority groups as innately deficient but looks at the societal structures that persist in marginalizing groups of citizens. As moral and ethical agents, school principals play a critical role in helping school communities understand the nuances and complexities of working within a culturally diverse organization that itself is situated in a broader social context.

Summary

The academic growth and development of students will continue to be the great responsibility and challenge of our nation's schools. Advances in scientific research continue to uncover deeper levels of understanding of how people learn. This exponentially growing body of knowledge must continue to be assessed and understood by education leaders so that they can ensure that our teachers and schools provide the best learning environments and experiences for students. At the same time, as resources continue to flow into the education sector, there will only be heightened degrees of accountability for learning. Schools and school leaders are charged with the tasks of carefully creating educational programs that meet high academic standards, utilizing research-based **learning theory** to guide instructional activities, and finding ways to motivate, honor, and engage a diverse student population.

A critical task for education leaders entails the alignment of local instructional programs with state standards and assessments—an issue also discussed in Chapter 9. This requires the collection of data surrounding how curricular units are constructed and how content is taught. Tools such as the Surveys of Enacted Curriculum provide insight on how school leaders might approach this complex task. Having considered the important issue of alignment between classroom instruction, standards, and assessments, one realizes that these determinations are in many ways a question of how to use the valuable resource of time most effectively. School leaders are in a position to help school communities grapple with the important issues of academic time, learning theory, and the reality of multiculturalism, as each has significant implications for the quality of educational environments and student learning.

Discussion Questions

1. In what ways has your work in education been influenced by the presence of academic standards and accountability mandates?
2. Many activities in schools consume time. Describe, or propose, an innovative use of time that increases the quantity and quality of instructional time while meeting the academic needs of a subgroup within your school community.
3. Describe the degree of instructional alignment among standards, instruction, and assessments in your school. What could a strategic leader do in your school or district to increase this alignment?
4. Which of the three learning theories discussed is most closely aligned with your philosophy or approach to teaching?
5. Explain a strategy that you could use to help a student's tacit understanding of a concept become more explicit.

6. As an educational leader, how can you raise the level of awareness regarding, and implementation of, contemporary learning theory in your school or district?

7. Choose a subject-specific lesson topic (e.g., vertebrate animals or conditional clauses), and discuss how you could ensure that the four components of the *How People Learn* framework are incorporated into the learning environment and experience.

8. In your career as an educator, what methods of motivating students have you found most effective?

9. Figure 8.8 depicts demographic projections of the teaching force and student population in 2025. What, if any, are the implications of the demographic disparity between teachers and students in your school and district?

10. Is there currently an overrepresentation of culturally or linguistically diverse students in programs for individuals with mild and moderate disabilities in your school? What might a strategic education leader do to assess this situation and ameliorate such an overrepresentation if one existed?

11. Describe one way that your school meaningfully embraces multiculturalism in the academic program.

12. ELCC Standard 3 emphasizes the important work that an education leader does to promote an efficient and effective learning environment. Considering the issues of time for instruction and multiculturalism raised in this chapter, how might a strategic leader engage the faculty and school community about these issues so as to improve the efficiency and effectiveness of the learning environment?

References and Suggested Readings

Bourdieu, P., Passeron, J.C., Nice, R., and Bottomore, T. (1990). *Reproduction in education, society, and culture.* Thousand Oaks, CA: Corwin Press.

Bransford, J., Brown, A. L., and Cocking, R. R. (Eds.). (1999). *How people learn: Brain, mind, experience and school.* Washington, D.C.: National Academy Press.
   This volume is the most comprehensive treatment of the topic of learning theory available today. The authors draw together decades of research in diverse fields of inquiry and harness these insights toward a unified theory of student learning.

Brown, H. J. (1992). *Live and learn and pass it on.* Nashville, TN.: Rutledge Hill Press.

Bryson, J. M. (1988). *Strategic planning for public and nonprofit organizations.* San Francisco, CA: Jossey-Bass.
   This book explains a number of approaches for helping leaders and managers of public and nonprofit organizations to fulfill their missions and to satisfy their constituents through strategic planning.

Clayton, J. B. (2003). *One classroom, many worlds: Teaching and learning in the cross-cultural classroom.* Portsmouth, NH: Heinemann.
   This volume provides a helpful and clear introduction to issues at the intersection of learning and multicultural settings.

Hoy, A. W. (2006). *Educational psychology* (10th ed.). Boston, MA: Pearson/Allyn & Bacon.
   This is an outstanding compendium on the myriad of insights that psychological research brings to bear on issues of learning.

Katona, G. (1967). *Organizing and memorizing.* New York: Hafner.

Kaufman, J. (Ed). (1993). *Planning theory: Commentary on Guy Benveniste's Mastering the Politics of Planning.* Milano, Italy: FrancoAngeli.

This newsletter journal shares and details expert reviews and opinions of Benveniste's text, a thought-provoking treatise that blends elements of public planning, management, and organizational development theory and also serves as an instructional primer covering a variety of political, managerial, and organizational skills and techniques.

Murphy, P. K., and Alexander, P. (2005). *Understanding how students learn: A guide for instructional leaders.* Thousand Oaks, CA: Corwin Press.

This volume synthesizes research primarily from the domain of educational psychology and discusses the topic of learning in practical terms for school leaders.

National Commission on Excellence in Education. (1983). *A nation at risk: The imperative for educational reform.* Washington, D.C.: U.S. Department of Education.

Notes

1. Goldberg, M. (1994). *Prisoners of time.* Report of the National Education Commission on Time and Learning.
2. Text and graphics in this section drawn from Blank, R. (2005), *Surveys of Enacted Curriculum: A guide for SEC state and local coordinators.* CCSSO SEC Collaborative Project.
3. This section of text from Bransford, J., Brown, A., and Cocking, R. (Eds.). (1999). *How people learn: Brain, mind, experience and school.* A report of the National Academy of Sciences.
4. Bransford, J., Brown, A., and Cocking, R. (Eds.). (1999). *How people learn: Brain, mind, experience and school.* A report of the National Academy of Sciences.
5. Gardner, H. (1983). *Frames of mind: The theory of multiple intelligences.* New York: Basic Books.
6. It is recognized that the meanings of the terms *race* and *ethnicity* are overlapping and defined by the context in which they are used. Racial categories used by the U.S. Census and others have varied widely, and the terms *race* and *ethnicity* are often used interchangeably. Our emphasis here is that schools need to deal with cultural context in addition to racial identity.

CHAPTER NINE

Programs

LEARNING OBJECTIVES

By the end of this chapter, you should be able to

- understand the influence of *A Nation at Risk* and the No Child Left Behind Act on school programs;
- identify the role of the "standards and accountability" movement in American education;
- rate the efficacy of state academic standards;
- comprehend the importance of aligning standards, assessments, and instructional programs;
- employ mechanisms for assessing and enhancing school program content;
- identify links between K–12 and postsecondary programs.

The instructional program serves as a vehicle for the transmission of knowledge and skills that will prepare students for college and work. The school program serves as the foundation upon which academic and social experiences are constructed. The school program can also be seen as an anchor that links students to key domains of knowledge and ways of learning. As the combination of content, process, and context that makes up the academic experience, school programs are of central importance to the well-being of students and society. The leaders of our nation's schools are in a position to serve a variety of functions for school communities in the realm of school programs. Strategic education leaders can engage school programs by serving in the following capacities:

- interpreter of national, state, and district program requirements
- allocator of funds to various programmatic budgets
- aligner of school programs to state standards and assessments
- assessor of program efficacy in meeting student needs
- modifier of programs based on school and classroom data
- provider of professional development to enhance faculty delivery of the instructional program
- architect of school-level conditions and resources to support the school program

• protector of programmatic time
• celebrator of programmatic successes

To successfully serve in such a variety of capacities, education leaders must have a solid grasp of the many forces influencing school programs, be aware of mechanisms for assessing the efficacy of program **standards**, understand various approaches to enhancing school programs, and be aware of the dynamics involved at the intersection of K–12 schooling and postsecondary education. The provision of such knowledge is the aim of this chapter.

■ FORCES INFLUENCING SCHOOL PROGRAMS IN THE UNITED STATES

As described earlier in the book, one of the key attributes of strategic leadership is a continual assessment of the external context. This section of the chapter focuses on three influential, external forces that have shaped, and will continue to shape, school programs in our nation. These include *A Nation at Risk*, the No Child Left Behind Act (NCLB), and the standards and accountability movement. Prior to addressing each of these topics, it is helpful to understand the relative level of programmatic freedom enjoyed in the United States, as well as get a sense of illustrative programmatic issues that are determined at the state and local levels. Table 9.1 provides a measure of programmatic decision making at the federal level by comparing the United States with other nations in the G-8 group as measured by the presence of a national **curriculum** and exam.

TABLE 9.1 National Curriculum and Exam Policies in G-8 Countries

G-8 Country	National Curriculum?	National Exam?
Canada	No	No—some provinces have high school exit exams
France	Yes	Yes—for exit from lower secondary school, entrance to university
Germany	No—lander (states) determine curriculum	Yes—for entrance to higher education
Italy	Yes	Yes—for entrance to upper secondary school, receipt of high school diploma
Japan	Yes	Yes—for entrance to and placement in upper secondary school
Russia	Yes	Yes—for graduation from lower secondary school, receipt of secondary completion certificate
United Kingdom	Yes, with some local discretion	Yes—for receipt of general certificate of secondary education (age 16) and admittance to most higher education institutions
United States	No	No—some states have high school exit exams

Source: Center on Education Policy, 2006. *A public education primer.*

As Table 9.1 highlights, the United States is one of only three of the G-8 countries without a national curriculum and one of just two such countries without a national exam. Thus, while the federal role in education has expanded in the United States under NCLB, many key education decisions are still made at the state, district, and local levels. Examples of decisions typically made at the state level versus those made at the local level are provided in Table 9.2. Here we see evidence that several key decisions pertinent to the academic program are made at the local level, providing district and school leaders with

TABLE 9.2 Examples of Education Decisions Set at the State and Local Levels

Policies Typically Set by State Legislatures or State Boards of Education	Policies Typically Determined at the Local Level
Content	**Content**
• Standards for curriculum content	• Specific curriculum content and specific performance standards
• General accountability requirements for school district and student performance	• Choice of textbooks and other instructional materials
• Student testing requirements	• Decisions about promoting or retaining specific students
• General student promotion and retention policies	• Student discipline and truancy
• Graduation requirements, including whether to require students to pass an exit exam	
Teachers	**Teachers**
• Teacher preparation requirements	• Teacher hiring and collective bargaining
• Teacher licensing and certification requirements	• Teacher salaries and job requirements
• "Right to work" or other collective bargaining laws affecting teachers' unions	• Teacher professional development
Structure	**Structure**
• Number of years of compulsory schooling	• School schedule
• Compulsory school age requirements	• School grade configurations
• Whether to require districts to offer kindergarten	• School attendance zones
• Length of school year	• Class sizes
• Charter school requirements	
Finance, organization and facilities	**Finance, organization and facilities**
• Systems of financing public schools within the state	• Types of non-instructional services to be provided
	• Local taxing policies for education
	• Budgets and school funding
	• Construction, renovation, and use of school facilities

Source: Center on Education Policy, 2006. *A Public Education Primer.*

considerable responsibility in terms of how to organize content, structure time, and allocate resources.

A Nation at Risk

The 1983 report from the National Commission on Excellence in Education, *A Nation at Risk*, is among the most influential public policy documents in the history of American education. *A Nation at Risk* posited as its principal thesis that downwardly spiraling pupil performance had rendered the U.S. education system dysfunctional, thereby threatening the nation's technological, military, and economic preeminence. The report further asserted that only by elevating education achievement could the United States avoid subordinating itself to its educational superiors and economic competitors. In retrospect, it is apparent that the report was wrong on both counts.

The U.S. education achievement was no lower in 1983 than it had been at previous points in history, and the U.S. economy was not at any long-term risk, at least not due to an ineffective education system. Still, the repercussions of *A Nation at Risk* publication have proven to be of historic proportions. The report motivated more significant changes in the manner in which American K–12 public schools conduct business than virtually any event or condition preceding it. Although education practitioners and researchers contend that some of these changes were positive, other changes may be deemed harmful to the long-standing traditions of education in the United States.

From today's vantage point, the most positive result of the report seems to have been that it triggered a move away from measuring the quality of schools by the resources they receive to a place where school performance is judged by outcomes students achieve. This paradigm shift in perceptions regarding the relation of inputs to outcomes of education could, in the long run, render the nation's education system more effective for students and more useful for the larger society. For the nation to focus on student achievement rather than on school funding alone is a good thing. A second positive result was a bit more indirect. Since the 1980s, the United States has increasingly focused on the **achievement gap**, the failure of low-income and minority children to achieve at the levels of white middle class children. *A Nation at Risk* barely mentioned this issue, as it was concerned primarily with preventing damage to the nation's productivity and scientific and military prowess by improving the skills of graduates who would go on to work in technologically advanced industries. But the report's emphasis on test scores as a measure of the nation's strength inexorably led to a more intensive examination of the performance of students whose test scores were typically the lowest—socially and economically disadvantaged youth. So although it was not the publication's primary intent, it would be fair to credit the report with spurring a trend that also led to demands for improving education for children at the bottom of the achievement distribution.

While these outcomes are certainly positive, some results of the report can be judged as having a negative impact on our nation's education system. One was the federalization of education policy, a trend that accelerated with *A Nation at Risk* and that now threatens the creativity and diversity of local school systems that have been among the nation's greatest strengths. Another has been the willingness to define student achievement exclusively by standardized tests, a trend that was spurred by the report's flawed analysis of test score declines and that may have foreclosed reform of policies regarding other, equally important aspects of student achievement. A third was the "crowding out" of social reform by school reform, the belief that all of the nation's social problems can be solved by improving schools alone and an accompanying willingness to tolerate failures in other social institutions.

The powerful impact of the report was evident in the Gallup Poll's September 1983 confidence index for the public school system. Gallup queried respondents regarding their confidence in the public school system using a six-point scale, with points including A Great Deal, Quite a Lot, Some, Very Little, None, or No Opinion. In 1977, more than 50 percent of respondents expressed a high level of confidence in the public schools. However, five months after *A Nation at Risk* was released, this percentage plummeted to less than 40 percent.

Although the confidence index for public education dipped following the release of *A Nation at Risk*, education was routinely identified as the most important factor for determining America's future strength.

The response to *A Nation at Risk* was far from uniform, as some states proceeded at a more rapid and comprehensive pace than others. Early efforts were, in retrospect, simple minded. The initial phase of resultant reform was characterized primarily by efforts to render graduation and college entry standards higher and academic expectations for students more rigorous.

This first change wave, which lasted from 1983 to 1990, was characterized by states harvesting immediately available low-hanging education reform fruit such as longer school days and years, more required courses, fewer electives, more math and science and less shop math, and higher graduation requirements and college admission standards.

A second reform wave, which occurred from 1990 to 2000, emerged from two distinct theories of change, one constructed around systems theories and another around markets. The first involved aligning components of the education system, linking standards, statewide standardized student achievement tests, teacher licensing requirements, instructional materials, professional development, state capacity-building subsidies, performance ratings and school report cards, and positive and negative sanctions for achievement progress. This systemic reform, sometimes referred to as standards-based reform, will be described in a subsequent section of this chapter. Despite disproportionate attention rendered to the market-based reform strategy, it has had only marginal impact compared to that of standards-based reform. The market strategy contends that public education is a monopoly with all the deficiencies usually found in activities dominated by a single supplier, such as bureaucratic rigidity, customer insensitivity, reliance on outdated production techniques, and efforts to restrain other providers from coming to the market. The market education reform strategy has had success by influencing policy targeting open enrollment plans, **charter schools, magnet schools, voucher programs**, and **homeschooling**. These reforms in the 1990s attempted to transform education's proverbial roles, structures, and goals by detangling unrelenting problems and altering the fundamental way in which the education system is composed. Whether these attempts were effective or not, they still have reached only a small portion of the nation's nearly fifty million public school students.

The third wave, the condition that characterizes the time span from 2001 to the present and beyond, is dominated by the federal government accountability requirement embedded in the 2001 enactment of NCLB. The federal government's modern-day dominance of education policy is ironic. Not only is it contrary to the first 350 years of the nation's education history, it is also contrary to the first two decades of response to the publication of *A Nation at Risk*. The federal government was not a major policy player in early reform stages. In his first two years as president, Ronald Reagan's goals for education included abolishing the Department of Education and promoting school prayer and tuition tax credits, although he eventually became a cheerleader for change. President George H. W. Bush pushed the rock up the hill a bit further by urging governors to formulate a slate of national goals. President Clinton also urged high standards, promoted greater accountability for student and teacher performance, and supported selected bills that allocated more resources (e.g., class size reduction funding). Yet little was done at a federal level to initiate actual change by school districts. Only with the passage of NCLB in 2001 did the federal government become a major actor in the education reform scene. Interestingly, despite its tardy appearance on the education reform stage, the outcome-oriented paradigm represented by NCLB may prove to be the dominant factor in altering America's schools, consistent with the theme of *A Nation at Risk*.

No Child Left Behind

The No Child Left Behind Act (NCLB; technically Public Law 107-110) is a reauthorization by Congress of the 1965 Elementary and Secondary Education Act (ESEA; technically Public Law 89–10)[1]. This new statute is a reenactment of a historic piece of the War on Poverty legislation sponsored by President Lyndon B. Johnson. President Johnson deeply believed that household poverty prevented many American children from participating fully in the nation's riches and that a principal instrument for overcoming this deficit was to enable poor children to engage successfully in the education system. The ESEA, over its thirty-five-year operational history, appropriated to states, and through states to local school districts, in excess of $300 billion for what was known as compensatory educational services (Wong, 1999). Although the ESEA was a remarkably influential piece of federal policy and a powerful force for enabling low-income children to engage in schooling more productively, it did not propel a paradigm shift in American education. NCLB is clearly more influential and is reshaping the landscape on which every public school in the nation operates every day. Here is how.

The federal government's leverage on states, and through states on local school districts and schools, is twofold. First, the American electorate heavily endorses the purposes for which the NCLB stands. The act, although proposed by Republican president George W. Bush, won wide bipartisan support and was enacted in the Senate by a vote of 87 to 10 and in the House by 381 to 41, a clear mandate that no individual state can oppose. However, NCLB relies on another lever. It distributes billions in federal dollars to states, an amount sufficient to ensure that no state would willingly forfeit such resources. To gain funding, states must comply with the act's provisions. The act is large, more than 1,400 pages; however, it is the accountability provisions that are important in this discussion. By 2012, states must display sufficient improvement to ensure that students are performing at high levels of proficiency on achievement tests and that schools are closing achievement gaps between advantaged and disadvantaged students. If a school fails to comply with the act's requirements and to make **Adequate Yearly Progress (AYP)** toward the prescribed goals, formidable consequences are triggered. These consequences can include permitting parents of persistently low-performing schools to claim public resources and to opt for the placement of their children at other instructional institutions, including private schools. It is these outcome measures, and the influence they have over the flow of resources, that complete the loop and focus accountability on school outcomes rather than inputs.

So, although the federal role in education from the 1960s through 2001 was focused mostly on helping special groups of students, such as disadvantaged and disabled children, and addressing urgent national needs, such as improving math and science education, it was NCLB that broadened the federal role to encompass all students and all teachers of academic subjects. For example, the NCLB Act requires

- school districts to test annually and meet performance goals for *all* students in grades 3 through 8 and once in high school;
- all academic teachers to demonstrate they are **highly qualified** by having a minimum of a bachelor's degree in their subject or meeting other criteria of subject-matter competence;
- districts to monitor and close achievement gaps among different groups of students, such as racial/ethnic groups;
- nearly all **English language learners** and students with disabilities to take the same subject-area tests that meet the same achievement goals as other students.[2]

Every current educational practitioner, parent, and student has felt the effect of the NCLB Act. While the test-driven accountability has impacted the relative importance of various academic subjects and has narrowed measures of academic achievement, the act has directed greater attention to low-performing students and schools. Since the inception of NCLB, the Center on Education Policy, an independent nonprofit research and advocacy organization, has conducted a multiyear review of the effects of the act on American education. While the influence of NCLB on particular schools and districts varies, ten major effects of the overall act on our nation's public schools follow.[3]

- State and district officials report that student achievement on state tests is rising, which is a cause for optimism. For example, scores on state tests in reading and mathematics are going up, according to 75 percent of states and districts, and the achievement gap on these tests is narrowing or staying the same.
- Schools are spending more time on reading and math, sometimes at the expense of subjects not tested. For example, to find additional time for reading and math, the two subjects currently required to be tested under NCLB, 71 percent of districts are reducing time spent on other subjects in elementary school.
- Schools are paying much more attention to the **alignment** of curriculum and instruction and are analyzing test score data much more closely in order to inform instructional decisions.
- Low-performing schools are undergoing makeovers such as improving curriculum, staffing, and leadership, rather than the most radical kinds of restructuring. As restructuring impacts schools that have not met AYP for five years, the longer the law is in effect, the more likely it is that more schools may face restructuring.
- Schools and teachers have made considerable progress in demonstrating that teachers meet the law's academic qualifications, yet many educators question if this will really improve the quality of teaching. While nationally 88 percent of districts reported all teachers of core academic subjects were highly qualified at the end of the

2005–6 school year, problems still persist for **special education** teachers, high school math and science teachers, and teachers in rural schools who teach multiple subjects.

- Students are taking a lot more tests. For example, in 2002, fewer than twenty states had annual assessments in math and reading for grades 3 through 8 and once in high school. Today, every state in our nation has such tests.
- Schools are paying much more attention to achievement gaps and the learning needs of particular groups of students. NCLB's requirements that districts and schools be responsible for improving the academic achievement of each subgroup of students is directing attention to traditionally underperforming groups of students, such as those who are learning English, have a disability, are ethnic or racial minorities, or are from low-income families.
- The percentage of schools on state "needs improvement" lists has been steady but is not growing. Over the past several years, about 10 percent of all schools have been labeled as "in need of improvement" for not making AYP, with urban districts reporting greater proportions of their schools in this category than are suburban and rural districts.
- The federal government is taking a much more active role in public elementary and secondary education than in the past.
- NCLB requirements have meant that state governments and school districts have expanded roles in school operations, but often without adequate federal funds to carry out their duties. In order to carry out NCLB provisions, states and districts are assuming more duties related to expanded testing, the provision of assistance to schools, and the establishment and utilization of criteria to assess teacher quality. Thirty-six states and 80 percent of districts report a lack of sufficient staff and funds to implement these requirements.

As described earlier, the NCLB Act is a legacy of the Education Department's *A Nation at Risk* report. It also is a revolutionary federal enactment. Not only does it mandate a dominating accountability model for America's public schools, but it is revolutionary in terms of the federal government's involvement in education. For most of the three and one-half centuries since the enactment in 1647 of the Ye Olde Deluder Satan Act, U. S. public education has been dominated by a doctrine of state plenary authority mixed with the practical reality of local school district management discretion. The concept of local control, even if not always compatible with the plenary constitutional authority of state government over education, has been the secular theology of American education. NCLB alters this historical arrangement. However, the reality is that the standards and accountability measures mandated by NCLB are a new driving force in American education.

Standards and Accountability

During the past several decades, standards, assessments, and accountability, both for school programs and student performance, have emerged as important levers for the improvement of education in the United States. Under NCLB, states are building on the work they had already begun in the area of academic standards and are implementing challenging academic content and achievement standards in the core academic subjects of language arts, mathematics, and science. The articulation and implementation of rigorous academic standards provides clear direction for what all students should know and be able to do and establishes clear expectations for schools, teachers, students, and parents. In addition to academic standards, performance standards provide a mechanism to assess the degree to which all students are attaining academic achievement. Prior to NCLB, federal legislation required states to test student achievement at only three times throughout a student's tenure in the K–12 educational system. As this situation could result in a significant number of years in which student performance went undiagnosed, the NCLB legislation required states to enhance existing assessment systems.

The timeline for state implementation of academic content and student achievement standards is as follows:

- By May 2003, as part of a state's consolidated application, states must have challenging academic **content standards** in reading/language arts and mathematics to cover each of grades 3 through 8. Additionally, as required under the 1994 reauthorization of the ESEA, states must continue to have academic content standards for grades 10 through 12 in reading/language arts and mathematics.
- By the 2005–6 school year, states must develop academic content standards in science for elementary (grades 3 through 5), middle (grades 6 through 9), and high school (grades 10 through 12).
- By the 2005–6 school year, states must develop and implement student academic achievement standards in reading/language arts and mathematics for each of grades 3 through 8. As required under the 1994 reauthorization of ESEA, states must continue to have academic achievement standards for grades 10 through 12 in reading/language arts and mathematics.
- By the 2007–8 school year, states must develop and implement student achievement standards in science for each of the grade spans 3 through 5, 6 through 9, and 10 through 12.

Similarly, the timeline for state implementation of assessments of academic standards is as follows:

- Through the 2004–5 school year, states must administer annual assessments in reading/language arts and mathematics at least once during grades 3 through 5, grades 6 through 9, and grades 10 through 12.
- By the 2005–6 school year, states must develop and implement in each of grades 3 through 8 yearly, high-quality assessments in reading/language arts and mathematics that are aligned with a state's challenging academic content and achievement standards. The requirement for annual assessments in reading/language arts and mathematics at least once in the grade span 10 through 12 remains and has not changed from the 1994 ESEA reauthorization.
- By the 2007–8 school year, states must develop and implement at least once in each of the grade spans 3 through 5, 6 through 9, and 10 through 12 yearly, high-quality annual assessments in science that are aligned with a state's challenging academic content and achievement standards.
- A state's assessments in reading/language arts and mathematics must be used to make annual accountability determinations of how well all students in public elementary and secondary schools are learning and mastering the subject material reflected in a state's academic content and achievement standards.
- Student achievement on assessments must be included in state and district report cards.

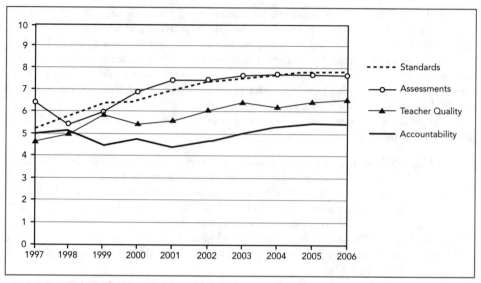

FIGURE 9.1 National Trends in Standards-Based Policy

Source: Editorial Projects in Education Research Center, 2006. www.epe.org/rc

A historical view of our nation's education landscape provides evidence that reform movements come and go, yet there seems to be no sign that the move toward standards-based accountability is slowing. To be sure, all fifty states are moving toward accountability systems that involve the establishment of clear and rigorous standards for student learning, assessing student performance on those standards, and administering a variety of incentives and sanctions related to performance. Figure 9.1 indicates the current trend in standards-based policies. The data in this figure are compiled by *Education Week* and are published in the annual *Quality Counts* report, which serves as a report card on public education in the realm of standards-based reform. This figure shows the national trend in state implementation of standards-based policies between 1997 and 2006. Specifically, the figure provides a fifty-state average in terms of adoption of rigorous content standards, as well as standards-based approaches to assessment, teacher quality, and accountability.

The graph displayed in Figure 9.1 was calculated by determining the degree to which states met the policy trend indicators described in Figure 9.2. Each state was assessed in each category, along a scale from 1 to 10, based on the degree to which the state provides evidence for meeting the specific indicators for each of the four domains of standards-based policies.

 CASE 5 REVISITED

Recall the struggle facing Fred Gomez to meet AYP at Carter Middle School. What impact have growing demographic variations and the subsequent instructional implications had upon your instructional program?

Standards
- State has adopted standards in the core academic subjects of English, mathematics, science, and social studies.
- English standards at all grade spans–elementary, middle, and high school–are clear, specific, and grounded in content.
- Mathematics standards at all grade spans are clear, specific, and grounded in content.
- Science standards at all grade spans are clear, specific, and grounded in content.
- Social studies standards at all grade spans are clear, specific, and grounded in content.

Assessments
- State tests go beyond multiple-choice items to include short-answer and extended-response questions.
- State English tests are aligned with state content standards.
- State mathematics tests are aligned with state content standards.
- State science tests are aligned with state content standards.
- State social studies tests are aligned with state content standards.

Accountability
- State provides report cards for all public schools.
- State imposes sanctions on low-performing schools.
- State provides rewards to high-performing or improving schools.
- State took part in the most recent cycle of the state-level National Assessment of Educational Progress.
- Student promotion is contingent on performance on statewide exams.
- High school graduation is contingent on performance on statewide exit or end-of-course exams.

Efforts to Improve Teacher Quality
- State requires a college major in the subject taught for initial teacher licensure at the high school level.
- Teachers must pass a basic-skills test for initial licensure.
- Teachers must pass a test of subject-matter knowledge for initial licensure.
- Teachers must pass a test of subject-matter pedagogy for initial licensure.
- State provides licensure incentives for teachers who earn certificates from the National Board for Professional Teaching Standards (NBPTS).
- State provides financial incentives for teachers who pursue or earn certificates from the NBPTS.
- State requires and finances mentoring for all novice teachers.
- Prospective educators must complete 11 or more weeks of student teaching.

FIGURE 9.2 Indicators of Standards-Based Policy Implementation

Source: Editorial Projects in Education Research Center, 2006. www.epe.org/rc

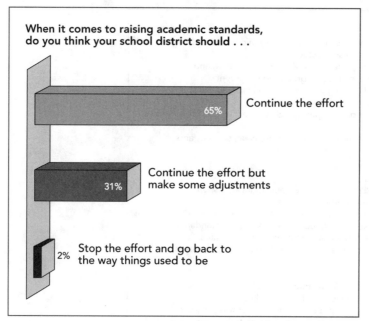

FIGURE 9.3 Data Regarding the Continuation or Termination of Approaches to Raising Standards

Source: Public Agenda, *Reality Check 2006.*

During the 2005–6 school year, Public Agenda, a nonpartisan nonprofit organization, continued its work of expanding community and parent engagement in public education by helping citizens understand important education policy issues. In its *Reality Check 2006* publication, Public Agenda sought to determine if the support for standards-based school initiatives is holding steady or fading. Results of a Public Agenda survey produced the following results depicted in Figures 9.3, 9.4, and 9.5.

The results provided in Figures 9.3 through 9.5 indicate that the vast majority of parents and students continue to support academic standards. A full eight out of ten students say that requiring students to meet higher standards for graduation and promotion is a good idea. Clearly, most parents (86 percent) find their own district to have been "careful and reasonable" in its efforts to raise standards, and virtually none (2 percent) believe that schools would be better if districts returned to the policies of the past. While these perception data provide one important picture of the standards-based accountability terrain, studies have only recently targeted the effectiveness of the standards-based reform movement, and one cannot yet draw accurate conclusions from these initial findings. This brings us to the important topic of assessing the efficacy of standards.

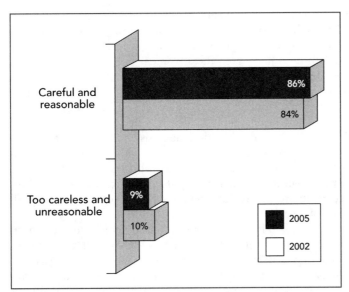

FIGURE 9.4 Data Regarding School Approaches to Raising Standards

Source: Public Agenda, *Reality Check 2006.*

■ PERSPECTIVES ON ASSESSING THE QUALITY AND ALIGNMENT OF STATE STANDARDS

There is no doubt that state and locally developed standards play an important role in American public education. Due to the current reach of standards into the domains of school programs, assessments, and efforts to improve teacher quality, many organizations

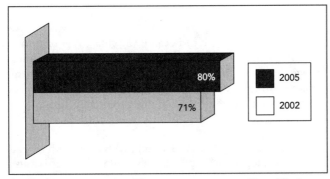

FIGURE 9.5 Student Responses Regarding High Standards

Source: Public Agenda, *Reality Check 2006.*

have begun to research the effects of standards and assess the efficacy of standards in meeting the valued ends of our education system. This section of the chapter highlights the findings of three organizations that have conducted nationwide, state-level assessments of the quality of standards and have rated the alignment between state standards and assessments. These include the American Federation of Teachers, *Education Week*, and the Fordham Foundation.

As will become evident, there are similarities and differences in the findings of organizations that review and assess state standards. Although it is beyond the scope of this chapter to provide a detailed analysis of the evaluation methods employed by each organization, it is important to note that, although there is disagreement among reviewers regarding which states have high-quality and which states have low-quality content standards, there is more agreement than not. That is to say that a comparison of the three reviews produces positive correlations. Before describing the reviews of the three organizations, two points provide helpful background knowledge.

The first is that there is no standard language or model for content standards. This is a product of the fact that standards are developed at the state level. As such, there is considerable difference in terminology, content, and format of state standards. For example, in the domain of terminology, a variety of terms are used to describe expectations for student learning, including standards, goals, outcomes, proficiencies, **curricular frameworks**, and benchmarks. Due to the lack of consensus among state standards, when one reviews standards, one is confronted with an array of documents that vary in terms of language, depth, length, scope, organization, and specificity.

The second point involves the issue of optimal specificity in the design of standards. Specificity is important because standards are meant to delineate the particular content to be covered, and what exactly students should know and be able to do upon interacting with the content. A high degree of specificity allows teachers and principals to compare the school program and student achievement to particular standards. Yet increasing the specificity of standards runs up against the ideal of professional autonomy, natural variations among school interests and teaching strengths, and the desirability of tailoring the curriculum to local needs.

American Federation of Teachers

In 1995 the American Federation of Teachers (AFT) became the first organization to examine state content standards. Between 1995 and 2001, this effort led to the publication of an annual report, *Making Standards Matter*. The most current report on this topic published by the AFT, *Smart Testing: Let's Get It Right* (2006), focuses on two key areas: the strength of state content standards and the alignment of state tests to the content standards.

Assessing the Strength of Content Standards. The AFT examined the strength of state standards along four dimensions. To be judged "strong," a state's content standards must

- be detailed, explicit, and firmly rooted in the content of the subject area to lead to a common core curriculum;

TABLE 9.3 Example of Strong and Weak Standards Based on AFT Criteria

	Strong Standards	Weak Standards
Reading	Students should apply knowledge of word origins, derivations, synonyms, antonyms, and idioms to determine the meaning of words and phrases. *(Grade 4)*	Students should be able to construct meaning through experiences with literature, cultural events, and philosophical discussion. *(No grade level indicated)*
Mathematics	The student will differentiate between area and perimeter and identify whether the application of the concept of perimeter or area is appropriate for a given situation. *(Grade 5)*	Students should become mathematical problem solvers. To develop these abilities, students need the experience of working with diverse problem-solving situations. *(No grade level indicated)*
Science	Students should be able to describe the basic process of photosynthesis and respiration and their importance to life. *(Grade 5)*	Students should be able to use basic science concepts to help understand various kinds of scientific information. *(Upper elementary)*

Source: American Federation of Teachers, (2006). *Smart Testing: Let's Get It Right.* AFT Policy Brief.

- contain particular content that is essential to a solid grasp of the subject area;
- provide attention to both content and skills;
- be articulated for the following individual grades and subjects: math (grades 3 through 8 and once in high school), English (grades 3 through 8 and once in high school); and science (once at each level—elementary, middle, and high school), for a total of seventeen content areas.

The AFT asserts that in general, strong content standards provide clear guidance to teachers, developers of curricular and assessment materials, and textbook publishers regarding the central knowledge and skills students should learn at particular grade levels. For illustrative purposes, Table 9.3 provides examples of standards deemed strong and weak by the AFT. In their analysis, the AFT examined only the standards documents posted on state websites, and in order to be judged as having strong content standards across the board, a state had to meet the AFT criteria in each of the seventeen content standard areas that correlate to NCLB-tested subjects and grades. Table 9.4 depicts the state-by-state content standards that met the AFT criteria for being strong.

As summarized in Table 9.4, here is where the AFT found states to be in 2006 in terms of strength of their content standards.

- A majority of states had content standards in each grade level and subject area required by NCLB.
- More than one-third of states had strong content standards in every grade and subject.

Table 9.4 Content Standards That Meet the AFT Criteria for Being Strong

	Reading							Math							Science*			% of Strong Standards
	3	4	5	6	7	8	hs	3	4	5	6	7	8	hs	e	m	hs	
Alabama	✓	✓	✓				✓	✓	✓	✓	✓	✓	✓	✓	✓	✓	✓	82
Alaska	✓	✓		✓			✓	✓	✓	✓	✓	✓	✓	✓	✓	✓	✓	82
Arizona	✓	✓		✓				✓	✓	✓	✓	✓	✓	✓	✓	✓	✓	76
Arkansas	✓	✓	✓				✓	✓	✓	✓	✓	✓	✓	✓	✓	✓	✓	82
California	✓	✓	✓	✓	✓	✓	✓	✓	✓	✓	✓	✓	✓	✓	✓	✓	✓	100
Colorado						✓									✓		✓	18
Connecticut								✓	✓	✓	✓	✓	✓	✓	✓	✓	✓	59
Delaware								✓	✓	✓	✓	✓	✓	✓	✓	✓	✓	59
District of Columbia	✓	✓	✓	✓	✓	✓	✓	✓	✓	✓	✓	✓	✓	✓	UD	UD	UD	82
Florida	✓	✓						✓	✓	✓	✓	✓	✓	✓	✓	✓	✓	71
Georgia	✓	✓	✓	✓	✓	✓	✓	✓	✓	✓	✓	✓	✓	✓	✓	✓	✓	100
Hawaii								✓	✓	✓	✓	✓	✓	✓	✓	✓	✓	59
Idaho	✓							✓	✓	✓	✓	✓	✓	✓	✓	✓	✓	65
Illinois															✓	✓	✓	18
Indiana	✓	✓	✓	✓	✓	✓	✓	✓	✓	✓	✓	✓	✓	✓	✓	✓	✓	100
Iowa																		0
Kansas								✓	✓	✓	✓	✓	✓	✓	✓	✓	✓	59
Kentucky				✓				✓	✓	✓	✓	✓	✓	✓	✓	✓	✓	65
Louisiana	✓	✓	✓	✓	✓	✓	✓	✓	✓	✓	✓	✓	✓	✓	✓	✓	✓	100
Maine								✓	✓	✓	✓	✓	✓	✓	✓	✓	✓	59
Maryland						✓		✓	✓	✓	✓	✓	✓	✓	✓	✓	✓	65
Massachusetts	✓	✓	✓	✓	✓	✓	✓	✓	✓	✓	✓	✓	✓	✓	✓	✓	✓	100
Michigan	✓	✓	✓	✓	✓	✓	✓	✓	✓	✓	✓	✓	✓	✓	✓	✓	✓	100
Minnesota								✓	✓	✓	✓	✓	✓	✓	✓	✓	✓	59
Mississippi	✓	✓	✓	✓		✓		✓	✓	✓	✓	✓	✓	✓	✓	✓	✓	88
Missouri				✓				✓	✓	✓	✓	✓	✓		✓	✓	✓	59
Montana																✓	✓	12
Nebraska						✓		✓				✓	✓			✓	✓	35
Nevada	✓	✓	✓	✓	✓	✓	✓	✓	✓	✓	✓	✓	✓	✓	✓	✓	✓	100
New Hampshire								✓	✓	✓	✓	✓	✓	✓	UD	UD	UD	41
New Jersey	✓	✓	✓	✓	✓	✓	✓	✓	✓	✓	✓	✓	✓	✓	✓	✓	✓	100
New Mexico	✓	✓	✓	✓	✓	✓	✓	✓	✓	✓	✓	✓	✓	✓	✓	✓	✓	100
New York	✓	✓	✓	✓	✓	✓	✓	✓	✓	✓	✓	✓	✓	✓	✓	✓	✓	100
North Carolina	✓	✓	✓	✓	✓	✓	✓	✓	✓	✓	✓	✓	✓	✓	✓	✓	✓	100
North Dakota	✓	✓	✓	✓	✓	✓	✓	✓	✓	✓	✓	✓	✓	✓	✓	✓	✓	100
Ohio	✓	✓	✓	✓	✓	✓	✓	✓	✓	✓	✓	✓	✓	✓	✓	✓	✓	100
Oklahoma	✓	✓	✓				✓	✓	✓	✓	✓	✓	✓	✓	✓	✓	✓	82
Oregon	✓	✓						✓	✓	✓	✓	✓	✓	✓	✓	✓	✓	76
Pennsylvania	✓							✓	✓	✓	✓	✓	✓	✓	✓	✓	✓	65
Rhode Island								✓	✓	✓	✓	✓	✓	✓	✓	✓	✓	59
South Carolina	✓		✓					✓	✓	✓	✓	✓	✓	✓	✓	✓	✓	71
South Dakota	✓	✓	✓	✓	✓	✓	✓	✓	✓	✓	✓	✓	✓	✓	✓	✓	✓	100
Tennessee	✓	✓	✓	✓	✓	✓	✓	✓	✓	✓	✓	✓	✓	✓	✓	✓	✓	100
Texas								✓	✓	✓	✓	✓	✓	✓	✓	✓	✓	65
Utah				✓	✓	✓		✓	✓	✓	✓	✓	✓	✓	✓	✓	✓	76
Vermont	✓							✓	✓	✓	✓	✓	✓	✓	✓	✓	✓	65
Virginia	✓	✓	✓	✓	✓	✓	✓	✓	✓	✓	✓	✓	✓	✓	✓	✓	✓	100
Washington	✓	✓	✓	✓	✓	✓	✓	✓	✓	✓	✓	✓	✓	✓	✓	✓	✓	100
West Virginia	✓	✓	✓	✓	✓	✓	✓	✓	✓	✓	✓	✓	✓	✓	✓	✓	✓	100
Wisconsin						✓		✓						✓	✓	✓	✓	35
Wyoming	✓	✓	✓	✓	✓	✓	✓			✓	✓	✓			✓	✓	✓	76

UD = under development

* NCLB required states to develop science standards at each of the three grade levels by 2005–6.

Source: American Federation of Teachers. *Smart Testing: Let's Get It Right.* (2006) AFT Policy Brief.

- Of all the content standards reviewed across states in the NCLB-related subjects, 75 percent met the AFT criteria for being strong.
- States had the strongest standards in science, with 95 percent of standards meeting the criteria for being strong.
- States had strong standards in math, with 87 percent of standards meeting the criteria for being strong.
- The weakest content standards were in reading, with just 40 percent of states meeting the criteria for being strong. Of note, 21 percent of reading standards reviewed repeated the same reading standards in three or more grades. This redundancy does not enable teachers or assessment developers to know what is expected of students in reading in sequential grade levels.

Judging the Alignment of Standards and Assessments. In order for a state to determine if students are meeting content standards, assessment tests must sample from the content specified in the standards. Without a degree of alignment between standards and the content of assessments, one is not able to determine accurately the degree to which teachers and schools are helping students master the content contained in the standards. The AFT has reviewed each of the NCLB-related tests administered by a state and has analyzed the degree to which these tests are aligned with state standards. In total, the AFT sample included 861 content-standards documents and information pertaining to 833 state tests across the fifty states and District of Columbia. To meet the AFT criteria for alignment, a state must

- have strong content standards;
- provide evidence of alignment between the standards and assessments for each NCLB-related grade and subject. Evidence included test and item specifications, test blueprints, test development reports, or assessment frameworks;
- post the alignment evidence on the state website in a transparent manner.

This analysis was conducted because while much emphasis has been given to the construction of tests that comply with the NCLB legislation, less attention has been given to the alignment of those tests to standards or to the transparency about which standards are assessed. Table 9.5 provides an overview of the findings regarding test alignment to content standards. Here one notes that many states continue to struggle in aligning their tests with strong content standards, as only eleven states met the AFT criteria for alignment in all subjects and grade levels. By subject, twenty-six states have aligned math tests, twenty-three have aligned science tests, and just thirteen have aligned reading tests across all grades tested. There was also variation in the number of state content standards that specified which particular standards would be assessed by the state. For example, fourteen states specified which math standards would be tested, twelve specified the reading, and ten specified the science standards that would be tested. Of the 833 state-administered tests, 52 percent were based on strong content standards. Specifically, 69 percent of all science tests were based on strong standards, 61 percent of math tests, and 39 percent of reading tests were based on strong standards.

TABLE 9.5 Tests That Meet AFT's Criteria for Being Aligned to Strong Content Standards

	Reading							Math							Science*			% Aligned as Required for NCLB '05–'06
	3	4	5	6	7	8	hs	3	4	5	6	7	8	hs	e	m	hs	
Alabama	✓	✓	✓					✓	✓	✓	✓	✓	✓		UD	UD		60
Alaska	✓	✓		✓		✓		✓	✓	✓	✓	✓	✓	✓	UD	UD	UD	79
Arizona	✓	✓		✓				✓	✓	✓	✓	✓	✓		✓	✓	✓	76
Arkansas															UD	UD	UD	0
California	✓	✓	✓	✓	✓	✓	✓	✓	✓	✓	✓	✓	✓		✓	✓	✓	100
Colorado			✓												✓		✓	18
Connecticut																		0
Delaware																		0
District of Columbia															UD	UD	UD	0
Florida	✓	✓						✓	✓	✓	✓	✓	✓		✓	✓	✓	71
Georgia	✓	✓	✓	✓	✓	✓					✓				UD	UD	✓	60
Hawaii																		0
Idaho								✓	✓	✓	✓	✓	✓	✓	✓			47
Illinois																✓		6
Indiana	✓	✓	✓	✓	✓	✓	✓	✓	✓	✓	✓	✓	✓	✓	✓	✓	UD	100
Iowa																		0
Kansas								✓	✓	✓	✓	✓	✓		✓	✓	✓	59
Kentucky		✓						✓	✓	✓	✓	✓	✓		✓	✓	✓	65
Louisiana	✓	✓	✓	✓	✓	✓	✓	✓	✓	✓	✓	✓	✓		✓	✓	✓	100
Maine																✓		6
Maryland					✓			✓	✓	✓	✓	✓	✓		✓	✓	✓	65
Massachusetts		✓			✓	✓		✓		✓				✓	✓	✓	✓	53
Michigan								✓	✓	✓	✓	✓	✓					35
Minnesota								✓	✓	✓	✓	✓	✓		✓	✓	✓	59
Mississippi	✓	✓	✓	✓		✓		✓	✓	✓	✓	✓	✓		✓	✓	✓	82
Missouri															✓	✓	✓	18
Montana																		0
Nebraska			✓						✓						✓	✓	✓	29
Nevada	✓	✓	✓	✓	✓	✓	✓	✓	✓	✓	✓	✓	✓	✓	✓	✓	✓	100
New Hampshire								✓	✓	✓	✓	✓	✓	✓	UD	UD	UD	50
New Jersey			✓					✓	✓	✓	✓	✓	✓		✓	✓		53
New Mexico	✓	✓	✓	✓	✓	✓	✓	✓	✓	✓	✓	✓	✓		✓	✓	UD	100
New York	✓	✓	✓	✓	✓	✓	✓	✓	✓	✓	✓	✓	✓		✓	✓	✓	100
North Carolina	✓	✓	✓	✓	✓	✓									UD	UD	UD	43
North Dakota															UD	UD	UD	0
Ohio	✓	✓	✓	✓	✓	✓		✓	✓	✓	✓	✓	✓	✓	✓	✓	✓	100
Oklahoma	✓	✓	✓					✓	✓	✓	✓	✓	✓		✓	✓	✓	82
Oregon	✓									✓		✓			✓	✓	✓	76
Pennsylvania	✓		✓						✓		✓				✓	✓	✓	53
Rhode Island								✓	✓	✓	✓	✓	✓	✓	UD	UD	UD	50
South Carolina	✓			✓											UD	UD	✓	20
South Dakota	✓	✓	✓	✓	✓	✓	✓								UD	UD	UD	50
Tennessee	✓	✓	✓	✓	✓	✓	✓	✓	✓	✓	✓	✓	✓		✓	✓	✓	100
Texas						✓		✓	✓	✓	✓	✓	✓		✓	✓	✓	65
Utah								✓	✓	✓	✓	✓	✓		✓	✓	✓	59
Vermont	✓							✓	✓	✓	✓	✓	✓	✓				47
Virginia	✓	✓	✓	✓	✓	✓	✓	✓	✓	✓	✓	✓	✓		✓	✓	✓	100
Washington	✓	✓	✓	✓	✓	✓	✓	✓	✓	✓	✓	✓	✓		✓	✓	✓	100
West Virginia	✓	✓	✓	✓	✓	✓	✓	✓	✓	✓	✓	✓	✓		✓	✓	✓	100
Wisconsin															✓	✓	✓	18
Wyoming																		0

UD = under development

*=Science testing under NCLB isn't required until 2007–8.

Source: American Federation of Teachers. *Smart Testing: Let's Get It Right.* (2006) AFT Policy Brief.

TABLE 9.6 State-by-State Analysis of Alignment between Tests and Strong Content Standards

Percent of State Tests Aligned to Strong Content Standards					
100%	75-99%	50-74%	26-49%	1-25%	0%
1. California	1. Alaska	1. Alabama	1. Idaho	1. Colorado	1. Arkansas
2. Indiana	2. Arizona	2. Florida	2. Michigan	2. Illinois	2. Connecticut
3. Louisiana	3. Mississippi	3. Georgia	3. Nebraska	3. Maine	3. Delaware
4. Nevada	4. Oklahoma	4. Kansas	4. North	4. Missouri	4. District of
5. New Mexico	5. Oregon	5. Kentucky	Carolina	5. South	Columbia
6. New York		6. Maryland	5. Vermont	Carolina	5. Hawaii
7. Ohio		7. Massachusetts		6. Wisconsin	6. Iowa
8. Tennessee		8. Minnesota			7. Montana
9. Virginia		9. New Hampshire			8. North Dakota
10. Washington		10. New Jersey			9. Wyoming
11. West Virginia		11. Pennsylvania			
		12. Rhode Island			
		13. South Dakota			
		14. Texas			
		15. Utah			

Source: American Federation of Teachers. *Smart Testing: Let's Get It Right.* (2006) AFT Policy Brief.

Table 9.6 provides an additional view of state-by-state performance in aligning tests to content standards. Here one sees that eleven states met the criteria for both having strong content standards and documenting in a transparent manner that their tests are aligned with the standards in each of the NCLB-required grades and subjects. Thirty-one states were at least halfway along in terms of providing evidence of alignment between assessments and strong standards. The states that had the lowest percentage of alignment fell short either by not providing test documents online or by failing to demonstrate alignment between tests and standards in a transparent manner, particularly in reading. With 74 percent of content standards across states being strong, but with only 52 percent of tests aligned to strong standards, the AFT concludes that states are doing a better job in developing content standards than in using them to drive aligned assessment. In nearly half the cases, testing unaligned to strong standards was driving accountability systems in our nation. As such, it is important for state, district, and school leaders to assess the quality of pertinent state standards and assessments and work toward enhanced alignment and cohesion between these important components of the academic program.

Education Week

Each year since 1997, *Education Week* had published *Quality Counts* to help monitor state progress in adopting the core elements of standards-based reform. The information for this report is gathered primarily from surveys conducted by the Editorial Projects in Education Research Center. The four domains of standards-based reform that the *Quality*

Counts report focuses on include establishing standards for what students should know and be able to do, aligning assessments to those standards, implementing accountability measures, and providing supports to improve teacher quality. You will recall that the indicators for these four domains are provided in Figure 9.2. Using the ten indicators for standards and assessments listed in Figure 9.2, each state is assessed on a scale of 1 to 10. Of the composite score, 40 percent of the grade is determined by a state's performance in the realm of standards, 30 percent is determined by the types of assessments used, and the remaining 30 percent is determined by the degree of alignment between standards and assessments. Scores for each of the fifty states are provided on each of these components in Tables 9.7, 9.8, and 9.9, respectively.

In each of these three tables we find data that both align with the review conducted by the AFT and provide an alternate assessment. One primary reason for such disparities involves different criteria used to measure the degree to which standards are "strong," "clear," and "aligned." For example, the AFT requirement that both standards and assessments be posted on websites in order to be considered aligned is not a criterion in the *Quality Counts* approach. This is but one factor in the differences between the AFT and *Education Week* assessments of the percentage of states with tests aligned with standards. The two approaches also tackle the issue at different levels of disaggregation. For example, AFT conducted a grade-by-grade analysis, while the *Quality Counts* report lists results aggregated at the elementary, middle, and high school levels.

The Fordham Foundation

In 2006, the Fordham Foundation, which is a research and advocacy organization, conducted an analysis of state academic standards. The 2006 report was the first comprehensive review of this topic since 2000, just before Congress enacted NCLB. In 2000, the Fordham Foundation found the average grade for state academic standards across all subjects to be a C-minus. The 2006 report contends that while thirty-seven states have upgraded their state standards in at least one NCLB-related subject area since 2000, the overall quality of state academic standards is still mediocre, with a national average of C-minus and with two-thirds of the nation's K–12 students attending schools in states with standards rated C, D, or F. The Fordham Foundation examined state standards in five subjects: language arts, mathematics, science, U.S. history, and world history. In each domain, reviewers scored standards regarding the degree to which they were clear, rigorous, and right-headed about content. Between 2000 and 2006, the Fordham Foundation found math standards generally worsened, while language arts standards generally improved, with science and history standards staying the same. During this time span, the four states that significantly improved their standards were Indiana, New York, Georgia, and New Mexico. Additionally, the five states that made the least progress include Utah, Nebraska, New Hampshire, and Wisconsin. The 2006 review produced perfect scores for three states: Indiana, California, and Massachusetts. Table 9.10 provides a summary of the Fordham Foundation ratings of state content standards in 2006.

Comparison of the data provided by the Fordham Foundation in Table 9.10 yields both similarities and differences to other approaches to evaluating standards. Again, one

TABLE 9.7 *Quality Counts* Scores for State Standards

	Overall Grade for Standards and Accountability		State Has Adopted Standards in the Core Subjects (2005-06)	State Has Standards That Are Clear, Specific, and Grounded in Content (2005)				State Has a Regular Timeline for Revising Standards (2005-06)
				English/ Language Arts	Mathematics	Science	Social Studies/ History	
Louisiana	A	98	✓	ES MS HS	ES MS HS	ES MS HS	MS HS	✓
New York	A	97	✓	ES MS HS	ES MS HS	ES MS HS	ES MS HS	
Massachusetts	A	96	✓	ES MS HS	ES MS HS	ES MS HS	ES MS HS	
South Carolina	A	96	✓	ES MS HS	ES MS HS	ES MS HS	ES MS HS	✓
Indiana	A	95	✓	ES MS HS	ES MS HS	ES MS HS	ES MS HS	✓
Florida	A	94	✓	ES MS HS	ES MS HS	ES MS HS	ES HS	✓
New Mexico	A	94	✓	ES MS HS	ES MS HS	ES MS HS	MS HS	✓
West Virginia	A	94	✓	ES MS HS	ES MS HS	ES MS HS	MS HS	✓
Maryland	A−	92	✓	ES MS HS	ES MS HS	ES MS HS	MS HS	✓
Georgia	A−	91	✓	ES MS HS	ES MS HS	ES MS HS	MS HS	✓
Ohio	A−	90	✓	ES MS HS	ES MS HS	ES MS HS	MS HS	
Oklahoma	B+	89	✓	ES MS HS	ES MS HS	ES MS HS	HS	✓
California	B+	89	✓	ES MS HS	ES MS HS	ES MS HS	ES MS HS	
Kentucky	B+	89	✓		ES MS HS	ES MS HS	MS HS	
Illinois	B+	88	✓	ES MS HS	ES MS HS	ES MS HS	MS HS	
Hawaii	B+	87	✓	ES MS HS	ES MS HS	ES MS HS	MS HS	✓
Delaware	B+	87	✓	ES MS	ES MS HS	ES MS HS	MS HS	
New Jersey	B+	87	✓	ES MS HS	ES MS HS	ES MS HS	MS HS	✓
Colorado	B	86	✓	ES MS HS	ES MS HS	ES MS HS	MS	✓
Virginia	B	85	✓	ES MS HS	ES MS HS	ES MS	ES MS HS	✓
Michigan	B	85	✓	ES MS	ES MS HS	ES MS HS		
North Carolina	B	84	✓	ES MS HS	ES MS HS	ES MS HS	HS	✓
Idaho	B	84	✓	ES MS HS	ES MS HS	ES MS HS	HS	
Alabama	B	84	✓	ES	ES MS HS	ES MS	MS HS	✓
Tennessee	B	84	✓	ES MS	ES MS HS	ES MS	ES MS	
Washington	B	83	✓	ES	ES MS HS	ES MS HS		✓
Arizona	B	83	✓	ES MS HS	ES MS HS	ES MS HS	ES MS HS	
Vermont	B−	82	✓	ES MS HS	ES MS HS	ES MS HS		✓
Wisconsin	B−	82	✓	ES MS HS	ES MS HS			
Pennsylvania	B−	81	✓	ES MS HS	ES MS HS	ES MS HS	ES MS HS	✓
Nevada	B−	81	✓	ES MS HS	ES MS HS	MS HS	MS HS	✓
South Dakota	B−	81	✓	ES MS HS	ES MS HS	ES MS HS	ES HS	✓
Connecticut	B−	80	✓		ES MS HS	ES MS HS	MS	
Texas	B−	80	✓	ES HS	ES MS HS	ES MS		✓
Arkansas	C+	78	✓	ES MS	ES MS HS	ES MS HS		✓
Oregon	C+	78	✓	ES MS HS	ES MS HS	ES MS HS	MS HS	✓
Mississippi	C+	78	✓	ES MS	ES MS HS	ES MS		✓
Minnesota	C+	77	✓	ES MS HS	ES MS HS	ES MS HS	MS HS	✓
Utah	C+	77	✓	ES MS HS	ES MS HS	ES MS HS	ES HS	✓
District of Columbia	C+	77	✓	ES MS HS	ES MS HS	ES MS HS	HS	
Rhode Island	C	75	3 Subjects		ES MS HS	ES MS HS		
Maine	C	74	✓	MS HS	ES	ES MS HS		✓
Kansas	C	74	✓	ES MS HS	ES MS HS	ES MS HS	MS HS	✓
New Hampshire	C	73	✓	MS	ES MS HS	ES MS HS	MS HS	✓
North Dakota	C−	72	✓	ES MS	ES MS HS	ES MS HS		✓
Alaska	C−	71	✓		ES MS HS	ES MS HS		
Missouri	D+	69	✓		ES MS HS	ES MS HS	MS HS	
Nebraska	D	66	✓	HS	ES MS HS	ES MS HS	MS HS	
Wyoming	D	65	✓		ES MS HS			✓
Montana	D	63	✓			MS HS		✓
Iowa	F	33						
U.S.	−	−	49	−	−	−	−	32

Source: Education Week. Quality Counts, 2006. Editorial Projects in Education

TABLE 9.8 Types of Assessments

Assessments [30% of Grade]		
Types of Statewide Tests Required (2005-06)[1] Aligned to State Standards		
Test Custom-Designed to Match State Standards (CRT)	Augmented/ Hybrid Test	Off-the-Shelf/ Norm-Referenced Test (NRT)
✓	✓	
✓		
✓		
✓		
✓		
✓		✓
✓		✓
✓		✓
✓	✓	✓
✓		✓
✓		
✓		
✓	✓	✓
✓	✓	
✓	✓	
	✓	
✓		
✓		✓
✓		
✓		
✓		
✓	✓	✓
✓		
✓	✓	✓
✓	✓	
✓		
✓		✓
✓		
✓		
✓		
✓	✓	✓
✓		
✓		
✓		✓
✓		✓
✓	✓	✓
✓		
✓		✓
✓		
✓		✓
✓	✓	
✓		✓
✓		
✓		
	✓	
✓	✓	✓
	✓	
✓		
✓		
✓		✓
		✓
44	**13**	**18**

Source: Education Week. Quality Counts, 2006. Editorial Projects in Education.

TABLE 9.9 Alignment of Standards and Assessments

Alignment [30% of Grade]					
	Subject in Which State Uses Assessments Aligned to State Standards (2005-06)				State Standards-Based Tests Have Undergone an External Alignment Review Since 2001 (2005-06)
	English/ Language Arts	Mathematics	Science	Social Studies/ History	
LA	ES MS HS	ES MS HS	ES MS HS	ES MS HS	✓
NY	ES MS HS	ES MS HS	ES MS HS	ES MS HS	
MA	ES MS HS	ES MS HS	ES MS HS		✓
SC	ES MS HS	ES MS HS	ES MS HS	ES MS	✓
IN	ES MS HS	ES MS HS	ES MS		✓
FL	ES MS HS	ES MS HS	ES MS HS		in process
NM	ES MS HS	ES MS HS	ES MS HS		✓
WV	ES MS HS	ES MS HS	ES MS HS	ES MS	✓
MD	ES MS HS	ES MS HS	HS	HS	✓
GA	ES MS HS	ES MS HS	ES MS HS	ES MS HS	✓
OH	ES MS HS	ES MS HS	HS	HS	
OK	ES MS HS	ES MS HS	ES MS HS	ES MS HS	
CA	ES MS HS	ES MS HS	ES MS HS	MS HS	✓
KY	ES MS HS	ES MS HS	ES MS HS	ES MS HS	in process
IL	ES MS HS	ES MS HS	ES MS HS		✓
HI	ES MS HS	ES MS HS			
DE	ES MS HS	ES MS HS	ES MS HS	ES MS HS	✓
NJ	ES MS HS	ES MS HS	ES MS		✓
CO	ES MS HS	ES MS HS	ES MS HS		✓
VA	ES MS HS	ES MS HS	ES MS HS	ES MS HS	✓
MI	ES MS HS	ES MS HS	ES MS HS	MS HS	✓
NC	ES MS HS	ES MS HS	HS	HS	
ID	ES MS HS	ES MS HS			✓
AL	ES MS HS	ES MS HS	HS	HS	✓
TN	ES MS HS	ES MS HS	ES MS HS	ES MS HS	
WA	ES MS HS	ES MS HS	ES MS HS		✓
AZ	ES MS HS	ES MS HS			✓
VT	ES MS HS	ES MS HS			
WI	ES MS HS	ES MS HS	ES MS HS	ES MS HS	✓
PA	ES MS HS	ES MS HS			✓
NV	ES MS HS	ES MS HS	ES MS		
SD	ES MS HS	ES MS HS	ES MS HS	ES MS HS	✓
CT	ES MS HS	ES MS HS	HS		
TX	ES MS HS	ES MS HS	ES MS HS	MS HS	
AR	ES MS HS	ES MS HS			
OR	ES MS HS	ES MS HS	ES MS HS		✓
MS	ES MS HS	ES MS HS	HS	HS	✓
MN	ES MS HS	ES MS HS			✓
UT	ES MS HS	ES MS HS	ES MS HS		
DC	ES MS HS	ES MS HS			✓
RI	ES MS HS	ES MS HS			
ME	ES MS	ES MS	ES MS		
KS	ES MS HS	ES MS HS			
NH	ES MS HS	ES MS HS			
ND	ES MS HS	ES MS HS			
AK	ES MS HS	ES MS HS			✓
MO	ES MS HS	ES MS HS			✓
NE	ES MS HS				
WY	ES MS HS	ES MS HS			✓
MT	ES MS HS	ES MS HS			✓
IA					
U.S.	–	–	–	–	31

Source: Education Week. Quality Counts, 2006. Editorial Projects in Education.

TABLE 9.10 Fordham Foundation 2006 Ranking of State Standards across All Subjects

State	English	Math	Science	U.S. History	World History	Cum. GPA	Overall Grade	Rank	Rank (2000 Rank)
California	A	A	A	A	A	4.00	A	1	1 (1)
Indiana	A	A	A	A	A	4.00	A	1	1 (10)
Massachusetts	A	A	A	A	A	4.00	A	1	1 (8)
New York	B	C	A	A	A	3.40	B+	4	4 (21)
Georgia	B	B	B	B	A	3.20	B+	5	5 (21)
Virginia	B	C	A	B	A	3.20	B+	5	5 (10)
Arizona	B	C	B	A	B	3.00	B	7	7 (2)
South Carolina	B	D	A	C	A	2.80	B−	8	8 (3)
Alabama	A	B	F	A	C	2.60	B−	9	9 (5)
Minnesota	B	D	B	F	A	2.20	C+	10	10 (39)
Louisiana	A	C	B	D	F	2.00	C+	11	11 (14)
Maryland	C	C	B	C	D	2.00	C+	11	11 (10)
Oklahoma	C	C	F	B	B	2.00	C+	11	11 (21)
Illinois	B	C	B	F	D	1.80	C−	14	14 (26)
Nevada	B	C	D	C	D	1.80	C−	14	14 (14)
New Jersey	C	D	B	F	B	1.80	C−	14	14 (29)
New Mexico	D	B	A	F	D	1.80	C−	14	14 (47)
Texas	B	C	F	C	C	1.80	C−	14	14 (3)
West Virginia	C	C	B	F	C	1.80	C−	14	14 (14)
Colorado	C	D	B	D	D	1.60	C−	20	20 (29)
Delaware	C	F	C	B	D	1.60	C−	20	29 (14)
Kansas	C	F	F	B	B	1.60	C−	20	20 (14)
North Carolina	B	C	B	F	F	1.60	C−	20	20 (5)
South Dakota	B	C	D	D	D	1.60	C−	20	20 (8)
Tennessee	D	D	B	C	D	1.60	C−	20	20 (47)
Ohio	C	D	B	D	F	1.40	D+	26	26 (20)
Utah	C	D	C	C	F	1.40	D+	26	26 (10)
Rhode Island	C	F	C	*	*	1.33	D+	28	28 (34)
D.C.	C	D	C	F	D	1.20	D+	29	29 (7)
Mississippi	B	D	F	F	C	1.20	D+	29	29 (21)
Nebraska	C	D	F	C	D	1.20	D+	29	29 (14)
Idaho	B	D	F	D	F	1.00	D	32	32 (NA)
Kentucky	C	C	D	F	F	1.00	D	32	32 (38)
North Dakota	C	C	D	F	F	1.00	D	32	32 (47)
Oregon	B	D	F	D	F	1.00	D	32	32 (29)
Pennsylvania	C	D	C	F	F	1.00	D	32	32 (34)
Vermont	C	D	C	F	F	1.00	D	32	32 (36)
Michigan	D	C	D	F	F	0.80	D−	38	38 (39)
Maine	C	D	D	F	F	0.80	D−	38	38 (36)
Missouri	C	F	C	F	F	0.80	D−	38	38 (29)
New Hampshire	B	F	F	F	D	0.80	D−	38	38 (26)
Arkansas	C	F	D	F	F	0.60	D−	42	42 (45)
Connecticut	F	F	C	D	F	0.60	D−	42	42 (29)
Florida	C	F	F	D	F	0.60	D−	42	42 (21)
Washington	F	F	C	F	D	0.60	D−	42	42 (39)
Wisconsin	C	D	F	F	F	0.60	D−	42	42 (26)
Alaska	D	D	F	F	F	0.60	F	47	47 (42)
Hawaii	C	F	F	F	F	0.40	F	47	47 (44)
Montana	F	D	F	F	F	0.20	F	49	49 (43)
Wyoming	F	F	F	F	F	0.00	F	50	50 (45)
AVG. 2006	**C+**	**D+**	**C−**	**D+**	**D+**	**1.59**	**C−**	*	*
AVG. 2000	**C−**	**C**	**C**	**D+**	*	**1.72**	**C−**	*	*

Source: Finn, C. E., Jr., Petrilli, M. I., & Julian, L. (2006), *The State of State Standards 2006*, Washington, D.C.: Thomas B. Fordham Foundation, www.edexcellence.net/institute.

contributor to these disparities is the unique criteria and foci of different reviews. For example, the AFT emphasized clarity as a hallmark of solid standards, while the Fordham Foundation focused on content. Fordham reviewers sought to determine the extent to which states have identified a suitable body of knowledge and skills for students to master at a given grade level. While the Fordham Foundation analyzed standards along a variety of dimensions, for sake of comparison, the criteria for assessing the *quality* of state language arts standards are provided below.

- They are clear and specific.
- They are measurable (i.e., they can lead to observable, comparable results across students and schools).
- They are of increasing intellectual difficulty at each higher educational level and cover all important aspects of learning in the area they address.
- They index or illustrate growth through the grades for reading by referring to specific reading levels or to titles of specific literary or academic works as examples of a reading level.
- They illustrate growth expected through the grades for writing with reference to examples and rating criteria, either in the standards document or in other documents.
- Their overall contents are sufficiently specific, comprehensive, and demanding to lead to a common core of high academic expectations for all students in the state.

The Fordham Foundation contends that solid standards are the foundation upon which modern education reform rests. As such, good standards matter very much. The current analysis of state standards conducted by Fordham contends that states fall short for four main reasons.

- Consensus instead of vision. The committee approach to creating standards leads to unclear writing and educational confusion.
- The absence of real expertise. The inclusion of university-level subject matter experts in the development of standards would raise the content quality of standards.
- The persistent influence of 1990s-era national standards. Standards developed by organizations such as the National Councils of Teachers of Mathematics and English are not appropriate for modern state content standards.
- Myopic perspective. States should look beyond their own borders and learn from the outstanding standards developed by other states.

This cursory overview of data available from three recent efforts aimed at assessing the quality of state standards and the degree of alignment between standards and assessments most definitely invokes more questions than answers. Among other benefits, this debate clarifies the multiple perspectives a modern education leader must consider in order to have a thorough understanding of the standards terrain, which plays a formidable role in what is taught, what is tested, and how rewards and sanctions are levied. In the foreseeable future, there will likely be a variety of approaches to assessing the quality and alignment of standards and assessments. Ratings aside, standards matter because they are a dominant component of the educational landscape in American education. With the eminent reauthorization of NCLB in 2009, the role of standards-based accountability, and thus the consequence of quality standards aligned to assessments, is likely to persist in the future. Education leaders can act strategically to the benefit of school programs and student performance by facilitating alignment between high-quality state standards, assessments, and the local instructional program.

  CASE 6 REVISITED

> To what degree can pay-for-performance serve as a vehicle to enhance the alignment between state standards, assessments, and the instructional program? What are potential negative consequences of such change?

■ APPROACHES TO ENHANCING SCHOOL PROGRAMS

The previous section dealt with the important topic of state standards and the alignment of those standards to state-level assessments. Although it is imperative for school leaders to understand how state standards are constructed, rated, and assessed for alignment to state tests, an equally critical domain of knowledge and skill for school leaders occurs at the intersection of these statewide realities and the curriculum and instruction enacted in schools. State standards and assessments provide benchmarks and an accountability structure, while the instructional program serves as the vehicle responsible for ensuring student learning. This section of the chapter will focus on several school-level approaches to enhancing school programs. Specifically, this section deals with the issue of alignment between facets of the school program and state standards, provides insight about the use of instructional time in schools, and recognizes the importance of considering cultural diversity in the school program.

■ INTERSECTION OF K–12 PROGRAMS AND POSTSECONDARY EDUCATION

The transition between the compulsory world of K–12 education and either further education or entry into the workforce marks an important gateway in the life of every student. As evidenced in Figure 9.6, a growing number of students predict that they will graduate from high school and complete some form of postsecondary education. This trend in college aspirations is found among students in all ethnic/racial groups as well as within each socioeconomic status (SES). This is encouraging news, as the benefits of attending college are substantial. According to the U.S. Department of Labor, these include enhanced employment opportunities, greater adaptability to shifting labor and workplace demands, and higher earning potential, as depicted in Figure 9.7.

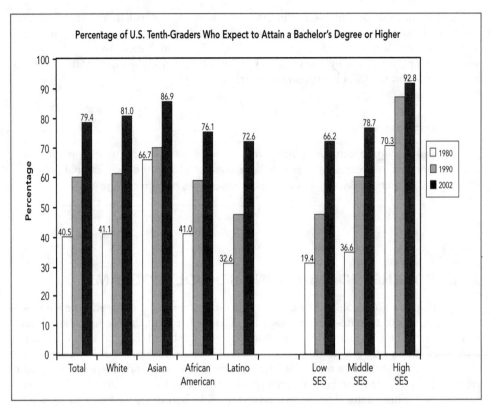

FIGURE 9.6 Student Expectations Regarding Postsecondary Educational Attainment

Source: U.S. Department of Education (2004)

While Figures 9.6 and 9.7 point to a recognition of the value of continued educational attainment and provide validation of the rewards of such attainment, currently too many students in our country are dropping out of the education pipeline. Figure 9.8 depicts a discouraging national picture. For example, a full third of the students who enter high school in our nation do not graduate. For several ethnic/racial groups, as well as lower socioeconomic groups, these dropout percentages can be as high as 50 percent. Of the students who enroll in college immediately following high school, only half will graduate college on time.

The picture portrayed in Figure 9.8 is especially troubling given the global economic shifts impacting our nation's workforce. The "flattening" of the world, explained in detail by Thomas Friedman in his book *The World Is Flat*, has serious implications for the kinds of knowledge and skills that will be required of citizens of the United States in order to

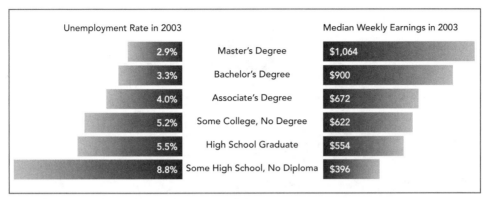

FIGURE 9.7 Influence of Educational Attainment on Unemployment and Earnings

Source: Bureau of Labor Statistics
Note: Earnings are for workers 25 and older for full-time wage and salary positions.

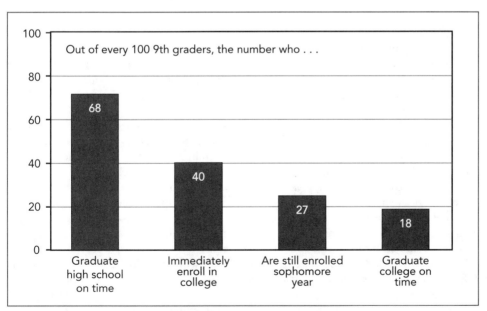

FIGURE 9.8 Student Trends in the Education Pipeline

Source: National Center for Public Policy and Higher Education, Policy Alert, April 2004.

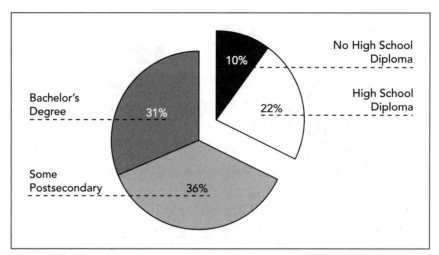

FIGURE 9.9 **Educational Requirements of New Jobs in the United States**

Source: Materials selected from "Standards for what? The economic roots of K–16 reform," Educational Testing Service, 2003. Reprinted by permission of Educational Testing Service, the copyright owner.

maintain a competitive edge in the global marketplace. The increased competition that results from a flattened world will only make the cut-out portion of the pie chart in Figure 9.9 smaller. This reinforces the tremendous importance of our nation's high school students being prepared to succeed in postsecondary education and the evolving workplace.

A critical issue, then, involves the degree to which high school students are prepared for college and the workforce. While nearly all education leaders are familiar with the *achievement* gaps that persist in our nation, more are beginning to focus on the *expectation* gap as well. In many states there is a large gap between what high schools expect of graduates and what colleges and employers demand. In order to address this important issue of alignment between high school policies and requirements for college and the workforce, a group of national governors and business leaders have established Achieve, Inc. Achieve is a bipartisan, nonprofit organization that helps states raise academic standards, improve assessments, and strengthen accountability to prepare all young people for postsecondary education, work, and productive citizenship. Along with forty-five governors, corporate CEOs, and K–12 and postsecondary leaders, Achieve has established the American Diploma Project Network—a coalition committed to aligning high school standards, assessments, graduation requirements, and accountability systems with the demands of college and the workplace. Achieve recently conducted a study of all fifty states along these dimensions, and the results are provided in Table 9.11.

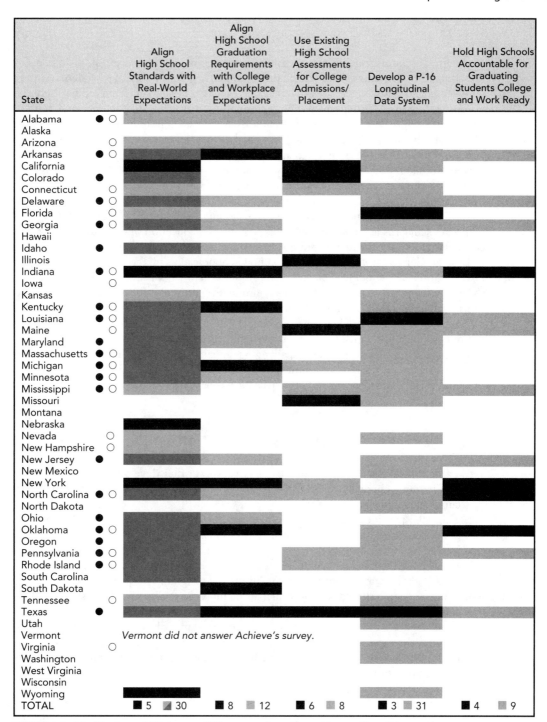

TABLE 9.11 National Picture of Expectation Gap Along Key Dimensions

▪ Policy in place   ▪ Plans to implement   ▪ In process of aligning standards

Source: Achieve survey results, 2006, www.achieve.org.

Summary

In the life of schools, the importance of the instructional program cannot be denied. Interaction with elements of the school program is the primary way that students acquire knowledge and skills. It is imperative that school leaders understand the increasingly important role played by federal policy, as exemplified by *A Nation at Risk* and the No Child Left Behind Act. The current standards-based accountability context is the result of federal influence. As a result of federal legislation, states have been required to articulate content standards for math, reading, and science. The efficacy with which states have undertaken this task varies widely, as noted by assessments of state standards conducted by the American Federation of Teachers, *Education Week*, and the Fordham Foundation.

A critical task for education leaders entails the alignment of local instructional programs with state standards and assessments. This requires the collection of data surrounding how curricular units are constructed and how content is taught. Approaches such as the Surveys of Enacted Curriculum provide insight on how school leaders might approach this complex task. Additionally, school leaders are in a position to help school communities grapple with the important issues of academic time and cultural diversity, as both have significant implications for the quality of educational environments. While attuned to these issues within the school program, school leaders must also understand the importance of preparing students not only to meet standards, but to be prepared for postsecondary education and the workforce. Each of these tasks represents challenging domains of leadership practice, and each directly influences the current and future lives of children and society, thus underscoring the imperative for capable, committed principals for our nation's schools.

Discussion Questions

1. Table 9. 1 compares the United States to several other developed nations in terms of a national curriculum and exam. Describe the pros and cons of having a national curriculum and a national exam.
2. Table 9.2 provides examples of policies set at the state and local level. Choose one policy set at the state level, and provide a rationale for why it would be preferable for it to be set at the local level.
3. From your experience, articulate one positive and one negative consequence that NCLB has had upon your school's instructional program.
4. To what degree should school principals be involved in ongoing discussion and decisions about state and local standards? Teachers?
5. From Figure 9.2, which of the four indicators of standards-based policy implementation has the most immediate impact on enhancing programmatic quality and elevating student performance? Which do you think has the potential to make the most enduring impact on these desired outcomes?
6. What would your responses be to the questions asked in Figures 9.3, 9.4 and 9.5?
7. Based on Tables 9.4 to 9.10, how does your state compare to neighboring states regarding high-quality standards and alignment between standards and assessments?

What recent initiatives have targeted any local or statewide deficiencies in these domains?

8. Figures 9.6 to 9.9 provide data regarding educational aspirations and attainment and link these outcomes with financial realities. Do you think school programs have kept pace with the needs of society? Who is being left behind? In what ways could school programs become more powerful preparation agents for helping students meet new social and economic realities?

9. What do you think will be your biggest challenge in meeting ELCC Standard 2, which emphasizes the stewardship of an effective instructional program?

References and Suggested Readings

Friedman, T. L. (2005). *The world is flat: A brief history of the twenty-first century*. New York: Farrar, Straus and Giroux.

Goodlad, J. I. (1984). *A place called school: Prospects for the future*. New York: McGraw-Hill.
    Based on *A Study of Schooling*, one of the most extensive on-the-scene educational investigations ever conducted, this report provides suggestions for significant improvement to American schools, beginning with the premise that they must be redesigned piece by piece and taking into consideration all aspects of schooling.

Jennings, J. F. (Ed.). (1993). *National issues in education: The past is prologue*. Bloomington, IN, and Washington, D.C.: Phi Delta Kappa International and the Institute for Educational Leadership.
    This volume, one in a series, seeks to present diverse perspectives on current major education issues at the national level, particularly as these issues have played out in the legislative process of the U.S. Congress. It focuses in particular on the continuity of the legislative and policy-making process and the impact of earlier discussions and debates on current education issues.

Jennings, J. F., Ed. (1995). *National issues in education: Goals 2000 and school-to-work*. Bloomington, IN, and Washington, D.C.: Phi Delta Kappa International and the Institute for Educational Leadership.
    This volume, another in a series, traces the Goals 2000: Educate America Act and School-to-Work Opportunities Act as they proceeded through the U.S. Congress and features essays that illuminate the policy-making process by explaining the development of important new national policies and by recounting the history of these two seminal pieces of legislation.

Lightfoot, S. L. (1983). *The good high school*. New York: Basic Books.
    In this book, Lightfoot, a prominent educator, provides vivid in-depth portraits of six exemplary American high schools that tell the reader something about the myriad definitions of educational success and how it is achieved.

Olson, L. (1988). Inside *A Nation at Risk*. *Education Week*, April 27.

Wong, K. K. (1999*). Funding public schools : Politics and policies*. Lawrence, KS: University Press of Kansas.

Notes

1. Public laws are numbered through a code. The first digits represent the Congress in which the law was enacted. The second digits represent the sequence in which the statute became law in that Congress. For example, the originally enacted Elementary and Secondary Education Act was Public Law 89-10. This denotes its being the tenth statute enacted by the eighty-ninth Congress.
2. Center on Education Policy (2002). *From the Capital to the Classroom: State and Federal Efforts to Implement the No Child Left Behind Act* (Washington, D.C.: Author, 2002).
3. Jennings, J., and Rentner, D. S. (2006), Ten big effects of the No Child Left Behind Act on public schools, *Phi Delta Kappan, 88*(2), 110-113.

CHAPTER TEN

Performance

LEARNING OBJECTIVES

By the end of this chapter, you should be able to

- identify varying approaches to assessing the performance of K–12 school students;
- comprehend mechanisms for assessing the performance of education leaders;
- engage with issues associated with evaluating school effectiveness;
- comprehend value-added performance measures;
- utilize national and international perspectives on educational performance.

Since the latter part of the twentieth century, the nation's K–12 public school system has been moving toward widespread adoption of standards and accountability strategies such as those vividly symbolized in the No Child Left Behind Act. Whereas the United States once routinely appraised schools by resources consumed, contemporary school performance increasingly is judged by learning produced. This important shift in American education to an outcome-based orientation is influencing the perspective and actions of education policy makers; state, district, and school officials; and parents. Yet to date, this performance orientation has failed to penetrate fully into the education profession.

The No Child Left Behind Act, along with many state accountability systems, contains sanctions for sustained low-performing schools. However, there are few incentives or disincentives for classroom instructors or school leaders to be judged by their performance in facilitating student academic achievement. Indeed, education is the largest single professional undertaking still devoid of significant performance rewards. Even government civil service workers increasingly come under modern performance-appraisal schemes. The lack of a performance orientation in education continues, although much is at stake. The direct financial cost of paying America's public-school teachers approaches $2 billion per school day, a figure that has been increasing faster than general price inflation for more than fifty years. On top of these dollars are the benefits that might accrue to students and societies if teacher expenditures were allocated in a more effective manner. Nevertheless, for now, the education system's quest for elevated outcomes, higher academic standards, enhanced instruction, practical **performance incentives**, and greater cost effectiveness has moved accountability and performance assessment from the periphery of concern and influence to a far more central role.

Current and future education leaders will likely operate within the context of an outcome-based accountability environment. Therefore, it is imperative that strategic education leaders have a solid understanding of various approaches to assessing the performance of students, teachers, principals, and schools.[1] Within this realm, school leaders also must be informed about the challenges and benefits associated with value-added performance measures, performance-based compensation models, and national and international comparisons of educational performance. The provision of such knowledge is the aim of this chapter.

Before jumping in, however, consider the following scenario. Although the summer Olympics are still two years away, Joe Spitz spots a posting at his high school about an upcoming talent development program for Olympic-hopeful swimmers. Though he has no relation to Olympic record holder Mark Spitz, Joe does enjoy swimming and has done a reasonable job of trying to stay in shape. So he decides to show up at the designated YMCA, sporting his favorite swimming trunks, in order to pursue his new dream of following his namesake to Olympic glory. As he nonchalantly strolls out to the pool deck, he is greeted by a swarm of very determined-looking kids wearing Speedos and nervous parents carrying clipboards and sporting stopwatches. At the sign-in desk, Joe is greeted by a very fit, middle-aged woman who is wearing what Joe thinks is an Olympic medal. She tells Joe that as a preliminary step, she will need to review his swimming stats. Joe sheepishly tells her that he does not have any. In fact, he did not even know what swimming stats were, unless they were what all the kids were wearing on their heads. Not knowing what to say next, he tells the woman that he is in pretty good shape, weighs only 105 pounds, and is really fast on his bike. To this, she pats him on the back and points out a swimmer in the far lane of the pool. She tells Joe that that Olympic hopeful is Suzie and that her swimming stats include a split time of 27 seconds on the 4×100, a resting heart rate of 54 beats per minute, a body fat composition of 12 percent, a tidal lung volume of 207 cc's, the ability to hold her breath underwater for 95 seconds at a heart rate 100 percent above the resting rate, a water resistance profile in the ninety-sixth percentile, and an average reflex time off the block of 0.42 seconds. With that, Joe slowly backs away from the sign-in booth but is comforted when he remembers another poster that he saw hanging at school—something about an intramural league developing, with no experience required.

■ ASSESSING THE PERFORMANCE OF STUDENTS

The No Child Left Behind Act created new standards of accountability that seek to increase the performance of all students. The ripple effect of this legislation has been felt at all levels of educational practice. On an annual basis, schools are now required by federal law to assess students in grades 3 through 8 in reading and mathematics, and in three grade levels in science, in order to determine the degree to which schools are making Adequate Yearly Progress (AYP). The ultimate performance target used to create AYP **benchmarks** is for all students to be proficient by the end of the 2013–14 school year. In order for a school to make AYP toward this ultimate goal, it must meet proficiency targets for *every* subgroup represented in the school and in *every* subject tested. Schools that consistently fail to meet these targets are sanctioned by experiencing federally imposed fiscal consequences and the prospect of losing students to available school choice options.

┌─┐
└─┘ CASE 5 REVISITED ───────────────────────────────────────

One of the most beneficial components of NCLB for Frank Gomez was the requirement to take a disaggregated view of student achievement. This illuminated achievement gaps between student subgroups, often along demographic lines. What story does disaggregated student data at your school tell? How can school leaders utilize this data to ensure that the needs of *all* students are being met?

This new era of educational accountability demands that assessments be capable of measuring student performance in attaining academic standards, informing educators' instructional practices, and determining the assignment of sanctions. Given the importance of these purposes, assessments should accurately reflect the work of students, educators, and school leaders in achieving federal and state academic standards. In light of the new accountability requirements, the question undoubtedly emerges as to whether existing assessments are capable of meeting these demands. To ensure this, one must understand the degree to which assessments are capable of measuring student attainment of academic standards and providing educators with information to make judgments regarding student performance. Given the central role of student performance in the current accountability context, it is important to understand the characteristics and uses of existing assessments of academic achievement. Toward that end, this chapter section will discuss several types of student assessments available to educators and highlight selected technical issues associated with assessing student performance.

Types of Student Assessments

Fortunately there are many ways to assess student performance; a single test, or a single type of test, certainly would miss the multipurpose nature of assessment in educational accountability. For example, externally derived achievement tests may be unable to measure the academic content and curriculum covered during a particular classroom unit, while classroom-based tests may be unable to assess systematically what students should know and be able to do concerning a specific academic standard. When utilized in concert, the various types of student assessments allow educators to make informed improvements to instructional practices and gauge the efficacy of such practices in regard to academic standards. The types of student performance assessment discussed in this section include **formative, summative,** standardized, nonstandardized, **norm referenced,** and **criterion referenced**.

Formative Assessments. Formative classroom assessments are frequent and ongoing evaluations of student progress. A primary purpose of formative assessment is to provide educators with an opportunity to collect continuing **feedback** regarding student performance and needs and thus make pedagogical adjustments within an instructional unit. The strength of formative assessment rests in the provision of targeted and timely feedback to students and teachers regarding academic progress. The use of multiple indicators provides a more accurate measure of student progress by allowing students multiple opportunities to demonstrate mastery of material. The degree to which formative assessments are helpful depends on the degree to which they are directly linked to classroom learning objectives. For example, if formative assessments are not sensitive to the actual learning occurring in the classroom, the frequency by which they are administered is of little value. Further, if adjustments are not made on the part of educators as a result of formative feedback results, this valuable information is underutilized.

In addition to guiding instructional decisions, formative feedback is beneficial in communicating expectations to students, providing parents and students with a measure of academic progress, encouraging student self-reflection, and motivating students to be more engaged in learning.

The Organization of Economic Co-operation and Development (OECD) is an international organization that provides a forum for democratic governments to compare policies and practices on economic, social, and environmental challenges. In 2005, the OECD conducted an extensive study of formative assessment practices in schools and found that the utilization of formative assessments in classrooms encouraged the following seven practices:

- The articulation of learning goals and the tracking of individual student progress toward those goals
- The systematic provision of information to students regarding their performance
- The establishment of a classroom culture that encourages collaboration and the use of assessment tools
- The active involvement of students in the learning process
- The adaptation of instruction to meet identified needs
- The use of multiple approaches to assessing student understanding

A rich array of data is available to teachers by virtue of daily interaction with students. Some of these formative data sources are more formal in nature, such as quizzes, homework assignments, and journal entries. Other sources of formative data are more informal, such as those gained through observation of student behavior or gleaned from conversations with students regarding their understanding of classroom material. Whether gained through formal or informal avenues, formative assessment provides a powerful mechanism for classroom teachers to ensure that learning environments are maintaining a high level of assessment- and learner-centeredness, as discussed in Chapter 8. When classroom teachers harness the power of formative assessment data to the creation and facilitation of instructional strategies, the enhancement of student performance is a likely outcome.

Summative Assessments. The two key distinctions between formative and summative assessments include timing and purpose. While formative assessments occur *during* an instructional unit, summative assessments occur at the *end* of a unit. Certainly, instructional units vary in duration and scope, and thus the purpose of summative assessments assists in distinguishing between the two. Whereas formative assessment can be used to refine instructional strategies, the purpose of summative assessments is to provide a final appraisal of student performance at the culmination of all the instructional activities associated with the given unit. Summative assessments are generally categorized as being either standardized or nonstandardized and norm referenced or criterion referenced. Each of these characteristics is described below.

Standardized Assessments. As discussed earlier, schools are being held accountable for student learning. One of the primary mechanisms used to assess student performance is standardized tests, which are constructed and administered in ways that minimize errors in measurement. For example, standardized tests are usually developed by a team of content and test development experts. Content experts ensure that test items adequately sample important content areas of the subject tested. This group will review curricula, textbooks, and standards throughout the nation, or a particular state if the test is state specific, in order to create test items that are aligned to key instructional content. The test development experts then select test items with the appropriate difficulty and discrimination levels, while seeking to avoid **item bias**. For example, in order to create a set of test items capable of discriminating between high and low achievers, norm-referenced tests may select questions that inadvertently bias against certain groups of students by covering culturally linked content or skills that are attained at home in addition to school.

Standardization of the test administration process is also important. This includes the use of uniform testing time, procedures, and testing environment. Uniformity in the administration process is a prerequisite for the fair comparison of scores. Following test administration, standardized tests are graded by machines or by raters who have undergone training to enhance consistency in the use of scoring rubrics. The purpose of a standardized test is to compare student performance either to that of a representative student group, also called a norm group, or to set criteria.

Norm-Referenced Tests. The purpose of many standardized tests is to provide a measure of an individual student's performance in relation to a norm group. Norm groups are representative, at the national or state level, of the demographic characteristics and academic capabilities of the broader population. Due to constant shifts in these dynamics, norm groups are updated every few years to ensure that the results of the representative group are kept current and meaningful. As a result, norm-referenced tests provide student performance scores that can be compared and ranked with a **sample** of the target population, such as a national sample of the grade level tested, a particular socioeconomic group, or a racial group. Norm-referenced test questions are generally **multiple choice** and are selected from different difficulty levels to distribute students along a normal bell curve. In other words, norm-referenced tests are constructed in a way that results in the representative norm group scoring in a pattern that matches the normal bell curve. This indicates that half of the norm group students scored below average, and half of the students scored above average. This representative sample of students thus provides a frame of reference for interpreting norm-referenced raw test scores. The results of norm-referenced assessment are generally reported using several scores that are derived from raw scores. While raw test scores provide the number of questions answered correctly, they must be converted into a derived score corresponding with the normal distribution curve in order to give the score meaning. Figure 10.1 displays the relationship of the normal bell curve to these norm-referenced derived scores.

Norm-referenced derived scores are often reported as **percentile ranks,** national stanines, normal curve equivalents, standard scores, and scale scores. Figure 10.1 and Table 10.1 are helpful in describing each of the derived scores. Table 10.1 is provided as an example of a student-level score report that might be associated with a norm-referenced test.

National stanines are scores based on the division of the normal curve into broad standardized intervals ranging from one to nine. (Hence the label "stanine," meaning standard nine.) Stanines ranging between one and three are considered below average, those between

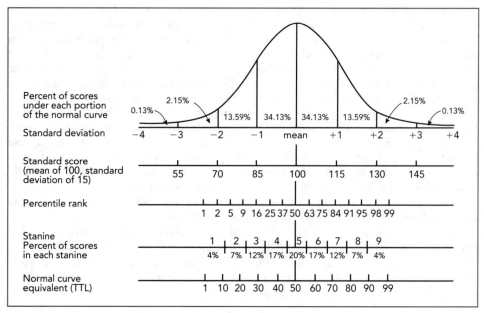

FIGURE 10.1 The Normal Curve and Its Relationship to Various Derived Scores

four and six are considered average, and those between seven and nine are considered above average. Given the relatively broad range of scores grouped into a stanine, it is impossible to observe small changes in performance. Additionally, stanine measures do not indicate if a score is at the top or bottom of a stanine group. Based on the national stanine scores presented in Table 10.1, one would conclude that this student falls in the average to above average range on various measures of reading ability.

National percentile scores contribute more specificity to determining how a particular student compares to a normed population. Percentile scores range from one to ninety-nine and represent the percentage of students in the norm group whose scores fall below the given student's test score. For example, the student in Table 10.1 scored at the

TABLE 10.1 Norm-Referenced Test Score Data

Test Sections	Derived Scores			
	National Stanine	Normal Curve Equivalent	Scale Score	National Percentile
Vocabulary	5	46	640	48
Reading comprehension	6	61	657	67
Language mechanics	7	72	663	84
Reading composite	6	63	654	65

sixty-seventh percentile in reading comprehension. This means that this particular student scored higher than 67 percent of the other students in the same grade level who took this test. Similar to stanines, the intervals for percentile scores are unequal. This means a higher percentage of scores are represented at the fiftieth percentile than at the ninety-ninth, following the bell curve distribution. However, the merit in both stanine and percentile scores is less in the specific placement of a student along a distribution than in assessing how students scored relative to the representative group.

Normal curve equivalent scores are similar to percentile scores in that they range from one to ninety-nine, yet they are based on an equal-interval scale. Therefore, unlike percentiles, a one-point interval change in a normal curve equivalent score has the same meaning throughout the scale. This means a movement from the fiftieth to the fifty-first equivalent score is equally difficult as an increase from the ninety-eighth to the ninety-ninth equivalent score. Normal curve equivalent scores also provide the benefit of having the same meaning across subtests. For example, a student who has normal curve equivalent scores of forty-six for vocabulary, sixty-one in reading comprehension, and seventy-two in language mechanics scored better on both the language and reading subtests than vocabulary.

Scale scores are derived by a mathematical transformation of raw scores. While scale score ranges depend on the particular test taken, they often span from 1 to 999. A benefit of scale scores is that they span all levels and grades of the test. This allows educators to measure the growth of a student from year to year on specific sections of tests. As such, by themselves, scale scores do not tell us much. In order to interpret the meaning of these scores, one either needs the student's scores from previous years or other students' scores to make comparisons.

As depicted in Figure 10.1, *standard scores* use the normal curve to report student performance in terms of how many standard deviations the test score is from the mean test score. In this figure, the mean score is set at one hundred and the standard deviation is fifteen.

Another form of the standard score is the Z score, which sets the mean score at zero and the standard deviation at one. Both of these standard scores provide students with a measure of their performance relative to the average score of the representative sample.

Criterion-Referenced Tests. While norm-referenced test data provide a measure of how well a student performs in relation to other students, criterion-referenced tests provide performance data on how well a student has mastered specific learning objectives. While the content covered by norm-referenced tests is generally broad and can be detached from local curriculum and instruction, criterion-referenced tests can be designed to reflect the knowledge and skills that students should know and be able to do in order to display understanding of particular domains of academic content. Criterion-referenced test items are not constructed to distribute students across a normal curve. Test items for each academic area are similar in difficulty level to provide an accurate index of individual mastery of content.

Criterion-referenced tests can be constructed at the classroom, school, district, state, and national levels. Many criterion-referenced tests are standards based, meaning they are aligned with the learning expectations of high-quality academic standards. Increasingly, criterion-referenced tests are being adopted at the state level to match state academic standards. Thus, it is important that education leaders at the school and district level ensure that the state tests have not omitted academic content that is important at the local level. Districts can contract with a testing organization to design criterion-referenced tests that are customized to local content and instructional goals. As it is likely that district or state standards-based tests will not cover all of the academic content pertinent to the local level, education leaders can support the development of classroom-level assessments to fill in the gaps.

Nonstandardized Assessments. While end-of-year standardized tests are one measure of student performance, learning is measured most frequently by teacher-made assessments that have undergone a process of standardized construction or administration. These non-standardized measures of performance are used as mechanisms for both formative and summative assessment of student mastery, of course objectives, and content material. As such, they are useful in providing assessments *for* learning and *of* learning. The information gleaned from classroom assessments can help teachers plan instructional experiences to facilitate content mastery. Thus, in addition to standardized tests, classroom-level assessments play an important role in data-based decision making, which will be explored in detail in Chapter 11.

Although classroom-based nonstandardized assessments do provide valuable insight regarding the progress of students in meeting particular learning objectives, these data also provide school leaders with insight regarding topics for faculty **professional development.**

Technical Issues Associated with Assessments

In order to ensure that student assessments exhibit the quality necessary to inform instructional practices and assign accountability consequences, tests must demonstrate **reliability** and **validity**. Test reliability indicates the internal stability of tests and provides information about how well test scores remain consistent from one testing instance to another. The rationale underlying reliability is that a test should produce the same score even if the student takes the test on a different day or is administered a different version of the test.

Test validity refers to the extent to which test items reflect a specific content domain. Validity ensures that the content covered accurately reflects the knowledge and skills that the test is supposed to measure. Together, reliability and validity help establish the underlying usefulness of student performance assessments. For example, long, multiple-choice tests bolster the reliability of test scores, while essay questions ensure greater validity in covering content. It is unlikely that any one test will have suitable levels of reliability and validity to make high-stakes accountability decisions.

Using multiple indicators of student performance provides more generalizable and accurate information. Therefore, school leaders and policy makers are encouraged to use multiple indicators of student performance when making important decisions about instructional practices and assigning sanctions or rewards. Chapter 11 tackles the important issue of how school leaders and teachers can utilize multiple types of data to guide instructional and organizational decisions.

▮ ASSESSMENT OF LEADERSHIP PERFORMANCE

Quality leadership is an essential component of successful schools. The utilization of thoughtful and appropriate ways to develop and assess school leaders can have an important influence on the quality of education leadership and ultimately the quality of education in our nation's schools. As such, practical and focused leadership evaluation holds great promise for providing educators with valuable information that can be used to improve leadership practice. Recognizing the decisive role played by principals, there have been multiple attempts to establish standards for school leaders. These standards seek to establish consensus within the field of education administration regarding the common body of knowledge and set of competencies, skills, dispositions, and language that will ensure quality preparation and development of school leaders. This section of the chapter will describe two of the most significant administrative standards and licensing efforts and will discuss recent progress in the realm of assessing administrator performance.

Administrative Standards and Licensing

The movement toward standards for student learning and for teacher instructional practice contributed to the sustained efforts to articulate standards for school leaders. Two of the primary ways that administrator standards have been used include the **accreditation** of graduation programs and the licensure of principals. Licensure and entry into the profession are granted based on candidates' successful completion of a preparation program and the passing of a test aligned to the standards. The two administrative standards that will be described below are those of the American Association of School Administrators and the Interstate School Leaders Licensure Consortium.

American Association of School Administrators. In 1983, the American Association of School Administrators (AASA) published *Guidelines for the Preparation of School Administrators*, which became the first widely recognized national effort to create consensus regarding a knowledge base and common set of competencies, skills, and dispositions needed to become a competent school principal. The AASA articulated seven competency and skill areas that became benchmarks for standards later developed by several state departments of education, university preparation programs, and professional administration associations. These seven AASA competencies for school principals include

- designing, implementing, and evaluating a school culture improvement program that utilizes mutual staff and student efforts to formulate and attain school goals;
- understanding political theory and applying political skills in building local, state, and national support for education;
- designing a systematic school curriculum that ensures both extensive cultural enrichment activities and mastery of fundamental as well as complex skills required in advanced problem solving and technological activities;
- planning and implementing an instructional program that includes learning objectives, curriculum design, and instructional strategies with the aim of facilitating high levels of achievement;
- designing **staff development** and evaluation systems to enhance the effectiveness of educational personnel;
- allocating human, material, and financial resources efficiently and accountably to ensure successful student learning;
- conducting research and utilizing findings in decisions to improve long-range planning, school operations, and student learning.

In addition to the seven competencies, the AASA articulated lists of specific skills to validate mastery of each standard. Further, the AASA provided a research rationale and mastery check for each of the seven competencies and related skills. To varying degrees, all subsequent efforts to create professional standards for school administrators rest on the research base of the AASA guidelines.

Interstate School Leaders Licensure Consortium. Established in 1994, the Interstate School Leaders Licensure Consortium (ISLLC) developed a set of national standards for school leaders, licensure assessments based on those standards, and professional development guidelines directly linked to the standards. The establishment of the ISLLC Standards was a project of the Council of Chief State School Officers (CCSSO) in partnership with the National Policy Board for Educational Administration (NPBEA).

The ISLLC Standards present a common core of knowledge, dispositions, and performances that help link leadership more directly to productive school practices and enhanced educational outcomes. The standards confirm the centrality of the principal's role in ensuring student achievement through an unwavering emphasis on learning-centered leadership. To serve as a philosophical foundation for the development of the ISLLC Standards, consortium members crafted several guiding principles. These principles assert that standards for school leaders should

- reflect the centrality of student learning;
- acknowledge the changing role of school leaders;
- recognize the collaborative nature of school leadership;
- set high aspirations, upgrading the quality of the profession;
- inform standards-based systems of assessment for school leaders;
- be integrated and coherent;
- be grounded on the concepts of access, opportunity, and empowerment for all members of the school community.

The ISLLC Standards[2] were created for the purpose of strengthening school leadership in several key areas, including improving preparation and professional development for school leaders, creating a framework for assessment of candidates for licensure, establishing a foundation for national recognition in certification programs, and creating criteria on which to base accreditation and program approval for institutions of higher education.

To date, ISLLC Standards have been adopted by forty-three states and have had a significant influence on the reform of preparation programs for school principals nationwide. Institutions of higher education have adopted curricular revisions for the preparation of school leaders directly linked to the ISLLC Standards. Encouraged by these efforts and having a desire for consistency among university preparation programs, the National Council for the Accreditation of Teacher Education (NCATE) aligned its accreditation standards for educational leadership preparation programs with the ISLLC Standards.

Though not without criticism, the ISLLC Standards do refocus the role of school principals squarely on instructional issues, as all six standards are firmly grounded in the key disposition that all students can attain academic achievement.

The ISSLC Standards state that a school administrator is an education leader who promotes the success of all students by

- facilitating the development, articulation, implementation, and stewardship of a vision of learning that is shared and supported by the school community;
- advocating, nurturing, and sustaining a school culture and instructional program conducive to student learning and staff professional growth;

- ensuring management of the organization, operations, and resources for a safe, efficient, and effective learning environment;
- collaborating with families and community members, responding to diverse community interests and needs, and mobilizing community resources;
- acting with integrity and fairness, and in an ethical manner;
- understanding, responding to, and influencing the larger political, social, economic, legal, and cultural context.

Taken together, the ISLLC Standards represent a depth and breadth of content that encompass the wide spectrum of knowledge and skills that school leaders can use as benchmarks for professional practice. Further, if these represent important domains of practice for school leaders, then it follows that such practice would need to be encouraged and evaluated.

Toward that end, a second initiative of the ISLLC consortium entailed the creation of the Collaborative Professional Development Process for School Leaders. In this process, school leaders are guided in the engagement of professional development activities that are

- linked to the ISLLC Standards;
- linked to the day-to-day work of the school leader;
- based on an assumption that school leaders are competent and, as professionals, routinely and in numerous ways improve their knowledge, dispositions, and performance;
- based on the supposition that the primary responsibility for professional growth ultimately rests with the school leader;
- based on the assumption that collaboration is required between a school leader and others in order to examine and reflect on leadership and to promote personal growth.

The collaborative ISLLC professional development process is implemented with the support of a school-based professional development team and combines individual professional development efforts with school-based improvement activities. In this way, the process promotes the personal and professional growth of school leaders. Along with the standards, the professional development process has been used to guide formal and informal performance appraisal programs for school leaders.

Assessing the Performance of School Leaders.[3] Recognizing that school leadership is an important component of student achievement efforts, standards and licensing competencies have been established to guide the development of school leaders. Additionally, recent strides have been taken to develop tools to assess and monitor leadership performance.

For example, in 2002 the Educational Testing Service (ETS) developed a framework for assessing leadership performance that utilizes a set of **rubrics** derived from the ISLLC Standards. These rubrics cover the core competencies contained in the six standards and address four important leadership themes:

1. a vision for success,
2. a focus on instruction,
3. the involvement of all stakeholders, and
4. a focus on integrity and ethics in leadership action.

For each standard and theme, benchmarks are specified and a principal is assessed as performing at one of the following four levels: rudimentary, developing, proficient, and accomplished.

In 2004 Douglas B. Reeves developed the Multidimensional Leadership Assessment which comprises performance-based rating scales along ten dimensions of leadership behavior. The dimensions include resilience, personal behavior, decision making, faculty development, student achievement, communication, time management, technology, leadership development, and learning. Each dimension is defined by several specific standards that are assessed at four levels of performance: not meeting standards, progressing, proficient (local impact), and exemplary (system-wide impact). The use of such standards-based models of principal evaluation grounds accountability in the practices and competencies important to lead schools in the current era of standards-based accountability.

At Peabody College of Vanderbilt University, educational researchers Andrew C. Porter, Ellen B. Goldring, and Joseph F. Murphy, in conjunction with the Wallace Foundation, have developed a framework for assessing learning-centered leadership titled the Vanderbilt Assessment of Leadership in Education (VAL-Ed). Functionally, this assessment will yield valid performance information that can facilitate both formative and summative evaluation of the behaviors of leaders and leadership teams. The VAL-Ed model of leadership assessment, highlighted in Figure 10.2, portrays how leadership might be assessed by utilizing the appropriate constructs of leadership assessment and situating leadership behavior within the larger context. The model shows leadership knowledge and

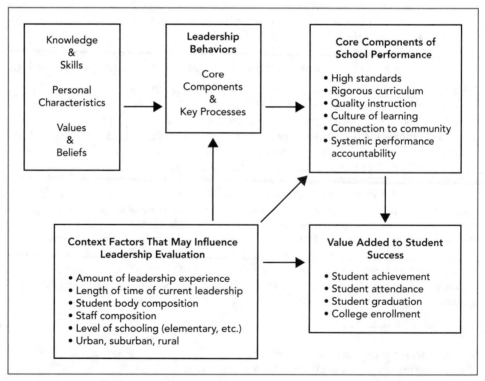

FIGURE 10.2 Model for Vanderbilt Assessment of Leadership in Education

Source: Porter, A.C., Goldring, E.B., Murphy, J., Elliott, S., N., & Cravens, X. (2006). A framework for the assessment of learning-centered leadership. New York, NY: Wallace Foundation.

skills, personal characteristics, and values and beliefs as precursors of the actual leadership behaviors exhibited by individuals or teams. These leadership behaviors, operationalized at the intersection of six leadership processes and six core components of school performance, are linked to dimensions of student success. Many leadership assessments exclusively focus on the knowledge, skills, and dispositions of leaders. The VAL-Ed assessment, however, focuses on the value-added improvements to student success that are the result of leadership behaviors. The leadership behaviors are assessed at the intersection of six core components of school performance and six key processes that together make up principal and team leadership. These components and processes are arranged in Figure 10.2 and described below.

The core components of school performance include

- High standards for student performance—There are individual, team, and school goals for rigorous student academic and social learning.
- Rigorous curriculum—Ambitious academic content is provided to all students in core academic subjects.
- Quality instruction—Effective instructional practices maximize student academic learning.
- Culture of learning—There are integrated communities of professional practice in the service of student academic and social learning. There is a healthy school environment in which student learning is the central focus.
- Connection to external communities—There are linkages to people and institutions in the community that advance academic and social learning.
- Systemic performance accountability—Leadership holds itself and others responsible for realizing high standards of performance for student academic and social learning.

The key processes of leadership include

- Planning—Articulate shared direction and coherent policies, practices, and procedures for realizing high standards of student performance.
- Implementing—Engage people, ideas, and resources to put into practice the activities necessary to realize high standards for student performance.
- Supporting—Create enabling conditions; secure and use the financial, political, technological, human, and social capital necessary to promote academic and social learning.
- Advocating—Act on behalf of the diverse needs of students within and beyond the school.
- Communicating—Develop, utilize, and maintain systems of exchange among members of the school and with its external communities.
- Monitoring—Systematically collect and analyze data to make judgments that guide decisions and actions for continuous improvement.

As Table 10.2 highlights, leadership behaviors are assessed at the intersection of each core component and process. For example, the extent to which the school leadership supports a culture of learning and implements systemic accountability will be assessed. Each cell in Table 10.2 will include a sample of leadership behaviors. Respondents will indicate the degree to which school leaders exhibit the appropriate behaviors. The VAL-Ed assessment process will include contributions from leader and team self-assessment, teachers in the school, supervisors, and potentially others in the school community. The assessment

TABLE 10.2 Vanderbilt Assessment of Leadership in Education:
Core Components and Key Processes

Core Components	Key Processes					
	Planning	Implementing	Supporting	Advocating	Communicating	Monitoring
High Standards for Student Performance						
Rigorous Curriculum						
Quality Instruction						
Culture of Learning						
Connection to External Community						
Systemic Performance Accountability						

Source: Porter, A.C., Goldring, E.B., Murphy, J., Elliott, S., N., & Cravens, X. (2006). *A framework for the assessment of learning-centered leadership.* New York, NY: Wallace Foundation.

feedback will provide leaders and leadership teams with a profile of performance in the key components and core processes.

For example, these data will illuminate if school leadership is especially effective in planning and implementing a rigorous curriculum or a bit weak on monitoring and evaluating instructional quality. The fact that leadership assessment is currently a topic of much academic and practical effort endorses the central importance of leadership in improving school performance and student achievement.

■ ASSESSING SCHOOL PERFORMANCE

In some ways, assessing school performance is comparable to an aggregate view of the levels of student, teacher, and principal performance at a given school. Yet in many ways this oversimplification does not do justice to the complex world of educational organizations. This section of the chapter provides education leaders with knowledge regarding several key issues associated with assessing school performance. Specifically, this section will discuss challenges to assessing school performance as a function of the average test scores of students by providing insight regarding the establishment of reliable aggregation across time, subjects tested, and student subgroups.

Time. One primary aggregation issue for school leaders to consider involves whether schools can and should be held accountable for a specific year's worth of performance data, or if such accountability should be based on several years of performance data. Accounting for the measurement error inherent in all tests, should schools be rewarded or punished based on yearly changes in measured proficiency? To compute annual changes, two successive years' average scores (each measured with a degree of error) are used to gauge changes in proficiency from one year to the next across different cohorts. The utilization of multiyear moving averages, which follow several cohorts over time, is one way to mitigate the instability of yearly comparisons of school performance. Additionally, an aggregate measure of school performance across cohorts over time is less likely to punish improving schools that are below performance targets for one subgroup in a given year. This is an important consideration given the fact that under the federal accountability system, schools that do not make Adequate Yearly Progress in every category are deemed failing. This issue is especially salient in school communities that have a high degree of racial heterogeneity and thus a large number of subgroups, each with a small sample size.

Aggregation of performance data over time mitigates fluctuation due to sensitive yearly comparisons between subgroups of small sample size, and thus provides a more accurate picture of student performance within subgroups. Balancing out these benefits of multiyear aggregation is the negative impact of lower scores for a longer period of time.

Another time-related challenge of using average test scores as a measure of school performance is the fact that these scores can be out-of-date. For example, the average test score of a group of students tested at the end of ninth grade reflects the accumulated learning that occurred during ninth grade and that which occurred during middle and even elementary school. Because of this, changes over time in average test scores can be quite unrelated to actual changes in school performance. It is possible that increases in middle school productivity can be high enough to outweigh declines in high school performance. This reinforces the importance of utilizing school performance indicators that provide current and accurate data, especially within a high-stakes accountability environment.

Subjects Tested. Currently the NCLB legislation requires annual testing and demonstrated yearly progress in both reading and math. As such, meeting high performance standards via multiple output measures in multiple curricular domains may be difficult for many institutions to attain. The introduction of science testing in the 2007–8 school year, as mandated by NCLB, adds another layer of accountability demands to schools. Unlike reading and math, the inclusion of science accountability testing is necessary in only one grade level per school division—elementary, middle, and high. Of course, the manner in which science tests are incorporated into state accountability systems will make a difference in the treatment of science, math, and reading in schools. With the inclusion of a third curricular domain in the accountability landscape, it will become increasingly important for education leaders to determine how multiple outcome indicators might be aggregated into a single indicator of school performance.

Student Subgroups. A third aggregation issue for school leaders to consider involves the manner in which student subgroups are used to compose a school-wide measure of performance. A core tenet of the NCLB legislation is that *all* student subgroups must be provided with an education that is adequate for meeting federal accountability standards. The federal NCLB legislation establishes student subgroups along racial, ethnic, and socioeconomic lines. Yet it is individual states that set the minimum subgroup size requirements for a subgroup to be counted in the school-wide accountability grade. As mentioned earlier, measurement errors become more acute as sample size decreases. Therefore, if subgroup size requirements are set low, there is an increased likelihood that the small subgroups could have a negative impact on the aggregate grade of a heterogeneous school.

On the other hand, higher subgroup size requirements minimize opportunities for measurement issues to influence the school-wide performance score, but at the same time exclude subgroups from counting. With so much at stake, school leaders are looked to as ambassadors able to engage district and state personnel in efforts to ensure appropriate and accurate representations of local school communities.

In addition to these aggregation issues, the use of average student scores as a measure of school performance poses several challenges. Average measures of student achievement reflect the contribution of both school and various nonschool inputs to the learning process. These nonschool inputs include the effects of student, family, and community characteristics, as well as prior levels of student achievement. It is possible that between-school comparisons of average student performance are more indicative of nonschool factors than are measures of actual school performance.

In this scenario, using average test scores as a measure of school performance would place schools serving a disproportionately high number of low-income students at a significant disadvantage. As all scores count toward the average, there is an incentive to measure the performance of those students who have high test scores. This pressure can result in active selection of students into courses or programs, inaccurate classification of students into special education or learning-disabled status, or unsupportive environments for those who might pull the average scores down. This scenario is another indicator of the challenging terrain facing educational leaders of our nation's schools.

The previous sections of this chapter have focused on issues of and approaches to assessing the performance of students, principals, and schools. Three additional performance-related topics will now be discussed. These include an overview of measuring academic performance in a value-added manner and a brief synopsis of national and international comparisons of educational performance.

■ VALUE-ADDED PERFORMANCE MEASURES[4]

The previous section on assessing school performance based solely on attained levels of achievement points to the need for complementary mechanisms of measuring the performance of teachers, principals, and schools. In contrast to traditional, cross-sectional examinations of trends in average test scores of students, **value-added** measures focus on the **longitudinal** growth of a given cohort of students from one grade level to the next. Value-added measures are derived from a statistical process that accounts for nonschool factors that contribute to growth in student achievement. As discussed earlier, the nonschool factors contributing to student achievement include student, family, and community characteristics, as well as prior student achievement. A core purpose of value-added measurement is to isolate the contribution that schools make to growth in student achievement. Depending on the level of analysis, the end result of this process is a value-added indicator that captures variances in educational productivity among policies, schools, programs, and instructors.

The rationale behind value-added measures of school performance is to level the playing field. For example, if one makes accountability decisions by relying exclusively on levels of student achievement, schools with higher beginning performance will have an advantage. Additionally, schools that serve a student population with higher levels of socioeconomic status or that serve more homogeneous student populations will likely have an advantage.

┌───

CASE 6 REVISITED

Recall the school board chair in Mountain Union School District who proposed a value-added approach to assessing the effectiveness of teachers. How might a shift from focusing on attainment levels to a value-added approach impact the perception of which schools are most successful and which teachers are most effective?

└───

On the other end of the spectrum, measures based on attained levels of achievement might not regard schools serving impoverished populations as successful, even if they are exceptional in bringing students from very low starting points up to higher levels of proficiency.

While for these reasons, value-added measures appear like an optimal and fair approach to assessing school performance, one must also consider the value in establishing high levels of expected attainment for all students.

In the past, not all students were expected to succeed in our nation's schools. Today, however, all schools and all students are being held accountable to the same standards, regardless of background characteristics or starting values of academic achievement. One must balance this ideal with the reality that a high correlation exists between aggregate levels of student test performance and background characteristics. While one does not want to fall prey to having different expectations for low-income or minority students, one must also acknowledge the equity concerns associated with evaluating schools by attained levels of achievement alone. Thus, the apparent answer is to use achievement levels in conjunction with value added or gain scores. Both measures are important.

The manner in which gain or value-added measures are calculated ranges from simple comparisons of average test scores from one year to the next, to complex multiple regression models that control for student and family background characteristics. All modes of value-added measurement require frequent testing of students, and a comparison of gains necessitates tests that can be compared from one grade level or one time point to the next. This, of course, requires a data system that is capable of tracking and linking student, family, and school-level variables to the appropriate achievement results. The logic of the value-added approach is illustrated in Figure 10.3, which compares test scores for students from two middle schools: Greenville Middle and Ashland Middle.

Each point on the graph represents test score data for a single student, with a student's seventh-grade math achievement represented by the score on the horizontal axis and the eighth-grade achievement noted on the vertical axis.

As one might expect, the general trend is that students at both schools who scored higher in seventh grade tend to have higher scores in eighth grade. Yet there is a systematic difference in eighth-grade achievement between the two schools. This is illuminated by fitting a regression line to the data for each school, which pictorially projects the pattern represented in the data. When one compares the regression lines of the two schools, it becomes clear that Greenville Middle School students, with the same level of achievement as Ashland Middle School students in seventh grade, scored approximately fifty points higher in eighth grade. These fifty points represent two things: the value-added difference in productivity between the two schools and possible differences between the

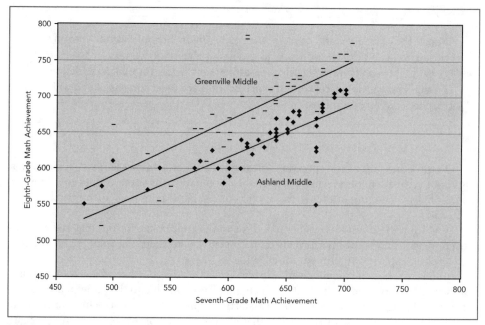

FIGURE 10.3 Value-Added Comparison of Math Achievement for Two Schools

schools in terms of nonschool factors related to growth in student achievement. This highlights the importance of including multiple control variables in value-added models. In so doing, value-added models provide an accurate estimate of the productivity of schools, programs, policies, and instructors in enhancing student achievement.

■ NATIONAL AND INTERNATIONAL ASSESSMENTS OF EDUCATION PERFORMANCE

The final section of this chapter provides education leaders with an overview of two prominent measures of national and international education performance. Specifically, this section describes the type of information made available to education leaders by the National Assessment of Educational Progress and the Trends in International Mathematics and Science Study.

National Assessment of Educational Progress

The National Assessment of Educational Progress (NAEP), also known as the Nation's Report Card, is a federally authorized survey of student achievement administered every two years to students in grades 4, 8, and 12. Since 1970, NAEP has tested a nationally representative sample of public and nonpublic students to assess their knowledge and skills in such subjects as mathematics, reading, writing, science, U.S. history, the arts, and foreign language. In 2001, the No Child Left Behind legislation required NAEP to collect data on specific student groups, based on race/**ethnicity,** gender, socioeconomic status, disability, and limited English proficiency.

Thus, data collected by NAEP provide a representative sample of student achievement for the nation, individual states, and subgroups of students. One of the primary objectives of NAEP is to track trends in student performance over time. While the NAEP is administered every two years in grades 4, 8, and 12, the NAEP long-term trend analysis is conducted every four years in math and reading for students who are 9, 13, and 17 years old.

Select results of the most recent NAEP long-term trend analysis, conducted in 2004, are provided in Figure 10.4 and Figure 10.5. While data are available for both reading and mathematics, the illustrative examples provided here will focus on mathematics to provide comparison to the **TIMSS** results presented later in the chapter. The results from NAEP assessments of mathematics proficiency, provided in Figure 10.4, indicate that the scores of 9-, 13-, and 17-year-old students were higher in 2004 than in 1973. Since the early 1970s, younger students have made greater strides on the math portion of the NAEP test than have older teenagers, whose scores have remained relatively stagnant. For example, between 1999 and 2004, average mathematics scores for 9- and 13-year-olds increased; however, no measurable changes in average scores were found for

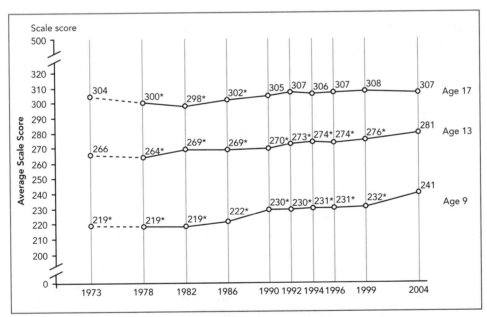

FIGURE 10.4 Trends in Average Mathematics Scale Scores for Students Ages 9, 13, and 17: 1973–2004

*Significantly different from the score in 2004.

Note: Dashed lines represent extrapolated data.

Source: U.S. Department of Education, Institute of Education Sciences, National Center for Education Statistics, National Assessment of Educational Progress (NAEP), selected years, 1973–2004 Long-Term Trend Mathematics Assessments.

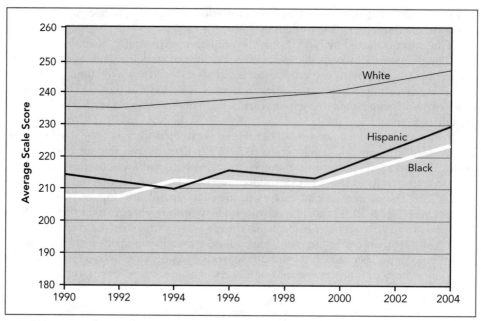

FIGURE 10.5 NAEP Long-Term Trend in Mathematics, Average Scale Score by Student Group, Age 9

Source: Compiled by authors from National Center for Education Statistics, http://nece.ed.gov/nationsreportcard/

17-year-olds. In the most recent interval, between 1999 and 2004, the average score in mathematics for 9-year-olds was nine points higher than in 1999, and for 13-year-olds, the increase was five points. These increases mark the largest single gains for these age groups since 1973.

Figure 10.5 extends the aggregate picture of mathematics trend data by illuminating variations in performance based on several race/ethnicity categories. Analysis of disaggregated NAEP trend data shows gains in average mathematics scale scores for each student group over time. Additionally, in terms of achievement gaps, black and Hispanic students have made improvements in their average scale scores and reduced the achievement gap with white students. For example, the gap between black and white students was 28 scale-score points in 1999 and has been reduced to 23 scale-score points in 2004.

Hispanic students have reduced the scale-score difference from 26 points in 1999 to 18 points in 2004. In addition to relative measures of student performance, Figure 10.5 also provides a picture of the progress each student group is making toward established proficiency levels. The NAEP achievement level descriptions and cutoff scores for grade 4 math are provided in Table 10.3.

Upon comparing the student performance data for each subgroup that are presented in Figure 10.5 with the achievement cutoff scores listed in Table 10.3, it is evident that white students on average are approaching the proficient level of performance in mathematics.

Specifically, the scale score of 247 demonstrated by white fourth-grade math students in 2004 is just two points shy of the cutoff score for proficiency. Although in 1999,

TABLE 10.3 NAEP Achievement Level Descriptions and Cutoff Scores for Grade 4 Mathematics

Level	Definition	Math Cutoff Scores
Basic	Fourth-grade students performing at the Basic level should show some evidence of understanding the mathematical concepts and procedures in the five NAEP content strands.	214
Proficient	Fourth-grade students performing at the Proficient level should consistently apply integrated procedural knowledge and conceptual understanding to problem solving in the five NAEP content strands.	249
Advanced	Fourth-grade students performing at the Advanced level should apply integrated procedural knowledge and conceptual understanding to complex and nonroutine real-world problem solving in the five NAEP content strands.	282

Source: Compiled by authors from National Center for Education Statistics, http://nece.ed.gov/nationsreportcard/

black and Hispanic students on average were scoring right at the basic level, the 2004 scores provide evidence that both of these student groups are making progress toward mathematics proficiency. In terms of achievement levels in mathematics performance, Figure 10.6 displays the percentage of our nation's students scoring at each performance level in fourth and eighth grade.

Here we see a promising trend at both the fourth- and eighth-grade levels; namely, that more and more students are performing at the higher achievement levels. For example, in 1990, over half of our nation's fourth-grade students were scoring below a basic level of understanding in mathematics. Fortunately, this percentage was cut in half by 2003, while at the same time, the number of fourth-grade students scoring in the proficient range increased from 10 percent in 1990 to 27 percent in 2003. While these trends are promising, analysis of the most current distribution of scores presented in Figure 10.6 provides a sobering challenge facing our nation's education leaders. One must keep in mind, however, that NAEP results are but one measure of academic performance. Figure 10.7 provides a comparison of the percentage of students meeting proficiency standards on NAEP with the percentage of students meeting proficiency levels on state standards-based assessments. In every state, the percentage of students meeting NAEP standards is lower than that of those meeting state standards. The range in differences in percent proficient ranges from 7 percent in South Carolina to 69 percentage points in Mississippi. Even in states where the highest percentages of students meet proficiency in reading on NAEP, such as Massachusetts, New Jersey, and Colorado, the percentage point differences between NAEP and state assessment pass rates are 50, 40, and 50, respectively.

This discrepancy points to varying degrees of difficulty inherent in such criterion-referenced tests as NAEP and standards-based state achievement tests. As described earlier in the chapter, criterion-referenced tests are based on content and performance levels from academic standards. Figure 10.7 indicates that the determination of such performance levels varies widely across states.

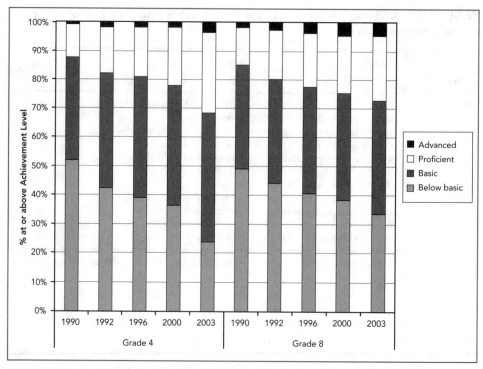

FIGURE 10.6 NAEP Performance Levels, Mathematics

Source: Compiled by authors from National Center for Education Statistics, http://nece.ed.gov/nationsreportcard/

Trends in International Mathematics and Science Study

Since its inception in 1959, the International Association of the Evaluation of Educational Achievement (IEA) has conducted a series of international comparative studies designed to provide educational practitioners, researchers, and policy makers with information about educational achievement and learning contexts. The Trends in International Mathematics and Science Study (TIMSS) is the largest and most ambitious of these studies ever undertaken, with data collected from forty-six countries in more than thirty languages in 2003.

The test, which is conducted every four years, produces data on fourth- and eighth-grade achievement levels and included over 15,000 schools and more than half a million students in 2003. All countries are required to draw random, nationally representative samples of public and private students and schools. In the United States, a total of 10,000 students participated in the 2003 test at the fourth-grade level, and 9,000 students participated at the eighth-grade level. TIMSS data can be used to track changes in achievement over time. Additionally, as the assessment is linked to the curricula of the participating nations, it can indicate the degree to which students have learned concepts in mathematics and science that they have encountered in school.

Table 10.4 provides an example of the type of ranking data supplied by TIMSS. Here one can see that in 2003, U.S. fourth-grade students scored 518, on average, in mathematics, exceeding the international average of 495. This places U.S. fourth-grade students ahead of their peers in thirteen of the twenty-four countries participating in fourth-grade testing and

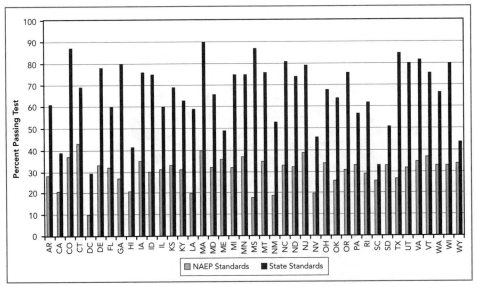

FIGURE 10.7 Comparison of Percentage of Students Passing NAEP and State Assessments in Elementary School Reading, 2003

Source: Compiled by Wong & Nicotera from McCombs, J. S., Kirby, S. N., Barney, H., Darilek, H., & Magee, S. (2004). *Achieving state and national literacy goals, a long uphill road: A report to Carnegie Corporation of New York.* Santa Monica, CA: RAND Corporation.

below their peers in eleven countries. In comparison to the other ten countries that are members of the Organization for Economic Cooperation and Development (OECD), U.S. fourth-graders outperformed their peers in mathematics in five countries (Australia, Italy, New Zealand, Norway, and Scotland) and were outperformed by their peers in the other five countries (Belgium, England, Hungary, Japan, and the Netherlands).

In addition to international comparative rankings, TIMSS data provide insight regarding the degree of change in scores over time. For example, Table 10.5 provides a picture of how the mathematics performance of fourth-grade students changed between 1995 and 2003. Here, one can see that in both 1995 and 2003 U.S. fourth-graders had an average score of 518 in mathematics. Fourth-graders in six other nations also showed no significant change in average mathematics performance over this period. In contrast, fourth-graders in six of the fifteen countries that participated in both 1995 and 2003 displayed a significant increase in average mathematics scores over this time period. Additionally, fourth-graders in two countries, Norway and the Netherlands, experienced a decrease in average mathematics achievement scores between 1995 and 2003.

The combination of comparative data and trend data allows nations to track their relative standings over time, as presented in Table 10.6. This figure reveals that although the average mathematics score of U.S. fourth-graders was 518 in both 1995 and 2003, the standing of the U.S. students relative to their peers in fourteen other nations was lower in 2003 than in 1995. For example, in 1995, U.S. fourth-grade students were statistically outperformed in mathematics by peers in four nations, and they outperformed peers in nine nations. In 2003, however, U.S. fourth-grade students were statistically outperformed in mathematics by peers in seven nations and only outperformed peers in seven nations.

TABLE 10.4 Average Mathematics Scale Scores of Fourth-Grade Students, by Country, 2003

Country	Average Score
International average	495
Singapore	594
Hong Kong SAR[1,2]	575
Japan	565
Chinese Taipei	564
Belgium-Flemish	551
Netherlands[2]	540
Latvia	536
Lithuania[3]	534
Russian Federation	532
England[2]	531
Hungary	529
United States[2]	**518**
Cyprus	510
Moldova, Republic of	504
Italy	503
Australia[2]	499
New Zealand	493
Scotland[2]	490
Slovenia	479
Armenia	456
Norway	451
Iran, Islamic Republic of	389
Philippines	358
Morocco	347
Tunisia	339

[1]Hong Kong is a Special Administrative Region (SAR) of the People's Republic of China.

[2]Met international guidelines for participation rates in 2003 only after replacement schools were included.

[3]National desired population does not cover all of the international desired population.

Note: Countries are ordered by 2003 average score. The test for significance between the United States and the international average was adjusted to account for the U.S. contribution to the international average. Countries were required to sample students in the upper of the two grades that contained the largest number of 9-year-olds. In the United States and most countries, this corresponds to grade 4. See table A1 in appendix A for details.

Source: International Association for the Evaluation of Educational Achievement (IEA), Trends in International Mathematics and Science Study (TIMSS), 2003.

■ Average is higher than the U.S. average

□ Average is not measurably different from the U.S. average

▨ Average is lower than the U.S. average

Source: U.S. Department of Education, National Center for Education Statistics, TIMSS 2003 highlights.

A final example of data available from TIMSS is provided in Figure 10.8. These data parallel the disaggregated results for student subgroups included in the NAEP data. Here one can see that no statistically significant change was detected in average mathematics achievement of U.S. fourth-grade boys and girls between 1995 and 2003. Yet one can see

TABLE 10.5 Differences in Average Mathematics Scale Scores of
Fourth-Grade Students, by Country: 1995 and 2003

Country	1995	2003	Difference[1]
Singapore	590	594	4
Hong Kong SAR[2,3]	557	575	18 ▲
Japan	567	565	−3
(Netherlands)[3]	549	540	−9 ▼
(Latvia-LSS)[4]	499	533	34 ▲
England[3]	484	531	47 ▲
(Hungary)	521	529	7
United States[3]	**518**	**518**	#
Cyprus	475	510	35 ▲
(Australia)[3]	495	499	4
New Zealand[5]	469	496	26 ▲
Scotland[3]	493	490	−3
(Slovenia)	462	479	17 ▲
Norway	476	451	−25 ▼
Iran, Islamic Republic of	387	389	2

[1]Difference calculated by subtracting 1995 from 2003 estimate, using unrounded numbers.
[2]Hong Kong is a Special Administrative Region (SAR) of the People's Republic of China.
[3]Met international guidelines for participation rates in 2003 only after replacement schools were included.
[4]Designated LSS because only Latvian-speaking schools were included in 1995. For this analysis, only Latvian-speaking schools are included in the 2003 average.
[5]In 1995, Maori-speaking students did not participate. Estimates in this table are computed for students taught in English only, which represents between 98 and 99 percent of the student population in both years.
Note: Countries are ordered based on the 2003 average scores. Parentheses indicate countries that did not meet international sampling or other guidelines in 1995. All countries met international sampling and other guidelines in 2003, except as noted. See NCES (1997) for details regarding the 1995 data. The tests for significance take into account the standard error for the reported difference. Thus, a small difference between averages for one country may be significant, while a large difference for another country may not be significant. Countries were required to sample students in the upper of the two grades that contained the largest number of 9-year-olds. In the United States and most countries, this corresponds to grade 4. Detail may not sum to totals because of rounding.
Source: International Association for the Evaluation of Educational Achievement (IEA), Trends in International Mathematics and Science Study (TIMSS), 1995 and 2003.
Rounds to zero.
▲ p < .05, denotes a significant increase.
▼ p < .05, denotes a significant decrease.
Source: U.S. Department of Education, National Center for Education Statistics, TIMSS 2003 highlights.

that the difference between boys' and girls' average mathematics scores in 1995 was four points, while in 2003 the difference grew to eight points.

Between the years 1995 and 2003, black students are the only subgroup of students to demonstrate statistically significant growth in average mathematics achievement scores. As a result, over these eight years, the gap in average scores between white and black fourth-grade students narrowed, from 84 points in 1995 to 69 points in 2003. In the same

TABLE 10.6 Average Mathematics Scale Scores of Fourth-Grade Students, by Country: 1995 and 2003

Country	1995	Country	2003
Singapore	590	Singapore	594
Japan	567	Hong Kong SAR[1,2]	575
Hong Kong SAR[1,2]	557	Japan	565
(Netherlands)	549	Netherlands[1]	540
(Hungary)	521	Latvia-LSS[3]	533
United States	**518**	England[1]	531
(Latvia-LSS)[3]	499	Hungary	529
(Australia)	495	**United States**[1]	**518**
Scotland	493	Cyprus	510
England	484	Australia[1]	499
Norway	476	New Zealand[4]	496
Cyprus	475	Scotland[1]	490
New Zealand[4]	469	Slovenia	479
(Slovenia)	462	Norway	451
Iran, Islamic Republic of	387	Iran, Islamic Republic of	389

[1]Met international guidelines for participation rates in 2003 only after replacement schools were included.

[2]Hong Kong is a Special Administrative Region (SAR) of the People's Republic of China.

[3]Designated LSS because only Latvian-speaking schools were included in 1995. For this analysis, only Latvian-speaking schools are included in the 2003 average.

[4]In 1995, Maori-speaking students did not participate. Estimates in this table are computed for students taught in English only, which represents between 98 and 99 percent of the student population in both years.

Note: Countries are ordered based on the average score. Parentheses indicate countries that did not meet international sampling or other guidelines in 1995. All countries met international sampling and other guidelines in 2003, except as noted. See NCES (1997) for details regarding 1995 data. The tests for significance take into account the standard error for the reported difference. Thus, a small difference between the United States and one country may be significant, while a large difference between the United States and another country may not be significant. Countries were required to sample students in the upper of the two grades that contained the largest number of 9-year-olds. In the United States and most countries, this corresponds to grade 4.

Source: International Association for the Evaluation of Educational Achievement (IEA), Trends in International Mathematics and Science Study (TIMSS), 1995 and 2003.

■ Average is higher than the U.S. average

□ Average is not measurably different from the U.S. average

■ Average is lower than the U.S. average

Source: U.S. Department of Education, National Center for Education Statistics, TIMSS 2003 highlights.

time period, there was no significant narrowing of the gap in mathematics scores between white and Hispanic students. Poverty level plays a visible role in the relative achievement levels of fourth-grade students.

In 2003, U.S. fourth-graders with the highest poverty level (75 percent or more eligible for free or reduced lunch) had lower average mathematics scores than their counterparts in public schools with lower poverty levels. The total variation in average mathematics scores of students in the lowest and highest poverty levels was 96 points in 2003. This

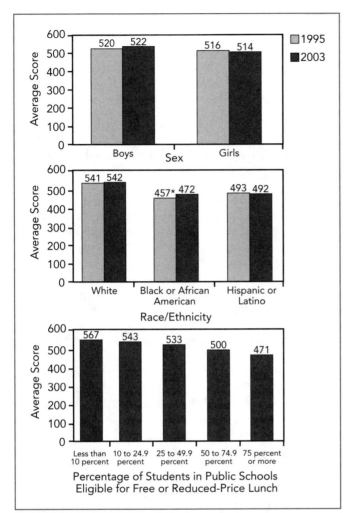

FIGURE 10.8 Average Mathematics Scale Scores of Fourth-Grade Students, by Sex, Race/Ethnicity, and Poverty Level: 1995 and 2003

*p<.05, denotes a significant difference from 2003 average score.

 Note: Reporting standards not met for Asian category in 1995 and American Indian or Alaska Native and Native Hawaiian or Other Pacific Islander for both years. Racial categories exclude Hispanic origin. Other races/ethnicities are included in U.S. totals shown throughout the report. Analyses by poverty level are limited to students in public schools only. The tests for significance take into account the standard error for the reported difference. Thus, a small difference between averages for one student group may be significant, while a large difference for another student group may not be significant. The United States met international guidelines for participation rates in 2003 only after replacement schools were included. See appendix A for more information.

Source: International Association for the Evaluation of Educational Achievement (IEA), Trends in International Mathematics and Science Study (TIMSS), 1995 and 2003.

Source: U.S. Department of Education, National Center for Education Statistics, TIMSS 2003 highlights

represents the greatest difference in average scores between any two student subgroups, thus reinforcing the important link between student socioeconomic status and educational performance.

Summary

Within the current accountability context of our nation's education system, it is imperative that education leaders have a solid understanding of the various ways in which the performance of students, teachers, administrators, and schools has been and can be evaluated. This chapter provided an overview of the important terrain of performance assessment in education. Specifically, it discussed the role of formative and summative assessment in determining levels of student performance. Here, the role of norm- and criterion-referenced tests were described, as were several types of derived scores and technical issues associated with assessment. When discussing the importance of assessing the performance of school leaders, special attention was given to the formative role of the ISLLC Standards in guiding administrator preparation, licensing, and development. Next, several challenges associated with evaluating the performance of schools were discussed, including issues inherent in the aggregation of student scores across time, subjects, and subgroups. The potential benefits and challenges of value-added performance measures were then described. Here, attention was drawn to the need for complementary approaches to assessing performance solely upon the basis of attained levels of achievement. Finally, insights from longitudinal, national, and international perspectives on education performance were shared. These data provide a view of how our schools are performing across the country and in comparison to other nations. The important topic of using school data to drive decision making is the focus of the following chapter.

Discussion Questions

1. List all of the various ways that student performance is assessed at your school. Are there any assessment approaches that you think should be added to this list?
2. On a scale of 1 to 5, with 5 being high, rate the degree to which teachers in your school utilize formative assessment to enhance instruction. As an education leader, what could you do to increase this level?
3. For your school, state the ways in which norm- and criterion-referenced tests are currently used to drive instructional decisions. Which type of assessment do you find more helpful in making such decisions?
4. Describe one benefit that normal curve equivalent scores provide that scale scores do not.
5. For classroom-based, end-of-unit tests, which do you think is more critical—reliability or validity?
6. In what ways have you experienced the influence of the ISLLC Standards?
7. Of the seven principles guiding the ISLLC Standards, which do you find most important and least important?
8. Choose one of the ISLLC Standards and provide a few examples of how you exhibit competency in this domain.

9. How might the VAL-Ed core components and key processes be useful to education leaders and leadership teams?

10. Comment on the strengths and weaknesses of value-added and attainment level modes of performance assessment.

11. How might NAEP and TIMSS data be useful to instructional decisions made in your school and district?

References and Suggested Readings

Eisenhart, M., and Borko, H. (1993). *Designing classroom research: Themes, issues, and struggles.* Boston, MA: Allyn & Bacon.

> This book centers on coordinating what is known from previous classroom research and working toward ideas, commitments, and guidelines that can inform future educational research efforts.

Flinders, D. J., and Mills, G. E. (Eds.). (1993). *Theory and concepts in qualitative research: Perspectives from the field.* New York: Teachers College Press.

> This volume invites the reader to reflect about the meaning of theory so that qualitative research can secure the kind of conceptual foundation it needs to withstand the scrutiny it deserves, and thus makes an important contribution both to the construction of that foundation and to the ways in which the complex social world we inhabit can be understood.

Hess, F. M. (2006). *Tough love for schools.* Washington, DC: AEI Press.

> In this book, the author explores the practical and political challenges of accountability, competition, excellence, and the public good and argues that real school reform requires new policies that enable public and private entrepreneurs to create new systems and schools, improve school management, reward excellence, harness advances in technology and knowledge, and devise strategies to draw new talent into the field.

Macpherson, R. J. S. (Ed.). (1987). *Ways and meanings of research in educational administration.* Armidale, Australia: University of New England.

> This text strives to demystify research and to unpack some of the associated metaphors of methodology, and it reveals through the work of selected researchers the significance of developments in the field of educational administration.

Osborne, D., and Gaebler, T. (1993). *Reinventing government.* New York: Plume.

> This book details the idea that government need not be a gigantic and inefficient bureaucracy but can instead tap into the power of the entrepreneurial process and the force of the free market.

Palumbo, D. J. (Ed.). (1987). *The politics of program evaluation.* Newbury Park, CA: Sage Publications.

> This text, one of a series, is particularly concerned with the politics of program evaluation in the context of the policy cycle of agenda setting, formulation, implementation, and termination, with evaluation at all stages. It also deals with political factors in the research process that relate to evaluation and utilization.

Porter, A. C., and Gamoran, A. (Eds.). (2002). *Methodological advances in cross-national surveys of educational achievement.* Washington, DC: National Academy Press.

Comprising papers prepared for the November 2000 public symposium held by the Board on International Comparative Studies in Education (BICSE), this book is a comprehensive assessment of methodological strengths and weaknesses of international comparative studies of student achievement.

Reeves, Douglas B. (2004). *Assessing educational leaders: Evaluating performance for improved individual and organizational results.* Thousand Oaks, CA: Corwin Press.

Notes

1. Due to the treatment of instructor assessment included in Chapter 13, the topic will not be included here.
2. The ELCC Standards, to which this book makes explicit reference, are built upon the ISLLC Standards. The two are essentially synonymous, with the ELCC Standards worded to serve as program accreditation standards.
3. This section draws upon the Framework for the Assessment of Learning-Centered Leadership. Authored by Porter, Goldring, & Murphy (2006) for the Wallace Foundation Grant on Leadership Assessment.
4. A reader may encounter the term *gain scores*. This is another means for appraising how much a student has learned over time. The distinction between a gain score and value added is subtle. A gain score is the achievement increment gained over a specified time period. Value added refers to the increment of achievement contributed by an instructor or school in excess of what would otherwise have been expected for that student given his or her social and economic circumstances and grade or age level.

CHAPTER ELEVEN

Data-Based Decision Making[1]

LEARNING OBJECTIVES

By the end of this chapter, you should be able to

- recognize the importance of data-driven decision making for education leaders;
- utilize a systematic process for making data-based decisions;
- use performance data in the design and operation of instructional programs and in guiding staff development;
- consider data infrastructure requirements to support school and district data-based decisions;
- identify various ways that school leaders can use data to guide program, personnel, and resource allocation decisions.

Within America's new era of heightened expectations for schooling, growing societal complexity, and increasing instructional sophistication, school leaders are looked to as individuals who can identify, define, and solve problems. While there are many approaches to making decisions and solving problems, a critical first step in solving problems is to identify and fully understand them, and one powerful mechanism for specifying and comprehending problems is to collect and analyze data. When strategic education leaders compile, assess, and utilize school and community data, they are in a better position to serve as catalysts for problem solving within school communities. While some problems clearly present themselves, others are not immediately evident or explicitly defined and thus must be discovered and fleshed out by careful analysis of data. Given the nation's current policy context, educators increasingly recognize the value of data and the need to obtain a greater comprehension of data analysis and decision making. The provision of such enhanced understanding is the aim of this chapter.

Consider for a moment what might be possible in American education if student-level performance data were systematically linked to corresponding grade-level and subject-area classroom teachers, and those data were linked to professional development allocations for those teachers, which were in turn linked to key classroom-level demographic indicators. While pondering this rhetorical question, consider the following two illustrative scenarios.

Mike McGee has been feeling a bit sluggish recently and decides to visit the local Veterans Administration hospital for a checkup. When accounting for habits and genetic factors, it is understandable that his level of anxiety is a bit high. Yet as each test is conducted, specialists have immediate access to the resultant data through a real-time local area network (LAN). These specialists, located in several separate buildings of the large hospital complex, are able concurrently to analyze and assess the test data and assemble a composite diagnosis for the patient. Throughout this process, nurses, who also have access to the test data and specialist analyses, are able to provide periodic updates and assurances to Mike. Results of early tests lead to subsequent follow-up analyses until all necessary data have been gathered. Within five hours of admittance, Mike McGee has undergone a thorough assessment and is provided with a data-based diagnosis crafted by a team of specialists. The diagnosis forms the basis of a plan of treatment that, fortunately, will remediate Mike's situation in a matter of weeks.

Karen Evans has been experiencing car trouble, and recently the check-engine light of her Lincoln Town Car has been illuminated. She rearranges her Monday work schedule to drop her car off at Friendly Auto for a checkup. However, the lead mechanic tells her that they only conduct diagnostic engine assessments on the last Thursday of each month. He warns that these reports, which are sent from the Friendly Auto headquarters, sometimes take a few weeks to arrive at storefront franchise locations. Further, he specifies that headquarters furnishes a report from these monthly diagnostic tests that lists all of the possible ailments for all of the cars at the garage on that given Thursday, making it difficult to pinpoint a specific problem with her car. Perplexed, Karen leaves Friendly Auto still uncertain if her car is capable of making the four-hundred-mile round-trip journey to a business conference later in the week.

Whether listening to the morning weather forecast, turning the radio dial to the afternoon traffic report, determining how to invest retirement funds, or keeping abreast of a favorite sports team, data keep citizens informed and appropriately influence decisions. Yet there are few twenty-first-century operations as outmoded as public school data systems. For example, which of the two scenarios above, Mike McGee at the VA hospital or Karen Evans at Friendly Auto, more closely resembles the data capacity of your school or district? What influence does this reality have upon the ability of school leaders to make well-informed, timely decisions?

In order to equip current and aspiring school leaders with increased knowledge of how to utilize data to make informed decisions, this chapter engages the challenging issue of (1) why it is important for school leaders to collect and analyze data, (2) how school data can be approached in a systematic manner, and (3) what specific types of data should be collected.

■ STRATEGIC APPROACHES TO DECISION MAKING IN EDUCATION

Why is data-based decision making so critical for school improvement? Why should school and district leaders turn to data to help inform leadership decisions? While there are many good answers to these questions, four key reasons will be provided here for why data-driven decision making is important.

First, however, we offer a working definition. Data-based decision making is the reliance for analyses and decisions upon systematically and reliably collected information regarding multiple performance and status characteristics of school operation. These facets can involve individual and collective student performance (e.g., academic achievement, attendance, extracurricular participation, or course taking), personnel (e.g., teacher characteristics, attendance, or professional development status), parents (e.g., participation, attendance at functions, responses to school communication), or fiscal matters such as spending within important categories (e.g., personnel, supplies, and instructional materials).

Careful collection, analysis, and utilization of data help schools to

- progress toward continuous student and organizational improvement;
- focus on and establish priorities for instructional and staff development efforts and monitor individual and collective progress;
- meet district, state, and federal accountability requirements;
- develop a sense of community through sustained collective learning.

Continuous Improvement

Systematic collection, analysis, and utilization of data can serve as a catalyst to propel organizational learning. School leaders can harness the regular information flow from data to sustain a culture of learning for both students and teachers within their schools. Data can provide leaders with continual **feedback** regarding mechanisms critical to supporting individual and collective learning in educational organizations.

In order for school leaders to sustain a culture of continuous improvement, questions such as the following should constantly be pursued: What are school and community data telling us? How can we change our practice in response to the data? What additional data need to be collected? How do data from standardized assessments compare with teacher-created measures of student performance and development? The greater degree of access that teachers and school leaders have to such information, the better able they will be to sustain cycles of inquiry that will enhance professional climate and organizational learning.

Focus Efforts and Monitor Progress

Multiple types and sources of data are necessary for a school leader to understand a school's strengths and weaknesses, set priorities for improvement, concentrate change efforts, and establish a baseline from which to monitor progress. As will become clear later in this chapter, data play an integral part in planning and implementing focused improvement strategies. School and district-level data are valuable tools to evaluate policies and programs, to develop and improve curricular offerings, and to monitor teaching and learning. Yet in many settings, this valuable tool is underutilized. Take, for example, Sunnybrook Elementary School.

At Sunnybrook, there are currently four isolated, supplemental reading initiatives in progress, five different reading textbooks are being used, and two quite different approaches taken to developing students' reading comprehension skills. Yet if detailed data were not collected on the reading program at Sunnybrook, one might be puzzled about the recent decline in reading scores. This is a good example of the fact that data are an excellent problem-finding tool. Yet one often does not have to look far to uncover a multitude of issues needing attention in schools. Here is where strategic education leaders can play a critical role in helping the school community approach problems in a systematic manner. Too often, schools and school systems try to do too much, and all at once.

One common problem in schools is a lack of programmatic focus and alignment. Strategic education leaders, however, are in a position to take a comprehensive view of programmatic data and thus assist schools in developing a more focused and integrated approach to instruction improvement. When used in this manner, data not only provide a valuable means of discovering school problems, but also provide the information necessary for a school to monitor progress in addressing those dilemmas.

Meet Accountability Requirements

Within the current policy environment, one of the most widespread reasons that data-based decision making is so important for school leaders is to meet accountability requirements. The No Child Left Behind Act (NCLB) legislation requires states and localities to collect, analyze, and report data on student demographics and achievement. Much of the accountability pressure that school leaders encounter is external; those outside the school such as district, state, and federal governing bodies determine benchmarks and standards. In order for school leaders to ensure they are meeting these external accountability requirements, they must use school data to answer questions such as, Is the school meeting various requirements outlined in the state standards? Are all students making Adequate Yearly Progress? What proportion and what subgroups of students are scoring at or above proficiency levels as determined by state achievement tests?

School leaders must also utilize data to ensure their school communities meet other forms of accountability. NCLB has enhanced the market accountability facing school leaders by requiring students enrolled in persistently failing schools to be given the option to transfer to more successful schools in their district. To address such competition-based pressure, schools need to be able to compare themselves with other schools and to highlight improvements as a vehicle to attract parents and students.

While market-based and externally imposed accountability systems attract most of the headlines, internal accountability is also an important domain influenced by data collection and analysis. Here, school groups develop goals based on local norms and aspirations for growth and then collect data to monitor instructional progress toward the school-based goals. As teacher motivation resides squarely within schools, where individual effort and collaboration can directly affect teaching and learning, internal accountability can play an important role in enhancing classroom practices.

 CASE 5 REVISITED

Principal Frank Gomez is concerned about his recent disaggregated student achievement data for many reasons. Foremost is the prospect that students will utilize vouchers to transfer out of Carter Middle School to other local schools that are making Adequate Yearly Progress. In what ways can Principal Gomez translate this market-based accountability into school-wide growth? What impact has competition for students had upon your school or district?

Build Community through Organizational Learning

Data can be an important lever for creating and supporting the professional relationships and sense of community at the center of organizational learning. An emerging view of teaching, referred to as the "new professionalism" of teaching, sees teaching as part of a communal endeavor, moving away from traditional egg-crate classroom autonomy toward new forms of interactive relationships with colleagues. Within and outside of schools, greater dialogue surrounding the collection and interpretation of data provides an opportunity to bridge the traditional divide that exists between key school actors and constituents—such as between middle school and high school teachers, parents and teachers, schools and businesses. Gone are the days when schools can serve an elite population subset. As such, it is imperative that schools take efforts to broaden the scope of what and who counts within the educational community. This necessary organizational learning is an excellent opportunity to build a sense of community inclusive of the growing demographic diversity facing schools.

■ SYSTEMATIC COLLECTION AND USE OF SCHOOL DATA

Having discussed several of the many good reasons why data-based decision making matters for school success, it is now important to situate data collection, analysis, and use within the context of an overall school improvement cycle. At its core, the reason for employing data in school decision making is to foster growth and improvement. A typical school improvement cycle is provided in Figure 11.1.

The systematic collection and use of data play key roles in school efforts aimed at continuous improvement. When one develops a school improvement plan, data can provide insight and focus for school goals. Data patterns can reveal strengths and weaknesses within the instructional program and thus provide excellent direction for growth. When one evaluates a plan, data allow the organization to assess whether the plan is being implemented as designed and to determine the impact of the plan on student achievement or other organizational goals. Of the three components of the school improvement cycle, evaluation is the domain where the process often deteriorates. Yet to secure continuous, synergistic school improvement, data-based evaluation is critical. Reflections upon the data provided throughout the evaluation process provide a basis for either adhering to an existing plan or modifying the plan better to meet organizational goals.

The utilization of data throughout the school improvement process, rather than relying upon intuition, tradition, self-reports, one-shot observations, or convenience to drive decisions, leads to benefits such as those highlighted in Table 11.1.

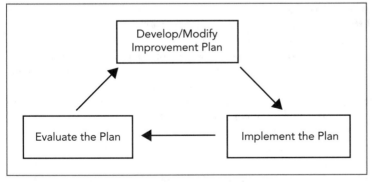

FIGURE 11.1 School Improvement Cycle

TABLE 11.1 Comparison of School Processes

Decision Making Based on Intuition, Inertia, Tradition, Self-Reports, Single-Shot Observations, Prejudices, or Convenience	Data-Driven Decision Making
Budgetary decisions based on prior practice, priority programs	Budget allocations to programs based on data-informed needs
Staff meetings that focus on operations and the dissemination of information	Staff meetings that concentrate on improvement strategies and issues raised by a local school's empirical data
Grading systems based on each teacher's criteria of completed work and participation	Grading systems based on common student-performance criteria that report progress on the standards as well as work skills
Scattered staff development programs	Concentrated collective and individual staff development programs as an improvement strategy to address documented problems/needs
Reports to the community about school events	Organized factual reports to the community about the learning progress of students
Periodic administrative team meetings focused solely on operations	Administrative team meetings that focus on measured progress toward data-based improvement goals

Although the particular manner in which data are collected, analyzed, and used varies from school to school, the key elements of an effective data-based decision-making program include (1) a data leadership team, (2) purposeful data collection and analysis, and (3) a plan for utilizing data to enhance instructional practice.

Data Leadership Team Appropriately Supported

In order for school and community data to be utilized effectively to enhance student learning, a number of infrastructure and support activities need to be in place. One important support is a data leadership team. A team, rather than an individual, is ideally suited for this work for a number of reasons. To begin, principals and other school leaders have been given a difficult charge: take an abundance of student and demographic data, provided from a variety of sources and in various formats, and turn these data into targeted information that can be used to enhance educational practice. The sheer magnitude of this task would make it difficult for even a "superhero" principal single-handedly to accomplish. Fortunately, discussions are richer and less biased, and potential solutions are more diverse and complete when numerous points of view are considered. When findings are ready to be presented, the dissemination of information benefits from a team that can ensure no constituent groups are overlooked. The tremendous effort needed to sustain a culture of continuous school improvement through data-driven decision making is much easier when tasks are divided among a team of committed people.

For these reasons, strategic education leaders should strive to develop a data leadership team. The goal of collaborative data teams is to cooperate in the design and analysis of data to improve the educational experiences and performance of students. These teams can exist in a variety of forms. They can be made up entirely of teachers, administrators, and various school specialists. Additionally, the teams may include members from the wider community, including parents, business leaders, and others with a vested interest in schools. These teams can be formed with a purposeful inclusion of members across grade levels or subject areas. Certainly, within a given school there may be multiple data teams— from a school-wide team with representatives from each grade level and curricular area to smaller grade-level or subject-area teams. Regardless of their composition, these teams all serve the purpose of successfully utilizing data to enhance the educational experiences and performance of students.

Time is one of the most important supports that the data leadership team and other staff members need in order to use data for decision making. To sustain the infusion of data into school improvement efforts, significant time is necessary to engage staff members with data on a continual basis. While many data-based activities can be embedded within faculty meetings, other activities, such as developing improvement strategies, will require substantial in-service or "release" time to construct thoughtfully. Monthly meetings will be necessary for a data leadership team that has primary responsibility for coordinating data collection, analysis, interpretation, and reporting efforts. School leaders can create time for these meetings through means such as providing substitute teachers for team members, or by arranging team members' schedules so that meetings can occur during planning periods, or by compensating team members for their time to meet after school hours.

In many ways, a data management system upon which school personnel rely for data will either provide a tremendous support for a data leadership team, or it will bring the data-dependent goals and intentions of school personnel to a grinding halt. One major assumption of the benefits of data-driven decision making is that **reliable**, timely, and accurate data will be available. So a primary step for strategic education leaders to take within the domain of data-based decision making is to assess the scope, quality, and availability of data to support instructional decisions. To assess the usability of existing data, strategic education leaders should examine data along the following five dimensions: (1) availability and accessibility, (2) timeliness and completeness, (3) accuracy, (4) consistency, and (5) alignment.

The *availability* of data refers to how easy it is for teachers and administrators to access student, teacher, and school-level data on demand. Is a special administrative code needed to access data? Are real-time data available, or is information only uploaded weekly or monthly? The *completeness* of data refers to how much pertinent information is available for analysis. Do some teachers and students have data files that are missing significant amounts of relevant demographic detail? What percentage of available student data is entered into the school data system? *Accuracy* and *timeliness* of data refers to how correctly student and faculty data are entered into the data system. How often do data files get updated? Are recent changes in student and teacher data profiles reflected in the available data? The *consistency* of data refers to the uniformity in which data are entered. Are all similarly situated special education students represented in the data system in the same manner? Are there differences in the way students of various **ethnicities** are represented in the data system? The *alignment* of data refers to the degree to which data can be linked to other data in the system. Are student-level data linked to faculty data? Are teacher demographic data linked to payroll data?

Data usability is a function of both the databases and data system utilized by a school or district. A database is an organized collection of information or data elements, stored electronically, that can be searched, sorted, reorganized, and analyzed rapidly. A data system is a collection of computer programs that facilitate the storage, modification, and extraction of information from a database. It is no surprise that both are integral to the provision of usable data for school leaders and teachers. Consider the degree to which your school data allow you to link teachers to students to educational activities at the elementary, middle, and high school levels. To what extent is your data management system able to link individual students to multiple teachers (such as in team teaching, shared positions, or multigrade teaming)? Does your data system link professional development data to teacher course loads and curricular responsibilities? If you can answer yes to these questions, your school benefits from usable data, likely a product of thoughtfully constructed databases and a high-quality data system. If not, efforts need to be undertaken by school and district personnel to construct a data system capable of accurately evaluating instructional activities and related outcomes.

Unfortunately, America's public schools do not uniformly code, collect, and assemble data with the instructional activities of classrooms linked to student performance. Something as important as linking individual students' test scores to their appropriate grade and subject-area teachers and then linking those data to key teacher-characteristic variables, school demographic variables, and resource levels can currently occur in only a few states and local school districts. At the local school level, strategic education leaders can provide a useful service to school communities by insisting on the availability of high-quality data. This begins by ensuring that usable data are entered into the system in a systematic manner; otherwise, the adage "garbage in, garbage out" may be all too true.

Purposeful Data Collection and Analysis

The acquisition and analysis of school data should be a planned and purposeful process. When data are collected in a purposeful manner, educators are better able to identify patterns of outcomes and design strategies to enhance student learning. Purposeful data collection and analysis are concerned with targeting identified needs and goals that are almost always linked to enhanced student and organizational performance. Currently, most data collection at the school level is externally driven and is primarily used to establish compliance with standards. By taking ownership of school data at the local level, school leaders can move beyond compliance to an authentic school improvement effort.

By focusing on domains of practice to which the school community is committed, school leaders can increase the likelihood that insights provided by data will have a sustained impact on teachers' instructional practice.

Purposeful data analysis is focused on using data to make decisions about programs and students. In order to make informed decisions about programs, data may need to be analyzed across multiple contexts or over multiple years. In order to make appropriate decisions about students, data may need to be analyzed across classes and teachers, **disaggregated** and drawn from multiple sources. For example, to determine how various student groups are performing in reading, one needs to collect data on student demographics, teaching practices, student learning (on both standardized and teacher-generated tests), and program features (such as classroom materials used and teacher proficiency with the curriculum) and analyze these data over a multiyear period. By moving beyond simplistic or token data analysis (examining one data source for one year) to in-depth, purposeful analysis (examining the interaction of multiple data sources over multiple years), educational leaders can determine the impact of their programs and practices and modify them to improve the performance of all students.

Student Achievement	**Demographic**
• Standardized tests • Norm-referenced tests • Criterion-referenced tests • Writing samples • Authentic assessments • Portfolio items • Teacher observation	• Enrollment • Attendance • Grade levels • Free and reduced lunch • Race • Ethnicity • Gender
School Program	**Perception**
• Texts and materials used • Library holdings • Technology • Curriculum • Supplemental programs • Content standards	• Community values • Beliefs • Attitudes • Satisfaction with program • Strengths and needs of school • Skill level of graduates

FIGURE 11.2 Multiple Data Types

As the example above illustrates, in order to collect and analyze data purposefully, one must consider multiple types of data. Four types of data are helpful to create the composite picture necessary for answering complex questions. These types of data include achievement data, demographic data, perception data, and school program data. These four types of data are highlighted in Figure 11.2, and each is described below.

Student Achievement Data. In many ways, student achievement data are the ultimate source of insight regarding educational program effectiveness. Fortunately, there are multiple forms of student achievement data in addition to that which is provided from standardized tests. Standardized achievement data are an example of annual, large-scale assessments. Additionally, educators can employ periodic assessment data and ongoing classroom assessment data to determine the efficacy of the instructional program. These three types of achievement data vary in purpose, frequency, type of feedback provided, and targeted audience. This information is summarized in Figure 11.3.

Annual, large-scale assessment data are designed primarily for accountability purposes, providing a broad indicator of school effectiveness. While these data can be of some use regarding curricular program efficacy, their utility is limited because these tests are designed to sample broad domains of student knowledge. As such, these assessments are insufficiently helpful when seeking to determine a specific area of student progress, and they provide only limited utility during a given school year.

Periodic, grade-level, and subject-specific assessments provide immediate results of student performance on key standards-based skills. These assessments can be used to establish entrance-level performance benchmarks for students at the beginning of a school year. By continuing to use these assessments throughout a school year, teachers and administrators can determine students' progress, as well as uncover strengths and weaknesses in particular content areas. These assessments are able to provide insight regarding which

Feedback	Assessment Type		
Purpose	Annual, large-scale tests	Periodic, grade level, and subject area	Ongoing classroom assessments
Frequency	Infrequent ⟵————————————⟶ Frequent		
Type	Broad ⟵————————————⟶ Specific		
Target	Community, policy makers, administrators, general accountability audience	Administrators, teachers	Teachers, students

FIGURE 11.3 Comparison of Assessment Types

students might need enrichment or special assistance during a school year. Additionally, by examining classroom or grade-level aggregate data, one is able to uncover patterns in content coverage or student success that may require alternate instructional strategies or content-specific professional development for a particular teacher. Ideally, these data are aligned with end-of-course assessments and standardized tests. In this way, one attains data on student and programmatic progress throughout a school year that are consistent with the perspective gained from annual, summative achievement tests.

Ongoing classroom-based assessments can be a powerful tool to help educators understand the depth of each student's knowledge and skills. In order for these data to bear fruit, however, the result must be used to make decisions for improving student achievement. Strategic education leaders must challenge teachers graphically to depict data from daily assignments in a way that clearly shows who is excelling, who needs enrichment, and who is performing on target. When data buried in grade books are charted, displayed, and utilized when constructing lessons, the richness of ongoing assessments is harnessed to the creation of responsive, student-centered learning experiences. The key here is how these formative data are used. If no instructional or programmatic modifications are made, then the potential benefits illuminated by data have been lost. Here again, data can pinpoint a problem, but solutions often require change in teacher practice.

Demographic Data. In an era of market-based accountability and increasing school choice options, school leaders must continue to develop a solid understanding of their communities. In some locations, this is tantamount to hitting a bull's-eye while riding a Brahma bull, as demographic conditions can be a swiftly moving target. To help facilitate this quest for community awareness, school leaders are advised to take a longitudinal approach to the endeavor. In this manner, an education leader can begin to view trends and make predictions. When determining which demographic data to collect, the goal is thoroughly to know the school population in order to clarify problems and needs. Dimensions of demographic data that should be collected include the following: neighborhood characteristics, parent involvement, behavioral and social problems of students, key demographic characteristics of students enrolled in school and their parents (e.g., age, gender, race, ethnicity, socioeconomic status), mobility patterns in and out of grades and schools, student transportation needs, and enrollment rates in special programs (e.g., ESL, special education, or after-school programs).

Collection and analysis of demographic data enable school leaders better to understand the social context in which students, parents, faculty, and administrators are situated. By assessing trends within the student population and analyzing factors outside of school that influence student learning, education leaders are better able to craft a purposeful, relevant, and responsive educational program.

School Program Data. Rich sources of information about the quality of programs in schools are often hidden in dusty binders or not contained in written documents at all, making this potential source of data difficult to collect and use. To guide the collection of program data, one might consider how successful school programs are in bringing about the academic excellence articulated in the school mission, goals, and content standards. At the outset of a school year, plans should be made to collect program evaluation data. The collection of these data throughout the school year, which can be seen as a form of action research, will inform decision making about programs, curricula, and supporting materials.

For example, if a school is concerned about the impact of the band program upon the academic performance of band members, one would collect information about the time demands of the instrumental music program, both within and outside of school, as well as assess students' success before, during, and following their involvement in the band. This latter assessment might be conducted both by looking at student grades and by interviewing students regarding their experiences with juggling academic responsibilities while in the band program. In this case, a mix of quantitative and qualitative data would provide a well-rounded picture of the impact that this program is having on the broader achievement level of students. The successful utilization of in-house program-level data may require a culture shift in some education organizations. The shift involves a commitment to examining educational practices thoroughly with a disposition to determining how such practices might be changed to benefit the academic performance of students.

Perception Data. A fourth type of data to collect and evaluate from various stakeholders in the school community is perception data. These data, similar to demographic data, are enlightening because they turn the attention of school leaders to the important ideas and opinions of the school community. It is no surprise that the opinions of parents and community members influence students profoundly. Therefore, it is essential that school leaders are aware of the perceptions of the school that exist in the community. In order to assemble a reasonably complete composite of perception data, school leaders should include the following members of the school community: students, parents, instructional and support staff, local businesses, school board members, regional colleges and universities, and other citizens with a vested interest in education. Perception data help school leaders understand such things as how the members of the school community feel about the school; how satisfied community members are with the educational programs; what community members perceive to be strengths and needs of the school; and what the community thinks about the knowledge and skills of graduates.

Mechanisms by which perception data can be gathered include surveys, polls, analyses of local newspaper editorials, and unsolicited letters to the school. These data, which are often seen as diffuse and intangible by members of the community, can be drawn together to provide a well-rounded and honest portrayal of school progress.

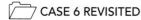

CASE 6 REVISITED

Considering Figure 11.2, how might the leader in the Mountain Union School District use the four types of data above to ensure a pay-for-performance plan is constructed that is tailored to the local context and community?

Using the Four Data Types. As achievement, demographic, program, and perception data are each unique forms of data, proper analysis will require slightly different methods. After the various types of data are analyzed through their own lenses, a next step is to bring key insights from each domain together to create a more holistic view. Because the primary emphasis in school improvement is on student learning, analysis of achievement data often forms the basis of school improvement plans and strategies. As a data leadership team sorts through additional data sources, patterns and relationships among the data may begin to emerge. Once these multiple perspectives are pulled together, it is important to step back from the fine-grained analyses and look at the composite picture from a distance.

At this stage, a summarizing and ranking of observed strengths and weaknesses from multiple data sources are beneficial. Based on all the data that have been studied and the patterns that have been observed, a data leadership team can synthesize the overarching problems that have been identified. In doing so, the data leadership team moves from data analysis to interpretation. As data are interpreted and understood within the context of the broader school program, they can inform questions about the instructional program to produce the desired results, whether they focus on increasing student performance in tenth-grade math or enhancing parental involvement in elementary school.

Crafting a Data-Based Plan to Enhance Practice

The time-intensive undertaking of collecting and analyzing multiple types of data in a purposeful manner, and the hard work of synthesizing and interpreting data, are wasted tasks if the data are not used to form a plan that will link these insights to appropriate programmatic and pedagogical changes. In some schools and districts, the problem with data-driven decision making is a lack of usable data. In other schools and districts, the problem is one of *having* too much data and not *using* it appropriately. This section provides instructional leaders with suggestions for using data to craft a plan for improvement by generating hypotheses, developing goals, designing strategies, defining evaluation criteria, and communicating with stakeholders.

Generate Hypotheses. One way to move closer to identifying root causes of student, classroom, or school performance problems is to generate hypotheses. A hypothesis is a possible explanation for observed patterns in data. Crafting a hypothesis enables school leaders and teachers to take specific actions aimed at enhancing, or somehow altering, patterns in data. In this way, generating hypotheses is a first step in determining the reasons for observed data patterns. To guide the generation of hypotheses, a data leadership team will create and ponder alternative explanations for why students are performing the way they are and consider what school practices and approaches are contributing to current levels of performance.

For example, considering that the previously mentioned Sunnybrook Elementary School has experienced consistent declines in student reading comprehension levels in grades 4, 5, and 6, the data leadership team proposed the following hypotheses:

- Hypothesis 1: The reading texts and workbooks are out of date and do not follow a logical, grade-by-grade sequence.
- Hypothesis 2: There are more ESL students in Sunnybrook classes each year, and their low level of English understanding dilutes scores.
- Hypothesis 3: Upper elementary teachers have not had sufficient training to teach the revised reading comprehension standards.

Having generated several hypotheses, the next step is to collect evidence to either support or reject these possible explanations. Certainly the kinds of data that are generated, analyzed, and interpreted prior to generating hypotheses will influence both hypothesis formation and subsequent evidence collection. For example, to uncover evidence pertinent to the hypotheses, one would conduct classroom observations, disaggregate achievement data by subgroups of students, and assess lesson plans and homework assignments. For illustrative purposes, data collection efforts linked to each hypothesis could produce such evidence as that highlighted below.

- Data-based evidence regarding Hypothesis 1: Current reading texts and workbooks used in grades 4, 5, and 6 were adopted between the years 1996 and 2000 from three different publishers.
- Data-based evidence regarding Hypothesis 2: Enrollment levels for ESL students at Sunnybrook do show slight increases in grade 6 but have been stable in grades 4 and 5.
- Data-based evidence regarding Hypothesis 3: All of the teachers in grades 4, 5, and 6 do have the appropriate reading credentials. However, neither the school nor the district has provided professional development activities for elementary teachers in reading comprehension during the past seven years.

Assessment of the illustrative evidence for each hypothesis would likely lead to the following conclusions. Hypothesis 1 would be accepted as a possibility, as the texts are both out of date and, since they are from three different publishers, potentially out of sequence. Hypothesis 2 would be rejected due to the fact that ESL levels have been stable for both fourth and fifth grade and only slightly increased in sixth grade. Hypothesis 3 would be accepted as a possibility, since no new professional development has occurred since the reading comprehension standards were revised.

Develop Goals. Obviously, the solution to be pursued is a function of the accuracy of any particular hypothesis. After data patterns have been interpreted and plausible hypotheses have been generated and tested, it is time to develop goals for improvement. When confronted with multiple problems and hypotheses, it is important to focus on developing goals for the most important or urgent issues first. Bear in mind that it is realistic for an education organization to focus on only three to five important goals at any one time. As such, the issue of prioritization cannot be overstated. The process of developing goals is about articulating desired outcomes, be they short term or long range. When developing goals, one must consider the capacities of both faculty and students and be cognizant of barriers that must be overcome. Human beings, by nature, can be quite resistant to change. Therefore, an educational leader must be able accurately to assess the institutional climate when considering a major change effort. A strategic education leader is able to assess the level of commitment to a goal and considers the resources necessary to reach the goal. Once a goal is set, many resources are deployed to attain the intended outcome. Therefore, crafting meaningful goals is an important endeavor. The following guidelines can assist in developing well-written goals:

- **S**pecific: Goals should be focused and clearly stated. A specific goal has a greater chance of being accomplished than a vague, general goal.
- **M**easurable: Goals should specify a desired outcome in tangible, quantifiable terms.
- **A**chievable: Goals should be able to be attained. The achievement of goals may require stretching, but leaders should avoid setting goals that are simply unrealistic.
- **R**esearch based: Goals should be directly linked to patterns observed in the data.
- **T**ime sensitive: Goals should reflect sensitivity to the urgency of the problem and the current status of the organizational culture.

To provide examples of school improvement goals, return to the two plausible hypotheses for the recent decline in Sunnybrook Elementary School's reading comprehension scores. The following is a potential goal statement targeting Hypothesis 1: To adopt an aligned set of reading texts and workbooks for grades 4, 5, and 6 by the fall of the 2008 school year so that by the spring of 2010, 80 percent of fourth-, fifth-, and sixth-grade students score at proficient or advanced levels in reading comprehension.

Similarly, the following is a goal statement targeting Hypothesis 3: To provide all Sunnybrook reading teachers with four days of in-service professional development regarding the revised reading comprehension standards during the 2008–9 school year so that by the spring of 2010, 90 percent of fourth-, fifth-, and sixth-graders surpass the **median** scale scores on the reading comprehension component of the state's annual, criterion-referenced assessment.

Design Strategies. Once well-specified goals have been formulated, it is necessary to determine what operational actions need to occur in order for the goal to be met. Goals, by themselves, are useless. Action-oriented strategies are necessary to move an organization toward intended outcomes. To determine the appropriate strategies for meeting a particular goal, a data leadership team might begin by brainstorming. The process of brainstorming provides a multitude of potential actions that might move the organization toward attaining a particular goal. In the brainstorming process, it is important to keep the hypotheses in mind, as specific strategies might flow naturally from these plausible explanations of organizational conditions. An additional source of potential action steps exists in the form of best-practice insights from other schools that have grappled with similar challenges. As another means of mitigating the tendency to focus on intuitive strategies, education leaders are encouraged to draw upon research-based and time-tested approaches.

When defining specific strategies, it is important to remember that these proposed actions are the vehicle by which an organization will move from where it currently stands to where it hopes to go. As such, it is important to consider the following guidelines when developing strategies. The strategy should be

- clear and understandable to all constituents;
- based on best-practice insights and mindful of the existing organizational culture;

- observable and measurable;
- targeted to one specific, attainable action that will lead to accomplishing the goal;
- broadly endorsed by data leadership team members;
- implemented and continually evaluated.

Strategies represent commitments to carrying out action. Therefore, it is important for school leaders to discuss the level of dedication and hard work that strategies will require. Additionally, it is helpful to establish timelines for strategies to be carried out and to assign duties to individuals who are responsible for specific strategy components. To the benefit of everyone involved, these arrangements must be noted on a documented version of the plan. It must be stressed that the absence of a written plan for attaining goals through the implementation and evaluation of strategies will significantly hinder improvement efforts.

To provide examples of defined strategies, return again to Sunnybrook School. The following is one of many possible strategies related to the goal statement for Hypothesis 1:

A reading comprehension committee, chaired by Ms. Jones, and including representatives from grades 4, 5, and 6, is charged with making textbook and materials adoption recommendations to the curriculum subcommittee of the school board by the end of next semester.

Similarly, the following is one possible strategy related to the goal statement for Hypothesis 3:

The district reading specialist will organize and conduct a professional development workshop for all reading teachers at Sunnybrook Elementary School during the November in-service day that will address the knowledge, skills, and competencies required of teachers by the new reading comprehension standards.

Define Evaluation Criteria. While strategies provide a vehicle for attaining the intended outcomes articulated in school goals, it is important to assess the degree to which goals are in fact being met; it is crucial to establish measures that will be used to evaluate the success of individual strategies. When determining these criteria, it is helpful to consider how the success of each strategy can be measured and what evidence will confirm the success of these actions. As an intermediate step, it is also significant to assess the degree to which individual strategies have been implemented. Without a clear understanding of the degree of implementation, one can never be certain if observed changes can be attributed to the reform strategy. Often the failure is not necessarily in the reform strategies themselves, but rather in the degree to which they were implemented.

To determine the impact that implemented strategies have had upon the educational organization, it is necessary to consider multiple data sources, as outlined earlier in the chapter. For example, to assess the degree to which the strategy pertinent to Hypothesis 3 was met, one would evaluate at least the following sources of data: standardized test scores, criterion-referenced assessments, faculty observation forms, evaluation data about staff development activities, select portfolio items, and grade-book entries. This example highlights the importance of establishing specific measures for each strategy. To the degree that goals and strategies are measurable, evaluation data will provide targeted insights regarding the degree to which the strategy was implemented and successful in creating the desired results.

Communicate with Constituents about Data. Communicating to a broad base of stake-holders about the purposes, results, and ongoing plans for data analysis is important for schools that want to sustain improvement efforts. Similar to communication about student progress and key school activities, communication about data-based findings should occur throughout the school year. It is not sufficient for stakeholders to receive sporadic or annual updates if a strategic education leader hopes to encourage greater understanding of and support for data-driven decision making.

Further, data leadership teams should discuss which particular data-based updates could be disseminated without a conversation and which warrant an opportunity for stakeholders to engage in a conversation about the results of data analysis. Such forums would provide an opportunity to discuss results, patterns, interpretations, and responses to trends illuminated by data. While affirming the school's commitment to the challenging process of utilizing data-driven decision making to enhance student performance, these efforts also endorse the commitment of school leaders to engaging the community in meaningful dialogue.

■ ANALYZING DATA INTEGRAL TO SCHOOL EFFECTIVENESS

Having described a systematic process for how education leaders can utilize data within the context of ongoing school improvement efforts, it is now important to provide practical examples of data analysis in domains important for school effectiveness. While there are many pathways to creating successful schools, they share the common theme of a school-wide focus on teaching and learning. Toward that end, strategic education leaders need to attend to the school's mission and goals, rigorous **content standards**, curricular and instructional alignment, teacher professional development, culture and climate for student learning, professional community of teachers, and school-community relations. In this chapter section, various sources of data that can be used to gauge how well a school is implementing select pathways to school improvement will be discussed. Examples of student achievement data analysis will also be provided. Together, these insights provide school leaders with important knowledge regarding the continuous monitoring and evaluation of progress toward achieving school goals.

Mission and Goals. For quite some time, educators have pointed to the importance of school mission and goals in guiding the activities of schools. Since the school mission and goals play a pivotal role for the organization, it is important that school leaders understand the degree to which these aspirations are being attained. A first step in this process is to consider the measurable components of the school mission. Next, one must determine what types and sources of data are currently available and what data must be collected in order to evaluate each component of the **mission statement**.

For illustrative purposes, consider the mission of Sunnybrook Elementary School.

> *The mission of Sunnybrook Elementary School is to provide a safe and nurturing environment with opportunities for all students to learn. All students will reach performance goals at or above grade level in reading, writing, mathematics, social studies, and science while demonstrating responsibility and self-control.*

When considering the measurable components of the Sunnybrook mission statement, the following three measurable goals come to the surface: (1) provide a safe and nurturing environment, (2) all students will reach performance goals, and (3) all students will demonstrate

TABLE 11.2 Mission Statement Planning Matrix

Mission Statement Components	What We Want to Learn from the Data	Data We Already Have	Data We Need to Collect	Sources of New Data	Who Should Be Involved in Data Collection
Safe and nurturing environment	Do students, parents, teachers, and staff feel school is safe and nurturing?	Number of discipline infractions, office referrals, suspensions, results from annual district parent survey	Input from students, parents, teachers, staff, and administrators	Student focus groups; parent town-hall meetings; faculty, staff, and administrator discussions	Student council, homeroom teachers, PTA, administrators
Perform at or above grade level in reading	Are all students meeting performance goals in reading?	End-of-year standardized tests, course grades, formative assessments	Level of reading in content areas, usage of library, time spent reading at home	Assignments in science and social studies, books checked out from library, accelerated reading, parent survey	Librarian, curriculum specialists, teams of teachers, PTA, administrators

responsibility and self-control. To guide the analysis of what data are currently available for each component and what data are needed, the matrix provided in Table 11.2 is helpful. As an example, two components of the mission are included in the matrix.

Here, one can see that data regarding the degree to which the school provides a safe and nurturing environment are currently available. However, before one can accurately assess the degree to which the school currently provides a safe and nurturing environment, more data are needed. The matrix encourages the specification of what additional sources of data are necessary and encourages discussion regarding who should be involved in data collection.

For example, where components of the mission are not being assessed by existing data, the leadership team may decide to construct data-gathering instruments to pinpoint these domains. If insufficient data exist regarding the degree to which students feel safe at school, an instrument can be crafted to address this issue directly. Typically, such surveys are constructed by asking specific questions and then providing a scale either to assess to what degree goals are being achieved or practiced or to assess the teachers', students', parents', and principals' level of satisfaction with goal achievement. For example, level of goal achievement can be measured using a four-point scale, such as "fully," "mostly," "somewhat," "not at all." One also can frame the questions around people's perceptions about how well the organization is doing to achieve goals, using scales such as "excellent," "good," "fair," and "poor." Armed with these insights, a data leadership team could follow the above-outlined steps to establish goals and strategies for collecting and analyzing the desired data in order to conduct a data-based assessment of the degree to which the school is attaining the components of the mission statement.

Professional Development. Given the rapid pace of change in contemporary educational policy and practice, the elevated expectations now held for schools, and the heightened focus on achievement of students, a renewed emphasis has been placed on professional development. Improving the operational and instructional capacity of teachers and other professionals should be a priority of schools and districts. By focusing on what works, school leaders can encourage professional development opportunities that empower teachers to make a positive impact on student performance. As described in Chapter 13, much research has been conducted on what makes professional development effective. As a means of assessing the quality of professional development experiences that teachers are participating in, and as a means of linking participation in professional development to the attainment of faculty goals, school leaders can use a data-gathering form like the one provided in Table 11.3. This form provides an example of how school leaders can assess the

TABLE 11.3 Professional Development Record

Teacher/Team Member	Annual Professional Development Goals	Focus of Professional Development Activities	Degree of Alignment with Correlates of Effective Professional Development
Jones	1.		___ Linked to student learning outcomes ___ Job-embedded
	2.		___ Ongoing and sustained, with follow-up ___ Incorporates authentic, active learning
	3.		___ Includes subject-matter content ___ Encourages reflection ___ Incorporates collaboration with colleagues ___ Measures impact on student achievement
Rodriquez	1.		___ Linked to student learning outcomes ___ Job-embedded
	2.		___ Ongoing and sustained, with follow-up ___ Incorporates authentic, active learning
	3.		___ Includes subject-matter content ___ Encourages reflection ___ Incorporates collaboration with colleagues ___ Measures impact on student achievement

degree to which faculty participation in professional development is linked to the correlates of effective professional development.

This form utilizes the nine components of effective professional development described in Chapter 13. Similar to this proposed model, an educational leader might create a template for each individual teacher, grade-level team, or departmental unit. The form includes a place for the teacher and leaders to discuss professional goals for the year. These goals will likely be linked to the mission and goals of the school, to state and school standards for a particular content area, and perhaps teacher evaluation data from a previous school year.

The column on the focus of the professional development will allow school leaders and teachers to track what particular domains of classroom experience are being targeted. This focus might include enhanced content knowledge (to help bolster low performance in a particular content domain from prior achievement-test results) or pedagogical techniques that may have a broader application. The final column of the sheet allows data to be collected regarding the degree to which individual teachers, teams, and an entire faculty are taking part in professional development experiences that are aligned with correlates of effective professional development.

Culture and Climate of Student Learning. Similar to the other domains of effective schools, it is important to set measurable goals regarding school climate. Yet before goals can be established and data collected, efforts to construct a shared vision of a safe and orderly school climate and culture must be established. In the absence of such consensus-building conversations, the collection and reporting of data will lose a measure of impact. The most efficient manner to collect information about the school's climate and culture is through surveys, which will capture respondents' perceptions, attitudes, and feelings. Survey data should include parents, students, teachers, and interested community members. It is important for a large percentage of each group to have the opportunity to respond. This will mitigate the skewed picture that might prevail if only the most vocally dissatisfied or involved and supportive members responded.

Many factors can impact respondents' opinions and feelings. These include the stress of starting a new school year, end-of-year testing anxiety, and so forth. Therefore, when collecting data regarding school culture over the course of several years, it is important to collect responses at the same time of year each year.

Consider again the mission of Sunnybrook School, which aspired to provide students with a safe and orderly environment. Figure 11.4 provides hypothetical data from the annual survey of student perceptions of the school climate.

Analyses of the results of the school climate survey illuminate an interesting condition. While nearly 95 percent of students believe students are well behaved, only 58 percent feel safe at school. These data indicate that students feel unsafe at school for reasons other than student behavior. The faculty and leadership at Sunnybrook are now equipped to deal more substantively with possible root causes of students' feelings regarding safety. In this case, the data do not necessarily provide an answer but do suggest a reframing of the question.

At Sunnybrook, data are routinely collected at school regarding discipline, such as in- and out-of-school suspensions, office referrals, and other pertinent infractions. These data are tallied and graphed as important indicators of the school climate. Figure 11.5 provides data regarding the number of office referrals for disruptive and violent behavior across

GOAL: 95% of respondents on an annual student survey will indicate that they

1) Feel safe at school	58.0%
2) Believe students are well behaved	94.6%
3) Know the rules for appropriate behavior and consequences for any infraction	92.2%

FIGURE 11.4 Sunnybrook Elementary School Climate Survey (Students)

four years. This figure suggests that the climate is becoming more disruptive at Sunnybrook, as there are increasing numbers of office referrals each year.

The graph in Figure 11.5 raises a number of questions. For example, is the increase in the number of office referrals a result of more students enrolled, more students being sent to the office, or a small number of students being sent to the office numerous times? Are some teachers more likely to send students to the office than other teachers? Ultimately, a discussion must occur throughout the school community about the discipline policy and behavioral expectations.

The next step is to dig deeper into the data. This is accomplished by disaggregating data at the individual-teacher and student levels. In this way, one is able to gain a deeper understanding of this issue that is of central importance to a positive school culture and climate. The disaggregated data is provided in Figure 11.6.

The disaggregated data begs the question: why is there such a difference among the teachers in the number and types of office referrals? Does the faculty have a uniform behavior system? Is it desirable to have misbehavior handled as much as possible in the classroom by the classroom teacher? Utilizing these data as a springboard for discussion, an

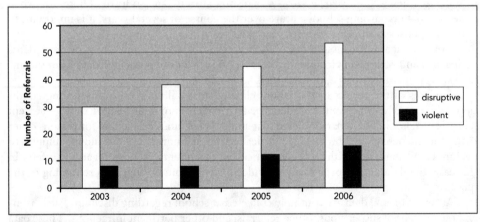

FIGURE 11.5 School-Wide Office Referrals for Disruptive and Violent Behavior

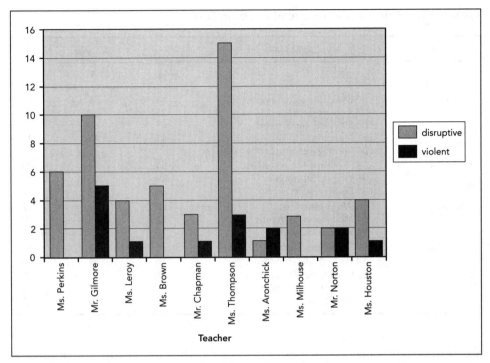

FIGURE 11.6 Office Referrals for Disruptive Behavior Disaggregated by Teacher

education leader might inquire about the various teacher intentions in sending students to the office. These types of questions can form a basis for careful deliberations among the school community, providing opportunities to clarify policies, set goals, and monitor progress on one of the key pathways to school improvement and student achievement; namely, a safe and orderly learning environment.

Criterion- and Norm-Referenced Achievement Data. Student achievement tests, whether they are criterion or norm referenced, are one of the main elements of both school improvement planning efforts and data-based decision making. Since the advent of NCLB, schools are increasingly being held accountable for student learning as measured by standardized achievement tests. As such, in this section demonstrating ways of analyzing key domains of data, it is important to include insights regarding the incorporation of standardized tests into data-based decision making.

As discussed in Chapter 10, criterion-referenced tests differ from norm-referenced tests in that they focus on assessing the performance of an individual as measured against a set standard or established criteria. Norm-referenced tests, on the other hand, assess achievement against the performance of others who take the test, namely, the norm group. Both are important indicators of student achievement, and thus examples of analyzing both criterion- and norm-referenced data will be provided.

Table 11.4 provides an example of school-wide achievement data that focus on student mastery of specific reading-related learning objectives at Sunnybrook Elementary

TABLE 11.4 Criterion-Referenced Reading Data

Test Area	Objective	Grade		
		4	5	6
Reading	01 Basic Understanding	44	58	69
	02 Analyze Text	35	37	70
	03 Evaluate and Extend	49	63	42
	Meaning	41	43	41
	04 Identify Reading Strategies			
Language	05 Sentence Structure	54	26	50
	06 Writing Strategies	39	30	37
	07 Editing Skills	34	49	57
Vocab	08 Word Meaning	37	37	37
	09 Multimeaning Words	17	36	79
	10 Words in Context	70	15	21
Lang Mech	11 Sentences, Phrases, Clauses	72	37	30
	12 Writing Conventions	38	55	64
Spelling	13 Vowels (Spelling)	41	32	21
	14 Consonants (Spelling)	52	53	6
	15 Structural Units	65	10	8

School. These hypothetical criterion-referenced test data are reported for students in grades 4, 5, and 6. The numerical data represent the percent of students in each grade level who have mastered content-specific objectives. For example, in fifth grade, 58 percent of students have mastered Basic Understanding, while in sixth grade 57 percent of students have mastered Editing Skills.

Criterion-referenced tests are crafted to assess the mastery of specific learning objectives and thus are often grade specific. Even so, the inclusion of multiple grade levels in Table 11.4 allows for a comparison of the percent of students who master particular objectives across fourth, fifth, and sixth grades.

On test items measuring multimeaning words (Vocab 09), the percent of students in the school that master the objective increased from fourth to sixth grade. Specifically, the percent of students increases from 17 percent in fourth grade to 36 percent in fifth grade and finally to 79 percent in sixth grade. However, there are several objectives in which the percent of students who master the objective decreases across the grade levels. For example, in vowels (Spelling 13), the percent of students who master the objective decreases from 41 percent in fourth grade to 32 percent in fifth grade to 21 percent in sixth grade. This is an example of a content area on which the principal and teachers should focus. Such problem areas will merit the collection of additional data and the construction of goals to increase student performance. It is important to remember that when comparing scores across grade levels with one year's worth of data, the comparison is among different groups of students. Thus, a next step would be to collect multiple years of data, so that one could follow the same groups of students across grade levels and thereby determine perennially challenging areas for particular grade-level teachers and teams.

While some educators are able to extract meaning from charts such as Table 11.4, others prefer a graphical representation of data. Therefore, an education leader or members of the data team can construct such graphs as depicted in Figures 11.7 and 11.8 below.

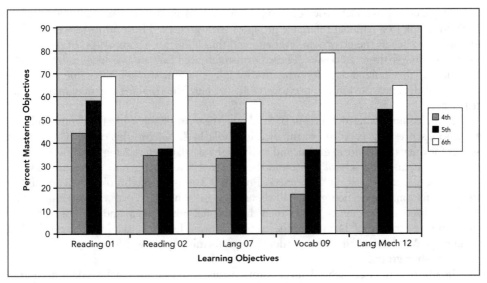

FIGURE 11.7 Trends in Increasing Reading Achievement across Grade Levels

Here, the trends of both increasing achievement across grade levels and decreasing performance are quite evident.

This exercise illustrates the fact that data do not always arrive in the most meaningful format. Just as one would encourage teachers to utilize a variety of techniques to communicate key points of a lesson, so too can a data team present data to the educational community in a variety of layouts.

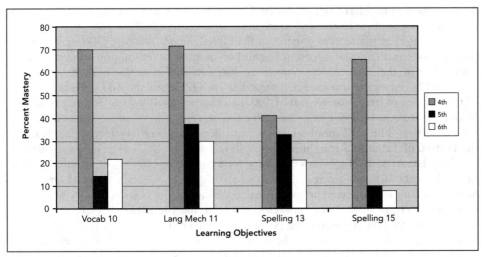

FIGURE 11.8 Trends in Decreasing Reading Achievement across Grade Levels

The data in Table 11.5 provide a comparison of the overall performance of sixth-graders at Sunnybrook to a national reference group of sixth-graders. These norm-referenced data are disaggregated at the classroom level and will thus allow for a comparison of the performance of three sixth-grade classes. These norm-referenced data are provided in the far right columns of the table. For reference, the middle columns include the same criterion-referenced data provided in the previous table, yet here the data are also disaggregated by teacher.

In the column labeled "Percent of Students Mastering Each Objective," one finds total school scores that correlate to the data in Table 11.4. Next to this category, one finds scores for the national norm group, and to the right are data referencing the difference between the sixth-grade school score and the national reference group. Here one notices that in every category except "Sentences, Phrases, Clauses" Sunnybrook scores are higher than the national reference group. For example, in "Analyze Text" Sunnybrook sixth-graders scored sixteen points higher than the national norm group and ten points higher in "Sentence Structure." Data from these columns would suggest that in all categories but "Language Mechanics" the sixth-graders are performing quite well in comparison to the national norm group.

In addition to these school-level comparisons, one can also analyze data disaggregated at the classroom level to gain a deeper understanding of the performance of sixth-graders at Sunnybrook. Jones, Robinson, and Smith are the sixth-grade teachers at the school. Based on data analysis, it is evident that a higher percentage of students are mastering the objectives in Jones's class than in Robinson's or Smith's classes. Additionally, a higher percentage of students in Jones's class are mastering objectives than both the school and national averages. Upon comparison of classroom-level data for Robinson and Smith, we see that a higher percentage of students are mastering the Reading and Vocabulary content areas in Smith's class than in Robinson's. However, a higher percentage of students in Robinson's class than in Smith's class are mastering the Language and Language Mechanics content areas. From this data analysis, it is clear that both Smith's and Robinson's classes would benefit from targeted support. These data also highlight opportunities for the teachers to work together to mentor and coach one another in areas of strength.

Moving on to the second portion of the table labeled "Average Objectives Performance Index (OPI)," one encounters another method of examining student performance data on the same content objectives. The data in this section of the table are presented as Objectives Performance Index numbers, or OPI numbers. An OPI is an estimate of the number of items correct out of 100, had there been 100 items for that objective. In other words, an OPI is a fancy name for the percent of items answered correctly for each objective. The OPI numbers are used to determine mastery levels. In the key at the bottom of Table 11.5 the three mastery levels and the OPI **ranges** are provided.

The data in the OPI columns also allow for a comparison of the sixth-graders at Sunnybrook to the national reference group of sixth-graders. Overall, the sixth-graders at Sunnybrook achieve mastery or partial mastery in all of the objectives. One will notice that the pattern of differences between the school and the national reference group is quite similar to data regarding the percent of students mastering each objective. The sixth-graders at the school perform better than the national average in the Reading, Vocabulary, and Language content areas. The sixth-graders at Sunnybrook perform at the same level or less than the national average only in Language Mechanics.

TABLE 11.5 Reading Performance by School and Teacher—Grade 6 Sunnybrook

	Percent of Students Mastering Each Objective						Average Objectives Performance Index (OPI)*					
	TEACHER						TEACHER					
	Total School	National Norm Group	Difference	Jones	Robinson	Smith	Total School	National Norm Group	Difference	Jones	Robinson	Smith
Reading												
01 Basic Understanding	69	54	+15	86	59	58	• 78	▪ 73	+ 05	• 87	▪ 73	▪ 74
02 Analyze Text	70	54	+16	55	55	65	• 79	▪ 72	+ 07	• 85	▪ 73	• 76
03 Evaluate/Extend Meaning	42	35	+7	27	27	31	▪ 67	▪ 62	+ 05	• 77	▪ 61	▪ 65
04 Identify Reading Strategies	41	33	+8	23	23	31	▪ 66	▪ 62	+ 04	• 77	▪ 60	▪ 63
Language												
05 Sentence Structure	50	40	+10	68	55	27	▪ 68	▪ 66	+ 02	• 76	▪ 68	▪ 62
06 Writing Strategies	37	29	+8	54	32	23	▪ 65	▪ 65	+ 03	▪ 72	▪ 64	▪ 61
07 Editing Skills	57	55	+2	75	64	31	▪ 73	▪ 73	00	• 81	• 76	▪ 63
Vocabulary												
08 Word Meaning	37	29	+8	46	27	35	▪ 63	▪ 60	+ 03	▪ 69	▪ 58	▪ 62
09 Multimeaning Words	79	71	+8	89	68	77	• 83	• 80	+ 03	• 87	• 80	• 84
10 Words in Context	21	16	+5	25	14	23	▪ 53	○ 49	+ 04	▪ 58	○ 49	▪ 53
Language Mechanics												
11 Sentences, Phrases, Clauses	30	33	−3	46	32	12	▪ 61	▪ 63	− 02	▪ 70	▪ 61	▪ 56
12 Conventions	64	64	0	82	59	50	• 77	• 76	+ 01	• 82	• 76	▪ 71
Number of Students	76	—	—	28	22	26	76	—	—	28	22	26

*Objectives Performance Index (OPI)** is the estimated number of items correct out of 100 had there been 100 items for that objective

Key: • Mastery (Range: 75–100 correct)

   ▪ Partial mastery (Range: 50–74 correct)

   ○ Nonmastery (Range: 0–49 correct)

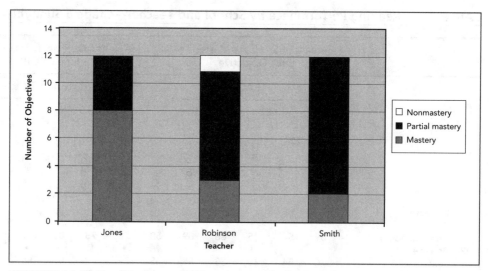

FIGURE 11.9 Comparison of Mastery Levels by Teacher

Analysis of the mastery levels of the three sixth-grade classes finds that Jones's students achieve mastery on eight of the content objectives and achieve partial mastery on four objectives. By comparison, Robinson's students achieve mastery on three objectives, and Smith's students achieve mastery on only two objectives. A comparison of this teacher-level data is provided in Figure 11.9.

Even though Jones's class has the highest performance levels, Figure 11.9 provides evidence that there is still room for improvement. The student achievement data presented in these tables and figures provide evidence that criterion- and norm-referenced standardized data can offer educational leaders, teachers, and data teams insight to spur goals for improvement in curricula, materials, and instructional strategies.

■ ANALYZING DATA INTEGRAL TO SCHOOL EFFICIENCY

To this point, little has been said regarding means for linking school data systems to financial and resource allocation issues. This silence does not reflect a level of significance. Rather, it is complexity that relegates the efficiency question to last.

A fully complete data system would track performance, demographics, program elements, and perceptions and link all of these to financial resource flows. The latter would principally be measures of teacher and other personnel time and the cost of that time. In addition, there could be other measures of supplies and expenses and, possibly, some capital costs. Over time, if one could determine a systematic relationship between resource flows and other measures such as student achievement, parent satisfaction, and student downstream success, then one could know better how to allocate resources in order to achieve these greater **cost-benefit ratios**.

However, in this chapter, we have not explored the financial linkages to data systems because it is an added level of complexity beyond the current capacity of most school districts. However, it is absolutely essential to provide, as part of the budgeting and accounting process, personnel costs, school by school. This would be an initial step toward determining which school programs cost the most or the least and beginning to align these data with student outcome data.

Summary

Well-informed decision making is a central component of successful school leadership. It is the process by which educational problems are articulated, analyzed, and addressed. However, as described in this chapter, the good intentions of education leaders are not sufficient to guarantee good decisions. Rather, successful solutions require data analysis and efficient action based on reflective collaboration and sound strategies. Decisions made by school leaders directly influence the instructional experience of students and thus ultimately impact the national and global landscape. As such, it is imperative that school leaders engage in reflective and systematic data analysis so that difficult decisions are made wisely. To do so requires education leaders to draw a school community together around a prioritized list of goals amidst the complexities of school life. The information in this chapter provides helpful action strategies for school administrators who are often confounded by the sheer pace and volume of their work. There are many approaches to problem solving within education organizations, yet all of them are enhanced by the utilization of data. While data-based decision making does not guarantee effective outcomes to educational challenges, it certainly improves the likelihood of such.

Discussion Questions

1. Four important reasons for engaging in data-based decision making were described in this chapter. Of these four, which do you feel is the primary reason stakeholders in your school community would cite? What might parents say? students? faculty? administrators?
2. Briefly critique the degree to which your current education organization is successfully pursuing the three components of the school improvement cycle provided in Figure 11.1.
3. In Table 11.1, comparisons are made between school processes guided by intuition versus data. Drawing on your experience, add two rows to this list, specifying how data *have* elevated or *could* elevate the way decisions are being made.
4. Comment on the current degree of usability of your school-level data, providing insight for how your data stacks up along each of the five dimensions.
5. Figure 11.2 provides examples of the various types of data school leaders can utilize to guide decisions. Choose one source of data from each quadrant and describe how those data are used to evaluate the quality of the instructional programs or organizational climate at your school.
6. Consider one of your personal or one of your school's current goals. Describe the degree to which the goal is SMART—specific, measurable, achievable, research based, and time sensitive.
7. List the ways that your school currently communicates with the community regarding the purposes and results of data collection and data-based decision making. Propose two additional methods.

8. Using Table 11.2 as a guide, evaluate your current educational organization's mission statement. What most notable or action-worthy insights emerged from this exercise?

9. Using Table 11.3 as a launching point, design a form that would help an education leader at your school analyze the grade level and subject area investments in professional development.

10. If you were the principal of Sunnybrook Elementary School and were presented with the data in Figure 11.6, what would your next steps entail? Would you conduct added analyses and create different displays using these data? What additional data would you collect regarding behavioral issues at your school?

11. To what degree are multiple formats of data available to teachers at your school? What concrete steps can be taken to facilitate this practice?

12. Imagine Figure 11.7 represents data for three teachers at your school. In addition to Figure 11.8, what ways would you present these data to these teachers? What additional analyses would you conduct? What graphic displays would be most preferred by or beneficial to your teachers?

13. Using school data to inform decisions and solve problems cuts across several ELCC Standards. Choose one component of one ELCC Standard, and describe how the utilization of data can help you be a more effective leader.

References and Suggested Readings

Baker, B., & Richards, C. (2004). *The ecology of educational systems: Data, models, and tools for improvisational leading and learning.* Upper Saddle River, NJ: Pearson Education.
    This informative book is written for those who need to understand education data and its place in school leadership and decision making. It provides a set of practical tools for data analysis and decision making using spreadsheet software and system dynamic models. A solid resource for all school administrators, especially those who plan budgets and report to school boards and their communities.

Goldring, E., & Berends, M. (2008). *Leading with data: Pathways to improve your school.* Newbury Park, CA: Corwin Press.
    This hands-on guidebook helps principals make meaningful data-based instructional decisions with confidence. In lay terms, the authors explain statistical and assessment information that administrators need to know: what types of data to look at, how to analyze the information, and how to use what they've learned from the data to make critical choices for their schools.

Notes

1. The authors wish to acknowledge the contributions and insights provided by Dr. Ellen Goldring, professor of education and public policy at Peabody College of Vanderbilt University.

PART FOUR

Power
The Application of Strategic Leadership

Section IV of the text builds on the knowledge from the previous three sections by providing a transition to the day-to-day operating activities in which strategic leaders engage. For example, Chapter 12 describes leadership roles and uses of power within education organizations. Chapter 13 concentrates upon selected topics pertinent to the central role of people for the success of schooling while Chapter 14 suggests ways that school leaders can usefully engage families and communities in the life of the school. Chapter 15 tackles the issue of constructing a professional philosophy of management along with other actions central to practicing leadership. Finally, Chapter 16 concludes this section by discussing how one can prepare oneself to be a strategic leader and to have a career as an education leader.

■ APPLICABILITY OF SECTION IV CONTENT TO ELCC STANDARDS

Content in Section IV of the text is aligned with all six of the ELCC Standards. Among other places, content in the chapters on practicing leadership are applicable to the development and implementation of vision, which is at the heart of ELCC Standard 1. Content in the chapters on people and preparation have direct links to ELCC Standard 2, which focuses on instructional programs and professional development issues. The chapters on power and practice link to the operational and resource management issues inherent in ELCC Standard 3. The chapter on partnering schools and communities deals squarely with the issue of engaging families and communities in the life of the school, the central theme of ELCC Standard 4. Within the content of the power and people chapters, attention is paid to the importance of personal ethics and consistent behavior, two dimensions of ELCC Standard 5. Finally, multiple chapters speak to the broader contextual factors that shape the implementation of leadership within schools, thus addressing ELCC Standard 6.

■ CASE STUDIES

 CASE 7

A Profile of Change

A Search for New Practices

University Charter School was located in an inner ring suburb of a major metropolitan geographic area. The school enrolled six hundred students. Its clientele included college faculty members, business executives, and working class parents.

The charter school board of directors comprised seven individuals, some of whom were there because of their political connections, others because of their access to money: their own or that of wealthy acquaintances.

Vince Cavanaugh was the charter school headmaster. He previously had operated a public middle school, and he was pleased to be free of the stifling regulatory culture that permeated the district in which he had been employed. Operating his own school, particularly a charter school with what he thought was a far wider range of leader discretion, was attractive to him. He wanted to be the head of a school to which he could impart his personality and his ideas. At least he thought that was his goal until he came fully to understand the forceful agenda of his board president, Harry Downer.

Harry was an *enfant terrible* who, upon succeeding beyond all prediction in the electronics industry, took education to be his hobby. Harry was wealthy, intelligent, highly educated, forceful, and successful. He was used to having his way, and who could argue with him? His way had proved to be remarkably successful in the past. Harry was impatient and had little ability to listen to, let alone understand, any views that were inconsistent with his own.

He came to be as powerful in the charter school leadership community as he had been in his startup electronics company. He was absolutely convinced that the private sector management techniques that had contributed to his business success would transfer productively into schooling. He believed in competition, performance incentives, data-driven decision making, and organizational goals and objectives. His hero was slash-and-burn, take-no-prisoners former General Electric executive Jack Welch.

Board president Harry liked Vince. To Harry, Vince had the making of a good leader. He was decisive, forceful, and had a keen eye for talent. Harry liked the way that Vince had managed the search for a school site, publicized the school opening and the recruiting of students and parents, and recruited and ultimately selected a carefully hand picked teaching staff. To Harry, Jim Collins, author of *Good to Great*, was the business theorist who mattered most, and by getting the good teaching staff, Harry thought Vince had complied with the first Collins rule: Get the right people on the bus, and they will drive the organization.

In addition to selecting Vince, Harry had insisted that the new headmaster be placed on a performance contract. Harry and Vince had agreed upon school goals for the first several years. If goals were achieved, then Vince was to receive substantial financial bonuses. It did not occur to Vince that what was good for the gander might be conceived as good for geese.

Before the school opened, Vince worked carefully with his new teachers. Cooperatively they designed the curriculum. They selected instructional technology and software. They developed school dress codes and discipline policies. They constructed grading practices and spent time reaching agreement upon what the new charter school would look like and feel like, and how it would operate.

Vince had selected players, and he was being careful to weld them into a team. He was proud of the high percentage of his new teachers who had earned master's degrees and the large number who were highly experienced instructors recruited from other settings. He was as strategic in his team building as a successful NFL coach.

University Charter School opened a year after its initial formation. It had a new faculty, a handpicked teaching staff, a thoughtfully constructed set of operating rules, a dedication to a cooperative culture for adults, and a supportive environment for students. It appeared on a course for success. Few schools were so well launched.

At the first board meeting in the initial operating year, Harry announced that the board would soon be considering a merit pay plan for the school's teacher workforce. This came as a surprise to Vince. A teacher-pay-for-student-performance plan was not inimical to his thinking, but he was not sure he wanted to implement such an incentive system so soon. He was first interested in launching the school successfully, and in his mind, that meant fostering the team environment. What would an incentive plan do to teacher cooperation? Could one have individual rewards?

When Harry initially unveiled the board's performance incentive plan, it contained these features: the bonus for high-performing teachers would be as much as 20 percent of their nine-month salary; only the top 10 percent of the teachers in the school would be eligible; bonuses would be awarded based on how many students scored above various test score cutoffs in each of the major subject matter areas; eligible teachers were those who taught mathematics, reading, science, and social studies; physical education teachers, art and music teachers, and other teachers of specialty disciplines were not eligible for bonuses, at least in the initial phases; nonteachers were excluded.

Vince was taken aback. The plan had not been discussed with him. His teachers were confused, frustrated, and angry. They did not hold Vince responsible for what they viewed as a breach of trust. However, they were distressed and planned a number of off-site meetings, without Vince, to determine their reaction.

Teachers also were frequently communicating with parents and were voicing their disaffection from the school. Parents, who quickly had come to identify with the handpicked teaching staff, felt isolated from the school's decision-making processes. Many parents believed in performance pay. However, they did not want to see their children's favorite teachers leave the school.

Vince knew he had to take the initiative. He had to act fast to display leadership. He was fearful that if enacted, the board's proposed incentive system would badly disrupt his carefully constructed team-teaching concepts. On the other hand, if he did not acquiesce to some form of teacher-pay-for-student-performance, he would jeopardize the board's confidence in him as a leader.

Discussion Questions for Case 7

1. Was there any way out of this situation? Could Vince regain his position as a leader?
2. Should Vince have resigned?
3. Should Vince have demanded that Harry quit as a board member?
4. Should Harry have demanded that Vince quit as headmaster?
5. Are there compromise pay-for-performance plans that might bridge the gap between individual merit and team member cooperation?

 CASE 8

A Teacher Union Official's Challenge

A Potential Profile of Courage

Peter Folio was a high school math teacher in a suburban school district. He had not done well in school, and that aroused compassion within him for students who themselves were not so successful. He nevertheless managed to graduate from high school and attend a community college. He joined the Marines and liked the structure and prestige of the Corps. He rose in the ranks of enlisted men and was comfortable with the hierarchy and culture around him. Moreover, he did not mind being a subordinate because he could see that his officers knew what they were doing and were often quite brave. He also liked the navigational and artillery training he received and the college tuition benefits he earned.

He served his term in the Marines and entered the state teacher college. He was part of the "Troops to Teachers" program that placed him on a fast track to be a teacher. Even though his grades would not prove it, he was good at, and always interested in, mathematics. It surprised him that his Marine training in navigation and artillery put him way ahead of his classmates in many mathematics classes. That is why he decided to take the extra courses that credentialed him to teach math.

Peter had grown up in a solid blue-collar neighborhood. His mother and father were Catholics, and he went to church as a youth, even serving, to his mother's delight, as an altar boy. He acquired a rather strong sense of right and wrong. He did not always do right, but he almost always knew what was the right thing to do. Peter had an embedded sense of morality to go along with his sympathy for the underdog. This morality had served him well in the structured world of the Marines.

Peter's father had been a plumber, and Peter grew up in a strong union family. Thus, once he was a classroom teacher, he rather easily gravitated toward becoming an active union member. He was proud of his local teacher union affiliate. He thought his fellow members were good teachers and, conversely, he was seldom favorably impressed with the school district administrative officials. They seemed to him always to be putting on false airs and brandishing their degrees and credentials from fancier colleges than his. They were not made of the same stuff as his Marine officers.

Peter remained a classroom teacher for seventeen years. He did go back to school at night and on weekends and obtained an administrative credential. He had little taste for administration, but the added college credits provided him with a higher place on the district's salary schedule. He needed the money. He had made a poor choice in getting married and now found himself divorced and raising two sons all by himself. He had his hands plenty full being a good teacher, taking care of his children, and striving to earn a living.

He found his friends among teacher union officials, and incrementally he assumed more and more union responsibility. He earned summer money by performing union duties and by learning the collective bargaining trade. In time, he was made a member of the union's collective bargaining team, and now he routinely sat on the opposite side of the table from the administrators whose pretense bothered him. He always strove to be down-to-earth in bargaining sessions, even a little salty, to prove that an Italian Catholic kid from a lower-middle-class neighborhood who had gone to community college had acquired just as much power as had they.

While Peter was a good teacher and a good union member, the remainder of his life was not perfect. He had gotten married and divorced again. His younger son had fallen in with a bad crowd and had been arrested for drug possession. His older son was doing well, but the college tuition costs were gnawing heavily at Peter's wallet. Peter needed more money, and he was not quite sure how to get it.

Peter was, by now, the second in command on the union bargaining team. He did not get to call all the shots, but he was informed regarding issues and influential when they caucused around a union position. Peter sometimes was surprised by the position of the union chief bargainer. On occasion, when Peter thought a strong stand was appropriate, he found his senior colleague rather quickly conceding to the administration on an issue.

Peter initially chalked these concessions up to his own naiveté. His senior had twenty years of bargaining experience, so who was Peter to question his judgment? Perhaps he was giving in more quickly on the small matters in order to hold a tougher position on the big stuff downstream.

As time progressed, Peter learned even more of the bargaining and union trade. He took night school courses on contracts. He attended national conferences. He began to understand the big picture of American education. In time, he even began to mellow a bit regarding his perception of the district's administrators. He came to understand better the pressures placed upon them also.

Still, as much as Peter liked his union role, and as much as he felt more confident regarding his understanding of public school systems, his need for added income did not lessen. He now had even more college tuition for which he was responsible. He wanted the best for his children, but he also liked his union responsibilities.

One evening, following a labor management meeting, the associate superintendent for administration asked Peter to have a drink with him. Peter enjoyed this relationship, one in which neither party ever crossed the line and made any deals that were outside the boundaries of what should be collectively bargained or publicly discussed. Mostly the two of them talked about politics, football, and the future of the district. Thus, Peter was surprised that night when his administrative counterpart offered him a job, a job in the district administration.

The associate superintendent was serious, and Peter was quite taken aback. He liked his union work. He liked his district. He was not quite sure how his union colleagues would accept his reversal of roles. He liked teaching and was not sure he wanted to get away from students. On the other hand, the added $20,000 in salary each year was terribly tempting. He had to pay those bills.

Peter expressed his appreciation for the offer and asked that he be able to think about it for several days. His counterpart assured him that he could have the time and that their mutual friendship would survive whatever decision Peter made.

Discussion Questions for Case 8

1. Have you ever been confronted with the opportunity to serve in several capacities in the same school or district? How did this impact your relationship with your peers?
2. To what degree are union leaders and district administrators on the same page in your district? On what issues are they most aligned and divided?
3. If you had to make Peter's decision, what would you do, and why?

CHAPTER TWELVE

Power

Decision Making and Implementation

LEARNING OBJECTIVES

By the end of this chapter, you should be able to

- understand the concept and application of power;
- identify sources of a leader's power;
- explain effective uses of power in leading an organization;
- comprehend approaches to power practically available to a strategic leader;
- react to limits on a leader's use of power.

Leaders must perform two essential functions. One, they have to make decisions. Making decisions, at least good decisions, involves knowledge, experience, wisdom, and courage. Making decisions does not necessarily involve power. Many foregoing portions of this book are directed at assisting leaders in defining an issue correctly, or at least defining it productively, by bringing appropriate information to bear upon possible solutions and then making good, well-informed decisions. Making decisions does not necessarily involve power.

Second, leaders have to enforce decisions or in some manner ensure that decisions are in fact carried out. Implementing decisions often involves issues of organizational change, overcoming inertia, and persuading others to alter past patterns of behavior and take risks. Change is at once simple and discouragingly complicated. The challenge for a leader is to persuade followers that the costs involved in not changing are higher to them than those involved in undertaking the change. Implementing decisions and striving to change an organization necessarily involve matters of power. A strategic education leader thus benefits from an understanding of several key facets of the operation of power in organizations. The provision of such insight is the topic of this chapter.

At the outset, it is important to be reminded that power comes in multiple forms and is displayed and deployed in multiple ways. Virtually every reader will have sensed the presence of a powerful person, be he or she a public officeholder, a highly successful or innovative corporate executive, an experienced and poised military officer, a commanding athlete, a stunning performing artist, or perhaps an unusually intelligent or influential individual.

In some sense, power is ineffable. It is everywhere, yet it is nowhere. It is difficult to identify. It is difficult to define, difficult to discuss with precision, and terribly troublesome to teach. Nevertheless, in an intuitive way, one often knows power when one observes it in action or when one is in the presence of a powerful person.

Power is also sometimes evident by its absence. Readers may have experienced an important, even a crucial, meeting in which, as a consequence of detrimental or confusing circumstances, immediate action is badly needed. An authentic leader, one comfortable with his or her power, will sense the situation is right for action. He or she will use power inherent in the position to do the right thing. However, even when such an urgent situation is palpably present, a timid leader may eschew action. It is in such vacuous circumstances that one can sense power by its absence.

Another version of the timid leader, one who is reluctant to exercise power, is the one who repeatedly panders to opinion or hides behind a cloak of collegiality and participatory management, even at times when bold ideas and forceful actions are clearly needed for organizational success or survival.

Repeated vacillation and acquiescence to or befuddlement in the face of uncertainty are other symptoms of an inauthentic leader, a leader for whom power is a problem rather than a solution. Discussions in this chapter will expand intuitive understandings and individual reader insights regarding power by describing its many facets and reviewing its possible applications.

Before turning to a set of definitions and descriptions, however, here is a time-honored observation. Often, after a modest amount of observation, it is relatively easy to identify the individual or individuals in an organization who possess power. This is the person, or these are the individuals, who most quickly and assuredly delegate authority. They know or sense their personal or professional power; they know it can be magnified many times over by the efforts and intelligence of others willingly enlisted in their cause. They are able, where and when appropriate, to share their power in service to the organizational purposes they hold important.

An able leader also may fully realize his or her own limitations and comprehend that his or her own deficiencies can be buttressed by carefully constructing compensating capacities through the contributed talents of those around him or her. Indeed, another sign of a secure, and often powerful, leader is the capacity to attract and retain talented individuals and enlist them in a collective cause. An effective leader has the patience to tolerate, indeed celebrate, those with more talent than he or she may personally possess on any particular dimension. It is the ineffective leader who is most likely to be afraid of appearing inept by comparison with others and is concerned about competition from surrounding individuals.

Regrettably, there is sometimes a converse. An individual, even one holding the nominal office and exercising the legal authority of a leader, can sometimes be spotted as weak, ineffectual, or possessing illusory or transitory power. If a leader is consistently unwilling to delegate authority, insists on making all decisions personally or reviewing all decisions made by others, and gives evidence of trusting few if any colleagues or subordinates, then his or her effectiveness, and possible hold on the position, is assuredly in jeopardy.

■ IMPORTANT DEFINITIONS AND DISTINCTIONS

Power is an ambiguous term. It is often used in common parlance as a slang proxy or a vulgar identifier to describe an amalgam of traits exhibited by an individual or group of individuals in positions of formal authority or who have accrued substantial informal influence.

CHAPTER FOURTEEN

Partnering Schools with Parents and Communities

LEARNING OBJECTIVES

By the end of this chapter, you should be able to

- recognize the theoretical and pedagogical significance of linking family and community with schools;
- apply practical approaches to engaging families and communities in student learning;
- utilize strategies for obtaining data regarding family and community involvement;
- develop strategic partnerships between schools and communities;
- respond to diverse community interests and needs;
- arrange communications among school, families, and the community.

A base of solid evidence confirms the utility of active family and community involvement as a contributor to student and school success. Provisions of the 2001 No Child Left Behind Act have particularly reinforced this desired condition. However, while practical experience, craft knowledge, policy mandates, and educational research combine to endorse the advantages of collaboration among schools, families, and communities, effectively coordinating among these agencies is challenging. The purpose of this chapter is to explore the theoretical and research-based underpinnings of home, community, and school linkages and to illustrate practical means by which this condition can be facilitated. It is important to note that strategic education leaders are relied upon not only to facilitate a thoughtful communications and outreach effort with external constituents, but also to communicate appropriately with internal constituents. While this chapter focuses on how education leaders can enhance community-based **stakeholder** engagement, many lessons from this discussion can be applied to internal communication efforts.

■ THEORETICAL AND EMPIRICAL RESEARCH CONSIDERATIONS

Joyce Epstein provides a theoretical framework that usefully guides thinking and research in the realm of community involvement (1995, 2001). She proposes a *theory of overlapping spheres*. In this abstraction, home, school, and community environments are "spheres of

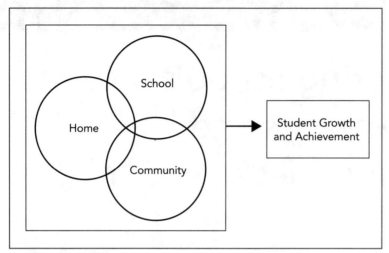

FIGURE 14.1 Spheres of Influence on Student Growth and Achievement

influence" that shape student growth and achievement. A greater degree of alignment among the three spheres will result in supporting endeavors acting synergistically to enhance student development. Conversely, the spheres can be pushed apart and made dysfunctionally distant when a gap exists between institutional policies and individual beliefs and practices. Ideally, there is a level of dynamic communication and collaboration among each of the three spheres that results in enhanced student achievement. Striving to achieve this alignment, as depicted in Figure 14.1, is one of the many challenging tasks facing educational leaders.

Epstein's spheres of influence are drawn closer together as interactions among schools, families, and the community become more frequent. However, it is important for leaders to maintain an appropriate balance among the spheres so they are aligned to maximize student achievement. Students receiving consistent reinforcement from the respective spheres are more inclined to grasp the importance of education and develop a strong commitment to their schooling.

The model of overlapping segments acknowledges that the individual zones operate independently of one another, yet most school initiatives can become more productive when the spheres collaborate. Schools, families, and communities are influential entities, yet they cannot guarantee successful students. While these spheres play a pivotal role in encouraging, directing, and stimulating a student's interest and desire to become successful, student initiative continues to be of crucial importance.

Students are an integral part of a school, family, and community partnership. They have a direct effect on the alignment of the spheres by serving as an intermediary between the school and their family. Students serve in this capacity as teachers frequently depend on them effectively to transmit important messages to their families. Students are more likely to cooperate in these situations if they are motivated and engaged in their education. A heightened level of commitment to educational excellence can occur when students

TABLE 14.1 Six Dimensions of Family Involvement for Grades 8 and 12

Type of Involvement	In Grade 8	In Grade 12
Parenting	—Expressing expectations about student's education —Limiting television viewing —Supervising time use and behavior	—Discussing interests, issues, and studies at school —Doing things together (shopping, vacations, movies, meals) —Supervising behavior —Knowing what courses student is taking —Supervising academic work
Communicating	—Parent-initiated contacts about academic performance —School-initiated contacts about student's academic program (courses, placement)	—School-initiated contacts about academic performance —Parent-initiated contacts on student's academic program —Parent-school contacts on post-secondary plans
Supporting School	Volunteering at school and fund-raising	Volunteering at school and attending school activities
Learning at Home	—Academic lessons outside school —Music or dance lessons —Discussions about school and plans for future	—Encouraging college —Encouraging high school graduation —Learning about postsecondary education —Taking on private educational expenses
Decision Making	Taking part in parent organization	Taking part in parent organization
Collaborating with Community	—Using community learning resources (like museum visits) —Taking part in community groups (scouts, sports)	Communicating parent-to-parent

believe that their school, family, and community genuinely care about their personal and academic well-being.

Table 14.1 provides a definition of community involvement by categorizing it into six dimensions. Joyce Epstein and colleagues at the Center on Family, School, and Community Partnerships synthesized this definition from an extensive review of the literature. Table 14.1 provides examples of the six dimensions of family involvement in both the eighth and twelfth grades.

Chadwick (2004) expounds on these domains by providing the following insights about the six dimensions of family, school, and community partnerships.

1. *Parenting*. Families must provide a healthy and safe environment at home that promotes learning and good behavior at school. Schools can provide information and training to support families in this endeavor.
2. *Communicating*. Families need information about school programs and school progress in a format that meets their individual needs.
3. *Volunteering*. Families can make significant contributions to schools, if schools can accommodate their schedules and interests.

4. *Learning at home*. Families can facilitate and supervise learning at home with the assistance of teachers.
5. *Decision making*. Families can have meaningful roles in the school decision-making process. This opportunity should be made available to all members of the school community, not just to those who have the most time and energy to devote.
6. *Collaboration with the community*. Schools can help families gain access to support services from other community agencies. Schools can also help mobilize families and other community groups in efforts to improve community life.

 CASE 5 REVISITED

You will recall the dilemma of Frank Gomez, principal of Carter Middle School. He is faced with a tough decision that has significant implications for his students and entire school community. In order to meet Annual Yearly Progress, the mean test score at Carter Middle must be elevated. Yet he is unsure if he should focus on those students near the proficiency threshold or those with the most significant needs. How might Frank draw upon the six dimensions of family and community involvement to craft a response that will not leave any children behind? Provide several practical examples of how Frank might engage families and the community to the benefit of the students at Carter Middle School.

In the research literature it is noted that all family members, including parents, siblings, grandparents, aunts, uncles, and "fictive kin" who may be friends or neighbors, often contribute in significant ways to children's education and development (Henderson & Mapp, 2002). This chapter focuses on community involvement, which, in addition to family involvement, includes the neighborhood and places around the school; local residents, who live in the area and may or may not have children in the school, but have an interest in the school; and local groups, such as businesses and churches, that are based in the neighborhood. Table 14.2 provides an extensive list of potential community partners.

Studies that seek to appraise the impact of community involvement on student performance use indicators such as the following:

- For young children: teacher ratings of school adjustment, vocabulary, reading and language skills, and social and motor skills
- Academic indicators: report card grades, grade point averages, enrollment in advanced classes, promotion to the next grade, and standardized test scores
- Attendance data, discipline data, participation in school clubs, sports, or other **extracurricular** activities

Henderson and Mapp (2002) reviewed fifty empirical studies of the impact of community involvement on student achievement and found the following benefits to be associated with community involvement in schools:

- Elevated grade point averages and scores on standardized tests or rating scales
- Enrollment in more challenging academic programs

TABLE 14.2 Prospective Partners for School-Community Collaboration

Community Partner Type	Specific Examples
Business/corporations	Local businesses, national corporations
Educational institutions	Colleges and universities, high schools, and other educational institutions
Heath care organizations	Hospitals; health care centers; health departments, foundations, and associations
Government and military agencies	Chamber of commerce, fire and police departments, city councils, and other local government agencies and departments
National service and volunteer organizations	Rotary club, Lions club, Kiwanis club, VISTA, YMCA, United Way, AmeriCorps, Urban League, etc.
Faith-based organizations	Churches, mosques, synagogues, other religious organizations, and charities
Senior citizen organizations	Nursing homes, senior volunteer and service organizations
Cultural and recreational institutions	Zoos, museums, libraries, recreational centers
Media organizations	Local newspapers, radio stations, public television, cable networks
Sports franchises and associations	Minor and major league sports teams, college sports teams and organizations
Other community organizations	Fraternities, sororities, foundations, neighborhood associations, alumni
Community individuals	Individual volunteers from the surrounding school community

Source: Adapted from Sanders, M. G. (2001) in Sanders (2006) *Building school-community partnerships: Collaboration for student success.* Thousand Oaks, CA: Corwin Press.

- More classes passed and credits earned
- Better attendance
- Improved behavior at school and at home
- Better social skills and adaptation to school
- Graduation and advancement to postsecondary education

In addition to these benefits, individual research teams have uncovered specific benefits of community involvement within specialized domains of schooling. For example, Arriaza (2004) found that school reform initiatives have greater chances of persisting when the community actively participates as an empowered change agent. In a longitudinal study on school attendance, several family-school-community partnership practices were associated with increases in daily attendance and decreases in chronic absenteeism (Epstein & Sheldon, 2002).

In a study of school engagement among Latino youth in urban schools, the following were found to enhance school engagement: teacher support, friend support, parent support, neighborhood youth behavior, and neighborhood safety (Garcia, Reid, & Peterson, 2005). Data from eighty-two elementary schools in an urban area indicate that, after controlling for school characteristics, the degree to which schools were working to overcome challenges to family and community involvement predicted higher percentages of students scoring at or above satisfactory on state achievement tests.

These findings should encourage school leaders to address obstacles to family and community involvement in order to realize the benefits of community partnerships for student academic performance (Sheldon, 2003). Additionally, findings suggest that subject-specific practices of school, family, and community partnerships may help educators improve students' mathematics achievement. For example, when controlling for prior levels of mathematics achievement, longitudinal analyses of elementary and secondary school data indicate that effective implementation of practices that encourage families to support their children's mathematics learning at home was associated with higher percentages of students who scored at or above proficiency on standardized mathematics achievement tests (Sheldon & Epstein, 2002).

■ STRATEGICALLY LINKING FAMILY AND COMMUNITY TO STUDENT PERFORMANCE

Families not only have direct influence upon student achievement through behavioral mandates and performance expectations, but also can have a subtle effect on achievement through student attendance and behavior. Students tend to remain in school for longer periods, perform better in school, and become interested in furthering their education in a postsecondary institution when families are committed to their educational experience.

A synthesis of studies on family and community involvement in schooling conducted by Henderson and Mapp (2002) finds that irrespective of a family's demographic characteristics or socioeconomic status, family involvement advances a student's learning experience. The literature also indicates that low-performing students and those at risk of failure can benefit greatly from family and community involvement.

Natural variation in support and involvement by families is one factor contributing to the widening achievement gap between students. After having synthesized the existing empirical studies in the realm of community engagement, Henderson and Mapp (2002) offered several specific suggestions regarding how schools and school leaders can engage communities for the purpose of enhancing student achievement. These suggestions include

- Adopt a family-school-community partnership policy. The philosophy behind it should see the total school community as committed to making sure that every single student achieves at a high level and to working together to make it happen.
- Identify target areas of low achievement. Work with families and community members to design workshops and other activities to give them information about how to help students learn. Provide materials for families to use at home and get ideas about how to help their children learn at school.
- Offer professional development for school staff on working productively with families and community members. Invite families and community members to attend.
- Assess the current family-school-community involvement program to determine how it is linked to learning. Work with faculty and community constituents to create activities that will foster a learning community.

From the studies reported in the National Center for Family and Community Connections (Henderson & Mapp, 2002) it is conclusive that different levels of family involvement have varying effects on student achievement at various age levels. For student achievement to be optimized, it is beneficial for schools to organize family involvement in a manner that engages families and students in activities that develop specific skills and knowledge. A recommendation is made for school leaders to create programs that support families in guiding their students' educational experience from preschool through high school. The programs are assigned to one of three categories and offer various practices and support levels to enhance student learning.

1. *Families of preschool children*
   - Home visits from trained parent educators with cultural backgrounds similar to those of the families or with knowledge of their culture
   - Lending libraries that offer games and learning materials to build skills at home
   - Discussion groups with other families about children's learning
   - Classes on how to stimulate children's mental, physical, and emotional development

2. *Families of elementary and middle school children*
   - Interactive homework that involves families with their children's learning
   - Workshops on topics that families suggest, like building their children's vocabulary and developing positive discipline strategies
   - Regular calls from teachers, not only when problems arise
   - Learning packets in reading, science, and math, as well as training in how to use them
   - Meetings with teachers to discuss children's progress

3. *Families of high school students*
   - Regular meetings with teachers and counselors to plan children's academic programs
   - Information about program options, graduation requirements, test schedules, and postsecondary education options
   - Explanations of courses students should take to prepare them better for postsecondary education
   - Information about financing postsecondary education and applying for financial aid (Henderson & Mapp, 2002)

As schools attempt to optimize students' learning opportunities, their reliance on families and the community can become more profound. As described by Henderson & Mapp (2002), some of the accomplishments that family and community organizing has encouraged include the following:

- Upgraded school facilities
- Improved school leadership and staffing
- Higher-quality learning programs for students
- New resources and programs to improve teaching and curriculum
- Funding for after-school programs and family support

▪ PRACTICAL CONSIDERATIONS IN LINKING SCHOOLS TO THEIR COMMUNITIES

The No Child Left Behind legislation updated the existing federal Elementary and Secondary Act **Title I** program by articulating expectations for schools and school districts in the realm of engaging families and communities. The National Center for Family and

Community Connections with Schools (2002) explains that all schools receiving Title I funds must abide by the following federal government education requirements:

- Develop a written parent involvement policy that is constructed and approved by parents. This policy must include how it will build a school's capacity to engage families, address barriers to their involvement, and coordinate parent involvement in other programs.
- Notify parents and the community about this policy in an understandable and uniform format.
- Use at least 1 percent of the school's Title I funds to develop a parent involvement program. The law defines parent involvement as activities that "improve student academic achievement and school performance."
- Describe and explain the school's curriculum, standards, and assessments.
- Develop a **parent-school compact**, or agreement, about how families and the school will collaborate to ensure children's progress.
- Provide parents detailed information on student progress at the school.

While studying the impact of home, school, and community partnerships on student achievement, Henderson and Mapp (2002) conclude that schools that succeed in engaging families from diverse backgrounds share three key practices.

- Focus on building trusting collaborative relationships among teachers, families, and community members
- Recognize, respect, and address families' needs, as well as class and cultural differences
- Embrace a philosophy of partnership where power and responsibility are shared

Educational researchers Hindman, Brown, and Rogers (2005) contend that community involvement in education has increased in the previous two decades as schools have formed partnerships with citizens and local businesses to provide volunteers, conduct fund-raising campaigns, and harness expertise to benefit students. While these initiatives promote student achievement, they have also been shown to help community members develop a sense of ownership in their schools. These researchers have found that when one seeks to involve community members in schools, it is important to tailor the specific message or request to the desired population.

One need only consider the different modes of community involvement portrayed in Table 14.1, along with the variety of school constituents to which these modes can be applied, as portrayed in Table 14.2, to understand the need to personalize requests to a target audience. During this process, schools and school leaders are also encouraged to identify potential barriers that could make community members reluctant to become involved (Hindman et al., 2005).

The Learning First Alliance (2005) recently conducted a study regarding how America's public schools can be promoted by the forging of relationships among key schools. Based on their research of successful family-school-community partnership approaches, the alliance has suggested the following approaches that school leaders can take to enhance the efficiency of their community engagement program:

- Describe how schools support family efforts to help children succeed. Help parents understand the curriculum and homework assignments. See that school meetings and events are scheduled at times that permit families to attend, and then publicize these efforts to the families and the community.

- Create a family-school-community compact that spells out how the school expects families to support their children's education and what families and community members should expect from the school.
- Work with parents to develop a list of volunteer activities, by school level. Create a clear job description for each activity, and provide an expected time commitment. Post this information on the school Web site, and publish it in the newsletter.
- Highlight and celebrate family volunteers at meetings, in the newsletter, and on the school Web site. Invite parents to share tips with you about how they support their children's education. Highlight the many ways that families and community members serve as partners in children's education.
- Make it easy for community members to ask questions, broach concerns, and offer ideas.

In the News

Superintendent Ernest Perlini acknowledged Wednesday night a very difficult month at Newington High School in the area of student conduct. In one week last month, police announced that they had foiled a school violence plot, were investigating a bomb scare and had seized a loaded weapon on school grounds. All three incidents led to arrests of Newington High School students.

During a board of education meeting Wednesday, at which some parents demanded better communication between school officials and the community, Perlini said he would be speaking with Police Chief Richard Mulhall over the next couple of weeks about possibly assigning a second school resource officer to Newington High, with potential duty at the middle schools.

A second security officer at the high school, along with improved communication technology, is being considered in light of recent, back-to-back events at the school that have troubled residents and town leaders.

On Feb. 14, junior Frank Fechteler, 16, was charged with two felony counts of manufacturing bombs after police found evidence that they say showed Fechteler planned to kill certain classmates with weapons that included shrapnel pipe bombs and a shotgun or semiautomatic rifle on April 10. The alleged plot has received national media attention.

Then Feb. 15, a few hours after Fechteler was arraigned in Superior Court in New Britain, a suspicious package was found on a school bus. The incident brought out the Hartford police bomb squad and a hazardous materials team to investigate, shutting down Garfield Street, where the Newington school bus garage is located, for more than five hours as authorities concluded that the package had no explosives. A 17-year-old Newington High student was recently charged with felony first-degree breach of peace in the case, after other students told investigators they saw him with the item on their school bus.

Rounding out the week, on Feb. 16, a 16-year-old Newington High student was arrested and charged with possessing a weapon at the school after students reported seeing a pistol tucked into his pants. The weapon turned out to be a loaded pellet gun, police said. Then last Friday, in what school administrators are calling a prank, someone called the main office from a room phone within the school and said "Oh my God" before hanging up. As a precaution, police were called, and at least a dozen officers and a SWAT team responded and did a full sweep of the school within 15 minutes, police and school officials said.

Town council member Jeff Hedberg, during a council special meeting with the board Monday, said the incidents represent "a crisis right now in town . . . . We have to face this."

On Wednesday night, Susan Mazzoccoli, a former board member, told school leaders that communication with parents needed to be more immediate, with contact information kept up-to-date. So far, Mazzoccoli said, she has not gotten a letter from Newington High about the power outage at the school last Thursday morning and a subsequent fire alarm—as students were taking the Connecticut Academic Performance Test—that led to a short school day.

"It can be extremely frustrating not to be in touch and learn things from the newspaper," Mazzoccoli said. Jeananne McMahon, another parent, told board members that letters should also be sent to the families of elementary and middle school children when something major happens at Newington High, since it is "a communitywide issue."

Newington High Principal Bill Collins said steps have been taken to improve communication at the school, such as working to install an Internet-based system that can make 6,000 phone calls to parents in a single minute, leaving a prerecorded message in the event of a school lockdown or other emergency. School administrators also plan to purchase a caller ID system that tracks the source of phone calls. The estimated cost of that system is $20,000, Collins said. But Perlini said that even with boosted technology and police presence, "we all have to recognize that our world has changed," and that he needs to be frank with parents who ask if their kids are safe.

By Vanessa De La Torre, "Board Urged to Improve Communication after Incidents," March 15, 2007, in the *Hartford Courant* (Connecticut).

The National Center for Family and Community Connections with Schools (Henderson & Mapp, 2002) has analyzed a broad array of family-school-community partnership programs to determine best practices. The authors have uncovered several key insights from existing literature. They cite a study conducted by Sanders and Harvey (2000) that identifies three key factors that contribute to successful community partnerships. These include a school's commitment to learning, a principal's support and vision for community involvement, and a school's willingness to engage in two-way communication with potential partners about their level and kind of involvement. One key issue in community engagement is how schools can best connect with families and community members from diverse cultural and class backgrounds.

Related to Epstein's theory regarding spheres of influence, Lareau and Horvath (1999) found that the greater degree of alignment between white, middle-class families and schoolteachers enabled white parents to work more easily with school staff than did parents from different ethnic or class backgrounds. Related to this, Scribner, Young, and Pedroza (1999) identified five best-practice strategies used by school staff in working collaboratively with Hispanic families and community members. These include building on the cultural values of Hispanics, stressing personal contact, fostering two-way communication, creating a warm school environment, and facilitating structural accommodations for family and community involvement.

While this study highlights the need for personalized approaches to engage constituent groups, several studies highlight an overarching need for schools and school leaders to ensure that partnership programs are integrated into a comprehensive approach to student achievement (Wang, Oates, & Weishew, 1995; Smrekar, Guthrie, Owens, & Sims, 2001). Effective programs to engage families and community embrace a philosophy of partnership where responsibility for children's educational development is a collective enterprise among families, school staff, and community members (Henderson & Mapp, 2002).

The processes of determining goals and establishing priorities benefit from the infusion of data in the decision-making process. As such, we next turn our attention to collecting data on community involvement.

■ COLLECTING DATA ON COMMUNITY INVOLVEMENT

While it is important to involve the community in data-based decision making, as was described in Chapter 11, it is also helpful for school leaders to understand how to collect data on family and community involvement in schools. Here we will discuss how school leaders might approach data collection for community engagement purposes.

1. Frame the Issue. While ultimately the goal of family-school-community engagement is enhanced student growth and achievement, there are many paths to this destination (Chadwick, 2004). Some schools and districts may need to conduct strategic planning to find an appropriate starting point for community engagement. The strategic planning process entails significant data collection efforts in a variety of domains, from fiscal to programmatic. A school or district will likely include community constituents in the strategic planning process. Once the strategic planning process has been conducted, a school leader might then involve a community engagement planning team to distill from the strategic plan the best mechanism to draw upon community resources to assist in the attainment of the goals outlined in the strategic plan. While student growth and achievement are the ultimate goals, preliminary activities may have a variety of foci. Sanders (2001) outlines four potential foci for partnership activities and provides sample activities for each. Table 14.3 synthesizes this information.

2. Identify Constituent Groups. Once an issue has been framed and a proposed destination has been articulated, a next step involves the identification of appropriate constituent groups to engage in the endeavor. Schools can collaborate with a broad range of community partners to implement activities that will enhance the local learning community and educational experience of students. As a reminder, Table 14.2 provides examples of this broad array of potential partners for school-community collaboration.

3. Understand Constituent Perspectives. In order to determine the appropriate community group to collaborate with on an initiative, it is important to understand the various perspectives held by these groups. As such, it is important that school leaders are acquainted with some options for measuring public opinion. While there are a variety of mechanisms

TABLE 14.3 Focus of Community Partnership Activities

Activity Focus	Sample Activities
Student centered	Student awards, student incentives, scholarships, student trips, tutors, mentors, job shadowing, and other student services
Family centered	Parent workshops, family fun nights, GED and other adult education classes, parent incentives and rewards, counseling and other forms of assistance
School centered	Equipment and materials, beautification and repair, teacher incentives and awards, funds for school events and programs, office and classroom assistance
Community centered	Community beautification, student exhibits and performances, charity and other outreach

to attain public information, it is important to use approaches that are appropriate for answering the questions at hand. For example, to get a broad picture of how a community feels regarding school safety, one would not need to conduct time- and resource-intensive phone interviews, but could hold an open forum to gather this information.

Opinion research comes in a variety of classifications based on the manner in which it is carried out, including scientific and unscientific, formal and informal, quantitative and qualitative, and probability and nonprobability (Gallagher, Bagin, & Moore, 2005). The authors explain that while the results of unscientific, informal, or nonprobability opinion research cannot be projected with statistical assurance to the total group from which the sample is taken, the results of scientific, formal, and probability research can. A few examples of how school leaders can collect unscientific opinion research will be briefly described, followed by a few examples regarding the collection of scientific opinion research via surveys.

Forums and conferences provide school leaders with a rough but important measure of how the school community feels about particular topics and can reveal areas of satisfaction and dissatisfaction. Often these forums allow school-based individuals or groups, be it the school leadership, teachers, or students, to present a proposed initiative or solution to an issue. After the presentation, members of the audience are given an opportunity to express their opinions and ask questions about the topic. Often an attempt is made to summarize the tone of the meeting and to gather a measure of how the group as a whole felt about the particular topic. This information can be quite useful in helping the school to determine the best course of action.

Advisory committees are established with the intent of including a balanced representation of interests expressed within the broader community. While a forum or conference can easily involve over a hundred individuals, an advisory committee comprises a much more manageable number of community members. This benefit is balanced by the danger of assuming that the full spectrum of ideas and beliefs present in the broader community are adequately represented on the advisory committee. Even so, the inclusion of a cross section of opinions from the broader community is a valuable asset to school reform initiatives.

Public opinion surveys are mechanisms for identifying community priorities regarding education that can provide precise, scientific data if conducted properly. As such, many schools and districts are utilizing survey data to guide decision making and to justify such decisions. Of course, the manner in which the survey is designed, utilized, and analyzed will have important implications for how useful the results are to school leaders. Before sending a survey to the school community, it is important that thought be given to the design of questionnaires, wording of questions, interview protocols, sampling techniques, data analysis, and reporting and use of the results.

Currently, the four most commonly used methods of gaining public opinion through survey techniques include personal interviews, phone interviews, mailed questionnaires, and drop-off/pick-up questionnaires. As technology continues to develop and become more widely used by all sectors of the community, two additional survey techniques are becoming more widely used. These include automated telephone questionnaires and Internet surveying via email or interactive Web sites. Gallagher, Bagin, and Moore (2005) have summarized the advantages and limitations of each of these six public opinion surveying techniques, and this information is provided in Table 14.4.

4. Develop Strategies to Encourage Constituent Action. Having acquired a base of insight regarding constituent perspectives in particular domains, it is next important to appropriately engage community members in strategies and actions related to current issues or challenges facing the school. When planning to engage community members in school endeavors, it is critical to understand the value proposition that we all calculate when considering spending our time on tasks. This value proposition is expressed below.

$$\frac{\text{Perceived benefit of involvement}}{\text{Perceived cost of involvement}} = \text{Perceived value of involvement}$$

School leaders are advised to seek ways to increase the perceived benefit of community involvement in education while decreasing the perceived costs of such involvement. One approach to such an aim might entail a movement of key school members out into the community (Chadwick, 2004). Although a limited number of community members may have the opportunity, or the luxury, of visiting the school campus on a given day, school leaders can meet the community members where they are, outside of the school environment. Businesses, community centers, and faith-based organizations are locations that can provide forums for school leaders to begin to engage, or reconnect, community members with the life of the school.

Table 14.2 provides examples of locations that school personnel can visit to engage members of the community or to tell the story of what is going on with the local public school system. Having made such good-faith efforts to meet the community where they are, school leaders might find that community members are more apt to see the value in becoming engaged in the local schools and more willing to support schools in terms of time, talent, and treasure. Aligned with this desire to bring community members into the school and to engage them more substantially in decisions impacting the instructional program and educational experiences provided to students, school leaders may include community representatives in the process of data-driven decision making.

■ DEVELOPING STRATEGIC COMMUNITY PARTNERSHIPS

Principals are charged with the challenging task of orchestrating a team comprising teachers, students, administrators, and support staff to create a positive learning environment contributing to student success. It is fitting for school leaders to be proactive in seeking ways to partner with diverse communities to establish beneficial relationships that will en-

Table 14.4   Advantages and Limitations of Six Public Opinion Surveying Methods

Survey Technique	Advantages	Limitations
Personal Interview	• High percentage of return • Highest probability of correct information • Possibility of obtaining additional information • Opportunity to clarify understanding for respondent	• Greater cost • Personnel training required • Increased time needed • Safety issues • Gaining access to interviewees
Telephone Interview	• Inexpensive • Shorter period of time needed • No transportation costs • Less personnel training needed • Opportunity to clarify understanding for respondent	• Unlisted phones • Some families do not have a phone • Easy for respondents to hang up • Answering machines • Caller ID devices
Drop-Off/Pick-Up Questionnaire	• High return in short period of time • Minimal training of personnel	• Transportation costs • Need many volunteers/workers • Possibility of irate citizen collecting many questionnaires and answering all of them
Mailed Questionnaire	• Mailing costs less than transportation costs • Possibility of reaching groups protected from solicitors • Increased candor from respondents	• Low returns • Total population not represented
Automated Telephone Questionnaire	• Covers a wide area • Interviewers not needed • No mail or distribution costs	• Expertise needed to format and record questionnaire • Representative sample difficult to obtain • Clarification of wording and meaning difficult to provide
Internet Surveying	• Can be less expensive • Can be faster • Broad area is reached • Automated tabulation • Email best for internal surveys	• Representative sample difficult to obtain • Response rate can be low • Web-site maintenance • Lack of uniform Internet access can lead to possible skewed results (e.g., socioeconomic status)

Source: Gallagher, D., Bagin, D., and Moore, E. (2005). *The school and community relations.* (8th ed.). Boston. Allyn & Bacon.

hance students' educational experience. In a principal's quest to form strategic alliances with various community partners, such as those outlined in Table 14.2, a school's mission and vision should always be taken into account. School leaders ought to assess the differing perspectives and intentions among community members to determine which partnerships are more practical, beneficial, and feasible for the school. It is advisable for schools to determine the desired outcomes of a partnership for students and the school, on an academic and social level, before entering into any formal agreements.

As one might imagine, effective school collaboration with communities is often more complicated than it appears. Principals frequently grapple with ways to identify the boundaries of their immediate community and struggle to decipher which techniques to utilize when developing strategic partnerships. In addition to these impediments, schools have to contend with several barriers that restrict successful school-community partnerships. Sanders (2006) collected data from 443 National Network of Partnership Schools that outlined obstacles schools would have to overcome in order to develop successful partnerships with communities. These pitfalls included

- Insufficient interest and participation from internal and external constituents
- Inadequate supply of community partners and resources available due to increased competition from other schools
- Time constraints on the part of school leaders to identify and contact potential community partners
- Ineffective leadership, which can deter school-community partnerships from progressing. It is critical to have a leader who can develop, coordinate, and maintain consistent interactions between a school and the community
- Lack of funding to support partnership initiatives and activities
- Difficulty of communicating in a timely manner and delivering the correct message across language barriers
- Vague outcomes specified in strategic plans

Schools typically have the luxury of being surrounded by an abundance of community partners with whom relationships can be formed. However, not all community members are compatible for schools. It is important for principals to consider thoughtfully which community members are strategically aligned with a school's plans, goals, and objectives. Chadwick (2004) emphasizes that the success of a school-community partnership hinges on the ability of school leaders effectively to recruit and partner with appropriate community members. As such, it is wise for principals to partner with community members who share similar interests and offer mutual respect for one another. As highlighted in Table 14.2, there are a multitude of prospective community partners with which a school can choose to collaborate. Below are three of the most common partners.[1]

1. Business Partnerships. Over the years, there has been a considerable increase in school-business partnerships around the country. This can be attributed to the potential for a mutually beneficial relationship between the two entities. Schools frequently receive additional funding while communities derive their satisfaction from making a difference in the lives of young adults. However, the partnership will attain desired outcomes and benefits only if the best interests of both parties are taken into account during the planning stages. Before implementing a detailed plan, school leaders and communities should pay particular attention to the *Guiding Principles for Business and School Partnerships*, outlined by the Council for Corporate and School Partnerships. The guiding principles for effective partnerships specify

- School-business partnerships must be built on shared values and philosophies.
- Partnership activities should be integrated into the school and business cultures.

- Partnerships should be defined by mutually beneficial goals and objectives.
- Partnerships should be driven by a clear management structure and detailed process.
- Partnerships should define specific and measurable outcomes.
- Partnerships should incur support at the highest level within the business and school.
- Partnerships should be developed with clear definitions of success for both parties.

When establishing school-business partnerships, it is critical that principals involve a cross section of constituents, including families, members of the school board, administrators, and teachers, in the planning and development phase. To ensure the success and longevity of a partnership, it is essential that these constituents have the ability to voice their opinions and become valuable team members in the collaboration process. Constituents who have a voice in the planning and development process are more likely to become enthusiastic and supportive of fostering community involvement. This positive attitude creates a trickle-down effect that encourages colleagues openly to welcome the opportunity to partner with the community.

In a school-business partnership, schools are the fortunate beneficiaries of funding for school initiatives, tutors, internships, guest lecturers, incentives, and sundry additional support services, all of which positively affect a student's learning environment. There are discernible advantages in a school-business partnership for schools, but one may question the rationale or incentive for businesses to collaborate with schools. The partnership between these two entities is not a one-sided affair as it often appears. Businesses have a vested interest in their surrounding schools for a number of reasons. They are committed to the well-being of schools, as a large portion of their workforce often comprises local high school and college graduates.

Business executives rely on schools, particularly K–12 schools, to provide students with a quality education that will prepare them with the necessary skills to perform effectively the tasks and assignments associated with their roles in the professional world. Through financial support and services that businesses provide schools, businesses become known as philanthropists, thereby augmenting the image of their organizations, while having a positive impact on the lives of young adults. Additionally, businesses also depend on schools to provide the community with various forms of entertainment, whether it is through activities such as school musicals, drama plays, or athletic events.

2. University Partnerships. Colleges and universities are increasingly partnering with schools and school districts to offer workshops on professional training and development. Higher-education institutions are also recognized for seeking and inspiring community involvement at various levels throughout campuses and in a manner that enhances the academic program. Increasingly, K–12 schools are being encouraged to call upon their post-secondary counterparts to share their expertise with principals and teachers regarding the effective development of school-family-community partnerships.

Establishing school-university partnerships can sometimes be difficult due to the bureaucratic channels that exist at both institutional levels. School leaders should look beyond the challenges posed by various forms of bureaucracy and resort to creative ways that will assist in making the relationship come to fruition. Once the two institutions have reached an understanding and a common vision has been shared, colleges and universities can collaborate with schools to enhance the level of college preparedness among high school students. School-university partnerships can assist in this effort by providing schoolteachers with instructional techniques on ways to improve students' cognitive abilities in multiple disciplines, including reading, writing, math comprehension, and problem solving.

One potential benefit of schools partnering with colleges and universities is the opportunities secondary students have to interact with college students and faculty, thereby becoming familiar with the resources and expectations associated with a university campus. College students will frequently serve as mentors and role models for schoolchildren, while developing friendships and meaningful relationships with these children. This exposure is particularly advantageous to students from low-socioeconomic families or urban schools who often doubt the value of furthering their education after high school. A school-university partnership has the ability to change student attitudes positively and provide them with the desire and aspiration to become college graduates.

3. Service-Learning Partnerships. Schools are more commonly becoming immersed in service-learning partnerships as many of today's youth have a limited sense of civic responsibilities. Through a student's constant exposure to service-learning materials and activities, schools aim to

- instill a value of civic engagement and leadership in students;
- foster an environment for students to apply service-learning principles within their lives and their communities;
- encourage students to participate actively in service-learning opportunities;
- provide students with a clear understanding of how to become effective civic-minded citizens.

As with business and university partnerships, service-learning partnerships should be carefully designed. Schools should become involved in projects and activities that will be productive and insightful for students. It is crucial that students do not become idle during the service-learning program but are engrossed in the activities, principles, ideals, and virtues of the program that will prepare them to lead a life of democratic citizenship.

Following completion of a service-learning project, it is important for students to be given an opportunity to reflect upon their experiences. A desired outcome of service-learning partnerships is that students will conceptualize their role in a community and become aware of their civic duties. Through a combination of knowledge and practical experience pertaining to civic engagement, students will become more informed citizens and inclined to contribute to the betterment of society and their community.

Responsiveness to Diverse Community Interests and Needs

The No Child Left Behind legislation that holds districts and schools accountable for student performance sounds encouraging, yet difficulties arise when they are charged with the same expectation—applying higher standards to enhance student achievement. Compared to suburban schools, urban schools have more difficulties in communicating, partnering, and collaborating with families to improve the educational experience for their students. To exacerbate matters, urban schools often lack the necessary capital—human and social—to provide their students with optimal learning opportunities. Despite the disparities that exist between suburban and urban schools, families and communities are vital resources to both types of schools, and much research has documented the benefit of such collaboration on student achievement.

The role of a family in a student's educational experience is profound. It is therefore important for teachers and school leaders to make a concerted effort to encourage families to participate actively in their children's schooling. One may question the value of family involvement, especially in cases where families may offer children conflicting messages or differing instructional techniques from those used by teachers. There is some validity in this ideology, but school leaders are addressing this issue and developing programs to educate families better on how to educate their students further at home. Securing a school-family partnership is an essential component of children's schooling, given that there is a definitive relationship between a student's learning potential and family involvement. With a family being able to influence student outcomes significantly, schools are constantly seeking ways to engage families and partner with them on multiple levels to enhance student achievement.

Chadwick (2004) suggests that a school's valiant attempts to communicate and educate families on the value of family participation are often underappreciated. As we witnessed earlier in this chapter, the perceived value of involvement is determined by comparing perceived benefit of involvement to the perceived cost of involvement. School leaders are fully aware of the significance of family involvement and the degree to which it influences student achievement. However, they cannot assume that all families are well versed on the implications of family engagement, or lack thereof, to children's social and academic development. It is valuable for schools to develop strategies that will increase the perceived importance and benefit of family involvement. These include

- providing ample notice to families when school events take place;
- creating festive events with food and entertainment to showcase student performances;
- conducting open houses and family meetings in conjunction with athletic events;
- communicating with families on a regular basis, highlighting student accomplishments, and sharing concerned student news;
- recognizing the role and importance of cultural differences among parental attitudes;
- offering workshops on personal and professional development for families. (Chadwick, 2004)

Hearkening back to Epstein's theory of overlapping spheres, one element that influences student achievement in school is the contrasting ways in which learning takes place at home. A student's environment outside of school, including neighborhood, peers, and language level, has a lasting impact on the potential for academic excellence. Unfortunately, communities with highly concentrated levels of poverty, criminality, addiction, and unemployment are often the same communities with decreased rates of high school graduation and college enrollment.

Along these lines, effective school leaders understand the importance of varying demographics within their schools, families, and community. It is important for principals to display their leadership prowess and strategically establish various outreach efforts to develop partnerships with community members who already have relationships and cultural knowledge of the community and its families. Successful leaders avoid operating in silos. Instead, they are efficient and effective through their willingness to partner with a cross section of people and organizations. It is vital that schools refrain from isolating themselves from the community, but rather become integrated into the communal fabric by forming strategic alliances with diverse partners (Sanders, 2006).

Sanders and Lewis (2005) discuss the value of a school's ability to accommodate the diverse needs and interests of its student population while upholding its academic standards. It is in a school's best interests to partner with multifaceted organizations, including families and communities, in order to relate better with unfamiliar cultures and negate any form of ethnocentricity. Gallagher, Bagin, and Moore (2005) emphasize the importance of school leaders' ability to address ethnocentrism and ensure that a school's internal constituents understand and respect families and communities with values and opinions that are different than their own. In order to include members from the full spectrum of cultures and ethnicities represented in a school community, school leaders are encouraged to develop a community involvement plan with the following qualities:

- School policies that address multiethnic diverse groups and full integration of these groups into the school environment
- Strategies to identify diversity within the school's internal and external constituents
- Approaches on how to build relationships with diverse groups and integrate them into the school environment
- Workshops that educate teachers and school personnel on different customs, norms, and beliefs of varying cultures
- A communication plan that addresses linguistic differences and what measures will be implemented to ensure an effective delivery of the intended message (Gallagher et al., 2005)

Communications in Addressing Families and the Community

Common sense dictates that the better informed families and the community are of a school's activities and direction, the more likely they are to become engaged and involved with a school. Communication functions in multiple directions. One-way communication keeps families and the community informed through traditional means such as newsletters, brochures, radio broadcasts, and television. Schools depend upon these means of communication to educate external constituents on current and future developments involving the school and its students. This strategy has its limitations as people receiving messages through these forms do not have the option of clarifying any misunderstandings or the ability to receive feedback on any comments they may have.

Through a two-way approach, schools can participate in discourse with families and communities on a personal level, either over the phone or face-to-face. One of the key components of communication, often overlooked by many, is the significance of being able to listen attentively. Perfecting the art of listening is a skill that is most beneficial to education leaders. As we have seen throughout this chapter, families and communities can serve as viable partners for schools and are willing to collaborate and support school leaders on varying initiatives. It is through the art of listening that school leaders are able to resolve conflicts admirably and to align community and family interests strategically with the school's mission and vision.

The flourishing of partnerships among schools, families, and communities is facilitated by a continual flow of communication among the respective groups. Two-way communication allows teachers an opportunity to abstract useful information from families regarding the learning environment at home and conditions or influences that may affect a student's behavior in the classroom. Teachers will gain insights into family interests, background characteristics, attitudes, beliefs, socioeconomic status, and a family's perceived benefit of involvement in their children's schooling. Based on this information, teachers can develop a deeper appreciation and understanding of their students and enhance their potential for success.

Through communication channels, teachers can provide families with meaningful information on strategies that can be used at home to enhance the learning outcomes for their children. Effective two-way communication provides families with a sense of how their children interact with others in a school environment, how their children are performing in the classroom, and what measures need to be implemented to stimulate their children's growth and prohibit any foreseeable shortcomings.

 CASE 7 REVISITED

> You will remember principal Vince Cavanaugh, the leader of University Charter School, as well as board chair Harry Downer. Upon being surprised by Harry about a merit pay system, teachers planned several off-campus meetings, and community members were concerned that some of the best and brightest teachers might leave the school. It is safe to say that Vince has a public relations problem on his hands that requires immediate attention. How does this scenario evidence a breakdown in school-community communications? What are some potential communication strategies that might help Vince remediate the situation and use it to draw the school community together?

Visible results are obtained only when teachers and families actively collaborate with one another to establish activities and follow-up procedures that promote a student's advancement in education. Unfortunately, there are teachers who are skeptical of partnering with families. This fear arises as teachers believe that a teacher-family partnership allows families an opportunity to intrude and impose their views on how instruction should take place in the classroom. Two-way communication is critical in circumstances like this, as teachers can openly converse with families, set boundaries, and discuss best practices for collaboration. Teachers can express what works best for them and determine how a family's strengths and expertise can be best utilized to enhance student learning. Teachers will acknowledge and respect the opinions of others, but a time may come when teachers will be unable to accommodate certain initiatives proposed by families.

Schools may enhance their communication efforts by encouraging families to participate in a variety of school activities and services. School leaders and teachers who are effective communicators and provide multiple opportunities for families to become involved with the school will reap the rewards of a unified partnership. This partnership can develop through the following:

- *Family visits.* These provide families with an understanding of how the school operates, what instructional materials and techniques are being used in the classroom, and the behavior patterns of their student. Family visits are most helpful to teachers in communicating with low-socioeconomic families. Visual aids are commonly used during these visits to illustrate curriculum design and educational goals.
- *Family conferences.* These offer families an opportunity to participate in a one-on-one conversation with teachers to evaluate the progress of their student. Teachers use this environment to inform families of a student's performance, which may be positive or negative, and it is during these latter occasions when families may become aggravated

and expressive. When situations like these arise, teachers should resort to the art of listening, and once a family has conveyed their discontent, then resourcefully and constructively communicate an appropriate message to the family. All family conferences should end on a productive note with the student's best interests in mind.

- *Study and discussion groups.* These have become more desirable as family involvement with schools proliferates. Teachers coordinate these groups to better educate families on advanced instructional methods, school projects and events, and student behavior patterns.
- *Family-teacher associations.* The purpose behind these groups is to have families, teachers, and school leaders congregate to collaborate on initiatives that will advance the school's image in the community, while enhancing the educational experience for all students. (Gallagher et al., 2005)

Principals and teachers are primarily concerned with communicating with families, but it is important for schools to establish lines of communication with a variety of stakeholder groups in their communities. Schools have a greater chance of experiencing community support when a consistent and systematic flow of communication occurs between the school and community, rather than the school's calling upon the communities only during times of need or crisis. Compelling communication strategies will allow schools to foster partnerships with communities while educating them on the school's initiatives and needs. Through effective leadership and communication, schools can instill a high level of confidence within the community. Once a community witnesses a school's commitment to educating future leaders through its commitment to educational excellence, the community will become more inclined to offer time, talent, and treasure to support school initiatives.

Families and the community appreciate being informed of proposed school plans and often feel compelled to contribute to, or in some cases demand to be involved in, the decision-making process. Principals need to take these attitudes and beliefs into account before making executive decisions that will significantly affect students, teachers, families, or the community. An effective communication system will keep families and the community abreast of the latest school news and provide them with opportunities to voice their opinions. Through this type of engagement, families and the community will develop a sense of belonging with the school and gain an in-depth appreciation of the challenges and opportunities a school may face. In turn, school leaders will understand what areas of involvement are most suited to various community members and how the two entities can best be paired together (Gallagher et al., 2005).

Summary

The variety of interactions between schools and various community constituents discussed in this chapter represents the dual focus that is required to lead education organizations strategically. While attending to the daily operations of the instructional program, school leaders must also be constantly engaged with life outside of school doors. This chapter provides leaders and aspiring school leaders with insights regarding various benefits of engaging families and communities in the life of the school. Strategies for harnessing community resources to the benefit of schools were discussed, as were mechanisms for collecting data on family and community involvement. As our nation's schools increase in diversity, this chapter provides insights regarding the manner in which school leaders can be responsive to diverse community interests and needs. Formal and informal communication strategies are often bridges that bring various school constituents together. As such, strategies for crafting compelling communications are provided as are insights regarding effective use of community resources for the benefit of student growth.

Discussion Questions

1. Describe the impact that No Child Left Behind has had upon the way in which your school or district engages families and community groups.
2. From your experience as a teacher or administrator within your current school, take a moment and rank six dimensions of family-school involvement in order of importance.
3. List one concrete way that you have seen family and community involvement enhance student performance in your school.
4. Utilizing Figure 14.1 as a guide, depict the degree of overlap among the *spheres of influence* as they currently exist in your school.
5. On a scale of 1 to 10, rate your current education organization on the degree to which it accomplishes this four-step process:
   - Frame the issue.
   - Identify constituent groups.
   - Understand constituent perspectives.
   - Develop strategies to encourage constituent action.
6. If you listed the number of events that would fit in each category of Table 14.3 for the current school year, how evenly balanced would the categories be? Should they be balanced? Explain.
7. Of the prospective partners for school-community collaboration listed in Table 14.2, which three hold the most promise for positively influencing student growth and performance in your school?
8. Of the six public opinion survey techniques described in Table 14.4, which, if any, does your school currently utilize? How might the current techniques be enhanced at your school in relation to this table?
9. Recalling the value proposition of perceived benefit divided by perceived cost, describe how you might help increase the perceived value of family or community involvement in your school.
10. Rate your current school on the degree to which the full array of diverse constituents is purposefully engaged in the life of the school. Then, describe which of the five qualities of community involvement plans might help your school improve the most.
11. ELCC Standard 4 articulates several different ways that school leaders should engage the community. Do you, or will you, find it more challenging to respond to diverse community interests and needs or to mobilize community resources on behalf of the school?

References

Arriaza, G. (2004). Changing schools for good: A study of school culture and systems. *Journal of Education and Society 22*(2), 5–21.

Arriaza, G. (2004). Making changes that stay made. School reform and community involvement. *The High School Journal, 37*(4), 10–24.

Chadwick, K. G. (2004). *Improving schools through community engagement: A practical guide for educators.* Thousand Oaks, CA: Corwin Press.

The Council for Corporate and School Partnerships. (n.d.) *Guiding principles for business and school partnerships.* Retrieved March 22, 2007, from www.corpschoolpartners.org/pdf/guiding_principles.pdf.

Epstein, J. L. (1995). School, family, and community partnerships: Caring for the children we share. *Phi Delta Kappan, 76,* 701–712.

Epstein, J. L. (2001). *School, family, and community partnerships: Preparing educators and improving schools.* Boulder, CO: Westview.

Epstein, J. L., & Sheldon, S.B. (2002). Present and accounted for: Improving student attendance through family and community involvement. *The Journal of Educational Research, 95,* 308–318.

Gallagher, D., Bagin, D., & Moore, E. (2005). *The school and community relations* (8th ed.). Boston: Allyn & Bacon.

Garcia-Reid, P., Reid, R. J., & Peterson, N. A. (2005). School engagement among Latino youth in an urban middle school context: Valuing the role of social support. *Education and Urban Society, 37,* 257–275.

Henderson, A. T., & Mapp, K. L. (2002). *A new wave of evidence: The impact of school, family, and community connections on student achievement.* Annual synthesis. Austin, TX: National Center for Family & Community Connections with Schools, Southwest Educational Development Laboratory.

Hindman, J. L., Brown, W. M., & Rogers, C. S. (2005). Beyond the school: Getting community members involved. *Principal Leadership, 5*(8), 36–39.

Lareau, A., & Horvath, E. M. (1999). Moments of social inclusion and exclusion: Race, class, and cultural capital in family-school relationships. *Sociology of Education, 72,* 37–53.

The Learning First Alliance. (2005). *A practical guide to promoting America's public schools: Values, vision and performance.* (Updated and expanded August 2005).

National Center for Family & Community Connections with Schools. (2002). Austin, TX: Southwest Educational Development Laboratory. www.sedl.org

Sanders, M. G. (2001). The role of "community" in comprehensive school, family, and community partnership programs. *Elementary School Journal, 101(1),* 19–34.

Sanders, M. G. (2006). *Building school-community partnerships: Collaboration for student success.* Thousand Oaks, CA: Corwin Press.

Sanders, M. G., & Harvey, A. (2000). *Developing comprehensive programs of school, family and community partnerships: The community perspective.* Paper presented at the annual meeting of the American Educational Research Association, New Orleans.

Sanders, M. G., & Lewis, K. C. (2005). Building bridges toward excellence: Community involvement in high schools. *The High School Journal, 88(3),* 1–9.

Scribner, J. D., Young, M. D., & Pedroza, A. (1999). Building collaborative relationships with parents. In P. Reyes, J. D. Scribner, & A. P. Scribner (Eds.), *Lessons from high-performing Hispanic schools: Creating learning communities* (pp. 36–60). New York: Teachers College Press.

Sheldon, S. B. (2003). Linking school–family–community partnerships in urban elementary schools to student achievement on state tests. *The Urban Review, 35(2)*, 149–165.

Sheldon, S. B., & Epstein, J. L. (2002). Improving student behavior and school discipline with family and community involvement. *Education and Urban Society, 35*, 4–26.

Smrekar, C., Guthrie, J. W., Owens, D. E., & Sims, P. G. (2001). March toward excellence: School success and minority student achievement in Department of Defense Schools. A report to the National Education Goals Panel. Washington, DC: National Education Goals Panel. (ED 459 218).

Wang, M. C., Oates, J., & Weishew, N. L. (1995). Effective school responses to student diversity in inner-city schools: A coordinated approach. *Education and Urban Society, 27(4)*, 484–503. [Also published in 1997 in Haertel, G. P., & M.C. Wang (Eds.), *Coordination, Cooperation, Collaboration* (pp. 175–197), Philadelphia, PA: the Mid-Atlantic Regional Educational Laboratory at Temple University.]

Suggested Readings

Brandt, R. S. (Ed.). (1979). *Partners: Parents and schools.* Alexandria, VA: Association for Supervision and Curriculum Development.

   In this book, the authors review some of the premises and practices of parent participation, analyze related assumptions, report on parents' perceptions of the curriculum and school, examine the constitutional and legal basis of the parent role for power sharing, and suggest ways the relationship could be more productive.

Chadwick, K. G. (2004). *Improving schools through community engagement.* Thousand Oaks, CA: Corwin Press.

   This text addresses questions about how to harness public interest in education, is a source of methods and strategies for educators to initiate action, and provides a framework that education leaders can use in designing and implementing initiatives to engage the public more effectively.

Chibucos, T. R., and Lerner, R. M. (1999). *Serving children and families through community-university partnerships: Success stories.* Norwell, MA: Kluwer Academic Publishers.

   This work presents several dozen exemplary "success stories" of community-university partnerships that serve to enhance the lives of children, youth, and families and illustrates the ways in which universities and colleges are using their learning resources in ways that more directly benefit society.

Hiatt-Michael, D. B. (Ed.). (2005). *Promising practices for family involvement in schooling across the continents.* Greenwich, CT: Information Age Publishing.

   This monograph represents a seminal examination of the relationship of families to the education of their children across the globe, and its intent is to generate new avenues for educational research and practice in the field of family-school-community involvement.

Lyons, P., Robbins, A., and Smith, A. (1982). *Involving parents: A handbook for participation in schools.* Ypsilanti, MI: The High/Scope Press.

   A result of the Study of Parental Involvement in Four Federal Education Programs, this text is a professional guide to effective parental involvement in school activities.

Minar, D. (1966). The community basis of conflict in school system politics. *American Sociological Review* 31: 824–835.

This article analyzes aggregate voting data on referenda and elections in suburban school districts and reveals substantial relationships among participation, tendency toward negative voting, and certain social characteristics. It also explores key findings indicating the impact of conflict-management skill availability.

Rioux, J. W., and Berla, N. (1993). *Innovations in parent & family involvement.* Princeton Junction, NJ: Eye on Education.

This book reveals the results of a national search for exemplary parent and family involvement programs and provides strategies and tips for planning and implementing such programs.

Sanders, M. G. (2006). *Building school-community partnerships.* Thousand Oaks, CA: Corwin Press.

This book, an insightful text that serves as a source for educators seeking to establish school-community partnerships to achieve goals for their schools and the students, families, and communities they serve, emphasizes the importance of community involvement for effective school functioning, student support and well-being, and community health and development.

Notes

1. This description of school-community partnerships is a distillation of ideas provided by Sanders (2006). *Building school-community partnerships: Collaboration for student success.* Thousand Oaks, CA: Corwin Press.

CHAPTER FIFTEEN

Practicing Strategic Leadership

LEARNING OBJECTIVES

By the end of this chapter, you should be able to

- craft a personal leadership persona and style;
- identify core values relevant to leadership;
- construct a professional philosophy of education and of management;
- set priorities for leadership action;
- comprehend considerations in deploying people, resources, and time;
- communicate with a spectrum of audiences;
- employ leadership symbols and follower impressions;
- conduct difficult conversations with colleagues, subordinates, and upperlings;
- understand the significance to a leader of personal ethics and consistent behavior.

This book, consciously, emphasizes the conceptual knowledge and strategic understandings needed by a leader effectively to determine and shape organizational direction. However, the book stresses not only the right things to do, but also the crucial importance of doing things right. Leaders need to learn and think, and they also need to act. Systematic reflection is an important avenue for learning and thinking. Reflection is the self-conscious and constructively critical examination of one's past professional experiences and personal reactions to or as a result of those experiences. By contemplating their past performance, leaders can determine what is important and how well they are improving. Self-examination is good. In addition, leaders can learn from the feedback they receive from others, from comparing their performance to that of peers, and from reading widely about leaders in other spheres and placing themselves in similar circumstances and second-guessing their historical antecedents.

However, it is ultimately via actions that leaders give vent to their vision and begin to implement that which they believe is needed for the long-run well-being of their organization and its clients. But what actions should a leader take? What activity and what behavior are most important in an effort to guide and change one's organization? This chapter concentrates on answering questions such as these. Here concepts and concrete conditions are considered, and then insights are offered on how to convert these into conscious plans and behaviors. Advice is provided regarding matters such as self-consciously constructing a personal leadership style; formulating thoughts regarding learning and schooling; crystallizing views regarding management; distilling the professional side of oneself into an effective résumé; effectively managing time; communicating interpersonally and institutionally; presenting a professional image; and holding difficult conversations with colleagues, subordinates, and even bosses.

▪ SHAPING ONE'S LEADERSHIP STYLE

In large measure, more than position, purpose, persona, poise, professionalism, education, intellect, morality, appearance, manner of communicating, attire, and day-to-day behavior, an individual in a leadership role will be defined, appraised, and known by his or her leadership style.

What Is Leadership Style? As introduced in Chapter 2, leadership style refers to the composite of and interactions among all the above-listed personal and professional traits and components. It is this mosaic of attributes and actions that makes up the stuff of leadership and the reality of a leader. In some instances, an individual's personal, physical, and professional facets fit comfortably in a self-reinforcing amalgam of attributes and actions, and successful leadership is the result. Conversely, sometimes leaders display traits and carry out behaviors that are inauthentic. In these falsely constructed, ill-conceived, or flawed efforts at crafting a leadership style, the composite is inconsistent, the sum of individual leadership components is not synergistic, and all the parts do not equal an effective whole. Followers have the ability rather quickly to discern what is real and what is unreal in a leader. Hence, it behooves a reader to pick and choose and to weld together a leadership style that is congruent and fits with what one genuinely believes and can consistently do.

However, developing a leadership style is far from a casual or one-time undertaking. It involves a complicated process entailing observation, reflection, practice, trial, and reformulation. In some ways, it is a time-consuming process and a never-ending search. A good leader is a work in progress. Modeling oneself after others, or facets of others, is one useful means to assembling a leadership style. Below are some illustrative leadership models taken from history.

George S. Patton, a remarkably successful World War II U.S. general, was flamboyant, goal oriented, fiercely patriotic, and highly religious. He believed he was predestined from on high for leadership, possessed a steely discipline, was given to quick judgments, and was steadfastly loyal to subordinates. He also demanded the highest possible performance from those who worked for him. No other field commander matched his World War II results. Might he be your role model?

Eleanor Roosevelt, a shy, awkward, somewhat emotionally mistreated child, starved for adult recognition and peer acceptance, grew into a woman with great sensitivity to the underprivileged of all creeds, races, and nations. When Mrs. Roosevelt came to the White House in 1933, she likely understood social conditions better than any of her First Lady predecessors, and she transformed the role of presidential spouse into presidential partner. She never shirked official entertaining and greeted thousands with charming friendliness. She also broke precedent to hold press conferences, travel to all parts of the nation, give lectures and radio broadcasts, and express her opinions candidly in a daily syndicated newspaper column, "My Day." Might she be your role model?

Jack Welch was the CEO of General Electric for twenty years during the latter part of the twentieth century. Under his leadership the value of the corporation soared by billions of dollars. He made many more billions for the owners of GE stocks, and ten thousand GE employees became real live millionaires on his watch. He pioneered new management strategies including intolerance for failure, set production standards with zero defect acceptance, and imposed a seemingly ruthless requirement that the lowest-rated 10 percent of all managers be released from the company each year. Since his tenure as GE's CEO, literally dozens of high-ranking Welch protégés migrated as CEOs to other private-sector firms where they implemented his management methods to great effect. What part of Jack Welch's style might fit you?

Harry S. Truman, who unexpectedly inherited the presidency following Franklin Delano Roosevelt's death, was self-effacing and genuinely humble and was raised in a nondescript middle-class home and had an undistinguished career as a farmer, military officer, businessman, and low-level public official. Yet despite such an inauspicious back-ground, he gained election to the U.S. Senate, and upon rising from vice president to commander-in-chief, rendered some of the most important decisions in the history of America, including the dropping of the atomic bomb on the Japanese homeland and con-structing the principal defense to the aggressive Cold War actions of the former Soviet Union. Does his self-effacing but effective leadership manner fit you?

Mother Teresa, who grew famous for selflessly ministering to lepers, the homeless, and the poorest of the poor in the slums of Calcutta, joined the Sisters of Our Lady of Lareto in 1928. For seventeen years, she taught school and performed charity work throughout the nation of India. In 1950, she founded the Missionaries of Charity, a new order devoted to helping the sick and poor. During the next fifty years, the order grew to include branches in more than one hundred cities around the world, and Mother Teresa became a worldwide symbol of charity, meeting with Princess Diana and many other pub-lic figures. In 1979, Mother Teresa was awarded the Nobel Prize for Peace, and in 1985 she was awarded the Medal of Freedom from the United States. Is her lead-by-doing and servantlike leadership approach appealing to you?

William Jefferson Clinton, president of the United States from 1992 to 2000 and hus-band of New York State U. S. senator Hilary Rodham Clinton, was among the nation's most charismatic presidents. His commanding presence, personal bearing, speaking eloquence, engaging personality, spectacular grasp of complexity, and ability to communicate with mul-tiple audiences were highly evident and striking traits. Regrettably, other than balancing the federal budget, championing welfare reform, and advocating for the North American Free Trade Agreement, he left virtually no legislative legacy as president. His term as president is characterized and chronicled by historians principally as squandered opportunity. Instead of towering accomplishments, such as those amassed by Washington, Adams, Lincoln, and the Roosevelts, Clinton will likely be remembered for a stream of unfortunate moral lapses and indelicate personal behaviors, activities outside the zone of follower tolerance.

Martin Luther King Jr.'s leadership actions altered the social and legal landscape of America. His ability to communicate and his strategic interventions elevated issues of race relations and civil liberties to the top of the nation's policy agenda. He informed himself regarding and then consciously adapted the nonviolent tenets of Henry Thoreau and Mahatma Gandhi. When Martin Luther King engaged in civil disobedience in an effort to secure racial justice and equal rights, it was a conscious action taken in pursuit of a larger goal. Within his civil rights organization, an organization that he personally founded, there were followers who routinely criticized his pacifist "turn the other cheek" philosophy. They preferred actions that were bolder, confrontational, and on occasion, inviting of retaliatory violence. Of course, among those in the larger society who opposed him, his purposes and practices were even more unacceptable. Still, despite having to maintain a course of nonviolence, in opposition to some of his followers' wishes and as an enemy of much of the nation's power structure, he adhered to his beliefs and ultimately achieved unparalleled success. Martin Luther King's style is the embodiment of strategic leadership.

Ronald Reagan could hardly seem more different from Martin Luther King. Their childhoods, their purposes, their friends, their eventual lifestyles, and their philosophies were in many ways counter opposites. Yet ironically, each was an absolutely world-class strategic leader. Reagan was renowned for keeping what for most presidents was a relaxed daily schedule. However, he was a master at setting priorities, selecting able staff, and delegating authority, relentlessly staying on task and maintaining a consistent course of strategic action. More than any other single individual, his perspicacity, policies, and persistence were responsible for undoing the hegemony of the former Soviet Union.

Self-Consciously Constructing a Leadership Style

While much can be learned from historical leaders serving in a variety of contexts, style is in large measure situational. An NFL quarterback will act differently than the chair of the Joint Chiefs of Staff, a high school principal, a teacher union leader, or a district superintendent. Each occupies a different societal niche and plays a different workforce or professional role; the situational requirements and follower expectations attract individuals with different qualifications, interests, and styles. Still, assuming some degree of situational commonality, from what elements and experiences can a leader or aspiring leader consciously construct his or her leadership style?

Style is amenable to active and thoughtful shaping and reshaping. One's leadership style need not—indeed should not—be an unexamined accident of history. When under conscious construction, leadership style is an amalgam of personal characteristics and capacities blended into day-to-day reality, through a formulation of experience, observation, reflection, trial and error, and reformulation. The challenge to a leader or aspiring leader is to render this amalgam willful and purposeful, not accidental. One's leadership style, to the extent reasonably possible, should be a complex composition of personally preferred and carefully crafted qualities and abilities, not an unedited summation of a crazy-quilt set of random life experiences.

Indeed, one of the largest distinctions between organizational leaders and many of their followers is that the former more likely have given consistent and self-conscious consideration to themselves and their careers. Too often, followers occupy subordinate roles not for lack of ability or by conscious choice, but rather because they have, perhaps unthinkingly, acquiesced to their life circumstances, rather than engaging with their conditions and striving to shape and continually reshape their lives. One should not take life as a given or see events and outcomes as inevitable. *Situation plus individual attitude can shape outcomes.*

The following categories make up the resources to which an active constructor of leadership style can turn, and return. One needs to remember, however, that a leadership style is not static, a condition once formulated and thereafter set for all time. Rather it is a process of continually determining and reinventing oneself.

Examined Experience. When in the past you were in leadership circumstances, even from elementary school, how did you act and how satisfied are you currently with the outcomes of those past actions? Would you modify your leadership style as a consequence of past actions you have taken and upon which you now believe improvement can be based? While looking back to lament is often an empty exercise in self-pity, looking back to learn can be productive. As the wise saying warns, the unexamined life is not worth living.

Observation. How do other leaders act? Do they do something you would like to do? Do they do something you know is ineffective and you would wish to avoid doing? Positive and negative models, as evident in the behavior of others, can both be useful. An experienced leader observes other leaders constantly, seeking clues regarding how better to improve his or her own performance. A reader should seldom listen to a speech, observe a debate, hear a lecture or presentation, participate in a meeting, or engage in a conversation with an upperling without having split vision, listening to and engaging with the content and appraising the leadership behaviors and methods being used. These observations of leaders should not be narrowly focused or sensitive only to leader nuances. Watch not only the leader but also the reactions of followers to whatever the leader has done.

Actively Searching for Models. It is not only the passive observation of leaders with whom one is in personal contact that can be useful. In addition, one can actively seek other models to observe. This can be done principally through reading biography and watching films or television footage of leaders in action. It is fruitful to engage in an active search for models, expanding the realm of leaders with whom one can engage and with which one can compare, even if vicariously, in order to find leadership components that one would like to weave into the tapestry of one's own leadership style.

Practice. Adolf Hitler rehearsed his public speeches tirelessly. He sought and consciously constructed physical and ceremonial circumstances in which his message would be maximally received by followers. He was a master, however evil a master, of communication and persuasion. However, it did not come naturally to an individual whose early life had been filled with mediocrity and failure. By conscious resolve he molded himself into an awesome machine frighteningly capable of manipulating large-scale public and follower opinion. Whereas one would hope that a leader's ends were moral, Hitler is nevertheless a good example of the self-conscious crafting of individual action, through practice and trial and error, to mold an effective leader. Of course, one should note that as time progressed and the gap between Hitler's rhetoric and his actions and the gap between his professed purposes and the reality of day-to-day German life widened, no amount of speechifying and media manipulation could voluntarily persuade followers; it was only through force, intimidation, and intrigue that he maintained his leadership position.

Outside Criticism. One can shape and reshape leadership style through conscious solicitation of **constructive feedback** from knowledgeable observers. Such observers may be friends, family members, upperlings, subordinates, and so on. They can even be formally arranged. There exist executive coaches, individuals who specialize, usually for money, in helping shape leadership style. The important point is that the observer providing feedback should be in a position to know what you as a leader have actually done and are striving to accomplish, and not be so subject to intimidation or reprisal that the individual critic is unable or unwilling to provide honest feedback.

Reflection. One's most capable critic can be oneself. Continually subjecting one's own actions to constructively critical self-examination can be useful. After a meeting, after a presentation, after a difficult conversation, after having met a superior, one should wonder: How did I do? Could I have done something differently that could have been better? Could my ends have been achieved more forcefully had I acted differently?

An individual incapable of honest self-appraisal is unlikely to be an effective leader. A word of caution is in order, however. One can become so self-absorbed in reflecting upon one's own actions as to become paralyzed, resulting in indecision and inactivity for fear of behaving in a less than fully effective manner. Such obsessive behavior is a symptom of self-examination taken to excess.

▪ CONSTRUCTING PROFESSIONAL PHILOSOPHIES

An education leader is often called upon to explain his or her philosophy regarding learning, management, and the links between the two. This is particularly true in job interviews and public settings. The precise nature of one's philosophy and all of its individual components is seldom as important as having a coherent view of how learning takes place and how schools as organizations should be managed to maximize learning. Of course, whatever one's views about such matters, of central importance is that they are internally consistent and one is prepared as a leader to act upon these views. While it comes down to the individual

Questions Illustrative of One's Philosophy of Education and Instructional Management

What is the mix of subjects and skills that you think students need to know at varying age and grade levels?

How best do you believe students can learn that which you specify as important?

Through what medium and means is reading best taught?

Do you have a view regarding the mix of **direct instruction** versus **situated learning**?

What role does technology, such as computer-assisted instruction, have in a school or district in which you would be engaged?

Are there any particular pedagogical approaches of which you are especially enamored and which you would recommend for adoption in a district? Can you cite any evidence regarding the effectiveness of those programs?

Do you have a view regarding the utility of **ability grouping** of students for instructional purposes?

What do you contend is the best way to enable non-English-speaking children to learn English quickly?

For what characteristics or qualifications have you come to look in hiring or rehiring teachers? Are there any teacher-training techniques in which you have particular confidence?

What is the role, in the school or district you would create and operate, for professional development of teachers?

Are there more cost-effective strategies for enhancing student achievement than the costly method of reducing class sizes?

What do you believe is the optimum enrollment size for an elementary school?

Do you have a philosophy regarding the middle school years? Would you have students in middle schools taught by specialized teachers?

How much homework should be assigned to students in the elementary years?

involved to construct his or her personal philosophies regarding learning and management, there are dimensions to which one might fruitfully give consideration in the design process. The boxed questions above are illustrative of the kind you can expect in job interviews and in prequalification questionnaires for education leadership positions. These are also the types of questions that your references will be asked to comment upon in their recommendations regarding you.

A job interview itself is not the place extemporaneously to formulate such an important part of one's leadership portfolio or knowledge arsenal. Prior consideration and even rehearsed presentations regarding one's philosophical predispositions are good ideas.

Time to Reflect

Write a two-page essay of instructional philosophy suitable for inclusion with your résumé in seeking a leadership position as a principal, superintendent, or other education leader. Take into account questions such as those listed in the text box on philosophical matters.

■ SETTING PERFORMANCE PRIORITIES

If you do not know where you want to go, any road will take you there. Witness the following vignette regarding a true-to-life education leader whose name has been disguised.

The Wondrous and Wishful, but Wayward, World of William Winston

Bill Winston was the superintendent of a large southern school district. He had had the typical administrative career, advancing from classroom teacher to counselor, to assistant principal, to principal, to central office administrator, and then he moved through a number of superintendencies from smaller to larger districts. He was articulate, gregarious, energetic, and absolutely committed to children and their well-being. He liked being a leader, and he wanted to do well. Bill wanted always to do the right thing. However, he was about to be fired, and for good, even if perplexing to him, reasons.

Bill liked everyone, and he desperately wanted everyone to like Bill. He sought approval when he should have pursued respect. He prided himself on his open door policy. He was personally accessible, to a fault. He permitted others to intrude on his time. He eliminated the administrators between himself and the district's approximately one hundred principals. He supervised all principals, which, of course, meant he did not supervise any of them. He never met an idea or a person he did not like. Therefore, every idea and every individual was of equal value. He had no priorities. Every possible action was as significant as every other possible action. Every interaction with another individual was as valuable to him as any other interaction. The result was that his energies, his ideas, his authority, his advice, and his time were splintered. He could accomplish little because he strove to accomplish everything. He was ethical, idealistic, generous, selfless, likeable, and useless. He was the antithesis of a strategic leader. His district made no progress toward the goals set for him by the school board. They terminated his contract. Bill just did not get it. Even his firing baffled him.

In order to overcome any possibility of acting in the feckless manner illustrated above, an effective leader should consider carrying two, possibly three, small cards in his or her shirt or blouse pocket. The cards should be ever present, even if not visible to others. One card should contain up to approximately six organizational goals. Every day a leader should examine these, read them on the way to work, and determine what of his or her intended activities that day will likely contribute to the accomplishment of which of these goals. If the day's activities do not in some significant way align themselves with accomplishment of goals, then the day may be wasted, and the time spent may have better been directed toward other activities.

Card 1: School Goals

90th percentile on state academic tests
90 percent graduation rate
No achievement gap by race
90 percent daily attendance
Zero expulsions and suspensions
90 percent parent engagement

Card 1 illustrates a possible set of goals for Howard Hiller, principal of Martin Luther King Middle School.[1] These goals are the crystallization of his aspirations for his school. Here you can see that Howard is concentrating heavily on high academic performance. Note, importantly, that each of Howard's goals is quantifiable and measurable. Take a moment to consider which of his goals are ends and which are means.

Being Mindful of Means

A second card should list the principal management strategies in which one believes and that one strives continually to implement. Presumably, these management strategies are the major means through which one can achieve the above-mentioned organizational goals. These too will serve as everyday considerations to guide action.

Card 2: Decision Guides

Academics First
Hire the Best
Empower Subordinates
Appraise Fairly
Reward Results
Anticipate Change

Card 2 lists Howard's decision guides. These are the most important management priorities by which he chooses to achieve his previously specified organizational goals. These decision guides are what he believes will enable him continually to renew his organization and facilitate his school's sustained success. As with the card on school goals, adherence to these guidelines is objectively verifiable.

Personal Values

The third card should be a set of personal beliefs. These are not so much about the organization as they are about the leader himself or herself. These are preferred personal values that guide actions. Cards 1 and 2 are organizationally focused, where a leader says to himself or herself, I want my organization to be a success (as defined by my Card 1 goals), and I think I know how to get there (as displayed in my Card 2 decision guidelines). However, in my own actions I want to be true to my values as expressed in Card 3.

The personal values expressed in Card 3 should be adhered to regardless of organizational context. They are personal attributes every bit as much as leader attributes. They should be as applicable in Howard's personal life, with his family, friends, and others with whom he regularly interacts, as in his professional life, with his school colleagues and employees.

Card 3: Personal Values

Honesty
Professionalism
Collegiality
Optimism
Helpfulness
Humility

In Card 3, Howard has listed personal attributes that are important to him. These are the traits by which he ideally prefers to act and the manner in which he would like his peers and those who work for him to think of him. These are aspirational. It is unlikely that Howard, or anyone else, is sufficiently disciplined or constantly diligent to the degree of 100 percent compliance with his own high code of conduct. Few individuals always match their aspirations. Still, having the code is a larger guarantee of consistent and thoughtful action than not having such a code.

Progress toward Card 1's organizational goals is measurable. Adherence to Card 2's decision guides is verifiable. Compliance with Card 3's personal values is known fully only to oneself.

 FLASHBACK TO CASE STUDIES

Each of the case studies presented in this book has a primary actor. Select any two of them, Daniel Bowles, Richard Ray, Shannon Cantrell, Vince Cavanaugh, Mary Kay Porter, Cameron Campbell, Frank Gomez, or Peter Folio, and construct a goal card for each individual. Place yourself in the protagonist's shoes and deduce what his or her goals were, or perhaps should have been.

Putting Life into Practical Priorities

Assuming that you, the reader, now have a sense of self and how you want to act and be perceived as a leader and further that you have a sense of that which you would like to accomplish, then just what should you do? How, concretely, should you begin to move from a sense of what should be done to actually doing it? Such is the purpose of this section. *Your principal tools are people, money, and time.* It is not sufficient for strategic leaders to look at these resources as either/or. An effective leader must orchestrate all three.

People

Chapter 13 concentrates on the topic of people, and there is no need here to duplicate the personnel principles described in that setting. There are only four simple, but remarkably practical and powerful, messages to be emphasized here.

- No leader can perform effectively without the help of others. Converting intent into reality calls upon the commitment, knowledge, and skills of others.
- Selecting, motivating, and appraising those "others" is one of the most important practical tools at the disposal of a leader.
- Empower those who work for you. If you are not prepared to delegate sufficient authority to "others" so that they can freely and fully do their assigned job, then you have wasted your resources in hiring them. If you cannot trust subordinates to do their job, then you might as well do it yourself.
- Act consistently. Being predictable is not the same as being personally boring. Subordinates have to be able to predict a leader's values, preferences, action styles, and priorities. If a leader is not reasonably predictable, then subordinates cannot easily act in his or her stead. The outcome of inconsistency is to create fear and anxiety among subordinates. They will react by always deferring decisions to you as leader or checking with you before taking actions. Being predictable means taking responsibility for your decisions and your mistakes. To blame a subordinate for a mistake you made is not only cowardly; it will redound to your deficit because you will be seen as dishonest and untrustworthy. Once you are perceived as untrustworthy, able subordinates will abandon the organization as soon as they reasonably can. Timid leaders generate timid subordinates. Timid leaders and timid subordinates, together, create a timid, do-nothing organization.

In the News

Contract provisions that force principals to hire teachers they do not want are hampering efforts to build a strong corps of teachers for urban schools, a report contends. In a study of collective-bargaining agreements in five large cities, the New Teacher Project calls for revising rules that allow senior teachers to take their pick of job openings, while novices are the first to be cut and can be "bumped" from their jobs by colleagues with more seniority.

The New York City-based nonprofit group, which works with districts and states to recruit and train teachers, urges allowing principals to hire the teachers that best "fit" their schools, regardless of seniority.

Maintaining current practices allows mediocre tenured teachers to move school to school, while high-performing novices are treated as expendable, says the report, released November 16. It also discourages strong leaders from taking principalships, the report argues, because they lack the power to assemble the teams of their choice, yet are held accountable for results.

While such work rules were adopted some four decades ago as sorely needed protections from arbitrary management practices, changing times now demand a changed approach, the report's primary author, Jessica Levin, said in an interview. "These changes follow naturally from the emphasis on standards-based reform, highly qualified teachers, and strong accountability," she said. "How do you get from A to B? It's hard for us to imagine meaningfully getting there unless schools can create high-quality teams of teachers."

N.Y.C. Example

Some of the New Teacher Project's recommmendations were incorporated into New York City's recently adopted teacher contract. Schools Chancellor Joel I. Klein brought the group in to examine teacher-hiring practices, and asked it to share the findings with an arbitration panel as the contract was being negotiated. The final contract eliminates bumping and gives principals the final say in whether they hire transferring teachers and "excessed" teachers—those whose jobs have been cut.

The New Teacher Project's study examined New York, San Diego, and three unnamed systems. Across those five, 40 percent of school-level vacancies, on average, were filled by voluntary transfers or by teachers whose jobs in other schools had been cut. In a Midwestern district, that figure rose to 60 percent.

Nearly 80 percent of the principals in San Diego, and 31 percent of those in New York, completed surveys about staff-hiring procedures. Nearly two-thirds of those responding in San Diego, and more than half those responding in New York, said they did not want one or more of such teachers in their schools. Forty percent of the principals interviewed in New York, and one-quarter of those interviewed in San Diego, said they had encouraged a weak teacher to transfer or had placed one on an "excess" list. Conversely, many principals said they had hidden vacancies from the central office to avoid taking teachers who had lost their jobs in other schools or were transferring voluntarily. Nearly half the principals interviewed in San Diego, for example, reported having done so.

The New Teacher Project recommends eliminating voluntary transfers' automatic rights to jobs in other schools, giving them instead a two-week period in early spring when they could get "preferential review" by principals. After that, schools could freely choose whom they hire.

Teachers who have been cut also should get a preferred-review period and ongoing chances to apply for other district jobs, but should not be forced on unwilling principals, the report says. Newer teachers should not be bumped by more senior colleagues, it says.

Districts also must come up with better ways to evaluate teachers, based in part on their performance with students, and ways to reward successful senior teachers, such as with more responsibility, more pay, and a meaningful career ladder, it says.

Proposals Critiqued

Julia E. Koppich, a San Francisco-based author and consultant on teacher-union issues, said she welcomes steps to make seniority less pivotal in teacher hiring, such as those Cincinnati, Seattle, and New York have taken. But giving unfettered hiring authority to principals should be avoided, she said.

Teachers should help decide who is hired at their schools, she said, and some form of appeals process should exist for senior teachers who are not chosen by a given school, including a justification for why they were not chosen.

She also criticized the report for ignoring the roles that district leaders play in forging union contracts. She said principals are often inclined to blame "the system" instead of skillfully documenting teachers' shortcomings. "To blame the union for inefficient transfer and assignment procedures is only placing half the blame," Ms. Koppich said. Antonia Cortese, the executive vice president of the 1.3 million-member American Federation of Teachers, said the report "completely misses the mark" in its approach to retaining new teachers, many of whom leave schools within five years.

Solving the problem, she said in a statement, would entail putting more emphasis on peer mentoring and other supports for teachers, rather than on management issues such as how districts arrange transfers.

Adam Urbanski, a Rochester-based union leader who has been a leading voice for change as the director of the Teacher Union Reform Network, was so angry about the report that he resigned from the New Teacher Project's board of directors. Forcing well-qualified, accomplished teachers to compete for jobs "on the same foot" as novices or outsiders sends the message that "meritorious service doesn't count much," he said.

From Gerwertz, C., Report Blasts Teacher Hiring in City Districts, *Education Week*, November 30, 2005.

Money

Educators are sometimes uncomfortable and reticent in dealing with money matters. They seldom have been trained regarding finance. If a reader recognizes this phobia, then strive to overcome it. An agency's budget process provides a crucial lever for organization influence and change. Only vision and people come first as levers for reshaping an endeavor.

Here are productive steps to pursue in order to take advantage of an organization's budget process as a means for understanding and then influencing the overall organization. Keep in mind that the following steps will likely meet with resistance, as budgeting is far more a political and social than a technical undertaking.

- Insinuate yourself in your organization's budget-planning process to occupy a place at the center of this endeavor. When you have a full budgetary understanding and the organization, through its resource allocation, is pursuing the path specified by your vision, you can then return the reins of budgeting to subordinates.
- Ensure that you are fully in the information loop regarding important budget-planning matters, such as enrollment projections, teacher turnover and recruitment projections, class size assumptions, facility needs, revenue projections, and alterations in government funding procedures.

- Inform yourself regarding federal government regulations pertaining to any program, school, department, or related activity for which as a leader you have responsibility. While the federal funding will not always be a large amount, regardless of magnitude, the federal funding is likely to be the tail that wags your organizational dog. Knowing the rules is crucial, or otherwise the forces of inertia will rely upon them to claim change is impossible.
- Become technically informed regarding any formulaic distributional or allocation decision rules relied upon by your organization to distribute resources from the managerial center to the operating periphery. Such distribution formulae tend to have a coloration of rationality and technical certainty to them when, in fact, they are almost always speculative and arbitrary. To the extent to which you can, and it may take time, rearrange these distributional criteria to more closely link resources with accurate measures of need and in a manner that is able to reward performance.
- However gradually, strive to move your organization away from employee salary arrangements that bear little or no relationship to performance and student achievement (e.g., certificates or credentials possessed, years of instructional experience, and units beyond the bachelor's degree), and establish an incentive system that rewards instructional skills, successful teaching, and elevated student performance.
- Maximize budgetary discretion for subordinates in whom you have confidence. It is a means for empowering them and unleashing their creativity. In effect, as a leader you are trading a conventional but unproductive role of prescribing processes for an emphasis on outcomes. It thus follows, of course, that accurately appraising outcomes is a part of the process thereafter.
- Pursue efficiencies and organizational incentives. For example, place substitute teacher budgets at individual schools, and permit the unused funds to be rolled over into a subsequent budget year and used for other purposes at the discretion of teachers and principals. Such small actions have been found to reduce teacher absenteeism. Treat utility budgets similarly. Arrange budgets to shape behavior. For example, when utility budgets are placed at individual work sites and carryover of unexpended funds is permitted, employees are motivated to conserve power, heat, and so on. Permit them to apply such surpluses to instructional programs.

Time

Time is the most elusive of a leader's resources. It is utterly irretrievable. Once used, it is gone. It cannot be stockpiled. Because of its scarcity, it is a leader's most valuable personal resource, and its deployment should be undertaken with considerable care. Thus, how is a leader's time best used?

There are limited hours in a day. One learns periodically of individuals alleged to need little or no sleep. Generally, sleep deprivation is not a productive way to solve the time scarcity problem. Similarly, time must be set aside for logistical reality such as shopping, personal chores, physical exercise, interaction with family and friends, and, on occasion, vacation. The latter can be a point of remarkable rejuvenation and should not regularly be foregone on grounds that one is too busy. It is often during time off for recreation that significant new and creative perspectives emerge regarding one's work.

A leader can routinely expect to work fifty to sixty hours per week. If working this much or this hard is not part of a reader's life plan, then he or she might well reexamine his or her motives in seeking a leadership position. Long hours are simply part of the territory of assuming added organizational responsibility.

Assuming a fifty-week work year, this means that there are in the neighborhood of 2,500 to 3,000 hours per year to be allocated to matters related to work. However, one cannot assume that all of this is time at a leader's absolute discretion.

For public officials, as for most education leaders, a question regarding "how to spend one's time" is somewhat rhetorical. There is an air of unreality to it. That is because a large part of a principal's job, a superintendent's role, or a teacher leader's position is unpredictable and subject to the flow of contextual events. A principal, a superintendent, and others of their ilk often are in reactive positions. Their time is not fully under their control. A private sector CEO such as GE's Jack Welch can determine with far greater certainty how to spend time. Even here, however, he or she must on occasion react. The stock market can plummet, an employee can unexpectedly run amok, a natural disaster can occur, and the CEO will have to drop all else and pay attention.

For a school official, a predetermined calendar of events can easily fall prey to a public disaster, a school bus accident, a racially motivated conflict, a violent act at a school, the misbehavior of a school official or teacher, or the unpredictable actions of a crazed individual or criminal element such as was made famous by the shootings at Columbine High School, outside of Denver, Colorado. An interruption can occur for something so mundane as the mayor phoning and expressing a desire to have lunch that day because he has something he would like to discuss.

When faced with unpredictable conditions to which one is expected to react, how does one plan a rational allocation of one's time? Here are some ideas.

A public service leader should know that he or she is unlikely to be able to fill an entire day's or week's schedule with predetermined appointments, presentations, conversations, classroom visits, central office conferences, and so on, and realistically expect that such can happen for a fluid, uninterrupted ten-hour span during the day. Rather, a leader might think in an alternative fashion.

A leader should consider flexible or block scheduling. That is, think of time in macro modules of a day, a week, a month, and a year. Consider disaggregating goals and activities and fitting them to available time blocks. The result is a distributed focus.

Block Scheduling. Here is a somewhat overly simple illustration of how a leader might think of utilizing block scheduling. Imagine that there are three major functions during the day, a week, a month, and so on. One function is to achieve a predetermined organizational goal. Disaggregate the actions needed to fulfill such a goal into component parts that lend themselves to incremental action. Fit the increments into your predetermined schedule over a period of time.

For example, elevating student performance in one's school to the ninetieth percentile on state achievement tests can be taken as a goal. Assign 30 percent of your discretionary time to activities aligned with this goal. However, do not be insistent upon precisely what 30 percent of your time that will be. Also, do not assume for a moment that the 30 percent will be routine or uninterrupted.

Now, imagine further that a part of a leader's job is to react to conditions that are not always predictable. Simply assume in your daily, weekly, and monthly block schedule that about a third of your time is going to be occupied by unpredictable and uncontrollable events. If few or no emergencies or urgent conditions come about, then use the unanticipated free period productively to undertake actions consistent with your larger goal, elevating student achievement, for the block of time involved.

Finally, in order to maintain one's organization and just manage the status quo, it is necessary to engage with employees and subordinates and keeps one's ear to the organizational ground. Here the technique of "management by walking around" is useful. One can allocate the remaining time block to engaging in this activity.

Walking Around. This need not be done at the same time each day or each week. Indeed, there are advantages to moving through one's organization at different points in the daily or weekly cycle of events. Often if you walk around your school, or drive around your district, at the same time each day or each week, you encounter only the same individuals. Also, your visits become predictable, and those you meet with have anticipated or even prepared for your arrival in advance. You are less likely to encounter them at candid moments. By relying upon a more random schedule, you may expand the spectrum of employees, subordinates, students, and clients you encounter, and you may expand the sample of their work lives and behavior you are able to observe.

The point of walking around is to engage with people wherever possible and, not disrupting instruction, to talk to as many individuals as you can. The agenda is not formed or formal. Topics are what are on people's mind. In the course of the conversation a leader should continually be attuned to events and conditions that appear to be emerging with which he or she may subsequently have to deal. It may also be a time when a leader can inspire subordinates and provide them with added information useful to their performance of assigned tasks. Being visible, sharing insights, commiserating where appropriate, congratulating when there is something to celebrate, making note of what needs to be fixed or added are all events that provide subordinates with a sense that their leader is present and cares.

A leader should not feel guilty, as if he or she were wasting time, when walking around and interacting with subordinates and clients. It is somewhat easy to feel guilty about such actions because for most leaders it is enjoyable. Talking to people is an activity from which many leaders themselves derive energy. However, there is an important balance here. Too much time in the field almost assuredly means too little time devoted to focused efforts at improvement and too little time devoted to reflection.

Gimmicks. What time of day should a leader do what? Some claim to be more alive early in the morning; others claim to be better later in the day. Whatever your circadian rhythm, it makes most sense to tackle that which you find most challenging at the time of day you feel most alert. That leaves for consideration the issue of paperwork. There is a quantum of paperwork, virtually no matter what one's role. Some corporate CEOs claim to hold all meetings while everyone is standing. No sitting is permitted. The proclaimed consequence is that meetings are more focused, everyone allegedly gets to the point quickly, decisions are made more expeditiously, and gossip and informality are reduced to a minimum. This idea is silly. If the decision is where to go to lunch or what team to back at a tournament, then fine. However, if the issue is where geographically to locate a new school, which candidate to employ as a new principal, or which textbooks to use in elementary mathematics instruction, the topic justifies sitting down and taking the issue seriously.

A former Dallas, Texas, superintendent gained a measure of media fame by claiming he never touched a piece of paper more than once. Presumably to read a memo, a notice, a letter, a request was immediately for him to formulate a response. Such probably is foolish. Some, usually trivial, items can be disposed of rapidly. Others are deserving of careful consideration and added thought.

Strive to avoid falling victim to ill-conceived work gimmicks claiming to save time. Consider having three boxes on the corner of your desk: "In," "Out," and "Baffled." The latter is for items and issues for which you do not have an immediate response. Take some time. Noodle the issue. Over time, solutions may appear. Eventually, you will need to take action, and that may, in some instances, prove uncomfortable. However, at least give yourself the benefit of time to reflect upon possible answers.

Time to Reflect

Can you think of downsides to managing by walking around? How available do you think a leader should make himself or herself to subordinates? Does one's position in an organization dictate availability? Should a principal or superintendent specify office hours when anyone can drop by to talk about anything?

▮ COMMUNICATING PURPOSES, CREATING IMPRESSIONS, CONFRONTING CONFLICT

Leaders make decisions. They create vision, determine priorities, select subordinates, and allocate resources. However, once they have determined the right thing to do, virtually all else a leader accomplishes will likely take place by persuading others to take action. Leaders are badly handicapped, probably hopelessly handicapped, if unable effectively to communicate preferences to audiences such as the general public, parents, professional peers, and subordinates and persuade them of the utility of pursuing necessary tasks.

By creating a favorable impression, particularly from the outset, a leader may establish a predisposition among targets of communication, a predisposition that can assist in gaining acceptance of the message, making **persuasion** easier. However, sometimes a favorable impression and effective communication are insufficient. Sometimes something goes wrong, and an uncomfortable conversation is a necessity. These difficult exchanges can operate two ways. One can initiate them, or one can be the target or recipient of someone else's negative judgment. Regardless, there are ways to handle unpleasantness that defuse the negative and may even salvage something positive. Confrontation need not result in irresolvable conflict and can, on occasion, be converted to a constructive outcome. This section is about these and related topics.

Communicating Purposes

Harvard psychologist Howard Gardner situates communication at the heart of effective leadership.[2] His assertion is that effective leaders, particularly public leaders, have an unusual capacity to frame stories that fall upon followers' ears with the ring of authenticity. A story, speech, or message that resonates with the recipients' reality has a chance of triggering allegiance and agreement. These stories enable a follower to identify with the leader personally or with the leader's purposes. The more effective the story, the wider the believing audience and the more intense the possible follower commitment.

Communication can take at least three forms: oral, written, and informal or nonverbal. As a leader, or aspiring leader, one should consciously craft an ability to speak effectively to audiences, both large and small. It will take practice, and there are ways to gain help. This is another place where watching and analyzing the styles of others can be of assistance. Still, regardless of how acquired and honed, effective public speaking is a must for a leader.[3]

Second, one should hone writing skills. Different audiences necessitate different writing formats and styles, and this is not the place to identify and review each of the various kinds. Suffice it to say that an administrative memorandum to subordinates is different from a congratulatory letter to a recent high school graduate or the winner of a teacher of the year award. Most writing is intended to be persuasive, either of action or of feeling. However, audience matters greatly. A budget message based solely on emotion and devoid of facts is less likely to be effective than one that stresses fiscal conditions and likely budgetary trajectories. A reader might keep in mind the difference between the Declaration of Independence, intended to inspire, and the U.S. Constitution, intended as a charter or regulatory document. The former was lofty and vague; the latter was declarative and specific.

Handwritten notes, for selected purposes, convey a special message, and a reader should consider his or her ability to undertake this medium. Good penmanship is ever more rare. Still, a handwritten note at a special time of commendation, commiseration, or celebration can have a disproportionate effect upon a recipient. What it says is important, but the medium is here also the message. Taking the time to render communication personal means that you, the leader, thought sufficiently of the recipient that you were willing to allocate your personal time to the matter.

Nonverbal and Informal Communication. This topic is accorded special emphasis here because of the capacity for a leader to underscore or undo much by mindlessness. One can harm that which is good by thoughtlessly conveying a separate or antithetical message through informal activities and nonverbal actions such as body language. Anyone doubting this should watch an accomplished elected official such as former president William Clinton weave his way through an audience, shaking hands, exchanging pleasantries, and conveying to virtually each individual that he or she is special to him. A picture of concern and engagement emerges that would be almost impossible otherwise to convey in writing or in spoken words alone. Conversely, attending a major meeting and acting in a callous or flippant manner can convey, even if mistakenly, to those present that you as a leader are unengaged in the activity that is taking place.

Influencing Follower Impressions

Others inevitably will have an impression of you as a leader. It may be a snap judgment. It may be modified over time, as an observer gathers more evidence and has more interactions. It may be a superficial, unflattering, or incorrect impression. Nevertheless, observers and those with whom leaders interact will form an impression. Consequently, given this inevitability of follower judgment, it is advantageous consciously to strive to shape impressions, to create a favorable predisposition. Creating a favorable impression is analogous in marketing to creating brand identification and brand loyalty. A leader can benefit from a wellspring of favorable regard, which proves invaluable to counter or dilute the inevitable episodic downturns when events and results are less than what the leader would want.

There are many means by and material components of which a favorable image can be constructed. What follows is intended to be illustrative, not exhaustive. Also, what follows assumes that the characteristics of leadership and the leader being promoted are authentic. They are actions and attributes the leader aspires to in the construction of image, but to be an authentic and successful image, the underlying facts, portrayals, and interpretations need to be accurate.

Within the text box are a set of activities and items that are grist for constructing a leadership impression. These are the vehicles from which an image or persona can be constructed. The content or coloration to be placed within each vector is a matter of selection for the individual leader. However, below is a list of image-shaping vectors contributing to follower impressions and amenable to shaping.

Vectors of Personal Impression (Initial and Lasting) Amenable to Influence

Web site appearance and content
Personal résumé[4]
Office and personal stationery
Telephone answering and messaging protocols
Office (and outer office) size and décor
Office staff greeting and behavior
Personal handshake, greeting, eye contact, and recollection of names
Bearing, posture, projection of energy level
Personal attire and its condition (shoes shined, tie tied, accessories matching)
Office trappings (books, awards, diplomas, photographs)
Evidence of connection to persons of power and to luminaries
Evidence of public and professional recognition and office holding
Media management and publicity
Use of language
Evidence of tastes
Public and professional venues where seen by others
Humility and self-effacing demeanor
Humor
Compassion

Difficult Conversations

Regardless of a leader's success, image, or preferences, sometimes something goes wrong. If the "wrong" is a function of a person's errors or systematic failure to perform, then a difficult interpersonal conversation may be in order. If the failing individual is aware of the shortcoming or willing to acknowledge the deficiency, then the conversation may be less difficult in that he or she may be apologetic and not defensive. Nevertheless, it usually is a good idea to discuss the failure so as to ensure that the individual understands that you, as leader, are mindful of the deficiency, and, whereas you are perhaps forgiving, you still do not want the incident or phase to go unnoticed. It is important to discuss it to ensure that it is understood as failure and is not to be repeated. Moreover, open acknowledgment of and discussion around failure may be cathartic for all involved, even for the overseeing leader. Finally, discussions of failure may lead to corrections that benefit both individuals and the entire organization.

If you anticipate that the failing or deficient individual is unaware or will be defensive, then your posture should be firm, convincing, and possessed of fact after fact after fact. Your records of failing, or multiple failures, and your ability to convey the records must be resolute. If you have any reason to believe that the conversation will become confrontational and that threats or retribution may be implied, you should arrange for a witness to be present or within earshot.

What if the difficult conversation is about you? What if you as a leader or aspiring leader are perceived as having made an error, an error of sufficient consequence to warrant a conversation or some kind of corrective action? In such an instance, you should play out the conversation in your mind in advance of the actual event. If you believe you are in some way at fault, either deficient or contributing to deficiency, then it is almost always best to acknowledge the condition and put forth means by which the situation can be reversed and avoided in the future. The rule of thumb by which you should act is to imagine yourself in the accuser's role and behave in a manner you would wish to see in the event roles were reversed.

Discussions Regarding Termination

Generally, though there are exceptions wherein an individual is thick skinned and insensitive to what he or she has done or what is going on around the individual organizationally, most individuals understand when they are performing poorly. The more defensive they are regarding criticisms of their performance, the more likely it is that they are aware of their deficiencies. Still, on occasion, the difficult conversation is about them and letting them know that they are fired. When it comes to firing public employees, there is no substitute for detailed, accurate, and unambiguous records to bolster the difficult conversation.

■ LEADER ETHICS AND CONSISTENT BEHAVIOR

Ethical issues are sometimes difficult for leaders. So is consistent behavior. This is because there can exist an inherent tension among many of the traits and qualities that render a leader effective and ethical and consistent in the realm of personal behavior. Moreover, ironically, the more successful a leader becomes, often the more attractive the opportunities to behave unethically. Once accruing power, overcoming adversity, and tasting success, it is tempting to deviate from one's previously determined path and seek personal gain. A leader's long-run effectiveness may well stem from his or her ability to resolve these tensions and resist such temptations.

To gain acceptance for an idea, in order to mobilize support for the pursuit of a vision, a leader may well develop traits of unusual persuasion and trustworthiness. These very traits, so crucial to leader success, need deviate only by but a few degrees before they can be distorted to the pursuit of personal and unethical ends. Witness, again, the persuasive prowess of Hitler. The problem was the ends he pursued. Had he pursued world peace, he might have been one of the greatest moral figures of all time. Moreover, the gregarious charm that may enable a leader to mobilize support for otherwise difficult-to-accomplish goals can be misdirected toward personal gain or short-run selfish pleasure. This was a weakness of President William J. Clinton.

> *Constant personal vigilance and self-criticism form the first line of defense regarding unethical leader behavior. An internal gyroscope is a far more effective guide to ethical behavior than detailed knowledge of a complicated set of external strictures.*

Often it is nuanced issues that pose the greatest ethical challenges to a leader. Stealing organizational assets for personal gain, embezzlement, and perpetrating personal or physical harm upon others are well-understood felonies and constitute a clear path to personal destruction. Overt and obvious crime almost invariably leads to a leader's downfall. However, it is the gray areas where judgment becomes more clouded, and it is in the interstices of indecision that the ethical standards of a leader more likely will be tested.

Below is an illustrative list of gray areas, leadership decision dimensions, not immediately subject to the scrutiny of others, but that can contribute to a leader's ethical decay. In each of the following instances there is, conceivably, a reason for a leader to distort the truth or to be misperceived as having acted appropriately. As such, each of the following illustrative dimensions involves matters of judgment important for a strategic education leader to consider:

- Possibly withholding or distorting information needed by others to judge a leader's performance or an organization's success
- Taking, perhaps unduly taking, credit for the accomplishments of others
- Appropriating, or perhaps misappropriating, organizational assets for personal comfort or individual material gain
- Invoking organizational authority in behalf of, perhaps, inappropriate purposes
- Possibly taking advantage of insider knowledge to advance personal, rather than organizational, goals
- Using one's position of authority, maybe unfairly, to extort material items or personal favors from others

▊ UNSUNG SIGNIFICANCE OF PREDICTABLE LEADER BEHAVIOR

In addition to acting ethically, it is important that a leader's behavior be consistent or, within reason, even predictable. If a leader is given to unexplainable mood swings and shifts in outlook, if the same behavior from a subordinate provokes widely different reactions in a leader from time to time or from person to person, if the criteria being used to judge proposals for action or personal performance vacillate from one moment to the next or from one subordinate to the next, then a leader is contributing to an atmosphere of emotional instability. In such circumstances, organizational instability may not be far behind.

When surrounded by instability or unpredictability, subordinates will minimize personal risks and react by curtailing initiatives and creativity. In an effort to reestablish equilibrium, to render their working culture stable, employees will revert to rigid rules, a condition that inevitably diminishes the capacity of an organization to elevate its overall performance. Such debilitating conditions can be avoided by the conscious efforts of a leader to establish and maintain a predictable pattern of action and style.

Summary

In this chapter, readers learn about the process of strategic leadership within educational institutions. As a whole this chapter focuses on how a leader can balance the key attributes of learning, thinking, and acting to develop an effective leadership style. This chapter gives specific advice regarding matters such as self-consciously constructing a personal leadership style; formulating thoughts regarding learning and schooling; crystallizing views regarding management; distilling the professional side of oneself into an effective résumé; effectively managing one's time; communicating interpersonally and institutionally; presenting a professional image; and holding difficult conversations with colleagues, subordinates, and even bosses. Resources were identified for the development of leadership style, including examined experience, observation, actively searching for role models, practice, external criticism, and reflection. This chapter identifies the importance of setting priorities to determine organizational direction and provides strategies to assist education leaders in this endeavor.

Discussion Questions

1. Consider the organization at which you are currently employed. Spend a few moments constructing a goal card for this institution. Based on your experience with the organization, create a card of decision guides that would help the institution achieve these goals. Finally, create a card of your personal values that guide your actions, both within and outside of your current organization.

2. Recall a few instances of employment hiring successes or failures, whether by you or other leaders you have known. Is there anything, upon reflection, that you can see was undertaken correctly or incorrectly during the hiring process? Are there actions, in retrospect, that would have made the selection of employees more effective for the particular position within the organization?

3. List approximately five or six questions that you could ask of a budget official that would begin to situate you, as an education leader, within the central activities of an organization's resource-allocation decision-making process.

4. What do you now feature in your professional résumé? Can you imagine changes that you might productively undertake in order better to convey your strengths to a potential employer?

5. Imagine that a subordinate has repeatedly failed to accomplish agreed-upon achievement goals for his or her school or department. Script your part, as a leader, in a difficult conversation with a subordinate.

6. To what degree would you offer unsolicited criticisms of a colleague's administrative performance if doing so held the prospect of providing you a competitive advantage in filling an upcoming leadership position?

7. To what degree do you feel that your colleagues would describe your professional behavior as consistent and predictable?

8. One ELCC Standard is devoted entirely to school vision, thereby endorsing the importance of this element. To what degree is your personal vision or philosophy of leadership in alignment with your school or district vision?

References and Suggested Readings

Beeman, T. E., and Glenn, R. (2005). *Leading from within*. Franklin, TN: Providence House Publishers.

  The authors, two health-care executives who use examples from their own careers and personal experiences, make the case that having a spiritual frame of reference can benefit companies and nourish the leaders who shepherd them. They also outline twelve spiritual concepts that senior management in all industries can use to lead and live by.

Bennis, Warren. (1989). *Why leaders can't lead*. San Francisco: Jossey-Bass, Inc.

  In this book, the author exposes the hidden forces in organizations and in society at large that conspire against good leadership and offers advice on what leaders in all arenas can do to identify, attack, and overcome these forces and effectively take charge.

Blanchard, K. (2007). *Leading at a higher level*. Upper Saddle River, NJ: Pearson/Prentice Hall.

  This book translates decades of research and years of global experience into simple, practical, and powerful strategies to equip leaders at every level to build organizations that produce bottom-line results.

Burns, J. M. (1978). *Leadership*. New York: Harper & Row.

  In this work, the author presents a theory of leadership as a dynamic reciprocity between ordinary people or "followers" and political and ideological "leaders" that thrives on conflict and demands no consensus, basing this political-psychological theory on biography, history, and analysis of findings in social and behavioral sciences.

Dubrin, A. J. (2001). *Leadership: Research findings, practice, and skills* (3rd ed.). Boston, MA: Houghton Mifflin Company.

  This text is designed to provide an overview of the voluminous research literature about leadership, to give a feel for how leadership is practiced, and to help the reader gain insights and information to enhance his or her own leadership skills.

Howell, J. P., and Costley, D. L. (2006). *Understanding behaviors for effective leadership* (2nd ed.). Upper Saddle River, NJ: Pearson/Prentice Hall.

  Written by authors with over twenty-five years of leadership/teaching experience, this text emphasizes that leaders' effectiveness is determined by what they do and is organized in a simple commonsense structure that describes current knowledge on actual behaviors of effective leaders.

Kouzes, J. M., and Posner, B. Z. (1987). *The leadership challenge*. San Francisco, CA: Jossey-Bass, Inc.

  In this book, the authors show that leadership is not the private preserve of a few charismatic men and women, but a learnable set of practices that virtually anyone can master, and examine the experiences of five hundred middle- and senior-level managers at their personal best.

Lawler, E. E., III. (1986). *High-involvement management*. San Francisco, CA: Jossey-Bass, Inc.

  In this book, various participative management approaches are analyzed, and the author details how each major approach works; describes the strengths, costs, and savings of each; and offers guidelines for implementation.

Wren, J. T. (Ed.). (1995). *The leader's companion*. New York: The Free Press.
    This book serves as a guided introduction to the rich and diverse perspectives on leadership through the ages and throughout the world.

Notes

1. The following text boxes are illustrative. They are not intended to be emulated, only illustrative and provocative. An individual reader's cards might well be very different. Moreover, what is on the cards is not as important as having given thought to their content. One's cards should not be fixed for all time. They should change as one's goals change, as one's job changes, as one's vision changes, or as one's personal circumstances change.
2. Gardner, H., with the collaboration of Laskin, E. (1995). *Leading minds: An anatomy of leadership*. New York: Basic Books. Basic Books Paperback with a new introduction, 1996.
3. One of the most moving and effective public speeches of all time is Abraham Lincoln's Gettysburg Address. Every reader should familiarize himself or herself with the wording, cadence, and precision of this uplifting set of remarks. Also, a reader can learn quickly the difference between a consciously inspirational set of remarks and a declarative or analytic speech by going to the Web site that follows and viewing the consequence of turning Lincoln's Gettysburg Address into a modern PowerPoint presentation. For some purposes, PowerPoint is inappropriate. www.norvig.com/Gettysburg/index.htm
4. There is no perfect résumé. If you are well educated but lack experience, stress education. If you are experienced but not schooled, stress experience. Build your résumé around your strengths. The one must is contact information—address, title, phone number(s), email address, and possible references.

CHAPTER SIXTEEN

Preparing to Be a Strategic Education Leader

LEARNING OBJECTIVES

By the end of this chapter, you should be able to

- understand education leadership as a profession;
- comprehend why strategic leadership necessitates preparation different from that of the past;
- identify the demand for education leaders;
- understand remuneration for education leaders;
- recognize opportunistic and activist paths to leadership positions;
- explain the return on investment for leadership training.

Despite its complexity, periodic setbacks, and accompanying hardships and heartaches, serving successfully as an education leader offers clear rewards and a distinct possibility of substantial lifelong fulfillment. The public generally thinks well of the education profession. Upward professional and administrative mobility is possible, and ambition and courage often are rewarded with professional recognition and higher levels of career responsibility. Colleagues often are appreciative of what one strives to accomplish. The pay is good; often surprisingly better than one might think. Also, education is an occupational field that has a good, even if not entirely perfect, record of drawing upon the talents and energies of women and minorities.

Perhaps most important, however, succeeding as an education leader is filled with opportunity for innate satisfaction. At the end of many school days, certainly at the end of a school year and an entire school leader's career, there is the chance to reflect upon efforts one has made to enable America to be a more perfect union, to come closer to the aspirations we as a society hold for ourselves and for our fellow citizens. Moreover, there is often substantial fulfillment in having acted as a successful **mentor** for younger individuals, be they students or subordinates in organizations. Not every vocation has such opportunities. To manufacture, sell, and repair widgets, or to engage in many other service-sector endeavors, does not always offer an opportunity for such personal fulfillment, career recognition, or financial security.

■ POSITIVE TRAJECTORY OF EDUCATION LEADERSHIP AS A PROFESSION

For an aspiring school leader or one already fulfilling the role, it should be understood that what is expected of leadership positions today is vastly more complicated than has been the case historically. To be sure, in an earlier era, lead teachers or principals chopped wood for school stoves, repaired school roofs, cleaned schools themselves, drove school buses, and perhaps even boarded on a rotating basis in parent homes in lieu of wages. Perhaps there has never been some bucolic or halcyon era when education leaders had it physically or materially easy. Yet at least today, a principal or central office administrator generally can call upon the assistance of others to complete some tasks and share the load of keeping schools operating.

Education leadership, like teaching itself, is becoming more of a profession. Progress toward professionalism is not everywhere uniform, and on occasion, there is a slip backward. For example, there has been an awesome late-twentieth-century proliferation in the availability of inexpensive and low-quality doctoral degree programs that probably have set the profession back and contributed to a public perception of educational administration as an intellectually flabby field. Conversely, however, through the promulgation of more uniform certification standards across states, the ELCC standards around which much of this book is oriented, professional administrators have been proclaiming with greater success what it takes to operate a successful school and what a successful school leader needs to know and be able to do.[1]

There are additional indicators of growing professionalism. For example, the paper-and-pencil instrument developed by Porter, Goldring, Murphy, and Elliot, which is capable of predicting or identifying successful administrative behavior, is a large step forward.[2] Drawing on twenty-five years of experience conducting social science research at Peabody, the application of Bickman's theories of professional feedback to education leadership portends of greater knowledge regarding leadership preparation and professional development. Finally, the conduct of the first-ever set of randomized field trials, or experiments, on principals' and superintendents' performance by Peabody researchers is suggestive of a more empirical base for future leadership preparation and leadership behavior.

■ MULTIPLE CHALLENGES OF TWENTY-FIRST-CENTURY EDUCATION LEADERSHIP

It is propitious that education leadership is becoming more professional. The societal and technical challenges are demanding more of the profession. When considered within a historical context, what is it about twenty-first-century American schools that renders them more complicated and challenging to manage and change than ever before? Answering this question is in large measure the mission of this book and all the books in the Peabody Education Leadership Series. Previous sections of this volume provide detailed responses; however, the summary answer is sixfold: (1) intensified public expectations for performance, (2) elevated societal resources invested in education and a desire for higher returns on that investment, (3) an expanded scope of societal conditions to be taken into account when instructing students, (4) a more sophisticated technology of instruction, (5) a far more comprehensive policy and regulatory environment and manner of performance oversight, and (6) conditions of awesome organizational scale, distance, and diversity.

Expectations. Today, America expects more of its schools than ever before in history. In an earlier era, it was sufficient that students attend school. A lot of learning was not necessarily expected. The nation could operate, and operate quite well, on the energies and talents of approximately 10 percent of its citizens being well educated. This educated elite staffed and operated the government, universities, military, and business. There were many, and often high-paying, craft and manufacturing opportunities for those who were not well educated or who had not even graduated from high school.

For example, until the 1990s automobile assembly workers routinely earned high wages, sufficient to propel them into the middle class and guarantee them a comfortable and relatively early retirement. This was true even though their jobs required little by way of detailed knowledge or analytic activity. Such jobs have now markedly declined in number. There were 90,000 fewer auto industry jobs in 2007 than in 1997. The Ford Motor Company reduced its workforce by 37,000 in 2006 alone. This is massive restructuring in an effort to become profitable and globally competitive. Some good jobs still exist, but increasingly they are offshore, in other nations. By contrast with the past, a modern assembly-line worker often controls millions of dollars in capital equipment (e.g., robots) that require sophisticated programming and high levels of technical maintenance. Employers are willing to pay fairly for such talent. They even are willing to provide advanced training. However, learning the new trade requires a good education. High school dropouts seldom qualify for the training needed.

The modern U.S. military also is instructive. Today's army is a complex set of activities requiring extensive and constant training, understanding of high-tech vehicles and weapons, and remarkable degrees of field officer and soldier on-the-ground discretion. The combination of these conditions renders the military no longer a place for dropouts and low-initiative individuals seeking a comfortable life within the boundaries of known rules.

Economic and technological changes have vastly altered former scenarios. Now, manufacturing and service competition is worldwide. Ideas, capital, and even talent move around the globe at the speed of light or, in the instance of people, with the speed of jet transports. Creativity, talent, and capital now know few national boundaries. No longer can America—or any other nation—plan its future in isolation. Financial well-being for individuals and households, and to a degree for the entire nation, now depends upon a workforce and military acquiring higher levels of knowledge and abilities than were ever contemplated in any other time. Where once a people prospered by virtue of what they derived from the ground, today their well-being is more a function of what they can derive from the mind.

This economic manifest destiny must be coupled to the similar escalation that has occurred among civic issues. To serve on a jury today, to be an informed voter, and to make good judgments as parents call upon individuals to have vastly more information and understanding. Thus, for economic, international, and civic reasons, America has come to expect more of its schools and is judging them by a new and far higher standard.

This new standard no longer is satisfied with measuring how much money flows to a school. The new standard expects schools to utilize resources well and to achieve results measured in terms of student performance. Whereas it once was possible to appraise the quality of a school by resources received, today schools are judged by academic results they achieve.

Resource Magnitude. School expenditures have increased mightily over time. Professional educators often lament a shortage of needed revenues. This is to be expected. They want the best for their students, parents, teachers, and other employees. They want class-rooms complete with all that it takes to teach students. Still, a modern school leader must understand that America funds its schools to a high standard. K–12 schooling was ac-corded more than $600 billion in 2007. This is close to $3.5 billion per operating school day. With such a large share of public resources now directed at schooling, the public un-derstandably expects a high academic-achievement return on its investment.

Societal Complexity. School leaders are expected to convert resources effectively to in-struction and to motivate and supply students with whatever they may reasonably need to learn. This may mean ensuring a child's nutritional and health needs, assisting physically or mentally disabled students, or providing opportunity for language-deficient students to learn English and then learn academic subjects in English.

However, the nature and complexion of American society is not static. Our nation has always been one of immigrants. We have always had students impacted by financial poverty, physical disability, and language deficiency. In some manner, tobacco, contra-band drugs, and alcohol have always been problematic in the adolescent culture. However, saying that there is little that is new ignores the interactions, magnitudes, and amplitude of these conditions today. Moreover, on important dimensions today's societal conditions are not simply more of the past painted on a larger canvas. There are qualitative differ-ences. Indeed, up until the latter quarter of the twentieth century, public schools were not legally obligated to instruct handicapped, illegal immigrant, language deficient, or a num-ber of other categories of challenging students. However, as the significance of education for individual and societal well-being has intensified, the policy system has expanded the legal and practical scope of those that schools must instruct.

Instructional Sophistication. Another part of the modern challenge regarding leadership complexity is the technology of modern instruction itself. More is known regarding how students learn and how productively they might be taught. A "systems" approach to learn-ing has emerged since the late twentieth century, and an education leader must know its components and how they mesh. New developments in cognitive science research continue to further our understanding of the complex dynamics involved in teaching and learning.

Additionally, technological advances continue to open new possibilities for teaching and learning. During the past two and a half decades, the evolution of personal computers, the increasingly sophisticated and widespread use of multimedia tools, and the exponential growth of the Internet have initiated new opportunities to enrich the learning process. While overhead projectors were at one time cutting-edge technology to a host of teachers nearing retirement age, the next generation of teachers is being raised in a wireless, vir-tual, and digital world. The successful harnessing of new developments from such fields as cognitive science, brain imaging, and technology and their appropriate application to the continued development of school leaders at various stages in their professional careers will be a major challenge facing educational leaders for years to come.

Policy and Regulatory Oversight. Because so much now is expected of the education system, because the stakes have become so high, because resources invested are now so vast, and because the technology of instruction has become so complicated, the policy and regulatory environment imposed on schools and school leaders through government, the judicial system, and clients has intensified. This regulatory environment stems from ac-tions of both executive and legislative branch officials and the judicial system. It emanates from local, state, and federal governments. An education leader ignores this regulatory mosaic at great peril. It is part of the knowledge base one needs to perform effectively in today's complicated education context.

Organizational Scale. Once, America had 127,000 school districts and approximately 200,000 schools. Through a century of consolidation and reorganization efforts, the number of districts has been reduced to a few more than 14,000. The number of schools has been reduced to 100,000. Simultaneously the U.S. school population has expanded by an exponential factor. At the beginning of the twenty-first century, there are in excess of 53 million school children, 90 percent of whom are enrolled in public schools. These enrollments are expected to continue to grow. The result is that today's K–12 education organizations, districts, and schools are larger than ever before in history. Moreover, there is an extraordinary concentration of students in a small number of these districts and schools. Twenty-five percent of America's students attend school in only 1 percent of these districts, and 50 percent attend school in only 5 percent of these districts. Such concentrations have created unusually large bureaucratic school organizations, many of which are rule bound and resistant to change.

Time to Reflect

- What do you find to be the most challenging and rewarding aspects of education leadership as a profession?
- Of the six key challenges facing twenty-first-century education leadership, which ones do you feel most prepared to surmount? Why?
- How can you develop your professional expertise to meet the key challenges facing twenty-first-century education leadership that currently sound most daunting to you?

■ THE PATH TO LEADERSHIP IS EVOLVING

A strategic leader, or a professional educator who aspires to yet greater responsibility, should take the following into consideration: old models of accruing college graduate courses and acquiring state credentials are unlikely soon to disappear. Programs of this nature, at night and on weekends at local state university campuses, have served many parts of the nation well, and they are likely to persist. However, this type of part-time training may not, at least by itself, any longer suffice for the rapid advancement and acquisition of added responsibility that particularly ambitious individuals might prefer.

The nation's schools appear to be on a path toward far greater consideration of student achievement results than at any other time in American history. This output orientation, an orientation that in large measure motivates this book on strategic leadership, is unlikely to melt away soon. The No Child Left Behind legislation has raised the stakes of educational outputs and set the goal of education to include all students. As such, knowing how to render our schools more productive, and thus inducing higher levels of achievement for all students, is now the challenge. Interestingly, few or none of the other leadership challenges—conventional matters such as **community relations,** budgetary legerdemain, or matters of law and student discipline—have disappeared. It is not that the leadership job has changed direction so much as it simply has become more complicated and freighted with more intense and elevated expectations.

■ GREAT DEMAND FOR LEADERS, AND NEW LEADERS, IN EDUCATION

In the United States, there are approximately 10,000 public school superintendents[3] and 100,000 public school principals. In addition, there are another 300,000 positions for associate and assistant superintendents; assistant principals; program coordinators; central office officials of various kinds; county, state, and federal education administrators; legislative staff positions; and a host of education leaders in philanthropic foundations and community agencies. Additionally, there are tens of thousands connected with nonpublic schooling, as administrators and leaders of different kinds. Finally, a reader should be mindful of the fact that U.S. school enrollments are increasing, and as a consequence many new schools are opening each year.

At a minimum, 10 percent of these various education leadership positions become available each year. This translates to forty to fifty thousand annual leadership openings. This does not mean that forty to fifty thousand new or relatively inexperienced individuals enter educational administration each year. Individuals who move vertically or laterally from one administrative opening to another fill many of the openings. The absolute entry-level number of positions may be in the 10,000 to 20,000 range. Still, if one is upwardly aspiring, ambitious, and willing to make short-run sacrifices of time, resources, and effort, there are multiple opportunities for long-run reward in the form of influence, prestige, material well-being, security, and personal satisfaction.

■ LEADING LEARNING AND IMPLEMENTING POLICY: THE NEW PROFESSIONAL PRACTITIONER PARADIGM

Managing a modern school, or a school district, for academic achievement is a far different and more daunting challenge than pursuing past paths of ensuring student control, parental acquiescence, community pride, and political stability. The professional skills and understanding that drive high levels of academic achievement involve technical and professional complexities such as

- knowledge of human learning;
- understanding of curriculum objectives;
- familiarity with modern performance measurement;
- comfort with managing by data;
- a feel for organizational complexity;
- conscious attention to leadership dynamics;
- appreciation of policy imperatives;
- comprehension of legal underpinnings;
- strategies for community and political engagement;
- understanding of budgetary processes and the empowerment they entail;
- integration of technology into both management and instruction;
- a sustained sense of the significance of public information, community relations, and the ever-evolving external context.

▪ CAREER PREPARATION CHANGES NECESSITATED BY STRATEGIC LEADERSHIP

Seeking preparation as a strategic leader imposes great burdens on an aspirant. An effective modern education executive must possess the ability continuously to (1) reexamine and, where appropriate, reshape an organization's purposes and mission, (2) assess a changing external environment and its possible impact on the organization, (3) interpret external and internal forces and deduce their consequences for the organization's day-to-day operation, (4) cooperate with others in the determination of appropriate new directions, (5) motivate colleagues and mobilize coalitions in the pursuit of organizational goals, (6) appraise the organization's progress in meeting objectives, and (7) where justified, undertake midcourse corrections. It is the job of a strategic leader to ensure that the steps in this continuous improvement cycle are taken effectively. It imposes a heavy leadership burden, particularly in education where, for decades, the prevailing paradigm has been process, not product. This drive for sustained improvement characterizes a modern organization, private or public. These are not abilities that simply can be forcefully commanded to exist or willed into being within individuals or that can be assumed to evolve in the normal flow of a professional career. Their acquisition must be conscious and cultivated. At the least, the following fields of knowledge are necessary in constructing a comprehensive personal and professional foundation for strategic leadership action.

Broad Knowledge Base. There is no substitute for this foundational component. Individuals devoid of a broad understanding of literature, history, political theory, physical and life sciences, economics, behavioral and social sciences, and the arts are handicapped in their ability to make sense of what is transpiring around them. Only a comprehension of the world's rich historical and cultural tapestry can provide a backdrop against which to make informed personal, professional, and organizational judgments. An effective liberal arts education enables a strategic executive to impart meaning to rapidly evolving events and conditions that might otherwise appear random and chaotic. A liberal education provides perspective, offers informative analogies, assists in assigning priorities, shapes values, and enhances communication. This fundamental knowledge is also intended to encompass crucial skills such as the ability to speak Standard English, write coherent paragraphs, count in a sophisticated way, and speak in a fluid, forceful, and correct manner.

Professional Knowledge. Strategic education leaders need to comprehend a body of professional knowledge for at least two reasons. First, it will inform their executive decisions and actions. Second, it will enhance their legitimacy and elevate their standing with those they lead and those who are served by their institutions. This professional component has three social and behavioral science dimensions.

Education Foundations. First is an understanding of the psychological, sociological, and anthropological foundations of education. Cultural patterns, social stratification and mobility, principles of human development, and racial dynamics are illustrative of critical social science understandings for a strategic leader. Also, an appropriate knowledge of learning theory and instructional practice is crucial. Finally, an understanding of fundamental components of school and college curricula is necessary as a professional cornerstone.

Institutional Knowledge. Strategic leaders are obligated to influence the direction of their institutions. Knowing where you are and where you have been facilitates knowing where to go. Hence, there is a need for strategic education leaders to be fully informed regarding such institutional matters as the history of education, organizational sociology, educational law, governance, and school finance.

Decision Knowledge. Gathering and analyzing information about an institution's external environment and its internal performance are critical functions for a strategic leader. Conducting these activities in a successful manner requires an understanding of important information-gathering and analytic techniques stemming from economics, statistics, survey research, testing, and accounting. Included here is knowledge on technical dimensions such as the logic of inquiry, experimental and quasi-experimental design, extrapolative or projection techniques, measures of central tendency and dispersion, probability theory, production functions, ratio studies, quantitative and qualitative evaluation, opinion polling, survey research, standardized testing, and psychological measurement.

There exists more than one means for acquiring the above-proscribed knowledge base. The details of acquisition can differ from nation to nation and upon the operating circumstances in specific jurisdictions and institutions. Also, the mix of preparation experiences (e.g., time allocated to classroom and online instruction, supervised practice, and apprenticeship) is not appropriate for debate here. Suffice it to say that while there is little about strategic leadership that restricts its practice to superheroes, there is also little about it that one is intuitively capable of performing. Thus, regardless of the specific sequence and arrangement of experiences, professional preparation of the most rigorous level will be necessary in order for education leaders to derive full advantage of the endeavor's potential.

Experiential Knowledge. The preparation of strategic leaders also requires an opportunity for examined experience. A conventional internship seldom will suffice. Careful selection of an appropriate mentor and model is a good beginning. However, thereafter, training institutions must ensure that leaders in the making are systematically encouraged to reflect upon the practices they see around them and speculate regarding the means by which they could be improved.

 CASE 5 REVISITED

> Recall Frank Gomez, the principal of Carter Middle School, a school which had not met Adequate Yearly Progress for two years in a row. Given Frank's perspective on NCLB and his preference for dealing with this dilemma on his own, how would you suggest he go about enhancing his professional, institutional, decision, and experiential knowledge bases so that he can lead his school out of this current predicament?

In most industrialized societies, the selection and preparation of school administrators rest upon a fundamentally flawed set of organizational dynamics and inappropriate career incentives. Becoming a school administrator frequently is looked upon as a release from the difficult work, lower status, and stifling career conditions of being a classroom teacher. Most school administrators are former classroom teachers. That in itself may be good. For it to be otherwise would deprive education leaders of an intense practical understanding and core knowledge of the institutions for which they are responsible; lacking this could potentially erode their legitimacy with followers.

The difficulty, rather, is that in the most frequent model of upward administrative mobility, existing promotion incentives subvert the professional significance of teachers and inject inappropriate perceptions and dysfunctional organizational dynamics into schools. Administrators too easily can come to perceive teachers not as a cadre of generally able equal-status professionals deserving of informed and collegial leadership but, instead, as an aggregate of alienated risk-aversive employees, many of whom possess too little ambition to achieve any status other than being a classroom teacher. Thus, instead of being productively engaged institutions comprising cooperative, self-confident colleagues occupying important but separate roles, schools too frequently run the risk of being hierarchically oriented bureaucracies comprising overly authoritative administrators responsible for coordinating a loosely coupled corps of less-than-fully-cooperative civil servants.

Where they exist, these dysfunctional dynamics are exacerbated by the widespread tendency to treat administrator preparation as a part-time undertaking. The overwhelming proportion of education administrators-in-training are practicing teachers who hope the acquisition of added college graduate school credits and an appropriate government-specified license will place them in the queue for an administrative position and more immediately result in a salary increase. The budgeted resources of administrator preparation institutions are almost always tuition dependent. Thus, they seldom are in a sufficiently secure position as organizations to exercise high standards, either for initial admission or final program completion.

> *Administrator preparation in education is almost universally characterized by low costs, part-time participant commitment, and institutional standards dictated by financial dependence on tuition.*

This in no way should be construed as an assertion that educational administrators are uniformly incompetent. Quite the opposite. The vast majority of education leaders exhibit remarkable leadership under conditions far more trying than most other public or private executives encounter. Nevertheless, it seldom is their professional preparation to which success can be attributed. These dismal conditions have been widely chronicled, and thoughtful solutions have been proposed with great frequency. Their implementation almost always is impeded, however, by the unwillingness of governments either to impose greater costs on administrator trainees, or increase the resource burden to the public.

In the News

Impatient to prepare better-qualified school leaders, a growing number of states are giving their universities an ultimatum: Redesign your preservice programs, or get out of the business of training school administrators. State policymakers in Alabama, Kentucky, and Tennessee have moved in recent months to require graduate programs in education leadership to meet new standards. Iowa and Louisiana already have done so, prompting a few programs to go off-line.

The aim is to prod universities to produce principals who are better equipped to lead school improvement.

In response, many programs are working with school districts jointly to select administrator-candidates and to create new courses with more field-based experiences. Analysts say the policy push reflects a new recognition that most education schools are unlikely to update their programs on their own. Kathy O'Neill, who directs leadership initiatives at the Southern Regional Education Board, said state action is needed.

As states complete the process of requiring such programs to redesign themselves, they're learning more about the challenges involved. Education schools often say getting adequate district participation in the recruitment and support of principal-candidates can be a problem. But many education school leaders see value in the effort. Cleveland Hill, who recently retired as the dean of the education college at Nicholls State University in Thibodaux, La., said the possibility of being shuttered helped convince others at the university of the need to change. "Once you go through the process, and look back, you realize this was a very tough thing to do, but probably the only way it could have gotten done," he said. "If we hadn't had that push from the top, it wouldn't have happened."

Changing the Rules

States are driving the retooling by changing requirements for programs that qualify people for school administrator licenses. In general, states doing so are moving from stipulations that certain courses be taught to mandates that specific skills be mastered. In 2003, for example, Louisiana called on all of its universities that prepared administrators to submit proposals for new training programs that focused on skills such as data-driven decision-making, parent engagement, and leadership of staff development.

Of the 15 that submitted plans, only one—the University of Louisiana at Monroe—was fully approved off the bat. Nine were approved conditionally. And five were sent back to the drawing board, in some cases more than once, by the state's summer 2006 deadline. Nathan M. Roberts, the director of graduate studies in education at the University of Louisiana at Lafayette, said the changes demanded were significant. His program—one of the first to submit a proposal—was approved conditionally, though it had been working on a redesign for years with the SREB.

The SREB redesign network, which includes 11 universities, is funded by the New York City-based Wallace Foundation, which also underwrites coverage of leadership in *Education Week*. A number of states also use Wallace grants to support redesign efforts. Mr. Roberts said that in the old structure, Lafayette didn't consult with districts about whom to admit. Students took courses largely in whatever order fit their schedules. And many, he admits, sought the master's degree simply to earn more money, not because they wanted to become administrators. "So I'm producing these numbers, but I know it's not going to help the district," Mr. Roberts said.

"Working with individual institutions, we just didn't see there would be the capacity or total will to make this happen," said Ms. O'Neill, whose Atlanta-based group leads a 5-year-old network of universities engaged in the redesign of principal preparation. Some state policymakers also took notice when Arthur E. Levine, the former president of Teachers College, Columbia University, issued a sharply critical review of the nation's university-based programs to prepare administrators in a report 18 months ago.

In the university's new program, which was launched a year ago, faculty members work with district leaders in picking from among applicants. Students take their courses in a specified sequence, and in a cohort, over two years. Classes stress assignments to be completed in the field. Gwen Antoine could be a poster child for the program. The curriculum director at Jeanerette Middle School in Iberia, La., had been taking graduate-level courses in administration on and off at Lafayette for about a decade when she heard about the new program.

Nothing that I had learned in those courses prepared me, or gave me any inkling of what to expect once I became an administrator," she said. "It was research, theory, just listening to professors lecture, and regurgitating information that wasn't really useful."

Now in her second year in the new program, Ms. Antoine often applies what she's learning. For instance, she's doing a study for one of her classes on the effects of benchmark testing to gauge students' progress throughout the year—a schoolwide initiative she's leading. Ms. Antoine said she likes being in a cohort of 18 people. "It forces you to stay in the program," she said. "If you want a master's degree, you have to do it on the university's terms, which I like, because every course builds on the last one."

Some Programs Closed

States are finding, however, that such overhauls take more effort than initially thought. Louisiana first told its universities to submit redesign proposals by 2004, but extended its deadline after campuses struggled to meet it. "[At first], they were taking their existing courses, and looking to see how the standards could fit them, which is not

what we wanted to happen," said Jeanne M. Burns, the state's associate commissioner for teacher education initiatives, who helped to lead the effort.

A sticking point has been involving local school districts. University leaders say some districts don't devote enough time to recruiting candidates, and some are reluctant to allow classroom teachers in the universities' programs enough time to do fieldwork during the day.

"The onus has been on the universities to redesign, and to get the districts to understand their role," said Frederick Dembowski, who chairs the department of educational leadership and technology at Southeastern Louisiana University in Hammond. Some districts have been supportive, however. The 6,300-student Evangeline Parish district pays tuition for its staff members in the redesigned program at the University of Louisiana at Lafayette. District leaders say they have a shortage of potential principals.

A few universities haven't been able to meet their states' new expectations. Buena Vista University in Storm Lake, Iowa, and Centenary College in Shreveport, La., were not approved by the states' deadlines, and so cannot admit new students to their programs. Both are small, private institutions. Sue N. Hernandez, the chairwoman of the education department at Centenary, said to meet the state's criteria would have required hiring more full-time faculty. Many of the instructors in the college's educational leadership program have been adjuncts. "It just didn't make sense to increase the size of our faculty in this department," she said.

Two other institutions in Iowa faced a similar fate: St. Ambrose University in Davenport and Loras College in Dubuque were told that their administrator-preparation   programs didn't pass muster, largely because they lacked enough full-time faculty. Both Roman Catholic institutions on the state's eastern edge, they decided to pool their resources. They hired a faculty member from Louisiana, who had helped a university there redesign its preparation of school leaders, to set up a joint program.

The new partnership won state approval late last year, after two years in which St. Ambrose and Loras couldn't take new candidates. Robert Ristow, the dean of the education college at St. Ambrose, admits frustration at having been shut down, but said the principals now prepared there will be better for it.

"I firmly believe that our program is on much more solid ground than it was previously," Mr. Ristow said. "It was a shocker," he said of the state's action. "It was, 'These are the standards; you've got to meet them.'"

From Archer, J., States Get Tough on Programs to Prepare Principals, *Education Week*, October 18, 2006.

■ EDUCATION LEADER REMUNERATION

Education leaders, be they strategic or conventional in their orientation, seldom are found among the super rich, at least not if their professional remuneration is the source of their wealth. Conversely, educators seldom are poor. Education leaders are particularly comfortable materially when various benefits such as health insurance, pensions, and employment security are taken into account.

Leader pay in education is almost always a function of four conditions: (1) enrollment size of the organization for which one has administrative responsibility, (2) level of administrative responsibility, (3) affluence of residents and housing prices in the community being served, and (4) geographic region involved.

A reader should take note of what is not included in the foregoing listing. The academic performance of one's organization seldom is explicitly taken into account in appraising an education leader. It may be a component of a leader's overall assessment, but it is seldom a specifically measurable evaluation dimension.

However, the missing link between administrator pay and academic performance may be changing. As academic achievement has escalated in the consideration of school evaluation, performance pay for administrators has increasingly been placed on the table. States as disparate as Alaska, Florida, Iowa, and Texas enacted administrator performance pay provisions in 2006. Also, the federal government began to offer inducements for performance pay experiments in 2006. As of this writing, it is not clear that these performance pay projects and experiments will persist. Similar ideas arose in the 1970s and subsequently disappeared. Still, pay for performance for educators is something worthy of sustained observation as strategic leaders continually scan their operating environments.

All other things being equal, principals and superintendents in large enrollment districts are paid more than in medium-size and small districts and schools. Principals are paid more than assistant principals, superintendents more than assistant superintendents, and so on. Eastern- and especially Northeastern-area school administrators are paid

TABLE 16.1 National Mean Annual Salary by Position, Work Year, and Community Type

Administrative Position	Days Worked	National Mean	Large Urban	Suburban	Small Town	Rural
Superintendent	239	$116,244	$172,387	$148,698	$108,137	$91,618
Assistant Superintendent	237	$ 96,771	$110,913	$116,333	$ 87,515	$86,457
Principal (Senior High)	233	$ 84,515	$ 96,288	$103,429	$ 81,879	$71,679
Assistant Principal (Senior High)	221	$ 70,983	$ 73,507	$ 84,252	$ 67,145	$64,689
Teacher	187	$ 46,953	$ 48,640	$ 54,678	$ 45,810	$42,533
Secretary	220	$ 30,077	$ 37,552	$ 38,780	$ 31,536	$30,587

Source: Selected ERS summary data for 2005–6.

higher salaries and face higher costs of living than their counterparts in the South and Southwest. Finally, regardless of school or district enrollment size or geographic region, a superintendent or other administrator in a posh suburb, such as Scarsdale, New York; Evanston, Illinois; or Palo Alto, California, is likely paid more than his or her counterpart in a less affluent community.

It is to the Education Research Service (ERS) of Alexandria, Virginia, that one most regularly turns for factual information regarding education administrator salaries.[4] This organization is a nonprofit agency that specializes in collecting and analyzing administrator salary information. The agency derives its data from annual surveys sampling school districts of all sizes and locations within the nation. Each year, ERS issues a report comparing salaries for varying administrative positions, ranks, district size, regions, and so on.

Any salary data are outmoded quickly by larger economic conditions and time trends. Hence, more important than the actual administrative salary figures in Tables 16.1 and 16.2 are the magnitudes and the relationships between functions and locations.

TABLE 16.2 Education Administrator Executive Pay Comparisons

Occupation Category	Annual Salary	Comment
High School Principal	$84,000	High fringe benefits and generally shorter work year
Military Officer	$120,000	Highly selective/high pressure/early retirement
Government Official	$69,000	Low selectivity/early retirement/job security
Private Sector Manager	$88,000	High pressure/low job security
College Official	$79,000	Low pressure/high job security
Private Sector CEO	$140,000	Low job security/high pressure/long hours

Source: Selected ERS summary data for 2005–6.

■ PATHS TO PROFESSIONAL LEADERSHIP POSITIONS

Locals and Cosmopolitans. Prior observation regarding educational administrators has identified two categories: those who are locals and those who are cosmopolitans. The former tend to be oriented more toward their immediate community, often the community in which they were raised or went to college. The latter are characterized by a broader geographic and professional perspective. The latter are more willing to relocate geographically and take the larger profession, more than their immediate local community, as their reference point for career success.

The differences in outlook appear not to follow so much from different individual levels of talent or ambition, as both classifications may be able and eager to get ahead, and both may be willing to assume added leadership responsibility. Rather, their approaches to their careers may be different. For purposes of discussion here, a different distinction is made between those potential leaders who are upwardly aspiring through preparation and opportunism and those who are upwardly aspiring through planned paths, ambition, and activist pursuit of promotion. While a few individuals may resonate with just one of these pure types, most of us fall somewhere between the ends of the continuum.

Opportunists and Activists. There appear to be at least several characteristics of note distinguishing career opportunists from ambitious activists. Characteristics of activists include a personal sense of urgency, existence of a life or career plan, need for fame and visibility, propensity for being proactive rather than reactive, and an individual willingness to assume risks. In the career scenarios that follow, a reader can sense the differences. However, there is no judgment being imposed here. Individual lives are different, and there are almost always multiple conditions to be considered, such as one's spouse and his or her ambitions and needs, one's extended family, and the presence of other personal interests such as hobbies and geographical preference.

Opportunist Path to Educational Leadership. The conventional opportunist path almost always begins with one first becoming a classroom teacher. The choice to be a teacher is interesting in itself. While not universally applicable, the common perception is that individuals become teachers not so much from predetermined, deliberate, rational, and long-standing conscious choice, but rather by successive elimination of other career alternatives. They are teachers because they ended up being teachers.

Covert Incentives. For many teachers, once employed in a school, the conventional American education incentive system becomes apparent. Those educators who make more money, garner more prestige, have more power, have better control over their time, and have more interactions with high-status adults are not classroom teachers but others who are administrators or specialists of one kind or another. For some upwardly interested classroom teachers, the siren song of ascending mobility is irresistible, once heard or seen.

Overt Incentives. An individual teacher's possible personal preference for upward mobility is reinforced by the widespread school district practice of paying classroom teachers a higher annual salary if they accrue added credentials or certificate and college credits in addition to their bachelor's degree. Often districts do not specify or enforce any provision that postbaccalaureate professional college courses need be related to the grade level or subject assignment of a teacher. Hence, a high school mathematics teacher, for example, enrolling in administrative preparation courses usually carries as much additional credit for the individual's salary as does taking additional mathematics courses. This financial reward dynamic, no doubt, at least partially explains the fact that there is a larger pool of administratively certified individuals than there is an active pool of applicants for administrative openings. America's education system has no shortage of individuals qualified as school administrators, at least formally qualified individuals, as determined by state credentialing standards.

Formal Preparation. Professional administrative preparation courses are widely available. Most state public college and university systems and private institutions offer such graduate courses. They frequently are offered on multiple campuses of a state system. Indeed, they may be offered in community extensions of state university campuses. Further, if not offered by easily accessible public institutions, they are offered widely by multiple and nationally operating private institutions. Many of these offer degrees online or through other distance learning means. There is no shortage of supply when it comes to administrator preparation courses.

For purposes of a conventional aspiring leader, one of the features of these frequently offered professional preparation courses is that the tuition fee, if public, is often very low. Also, these courses are almost always offered at convenient hours, in the evening and on weekends. Hence, an enrollee does not incur the biggest costs of all, opportunity costs. One can obtain much of the coursework required by state administrator certification at low costs, both in terms of tuition and not having to forfeit salary or other income from a regular job. Contrast this with the conventional path to becoming an attorney or physician, where the professional training is extensive, costly, and requires much time without a paying position.

Acquiring Experience. A conventional path necessitates pursuing college-offered courses consistent with an aspirant's state administrative credential specifications. However, that is only a part of the challenge. Once certified, or close to being certified, one needs to begin to acquire the active experience formative in becoming an effective leader. Almost invariably, this will necessitate a willingness to assume added tasks and to volunteer for duties beyond what is conventionally expected. Indeed, it is a mistake to believe that one can become any kind of education leader, even become the most humdrum of administrators, without displaying initiative or a willingness to go beyond what is expected immediately. Preparing oneself for leadership positions, even in a conventional path to power, requires displays of initiative.

Mentoring. Along the lines of the apprentice model, one can learn a tremendous amount about the real-world challenges and rewards of education leadership through a mentoring experience. While such an experience can be set up informally, many administrator programs require some degree of shadowing as a component of their formal program. While many leadership skills are transferable across levels of schooling and contexts, there is value in observing particular skills and approaches that are modeled in an environment similar to the one that you anticipate working within. One important component of mentoring experiences is reflective dialogue, whereby the mentee is able to articulate what has been observed and learned and is then provided feedback from the mentor.

Building a Professional Portfolio. One manner of building a professional portfolio is by employing Daniel Griffith's concept of gassing, which is the process of gaining the attention of superiors. An aspiring administrator needs to engage in such behavior. It can be done without being obsequious. It simply involves doing a good job at what one is expected to accomplish and offering to do more when so volunteering is appropriate. Upward mobility demands displays of leadership. Also, certification and subsequent applications for promotion will rest heavily upon evidence of administrative or leadership capacity. An ambitious individual needs to construct a record of leadership capacity. In large measure, volunteering for an opportunity to display one's ability is often the first rung on such an upward ladder.

Certification Tests. In addition to the host of course-specific tests required for graduation from a graduate-level program in education leadership, state- and district-mandated certification requirements are in place. Individuals seeking to acquire a principal or superintendent certification or license are required to pass a test such as the **Education Testing Service (ETS)/**Praxis School Leadership Series. These tests were developed to provide a thorough, fair, and carefully validated assessment for states to use as part of the licensure process for principals, superintendents, and school leaders. These tests reflect the most current research and professional judgment and experience of educators across the country, and they are based on both a national job analysis study and a set of standards for school leaders identified by the Interstate School Leaders Licensure Consortium. Each state agency that uses the School Leaders Licensure Assessment and/or the School Superintendent Assessment determines its assessment needs for principals, superintendents, and other school leaders based on legislated requirements and/or state policy. Typically the agency assembles a panel of principals, superintendents, other school leaders, and educational administration professors as appropriate to review the test specifications and make an initial determination of whether the assessment is appropriate for meeting that agency's goals. The test is then reviewed and validated for that state. If you are not sure you have the latest information regarding state licensing requirements, check with the Department of Education or Educational Licensure Board in the state where you plan to work.

References and Networks. It is necessary to begin to build a set of professional references and to become engaged in professional and social networks of interested individuals who can provide counsel and be of possible downstream assistance. Faculty members, in graduate-level courses where one has performed well, can serve as a good base for constructing a portfolio of professional references. Also, one must be alert to possible *king makers* on college educational administration faculty. There may well be a former superintendent or a particularly active professor when it comes to knowing superintendents around the region or in the nation, who can be an enormous job identification help if favorably disposed to do so.

Professional File. It is necessary to explore the resources of one's major university in establishing a professional file, one suitable for providing references and transcripts to prospective employers. In the formation of a professional file, testimony from friends, relatives, or high-placed individuals whose status or position has little or no bearing upon one's immediate professional aspirations should be avoided. A potential employer will see quickly that one is simply pulling rank, exercising political connections, or exploiting social status. Such actions run the risk of backfiring.

Activities such as participating in community associations, Rotary Clubs, and professional fraternities and sororities also offer a chance for making friends, building professional networks, and contributing to a portfolio of important references. Upperlings for whom one has performed well are another leg of a reference folio.

Ever Alert to Opportunities to Advance. Once technically qualified and having amassed a quantum of useful administrative experience, possibly through volunteering or accepting otherwise unwanted tasks, then an aspiring leader candidate must be ever alert to suitable employment openings. If geography is of consequence, then being particularly sensitive to openings in one's current or in nearby districts is in order. Also, there are online agencies and publications such as *Education Week* that routinely carry advertising for administrative openings. Finally, becoming acquainted with and perhaps having a file on record with an education-oriented professional executive search firm or headhunter is a good idea.

Activist Tracks. Some individuals may have the luxury of pursuing, or at least have a pre-disposition toward exploring, a faster track toward leadership positions. There is more than one way to adopt an aggressive personal posture toward an administrative career. What follows is an illustrative but not exhaustive list of fast-track options. Even here, however, a reader should understand that there might well be an advantage from having spent time as a classroom teacher. Such can contribute legitimacy to one's subsequent leadership aspirations. How long one should be a teacher is difficult to say. It may be only a two-year stint in a program such as Teach for America. Still, it is teaching, and it counts.

Advanced College Degrees. A master's degree has come to be expected of those seeking administrative leadership positions, and in terms of duration, the degree is relatively easy to obtain. Many institutions offer a master's degree in school administration, and at many of them admission is reasonably obtained. And, at least in many public institutions, the de-gree course of study is relatively inexpensive. This, in part, accounts for the low added pay and prestige premium attached to gaining a master's degree.

A doctorate, unlike a master's degree, offers a distinct advantage, particularly for an individual seeking to bypass some of the conventional steps to becoming a high-level leader. In education, particularly from a select few prestigious institutions, either an Ed.D., a doctor of education degree, or a Ph.D., doctor of philosophy degree, continues to accrue a premium in terms of recipient pay and prestige, and in placing one higher in the queue for leadership employment. A reader should understand, however, that the field of advanced degrees in education is in an apparent state of transition. One seeking a fast track into an administrative or leadership career should be aware of the controversy and perhaps select one's doctoral institution accordingly.

The Controversy. A 2005 nationwide report issued by former Teachers College president Arthur Levine[5] heavily criticized the doctor of education degree (Ed.D.) and recom-mended its abolition. The doctor of philosophy programs (Ph.D.) in education are often just as weak or ill conceived. Needed are not simply Ed.D. reforms, but program reforms across the entire spectrum of education's highest degrees. However, despite Levine's lament and a long list of supportive polemics by others, the Ed.D. remains a potentially valuable degree.

In some institutions, the education doctoral degree is a Ph.D. In others it is an Ed.D. In an earlier era, such confusion of purpose or direction did not matter. Old-style doc-toral programs in prestigious institutions such as the University of Chicago, Teachers College, Harvard University, and Stanford University, regardless of degree type, rou-tinely graduated individuals who, with facility, could manage a state education depart-ment, school or school district, philanthropic foundation, or high-level government or international program or could teach university courses. They moved with ease from high levels of professional scholarship and instruction to program leadership, from classroom to boardroom, and back again.

Not so today. Neither the world of leadership nor the realm of research permits such generality. Modern education research increasingly is characterized by a rigorous scientific paradigm entirely different than was true even five years ago. Experimentation and large data-set analyses are now the expected research mode. Measurement techniques such as regression analysis and hierarchical linear modeling, regularly used by epidemiologists, psychologists, and economists, are increasingly threshold quantitative skills for methodological competency. These are skill sets and understandings that take time to impart, require immersion in analyses and research, and are not learned by lecture alone.

That is only half the story. Now that the production of students' academic performance, no longer the institution's consumption of public resources, is the measure of K–12 school success, being an educational administrator is becoming a sophisticated professional and technical challenge. It no longer is simply a bureaucratically oriented or politically concentrated endeavor.

An analogy helps. Can physicians become researchers after attending medical school? Yes, but only in a limited sense. They can undertake selected analyses of patient treatments, sometimes even arranging for experimental conditions. However, they cannot delve into fundamental relationships between biochemical and physiological interactions, genetic research, or anatomical and mechanical processes without having far more intense disciplinary preparation than M.D. programs conventionally are able to provide.

Similarly, however, a Ph.D. candidate in, for example, biochemistry or physiology, would be almost completely unprepared to sit for a physician's various clinical and professional board examinations. The roles of researcher and practitioner now are sufficiently different that reciprocal certification and role reversal would be unthinkable, not to mention illegal.

What to Do? An ambitious activist fast-track leadership candidate should pay critical attention to the doctoral program to which he or she applies. Ensure that one has an opportunity to learn the strategic leadership skills described in the earlier part of this chapter. To miss such learning is perhaps to forgo the advantage that a doctorate can convey.

Special Programs. Several foundations, sometimes in cooperation with universities, sponsor fast-track professional training for individuals eager to assume high-level leadership positions in education. Some of these are for principals, while others are for superintendents, and both are stringent in their admission requirements. However, if admitted, such programs often provide remarkably valuable practical leadership preparation and, importantly, place one in important networks for subsequent job placement and career advancement.

Return on Investment. Assume a conservative lifetime annual salary increment, net of doctoral program or other preparation expenses, of $50,000 resulting from a successful effort to gain appointment to a leadership position. Assume this differential over a thirty-year administrative career. The lifetime earning increment is $1.5 million, net of advanced training preparation costs. If one undertakes such calculations for a higher-paying position such as a large-district superintendent, the return on investment (ROI) is twice as high,

$3.0 million. Whether using a low or high ROI calculation, and even using an aggressive present value discount rate of 4 percent (the annual inflation or investment rate depending upon assumptions), the financial return to striving successfully for a leadership position is high. This is not to mention the various parallel and psychic benefits (e.g., pensions and fulfillment) that often accompany leadership positions.

Summary

The final chapter provides guidance for those preparing to be strategic education leaders. This chapter begins by citing the many benefits associated with education leadership, including clear and consistent rewards, opportunities for personal fulfillment, and career recognition. Despite these benefits, the chapter gives warning to those who are unwilling to devote substantial time and energy to the profession, as many unforeseen challenges arise in this increasingly complex profession, all of which place great time, energy, and intellectual demands upon leaders and require a great deal of contextual adaptation. This chapter continues to explain how education leaders are expected not only to understand modern technology and educational research but also the policy and regulatory oversight mechanisms governing schooling. Given both the favorable market for education leaders and the rigorous demands for these positions, it is important that future leaders understand processes for acquiring the skills necessary to lead twenty-first-century education institutions.

Discussion Questions

1. When discussing the professional skills and understanding that drive high levels of academic achievement, twelve technical and professional complexities were listed. Choose two for which you feel especially proficient and describe the source of your expertise. Similarly, choose two that you do not feel especially comfortable with and describe how you will go about developing skills in these areas.
2. This chapter discussed the importance of professional, institutional, decision, and experiential knowledge. Describe the type of experience(s) that you think would best facilitate the development of these domains of expertise for aspiring education leaders.
3. Describe your current motivations for pursuing advanced study of education. What would you consider to be the greatest challenge to your current educational pursuits? What do you think will be the greatest benefits of completing your current program of study?
4. Along the continuum between locals and cosmopolitans, where do you currently fit? Is this your optimal placement? Why or why not?
5. Provide a rationale for why you would be seen as having taken either an opportunist or an activist approach to previous career decisions. Explain why or why not this will be the approach you will take in the future.
6. Education leadership preparation programs are one of the primary avenues by which one advances into a formal leadership role in education. What components of your preparation program do you think have had the greatest impact on preparing you to meet the leadership goals articulated in the ELCC standards?

References and Suggested Readings

Mullen, C. A. (2004). *Climbing the Himalayas of school leadership: The socialization of early career administrators*. Lanham, MD: Scarecrow Education.

>   This book provides insight into the first years of becoming a school administrator—an excellent guide to what to expect in the early stages of transitioning from the classroom to life as a school administrator.

Murphy, J. (1992). *The landscape of leadership preparation: Reframing the education of school administrators*. Thousand Oaks, CA: Corwin Press.

>   This book is designed to inform the debate on administrator preparation and to provide information for shaping new designs for administrator education.

Notes

1. See discussion in the Foreword and in Chapter 10 for detail on ISLCC and ELCC standards.
2. This statement references the Framework for the Assessment of Learning-Centered Leadership, described in Porter, A.C., Goldring, E.B., Murphy, J., Elliott, S., N., & Cravens, X. (2006). *A framework for the assessment of learning-centered leadership*. New York, NY: Wallace Foundation[0].
3. Many small districts share a superintendent. That is why there are fewer superintendents than there are operating school districts.
4. This may soon be changing. The National Center on Education Statistics is about to contract with the U.S. Bureau of the Census to undertake systematic data collection regarding educator salary and fringe benefit information.
5. Levine, Arthur, *Educating School Leaders*, Teachers College Record, March 2005.

Significant Education Finance Court Decisions

Abbeville v. South Carolina, 515 S.E. 2d 535 (2005).

Abbott v. Burke, 575 A. 2d 359 (N.J. 1990).

Abbott v. Burke, 693 A. 2d 417 (N.J. 1997).

Alabama Coalition for Equity v. Hunt, WL 204083 (AL 1993).

Board of Education of Levittown v. Nyquist, 408 N.Y.S. 2d 606 (N.Y. Sup. Ct. 1978).

Board of Education of Levittown v. Nyquist, 57 N.Y. 2d 27 (1982).

Brown v. Board of Education of Topeka, 347 U.S. 483, 74 S.Ct. 686, 98 L.Ed. 873 (U.S. 1954).

Buse v. Smith, 247 N.W. 2d 141 (Wis. 1976).

Campaign for Fiscal Equity v. State, 162 Misc. 2d 493 (N.Y.S. 1994).

Campaign for Fiscal Equity v. State, 187 Misc. 2d 1 (N.Y.S. 2001).

Campaign for Fiscal Equity v. State, 100 N.Y. 2d 893 (N.Y. 2003).

Campbell County School District v. State, 907 P. 2d 1238 (Wyo. 1995). Hereinafter Campbell I.

Campbell County School District v. State, 907 P. 2d 1238, 1274 (Wyo. 1995).

Charlotte-Mecklenburg v. Capacchione (2001), 99-2389.

Claremont School District v. Governor. 635 A. 2d 1375 (N.H. 1993).

Claremont School District v. Governor, 635 A. 2d 1375 (N.H. 1994).

Claremont School District v. Governor, 147 N.H. 499 (N.H., Apr 11, 2002) at 520.

Columbia Falls Elementary School District No. 6 v. State of Montana, WL 648038 (Mont. 2005).

DeRolph v. Ohio, 677 N.E. 2d 733 (Ohio 1997).

DeRolph v. Ohio, 728 N.E. 2d 99 (Ohio 2000).

Dupree v. Alma School District No. 30, 651 S.W. 2d 90 (Ark. 1983).

Edgewood Independent School District v. Kirby, 777 S.W. 2d 391 (Tex. 1989).

Eisenberg v. Montgomery County Schools (1999), 197 F. 3d 123.

Hancock v. Driscoll, No. 02-2978, (Sup. Ct. of Mass. at Suffolk, April 26, 2004). 2004 WL 877984 (Mass. Super.).

Helena Elementary School District v. State of Montana, 769 P. 2d 684 (1990).

Helvering v. Davis, 301 Dr. S. 619, 57 Sup. Ct. 904.

Horton v. Meskill, 332 A. 2d 113 (Conn. Super. 1974).

Horton v. Meskill, 376 A. 2d 359 (Conn. 1977). Hereinafter Horton II.

Kasayulie v. State, 3AN-97-3782 CIV (AK 1999).

Lake View School District, No. 25 v. Huckabee, No. 1992-5318 (Pulaski County Chancery Court, May 25, 2001).

Lake View School District, No. 25 v. Huckabee, 91 S.W. 3d 472 (AR 2002).

Lau v. Nichols (1973) 483 F. 2d (9OR., 1973); 94 S. C7 786 (1974). Sup. 866.

Lemon v. Kurtzman, 403 U.S. 602, 91 Sup. Ct. 2105. See also Leeman v. Sloan, 340 f. Suppl. 1356, 1972.

McDuffy v. Secretary of the Executive Office of Education, 615 N.E. 2d 516 (Mass. 1993).

McInnis v. Ogilvie, 394 U.S. 322 (U.S. 1969).

Mills v. Board of Education (1972).

Moore v. State of Alaska, No. 04-9756 Alaska Super. Ct. (2007).

Muellar v. Allen, 54 U.S. LW 5050.

Northshore School District v. Kinnear, 530 P. 2d 178 (Wash. 1974).

Papasan v. Allain, 106 U.S. 2932 (S. Ct. 1986).

PARC v. Commonwealth (1971), 834 F. Sup. Ct. 1257.

Parker v. Mandel, 344 F. Supp. 1068 (D. Md. 1972).

Pauley v. Bailey, 324 S.E. 2d 128 (W. Va. 1984).

Pauley v. Kelly, 255 S.E. 2d 859 (W. Va. 1979).

Robinson v. Cahill, 62 N.J. 473, 303 A. 3d 273 (N.J. 1973).

Roosevelt v. Bishop, 877 P. 2d 806 (1994).

Rose v. Council for Better Education, 790 S.W. 2d 186 (Ky. 1989).

San Antonio v. Rodriguez, 411 U.S. 1, 93 1278 (S. Ct. 1973).

Sawyer v. Gilmore, 109 Me. 169, 83 A. 673 (1912).

Seattle School District No. 1 of King County v. State, 585 P. 2d 71 (Wash. 1978).

Serrano v. Priest (1971).

Serrano v. Priest, 557 P. 2d 929 (Cal. 1976). Hereinafter Serrano II.

Serrano v. Priest, 569 P. 2d 1303 (1977). Hereinafter Serrano III.

Shaffer v. Carter, 252 U.S. 37, 40 S.Ct. 221 (U.S. 1920).

Skeen v. State, 505 N.W. 2d 299 (MN 1993).

Springfield Township v. Quick, 63 U.S. 56 (U.S. 1859).

State ex rel Anderson v. Brand, 313 U.S. 95.

State v. Board of Commissioners of Elk County (1899).

State v. Campbell County School District, 19 P. 3d 518 (Wyo. 2001).

Stuart v. School District No. 1 of Village of Kalamazoo, 30 Mich. 69 (1874).

Tennessee Small School Systems v. McWherter, WL 119824 (Tenn. Ct. App. 1992).

Tennessee Small School Systems v. McWherter, 851 S.W. 2d 139 (Tenn. 1993).

United States v. Butler, 297 U.S. 1, 56 Sup. Ct. 312.

Vincent v. Voight, 614 N.W. 2d 388 (Wis. 2000).

West Orange-Cove Cons. Indep. Sch. Dist. v. Neely, No. GV-100528 (Tex. Dist. Ct. Nov. 30, 2004, pet. filed).

Williston Public School District v. State (N.D. pending).

Young v. Williams, Cir. Ct. Div. II (2007).

Zelman v. Simmons-Harris (2001), U.S. Supr.Ct. 00–1751.

Glossary

Boldface numbers following entries denote the book chapter that provides context for the concept involved.

ability grouping (15) Arrangement whereby students are assigned to groups on the basis of aptitude testing or other judgments regarding performance or potential.

ability to pay (6) The principle of taxation that holds that the tax burden should be distributed according to a person's wealth. It is based on the assumption that, as a person's income increases, the individual or corporation can and should contribute a larger percentage of income to support government activities. The progressive income tax is based on the ability-to-pay principle.

academic standards (8) Degrees or levels of achievement. The "standards movement" began as an informal effort that grew out of a concern that American students were not learning enough and that American schools did not have a rigorous curriculum. The U.S. Congress adopted this concept more formally with its 1994 reauthorization of the federal Title I program.

accelerated learning (9) Combining adult learning theory and whole-brain learning theory in the learning environment to achieve a faster learning rate.

accommodations (10) Changes in the way tests are designed or administered to respond to the special needs of students with disabilities and English learners.

account code (6) A number classification of sources of revenues or purposes of expenditures in either a school district budget or in the reports that districts submit to a state's department of education. The account code classifies expenditures according to the types of items purchased or services obtained, and revenues by the general source and type of revenue.

accountability (8, 10, 13) The responsibility to justify and link money spent, decisions made, and activities performed by an individual or an institution.

accreditation (10) Credentials awarded by an authorized accrediting body that certify compliance with established standards of quality of practice, service, or production.

achievement gap (9) A consistent difference in scores on student achievement tests between certain groups of children and children in other groups. The data document a strong association between poverty and students' lack of academic success as measured by achievement tests.

ACT (10, 13) A set of college admissions tests and the organization that produces them, the American College Testing Program, located in Iowa City, Iowa. Most colleges now accept either the SAT or the ACT for admissions purposes.

action plan (3) A set of decisions regarding who is going to do what, by when, and in what order, so that the organization can reach its strategic goals. The design and implementation of action planning depend on the nature and needs of the organization. An action plan includes a schedule with deadlines for significant actions.

adaptive capacity (2) The ability of the organization to adapt to changing conditions in order to realize improved results. Some elements of adaptive capacity include an external focus; interdependent relationships and networks; and inquisitiveness and innovation.

added value (10) Additional benefit gained by the use of specific factors in teaching, learning, or administration activities.

adequacy (6) An approach to school funding that begins with the premise that the amount of funding schools receive should be based on some estimate of the cost of achieving the state's educational goals. This approach attempts to answer two questions: how much money would be enough to achieve those goals; and where would it be best spent?

adequate yearly progress (1, 9) An individual state's measure of yearly progress toward achieving state academic standards. Adequate yearly progress is the minimum level of improvement that states, school districts, and schools must achieve each year, according to the federal No Child Left Behind Act. This progress is determined by a collection of performance measures that a state, its school districts, and subpopulations of students within its schools must meet in order for the state to receive federal funding.

administrative costs of taxation (6) Costs related to administering the tax system.

ad valorem duties (6) Taxes on imported goods that are levied as a percentage of assessed value.

advanced placement (AP) program and AP exams (12) A

cooperative educational program between high school students and institutions of higher education that offers high school students the opportunities to complete college-level courses and earn college credit for them.

adverse or disparate impact (10) Criteria used to show that employment practices affect one group more harshly than another.

affective domain (8) The emotional aspect of experience and learning; a classification of objectives that focus on the development of attitudes, beliefs, and values.

agenda-setting (5) Controlling the focus of attention by establishing the issues for public discussion.

alignment (8, 9) The degree to which assessments, curriculum, instruction, textbooks and other instructional materials, teacher preparation and professional development, and systems of accountability all reflect and reinforce the educational program's objectives and standards.

alternate dispute resolution (7) An alternative to court adjudication that must be entered into voluntarily by all parties.

alternative assessments (10) Any of a variety of assessments that enable teachers to evaluate their students' understanding or performance; ways, other than standardized tests, to get information about what students know and where they need help, such as oral reports, projects, performances, experiments, and class participation.

alternative certification (13) An alternative method to qualify an individual to teach. Teachers generally require a college degree in education and a state certification to teach. Under the federal No Child Left Behind Act, states are encouraged to offer other methods of qualification that allow talented individuals to teach subjects they know.

alternative schools accountability model (10) An alternative way of measuring student performance in schools with primarily high-risk students—such as continuation schools or some county office of education schools—and schools with fewer than ten valid test scores.

American Federation of Labor and Congress of Industrial Organizations (AFL-CIO) (5) A large labor organization whose members are in and of themselves national unions, founded in 1886; it merged with its offshoot, the Congress of Industrial Organizations, to create the AFL-CIO in 1955.

Americans with Disabilities Act (ADA) (9) Prohibits discrimination based on a person's disabilities with regard to employment, programs, and services that are provided by private companies; commercial facilities; and federal, state, and local governments. The act also guarantees equal opportunity for people with disabilities in public accommodations, transportation, and telecommunications.

amicus curiae **(7)** Latin term for "friend of the court"; any person or organization permitted to participate in a lawsuit who would not otherwise have a right to do so. Participation is usually limited to filing a brief on behalf of one side or the other.

analysis (strategic analysis) (3) A systematic approach to problem solving. Complex problems are made simpler when separated into more understandable elements. This involves identification of purposes and facts, a statement of defensible assumptions, and the formulation of conclusions.

anchored instruction (8) A form of constructivism by which learning is tied to the students' real-world "anchors" (such as social or work experiences).

appeal (7) (1) The process by which a case is brought before an appellate court. (2) In legislatures: a member's challenge of a ruling or decision made by the presiding officer of the chamber. (3) A formal process within an organization by which an employee may question an upperling's decision, particularly a personnel decision or formal performance evaluation.

apportionments (6) Funds that federal or state governments distribute to local education agencies or other governmental units according to certain formulas.

appropriation (6) Provision of law that provides authority for local, state, or federal agencies to obligate funds and make payments out of the treasury for specified purposes. Appropriations for the federal government are provided both in annual appropriations acts and in permanent provisions of law.

appropriation acts (6) Annual legislative enactments, federal or state, approving allocation of specific amounts of government revenue to be spent by operating jurisdictions consistent with purposes described in detail in a pre-existing legislative authority (an authorizing act).

aptitude test (10) A standardized test measuring specific intellectual capabilities or other characteristics.

arbitrator (arbiter) (7) An impartial individual selected by major parties to a dispute who is empowered to make a determination concerning the issues in conflict.

assessed value (6) The value of land, homes, and businesses set by the county assessor for property tax purposes.

attributes (2) Characteristics or qualities or properties. Attributes of the leader fall into three categories: mental, physical, and emotional.

audit (6) An independent examination of the accounting records and other evidence relating to an agency's public or private operation to support the expression of an impartial expert opinion about the reliability of the agency's financial statements.

authentic instruction (8) Teaching that is meaningful to students. Focuses on higher-order thinking, depth of knowledge, real-world applications, and social interactions.

authoritarian culture (2) An organizational culture characterized by the holding of all power (decision making and information) at the top of the organization. The authoritarian organization seeks to maintain the status quo and forces workers to conform, never question or give feedback, play politics, and wait for orders.

authoritarian leadership (2) A style of leadership in which the leader tells the employees what needs to be done and how to perform it without soliciting their advice or ideas.

authority (3, 12) A form of power based on consensus regarding the right to issue commands and make decisions.

autocratic leader (2) A person in charge who retains most of the authority for himself or herself.

average daily attendance (ADA) (6) The total number of days of student attendance divided by the total number of days in the regular school year. A student attending every day would equal one ADA. ADA is not the same as enrollment, which is the number of students enrolled in each school and district. (This number is determined by counting students on a given day in October.) ADA usually is lower than enrollment due to factors such as students moving, dropping out, or staying home due to illness. The state uses a school district's ADA to determine its general purpose (revenue limit) and some other funding.

basic aid (6) The minimum general-purpose aid guaranteed by the state's constitution.

basic aid school district (6) The historical name for a district in which local property taxes equal or exceed the district's revenue limit. These districts may keep the money from local property taxes and still receive constitutionally guaranteed state basic aid funding.

behaviorism (8) A psychological theory that claims all mental states can be reduced to statements of observable behaviors. In learning theory, the claim is all learning is based on a stimulus-response relationship.

benchmark (10) An original set of performance-related data against which a later set is compared in order to measure progress toward an individual's or institution's specified outcomes or aspirations.

benefit-cost ratio (10) The ratio of the present value of benefits over the present value of costs.

benefit principle (6) A taxation principle whereby taxes are assigned on the basis of benefits received.

bias (10) Errors in statistical sampling or testing that are made by favoring some factors over others.

Bias reduces the overall validity of research. Also known as *item bias*.

bilingual education (9) An in-school program for students whose first language is not English or who have limited English skills.

block grant (6) An allotment of money that is the sum of multiple special-purpose funds combined into one. A block grant tends to have fewer restrictions on how the money is spent than the original, disparate funding streams had, and it often combines funds that have similar purposes.

block scheduling (9) A way of organizing the school day into blocks of time longer than the typical fifty-minute class period. Students take as many courses as before (sometimes more), but the courses either do not meet every day or do not run the entire school year.

Bloom's Taxonomy (8) An approach to ranking learning by the sophistication or depth of learning required or accomplished. A hierarchical framework of learning based on three domains: the cognitive, affective, and psychomotor. In the cognitive domain there are six levels of knowledge: knowledge, comprehension, application, analysis, synthesis, and evaluation. In the affective domain there are five levels: receiving phenomenon, responding to phenomenon, valuing, organizing values, and internalizing values.

bond measure (6) A method of borrowing employed by school districts to pay for a large capital investment, used in much the same way as a person who takes out a mortgage to purchase a home.

bonus/performance pay (13) Extra money for school district employees who perform extra duties or are considered exemplary.

***Brown v. Board of Education* (4, 7)** The case heard by the U.S. Supreme Court in 1954 in which racial segregation in public schools was held to be unconstitutional.

budget (6) A detailed documentation of estimated income and expenses that can be used as a tool for projecting revenue and expenditures for the ensuing fiscal year.

canons of taxation (6) Adam Smith's five desiderata for a prudent system of taxation were adequacy, certainty, efficiency, ease of administration, and equity.

capital outlay (6) Money spent for major physical changes to a school such as new buildings, renovations, reconstruction, or certain new equipment. These investments in the physical structure of a school are expected to last for a number of years.

Carnegie unit (8) The unit of time spent in a course over a year. Carnegie units are typically used to award credit in secondary schools.

categorical aid/categorical programs (6) Funds from the state or federal government granted to qualifying schools or districts for specific children with special needs, certain programs such as class size reduction, or special purposes such as transportation.

centralization (2) An organizational process by which upper-level management retains major decision-making authority, creates all major policies and programs, and preserves the authority to make significant changes.

certificated/credentialed employees (10) Employees who are required by the state to hold some type of teaching credentials, including most administrators and full-time, part-time, substitute, and temporary teachers.

chaos theory (2) A means of explaining the dynamics of sensitive systems that seeks to find the underlying order in apparently random data or apparently random systems; used especially to understand the functioning of dysfunctional organizations.

charisma (2, 12) A special quality of leaders, whose purposes, powers, personality, and extraordinary determination differentiate them from others.

charter school (9) A public school operated independently under a performance agreement with a school district, a county office of education, or the state board of education.

chief executive officer (2) An individual who hires, supervises, and evaluates staff and serves as a liaison between staff and board.

choice (1) The right of parents to be able to choose where to send their children to school.

Common Core of Data (6) The database of public school and school district data annually collected by the U.S. Department of Education's National Center for Education Statistics.

community relations (16) The planned, active, and continuous participation by an organization with and within a community, usually to maintain and enhance its environment to the benefit of both the organization and the community.

compliance (4) Within statutory limits and court interpretations, acts by an employer such as a school district or charter school to bring practices into line with state, federal, and local regulations.

consensus building (14) Creating consensus or agreement in groups through leadership and compromise.

consensus leader (2) The person in charge who encourages group discussion about an issue and then makes a decision that reflects general agreement and will be supported by group members.

consideration (7) The quid pro quo in a contract. In the context of a contract, some right, interest, profit, or benefit accruing to one party or some forbearance, detriment, loss, or responsibility given, suffered, or undertaken by the other.

consolidation (4) The act of creating a new corporation and extinguishing both of the consolidating agencies.

constituent relationships (14) The heart of an organization's work. Constituents serve on boards, participate in programs and evaluations, and inform strategic planning. They are the organization's most important public partners.

constructive feedback (15) Comments intended to highlight positive elements of a person's activities.

constructivism (8) A theory of learning that claims that people learn by constructing knowledge through social interactions with others.

content standards (11) Standards that describe what students should know and be able to do in core academic subjects at each grade level.

contingency theory (2) The contention that leaders are most effective when they make their behavior contingent upon situational forces, including group member characteristics.

continuous assessment (10) Ongoing evaluation of work during a course in which the scores earned count toward the final evaluation.

contracting out (4) The hiring of private organizations to provide public services.

cooperative learning model (8) An approach in which students share knowledge with other students through a variety of structures. Cooperative learning, as a phrase, originated in the 1960s with the work of David and Roger Johnson.

co-optation (5) Alliance building between an administrative agency and a clientele group in which the clientele group is allowed to influence agency policymaking, in return for which the clientele group tacitly agrees to support the general mission of the agency, provide it with political support, and defend the agency against assaults on its powers, programs, or budget.

core competency (8) Fundamental knowledge, ability, or expertise in a specific subject area or skill set. To be considered a core competency, a capability must be an essential part of an organization's offerings and it must describe a significant advantage in the marketplace.

cost-benefit analysis (11) A technique designed to measure relative gains and losses resulting from alternative policy or program options; emphasizes identification of the most desirable cost-benefit ratio, in quantitative or other terms.

cost-benefit ratio (11) The proportional relationship between expenditure of a given quantity of resources and the benefits derived therein; a guideline for choosing among alternatives, of greatest relevance to the rational model of decision making.

cost-of-living adjustment (6) An increase in funding for schools from the state or federal government due to inflation.

county office of education (4) The agency that provides, in general, educational programs for certain students; business, administrative, and curriculum services to school districts; and financial oversight of districts.

courage (1) The virtue that enables us to conquer fear, danger, or adversity, no matter what the context happens to be (physical or moral). Courage includes the notion of taking responsibility for decisions and actions. Additionally, the idea involves the ability to perform critical self-assessment, to confront new ideas, and to change.

credentialing/teacher preparation (10) A process implemented by the state commission on teaching credentialing to certify that teachers are well prepared to enter the classroom.

credit hour (9) A quantitative measure of instructional courses. See *Carnegie unit.*

crisis leadership (2) The process of leading group members through a sudden and largely unanticipated, intensely negative and emotionally draining circumstance.

criterion-referenced test (10) A test that measures specific performance or content standards, often along a continuum from total lack of skill to excellence. These tests can also have cut scores that determine whether a test taker has passed or failed the test or has basic, proficient, or advanced skills. Criterion-referenced tests, unlike norm-referenced assessments, are not created primarily to compare students to each other. The goal is typically to have everyone attain a passing mark.

critical incident (1) An event that triggers reflective self-examination and critical assessment of the event.

critical path (3) In project management, the sequence of events with the longest duration. The duration of the critical path determines the duration of the entire project. Any delay of a terminal element on the critical path directly impacts the planned project completion date.

critical thinking (8) A process whereby the learner considers a variety of possibilities and then chooses from those possibilities using unbiased, rational thinking.

critical thinking skills (8) The use of those cognitive skills or strategies that increase the probability of a desirable outcome. Describes thinking that is purposeful, reasoned, and goal directed.

cross-age tutoring (8) A type of instruction or assistance in which older students act as tutors to younger students. Often carried out in the form of a "buddy" program (e.g., all the fourth-graders in a school may have a first-grade "reading buddy" with whom they work).

culture (2) A learned pattern of customs, beliefs, and behaviors that are socially acquired and socially transmitted through symbols and widely shared meanings.

curriculum (9) The courses of study offered by a school or district.

curriculum alignment (8, 9) A match between the written, taught, and tested curriculum.

curriculum articulation (9) The extent to which curriculum builds and is vertically aligned through the grades for complex learning to take place.

curriculum framework (9) The blueprint for schools to use to implement the state-adopted content standards.

curriculum guide (8) A document that provides clear learning goals and objectives, pacing recommendations, and expected student learning achievements that are tied to state and local performance standards. Assessments, model lessons, and a listing of approved instructional support materials are included to provide comprehensive curriculum.

decentralization (6) Significant decision-making authority is delegated throughout the organization to lower operational levels.

decision analysis (11) A technique by which decisions are likely to be made sequentially and under some degree of uncertainty.

decision tree (11) A treelike diagram illustrating the choices available to a decision maker. Each possible decision and its estimated outcome are shown as a separate branch of the tree.

deductive inquiry (11) A form of inquiry with four basic components: presentation of a generalization, discussion of core elements of the generalization, student exploration of the elements, and student generation of relevant examples of the generalized concept.

de facto segregation (5) Separation (usually racial) that is neither the result of nor created by law but that exists in fact.

deferred maintenance (6) Major repairs or replacement of buildings and equipment. Declines in school funding over a number of years can lead many districts to delay preventive maintenance expenses in order to maintain education programs.

defined benefit plan (13) The dominant pension plan for public-sector employees. Financial contributions, a specified percent of annual salary, are paid into the pension fund each year by both employee and employer. An employee member is eligible for retirement benefits after having been vested, in keeping with a formula that considers years of service, often combined with employee age, resulting in a defined annual pension benefit that is a specified percent of annual salary at time of retirement. For example, a defined benefit plan may specify that an employee, after becoming vested, is eligible for a predetermined percent of annual salary that is a combination of years employed (30) and age (60), for 90 percent of annual salary at time of retirement.

defined contribution plan (13) The dominant mode of private-sector pension plans. Employees contribute a predetermined percent of annual salary into a tax-exempt investment retirement account (IRA). That amount is matched, partially or fully, by the employer. The corpus (individual and employer contributions plus investment return) is not taxable until the employee is eligible for retirement. At retirement, the pensioner owns the entire financial corpus and is taxed on

the amount he or she withdraws each year.

delegative leadership (2) A style of leadership in which the leader entrusts decision making to an employee or a group of employees. The leader is still responsible for their decisions.

Deming Cycle for Continuous Improvement (2) A visualization of the Continuous Quality Improvement process, usually consisting of four points—Plan, Do, Check, Act—linked by quarter-circles. The cycle was first developed by Dr. Walter A. Shewhart but was popularized in Japan in the 1950s by Dr. W. Edwards Deming.

democracy (4) From the Greek words for "people" (*demos*) and "power" (*kratos*). This concept has no single meaning. Theorists distinguish between "procedural" democracy (which is concerned with activities such as political participation, elections, and ways of taking power) and substantive policy outcomes (which are concerned with the educational, health, and economic consequences that government produces).

departmentalization (2) The process of combining jobs into work units and grouping similar work units.

developer fee (6) A charge per square foot on residential and commercial construction within a school district.

didactic instruction (8) A teaching style characterized as noninteractive and expository; teacher-centered instruction in which the teacher tells the student what to think about a topic. Used for the delivery of factual (not debated) information.

direct instruction (15) Teacher-centered instruction that includes lecture, presentation, and recitation.

disaggregated data (11) The presentation of data broken into segments (e.g., test scores for students from various ethnic groups instead of in the aggregate) for the entire student population.

discovery teaching (8) A constructivist approach in which students begin learning with an activity designed to lead them to particular concepts or conclusions. Students acquire basic and advanced knowledge in random order.

distance education (9) Education using strategies designed to deliver distance learning.

distributed leadership (2) A process by which the responsibilities of leading the instructional aspects of the school are shared among leadership team members. All members of the leadership team participate and are engaged in solving problems, monitoring student achievement, and planning for study groups and teacher meetings to support instructional practices in the school.

distributed learning (8) Providing a learning context by projecting the environment to the student, usually via information technology. The student may be on or off campus.

division of work (2) One of the fundamental principles upon which the science of administration is based; increased specialization in the organization of work in order to narrow the range of tasks for which each person is responsible, which in turn increases the need for administrative planning and coordination and raises the productivity of the organization as a whole.

double-loop learning (8) An in-depth style of learning that occurs when people use feedback to confront the validity of the goal or the values implicit in the situation.

dropout (11) A student who leaves school prior to completing a school year (e.g., in California, a grade-7-to-10 student who leaves school prior to completing the school year and has not returned by Information Day in October, when students throughout the state are counted and enrollment is determined). Students are not considered dropouts if they receive a General Education Development or state high school proficiency examination certificate, transfer to another high school or to a college, move out of the United States, are suspended or sick on a particular day, or will be enrolling late.

due process (substantive) (7) The Constitutional guarantee that no

person can be arbitrarily deprived of life, liberty, or property. Its essence is protection from arbitrary and unreasonable action.

economies of scale (4) Decreased average costs of production resulting from increased levels of production; attempts to reduce costs by increasing the number of items produced and sold or reducing the number of competing institutions.

education code (4) The body of law that regulates education in a state.

Educational Testing Service (ETS) (16) A nationwide organization that administers various types of educational and psychological tests, such as the National Assessment of Educational Progress.

effective tax rate (6) Tax rate calculated by dividing tax liability by a comprehensive measure of income.

e-learning (8) Learning activities based on any electronic format.

Elementary and Secondary Education Act (ESEA) (5) The principal federal law affecting K–12 education. The No Child Left Behind Act is the most recent reauthorization of the ESEA.

empowerment (2) (1) The expansion of capacities and choices. (2) The ability of all groups to exercise choice based on freedom and the opportunity to participate in, or endorse, decision making that affects their lives.

English Language Learner (9) A student who speaks one or more languages other than English and is developing proficiency in English.

equal protection clause of the 14th Amendment of the U.S. Constitution (7) A clause in the U.S. Constitution that says that no state shall "deny to any person within its jurisdiction the equal protection of the laws."

equalization aid (6) Funds allocated, on occasion, by the legislature to address perceived inequalities and raise the funding level of school districts with lower revenue limits toward the statewide average based on size and type of district.

equity (6) The belief that state governments have an obligation to

equalize students' access to educational opportunities and thus life chances.

ethnicity (10, 11) A classification in which members share a unique social and cultural heritage transmitted from one generation to the next.

excise tax (6) Tax applied to the sale of specific commodities.

executive session (4) A board meeting that, by law, is not open to the public, usually dealing with personnel matters, negotiations strategy, property purchase, or legal strategy; also referred to as a *closed session*.

ex-officio member (4) Usually a member of a school board or similar deliberative body holding a seat by virtue of holding another elective or appointive office, sometimes by virtue of former membership on the board or group. (*Ex officio* means "from or because of office" in Latin.) The person is usually a nonvoting member.

expectancy theory (2) A theory of motivation based on the premise that the amount of effort people expend depends on how much reward they can expect in return.

expenditures per pupil (6) The amount of money spent on education by a school district or the state, divided by the number of students educated.

experiential learning (8) Carl Rogers' theory that there are two types of learning: cognitive (memorizing or studying simply because work is assigned) and experiential (learning to satisfy the needs and wants of the learner). Studying a book with commonly used phrases in Norwegian is experiential if you are planning a trip to Norway, but the same activity is cognitive if you are taking a language class and the teacher assigns reading from the book.

extended-day programs (9) Programs that offer an organized activity or place for children to go after school every day and provide opportunities for them to learn. Also called *after-school programs*.

extracurricular (5) Activities of students, teams, or clubs that are not considered part of (and are therefore outside of) the school curriculum.

extrinsic reward (8) A reward to provide motivation that is outside the ongoing learning activity: gifts, accumulated points, and so on.

Family and Medical Leave Act (7) A federal law requiring employers covered by the act to grant eligible employees up to ten work weeks of unpaid leave a year for an employee's own serious health condition, to care for certain family members with serious health conditions, or following the birth or adoption of a child; employees returning from such leave are entitled to be restored to the same or a similar position.

Family Educational Rights and Privacy Act (7) A federal law that gives parents certain rights with respect to their children's education records.

federalism (4) A constitutional division of governmental power between a central or national government and regional governmental units (such as states), with each having some independent authority over its citizens.

feedback (10, 11) The process that permits multiple paths of communication between an employee and a supervisor for the purpose of modifying, correcting, and strengthening employee performance and results; any means by which a teacher informs a student about the quality or correctness of the student's products or actions.

flow chart (3) A graphical representation of the flow of a process, generally using symbols to depict the step-by-step sequence of operations, activities, or procedures. Typically flow charts include icons showing particular processes or steps, and arrows indicating paths.

formative assessment (10) Any form of assessment used by an educator to evaluate students' knowledge and understanding of particular content and adjust instructional practices accordingly toward improving student achievement in that area.

formative evaluation (10) A testing process involving a series of events as a course develops, with the intention of assessing progress in a regular manner.

free/reduced-price meals (6) A federal program to provide food—typically lunch and/or breakfast—for students from low-income families.

Gantt Chart (3) The summary of a work plan presented in the form of a chart showing the major activities planned in their chronological sequence, as well as the week or month in which they will be conducted, and the person responsible for carrying them out. This chart often includes a list of resources that will be necessary to carry out the activities.

gap analysis (3) An evaluation of differences between the organization's current position and its desired future. Gap analysis results in the development of specific strategies and allocation of resources to close the gap.

"garbage can" theory of organizational choice (2) A theory of organizational decision-making applicable to organizations whose goals are unclear, technologies are imperfectly understood, histories are difficult to interpret, and participants wander in and out; such "organized anarchies" operate under conditions of pervasive ambiguity, with so much uncertainty in the decision-making process that traditional theories about coping with uncertainty do not apply.

general fund (6) The primary legally defined fund used by the state and school districts to differentiate general revenues and expenditures from those placed in other funds for specific uses.

general-purpose funding (6) Money granted to school districts for general purposes. For example, California school districts receive general-purpose money based on a per-pupil revenue limit. They have discretion to spend this money as they see fit for the day-to-day operation of schools—including everything from salaries to the electric bill—within the constraints of certain laws and contracts with employees.

genetic epistemology (8) A theory proposed by Jean Piaget. It stated that children pass through various stages of cognitive development. For example, during very early stages, children are not aware of the permanence of objects, so hiding an object causes the child to lose interest. Once the child has acquired the ability to think of the object as still existing even when out of sight, the child will begin to look for the missing object.

gestalt theory (8) Max Wertheimer's theory that deals with the nature of whole problems or concepts. Gestalt theory stresses the importance of the relationship between objects in a group and the relatedness of concepts. Gestalt is about "the big picture" and originated as a response to the traditional scientific approach of breaking things down into their component parts and seeking understanding by analyzing the parts.

gifted and talented education program (9) A program that provides supplemental, differentiated, and challenging curriculum and instruction to public school students who are deemed by their districts to be intellectually gifted or especially talented in leadership or visual and performing arts.

goal (1) A desired outcome or intention. If expressed in the correct form, it may be described as an objective.

governance (4) The structure and policies for decision making that include board, staff, and constituents. Governance, in the nonprofit sector, refers to the actions of the board of directors of an organization with respect to establishing and monitoring the long-term direction of that organization. On the national level, governance is the exercise of political, economic, and administrative authority in the management of a country's affairs at all levels. Governance is a neutral concept comprising the complex.

grade-level team (13) A system involving the assignment of a group of staff for course teaching so that individual staff receive peer support and particular strengths can be exploited; two or more teachers cooperatively planning, teaching, and evaluating the progress of their students.

Head Start (9) A federal program, established as part of President Lyndon Johnson's anti-poverty agenda, that provides economically disadvantaged preschoolers with education, nutrition, health, and social services at special centers based in schools and community settings throughout the country.

heterogeneous grouping (9) Organizing students of varying achievement levels or needs in the same classroom (the opposite of homogeneous grouping).

heuristic learning (8) A process by which conditions are established that allow students to encounter information and derive their own conclusions. Also called *discovery learning*.

higher-order thinking skills (HOTS) (9) Any thinking that goes beyond recall of basic facts. The two key reasons to improve higher-order thinking skills are to enable students to apply facts in order to solve real-world problems and to improve retention of facts. In addition to the basic meaning of higher-order thinking skills, HOTS also refers to a specific program designed to teach higher-order thinking skills through the use of computers and the Socratic method.

highly qualified teacher (9, 13) According to the No Child Left Behind Act, a teacher who has obtained full state teacher certification or has passed the state teacher licensing examination and holds a license to teach in the state, holds a minimum of a bachelor's degree, and has demonstrated subject area competence in each of the academic subjects in which he or she teaches.

high-stakes test (13) A test that results in some kind of consequence for those who score low, some kind of reward for those who score high, or both. For example, students who pass a high school exit exam typically receive a diploma, while students who fail do not.

homeschooling (9) Provision of compulsory education in the home as an alternative to traditional public/private schooling, often motivated by parental desire to exclude their children from the traditional school environment.

homogeneous grouping (9) Organizing students for instruction on the basis of one or more common characteristics. Most frequently, homogeneous groups are created on the basis of student achievement.

horizontal equity (6) Arrangement whereby all individuals with identical abilities to pay are assigned identical tax burdens.

hoshin planning (3) A Japanese strategic planning process in which a company develops up to four vision statements that indicate where the company should be in the next five years. Goals and plans are developed based on the vision statements. Audits are conducted periodically to monitor progress.

impact aid (6) The federal program that provides funds to districts with children whose families live or work on federal property, such as military bases or Native American reservations. Funded through Title VIII of the No Child Left Behind Act, this program is also called *Public Law 81-874*.

incidence of taxation (6) The specification of just who ultimately pays a tax. Although the personal income tax falls on the individual taxpayer, the incidence of other taxes depends on the elasticity of demand. The more inelastic the demand, the more likely the tax is paid by the consumer.

incrementalism (5) The notion that public policy is usually brought about through small, piecemeal alterations. Called *salami tactics* by William Safire, incrementalism is said to be typical of pluralism, where the many veto groups make it difficult to enact major synoptic change.

independent learning (8) Self-directed learning independent of any teaching or formal guidance; learning completed by an individual without the assistance of an instructor. A term often mistakenly used to mean individual learning.

individual differences (8) Unique characteristics of individuals that have an impact on how they learn.

Individualized Education Program (IEP) (9) A plan developed for a specific student that outlines what that student needs to learn in a specified period of time and what special services need to be provided based on the student's ability. Special education students have IEPs that sometimes require exemptions from tests or accommodations for testing such as an exam in Braille.

inductive thinking (8) Analyzing individual observations to come to general conclusions. Proceeding from facts to the "big picture."

inflation factor (6) An increase in funding for schools from the state or federal government to compensate for inflation.

information flow table (3) A chart showing the types of information that will be collected, how the information will be collected and reported, who will collect it, to whom it will be submitted, how it will be used, and the level of detail required. The purpose of the chart is to ensure appropriate flow of information in the correct sequence and to communicate to staff how the information system functions.

infrastructure (2) The basic equipment and structure required for a particular system to function (e.g., systems of transportation, communications, and public utilities that are believed to be crucial to a nation's economic competitiveness).

inquiry-based learning (8) Learning methodology under which students are presented a problem to solve using knowledge and skills they have acquired or need to develop.

intelligence quotient (IQ) (13) A scale unit used in reporting test scores that attempt to measure "general intelligence." It represents a ratio between tested mental age and chronological age.

interest groups (5) Associations of individuals who share a common goal and work to promote their common interest.

International Baccalaureate (IB) Program and Examinations (9) A rigorous international program of study that originated in Switzerland. To be eligible for an IB exam, students must be enrolled in a school that has been accredited through the IB accreditation process and must be taking the course for which they plan to take the exam. In the IB system, the exam will count for 75 percent of the course grade. Students can earn college credit from many universities for IB courses if their exam scores are high enough.

interstate commerce (4) The power to regulate the flow of goods across state or national boundaries that was awarded to Congress in Article I, Section 8, Clause 2 of the U.S. Constitution and became the legal foundation for many federal programs during and after the New Deal. At various times federal action has been nullified because the commerce in question was intrastate or because the activity being regulated was deemed to be noncommercial in nature. The subject of *U.S. v. E.E. Knight Co.* (1895).

intrinsic reward (or reinforcement) (8) Motivating events that occur as a natural part of the learning experience.

Iowa Test of Basic Skills (10) General achievement tests designed to measure how well a student has learned the basic knowledge and skills that are taught in elementary and middle schools in areas such as reading and mathematics.

iron triangle (5) A coalition of interest groups, agency personnel, and members of Congress created to exert influence on a particular policy issue.

issue networks (5) Open and fluid groupings of various political actors (in and out of government) attempting to influence policy.

item bias (10) See *bias*.

joint school districts (4) School districts whose boundaries cross county lines.

just-in-time learning (8) Learning completed at the time knowledge or skills are necessary to complete a specific task.

K–14 (4) Kindergarten through community college.

kaizen (2) Japanese term for improvement. It involves both workers and managers.

Kolb's learning cycle (8) A learning model presented by David Kolb that identifies four stages in the learning cycle: concrete experience, observations and reflections, formation of abstract concepts and generalizations, and testing implications of concepts in new situations.

leadership (1) (1) The process of motivating and influencing others to strive willingly and enthusiastically toward the achievement of the orga-

nization's mission. (2) Implementing coaching and facilitating skills to e courage employees to improve their work and strive to do their best. (3) Improving the organization through change.

leadership style (15) The relatively consistent pattern of behavior that characterizes a leader.

learning (8) An internal process in which the individual's cognitive structures are modified by experience.

learning contract (8) A form of individualized, active learning in which the student proposes a course of study to satisfy an academic requirement and a teacher checks and approves the contract. The student typically works independently until assistance is needed from the teacher, at which point it is the responsibility of the student to ask for help.

learning organization (2) An organization that looks for meaningful solutions, then internalizes those solutions so that it continues to grow, develop, and remain successful. Learning organizations incorporate ideas from many sources and involve a variety of people in problem solving, information sharing, and celebrating success.

learning style (8) One of the various and unique ways in which individuals learn and process information. Although each of us learns differently, we can categorize an individual's strengths and weaknesses for a number of different factors that affect the way we learn. It is possible to refer to someone as a "visual learner" or a person who prefers "step-by-step" directions. By assessing and then planning for each student's individual learning style, a teacher can improve the chances that each student will learn.

learning theory (8) A theory explaining the learning process by reference to a particular model of human cognition, development, or something else.

legitimacy (5, 12) The degree to which a leader's, an organization's, or a government's procedures for making and enforcing laws are acceptable to those to whom they will apply. A legitimate system is legal, but more importantly, citizens believe in its ap-

propriateness and adhere to its rules. Legitimacy is closely tied to governance; voluntary compliance with laws and regulations results in greater effectiveness than reliance on coercion and personal loyalties.

levy (6) Total sum to be raised by a tax; or the legislative measure by which an annual or general tax is imposed. Also known as *tax levy*.

local control (6) The presumptive base of education governance in the United States. In the absence of explicit state or federal constitutional or statutory regulation, the presumption is that the local school district has decision-making authority over an issue.

longitudinal data (10) Data that are tracked over time; for example, achievement data for a specific student or group of students. In education, the ability to track students as they progress through the school system is seen as important for evaluating the contribution schools, specific programs, and teachers make to student performance, and for accurately tracking the progress of specific subgroups of students.

Machiavellians (2) People in the workplace who ruthlessly manipulate others. Taken from Machiavelli's classic writing *The Prince*.

magnet school (9) A school that places special emphasis on academic achievement or on a particular field such as science or the arts, designed to attract students on a voluntary basis from all parts of a school district. Often used to aid in achieving diversity in the school population.

managed learning environments (9) A system, typically computer based, for organizing and evaluating information related to an educational endeavor, including the lessons, learning activities, and evaluations.

management by anecdote (2) The technique of inspiring and instructing group members by telling stories.

management by objectives (2) A management technique designed to facilitate goal and priority setting, development of plans, resource allocation, monitoring progress toward goals, evaluating results, and generating and implementing improvements in performance; a participative goal-setting process that enables a manager or supervisor to construct and communicate goals to each subordinate. At the same time, a subordinate is able to formulate personal goals and influence the department's goals.

management information system (11) A system designed by an organization to collect and report information on a program, allowing managers to plan, monitor, and evaluate the operations and performance of the whole program.

mandated costs (6) School district expenditures that are required because of federal or state law, court decisions, administrator regulations, or initiative measures. Since the passage of Proposition 4 (the Gann Limit) in 1979, the California constitution has required the repayment of mandated costs to school districts.

manipulatives (8) Objects used in the classroom to allow students to make connections to concepts through touch. Examples include a bag of beans for counting or a microscope for scientific inquiry.

master teacher (13) An individual who possesses demonstrated, high-level teaching skills; a master teacher would be selected to serve as a supervising teacher or to lead a team teaching group. Sometimes known as a *lead teacher.*

mastery learning (8) A system in which all students are expected to achieve specified learning outcomes within a course segment and are engaged, without progression, until they do. Objectives for learning are established and communicated to students. Students progress at their own speed and continue to work until their performance indicates they have mastered each set of objectives.

matching funds (legislative) (6) Financial support program (usually a grant) through which the federal government seeks to create an incentive for developing needed programs at the state or local level by offering to match state or local funds allocated for the same purpose; private groups and foundations also offer matching funds.

median (11) A number in a series of numbers that has at least half the values greater than or equal to it and at least half of them less than or equal to it.

mediator (7) A person with whom parties in a dispute meet in an effort to reach a mutually acceptable decision. The mediator is an active participant in the discussions, but unlike an arbitrator, a mediator does not impose a decision on the disputants; rather, he or she actively attempts to help them find a solution that is acceptable to all parties.

mental models (8) Students' existing knowledge, which is organized into patterns or models that help them explain phenomena. Learning involves adding to or altering the learner's existing mental models.

mentor (10) A more experienced person who develops a protégé's abilities through tutoring, coaching, guidance, and emotional support; teacher and/or individual from the community who acts as guide along a student's educational journey. It can also apply to teachers who assist educators new to the field.

merit pay (10) Any of a number of plans to pay teachers and administrators on the basis of their demonstrated competence. Also known as *pay for performance.*

meta-analysis (8, 10) Statistical procedure for integrating the results of different studies.

metacognition (8) "Thinking about thinking." Learners monitor their own thought processes to decide if they are learning effectively. Taking a learning-styles inventory and then altering study habits to fit what was learned about preferences would be an example of a metacognitive activity.

micromanagement (2) The close monitoring of most aspects of group member activities by the manager or leader.

migrant education (9) Special federal funds for districts with students who are children of migrant workers.

mill (6) A unit of measurement of the level of taxation levied on property. One mill is one one-thousandth of the value of the property.

mind map (8) A diagram that shows the connections between different pieces of information or between different things that have been learned.

minimal competencies (8) Lowest level of knowledge or skill necessary for engaging in a task or admittance into a program.

mission (2, 11) An articulation, often in writing, of the primary aims of a group or institution. Also called *mission statement.*

motivation (8) The combination of a person's desire and energy directed at achieving a goal. It is the cause of action.

multiage grouping (9) The practice of having children of different ages in the same classroom, rather than assigning them to age-graded classrooms.

multiculturalism (8) The inclusion of a variety of cultures or ethnic groups.

multiple choice questions (10) A test format that provides students with several possible answers and asks them to identify the best possible answer.

multiple intelligences (8) A theory of intelligence developed in the 1980s by Howard Gardner, who defined intelligence broadly as "the capacity to solve problems or fashion products that are valued in one or more cultural settings." Gardner originally identified seven intelligences: linguistic, logical-mathematical, musical, spatial, bodily-kinesthetic, interpersonal, and intrapersonal. He later suggested the existence of several others, including naturalist, spiritual, and existential. According to Gardner, these intelligences exist in different proportions in everyone. The intelligences work together.

Myers-Briggs type indicator (10) An instrument for measuring a person's preferences using four basic scales with opposite poles. The four scales are (1) extroversion/introversion, (2) sensate/intuitive, (3) thinking/ feeling, and (4) judging/perceiving. The various combinations of these preferences result in fifteen personality types.

National Assessment of Educational Progress (NAEP) (10)
A national test given to students in specific grade levels in specific subjects every other year. A small sample of students representative of the state is tested. NAEP test scores can be compared to national averages.

National Board Certification (13) A certificate, awarded by the National Board for Professional Teaching Standards, attesting that a teacher possesses the skills and knowledge of accomplished teaching and meets the national board standards. To earn a certificate, the teacher must complete a rigorous two-part assessment. Most candidates spend approximately one hundred hours on assessment activities.

national school lunch program (6) A federal program to provide food—typically lunch and/or breakfast—for students from low- income families.

nationally administered tests (10, 12, 13)

IB (International Baccalaureate): An international series of exams based on a two-year program. All participants within the program are required to do coursework in at least two languages, experimental sciences, humanities, and mathematics.

AP (Advanced Placement) Tests: A series of voluntary exams based on college-level courses taken in high school. High school students who do well on one or more of these exams have the opportunity to earn credit, advanced placement, or both for college.

SAT (Scholastic Aptitude Test) (13):

SAT I—An exam used to gauge the verbal and mathematics reasoning skills of students. The SAT I is often used by colleges and universities to compare the skills of student applicants and to predict their future academic success.

SAT II—A set of tests that consists of a number of single-subject exams that measure content knowledge and skill level. Approximately 150 colleges and universities nationwide use the SAT II for admission and/or placement of students.

ACT (American College Testing) (10,13): A college entrance exam that covers English, mathematics, reading, and science reasoning. Similar to the SAT I exam, the ACT is often used by colleges and universities to determine a student's ability to complete college-level work.

NAEP (National Assessment of Educational Progress): Also referred to as the *Nation's Report Card.* A nationwide assessment of what America's students know and can do in various subject areas, including reading, mathematics, science, writing, history, geography, the arts, and other fields.

TIMSS (Third International Mathematics and Science Study): An international study conducted in 1995 and then revisited in 1999 that collected data on the mathematics and science achievement of students from the United States and other countries.

No Child Left Behind Act (NCLB) (3) The 2002 reauthorization of the Elementary and Secondary Education Act (ESEA). Originally passed in 1965, ESEA programs provide much of the federal funding for K–12 schools. NCLB's provisions represent a significant change in the federal government's influence in public schools and districts throughout the United States, particularly in terms of assessment, accountability, and teacher quality. It increases the federal focus on the achievement of disadvantaged pupils, including English learners and students who live in poverty; provides funding for innovative programs; and supports the right of parents to transfer their children to a different school if their school is low performing or unsafe.

normative decision model (2) A view of leadership as a decision-making process in which the leader examines certain factors within the situation to determine which decision-making style will be the most effective.

norm-referenced assessments (10) Assessments in which an individual or group's performance is compared to a larger group; evaluations or tests in which students are compared to each other. Usually, the larger group is representative of the crosssection of all U.S. students. The students with the best performance (on tests, presentations, etc.) receive the highest marks. Grades are distributed over a range (typically A through F), and not all students can receive the highest marks.

observational learning (8) Albert Bandura's learning theory stating that much human learning occurs through our observation of the behavior of others. This theory is now often called a "social learning" model or theory.

organizational culture (2) The written and unwritten rules that shape and reflect the way an organization operates.

organizational development (2) The tools and skills used to change an organization's structure that enable a board and staff to run a nonprofit organization effectively and efficiently. These include resource development, financial management, strategic planning, board recruitment and development, and communications.

organizational theory (2) The study of human organizations and groups.

organizational transformation (2) Fundamental organizational process changes.

outcome-based learning (8) A school reform structure that typically requires students to pass specific exit exams or pass exit performances by the time they finish the program. Instruction is adapted to guarantee that 30 percent of the students can meet these exit requirements.

outcome evaluation (10) An evaluation used to identify the results of a program's effort. This type of evaluation provides knowledge about (1) the extent to which the problems and needs that gave rise to the program still exist, (2) ways to ameliorate adverse impacts and enhance desirable impacts, and (3) program design adjustments that may be indicated for the future.

parent/school compact (14) Under the No Child Left Behind Act, a written agreement of shared responsibility that defines the goals and expectations of schools and parents as partners in the effort to improve student achievement.

Pareto management principle (2) An unproven but widely quoted management aphorism, sometimes called the 80/20 rule, that posits that 80 percent of everything accomplished productively in a system is done utilizing 20 percent of the available resources in people, time, and money.

participative leadership (2) A style of leadership in which the leader involves one or more employees in determining what to do and how to do it. The leader maintains final decision-making authority.

percentile ranks (10) One method of comparing a given child, class, school, or district to a national norm. Everyone who took the test outranks students in the first percentile. Students in the ninety-ninth percentile outrank everyone else. Students at the fiftieth percentile are exactly in the middle. Percentiles are ranks, not scores.

performance assessment (10) An assessment that requires students to generate a response to a question rather than choose it from a set of possible answers provided for them. Examples of performance assessments include essay questions, portfolios, and demonstrations. Also sometimes referred to as *alternative* or *authentic assessment*.

performance incentive (10, 13) Any incentive—monetary or other—used to encourage teachers, administrators, and other school staff to improve the academic achievement of their students.

performance pay (10) Compensation concept whereby an individual's pay is directly related to the individual's or the organization's performance.

persuasion (15) The act of influencing the opinions or actions of others through arguments and reasons.

planning (3) (1) Setting objectives and identifying methods of achieving those objectives. (2) A continuing process of analyzing program data, making decisions, and formulating plans for action in the future, aimed at achieving program goals.

planning-programming-budgeting system (6) Effort to connect planning, systems analysis, and budgeting in a single exercise.

plenary authority (4) Ultimate power. In education, the interaction of federal and state constitutional provisions cedes ultimate authority for the governance of public education to state authorities.

policy (5) A rule or governing principle pertaining to goals, objectives, and/or activities. Policy implies a predicted behavior, although an occasional exception may be tolerated and permitted. Policies establish boundaries around decisions, including which decisions may be made and which may not. These rules usually are published, along with the procedure for obtaining an exception.

policy analysis (5) An analysis used to assist managers and decision makers in understanding the extent of the problem or need that exists and to set realistic goals and objectives in response to such problem or need. It may be used to compare actual program activities with the program's legally established purposes in order to ensure legal compliance.

***polis* (5)** A Greek city-state.

political culture (5) Attitudes, values, beliefs, and orientations that individuals in a society hold regarding their political system.

political socialization (5) The process by which political culture is transmitted from generation to generation.

power (2) The ability to accomplish objectives, whether through force, cooperation, or the power of the integrative system. The system of identity and relationships that holds people together in groups.

practicing or professional ethics (15) The influence of moral values and principles on the conduct of an organization and its individual and institutional operations.

problem-based learning (8) Inductive teaching method that involves no direct instruction. The teacher poses an authentic (real-world) problem; students learn particular content and skills as they work cooperatively to solve the problem.

***pro bono* (7)** Provision of products or services at low or no cost. Also known as *pro bono publico*.

procedural due process (7) An orderly, established process or set of procedures (1) for arriving at an impartial and just resolution of a conflict between parties or (2) that must be followed before a person can be deprived of certain legal rights. In its most basic form, it includes the elements of notice and fair hearing.

productivity (6) The relationship between production of an output and one, some, or all of the resource inputs used to accomplish the assigned task. It is measured as a ratio of output per unit of input over time. It is a measure of efficiency and is usually considered as output per person per unit of time.

professional development (10, 13) The process of progressing in one's chosen career through continuing education and training; programs that allow teachers or administrators to acquire the knowledge and skills they need to perform their jobs successfully. Often these programs are aimed at veteran teachers to help them update their skills and knowledge.

proficiency (8) Mastery or ability to do something at grade level; the term is often used in relation to testing. A state's goal is for all students to score at "proficient" or "advanced" level.

programmed learning (8) A teaching method involving a preconstructed sequence of steps and associated feedback, based on the ideas of Skinner and/or Crowder. Now largely subsumed under computer-based learning.

progressive tax (6) One that taxes those with higher incomes at a higher rate.

property tax (6) A tax on local residential and commercial property that is part of a school district's income based on a formula that is usually set by the state legislature. These taxes, which vary by district, are part of the district's revenue limit income.

proportional tax (6) One that taxes everyone at the same rate.

Proposition 13 (4) A popularly enacted amendment to the California constitution passed by voter initiative in June 1978 that limits property taxes to no more than one percent of full assessed value (plus any additional rates approved by local voters, such as general obligation bonds). Annual increases in assessed value are capped.

Public Law 81-874 (PL 81-874) (6) The federal program that provides funds to districts with children whose families live or work on federal property, such as military bases or Native American reservations. (See Title VIII.)

Public Law 94-142 (PL 94-142) (4) A federal law that mandates a "free and appropriate" education for all children with disabilities.

pupil-teacher ratio/pupil-professional ratio (13) Average number of pupils per teacher in a school district or school.

Pygmalion effect (9) Effect that occurs when a managerial leader believes that a group member will succeed and communicates this belief without realizing it.

quality assurance (2) Internal and external processes for ensuring that the quality of an object or institution maintains a desired level.

quartile (11) One-quarter range of percentiles; a student with a test placement of seventy-five or more (out of one hundred) would be in the first or top quartile.

range (11) The difference between the smallest and largest values in a distribution.

rational model of decision making (2) Derived from economic theories of how to make the "best" decisions; involves efforts to move toward consciously held goals in a way that requires the least input of scarce resources; assumes the ability to separate ends from means, rank all alternatives, gather all possible data, and objectively weigh alternatives; stresses rationality in the process of reaching decisions.

recapture (6) State-enacted statutory provisions whereby school-district-generated tax revenues in excess of a specified per-pupil amount revert to the state for redistribution to districts of lesser wealth. A recapture provision implies that property tax is a statewide tax, the revenue distribution of which is at the state's discretion.

reconstitution (10) A drastic corrective action for a school whose students have performed poorly over time and have failed to improve. A reconstitution is marked by the replacement of the majority of the school's staff, as well as its principal.

referent power (2) The ability to influence others that stems from the leader's desirable traits and characteristics.

regressive tax (6) One that taxes those with lower incomes at a proportionately higher rate than those with higher incomes. In an absolute sense, this is a tax in which the rate falls as the taxable base increases, as with early Social Security. In a relative sense, it is a rise in total taxes paid as a percentage of one's income, as is the case with most property and sales taxes.

reliability (10, 11) The characteristic that same or similar results can be obtained through repeated experiments or tests. In relation to an examination or test instrument, a measure of the degree to which it gives consistent results when applied in different contexts.

remedial instruction (9) Procedure used to teach students whose performance is judged to be below normal in a given subject, remedying below-normal performance.

retention (9) The act or policy of holding students back from advancing to the next grade level if they do not meet established performance standards.

revenues per pupil (6) The total revenues from all sources allocated to K–12 education, divided by the number of students as determined, most often, by average daily attendance.

rubrics (10) Scoring guides that include descriptors for defined, succeeding levels of performance.

rule of law (7) Equal protection (of human as well as property and other economic rights) and punishment under the law. The rule of law reigns over government, protecting citizens against arbitrary state action, and over society generally, governing relations among private interests. It ensures that all citizens are treated equally and are subject to the law rather than to the whims of the powerful. The rule of law is an essential precondition for accountability and predictability in both the public and private sectors.

sampling (10, 12) In education research, administering a test to and analyzing the test results of a set of students who, as a group, represent the characteristics of the entire student population. Based on their analysis of the data of the representative sample, researchers, educators, and policymakers can infer important trends in the academic progress of an individual or group of students.

SAT (13) A test administered by the national College Board and widely used throughout the country as a college entrance examination. National and state averages of scores from the SAT I Reasoning Test (formerly called the Scholastic Aptitude Test) are published annually.

satisficing (2, 12) The process of decision making that characterizes most governmental action; a limited search through familiar patterns of behavior for a course of action that meets pre-established minimum standards of performance, rather than an exhaustive review of all alternatives in search of the optimal solution to a particular problem.

scaled score (10) An adjustment of raw scores that differentiates among the test items by, for example, giving more weight to difficult questions and less weight to easy questions across all grade levels. Unlike other types of scores, the scaled score has the same meaning in terms of achievement for each grade, making it the best indicator of a student's growth from one year to the next.

school board (4) A locally elected group, usually consisting of three or seven members, who set fiscal, personnel, instructional, and student-related policies. The number of board members relates to the size of the district. A school district governing board also provides direction for the district, hires and fires the district superintendent, and approves the budget and contracts with employee unions.

school-community partnership (14) Corporate community involvement, encompassing collaborative arrangements among schools, districts, and community-based organizations.

school district (4) A local education agency directed by an elected local board of education that exists primarily to operate public schools. In most instances, there are three types of school districts: elementary, high school, and unified. An elementary district is generally kindergarten through eighth grade (K–8); high school is generally grades 9 through 12; unified is kindergarten through twelfth grade (K–12).

school site council (4) Parents, students (high schools only), teachers, and other staff selected by their peers to prepare a school improvement plan and to assist in seeing that the planned activities are carried out and evaluated. Such a council is required when a school receives funding for a school improvement program (SIP) or through Title I.

scientific management (2) A formal theory of organization developed by Frederick Taylor in the early 1900s; concerned with achieving efficiency in production, rational work procedures, maximum productivity, and profit; focused on management's responsibilities and on "scientifically" developed work procedures, based on time-and-motion studies.

scope of bargaining (5) The range of subjects negotiated between school districts and employee organizations during collective bargaining; often scope includes matters relating to wages, hours, and working conditions. The Public Employment Relations Board is responsible for interpreting disputes about scope.

***Serrano v. Priest* (6)** A California court case—begun in 1968 and settled in the mid-1970s—that challenged the inequities created by the U.S. tradition of using property taxes as the principal source of revenue for public schools, saying the wide discrepancies

in school funding because of differences in district wealth represented a denial of equal opportunity.

servant leadership (2, 12) A leadership style in which the leader acts as a trusted servant, acting in the presumed best interest of his or her followers.

single salary schedule (13) An established plan for paying salaries to teachers, supervisors, and administrators according to a defined scale of increases that depends on length of service and amount of professional preparation. Also known as *single salary schedule.*

site-based management (2) A school management system in which certain authority is reallocated from a centralized organizational structure to its decentralized components—the individual schools. Site-based management usually preserves the role of the building principal in the organizational hierarchy. Also known as *school-based management.*

situated learning (8, 15) An educational theory by Jean Lave proposing that learning normally occurs in a specific context (i.e., with certain people or while performing certain tasks). Learning, then, involves both social interactions and interactions with the real-life materials and places where the knowledge would be applied. Variations of situated learning would include apprenticeships and cognitive apprenticeships.

situational leadership model (2) A model that explains how to match leadership style to the readiness of the group members.

social contract (4) An implicit component of a democratic government wherein citizens collectively agree, informally, to cede each individual's God-given personal authority to appropriately elected representatives who pledge themselves to act consistent with and in furtherance of the goals of the society's adopted governmental framework—its constitution.

span of control (2) One of the early principles of administration, which states that there is an upper limit to the number of subordinates

any administrator can directly supervise—generally set at twelve—and advises administrators to eliminate any violations of this principle by reducing the number of officials reporting to them either by merging certain offices or stretching out the hierarchy.

special districts (4) Local governments created for a specific purpose within a specific area.

special education (13) Programs to identify and meet the educational needs of children with emotional, learning, or physical disabilities. Federal law requires that all children with disabilities be provided a free and appropriate education according to an individualized education program from infancy until twenty-one years of age.

spiral curriculum (9) A strategy in which a subject is taught by visiting the same issues or concepts a number of times, initially with a simple treatment but then in progressively more depth.

staff development (10) The activities of an organization or supervisor that are designed to improve the skills, motivation, and qualifications of individuals within that organization.

stakeholder (14) One who has credibility, power, or other capital invested in a project and thus can be held to be, to some degree, at risk with it.

standards (9) Degrees or levels of achievement. The "standards movement" began as an informal effort that grew out of a concern that American students were not learning enough and that American schools did not have a rigorous curriculum. The U.S. Congress adopted this concept more formally with its 1994 reauthorization of the federal Title I program.

standards-based reform (5) A late-twentieth-century shift in education policy and school reform toward reaching consensus on and establishing standards for what students need to know and be able to do at each grade or developmental level. Although the momentum for standards-based education is well on its way, tension still exists over how much influence national, state, or local policymakers should have over setting the standards. Although a strong backlash to national control continues, a growing number of states are taking on this responsibility.

Stanford-9 (SAT-9) Also called the SAT-9 and officially known as the Stanford Achievement Test, Ninth Edition Form T, this test is published by Harcourt Brace Educational Measurement. It is a standardized, nationally normed, multiple-choice test that measures basic skills in math, reading English, and other areas.

state education agency (4) The agency primarily responsible for the supervision of a state's public elementary and secondary schools.

strategic leadership (1) The process of providing the direction and inspiration necessary to create or sustain an organization.

strategy (1) An integrated, overall concept of the methods that an organization will use to deliver services and implement activities in order to achieve its goals.

summative assessment (10) Assessment typically completed at the end of a learning period with the aim of providing a final evaluation of an individual's mastery of a knowledge or skill.

SWOT analysis (10) An analysis of an organization's strengths, weaknesses, opportunities, and threats.

tactical leadership (1) A leadership style used when the objective is very clear, a plan for achieving the objective has been developed, and the members of the collective effort are being led in the execution of the plan.

tax base (6) In one sense, that which is taxed, such as annual income, personal wealth or property, or the value of goods that are being imported or sold at retail. In another sense, the smaller dollar amount that is subject to taxation after all exemptions, exclusions, and income not taxed have been set aside. The difference between the apparent gross income and the remaining taxable income accounts for the difference between nominal and effective rates of taxation.

tax rate (6) The amount of tax paid for each increment of assessed value of property; the percentage of tax levied on something such as income or property. *Proportional rates* are the same regardless of the size of the base being taxed. *Progressive rates* grow as the taxable base becomes greater. *Regressive rates* grow smaller as the base increases.

tenure (13) A system of due process and employment guarantee for teachers. After serving a two-year probationary period, teachers are assured continued employment in the school district unless carefully defined procedures for dismissal or layoff are successfully followed. Tenure cannot be rescinded except for specified reasons.

Theory X and Theory Y (2) Two opposing assumptions about people at work that lead to opposing styles of management. Theory X assumes that most people hate work, avoid responsibility, prefer to be directed, and have to be controlled and coerced to put out a fair day's work; Theory Y assumes that people seek responsibility, demonstrate a high degree of imagination, and exercise self-direction if they have a creative, challenging job to which they can become committed.

Title I (14) A federal program that provides funds for educationally disadvantaged students, including the children of migrant workers. Funding is based on the number of low-income children in a school, generally those eligible for the free/reduced-price meals program. Title I is intended to supplement, not replace, state and district funds. The funds are distributed to school districts, which make allocations to eligible schools according to criteria stated in the federal law.

tracking (9) The practice of grouping students in curricular paths by achievement levels; for example, college preparatory or vocational.

transfer of learning (8) The application of principles or concepts learned in one context to another context.

tuition tax credit (6) A reduction in state or federal income tax to offset a specified amount of money for private education tuition.

***ultra vires* (7)** An action that exceeds the conferred constitutional powers of the actor. Literally, "beyond the power."

unification (4) Joining together of all or part of an elementary school district (grades K–8) and high school district (grades 9–12) to form a new unified school district (grades K–12) with a single governing board.

validity (10) The degree to which an investigation accurately assesses the specific idea that a researcher is investigating; the extent to which a measuring instrument or procedure serves the purpose for which it was designed.

value-added systems of accountability (10) Models that attempt to measure the value added by an individual teacher or school to students' performance over time.

vested (13) Eligibility status in a retirement plan; the specified time period that pension plan members must contribute to a system before being eligible for benefits.

visioning (1) A process by which an organization envisions the future it desires and plans how to achieve it. Through public involvement, organizations and communities identify their purpose, core values, and vision for the future, which are then transformed into a manageable and feasible set of goals and an action plan.

voucher (9) A promise of payment from the state for all or part of a student's education expenses at a school of the student's choice.

zero-base budgeting (6) A budget format that presents information about the efficiency and effectiveness of existing programs and highlights possibilities for eliminating or reducing programs by assuming that the minimum funding level for the agency is zero, thereby requiring agency administrators to justify all expenditures by the same standards of review that normally are applied only to new programs or increments above the base.

Index